Lecture Notes in Computer Scie

Commenced Publication in 1973
Founding and Former Series Editors:
Gerhard Goos, Juris Hartmanis, and Jan van Leeuwen

Aaron Marcus (Ed.)

Design, User Experience, and Usability

User Experience in Novel Technological Environments

Second International Conference, DUXU 2013
Held as Part of HCI International 2013
Las Vegas, NV, USA, July 21-26, 2013
Proceedings, Part III

 Springer

Volume Editor

Aaron Marcus
Aaron Marcus and Associates, Inc.
1196 Euclid Avenue, Suite 1F
Berkeley, CA 94708, USA
E-mail: aaron.marcus@amanda.com

ISSN 0302-9743   e-ISSN 1611-3349
ISBN 978-3-642-39237-5   e-ISBN 978-3-642-39238-2
DOI 10.1007/978-3-642-39238-2
Springer Heidelberg Dordrecht London New York

Library of Congress Control Number: 2013941914

CR Subject Classification (1998): H.5, H.1, J.3, H.3, K.4

LNCS Sublibrary: SL 3 – Information Systems and Application, incl. Internet/Web
and HCI

Typesetting: Camera-ready by author, data conversion by Scientific Publishing Services, Chennai, India

Printed on acid-free paper

Springer is part of Springer Science+Business Media (www.springer.com)

Foreword

The 15th International Conference on Human–Computer Interaction, HCI International 2013, was held in Las Vegas, Nevada, USA, 21–26 July 2013, incorporating 12 conferences / thematic areas:

Thematic areas:

- Human–Computer Interaction
- Human Interface and the Management of Information

Affiliated conferences:

- 10th International Conference on Engineering Psychology and Cognitive Ergonomics
- 7th International Conference on Universal Access in Human–Computer Interaction
- 5th International Conference on Virtual, Augmented and Mixed Reality
- 5th International Conference on Cross-Cultural Design
- 5th International Conference on Online Communities and Social Computing
- 7th International Conference on Augmented Cognition
- 4th International Conference on Digital Human Modeling and Applications in Health, Safety, Ergonomics and Risk Management
- 2nd International Conference on Design, User Experience and Usability
- 1st International Conference on Distributed, Ambient and Pervasive Interactions
- 1st International Conference on Human Aspects of Information Security, Privacy and Trust

A total of 5210 individuals from academia, research institutes, industry and governmental agencies from 70 countries submitted contributions, and 1666 papers and 303 posters were included in the program. These papers address the latest research and development efforts and highlight the human aspects of design and use of computing systems. The papers accepted for presentation thoroughly cover the entire field of Human–Computer Interaction, addressing major advances in knowledge and effective use of computers in a variety of application areas.

This volume, edited by Aaron Marcus, contains papers focusing on the thematic area of Design, User Experience and Usability, and addressing the following major topics:

- Designing for Safe and Secure Environments
- Designing for Smart and Ambient Devices
- Designing for Virtual and Augmented Environments
- Emotional and Persuasion Design

The remaining volumes of the HCI International 2013 proceedings are:

- Volume 1, LNCS 8004, Human–Computer Interaction: Human-Centred Design Approaches, Methods, Tools and Environments (Part I), edited by Masaaki Kurosu
- Volume 2, LNCS 8005, Human–Computer Interaction: Applications and Services (Part II), edited by Masaaki Kurosu
- Volume 3, LNCS 8006, Human–Computer Interaction: Users and Contexts of Use (Part III), edited by Masaaki Kurosu
- Volume 4, LNCS 8007, Human–Computer Interaction: Interaction Modalities and Techniques (Part IV), edited by Masaaki Kurosu
- Volume 5, LNCS 8008, Human–Computer Interaction: Towards Intelligent and Implicit Interaction (Part V), edited by Masaaki Kurosu
- Volume 6, LNCS 8009, Universal Access in Human–Computer Interaction: Design Methods, Tools and Interaction Techniques for eInclusion (Part I), edited by Constantine Stephanidis and Margherita Antona
- Volume 7, LNCS 8010, Universal Access in Human–Computer Interaction: User and Context Diversity (Part II), edited by Constantine Stephanidis and Margherita Antona
- Volume 8, LNCS 8011, Universal Access in Human–Computer Interaction: Applications and Services for Quality of Life (Part III), edited by Constantine Stephanidis and Margherita Antona
- Volume 9, LNCS 8012, Design, User Experience, and Usability: Design Philosophy, Methods and Tools (Part I), edited by Aaron Marcus
- Volume 10, LNCS 8013, Design, User Experience, and Usability: Health, Learning, Playing, Cultural, and Cross-Cultural User Experience (Part II), edited by Aaron Marcus
- Volume 12, LNCS 8015, Design, User Experience, and Usability: Web, Mobile and Product Design (Part IV), edited by Aaron Marcus
- Volume 13, LNCS 8016, Human Interface and the Management of Information: Information and Interaction Design (Part I), edited by Sakae Yamamoto
- Volume 14, LNCS 8017, Human Interface and the Management of Information: Information and Interaction for Health, Safety, Mobility and Complex Environments (Part II), edited by Sakae Yamamoto
- Volume 15, LNCS 8018, Human Interface and the Management of Information: Information and Interaction for Learning, Culture, Collaboration and Business (Part III), edited by Sakae Yamamoto
- Volume 16, LNAI 8019, Engineering Psychology and Cognitive Ergonomics: Understanding Human Cognition (Part I), edited by Don Harris
- Volume 17, LNAI 8020, Engineering Psychology and Cognitive Ergonomics: Applications and Services (Part II), edited by Don Harris
- Volume 18, LNCS 8021, Virtual, Augmented and Mixed Reality: Designing and Developing Augmented and Virtual Environments (Part I), edited by Randall Shumaker
- Volume 19, LNCS 8022, Virtual, Augmented and Mixed Reality: Systems and Applications (Part II), edited by Randall Shumaker

- Volume 20, LNCS 8023, Cross-Cultural Design: Methods, Practice and Case Studies (Part I), edited by P.L. Patrick Rau
- Volume 21, LNCS 8024, Cross-Cultural Design: Cultural Differences in Everyday Life (Part II), edited by P.L. Patrick Rau
- Volume 22, LNCS 8025, Digital Human Modeling and Applications in Health, Safety, Ergonomics and Risk Management: Healthcare and Safety of the Environment and Transport (Part I), edited by Vincent G. Duffy
- Volume 23, LNCS 8026, Digital Human Modeling and Applications in Health, Safety, Ergonomics and Risk Management: Human Body Modeling and Ergonomics (Part II), edited by Vincent G. Duffy
- Volume 24, LNAI 8027, Foundations of Augmented Cognition, edited by Dylan D. Schmorrow and Cali M. Fidopiastis
- Volume 25, LNCS 8028, Distributed, Ambient and Pervasive Interactions, edited by Norbert Streitz and Constantine Stephanidis
- Volume 26, LNCS 8029, Online Communities and Social Computing, edited by A. Ant Ozok and Panayiotis Zaphiris
- Volume 27, LNCS 8030, Human Aspects of Information Security, Privacy and Trust, edited by Louis Marinos and Ioannis Askoxylakis
- Volume 28, CCIS 373, HCI International 2013 Posters Proceedings (Part I), edited by Constantine Stephanidis
- Volume 29, CCIS 374, HCI International 2013 Posters Proceedings (Part II), edited by Constantine Stephanidis

I would like to thank the Program Chairs and the members of the Program Boards of all affiliated conferences and thematic areas, listed below, for their contribution to the highest scientific quality and the overall success of the HCI International 2013 conference.

This conference could not have been possible without the continuous support and advice of the Founding Chair and Conference Scientific Advisor, Prof. Gavriel Salvendy, as well as the dedicated work and outstanding efforts of the Communications Chair and Editor of HCI International News, Abbas Moallem.

I would also like to thank for their contribution towards the smooth organization of the HCI International 2013 Conference the members of the Human–Computer Interaction Laboratory of ICS-FORTH, and in particular George Paparoulis, Maria Pitsoulaki, Stavroula Ntoa, Maria Bouhli and George Kapnas.

May 2013
Constantine Stephanidis
General Chair, HCI International 2013

Organization

Human–Computer Interaction

Program Chair: Masaaki Kurosu, Japan

Jose Abdelnour-Nocera, UK
Sebastiano Bagnara, Italy
Simone Barbosa, Brazil
Tomas Berns, Sweden
Nigel Bevan, UK
Simone Borsci, UK
Apala Lahiri Chavan, India
Sherry Chen, Taiwan
Kevin Clark, USA
Torkil Clemmensen, Denmark
Xiaowen Fang, USA
Shin'ichi Fukuzumi, Japan
Vicki Hanson, UK
Ayako Hashizume, Japan
Anzai Hiroyuki, Italy
Sheue-Ling Hwang, Taiwan
Wonil Hwang, South Korea
Minna Isomursu, Finland
Yong Gu Ji, South Korea
Esther Jun, USA
Mitsuhiko Karashima, Japan

Kyungdoh Kim, South Korea
Heidi Krömker, Germany
Chen Ling, USA
Yan Liu, USA
Zhengjie Liu, P.R. China
Loïc Martínez Normand, Spain
Chang S. Nam, USA
Naoko Okuizumi, Japan
Noriko Osaka, Japan
Philippe Palanque, France
Hans Persson, Sweden
Ling Rothrock, USA
Naoki Sakakibara, Japan
Dominique Scapin, France
Guangfeng Song, USA
Sanjay Tripathi, India
Chui Yin Wong, Malaysia
Toshiki Yamaoka, Japan
Kazuhiko Yamazaki, Japan
Ryoji Yoshitake, Japan
Silvia Zimmermann, Switzerland

Human Interface and the Management of Information

Program Chair: Sakae Yamamoto, Japan

Hans-Jorg Bullinger, Germany
Alan Chan, Hong Kong
Gilsoo Cho, South Korea
Jon R. Gunderson, USA
Shin'ichi Fukuzumi, Japan
Michitaka Hirose, Japan
Jhilmil Jain, USA
Yasufumi Kume, Japan

Mark Lehto, USA
Hiroyuki Miki, Japan
Hirohiko Mori, Japan
Fiona Fui-Hoon Nah, USA
Shogo Nishida, Japan
Robert Proctor, USA
Youngho Rhee, South Korea
Katsunori Shimohara, Japan

Michale Smith, USA
Tsutomu Tabe, Japan
Hiroshi Tsuji, Japan

Kim-Phuong Vu, USA
Tomio Watanabe, Japan
Hidekazu Yoshikawa, Japan

Engineering Psychology and Cognitive Ergonomics

Program Chair: Don Harris, UK

Guy Andre Boy, USA
Joakim Dahlman, Sweden
Trevor Dobbins, UK
Mike Feary, USA
Shan Fu, P.R. China
Michaela Heese, Austria
Hung-Sying Jing, Taiwan
Wen-Chin Li, Taiwan
Mark A. Neerincx, The Netherlands
Jan M. Noyes, UK
Taezoon Park, Singapore

Paul Salmon, Australia
Axel Schulte, Germany
Siraj Shaikh, UK
Sarah C. Sharples, UK
Anthony Smoker, UK
Neville A. Stanton, UK
Alex Stedmon, UK
Xianghong Sun, P.R. China
Andrew Thatcher, South Africa
Matthew J.W. Thomas, Australia
Rolf Zon, The Netherlands

Universal Access in Human–Computer Interaction

Program Chairs: Constantine Stephanidis, Greece, and Margherita Antona, Greece

Julio Abascal, Spain
Ray Adams, UK
Gisela Susanne Bahr, USA
Margit Betke, USA
Christian Bühler, Germany
Stefan Carmien, Spain
Jerzy Charytonowicz, Poland
Carlos Duarte, Portugal
Pier Luigi Emiliani, Italy
Qin Gao, P.R. China
Andrina Granić, Croatia
Andreas Holzinger, Austria
Josette Jones, USA
Simeon Keates, UK

Georgios Kouroupetroglou, Greece
Patrick Langdon, UK
Seongil Lee, Korea
Ana Isabel B.B. Paraguay, Brazil
Helen Petrie, UK
Michael Pieper, Germany
Enrico Pontelli, USA
Jaime Sanchez, Chile
Anthony Savidis, Greece
Christian Stary, Austria
Hirotada Ueda, Japan
Gerhard Weber, Germany
Harald Weber, Germany

Virtual, Augmented and Mixed Reality

Program Chair: Randall Shumaker, USA

Waymon Armstrong, USA
Juan Cendan, USA
Rudy Darken, USA
Cali M. Fidopiastis, USA
Charles Hughes, USA
David Kaber, USA
Hirokazu Kato, Japan
Denis Laurendeau, Canada
Fotis Liarokapis, UK

Mark Livingston, USA
Michael Macedonia, USA
Gordon Mair, UK
Jose San Martin, Spain
Jacquelyn Morie, USA
Albert "Skip" Rizzo, USA
Kay Stanney, USA
Christopher Stapleton, USA
Gregory Welch, USA

Cross-Cultural Design

Program Chair: P.L. Patrick Rau, P.R. China

Pilsung Choe, P.R. China
Henry Been-Lirn Duh, Singapore
Vanessa Evers, The Netherlands
Paul Fu, USA
Zhiyong Fu, P.R. China
Fu Guo, P.R. China
Sung H. Han, Korea
Toshikazu Kato, Japan
Dyi-Yih Michael Lin, Taiwan
Rungtai Lin, Taiwan

Sheau-Farn Max Liang, Taiwan
Liang Ma, P.R. China
Alexander Mädche, Germany
Katsuhiko Ogawa, Japan
Tom Plocher, USA
Kerstin Röse, Germany
Supriya Singh, Australia
Hsiu-Ping Yueh, Taiwan
Liang (Leon) Zeng, USA
Chen Zhao, USA

Online Communities and Social Computing

Program Chairs: A. Ant Ozok, USA, and Panayiotis Zaphiris, Cyprus

Areej Al-Wabil, Saudi Arabia
Leonelo Almeida, Brazil
Bjørn Andersen, Norway
Chee Siang Ang, UK
Aneesha Bakharia, Australia
Ania Bobrowicz, UK
Paul Cairns, UK
Farzin Deravi, UK
Andri Ioannou, Cyprus
Slava Kisilevich, Germany

Niki Lambropoulos, Greece
Effie Law, Switzerland
Soo Ling Lim, UK
Fernando Loizides, Cyprus
Gabriele Meiselwitz, USA
Anthony Norcio, USA
Elaine Raybourn, USA
Panote Siriaraya, UK
David Stuart, UK
June Wei, USA

Augmented Cognition

Program Chairs: Dylan D. Schmorrow, USA, and Cali M. Fidopiastis, USA

Robert Arrabito, Canada
Richard Backs, USA
Chris Berka, USA
Joseph Cohn, USA
Martha E. Crosby, USA
Julie Drexler, USA
Ivy Estabrooke, USA
Chris Forsythe, USA
Wai Tat Fu, USA
Rodolphe Gentili, USA
Marc Grootjen, The Netherlands
Jefferson Grubb, USA
Ming Hou, Canada

Santosh Mathan, USA
Rob Matthews, Australia
Dennis McBride, USA
Jeff Morrison, USA
Mark A. Neerincx, The Netherlands
Denise Nicholson, USA
Banu Onaral, USA
Lee Sciarini, USA
Kay Stanney, USA
Roy Stripling, USA
Rob Taylor, UK
Karl van Orden, USA

Digital Human Modeling and Applications in Health, Safety, Ergonomics and Risk Management

Program Chair: Vincent G. Duffy, USA and Russia

Karim Abdel-Malek, USA
Giuseppe Andreoni, Italy
Daniel Carruth, USA
Eliza Yingzi Du, USA
Enda Fallon, Ireland
Afzal Godil, USA
Ravindra Goonetilleke, Hong Kong
Bo Hoege, Germany
Waldemar Karwowski, USA
Zhizhong Li, P.R. China

Kang Li, USA
Tim Marler, USA
Michelle Robertson, USA
Matthias Rötting, Germany
Peter Vink, The Netherlands
Mao-Jiun Wang, Taiwan
Xuguang Wang, France
Jingzhou (James) Yang, USA
Xiugan Yuan, P.R. China
Gülcin Yücel Hoge, Germany

Design, User Experience, and Usability

Program Chair: Aaron Marcus, USA

Sisira Adikari, Australia
Ronald Baecker, Canada
Arne Berger, Germany
Jamie Blustein, Canada

Ana Boa-Ventura, USA
Jan Brejcha, Czech Republic
Lorenzo Cantoni, Switzerland
Maximilian Eibl, Germany

Distributed, Ambient and Pervasive Interactions

Program Chairs: Norbert Streitz, Germany, and Constantine Stephanidis, Greece

Human Aspects of Information Security, Privacy and Trust

Program Chairs: Louis Marinos, ENISA EU, and Ioannis Askoxylakis, Greece

Julien Touzeau, France
Theo Tryfonas, UK
João Vilela, Portugal

Claire Vishik, UK
Melanie Volkamer, Germany

External Reviewers

Maysoon Abulkhair, Saudi Arabia
Ilia Adami, Greece
Vishal Barot, UK
Stephan Böhm, Germany
Vassilis Charissis, UK
Francisco Cipolla-Ficarra, Spain
Maria De Marsico, Italy
Marc Fabri, UK
David Fonseca, Spain
Linda Harley, USA
Yasushi Ikei, Japan
Wei Ji, USA
Nouf Khashman, Canada
John Killilea, USA
Iosif Klironomos, Greece
Ute Klotz, Switzerland
Maria Korozi, Greece
Kentaro Kotani, Japan

Vassilis Kouroumalis, Greece
Stephanie Lackey, USA
Janelle LaMarche, USA
Asterios Leonidis, Greece
Nickolas Macchiarella, USA
George Margetis, Greece
Matthew Marraffino, USA
Joseph Mercado, USA
Claudia Mont'Alvão, Brazil
Yoichi Motomura, Japan
Karsten Nebe, Germany
Stavroula Ntoa, Greece
Martin Osen, Austria
Stephen Prior, UK
Farid Shirazi, Canada
Jan Stelovsky, USA
Sarah Swierenga, USA

HCI International 2014

The 16th International Conference on Human–Computer Interaction, HCI International 2014, will be held jointly with the affiliated conferences in the summer of 2014. It will cover a broad spectrum of themes related to Human–Computer Interaction, including theoretical issues, methods, tools, processes and case studies in HCI design, as well as novel interaction techniques, interfaces and applications. The proceedings will be published by Springer. More information about the topics, as well as the venue and dates of the conference, will be announced through the HCI International Conference series website: http://www.hci-international.org/

General Chair
Professor Constantine Stephanidis
University of Crete and ICS-FORTH
Heraklion, Crete, Greece
Email: cs@ics.forth.gr

Table of Contents – Part III

Designing for Safe and Secure Environments

Designing for Smart and Ambient Devices

Designing for Virtual and Augmented Environments

Emotional and Persuasion Design

Part I

Designing for Safe and Secure Environments

Rap Backs: Continuous Workforce Monitoring to Improve Patient Safety in Long-Term Care

Fuad Abujarad[1], Sarah J. Swierenga[2], Toni A. Dennis[3], and Lori A. Post[1]

[1] Yale School of Medicine
New Haven, CT, USA
{fuad.abujarad,lori.post}@yale.edu
[2] Usability/Accessibility Research and Consulting
Michigan State University, East Lansing, MI, USA
sswieren@msu.edu
[3] Department of Licensing and Regulatory Affairs,
State of Michigan, Lansing, MI, USA
dennist@michigan.gov

Abstract. The Michigan Workforce Background Check (MWBC) system is a Web-based application that centralizes the screening process for job applicants at long-term care facilities by integrating the checking of registries and databases, and by providing secure communication between the system and state agencies. A key feature of the system is the rap back, which is a process whereby fingerprint images submitted by healthcare workers are maintained in a database and compared against arrest fingerprints to track subsequent criminal activity. Rap backs eliminate the need for subsequent fingerprinting to update criminal record information. A user-centered design process was used to create the interaction design during the development process, resulting in very few post-release adjustments and saved time and financial resources. Patient safety is improved due to this rap back process because unfit workers are immediately identified and removed from long-term care facilities.

Keywords: Criminal background checks, rap back, long-term care, health information technology, usability, user-centered design, patient safety.

1   Introduction

As the U.S. population ages, the number of adults residing in nursing homes and assisted living facilities is increasing dramatically, and the number of home health care service providers is rising to meet the need for home and community-based services. Elderly and disabled persons in long-term care (LTC) settings are vulnerable to abuse, neglect, and exploitation necessitating special protective measures by criminal justice, social services, and healthcare agencies [1-2]. In 2006, 28.6% of Michigan households with a family member in LTC reported that person having experienced one or more forms of abuse including physical, caretaking, verbal,

A. Marcus (Ed.): DUXU/HCII 2013, Part III, LNCS 8014, pp. 3–9, 2013.

emotional, neglect, sexual and material exploitation [3]. Elder abuse is increasingly an important public health topic given that the population aged 65 years and older is estimated to double by 2030 [3-4]. Criminal justice agencies are scrambling to identify programs aimed at reducing elder abuse in LTC. A report from the Office of Inspector General noted that 92% of healthcare workers in nursing homes have a criminal record [5].

One response by state and federal governments is to require pre-employment background checks for workers who have direct access to residents in nursing homes and other beneficiaries of federal funding in long-term care. Section 307 of the United States Medicare Prescription Drug, Improvement, and Modernization Act (MMA) of 2003 (PL 108-173) directed the Secretary of Health and Human Services to establish a program to identify efficient, effective and economical procedures to conduct background checks on prospective employees of long-term care facilities or providers with direct access to patients. From 2005-2007 Michigan was one of seven states that participated in this pilot study; Michigan partnered with nationally and internationally recognized experts in system development, usability and accessibility, and domestic violence research at Michigan State University to create a comprehensive system to check abuse and neglect registries and state and federal criminal history records of prospective employees [6]. Insights gained from conducting several usability-oriented focus groups, concept usability evaluations, expert user interface reviews, website accessibility compliance inspections, and formal usability testing with both providers and state analysts were incorporated into the design [7].

This project resulted in a state-of-the-art online system that established innovative communication protocols among the fingerprint vendor, the Michigan State Police, and the Michigan Workforce Background Check. This system reduced the turnaround time for background checks from six weeks to 48 hours and provided role-based user interfaces that were developed in collaboration with usability experts involved throughout the design process.

2   Rap Back Continuous Monitoring Process

Noncriminal background screening of workers plays a significant role in maintaining a safe and stable healthcare system [8-9]. Recently, local and national legislation has reflected these themes and demanded a broader and stronger pre-employment noncriminal background checks (Section 6201 of the U.S. Patient Protection and Affordable Care Act Pub. L. 111-148, 124 Stat. 119-124, Stat. 1025, enacted March 23, 2010; Michigan Compiled Laws §§ 330.1134a, 333.20173a, and 400.734b). More specifically, the legislation highlights the importance of performing noncriminal background checks on applicants who have direct contact with vulnerable populations. Each prospective new employee (i.e., applicant) is subject to a criminal history check. The applicant fingerprints are digitally live scanned and sent to the state police. Once the state police accept the fingerprint images, they are used to generate state and federal criminal history reports (See Fig. 1). The reports are sent to the Background Check system to be investigated by a background check state analyst.

Since April 1, 2006, providers have entered requests for 726,000 applicants. After initial registry checks and withdrawals, 515,000 prospective employees continued the process and had their fingerprints retrieved digitally under the Michigan Workforce Background Check program. The number of applicants disqualified based on the fingerprint results and rap back has reached 18,565. While the use of the criminal history report is the cornerstone in making employment eligibility determinations, its effect is limited to a single point in time. Frequently, applicants are hired without criminal histories and become criminal offenders post hire. An outdated criminal report cannot be used for future background check analysis since the applicant's criminal history record may have changed. Rap back, a process whereby fingerprint images submitted by health care workers are maintained in a database and compared against arrest fingerprint cards to track subsequent criminal activity, is an important feature of the Michigan background check system. To maintain an ongoing check of any updates on the criminal history for workers who have been fingerprinted for employment with long-term care employers, the system provides the Michigan Department of Licensing and Regulatory Affairs and the Department of Human Services details of new arrests and convictions. This information is used to determine if employees continue to be safe care providers.

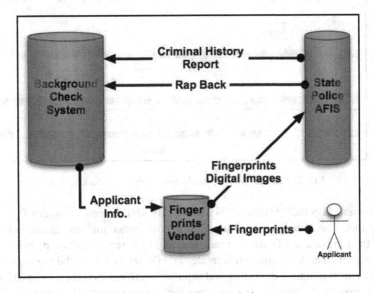

Fig. 1. The rap back process design

The rap back process eliminates the need for subsequent fingerprinting to update criminal record information, saving employers and the State of Michigan approximately $1.2 million annually and reduces the inconvenience of multiple fingerprinting for applicants and employers. The Michigan Workforce Background Check system is able to retrieve response data from the state police rap back system. This information is displayed on the dashboard for assessment by background check analysts with a summary to employers. Moreover the rap back interface on the

Michigan Workforce Background Check system uses web services to obtain and display the rap back messages.

The department is notified immediately when an arrest fingerprint matches prints in the healthcare worker database. A background check analyst can access the new criminal history records by logging into the analyst interface where the information is matched to employee records in the system. The electronic criminal history record is accessible as an attachment to the employee profile and can be viewed in a secondary window. The rap back screen was designed to provide relevant information to review and notify an employer of new felony arrests or convictions (see Fig. 2). The user interface is organized to match the analyst's workflow. Updated criminal history records can be reviewed, investigated and processed from the analyst's rap back screen with links to an automated document creation screen to notify the employer. The rap back module also contains archiving functionality to save records according to an established retention schedule, which eliminates the need for additional document management systems.

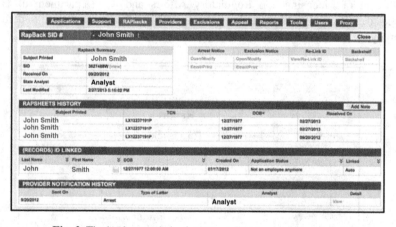

Fig. 2. The background check state analyst rap back screen

The system also includes the ability to quickly send E-mail messages for rap back notifications. The employers have the ability to designate multiple email addresses to receive the rap back notifications. Once the employer receives the rap back message, a final employment determination is made. To effectively utilize the rap back process, employers must maintain the hiring and separation information for all employees. The hire and separation dates are triggers that include or remove an individual from an employer's rap back system notifications, automatically validating the list of employees subject to rap back.

On average, the Michigan Workforce Background Check program processes 75,000 background checks per year with 80% of those submissions stemming from healthcare workers new to long-term care. Processing information received through the rap back for a workforce that has a high turnover rate and is projected to increase by at least 25% in the next five years created a challenge for a state that is facing hiring freezes and staff reductions. This is of concern for processes that are partially automated. In Michigan, the program staff consists of a program manager, three analysts and two administrative support staff. These employees are responsible for processing the initial criminal background checks and appeals and provide support for applicants and health care providers. The manual rap back process has significantly increased the work burden and resulted in 25-30 pieces of new information per day that must be reviewed to determine if an existing employee should be removed from service. Frequently, the new information requires additional investigation to make an accurate determination. In summary, while the rap back system is an important feature of patient safety, it is a labor-intensive activity. To this end, automating the rap back process resolves the work burden plus integrates the process within the existing background check system, and creates a secure, centralized electronic repository of criminal history information.

The state analyst has the option of sending notification messages via e-mail to notify LTC providers of relevant rap back findings. The provider is able to receive Arrest Notifications and Conviction Notifications. The Arrest Notification is sent when the LTC employee is arrested and the state analyst deemed this information relevant to the provider. Similarly, the Conviction Notification is sent when the LTC worker is convicted and the state analyst needs to notify the provider with convictions that are related to employment eligibility. At this point, the system sends an E-mail to the LTC provider prompting login that an important message is in their system. Once the provider logs into the system, the rap back notification message is prominently displayed on the provider dashboard. More notably, the provider dashboard changes to reflect that the user has an urgent message. Fig. 3 displays the provider dashboard without any notifications, while Fig. 4 displays the dashboard with notification.

Home	New Application	Search Applications	Reports	Manage Users

Choose a Facility: Usability Testing Facility for DHS

In Progress		Pending Results		Employability Results
APPLICANT ID	LAST NAME	FIRST NAME	PROFILE	CURRENT STATUS
A0000012	Launch	Soft	View	Fingerprints Overdue
A0000024	MSPDHSTest	New	View	Fingerprints Overdue

Fig. 3. The provider dashboard without rap back notifications

Home	New Application	Search Applications	Reports	Manage Users

Choose a Facility: Usability Testing Facility for MDCH

RAPbacks Why is this here? (RAPbacks Help)				
APPLICANT ID	LAST NAME	FIRST NAME	PROFILE	RAPBACK
A0000028	Vega	Maria	View	View Results

In Progress		Pending Results		Employability Results
APPLICANT ID	LAST NAME	FIRST NAME	PROFILE	CURRENT STATUS
A0000007	Reynolds	Robert	View	Fingerprints Overdue
A0000010	Steinfield	Michael	View	Fingerprints Overdue

Fig. 4. The provider dashboard with rap back notifications

3   User-Centered Design Approach to Rap Back Integration

The MWBC team initially met with end users to determine how many tasks in the rap back process should be automated and how to exploit existing functionality to minimize the costs of implementing the rap back. The usability expert conducted in-depth interviews with department analysts, who would have primary responsibility for processing rap back information and with the program manager who is an expert in the business process and system. The state analysts demonstrated how they process State rap backs, and how the long-term care providers (facilities) are notified. They identified aspects of the process that were candidates for increased automation and made recommendations for improving the rap back process that included electronic delivery of rap sheets and automatic linking with existing system records.

The recommendations resulting from the interviews were incorporated into user interface requirements for the new functionality, as well as a high-level user interface specification document. The development team created a working prototype that incorporated the desired interaction design for the new rap back module. As the rap back functionality became available in the test system, the analysts were encouraged to test out various use scenarios; feedback was folded into the design in an iterative fashion. The usability expert also conducted an accessibility inspection of the new functionality, ensuring its compliance with Section 508 standards. Because of the attention given to the interaction design during the development process, very few adjustments were needed after the rap back module was released into production. This saved considerable time and financial resources. More importantly, patient safety has increased because unfit workers are immediately identified and removed from LTC facilities.

4   Rap Back Impact

While many employers rely on pre-employment background checks to screen workers, there are few options for conveniently monitoring the criminal activity of workers after the hiring process. Applicants whose criminal behavior is not apparent at the time of hire may continue to offend after they are employed. Because criminal history records are often updated, a pre-employment background check contains information that is outdated and doesn't convey the relative risk of abuse, neglect and financial exploitation of the elderly and disabled. Monitoring criminal activity through rap back provides employers with updated information that allows for informed hiring and employment decisions, especially for employees recently convicted. Self-reporting is often a requirement for maintaining licensure or certification, but is not a reliable method for obtaining knowledge of an increased risk associated with employees who actively engage in criminal activity. Since April 1, 2006, approximately 3,400 employees were found to be unfit for continued employment in Michigan's long-term care facilities due to felony or misdemeanor convictions for offenses involving abuse, neglect, assault, theft and illegal use of controlled substances. Through the successful implementation of the rap back, employers can take action to remove or reassign these workers in order to eliminate the opportunity to harm or exploit our most vulnerable citizens.

References

1. Post, L.A., Salmon, C.T., Prokhorov, A., Oehmke, J.F., Swierenga, S.J.: Chapter 6 - Aging and Elder Abuse: Projections for Michigan. In: Murdock, S.H., Swanson, D.A. (eds.) Applied Demography in the 21st Century, pp. 103–112. Springer Science and Business Media B. V. (2008) ISBN: 1402083289
2. Post, L.A., Swierenga, S.J., Oehmke, J., Salmon, C., Prokhorov, A., Meyer, E., Joshi, V.: The Implications of an Aging Population Structure. International Journal of Interdisciplinary Social Sciences 1(2), 47–58 (2006)
3. Department of Health and Human Services, Office of Inspector General: Nursing Facilities' Employment of Individuals with Criminal Convictions. Report OEI-07-09-00110 (March 2011)
4. Cooper, C., Selwood, A., Livingston, G.: The Prevalence of Elder Abuse and Neglect: A Systematic Review. Age and Ageing 37, 151–160 (2008)
5. Grant, G.: Safeguarding Vulnerable Adults Over the Life Course. In: Katz, J., Peace, S., Spurr, S. (eds.) Adult Lives: A Life Course Perspective, pp. 230–237. The Policy Press, Bristol (2012)
6. Swierenga, S.J., Choi, J.H., Post, L.A., Coursaris, C.: Public Health Communication Technology: A Case Study in Michigan Long-term Care Settings. International Journal of Interdisciplinary Social Sciences 1(5), 115–124 (2007)
7. Swierenga, S.J., Abujarad, F., Dennis, T.A., Post, L.A.: Real-World User-Centered Design: The Michigan Workforce Background Check System. In: Salvendy, G., Smith, M.J. (eds.) HCII 2011, Part II. LNCS, vol. 6772, pp. 325–334. Springer, Heidelberg (2011)
8. Galantowicz, S., Crisp, S., Karp, N., Accius, J.: Safe at Home? Developing Effective Criminal Background Checks and Other Screening Policies for Home Care Workers. AARP Public Policy Institute (September 2010)
9. Blumstein, A., Nakamura, K.: Redemption in the Presence of Widespread Criminal Background Checks. Criminology 47(2), 327–359 (2009)

Join the Ride!
User Requirements and Interface Design Guidelines
for a Commuter Carpooling Platform

Katrin Arning[1,*], Martina Ziefle[1], and Heike Muehlhans[2]

[1] Human-Computer-Interaction Center, RWTH Aachen University, Theaterplatz 14,
52062 Aachen, Germany
{arning,ziefle}@comm.rwth-aachen.de
[2] ivm GmbH (Integriertes Verkehrs- und Mobilitätsmanagement Region Frankfurt Rhein-Main), Lyoner Str. 22, 60528 Frankfurt am Main, Germany
h.muehlhans@ivm-rheinmain.de

Abstract. Carpooling might be a solution for maintaining mobility and reducing traffic problems of cities. In order to exploit the potential of carpooling for congested cities, to enhance the awareness of carpooling platforms among commuters and citizens, and to improve the interaction with existing carpooling web solutions, user-centered research methods (focus groups and usability analysis) were applied to understand the key motivators, acceptance barriers, and design requirements associated with carpooling platforms. The diversity of potential commuter platform users regarding age, gender, carpooling- and Internet expertise was also considered.

Keywords: carpooling, requirement analysis, focus groups, usability analysis, acceptance.

1 Introduction

Maintaining mobility of its residents is one of the key challenges for cities in the 21st century. The high significance of car-related mobility also applies for older drivers because they live in better health conditions which allow them to drive longer, and because they were socialized in the age of the "mobile lifestyle," in which driving a car stands for independence, freedom, and activity [1].

Due to decreasing numbers of people living in households, the high number of commuters who live in outskirts and want to reach their workplace, and due to the rising number of people living in cities, traffic problems such as congestion (especially during rush hours) and accidents are increasing. Further consequences of these traffic problems are increased traveling time, fuel costs, environmental pollution, and human health effects (e.g., asthma) [2].

---

* Corresponding author.

A. Marcus (Ed.): DUXU/HCII 2013, Part III, LNCS 8014, pp. 10–19, 2013.

Carpooling might be a solution for the mobility and traffic problems of cities. The concept of carpooling is two or more persons sharing a car trip with the passengers contributing to the driver's expenses and might be a solution for mobility problems of cities by increasing vehicle occupancy [3]. When used as a substitute for a private car, carpooling has the potential to reduce the number of private car owners. Moreover, carpooling might exert effects on mobility behavior [4].

Several web-based carpooling solutions were developed in recent years, enabling potential drivers and passengers to find and arrange shared vehicle journeys. Although carpooling is not a novel concept [5] - first formal carpooling systems were established in the 70ies during the "oil shocks" - the actual usage and awareness of carpooling platforms among commuters in Germany is still quite low. The biggest carpooling platform in Germany ("Mitfahrgelegenheit.de") has more then 4 million registered members with more than 14.000 arranged journeys per day. Other carpooling platforms (e.g., "Mitfahrzentrale," one of the first online carpooling platforms in Germany, founded in 1998) have approx. 800.000 members.

In order to exploit the potential of carpooling for congested cities, to enhance the awareness of carpooling platforms among commuters and citizens, and to improve the interaction with existing carpooling web solutions, user-centered research methods were applied to understand the key motivators, acceptance barriers, and design requirements associated with carpooling platforms. Since the workforce in Western societies is aging due to the demographic change, the diversity of potential commuter platform users regarding age, gender, carpooling- and Internet expertise was also considered.

2   Method

An empirical multi-method approach was applied in order to derive user requirements and interface design guidelines for a commuter carpooling platform.

1. A requirements analysis was conducted using the focus-group approach (n = 20), which elicited user requirements for mobility platforms, usage motives, and acceptance barriers.
2. A usability analysis of a web-based carpooling platform was carried out (n = 50), which assessed web-navigation performance (effectiveness and efficiency), user satisfaction, sources of usability problems, and allowed to derive design guidelines for web-based carpooling platforms.

2.1   Requirement Analysis

Focus Group Interviews. In order to elicit user requirements for mobility platforms, usage motives, and acceptance barriers, focus group interviews were carried out. Focus groups are a qualitative research method, which are predominantly used in opinion and market research. A selected group of people takes part in an organized group discussion in order to obtain information about opinions and experiences about a specific topic [6]. The underlying idea of focus groups is that the group interaction helps people to explore and express their opinions during the discussion by exchanging experiences and opinions, commenting on each other, and jointly developing new ideas and concepts.

Procedure. A total of four focus group interviews were carried out. The group composition was age-specific (two focus-groups with younger and two with older participants) in order to give older participants enough opportunity to articulate their wishes and expectations. The focus groups started with a round of introductions and participants were informed about the general goals of our study and about the procedure of the focus group sessions. Also, the interview guideline was presented and participants were asked to answer the screening questions. Applying the brain-writing-method, participants were then asked to write down personal statements regarding requirements, usage motives, and barriers of carpooling platforms on paper cards. Following that, the group of participants discussed their statements about carpooling platform usage. The moderator of the focus groups collected and visualized novel or additional statements.

The Sample. A total of n = 20 participants aged between 20 - 70 years took part (M=35.65, SD =14.60, 40% females). Since the commuter platform was web-based, we asked about Internet experience among the participants. All participants had Internet experience; the majority (85%) used the Internet on a daily basis (10% 2-3x per week, 5% less than once per week). Looking at different usage purposes, 65% used the Internet for online-shopping, 60% for online-banking, 80% for travel bookings, 95% for looking up timetable-information, and 100% for looking up information. According to that, we assume that our participants had at least sufficient Internet experience to be interviewed about web-based carpooling services. Asked about carpooling experience, 40% had at least some experience with web-based carpooling platforms. In order to study the impact of individual user factors, we used the ratings of carpooling experience and Internet experience in order to create two between-factors with the levels low vs. high experience (referred to as "novices" and "experts").

Data Analysis. Participants' card statements were collected, transcribed, and categorized. Data was analyzed by nonparametric tests. In order to investigate statistical interactions between user factors and requirements, ANOVAs were applied.

2.2   Usability Analysis

Procedure. A usability analysis of a web-based carpooling platform was conducted which supplemented the findings of the requirement analysis phase. The usability study started with a preliminary interview in which demographic data and computer experience were assessed. Following that, participants had to perform seven experimental tasks, which represented standard functionalities of carpooling platform usage. The order of tasks was kept constant and was presented in the following sequence:

- Task 1: Free Search for a ride, i.e., finding a driver for a pre-specified trip.
- Task 2: Registration in the carpooling platform as John/Jane Q. Public. All participants received standardized information about personal data for registration (name, telephone number, email-address).
- Task 3: Search for a lift, i.e., finding a driver for a pre-specified trip.
- Task 4: Search for a car passenger for a specified trip.
- Task 5: Placing an add for a lift, i.e., participants had to add additional details about their identity (gender, residency), their car, time and frequency of rides, and preferred car passengers.
- Task 6: Ride costs, i.e., looking up information about travel costs.
- Task 7: Deleting the registration.

After task completion, participants had to fill in a post-questionnaire which assessed users' satisfaction with carpooling system interaction ("1 = very high satisfaction" to "6 = very low satisfaction") and usability problems (on a rating scale with "1 = no problem at all" to "4 = severe problem"), and a follow-up-interview took place.

Participants' web navigation data was logged by using the program Morae ®(TechSmith) and the following usability measures were derived according to the ISO norm 9241 [7]. For task effectiveness, the percentage of successfully solved tasks was summed up. As efficiency measure the time needed to process the tasks was measured. Additionally, the perceived ease of use carpooling interface as well as usability problems were surveyed. One test session lasted approx. 1.5-2 hours.

The Sample. In total, 50 participants took part in the usability study. Mean age was M=45.6 (SD= 9.7) with 47.4 % females and 52.6 % males. In order to study age effects, a between factor "age group" was created with two groups, "younger adults" (aged 18-30) and "older adults" (aged 45-72). Asked about their education, 39.5% reported to have higher education entrance qualifications. Furthermore, 23.7% have the certificate of secondary education, 21.1% the general certificate of secondary education, 13.2% a university degree and 2.6% the advanced technical college entrance qualification. All participants had computer usage experience. The majority of the participants (81.6%) reported to use their computer "daily," 7.9 % use it "2-3 times a week" and 10.5% use the computer "less than once a week". Two thirds of respondents (63.2 %) rate PC usage as "very easy," 23.7 % as "easy," and 13.2 % as "a bit difficult." In comparison, the Internet is used "daily" by 73.7%, "2-3 times a week" by 13.2%, "weekly" by 5.3%, and "less than once a week" by 7.9% of the respondents. Half of the participants (55.3%) perceive Internet usage as "very easy", 36.8 % as "easy", 5.3 % as "a bit difficult" and 2.6 % as "very difficult". Asked about the recent use of carpooling network services, only 7.9% reported having experiences with carpooling services (92.1% do not have experiences). These respondents used carpooling networks far "less than once a week" and were "fairly satisfied" with it. Since the majority of the sample did not have carpooling experience, this factor was not included as a between-factor in statistical data analysis of the usability study.

Data Analysis. Data was analyzed by ANOVAs and t-tests for unrelated samples for interval-scaled data and nonparametric statistics (Mann-Whitney-Test) for ordinal-scaled data; the level of significance was set at alpha = 0.05.

3   Results

3.1   Requirement Analysis

In this section, the results concerning motivators and acceptance barriers of carpooling platform usage, differences in acceptance patterns according to individual factors as well as general requirements for web-based carpooling·platforms are presented.

Key motivators of carpooling platform usage were financial motives (fuel cost savings, M = 5.55, SD = 0.61) in contrast to social (conversations and company in the car, M = 4.35; SD = 0.75), ecological (ecological consciousness, reducing pollution, M = 4.20, SD = 1.47), or job-related motives (professional exchange and networking opportunities, M = 3.05, SD = 1.19) that played a minor role in explaining carpooling acceptance (Fig. 1).

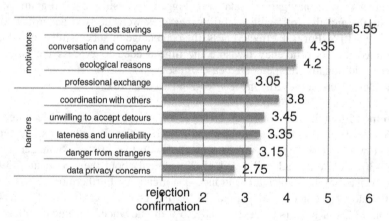

Fig. 1. Key motivators and barriers of carpooling service usage

As *key barriers* to carpooling platform usage we identified flexibility constraints (unwillingness to temporally coordinate with others (M = 3.8, SD = 1.4) or to accept detours (M = 3.5, SD = 1.4)). Further barriers such as lateness and unreliability, danger from strangers, and data privacy concerns received average ratings below 3.5, i.e., they were not perceived as barriers to carpooling service usage (Fig. 1).

The inclusion of *user factors* (age, gender, carpooling experience and internet experience) into the analysis revealed insightful differences in user-specific acceptance-patterns: Fuel cost savings were more important for male participants (M_{male} = 5.8, SD = 0.4, M_{female} = 5.1, SD = 0.6; F(1,9) = 8.77, p < 0.05), whereas female participants emphasized ecological advantages of carpooling (M_{male} = 3.9, SD = 1.6, M_{female} = 4.6, SD = 1.2; F(1,9) = 4.63, p < 0.1). Women also expressed a higher fear of strangers

(M_{male} = 2.6, SD = 0.9, M_{female} = 4, SD = 1.5; $F(1,9)$ = 7.24, p < 0.05) and higher concerns regarding the exposure of private data (M_{male} = 2.3, SD = 1.1, M_{female} = 4.5, SD = 1.3; $F(1,9)$ = 6.81, p < 0.05).

Moreover, ANOVAs revealed interactions between user requirements and interactions. The aspect of saving fuel costs was especially important for young carpooling experts, whereas this aspect was less important for older carpooling experts ($F(1,9)$ = 6.67, p < 0.05). A similar pattern was found for ecological advantages of carpooling: especially younger carpooling experts perceived ecological advantages as important, but this aspect was far less important for older carpooling experts ($F(1,9)$ = 11.13, p < 0.01). Regarding carpooling usage barriers we found that especially male participants were not willing to coordinate with others ($F(1,9)$ = 3.67, p < 0.1) or to accept detours during the ride ($F(1,9)$ = 3.98, p < 0.1). Interestingly, this finding was moderated by carpooling expertise: Carpooling experts were more flexible in accepting detours ($F(1,9)$ = 4.69, p < 0.1) and coordination efforts than novices ($F(1,9)$ = 5.11, p < 0.1).

Apart from motivators and barriers participants also discussed *general requirements* of carpooling platforms. Participants stated the following requirements:

  Costs:

- precise definition and high transparency of costs before the trip starts in order to prevent bargaining
- centrally organized invoice-service which issues an invoice about the trips on a monthly basis
- *Information on the carpooling web-interface regarding:*
- trip costs and cost calculation
- tax issues (e.g., tax deduction)
- insurance issues (e.g., liability for car accidents or delays)
- commuter etiquette (e.g., rights and duties of drivers and passengers, what to do in case of delays)
- *Service*
- document download with trip cost calculation information or informed consent regarding "joining the ride at own risk"
- link to route planner applications
- bonus system for frequent commuters
- rating system for friendly/unfriendly drivers
- parking discount or fuel vouchers
- road safety trainings
- more park and ride parking spaces
- *Security*
- personal data security is inevitable
- registration as prerequisite for carpooling service usage
- evaluation profile for carpooling members

To sum up, the requirement analysis revealed main motivators (fuel cost savings) and barriers (lack of flexibility regarding trip time or route coordination) of carpooling platform usage, which are important key levers when it comes to promoting and carpooling platform usage. Beyond, general expectations of potential carpooling users regarding costs, information, service, and security aspects were identified that should be considered in carpooling service design.

3.2   Usability Analysis

The following section reports users' general performance when interacting with the web-based carpooling platform and focuses on usability problems that were experienced by participants and related to task performance.

Task effectiveness: Participants successfully solved on average M = 4.2 (SD = 1.58) of six experimental tasks. A minority (2%) was not able to solve at least one task, 16% solved one task, 10% solved two tasks, 8% solved three tasks, five tasks were solved by 28% and 14% managed to solve all tasks successfully.

Task efficiency: Participants needed on average 17 minutes to solve the tasks (range 9 - 42 minutes). In comparison to the benchmark time of 3:31 minutes (when all tasks were consecutively solved by an expert), participants needed on average 14.30 minutes longer for carpooling platform interaction. These performance data results implicate that the interaction with the carpooling platform was neither highly effective nor efficient. This finding is corroborated by users' satisfaction ratings.

Satisfaction: Users' satisfaction was on average 2.57 (SD = 1.3), with ratings ranging from 2 – 5. In total, two thirds rated the interaction with the carpooling platform as "satisfying," but one third was not satisfied with the ease of use.

The inclusion of *users' age* revealed that older users achieved a lower task performance and faced significantly higher usability problems when using the carpooling web-interface (F(2,48) = 5.97, p < 0.00, Fig).

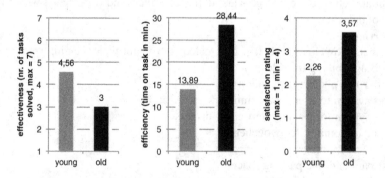

Fig. 2. Task performance (effectiveness and efficiency) and satisfaction ratings for younger and older users

Older users solved fewer tasks successfully (M = 3,0, SD = 2) in comparison to younger users (M = 4.6, SD = 1.2; F(2.48 = 6.17; p < 0.05), needed more time to work with the carpooling interface (M = 28.44 min., SD = 10.00) than younger users (M = 13. 9, SD = 3.3; F(2.48) = 37.76; p < 0.00) and reported a lower satisfaction

(M = 3.6, SD = 1.3) compared to younger users (M = 2.3, SD = 1.3; $F_{(2.48)}$ = 6.12; $p < 0.05$). Neither gender differences nor effects of the factor "Internet experience" were found for carpooling system interaction.

Based on users' experience of *usability problems* during carpooling system interaction, the most dominant usability problem was *navigational disorientation* using the web interface. Users reported that they lost orientation in the hypertext structure of the carpooling system (M = 3.2 on a scale with max. = 4, SD = 0.8), could not remember the location of specific functions (M = 2.4, SD = 0.7), had to navigate for a long time until they found the function they searched for (M = 3, SD = 0.7), and did not to know which navigation path to take within the carpooling system (M = 3,0, SD = 0.9). The second cluster of usability problems referred to *verbal labeling* issues in the carpooling interface. Users did not immediately understand the meaning of terms (M = 2.5, SD = 0.9) and perceived the naming of functions as incomprehensible (M=2.7, SD = 0.8). In contrast, *visual design* problems due to font size (M = 2.1, SD = 0.9), color (M = 1.8, SD = 0.7), or design element inconsistencies (M = 1.8, SD = 0.7) were not perceived to cause usability problems. Correlational analyses proved that task performance (effectiveness and efficiency) and user satisfaction were strongly influenced by disorientation and verbal labeling problems, but not by visual design issues (see Table 1).

Table 1. Bivariate correlations between task performance and satisfaction and usability problem indices (n = 50, ** = $p < 0.01$)

usability problems	effectiveness (no. of tasks solved)	efficiency (time on task)	satisfaction
disorientation	-.516**	.386**	.537**
verbal labeling	-.523**	0.262	.478**
visual design	0.233	-0.071	-0.072

4   Discussion

Understanding the preferences, attitudes, and user experiences of potential carpooling users is essential for the design and roll-out of successful web-based carpooling platforms which are one important measure in preventing traffic problems and gridlock in present and future urban environments. In the present study, user requirements, usability problems, and interface design guidelines were identified which led to a redesign of an existing web-based commuter carpooling platform. Moreover, the findings provide valuable input for marketing activities promoting carpooling activities.

4.1   User Requirements for Carpooling Platforms

The analysis of user requirements clearly showed that a rather small number of motives are involved in carpooling platform usage motivation. Motivators of carpooling service usage were rated higher than barriers, i.e., our participants were positively motivated and perceived more arguments for than against the using of a carpooling platform. Especially fuel cost savings were perceived as main advantage of carpooling usage. Accordingly, marketing activities should address this motive and emphasize the potential of fuel cost savings and carpooling platforms should contain a fuel cost savings calculator. The main argument against the use of a carpooling platform is the unwillingness to coordinate with others regarding departure time or trip route.

The requirement analysis also revealed that users distinctly differ in their motive patterns: Older participants reported a lower flexibility to adapt the trip time or route to other passengers' needs. Women put more emphasis on ecological advantages of carpooling platforms, but they expressed a higher fear of strangers and higher concerns regarding the exposure of private data. This shows that data security and privacy are highly sensitive topics in carpooling system design. One the one hand, users expect highest security standards in order to prevent personal data misuse, on the other hand, they also demand a high level of transparency and detailed explanations about which personal data is needed for which purpose.

Further requirements of potential users of carpooling platforms are extensive service functions, such as a cost calculator, an interactive map, a route planner, information regarding legal aspects and insurances. Moreover, potential users expect social media design components, i.e., a "commuter identity and community."

4.2   Usability Barriers and Design Recommendations for Carpooling Platforms

The usability analysis of a web-based carpooling platform showed that the majority of potential users was basically able to use core functionalities such as registration, looking for rides, or placing an add. However, reduced task performance and satisfaction – especially in older users - proved severe usability barriers in carpooling interface design. The assessment of usability problems allowed for an identification of the main causes of reduced system navigation performance.

The biggest usability barrier, navigational *disorientation* in hypertext structures, is a well-known problem [8]. Especially older users or those with restricted spatial abilities feel like getting lost in the hypertext structure and fail to successfully use the interface [9]. In the present study, older users also faced higher usability problems, which led to a reduced effectiveness, efficiency, and satisfaction when using the carpooling platform. Even younger users, who should represent the "best case" of a user group, did not reach perfect performance and satisfaction levels in the interface interaction. For a successful design of carpooling platforms we recommend *transparent search semantics and structures,* which follow the users' mental model. Interviews showed that users think first of trip route and destination (from A to B) when they use the carpooling platform before they think about roles as driver or passenger. Therefore trip offers should not be separated in trip offers and trip requests in the very beginning of the interaction process but the search task procedure should begin with finding and showing compatible trip profiles.

The second cluster of usability problems referred to *verbal labeling* issues. In order to promote a higher transparency of task steps and procedures, precise and clear verbal labels should be used which indicate the users' current position within a task sequence and within the overall system or hypertext structure. An example of an imprecise verbal label used in the carpooling platform is the link label "what carpoolers helps," which leads to information for calculating trip costs. Accordingly, verbal labels should be short, informative, and with keyword character in order to improve comprehensibility and system transparency.

The third usability barrier was related to *visual design factors*, which had – in comparison to the aforementioned barriers - less impact on carpooling system performance and satisfaction. One important factor is the spatial arrangement or coding of icons and buttons on the interface. When a user looks at a webpage, he/she not only perceives and encodes the content, but also the location of information or control elements on the webpage. When the user is searching for specific information, the user will assume to find similar information (e.g., horizontal or vertical arrangement of entry fields for route starting points and destination) at similar positions. In order to promote the recognition of information or control elements, the spatial location should remain constant. Further visual design aspects referred to animated banners and the use of colors, as especially older users reported a visual overload.

Acknowledgments. We owe gratitude to Oliver Sack, Jennifer Kabelitz, and Julia van Heek for research support.

References

1. Ball, K., Owsley, C.: Increasing Mobility and Reducing Accidents of Older Drivers. In: Schaie, K.W., Pietrucha, M. (eds.) Mobility and Transportation in the Elderly, pp. 213–250. Springer, Heidelberg (2000)
2. Levy, J.I., Buonocore, J.J., von Stackelberg, K.: Evaluation of the Public Health Impacts of Traffic Congestion: A Health Risk Assessment. Environ. Health 9, 65 (2010)
3. May, A., Ross, T., Grebert, J., Segarra, G.: User Reaction to Car Share and Lift Share Within a Transport "Marketplace". Intelligent Transport Systems 2(1), 47–60 (2008)
4. Meijkamp, R., Theunissen, R.: Car Sharing: Consumer Acceptance and Changes on Mobility Behavior Report. Netherlands, Delft University of Technology (1996)
5. Ben-Akiva, M., Atherton, T.J.: Methodology for Short-range Travel Demand Predictions: Analysis of Carpooling Incentives. Journal of Transport Economics and Policy 11, 224–261 (1997)
6. Krueger, R.A.: Focus Groups: A Practical Guide for Applied Research. Sage, Thousand Oaks (1994)
7. ISO - International Organization for Standardization: ISO 9241 - Ergonomic Requirements for Office Work with Visual Display Terminals (VDTs) (1998)
8. Kim, H., Hirtle, S.C.: Spatial Metaphors and Disorientation in Hypertext Browsing. Behaviour & Information Technology 14, 239–250 (1995)
9. Lin, D.-Y.M.: Age Differences in the Performance of Hypertext Perusal as a Function of Text Topology. Behaviour & Information Technology 22, 219–226 (2003)

SustainDesign – A Project with Young Creative People

Roby Attisano

DeSein – Design & Communication,
Messeplatz 1 Piazza Fiera , 39100 Bozen/Bolzano, Italy
roby@desein.it

Abstract. Roby Attisano and his team of „young creative minds" introduce their approach to the topic sustain design. After a period of long and intense work, two interesting and sustainable projects from two completely different areas emerged. The young students from the little North-Italian province of South Tyrol focused on sustainability in waste prevention issues and on consciousness-raising concerning gambling addiction. All work steps and developments on logos, campaigns, apps and much more will be presented hereinafter. Our main focus relied on interactivity, sustainability as well as the contact to other people. Answers to the question of all questions – „*can design contribute to sustainability?*" – were searched and possible solution processes were revealed.

Keywords: Sustain Design, Sustainability.

1 Sustain Design – A Project with Young Creative People

After I got to know Aaron Marcus during an education project in 2010, I met him in Berkeley in 2011 privately again.

I was reasoning with Aaron about „good" design and the challenges related to sustainability in the design industry. The discussion was sophisticated, passionate and highly inspiring. Problem-solving approaches, that should be studied and tested more precisely, came up. During that afternoon, a special connection developed between Aaron and me and at the end of our conversation he stated a unique invitation and said: „Roby, come to Las Vegas and make a guest speech at the DUXU 2013!"

For a graphic designer from South Tyrol like me, a golden opportunity: not only taking part, but also making a contribution to one of the world´s most important design conferences, is a great honor for me. It has filled me with pride, exitement and the will to accept this challenge. I´m also looking forward to exchange views and perceptions with my appreciated colleagues from around the globe. Since I don´t limit myself as a graphic designer in order to deal with all design disciplines and furthermore to share my knowledge with young students as a specialist teacher for design, the right topic of my speech was quite easy to define. I have decided against presenting one of my own projects. To me, it was of greater importance to include my

A. Marcus (Ed.): DUXU/HCII 2013, Part III, LNCS 8014, pp. 20–29, 2013.

students, so we have developed and elaborated this project together. The only input the students got from me was the main issue: Sustainable Design.

We live in a throwaway society. Far too often, things are created for disposable use only – but design can and has to do more. Good and modern design has to be sustainable. This task requires certainly more mental efforts and more courage in order to develop new approaches and to reveal new perspectives.

It didn´t take us too long to find the appropriate support for this forward-looking project at the academy, my colleagues from Marketing, German, English, 3D and Video realized the huge potential immediately. The project allows us a new and different way of teaching: theory and practice merge and powerful synergies with great learning potentials arise. The students learn theory through practice and testing. They also have to learn that mistakes are part of the learning process. In this way, the receptiveness of the young people is increasing many times over and the value of self-awareness for the acquisition of knowledge is getting more conscious. The fluent passages of the teaching subjects explain the necessity of „lateral thinking". I want to show the students, what it means to implement and accomplish a project with gut instinct, passion, capacity for suffering and endurance. They should experience, how versatile, also painful but in the end how satisfying our work as designers can be.

Shortly after the project started, the initial enthusiasm, passion and anticipation vanished. Self-doubts, difficulties in communication and concerns coursed through rapidly. The team dynamic was unbalanced and the energy of the working groups dwindled increasingly. Discussions have gone round in circles, achievements came to nothing and decisions were postponed more often.

Doubts and concerns spread amongst us teachers, who accompanied the project. Did we expect or demand too much from the group? Can they handle a project of this dimension at all? Very quickly it became clear, that the size and complexity of this project has been underestimated. This led to uncertainties and tensions.

The whole project evolved distressingly into a race against time. We always knew that our available time resources were limited, but we hoped, it would become a process with its own dynamics that leads the students to do extra work during their spare time and continue to work on the project. Unfortunately, this was not the case.

Piece by piece, through our decision support and assistance, we could regain the student´s confidence in themselves, the working groups and the project. We strengthened their faith in their own ideas and discussed the meaningfulness of those very same ideas. Step by step, we could finally archieve our common goal through hard work. Now and then we had the feeling of losing sight of our main focus, sustainability. But at some point we realized that we just had to take a closer look at the group in order to see that they were actually reflecting about sustainable considerations all the while. Their actions and designings were becoming increasingly sustainable. The students have definately changed for the better. Today they think and act more sustainable and affect their environment in a positive way.

Most certainly, we can´t affect the whole world with our projects and ideas, but we could prevail on eighteen students and six teachers to think, live and work in a more sustainable way and to let their environment conciously participate.

The students present their projects on the following pages themselves, only by this the text can remain honest and authentical. It´s about a well researched and demanding topic, though it´s no professional article in the proper sense. With this concept, the young students want to advance parts of their sustainability studies. They paid attention to a content-related structure and tried to ensure that the text leaves positive marks. In this sense I wish you all a lot of fun and sustainability while browsing in our projects.

Roby Attisano, grafic artist, South Tyrol

1.1   Why Sustainability?

Sustainability indicates the development, which is adjusted to the needs and requirements of today´s generations, without putting the satisfactions of needs of future generations at risk. The aim is to keep our planet as intact and sustained as possible for our posterity. Many large companies have a focus on these developments for years already and find thereby new ways for sustainable solutions. For us and our project, sustainability takes top priority within the scope of DUXU 2013. But we don´t want to keep it in mind for this brief moment of this presentation here in Las Vegas only. No!

We want to affect our future sustainably.

We want to raise awareness and galvanize.

We want to change views of people we can reach in the long term.

We want to leave traces, traces in the minds of people.

Traces that will not fade. Due to our individual diversities it was hard to agree on one single topic, so we decided to develop two different ones. We chose the subject areas **gambling addiction** and **environment.** Both topics are based on the main concept of Sustainable Design and will be developed in respect of sustainability.

1.2   What´s Wrong with Our Approach to Environment?

Just the thought of a world that has been destroyed and buried under huge piles of trash, a world, that has nothing in common with the planet we know and love anymore, makes us shiver.

Just the idea, that our grandchildren and great-grandchildren may not be able to see and experience the earth as we do, that they can no longer play outside, that they can´t see the sun and the sky anymore.

Just the thought, that our children can never drink water straight from the tab again and that tigers and bears are only known from books, makes us upset, but responsible at the same time. With every animal or plant species that becomes extinct, we bring nature a bit more out of balance. Our carelessness and wastefulness play, without any doubt, a big and shady part in this grave development. Every day, each and every one of us produces garbage. A sizeable part of this trash is only packaging material. So it seems that the thesis „ Garbage is nothing more than bad design" could come close to the truth in a sense. If we would be more mindful and conscious of reducing and decreasing our packaging materials, or if we would even find better ways how disposable packagings could be led to another, more sustainable purpose of use, we would have already archieved a reduction of future landfills. Each city and every community has to reconsider and rethink over and over again, from generation to generation, where our future garbage should be deposited or stored. But this is not as easy as it may seem. Waste storage is a very delicate issue, especially when you take sustainability into consideration. We definitely don´t want the next generation to build their homes on a contaminated landfill. Where garbage was deposited in the 1980ies, no clean water can seep into the ground any longer.

That leads, among other things, to a strong obstruction of the soil, with all its already known disadvantages for nature and environment. Furthermore, the redevelopment of old landfills causes huge and unavoidable financial expenditures. People in South Tyrol have realized decades ago that they have to find sustainable solutions to the waste problem. In our country it is self-evident by now that waste has to be disposed of separately. Glass, plastic, cans and paper are collected separately and recycled again. Organic waste can either be composted directly at home or brought to organic waste facilities, where for instance compost for the wholesale trade is being produced. Batteries and toxic waste is also collected separately.

In this way, „only" residual waste, which has to be incinerated or stored, remains. Any idea, where we shall put it in 20 years? For that reason sustainable waste disposal is already part of child education. We teach our children how to separate garbage properly and which garbage belongs in which garbage bin.

Parents, kindergardens and schools have been working hand in hand for years to improve the situation. „Garbage collection days" have been launched, where pupils and students from different communities and cities inspect hiking trails and other public spaces in order to pick up carelessly discarded trash.

Despite all this we see again and again, day after day, how much trash is carelessly discarded on the ground directly next to garbage containers, in the open countryside, or in places of silence and contemplation. Even in food stores you can watch how people rather pack each fruit or vegetable individually in plastic bags than to summarize and use fewer bags. Moreover, the packed goods are packed again.

Entrance areas of bars or office buildings are paved with regardlessly discarded cigarette butts. On hiking trails you can find garbage bags and used tissues.

If monthly a hundred people pass a resting spot for hikers, at least a hundred tissues lie there at the end of the month and already 1.200 at the end of one year. Why does everyone think, he or she is the only one who tosses a tissue to the ground? Waste collection areas and likewise the trash cans themselves would need a redesign. They should be located within easy reach and could be designed more attractiv in order to reverse the image.

People should love to go to waste collection areas, they shouldn´t be disgusted by old, dirty containers. The friendlier a collection area appears, the more likely people would go there and use it in order to dispose of garbage sustainably and properly. We are living in a fast moving time in the middle of a consumption-focused society. Nevertheless, each and everyone of us can contribute in helping designers find new, sustainable ways regarding product packaging issues. Usually it takes just a few steps to reach the nearest trash can and a simple handgrip ensures that the world is a bit longer the way as we know it today.

2   The Project "Each One Teach One"

2.1   The Situation in South Tyrol

In South Tyrol, waste has been collected and disposed of seperately for decades already. Appropriate educational efforts happen from an early age. But despite all that, it´s alarming to see what`s happening in our school alone: The schoolyards are often littered with trash after the breaks and incorrectly discarded garbage can be found in the provided trash bins every day. Student´s behaviors in dealing with garbage must be described as careless and apathetic. Many students just chuck everything, that is no longer needed, to the ground instead of bothering to dispose of the trash correctly only a few meters further. This thoughtlessness can be watched almost everywhere and it´s a cross-generational phenomenon. Everybody knows the right behavior pattern, no matter if you´re young or old.

Is it a question of laziness or indifference?

2.2   Our Aim

We decided to implement the project in a sustainable and social way. Everyone should be able to participate actively and give each other hints and ideas for a proper waste handling and also for protecting our planet. Our concept is about constantly sharing advices and ideas, where the students learn from each other instead of being consciously instructed. In this way we hope and expect that they are willing to reflect on their behavior pattern. We want to provide the opportunity for everyone to contribute with ideas, thoughts and opinions as an inspiration to others. This approach increases the participation rate. Our effort is to make this topic tempting for the people. With little effort and in small steps we are able to preserve the world for our posterity. We are confident that it would make sense to redesign waste collection areas. The idea is to make them more attactive. Due to the anticipation of redesigning these areas, through a possible interaction, we could even convince reluctant persons that sustainable waste separation can be fun.

2.3   Research and Planning

In order to perceive all difficulties concerning our issue, we have observed and analyzed the behavior of our students in dealing with waste. We talked to people from different age groups, how they deal with garbage. In order to design our print products and implement our actions, we want to make shure that the appearance is exceptional, fresh and modern. For a period of three months we collected the garbage that was improperly disposed of at our school and documented these misconducts. The installation of a „garbage road" should make the students conscious of how much trash accumulates immediately, though there are plenty of trash bins standing by for a proper waste disposal at every turn. For now the garbage road was solely realized at our school, but it could be extended to public spaces any time. The garbage road arouses attention, provokes and offers space for actions and reactions. In this way we will get the chance to share information in order to start an exchange of ideas. The whole thing could be based on the principle of the famous parlor game „Chinese whispers": „Did you already know...and spread the information!" A big challenge is the age limit: everyone learns from one another. No matter, how old the person is, wether eight or eighty years old – everybody can learn something from the other. In this way, we as designers are greatly challenged. Our design, the content and all relevant information must be structured and designed in a way, that they are applicable to all age groups. Keeping the participant´s inhibition level low or offering them an enticement in order to get them involved, is another principle. We want to touch people´s hearts, address them and evoke something in them. „Each one teach one" relies on learning with and from each other. We asked two members of „Be the Change", that´s a group of people who put themselves out for an environmentally sustainable, socially equitable and meaningful existance on this planet, to perform a „wake up call" with us. We believe, the uniqueness of our project lies in the fact that we give each individual the opportunity to participate and to learn from each other. We support our project with video and audio recordings to capture the developments and to document our work.

2.4   Our Problem-Solving Approaches

We also use social networks for the project, where we have the opportunity to create a place of exchange and get-together. The participants come together in these networks and share their experiences. For younger audiences we focused on garbage recyling by building useful objects.

For a coherent look we developed a campaign logo, whose principal element is the geometric shape of a triangle. The rarely used triangle increases the logo´s potential of attention clearly, because it is in contrast to the common rectangular and circular shapes. It stands for stability and durability. Our triangle has rounded edges, that distinctly underlines the positive signal effect.

Our triangle points to the right, which is equivalent to „forward". Firstly, this has a positive effect on the viewer and additionally it arouses the association with a start button, the PLAY button that we can find on technical devices. This association gives our logo triangle a powerful meaning. It stands for the beginning of a new future, the start of becoming a society of health and sustainability. This signal effect gives us the feeling of something is not ending here, something is starting. It builds on our goal of „spreading the word" and invites to participate. Our campaign logo consists of six colours. We have deliberately included two green tones. The colour green occurs in all shades and variants in nature and has an additional beneficial effect. In the traffic light system, green means „go ahead" and signifies the permission to take off. This brings us one step closer to our „start button". Our researches have shown that in America the colour green is hardly used in advertisements. That surprised us a lot because in Italy many use this color in order to appear more green-minded and eco-sensitive. Besides: Green is also the colour of hope.

In order to persuade people, especially young people, to commit themselves to environmental issues, we need to attract their attention. On the basis of this perception we have initiated the garbage road campaign „glorious mess". Several projects related to the topic „touching arts"followed. The viewer can see, feel, touch and comprehend art that is made from recycled materials. One idea and example are our „bottle pictures". We construct mobile walls in school buildings, on which different kinds of bottle caps are fixed. The students can screw their empty bottles onto these walls. Through the different shapes, colors and sizes constantly new and ever-changing pictures emerge. Discussions, actions and reactions result from this initiative.

Special theme installations can be created. In gastronomical facilities for instance these bottle pictures could symbolize forks or a chef´s hat. Action, participation and creativity of all participants will be included and utilized. Another approach will be furniture design. The students miss additional seating possibilities in school´s hallways and recreation rooms. There is also a shortage of coat racks and the garbage containers could be more appealing. We want to dabble ourselves in furniture designing in order to find ways to produce these items from recyclable materials.

3   Why Is Compulsing Gambling Dangerous?

Gambling, in other words: playing on computers or with gaming consoles, is contemporary and omni-present for us young people. Nowadays, we are used to have access to the internet and to online games everywhere and anytime, the choice of games has become incalculable. At the beginning, most of the people just play for the fun of it. Then they become ambitious and play with increasing frequency. Today we go less often a football field to work off, we rather sit at home alone at our computers to spend hours on the alleged relaxing.

More and more people start to play for money at some point. The sums, which are gambled away on a single day, are alarming. Monthly salaries are quite often gambled away in just half an hour. At this moment, the players don´t think about their living expenses. What happens when the first negative effects set in? When we started our researches, we found out that this issue is ubiquitous and hotly debated at the moment. Headlines like „Ban on slot machines in bars" or „Ex-gambling addict writes book about her experiences" dominate the local press. The human need for security is understandable and comprehensible. Money provides security. According to that, the multiplication of money has top priority. The more money you accumulate, the more you consider yourself save. In these efforts, many people slide into addiction. „Game over" doesn´t always mean that it´s over, it´s much more an invitation to continue playing. You want to prove yourself that you´re not a loser. The losing streak must at some point become a winning streak. Big profits attract attention. People very often don´t just lose their hard earned money, they don´t shy away from raising a credit. Then the debt trap snaps shut. Gamblers mostly act in secret, don´t tell anyone about their debts and want to regain control without the help of others. Gambling addiction reaches the climax when family members and friends being robbed in order to finance the addiction.The secret-mongering leads to social isolation. Gambling addicts seclude themselves and want to solve the problems, which are not really problems for them, alone. They start to neglect their families and friends, though they surely know that social contacts provide stability in life. Friends and family can help when live becomes difficult. The characters from computer games can´t be of any help when you´re in trouble. None of these virtual friends comforts you or takes you by the hand, no slot machine claps you on the shoulder, cheers you up or pulls you out of your depression.

Playing is a part of live, a part of growing up. Through learning by playing, children and young adults grasp a lot of what they need later on. Playing with other individuals is an important part of human development, it strengthens us in our social skills and increases self-confidence. In recent years, digital games and game consoles for kids and teenagers have been spreading like wildfire. Today kids don´t play „cowboys and indians" or run around in the woods to collect pine cones anymore.

Doubtful about this development is the fact that digital games must be played most often alone and undisturbed. The teenagers lose their contact to the outside world and neglect their social contacts. Even the perception of time is distorted heavily, so they increasingly lose track of time. Playing on the computer for hours and days is the negative outcome. While kids previously had to go home from the playground at nightfall, today´s games don´t require any natural time limits.

We want to inspire young people to spend less time playing computer games or slot machines, we want them to spend more time with real people. We don´t want them to throw away their lives or to neglect their families and friendships. We want them to change their attitude to live. We want to advise them against addiction and underline the importance of dealing with real people in a real world.

4   Plato´s Allegory of the Cave and Gambling Addiction

When we exchanged views with Martin Osen about gambling addiction in combination with shadows, he told us about the well-known „allegory of the cave". The shadow, equal to a dark companion, that symbolizes gambling addiction, reminds strongly of Plato´s allegory of the cave. Human beings, who live in constant darkness, merely perceive their own shadows. Everything else is unreal and wrong for them.

Their behavior pattern reminds us of gambling addicts who are detached from reality. The shadow becomes their reality. With the idea of an abstract world, Plato refers to people´s narrowmindedness, obstinacy and credulity. In this „parallel world", addiction becomes reality, and people who live in this illusory world, become the shadow of their former self.

5   The Shadow Project

5.1   The South Tyrolean Situation

Many people spend most of their leisure time with gambling on vending machines or with playing computer games, they waste valuable time they rather could spend with their family or friends. The numbers of recently diagnosed gambling addicts and people at risk for addiction in our country are constantly increasing. This disease is still declared taboo and nobody likes to talk about it publicly. Compared with alcohol or drug addiction, you hardly find any educational material concerning gambling addiction. This addiction is hardly accepted and often takes place in secret. Affected people keep silent, because they refuse to believe the problem for a long time and feel ashamed later on. We are sure that these factors facilitate the addiction.

5.2   Our Goal

We want to address young people in order to keep them from using slot machines or money-guzzlers to spend more time with their families and friends. They should realize that they need their social contacts like the air we breath. Friends and family give us wonderful moments, safety and security. In the long term fortune and happiness most likely can be found within family and friends. Kids should know, that temperate playing is allright and beyond dispute, but they shouldn´t forget about their social environment.

5.3   Research and Planning

Besides theoretical researches in books and newspapers we took to the streets with open eyes and open ears. We sat in bars and casinos, whatching people´s approach to both, machines and human beings around them. I remember the incident in the middle of the night, when I saw a young mother gambling on a slotmachine while her five year old daughter was sitting next to her half asleep just waiting to go home…we see clearly that social responsability must be the key to success.

Parallel to the attitude survey we began to examine different light sources and locations. We wanted to find out how shadows of different light sources really look like and which influencing factors have an effect on the intensity and shape of the shadow. It shows that space has an enormous influence on shadows, shadows cannot exist without space. Shadows can adapt themselves to space, no matter if it´s open or confined space and which building materials were used. We tried to understand how light, shadows and space are related to each other in order to work with these components purposefully. After we had finished our studies, we began to illustrate shadows analogously and digitally. We experimented with various shapes and combinations. We printed digital templates, cut them into shape and produced stencils that are suitable for shadow theatres. Then we tried to find suitable light sources, which could be used by everyone and everywhere to cast shadows by the help of our stencils. We noticed that the daylight was not ideal for casting shadows, the light was too scattered and the stencils were too small. Various lamps were out of the question, who constantly carries around a torch?

Just when we wanted to discard the idea of casting shadows, we spotted the flash on one of our cellphones. We experimented around and lastly found the optimal solution: Today, almost every cellphone has an integrated flash. Our target groups have their cellphones always within reach and could easily cast shadows with their integrated flashes and appropriate stencils.

In support of the recognition value we created a campaign logo. This logo will be placed on all advertising materials and serves as a mark simultaneously. The logo consists of shadows, which are arranged according to the golden grid system. No logo illustration is identical to another, in that way the logo stays in motion and looks exciting and interesting. Players demand varieties, which we provide them in order to get them interested in our project. All logo illustrations have similarities that ensure recognition. They are all quadratic and the colour scheme, that consists of dark colours, black and white, also remains steady. The logo lettering „The Shadow" runs through all illustrations and always stays in the same font and font colour.

5.4   Our Problem-Solving Approaches

As a particular implementation, we have thought of shadow plays that will be implemented analogously. In this way, stencils, memory cards and classical games, that were formerly played by two people very often, emerged. On all these advertising materials, information on gambling addiction can be placed discreetly in order to inform about the disease. Thereby we firstly cause a debate about gambling addiction and secondly, we ensure that two people can spend time together playing a haptic game. We have to assume that gambling hall operators and bar owners will have little interest in supporting our campaign against gambling addiction. Therefore we have to operate publicly in order to gain people´s attention. Public areas around gambling facilities would be perfect for spreading the information.

Currently we are working on the idea to project real shadows of passers-by with the help of strong light sources onto the street. Next to it, the passers-by should read a catchphrase like „Take a picture with your shadow" and at the same moment we inform about our campaign.

In the digital scope we create an app to detect the severity of the addiction. The users should declare, how many hours they played and how much money they won or lost. Based on these data, the app generates the appearance of a shadow. The higher the numbers are, the more demonic the shadow appears. If the numbers are low and the user gambles less, the shadow gradually returns to its natural shape.

Using Virtual Reality to Examine Hazard Perception in Package Design

Hande Ayanoğlu[1,2], Francisco Rebelo[1,3], Emília Duarte[1,4],
Paulo Noriega[1,3], and Luís Teixeira[1,3]

[1] Ergonomics Laboratory, Faculdade de Motricidade Humana, Universidade Técnica de Lisboa.
Estrada da Costa, 1499-002 Cruz-Quebrada, Dafundo, Portugal
[2] IDEAS, Dipartimento di Industrial Design, Ambiente e Storia, Seconda Università degli Studi
di Napoli, Aversa (CE), Italy
[3] CIPER – Interdisciplinary Center for the Study of Human Performance, Universidade Técnica
de Lisboa. Estrada da Costa, 1499-002 Cruz-Quebrada, Dafundo, Portugal
[4] Unidcom, IADE, Creative University, Av. D. Carlos I, 4, 1200-649 Lisbon, Portugal
hande.ayanoglu@gmail.com, emilia.duarte@iade.pt,
{frebelo,pnoriega,lmteixeira}@fmh.utl.pt

Abstract. Informing users about the correct hazard level associated with products can be one of the most important measures to help promote user safety while they handle hazardous household chemicals. The aim of this paper is to present pilot study's results about the effectiveness of using a VR-based methodology to examine the influence of a container's features (e.g., shapes) on the users' perception of hazardousness. Previous works have mostly used 2D drawings for this type of study. Issues which may compromise the quality of future experiments: e.g., adequacy of VR devices, interaction quality, simulator-sickness, procedure and quality of the instruments (i.e., questionnaires) are discussed. Despite the fact that the key experiment has not yet been completed, very promising results have been obtained, suggesting that the VR simulator and the methodology adopted may provide a successful evaluation of the packages' hazardousness.

Keywords: Package Design, Virtual Reality, Virtual Prototyping, Hazard perception.

1 Introduction

Although extensive research on packaging has been conducted in the fields of marketing [1–4], product and graphic design [5–8], little attention has been given, in the field of Ergonomics [9–11], to the packages' power to induce safe human behaviors (e.g., to read a warning before handling an object).

This study is concerned with packages for household hazardous liquids. If packages of household products are poorly designed, users may make wrong assumptions about their contents, and therefore, may not perceive the real level of hazard while interacting with it. Furthermore, it is not realistic to assume that it is possible to design-out all hazards from all the packages.

A. Marcus (Ed.): DUXU/HCII 2013, Part III, LNCS 8014, pp. 30–39, 2013.
© Springer-Verlag Berlin Heidelberg 2013

According to a User-Centered Design approach, in order to ensure that the users' abilities and needs are considered in the design process since the earlier stages of development, the potential users must be actively engaged in the design process [12, 13]. Prototyping offers the potential user the opportunity to observe and examine different product alternatives, with diverse levels of detail, and then compare them with the defined requirements. There are two forms of prototyping that are commonly used [14]: physical and virtual prototyping. With physical prototypes, users can feel the products' weight, as well as differentiate textures and temperatures, among other properties. However, physical prototypes may take a long time to be produced, the materials used might not be the same as in the final product and a new prototype must be built for each modification, which makes it an expensive procedure. This does not happen with virtual prototyping, since most changes (e.g., shape, color, texture) are easily achievable in a virtual object. Conversely, due to technological limitations, virtual prototypes do not yet allow users' to sense the products' physical properties in a realistic manner.

Most of the previous studies about packages used 2D drawings or pictures to express the shape of a package's taste (e.g., [15]), to express a visual form's scent or sound (e.g., [16]) or to analyze if shapes and colors influence hazard perception (e.g., [11, 17]). However, since 2D drawings cannot show all the objects' details, users may get a wrong impression. A Virtual Reality (VR) simulation can be an effective way to present scenarios that facilitate effective interaction between users and products [18]. In this manner, the observation of 3D virtual prototypes may be more effective than 2D drawings, and also increase a study's validity.

As such, VR could be used to visualize the 3D prototypes. For that, some criteria need to be followed to ensure the best simulation quality. In this study, the first criterion considered was the easiness to discern the details of the 3D prototypes. Other criteria were that participants should be able to easily observe the packages, as well as freely navigate in the Virtual Environment (VE). The VE should be presented in stereoscopy in order to provide the participant with depth information. The participant needs to be in control of what they want to observe (possibility to navigate and change their point of view in the VE). The task that participants need to fulfill inside the VE should not be so complex that it prevents them from replying verbally to questions while they are interacting with the VE.

Considering all these criteria, the purpose of this study was to examine the feasibility and adequacy of a VR-based methodology to study the influence of packages' features (i.e., shape) on the users' perception of hazardousness when exposed to diverse household packages with chemical substances.

2   Method

2.1   Design of the Study

This study used a within-subjects design. The measure of interest was the VR-based methodology's feasibility and adequacy according to the criteria that were defined.

Additionally, measures regarding the simulation (i.e., if participants can observe the packages from different viewpoints, walk freely in the VE), the interaction with the equipment (e.g., 3D glasses, mouse), instruments (i.e., verbal questionnaire) as well as simulator sickness, were collected through a follow-up questionnaire.

2.2   Sample

The sample consisted of 10 undergraduate students (5 males and 5 females), ranging in age from 18 to 24 years old (mean age = 21.6, SD = 1.5 years) from the Technical University of Lisbon, Portugal.

2.3   Experimental Settings and Virtual Environment

A Lightspeed DepthQ 3D Video Projector presented the VE with the 3D prototypes. The virtual prototypes were designed using Rhinoceros and then exported to Unity. MacNaughton Inc's APG6000 shutter glasses were used to see the VE in stereoscopy. Participants were free to visually explore the prototypes by navigating in the VE using a mouse. Pressing the left button of the mouse allowed the participants to move forward and the right button to move backwards. By completely moving the mouse, the participants were able to control their point of view.

The projected image size was 1.72m (horizontal) by 0.95m (vertical) with an aspect ratio of 16:9. The observation distance between the screen and the participant was 1.50 m, resulting in a 35.2° of a vertical field-of-view (FOV) and 59.7° of a horizontal FOV. Participants remained standing during the experiment. The researcher stood with the participant inside the room, which was darkened to prevent any external light interference. There was no sound in the VE.

The VE was a closed room, measuring 6.6m by 6.6m, containing a table (260 cm length, 30 cm depth and 90 cm height) in the middle. The packages were placed on the table standing 20 cm away from each other. When the simulation began, the participant's view was as if they were standing 1m away from the table. Each package was associated to a letter, from A to H, so that their identification was easier and accurate.

2.4   Procedure

Participants were asked to sign an informed consent form before starting the experiment. Subsequently, the researcher explained how the equipment and the experiment worked.

Before the test, participants became familiarized with the VR devices and the task by practicing in a training VE, which was similar to the one to be used for the experiment, but with 3D geometrical objects being displayed instead of packages. After they declared they felt able to do the test, the experimental session began. At this point the researcher stressed that they could stop the experiment at any time without any prejudice. After the experimental session, the participants were given a follow-up questionnaire. More detailed information about the training and the experiment are as follows:

Training. Participants were placed in a training VE so that they could familiarize themselves with the equipment and the task. The training VE was a closed room where different 3D objects (e.g., sphere, cylinder, cone, cube) were located on a table. The researcher asked the participants to observe the 3D objects, and then informed them that they could walk around the table. While observing the 3D objects, the participants were asked to verbally reply to the researcher's questions. If they were able to accomplish the task (examine the 3D objects and reply to the questions without showing any signs of simulator sickness) they were considered able to do the experiment.

Experiment. In the experimental stage, participants were given a scenario and a task before the simulation started. As such, the cover story used and the task, were as follows:

Cover Story.
Imagine that your friend is moving to a new house and he/she asks you to help unpack and to organize liquid household products' packages according to their level of hazard (e.g., how poisonous can the content be when drunk, how toxic can it be when inhaled, or how irritant/harmful can it be if it comes into contact with skin).

Task.
Observe the packages and reply to the questions.

When the simulation started, eight containers were presented on a table, as depicted in Figure 1. Participants were asked to observe the packages and to reply orally to the researcher's questions (the researcher took notes of the answers).

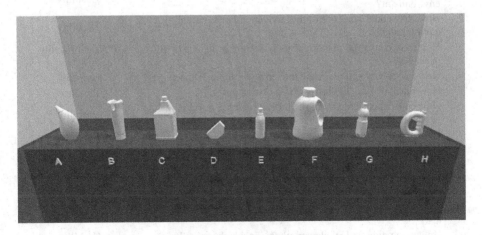

Fig. 1. Screen shot of the VE

2.5   Measures

In the present study, a two parts questionnaire was used. The first part, which was to be responded immediately after observing the prototypes, intended to evaluate the influence of the packages' features on the perception of hazard. The questions were adapted from the questionnaire that was developed by Wogalter and colleagues [11, 19]. There were 6 questions as shown in Table 1, divided equally into two sets: package selection and package rating. There were two different kinds of questions to check if the participants were able to verbally reply to them. On the package selection set, participants had to select one package out of the eight packages. On the package

Table 1. Questionnaire Part I

	Selection Questions
1.	Based on the shape of the package, which one do you think has the most hazardous contents?
2.	Based on the shape of the package, which one do you think is the most hazardous package?
3.	Based on the shape of the package, which one do you think has the most hazardous content when children enter in contact with it?
	Rating Questions
4.	Based on the shape of the package, how familiar are you with this package?
5.	Based on the shape of the package, how hazardous would it be to drink its contents?
6.	Based on the shape of the package, how cautious would you be when handling this package?

Table 2. Questionnaire Part II

	Questions	Category
1.	How easy could you control the point of view in the virtual environment?	Usability
2.	How easy could you control the navigation in the virtual environment?	Usability
3.	How easy could you explore/visually search the details of 3d packages?	Physical Fidelity
4.	How easy could you associate the letters with the 3D packages?	Usability
5.	How much did the 3d glasses cause distraction?	Presence
6.	How conscious were you of the mouse presence during the simulation?	Usability
7.	How much did the mouse cause distraction?	Presence
8.	How much did the shadows of the packages cause difficulty on observing details of the packages?	Physical Fidelity
9.	Were you able to concentrate in the questions asked instead of being concentrated on the interaction devices?	Performance
10.	How easy was to reply the questions asked verbally during the test?	Performance
11.	How much did you feel claustrophobic inside the room?	Usability

rating set, participants were requested to rate the 8 packages, according to the three questions, using a 9-point Likert type scale [20], with 0 indicating the minimum quantity and 8 indicating the maximum of the dimension.

The second part consisted of a written questionnaire, shown in Table 2, asking to rate issues related to the quality of the participants' interaction with the equipment (e.g., 3D glasses, mouse), instruments (i.e., verbal questionnaire) as well as simulator-sickness in a Likert type scale. The first eleven questions used a 7-point Likert type scale: (1) very easy/low/little to (7) very hard/high/much; whereas questions about simulator-sickness had a 4-point scale: (1) absent, (2) slight, (3) moderate and (4) severe.

The questions were created according to these categories: physical fidelity (how well the VE emulates the real world), usability of VE and interaction devices, performance of the participant (accomplishment of the task), presence (whether the participant was distracted with the equipment) and simulator-sickness [21].

3   Results

3.1   Questionnaire Part I – Package Evaluation

According to the results, it can be seen that all the participants were able to reply orally to all of the questions, while they were interacting with the VE.

Selection Questions. The frequency distribution for each package that was chosen, across the three selection questions, is depicted in Table 3.

Packages that were most often perceived as having the most hazardous content (Question 1) were packages F, C and H. In what regards the most hazardous package itself (Question 2), the three most chosen packages were F, D and E. Surprisingly, package F was not perceived as containing a hazardous substance for children (Question 3). In this context, the packages most chosen were C, B and E, while packages A and G were never chosen as being the most hazardous.

Table 3. Frequency distribution of packages selection across questions

	Packages							
	A	B	C	D	E	F	G	H
Question 1	0 (0%)	0 (0%)	3 (30%)	0 (0%)	1 (10%)	4 (40%)	0 (0%)	2 (20%)
Question 2	0 (0%)	0 (0%)	1 (10%)	2 (20%)	2 (20%)	3 (30%)	0 (0%)	1 (10%)
Question 3	0 (0%)	2 (20%)	3 (30%)	1 (10%)	2 (20%)	0 (0%)	0 (0%)	1 (10%)

Rating Questions. The mean ratings and standard deviation, for the rating questions, are shown in Table 4.

The data show that the three most familiar packages (Question 4) were G, F and E, while the less familiar were A, H and D. Regarding ingestion hazard (Question 5) packages C, F and B elicited high hazard ratings, while packages D, E and G elicited

Table 4. Mean ratings and standard deviation (SD) for the three questions across packages

	Packages							
	A	B	C	D	E	F	G	H
Question 4	2.50 (2.16)	2.60 (2.87)	5.60 (2.01)	0.30 (0.64)	6.80 (1.60)	7.30 (1.19)	7.40 (1.50)	0.80 (0.75)
Question 5	5.00 (2.24)	5.40 (1.80)	7.00 (1.55)	4.20 (2.18)	3.10 (2.88)	6.10 (2.81)	2.30 (3.52)	5.00 (2.57)
Question 6	5.30 (2.61)	4.10 (2.07)	5.90 (2.21)	4.70 (1.55)	2.70 (2.24)	5.40 (2.94)	1.70 (2.28)	5.30 (2.28)

low hazard ratings. The packages perceived as having high level of hazard when handled were C, F and A, while packages B, E and G had a lower relation with handling packages

3.2   Questionnaire Part II – Simulation Evaluation

The results of the second part of the questionnaire, according to the categories defined, are shown in Table 5 and Table 6.

Table 5. Mean ratings and standart deviation for the subjective questions regarding simulation

Question	1	2	3	4	5	6	7	8	9	10	11
Mean	2.20	2.70	2.70	1.40	1.70	3.00	1.50	1.40	5.50	3.10	1.30
(SD)	(1.08)	(1.00)	(1.35)	(0.92)	(0.64)	(1.18)	(0.50)	(0.66)	(1.75)	(1.22)	(0.64)

Note 1. The response format was a 7-point Likert type scale, from 1 to 7. Lower means are better except for the question 9.

Table 6. Mean ratings and standart deviation for simulator-sickness conditions

	Conditions				
	Mean	(SD)		Mean	(SD)
Generalized Indisposition	1.1	(0.3)	Difficulty in concentrating	0.5	(0.5)
Tiredness	0.2	(0.4)	"Heavy head"	0.4	(0.9)
Headache	0.2	(0.4)	Blurry vision	0.4	(0.49)
Eyestrain	0.7	(0.64)	Open eyes dizziness	0.1	(0.3)
Difficulty maintaining focus	0.3	(0.46)	Closed eyes dizziness	0.2	(0.4)
Increase in salivation	0.1	(0.3)	Vertigo	0.0	(0.0)
Sweat	0.0	(0.0)	Abdominal discomfort	0.0	(0.0)
Nausea	0.2	(0.4)	Burp	0.0	(0.0)

Note. The response format was a 4-point Likert type scale, from 1 to 4.

By analyzing the data according to category it is possible to see that for physical fidelity, participants felt that it was easy to distinguish the packages' features (Question 3), and that the presence of shadows did not cause difficulty in distinguishing such features (Question 8).

For the usability category, the point of view (Question 1) and navigation (Question 2) were found easy to control. Participants were also able to easily match the letters with the packages (Question 4) and they did not feel claustrophobic inside the VE (Question 11). An almost average number of participants claimed that they were aware of mouse presence (Question 6).

Considering the data gathered for performance questions, participants were able to concentrate on the questions that were asked while they interacted with the devices (Question 9). At the same time, participants considered that they could verbally reply to the questions that were asked during the simulation (Question 10).

According to the presence category, the distraction caused by the mouse (Question 5) and 3D glasses (Question 6) were low during the simulation.

Finally, regarding simulator-sickness (see Table 6), participants reported a minimal level of sickness symptoms. Possible explanations for this could be because the experiment made use of a large screen projection instead of head-mounted display, the reduced dimensions of the VE, as well as its low level of visual complexity, reduced motion of users and objects, the simple task to be performed, and the short amount of time spent inside the VE [22].

4 Conclusion

Measurement of users' perceptions of packages' hazardousness can be limited by methodological constraints, such as the extent to which the experimental scenario mimics real-world situations. Virtual Environments (VE) can be used as research tools to avoid such limitations. In this context, this paper presents a pilot study concerning Virtual Reality (VR) adequacy/feasibility to examine the influence of packages' shape on the users' perception of hazardousness.

It is important to note that, unlike previous studies, which used 2D drawings, the data presented here was gathered from 3D virtual prototypes observed in a VE. Due to the details that cannot be seen in 2D drawings, users may get a wrong impression about the packages' correct shape. Thus the use of 3D prototypes in VR could enhance the packages' perception due to several factors such as: details, stereoscopic view, perspective actualization, navigation in the environment and presence.

The results attained in this pilot study, indicate that participants were able to make a perceptual judgment of the 3D packages' hazardousness, as well as to evaluate their level of familiarity. Considering a specific example, Package G (a water bottle) was rated as the most familiar package from the set and, at the same time, the one with the less hazardous content.

Responses to the simulation quality assessment questionnaires indicate that the VR-devices and the VE used in the experiment did not negatively affect task performance. Participants did not report they were distracted by the presence of the interaction devices, nor an increased difficulty in using them to perform the task. The visual inspection of the packages was easy and accurate enough to the required level of detail. Also, results revealed that participants did not report many symptoms of simulator-sickness, or any light symptoms. Apparently, the option of having the participants replying orally to the questions, posed by the researcher, was adequate and did not increase task difficulty.

Though generalizing results from a pilot study is risky at best, our results suggest that VR can be successfully used to assess users' perceptions about packages' hazardousness. Clearly, further investigations are required. In terms of future work, since this pilot study provided promising results, a larger sample and a more detailed questionnaire, related with hazard perception, shall be used. Furthermore, the next step shall examine other features of the packages beyond shape (e.g., color, texture, material).

Acknowledgements. A PhD scholarship from Italian Government supported this study, which was developed in the scope of a Research Project financed by FCT (PTDC/PSI- PCO/100148/2008).

References

1. Creusen, M.E.H., Schoormans, J.P.L.: The different roles of product appearance in consumer choice. Journal of Product Innovation Management 22, 63–81 (2005)
2. Bloch, P.H.: Seeking the ideal form: product design and consumer response. The Journal of Marketing 59, 16–29 (1995)
3. Orth, U.R., Malkewitz, K.: Packaging design as resource for the construction of brand identity. In: Proceedings of 3rd International Wine Business Research Conference, pp. 6–7 (2006)
4. Chen, X., McKay, A., De Pennington, A., Chau, H.H.: Package shape design principles to support brand identity. In: 14th IAPRI World Conference on Packaging, pp. 1–14 (2004)
5. Langley, J., Janson, R., Wearn, J., Yoxall, A.: "Inclusive" design for containers: improving openability. Packaging Technology and Science 18, 285–293 (2005)
6. Overbeeke, C., Peters, M.: The tastes of Desserts' Packages. Perceptual and Motor Skills 73, 575–583 (1991)
7. Schneider, K.: Prevention of accidental poisoning through package and label design. Journal of Consumer Research 4 (1977)
8. Wogalter, M.S., Magurno, A.B., Scott, K.L., Dietrich, D.A.: Facilitating information acquisition for over-the-counter drugs using supplemental labels. In: Proceedings of the Human Factors and Ergonomics Society Annual Meeting, pp. 732–736. SAGE Publications (1996)
9. Laughery, K., Wogalter, M.S.: Warnings and risk perception. In: Salvendy, G. (ed.) Handbook of Human Factors and Ergonomics, pp. 1174–1197. Wiley, New York (1997)
10. Leonard, S.D., Wogalter, M.S.: What you don't know can hurt you: household products and events. Accident; Analysis and Prevention 32, 383–388 (2000)
11. Wogalter, M.S., Laughery, K.R., Barfield, D.A.: Effect of container shape on hazard perceptions. In: Human Factors Perspective on Warnings. Selections from Human Factors and Ergonomics Society annual meetings, 1994-2000, vol. 2, pp. 231–235 (2001)
12. Von Hippel, E.: The sources of innovation. Oxford University Press (1988)

13. Christensen, C.M.: Innovator's Dilemma:When new technologies cause great firms to fail. Harvard Business School Press Books (1997).
14. Wang, G.G.: Definition and Review of Virtual Prototyping. Journal of Computing and Information Science in Engineering 2, 232 (2002)
15. Smets, G.J.F., Overbeeke, C.J.: Expressing tastes in packages. Design Studies 16, 349–365 (1995)
16. Smets, G., Overbeeke, C.: Scent and sound of vision: Expressing scent or sound as visual forms. Perceptual and Motor Skills 69, 227–233 (1989)
17. Serig, E.M.: The influence of container shape and color cues on consumer produckt risk perception and precautionary intent. In: Wogalter, M.S., Young, S.L., Laughery, K.R. (eds.) Human Factors Perspective on Warnings. Selections from Human Factors and Ergonomics Society annual meetings, 1994-2000, vol. 2, pp. 185–188. Human Factors and Ergonomics Society (2001)
18. Rosson, M.B., Carroll, J.M.: Usability engineering: scenario-based development of human-computer interaction. Academic Press (2002)
19. Wogalter, M.S.: The Relative Contributions of Injury Severity and Likelihood Information on Hazard-Risk Judgments and Warning Compliance. Journal of Safety Research 30, 151–162 (1999)
20. Likert, R.: A technique for the measurement of attitudes. Archives of Psychology 22, 1–55 (1932)
21. Kennedy, R.S., Lane, N.E., Berbaum, K.S., Lilienthal, M.G.: Simulator Sickness Questionnaire: An Enhanced Method for Quantifying Simulator Sickness. The International Journal of Aviation Psychology 3, 203–220 (1993)
22. Ruddle, R.A.: The effect of environment characteristics and user interaction on levels of virtual environment sickness. IEEE (2004)

Multi-touch Based Standard UI Design of Car Navigation System for Providing Information of Surrounding Areas

Jung-Min Choi

Seoul National University of Science and Technology,
Department of Design, Seoul, Korea
jmchoi@seoultech.ac.kr

Abstract. Recognizing current location and surrounding areas is one of the default tasks to utilize car navigation systems. Due to the information and communication technologies, features in in-vehicle navigation systems are getting complicated and require more drivers' visual attention. This research aims to develop UI design for enhancing drivers' performance in the situation of recognizing and exploring surrounding areas with car navigation systems. In order to make drivers' eyes on the road, a standard feature definition and efficient operation methods are required. First of all, standard features are defined by analyzing top-selling navigation systems in Korean market. Drivers' can get route guidance from their in-vehicle system and personal handheld devices. However, the differences amongst the systems make drivers confused and waste time. The development of standard features of car navigation systems can reduce drivers' cognition load. Secondly, multi-touch interaction methods and drivers' behaviors are investigated in order to develop basic rationale to introduce multi-touch operation to a car navigation system. Current systems in market except smart applications adopt tactile and single-touch based interaction methods. These methods require more visual workload than multi-touch based methods in certain cases. User research has been conducted in tandem with researches of standard features and multi-touch interaction to figure out problems and their needs regarding to exploring surrounding areas in relation to current location. As results of this research, TF (Task Flows) of a multi-touch based standard UI design is suggested. The UI design can offer more values to drivers in terms of the amount of information with efficient and less eyes-on-the-system operations.

Keywords: in-vehicle information system, touch-based interaction, location-based service, interaction design.

1 Introduction

1.1 Background and Goal

Nowadays, IVIS (In-Vehicle Information System) offers an increasing number of information and functions for enhancing drivers' experience. Sometime, those features require drivers' visual attention and decrease their driving performance. When

A. Marcus (Ed.): DUXU/HCII 2013, Part III, LNCS 8014, pp. 40–48, 2013.

using a navigation system in IVIS, it is very critical to recognize current location and surrounding areas for route guidance features. Current location of a person works as a reference point to search the location of a target in relation to current location by forming a spatial mental model of a target space. The clear overview of current location and other spots from the current location is important for other situations when people navigating in indoor spaces, public and outdoor spaces, and even cyber spaces such as an internet space. In driving situation, the failure of figuring out driving route would make a driver distracted and cause an accident in the worst case. The poor quality of information delivery and complicated operation procedure of using IVIS make drivers' are the sources of the accident. Nowadays, IVIS (In-Vehicle Information System) comes into wide use more and more, thus a driver-oriented UI for navigation systems is required. This research aims to develop UI design for enhancing drivers' performance in the situation of recognizing and exploring surrounding areas with car navigation systems. In order to make drivers' eyes on the road, a standard UI is developed by defining standard features and efficient operation methods.

1.2   Process and Methods

The process of design a standard UI of car navigation system consists of four phases: In phase 1, Understanding issues in visualization of current location, existing problems are investigated in order to elicit drivers' needs with Nethnography and FGI.

In phase 2, Function definitions, comparing with commonly used IVIS in Korean market, the main features are summarized with three different modes: map view mode, route view (driving direction) mode, neighborhood searching mode.

Phase 3, Investigation of multi-touch interaction, multi-touch interaction methods have been collected from many digital artifacts and applications. With this data, a reference table is developed by filtering feasible methods in driving context.

In phase 4, Multi-touch UI proposal, the proposal is designed by developing simplified UI and mapping multi-touch interactions onto the corresponding-behaviors-triggered features. A new UI design of a car navigation system is developed to demonstrate the concept of this research, and is discussed, compared with an existing design. In addition, the possible results of applying this standard UI to other systems in IVIS are discussed by reviewing use case scenarios.

2   Understanding Driving Experience

2.1   Nethnography

To capture issues in the use of car navigation systems, users' comments on car navigation systems on internet sites such as dcinside.com, and power blogs have been collected [1]. The common postings on this research topic are as below: 1) occasionally, my eyes are one screen to figure out that images on the screen indicate to which one around me. If I fail to do that, I cannot start to use route guidance system. 2) I am very familiar with multi-touch operation due to my smartphone, so sometimes I try to manipulate my IVIS as I do to my smartphone. 3) Sometimes, I want to stop by restaurants, rest areas, and/or attraction points nearby. However, it is not easy to explore surrounding areas around my current location. 4) It is very hard to click the right button on the screen because the size of a button is relatively small and a car swayed usually.

2.2   FGI

FGI method is also used to capture users' driving experience with details [2]. Twenty four interviewees were participated in the discussion, and the interviewees are divided into two sub-groups. Sixteen are general user group who utilize default and general features in products. Other eight expert user group who are a kind of early adaptors and/or lead users. Each sub-group is divided into two sub groups for effective and in-depth discussion. Basic questions in proceeding scenarios are as follows: 1) which features in IVIS are not comfortable, and when, 2) why certain features do not work and how to improve the issues, and 3) which future features will be available for enhancing driving performance with the use of IVIS. Figure 1 shows the summary of Nethnography and FGI at the first phase.

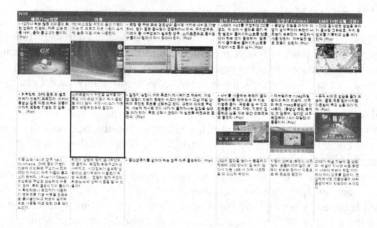

Fig. 1. Summary of Results from Nethnography and FGI

3   Standard Feature Definition

3.1   Approach

Standard features commonly used in most IVIS systems are defined by comparing popular IVIS products and Apps in Korean market. Four products and three Apps are selected from top-ranked selling items. There are three modes in relation to drivers' current location as shown in Figure 2. 1) Map view mode is the default that displays a driver's current location without specific destinations. 2) Route view mode (driving direction) will be activated when a drive selects a destination and IVIS starts to guide the route. 3) Neighborhood searching mode will be activated when a driver want to look around the current location.

Fig. 2. Screenshots of Map view mode (left), Route view mode (middle), Neighborhood searching mode (right)

3.2 Map View Mode

First of all, it is very important to calibrate his/her the current location to the point in the map in IVIS. If a driver fails to do that, IVIS will be useless. Some features in

Table 1. Common Features in Map View Mode

Feature	Aftermarket Products				Apps in Smartphone			Note
	Atlan 3D	Thinkware	Gini	Mappy	Olleh Navi	GoGo 3D	Tmap	
Main Menu	O		O	O	O	O	O	
Recent Search							O	
Navi Menu		O	O					
Search (Route, Destination)		O		O	O			Touch
Name of Current Location	O	O	O	O	O	O	O	
Eco Point	O	O						
GPS	O		O	O		O	O	
Clock	O		O	O	O	O	O	
Compass	O	O		O		O	O	Mode Change
Zoom +/-		O	O	O	O	O	O	Touch
Scale	O	O	O	O	O	O		Touch
TPEG	O		O	O	O			
View Change	O		O		O			Touch
Save Spot		O						Touch
Scroll Map	O	O	O	O	O	O	O	Touch
Mode Change				O				Compass Touch
Volume				O	O			

IVIS such as zooming, scrolling map around can support to recognize the current location inside the map in IVIS. Table 1 shows the common features in Map view mode and in which features multi-touch interactions can be applied for reducing operations in the use of IVIS.

3.3   Route View (Driving Direction) Mode

When a driver chooses a certain destination, Route view mode will start. In this mode, a driver wants to expect when he/she has to change lane and/or route, how far from starting point and destination, etc. The quality of information representation is very important in this mode. Table 2 shows the common features in Route view mode and in which features multi-touch interactions can be applied for reducing operations in the use of IVIS.

Table 2. Common Features in Route View Mode

Feature	Aftermarket Products				Apps in Smartphone			Note
	Atlan 3D	Thinkware	Gini	Mappy	Olleh Navi	GoGo 3D	Tmap	
Diverging point Info.	O	O	O	O	O	O	O	
Lane Info.	O	O	O	O	O			
Searching options (Tollway, Fastest, Shortest, etc.)	O		O	O				Touch
Distance to Destination	O	O	O	O	O		O	
Time to Destination (Arrival Time)	O	O	O	O	O	O	O	
Travelled Distance		O				O		
Travelled Time	O							
Name of Destination	O	O	O	O	O	O	O	
Traffic Sign	O	O	O	O	O	O	O	

3.4   Neighborhood Searching Mode

While driving, sometimes a driver wants to look around the current location. Searching restaurants, rest areas, gas stations, etc. are common situations. In this situation, it is important to explore the map in IVIS without distracting a driver's attention too much. Reducing operation time can a solution for this situation. In this sense, introducing multi-touch interaction is a good idea. Table 3 shows the common features in Neighborhood searching mode in which features multi-touch interactions can be applied for reducing operations in the use of IVIS.

Table 3. Common Features in Neighborhood Searching Mode

Feature	Aftermarket Products				Apps in Smartphone			Note
	Atlan 3D	Thinkware	Gini	Mappy	Olleh Navi	GoGo 3D	Tmap	
Back to Current Location	O	O	O	O	O	O	O	Touch
Set as Start	O	O	O	O	O	O		Touch
Set as by way of destination	O	O	O	O		O		Touch
Set as Destination	O	O	O	O	O	O	O	Touch
Get Direction	O	O	O	O				Touch
Save spot	O		O	O			O	Touch
Control to Scroll Map	O							Touch
Adjust angle of Map		O						Touch

4   Multi-touch Interaction

4.1   Potential for Application

With the wide spread of smart phones, people tend to take multi-touch interaction as a matter of course. Multi-touch enables users to operate a system with two or more points of contact with the surface [3, 4]. However, interaction design of IVIS seems behind this trend because the character of car industries is relatively conservative. When they introduce new technology into their products, they have to consider the safety issues. Not to make a drivers' gaze distracted can guarantee his/her safety while driving. According to an experiment with tactile, touch, and gesture interaction, touch interaction leads to fast and efficient task completion for in-vehicle system [5]. There is potential to introduce multi-touch interaction into IVIS because it can reduce operation time with less focus on screen.

4.2   Application Types

Table 1 shows the selected multi-touch gestures in smart phones and touch-enabled OS systems that have potential to be applied. When selecting appropriate interaction types, three criteria are considered. First, the interaction must be performed using one hand. Two hand interaction methods such as rotate do not work. Second, the consistency of behaviors between features in IVIS and multi-touch interaction. For example, 'Drag,' the movement of fingertip over surface without losing contact in Table 4, has the analogy of behaviors for scrolling map in Table 3. In this way, Table 4 is suggested. Not to require visual reference point is the last one. The benchmark systems in Table 1, 2, and 3 requires visual reference point when a driver interacts

Table 4. Applicable Multi-Touch Interactions for IVIS

Type	Symbol	Description
Tap		Move to the point
Double Tap		Back to current location
Hold (Press)		Activate context menu (Long Tap)
Flick		Slow scrolling map
Drag		Adjust 3D angle with Hold
Pinch/ Spread		Zoom in/out
Multi-Finger Drag		Quick scrolling map

with them. Zooming is an example. In order to zoom in and/or out, a driver has to take a look the screen and find buttons. However, 'Pinch/Spread' in Table 4 requires less drivers' attention. He/she can zoom in and/or out with contacting on any surface of the screen, so he/she can save time to find the right buttons.

5   UI Design Concept

The standard features are summarized as shown in Table 5 by referring to Table 2, 3, and 4. The table explains main features and sub-features in each main category.

Table 5. Summary of Standard Features

Main Feature	Sub-Feature
Main menu	Main Menu, Destination, Map Menu, Navi Menu, POI, TPEG will appear if tap any spot on the screen
Map Menu	Start Guidance, Set Destination, Delete Destination, Detail Route, Multiple Route, Cancel Guidance

Table 5. (*continued*)

Recent Search	No sub-menu
Navi Menu	Features for navigation control
Search (Route, Destination, etc.)	No sub-menu
Name of Current Location	On the bottom of screen
GPS	Always on status bar
Clock	Always on screen
Compass	Always on screen
Zoom in/out	Will be replaced with Pinch & Spread
Scale	Will be simplified with Press & Drag
TPEG	No sub-menu
View	Will be replaced with Two-Finger Rotate, Double Tap
Bookmark	Will be simplified with Long-Press
Map scrolling	Will be replaced with Flick, and Two-Finger Flick
Mode Change	Will be activated by Pressing over compass icon
Volume	Always on status bar
POI	Will be activated by Search options

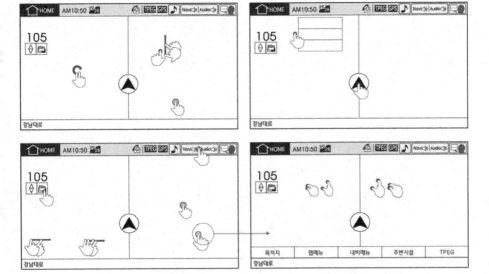

Fig. 3. Screenshots of multi-touch based UIs

6   Discussion

This study has attempted to develop a standard multi-touch based UI for the core of car navigation systems. From the reviews using paper prototypes with five participants, they give positive responses in terms of faster operation with less visual attention. In terms of how to recognize which multi-touch interactions are behind the screen, the more sophisticated UI concepts are required. For the standard navigation menus on the bottom, they have various comments depending on their systems. In order to evaluate the menus, new evaluation criteria and methods are required. For example, learning effects and faster task completion can be criteria for evaluating how to organize features and information in driver-oriented way. For the further development, working simulators will be developed and usability test will be conducted with scenarios.

References

1. http://www.dcinside.com/
2. Goodman, E., Kuniavsky, M., Moed, A.: Observing the User Experience, 2nd edn. A Practitioner's Guide to User Research, pp. 141–178. Morgan Kaufmann (2012)
3. http://www.billbuxton.com/multitouchOverview.html
4. http://www.touchuserinterface.com/
5. Bach, K.M., Jæger, M.G., Skov, M.B., Thomassen, N.G.: You can touch, but you can't look: interacting with in-vehicle systems. In: CHI 2008: Proceedings of the SIGCHI Conference on Human Factors in Computing Systems, pp. 1139–1148 (2008)

Designing Technology for Older People – The Role of Technical Self-confidence in Usability of an Inclusive Heating Control

Nicola Combe[*], David Harrison, and Hua Dong

School of Engineering and Design, Brunel University, Uxbridge, UB8 3PH
niccombe@gmail.com

Abstract. The ageing population of the UK is providing a large market opportunity for inclusive products and services. Yet older people are often excluded from using new technology due to inadequate consideration of their needs during the design process. This study focused specifically on including older people (aged 50-80) in the testing of a novel heating control interface under development. Recent studies have used two scalar methods to assess self-confidence; building upon this a technical self-confidence questionnaire was developed and completed by participants prior to attempting a usability task using the prototype. This study found that high technical self-confidence was inversely correlated to successful task performance. The participants who rated themselves as most technically self-confident were not successful in completing the task. Whereas, participants that rated themselves less confident had greater success completing the task. In general older people reported high levels of technical self-confidence and they were found to be willing to engage with the technical prototype. This highlights the high expectations of the older users group to be able to effectively engage with new technological systems. Designers should aim to instil further confidence amongst older users and provide systems that both support and include older people.

Keywords: Inclusive design, usability testing, older people, technical self-confidence, technology.

1   Introduction

Inclusive interaction design has become increasingly significant in recent years, specifically in relation to product and mobile interfaces. In 2010 Langdon and Thimbleby introduced a special issue of Interacting with Computers with a discussion of the main theme 'Inclusion and Interaction'. The need for such a special issue was highlighted by the fact that although designing products for customers the 'user' is often not defined specifically. This can lead to designers basing their work on their

---

[*] Corresponding author.

A. Marcus (Ed.): DUXU/HCII 2013, Part III, LNCS 8014, pp. 49–56, 2013.
© Springer-Verlag Berlin Heidelberg 2013

own, somewhat limited, experiences (Langdon and Thimbleby, 2010). The main criticism of existing usability studies is the common focus on testing in laboratory settings using only student participants, often under 30 years old.

Designing technology for older people can present unique challenges due to declines in motor, cognitive and sensory function associated with the ageing process. This paper presents a usability study, which examined whether older people (aged 50-80) were successful in interacting with a prototype heating control interface and whether their reported technical self-confidence influenced success.

As Coleman (2003) argues that an accessible product is not necessarily inclusive, similarly Abascal and Nicolle argue, "even if the services are accessible...it is also important that users can perform those tasks easily, effectively and efficiently" (pp. 486, 2005) through the user interface. Langdon and Thimbleby (2010) concluded that there is a need for increased knowledge transfer from inclusive design to the human-computer interaction (HCI) community to help design more inclusive interactions.

Several studies have recognised that older users may have difficulties interacting with heating controls and energy management interface (Combe et al., 2012, Meier et al., 2011, Caird and Roy, 2008, and Freundenthal and Mook 2003). The realisation that older users in particular may struggle to use product interfaces was also recognised by Zhang, Rau and Salvendy (2009) and Sauer, Wastell and Schmeink (2009). When using a smart home interface to control a range of energy consuming activities within the home, older users took longer to complete tasks and made more errors than younger users (Zhang, Rau and Salvendy 2009).

Recent studies have used two scalar methods of assessing self-confidence; Subjective Technical Competence (STC) used by Arning and Ziefle (2007) and the Affinity to Technology scale by Wolters et al. (2010). Wolters et al. (2010) found that older users who had a high level of affinity to technology had increased rates of task success when using a voice controlled smart home interface. Arning and Ziefle (2007) found a strong association between STC and completion of a task effectively and efficiently amongst the older participant group. Older people reported significantly lower levels of confidence compared with the younger participants of their study. This study aims to investigate whether the self-reported technical confidence of older people influenced the task success rate when using a novel heating control interface prototype. It was hypothesised that older people who reported high technical confidence would have successful interactions with the prototype system.

2   Method

This study tested a prototype heating control with a group of older adults who gave their informed consent to the study and received no payment or reward for taking part. The Brunel University School of Engineering and Design Ethics Committee approved the study. Firstly, the study collected demographic data and participants answered a set of paper based technical self-confidence questions. The participants were then asked to interact with the prototype by programming some example settings and their success was noted. Once collected the technical self-confidence scores were compared to both task success and other demographic factors.

There were 16 participants aged 52-78 (mean = 68.6 years, male = 7, female = 9), who were recruited through the Brunel Older People Research Group. Of the participants, 12 users said they currently had a digital programmable thermostat at home, however this should be treated with caution. Peffer et al. (2011) cited large inaccuracies in reporting whether households had a manual or programmable thermostats as the terms can cause confusion amongst lay users (Energy Information Administration 2010 and 2011).

2.1   Technical Self-confidence

The technical self-confidence questions were based on the Subjective Technical Competence (STC) scale used by Arning and Ziefle (2007) and the Affinity to Technology scale used by Wolters et al. (2010). The STC scale used by Arning and Ziefle (2007 & 2009) is a shortened version of the original German questionnaire from Beier (1999) containing eight statements. The participant then rated the statements from 1 to 5 as to whether they totally disagree (1) or totally agree (5), giving them a maximum score out of 40. The Affinity to Technology scale used by Wolters et al. (2010) was tailored to home appliances and voice control as an interaction style. Of the 10 statements 7 more generic statements could be applicable for this study. Of these statements, 3 are a negative version of the previous statement to highlight general disinterest with technology. The statements the participants were asked to rate were:

1. Technology has always fascinated me
2. I really like to try out new gadgets
3. I successfully cope with technical problems
4. Even if problems occur, I continue working on technical problems
5. I really enjoy solving technical problems
6. Up to now I managed to solve most of the technical problems, and I am not afraid of technical problems in future
7. I feel uncomfortable and helpless about using technical devices
8. Technical devices are often not transparent and difficult to handle
9. When I solve a technical problem successfully, it mostly happens by chance
10. Most technical problems are too complicated for me to deal with

2.2   Usability Task

The usability task, shown in Table 1, involved programming the control prototype and it was noted whether the participants were successful, used the help features, and any points of confusion during the interaction.

Table 1. Usability Task Settings

Day	Time (12 hour clock)	Time (24 hour clock)	Temperature
Monday - Friday	7am-9am	07:00-09:00	19°C
	4pm-11pm	16:00-23:00	21°C
Saturday & Sunday	7am-9am	07:00-09:00	19°C
	6pm-10.30pm	18:00-22:30	21°C

2.3   Data Analysis

For the analysis of the results, two statistical methods were used to establish significance. Observed user exclusion was compared to expected exclusion, based on previous analysis published in Combe et al. (2012), and was evaluated using Chi-square tests. Correlations were evaluated using Pearson's product-moment correlation coefficient for parametric variables.

3   Results

Firstly, the results of the usability testing and task success of participants are reported before correlations between technical self-confidence and success and technical self-confidence and age are explored.

3.1   Task Success

In terms of task success, 9 of the 16 older users were able to programme the prototype for two heating periods on the weekdays and two on the weekends. This gave a success rate of 56.3% for the older participants. Despite the improved success rate, a Chi-square goodness-of-fit test discerned there was still a significant difference between the observed and expected exclusion of the older age group ($p < 0.01$ as $X^2 = 13.204$ and df = 1).

3.2   Technical Self-confidence and Task Success

Technical self-confidence data was gathered prior to attempting the task using the prototype. Interestingly, older users who rated themselves as most technically self-confident were not successful with the task. Participants that rated themselves less confident had greater success, with 3 of the 4 participants that rated their technical self-confidence less than 50% being successful with the task. These participants also performed quicker with an average task time of 3 minutes 40 seconds compared with 6 minutes 28 seconds for users with technical self-confidence scores above 50%.

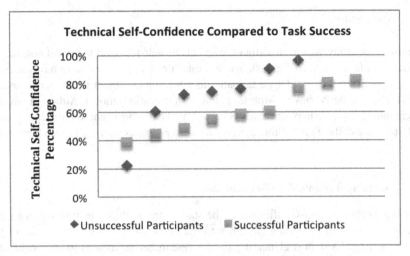

Fig. 1. Task Success vs. Technical Self-Confidence

3.3   Technical Self-confidence and Age

Overall, there was a negative correlation between age and technical self-confidence, with self-confidence decreasing with age ($r = -0.229$, $n = 31$ and $p=0.215$). This negative correlation was small and did not reach levels of statistical significance. Of the unsuccessful older participants, 6 out of 7 rated their self-confidence highly (above 60%). Participants with a high technical self-confidence appeared to be less patient and got frustrated quickly with the prototype. Highly confident older people were also less tolerant of error messages. Only the participant with the lowest technical self-confidence score of 22% was also unsuccessful.

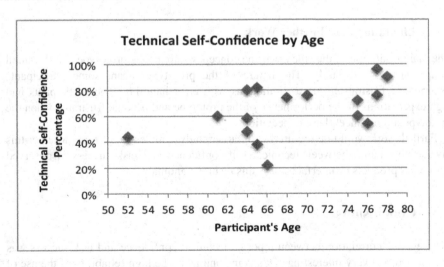

Fig. 2. Age vs. Technical Self-Confidence

4　Discussion

The aim of the study was to investigate whether the self-reported technical confidence of older people influenced the task success rate. Prior experience may have affected task success as only one older participant did not use a computer at all and 13 used a computer on a daily basis. Mobile phone usage varied more. Although all the participants had a mobile phone, only 8 used it on a daily basis and 6 participants used it only to make calls. This technical experience may have contributed to success in the task.

4.1　Assessing Technical Self-confidence

Assessing Technical Self-Confidence at the start of the usability testing was a simple and effective way of providing insight into the perception of the user, ahead of the usability testing. Even at a glance it gave the researcher an idea as to how confident the participant was using a technical prototype prior to the testing. This could be useful when including older people in a study sample so that the researcher could support less confident participants in an appropriate manner.

One issue experienced with the application of the scales was some users asked for clarification of the statement "Even if problems occur, I continue working on technical problems". This was considered to be less readable among participants and may be due to the translation for the original German statements. Perhaps this could be reworded for clarity in future use.

Analysis of the completed scales was straightforward, however it was less clear as where the thresholds for high and low confidence should be. This was determined by the researcher as high, over 50% and low, under 50% however further work could refine this definition.

4.2　Limitations and Further Work

The main limitation of the study was the concept nature of the prototype and the small sample size of the study. The nature of the prototype meant some participants experienced frustration due to limitations with error handling. The participants had high expectations of the performance of the prototype and became frustrated when the prototype did not meet these expectations.

Further work would be required with larger study samples to examine whether this inverse correlation between technical self-confidence and task success is observed with other products or interfaces or is this result an anomaly.

5　Conclusions

The negative correlation between reported technical confidence and task success was unexpected, yet very interesting. This is in contrast to the high reliability of the use of such scales reported by both Beier (1999) and Arning and Ziefle (2009). The reported confidence of the older people was generally high and highlights that older people expect to be able to interact with systems successfully.

Designing technical systems which give older people positive experiences may improve their technical confidence overall with other systems. With a rapidly ageing population in the UK there is a growing market for technological products, which are both usable and inclusive of older users' needs.

The reported high perceptions of confidence amongst older people should challenge designers' perceptions of older people. This is applicable in the context of both users of technological products and willing participants in usability studies. For designers it would be useful to examine the factors of interactions: which affect the confidence of older people? This leads to the further research questions: does reducing exclusion of older users increase their technical self-confidence? And what design factors can instil confidence within older people?

Acknowledgements. The authors would like to acknowledge both the ESPRC and Buro Happold, who funded this research, and the participants who gave up their time to take part in the study.

References

1. Abascal, J., Nicolle, C.: Moving towards inclusive design guidelines for socially and ethically aware HCI. Interacting with Computers 17(5), 484–505 (2005), doi:10.1016/j.intcom.2005.03.002
2. Arning, K., Ziefle, M.: Effects of age, cognitive and personal factors on PDA menu navigation. Behaviour & Information Technology 28(3), 251–268 (2009)
3. Arning, K., Ziefle, M.: Understanding age differences in PDA acceptance and performance. Computers in Human Behaviour 23(2007), 2904–2927 (2007)
4. Beier, G.: Locus of control when interacting with technology. Report Psychologie 24, 684–693 (1999)
5. Caird, S., Roy, R.: User-Centred Improvements to Energy Efficiency Products and Renewable Energy Systems: Research on Household Adoption and Use. International Journal of Innovation Management 12(3), 327–355 (2008)
6. Coleman, R.: Living Longer. In: Clarkson, J., Coleman, R., Keates, S., Lebbon, C. (eds.) Inclusive Design: Design for the Whole Population, 1st edn., pp. 120–142. Springer, London (2003)
7. Combe, N., Harrison, D., Craig, S., Young, M.S.: An investigation into usability and exclusivity issues of digital programmable thermostats. Journal of Engineering Design 23(5), 401–417 (2012), doi:10.1080/09544828.2011.599027
8. Etchell, L., Girdlestone, N., Yelding, D.: Taking control: a guide to buying and upgrading central heating controls, London (2004), http://www.ricability.org.uk/consumer_reports/at_home/Taking_control/ (accessed on February 28, 2012) (retrieved)
9. Freudenthal, H.J., Mook, A.: The evaluation of an innovative intelligent thermostat interface: universal usability and age differences. Cognition, Technology and Work 5, 55–66 (2003), doi:10.1007/s10111-002-0115-6

10. Langdon, P., Thimbleby, H.: Inclusion and interaction: Designing interaction for inclusive populations. Interacting with Computers 22(6), 439–448 (2010), doi:10.1016/j.intcom.2010.08.007
11. Meier, A., Aragon, C., Peffer, T., Perry, D., Pritoni, M.: Usability of residential thermostats: Preliminary investigations. Building and Environment 46(10), 1891–1898 (2011), doi:10.1016/j.buildenv.2011.03.009
12. Peffer, T., Pritoni, M., Meier, A., Aragon, C., Perry, D.: How People Use Thermostats in Homes: A Review. Building and Environment 46, 2529–2541 (2011), doi:10.1016/j.buildenv.2011.06.002
13. Sauer, J., Wastel, D.G., Schmeink, C.: Designing for the home: A comparative study of support aids for central heating systems. Applied Ergonomics 40, 165–174 (2009)
14. Wolters, K.M., Engelbrecht, K.-P., Gödde, F., Möller, S., Naumann, A., Schleicher, R.: Making it easier for older people to talk to smart homes: the effect of early help prompts. Universal Access in the Information Society 9(4), 311–325 (2010), doi:10.1007/s10209-009-0184-x
15. Zhang, B., Rau, P.P., Salvendy, G.: Design and evaluation of smart home user interface: effects of age, tasks and intelligence level. Behaviour and Information Technology 28(3), 239–249 (2009)

Effects of In-Car Navigation Systems on User Perception of the Spatial Environment

Mehmet Göktürk and Ali Pakkan

Gebze Institute of Technology, Turkey
{gokturk,pakkan}@gyte.edu.tr

Abstract. This study aims to understand how navigation devices affect driver's awareness of the environment. The hypothesis of this study suggests that use of in-car navigation systems diverts driver's attention from outside of the car to the inside where external objects are less likely to be recognized. These objects may include landmarks, buildings, traffic signs and even pedestrians. Further, internet connected navigation devices cause the amount of information presented to user become very large in size during driving. This study conducted a multiuser field experiment in order to understand basic effects of in-car navigation systems on user perception of external world outside of the car. It was also hypothesized that technology aptitude of driver has significant contribution on how these devices affect user's perception. Results suggested that in-car navigation systems has adverse effects on external world perception. Technology aptitude of the driver played significant role on navigation device interaction as well.

Keywords: navigation system, situatonal awareness, technology aptitude, driving aids.

1 Introduction

The tremendous increase in the use of in-car navigation systems requires attenion for studying driver behaviour and way finding strategies in typical car driving task. The widely accepted popular belief is that navigation devices weaken environmental and situational awareness of driver as compared to driving without a navigational aid. There are numerous incidents where navigation devices are the main cause. In one of them, a car driver, fully obeying the orders given by the in-car navigation system, teetered on the edge of a cliff and and only could come to a stop and realized that he was in wrong path by hitting a fence [1]. In another interesting incident, a Belgian woman blindly drove 900 miles across Europe as she followed broken GPS instead of 38-miles to the station[2].

These incidents certainly not in parallel with the designs and predictions of the device manufacturers may suggest that GPS devices are incapable and disembodied understanding of the environment as Lorimer et al. argue [3]. On the other hand, some researchers believe that the use of in-car navigation systems brings new and constructive levels and opportunities into driving experience [4]. Donald Norman's

A. Marcus (Ed.): DUXU/HCII 2013, Part III, LNCS 8014, pp. 57–64, 2013.
© Springer-Verlag Berlin Heidelberg 2013

famous "Cautious Cars and Cantankerous Kitchens" article draws attention to how an ultimate car should behave avoiding such incidents.

When there is nobody helping along, people count on their sense of orientation and past experiences. They keep the landmarks in mind, for example: "Take the first left, after the hospital". With in-car navigation systems, this approach has been changed, and turned into listening to the device and obeying the commands it gave: "Get ready to turn left in 100 meters". At first glance, this can be considered as a small change, but it is obvious that this situation has the potential to modify whole driving experience as can be seen in previously made studies [4-6].

1.1   Purpose

The main purpose of this study is to determine behavioral changes of driver interacting with the environment inside and outside of the car. Moreover, it is known that with different user profiles, different results are obtained as there is no unique type of driver profile[6]. Since these systems include increasing technological features in time, technology aptitude of driver is chosen as one of the variables in this study. Finding out the changes in the interaction with the environment, due to in-car navigation systems on drivers who have technology aptitude and who do not is the main purpose of the study.

First, the change in driving experience, the level of the change, and finally pros and cons of the change are investigated and studied. To this purpose, the expected outputs are as follows:

- To get general ideas of users about in-car navigation systems and positive and negative experiences that they had while using the system.
- To find out the real value of the certain features of the in-car navigation systems to the user.
- To determine the user needs, requests and expectations that can be input for device manufacturers.
- To analyze the levels of role in interaction and environmental perception of the user technology aptitude.

2   In-Car Navigation Systems

As Mark Weiser [7] foresaw 20 years ago, computers take much more place in our daily life today. In-car navigation systems, with advanced technological features can be considered as computers with features such as internet connection, backup camera, audio and video player in addition to their standard features as compass, navigation and positioning aids with a few meter accuracy [8]. According to a market research about the in-car navigation systems, by iSuppli, it was estimated that 114 millions of portable navigation devices and 57.8 millions of GPS enabled smartphones were in use worldwide in 2009 [9]. By 2012 the number of smartphone navigation application users has grown to 160 million whereas personal navigation devices totals to 150

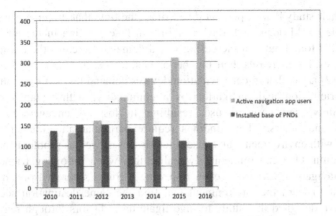

Fig. 1. PND and smartphone navigation application use worldwide (millions)

million. It is also worth to mention that worldwide smartphone sales was 700 million in 2011 with 33 million PNDs. Figure 1 shows the change of realized and estimated numbers of PND (Portable Navigation Device) and smartphone navigation applications in use.

A list of guidelines that a navigation device should have is as follows:

- Efficiency in time and mileage [5].
- Assurance of driving safety [5].
- Turn-by-turn guidance with voice instructions [13].
- Quickly accessible and easy-to-use control interface [13].
- High location not to distract driver [14].
- Delivery of valuable information such as landmarks and distance to nearest turn with voice guidance [15].

2.1   Change in External Perception

As several examples given in previous sections [1] [2], navigation products may not create the expected outcomes all the time. Guidance and routing features that are developed for the comfort of user can cause several problems due to obeying without situational awareness. Nevertheless, in-car navigation systems are perceived as an important assistant that increases safety of driver: *"I never feel like getting lost anymore"*, (Participant 9). It is definite that system manufacturers have taken safety, user needs and satisfaction into consideration with high priority. However, business competition and high user expectations force manufacturers to market some features before they reach maturity. *"It led me to a closed road, I tried to find the correct road more than half an hour"*, (Participant 4).

There are number of studies on the effects of in-car devices, such as navigation systems, focusing on user interaction within the environment. Horrey et al. [10]

showed in their study that as percent dwell time (the time that drivers spend looking) at the outside world decreased, the variability in lane position increased. Tsimhoni and Green [11] found out that increasing visual demand decreases the duration of in-vehicle glances, but increases their number as well as the time between them. Aporta and Higgs [12] argue that in-car navigation devices demand less skill and attention by providing orientation and navigation as a commodity, with instant availability, ubiquity, safety, and ease of use, resulting in loss of engagement with the environment and others. Their findings require particular attention since loss of engagement with environment can cause safety issues as well as problems in reaching final destination. One can immediately realize that when following friend's verbal directions, navigation devices or even following a friend's car in front, it becomes very difficult to learn the environment and find the same destination second time later. We have designed this study to investigate these factors through real life field experiments.

2.2   Measurement of User Perception

A two stage study was applied to measure the changes in user perception within the environment. In the first stage, participants were asked to fill in the survey [16], which was developed to measure their knowledge and experiences about in-car navigation systems. In the second stage, participants drove a car that was equipped by two video cameras. One of the cameras was focused on the eye of the driver, and the other camera was focused on the navigation device and the road together. Participants, who were chosen amongst friends and colleagues, consisted of 10 people of which 5 had technology aptitude and 5 did not have. Technology aptitude was determined based on participants' verbal declarations about themselves.

While the survey study helped to obtain quantitative data, the driving study made it possible to obtain both quantitative and qualitative data. Both data has been investigated, compiled carefully and divided into common groups.

3   Results

Participants consisted of mostly men (% 70) and married (% 60) people. The mean age of the participants that have technology aptitude was 32, whereas it was 55 for the participants that don't have. The general mean age was 43. Evaluations were grouped based on technology aptitude and therefore in the following figures, series names were given accordingly.

In-car navigation system usage seemed to be affected by the familiarity with the environment, as seen in Figure 2 and Figure 3. The use of PND in an unfamiliar environment for participants that have technology aptitude was % 80, whereas it was % 100 for the participants that don't have. In a familiar environment, there were some occasional usages by the participants that have technology aptitude, whereas, the other half of the participants cited that they didn't ever use it, or used it very rarely.

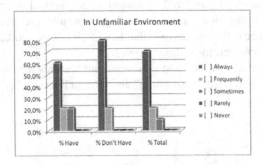

Fig. 2. Usage in unfamiliar environment

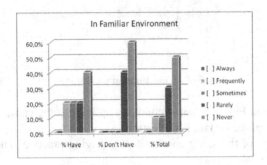

Fig. 3. Usage in familiar environment

The satisfaction of the participants about the route suggested by in-car navigation system was measured and results are presented in Figure 4. According to results, the participants that have technology aptitude are % 80 satisfied about the route and think that their personal decision and system suggestion match and so that they are convenient, whereas it's % 60 for the other participants that don't have technology aptitude.

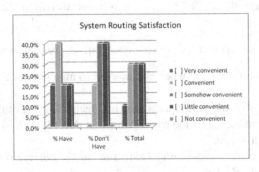

Fig. 4. System routing satisfaction

In the measurement of preferred communication method with the navigation system, participants that don't have technology aptitude preferred mostly voice communication, whereas the participants that have technology aptitude preferred both voice and display communication almost equally.

Participants indicated that the most two important features that should exist on an in-car navigation system were "Positioning" and "Route Planning" (Figure 5).

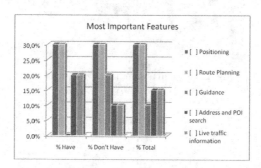

Fig. 5. Two most important features

It is clearly seen in Figure 5 that, technology aptitude is the cause of difference on relative importance of the certain PND features.

The second stage of the study consisted of a driving practice. The results of this stage are summarized as follows:

- Glances at navigation system: The participants that have technology aptitude glanced 2.8 times (σ: 0.8), whereas the participants that don't have technology aptitude glanced 1.4 times (σ: 0.5) at navigation system, mean glance number was 2.1 (σ: 0.9).
- Landmark notice: One of the most significant results of this study is the effect on landmark recall performance. The participants were asked whether they noticed 10 pre-selected landmarks. As the navigation system was on, the participants noticed 2.4 (σ: 1.2) landmarks, but as it was off, the participants noticed 1.4 (σ: 0.9) landmarks. Namely the use of navigation systems decreased the landmark recall rate by 42%.

Also throughout the experiments, following observations were obtained:

- Participant felt uncomfortable when she was led to an alley instead of highway by the system.
- It was measured that the participants that had technology aptitude looked at the system 3 times a minute, and the participants that don't have looked at the system once a minute as average.
- Participants indicated "*validation of being still on the correct route*" as the main reason to look at the device.

- Participant took the first right with the command: *"Get ready to turn right in 100 meters"*. But it wasn't the right one yet. The distance perception of user is probably not matched with the navigation device estimation.
- Participant commented: *"In my navigation system the traffic message channel (TMC) support is enabled, but municipality still doesn't provide service"*.
- Participant indicated that system was kind of enjoying him, and used it even in familiar environment.
- Participant was about to make an accident while programming navigation system during the drive.
- Participant indicated that using in-car navigation system prevented him from asking other people or finding on a map and so that provide a more comfortable and enjoyable transportation.

4 Conclusion

According to the results of this study we conclude that in-car navigation systems affects users perception of the spatial environment from many viewpoints. At the end of the study that consisted of two stages, survey and driving, it is observed for both participant groups that using in-car navigation system causes disengagement from the external spatial environment, being unaware of environmental objects. Furthermore, some security risk was observed due to looking at the device. It is found out that the trust of participants that don't have technology aptitude in the system is less than the participants that have, nevertheless they used it in unfamiliar environment by a high percentage. It is concluded that in-car navigation systems are successful by means of basic functionalities, but they lack support on safe driving.

Besides, additional functions such as points of interests (POI), backup camera and Internet queries of flights or weather, make the system more effective. And the system presents a social dimension and can be positioned as an entertainment tool, mostly for participants that have technology aptitude. Therefore, it is foreseen that the in-car navigation systems can provide much more than what they provide currently. With technological development they will be used by more people and will be a part of daily life.

The market shift towards navigation enabled smart phones open new opportunities for application and service providers. Extended traffic information, communication with nearby drivers, integration of search engines and online information sources along with highly skilled voice assistants will bring new ways of user interaction within the car. As these happen, measures to keep driver connected with the external spatial world outside of the car should be seriously considered.

It is also understood that technology aptitude is an important parameter that affects user perception, therefore, device manufactures can be suggested to develop customized designs for different levels of technology aptitudes according to fundamental human computer interaction principles.

It must be stated that due to serious difficulties in conducting in-car experiments, only 10 participants were participated to the study and further experiments are suggested to increase statistical significance.

References

1. Glazebrook, M.: GPS Leads Driver to Cliff's Edge. Asylum.com AOL Inc., USA (March 2009), http://www.asylum.com/2009/03/26/gps-leads-driver-to-cliffs-edge/
2. Daily Mail Online (February 24, 2013), http://www.dailymail.co.uk/news/article-2262149/Belgian-woman-67-picking-friend-railway-station-ends-Zagreb-900-miles-away-satnav-disaster.html
3. Lorimer, H., Lund, K.: Performing facts: finding a way over Scotland's mountains. The Soc. Review 51(s2) (2003)
4. Leshed, G., Velden, T., Rieger, O., Kot, B., Sengers, P.: In-car GPS navigation engagement with and disengagement from the environment. In: Proc. CHI 2008, Florence, Italy (2008)
5. Svahn, F.: In-car navigation usage: An end-user survey on existing systems. In: Proc. IRIS 27, Falkenberg, Sweden (2004)
6. Al Mahmud, A., Mubin, O., Shahid, S.: User experience with in-car GPS navigation systems: comparing the young and elderly drivers. In: MobileHCI 2009, Bonn, Germany (2009)
7. Weiser, M.: The Computer for the 21st Century. Scientific American, USA (1991)
8. PNT: How accurate is the Global Positioning System? Space-Based PNT, Washington, USA (October 2009), http://pnt.gov/public/faq.shtml
9. Arghire, I.: GPS-Enabled Smartphones to Kill PNDs Will lead on the navigation market by 2014. iSuppli, Softpedia.com SoftNews NET SRL (September 2009), http://news.softpedia.com/news/GPS-Enabled-Smartphones-to-Kill-PNDs-120729.shtml
10. Horrey, W.J., Wickens, C.D., Consalus, K.P.: Modeling Drivers' Visual Attention Allocation While Interacting With In-Vehicle Technologies. Journal of Experimental Psychology: Applied 12(2), 67–78 (2006)
11. Tsimhoni, O., Green, P.: Visual demands of driving and the execution of display-intensive in-vehicle tasks. In: Proceedings of the Human Factors and Ergonomics Society 45th Annual Meeting (2001)
12. Aporta, C., Higgs, E.: Satellite culture - global positioning systems, Inuit wayfinding, and the need for a new account of technology. Current Anthropology 46(5) (2005)
13. Burnett, G.E.: Usable Vehicle Navigation Systems: Are We There Yet? In: Proceedings of Vehicle Electronics Systems 2000 European Conference and Exhibition. ERA Technology Limited, Leatherhead (2000)
14. May, A.J., Burnett, G.E., Joyner, S.M.: Integrating a Route Guidance Display within a Vehicle: Safety Implications of Display Position. CEC EUREKA PROMETHEUS Programme BRIMMI CED 9: Dual Mode Route Guidance, Report 5.2. HUSAT Research Institute, Loughborough (1995)
15. Green, P.: In-Vehicle Information: Design of Driver Interfaces for Route Guidance. TRB Annual Meeting, Washington, USA (1996)
16. Pakkan, A.: GPS In-car Navigation System Usage Questionnaire. GYTE, Turkey (January 2010), http://alipakkan.blogspot.com/2010/01/anket-calsmas.html

Analysis and Evaluation of Wireless Ad Hoc Network Performance for a Disaster Communication Model and Scenarios

Koichi Gyoda

Shibaura Institute of Technology, 3-7-5, Toyosu Koto-ku Tokyo 135-8548 Japan
gyoda@shibaura-it.ac.jp

Abstract. When a large-scale disaster occurs, the telephone network and the cellular phone network may not be able to be used because of the hardware destruction and/or congestion. The wireless ad hoc network is expected to be a means of communication in such cases because it can be configured without network infrastructure. One of the most important problems in the wireless ad hoc network is maintaining high connectivity by autonomous routing according to the movement of the terminals. Another important problem is reducing the power consumption of the mobile terminals because the power resource of each mobile terminal is limited. In this study, it is aimed to solve both these problems and try to clarify the relationship between the quantity of routing packets and the data arrival rate when packet transmission intervals are changed in our model by use of a network simulator. The parameter values of Ad hoc On demand Distance Vector (AODV) protocol also changed to improve the network performance. Three communication scenarios termed the two-way communication, the one-way data delivery, and the browsing that could occur in disaster situations are used.

Keywords: Disaster communications, Ad hoc network, AODV.

1 Introduction

Recently so many earthquakes have been occurred all over the world. Especially, the great East Japan Earthquake on March 11th 2011 caused extensive damage including more than 18,000 people died or was missing, more than 38,000 houses were fully or partially destroyed, and the cutting of lifelines by not only earthquakes but also subsequent tsunami waves. In the fixed telephone network, maximum about 1.9 million lines were out of service. In the cellular phone network, maximum about 29,000 base stations stopped transmitting/receiving. It took more than 40 days to fully restore both fixed telephone and cellular phone networks. In addition, the cellular network experienced enormous voice call volume (maximum 50 or 60 times as much as normal) and restriction of 70% to 90%. Text messages faced much milder congestion, with only a 30% restriction. However, text messages service could not be used in the disaster area where the base stations were corrupted.

A. Marcus (Ed.): DUXU/HCII 2013, Part III, LNCS 8014, pp. 65–74, 2013.

It was also estimated that more than 5 million people had difficulty getting home on March 11th 2011 mainly in a metropolitan area of Japan. It is important to provide necessary information for such people from the standpoint of secondary disaster prevention.

We have been researching the performance of a wireless ad hoc network that can function without infrastructure in order to provide a means of communication when the existing infrastructure cannot be used in a time of disaster. When the wireless ad hoc network is configured with only a portable terminal, a difficult problem arises in maintaining the communication route while corresponding to the movement of the user terminals. An additional problem is decreasing the number of sending packets to control the network because of the limitations of the power resources of the terminals.

In this paper, we consider three communication scenarios that could occur in disaster situations. They are termed two-way communication scenario, one-way data delivery scenario, and browsing scenario. Performance of the ad hoc network protocol in these scenarios is evaluated with a model that simulates an actual Japanese city.

In the two-way communication scenario, we examine how changing the parameters of data transmission and routing affect the data arrival rate and the quantity of routing packets. In the one-way data delivery scenario, we analyze the effect of changing the data transmission interval on the data arrival rate. In the browsing scenario, we analyze the effect of changing the data transmission interval and the size of requested data size on the data arrival rate. It also examined how changing the parameters of routing protocols on the data arrival rate.

2 Communication Scenarios That Model Disaster Communication

We constructed three communication scenarios based on some actual service models: a two-way communication scenario, a one-way data delivery scenario, and a browsing scenario. In the two-way communication scenario, all terminals in the network can send and receive data packets. This scenario assumes the existence of real-time communication means such as telephones and messaging devices, which can exchange text regarding safety confirmation in real time. Figure 1(a) shows a graphic representation of the two-way communication scenario.

In the one-way data delivery scenario, only one terminal can transmit original data, and the other terminals in the network can receive or relay the data. Figure 1(b) graphically portrays the one-way data delivery scenario. This scenario assumes that disaster information will be delivered from the disaster headquarters to the victims.

In the browsing scenario, an immobile terminal acts as an http server. Other mobile terminals act as clients. Figure 1(c) shows a graphic representation of the browsing scenario. This scenario assumes that disaster information will be delivered from the server in the disaster headquarters to the victims' terminals on demands. It also will be available to assume that the SNS (Social Networking Service) is used to exchange information in the disaster area.

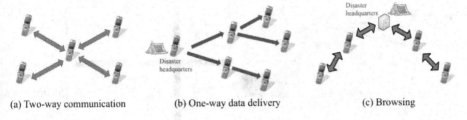

(a) Two-way communication   (b) One-way data delivery   (c) Browsing

Fig. 1. Communication scenarios

3   Details of the Simulation Model

We constructed a "real city" model by simulating an actual Japanese metropolitan area, as shown in Figure 2. This real-city model uses thick lines to represent main streets (20 m in width) and thin lines to represent side streets (5 m in width). We assume that a major street consists of two one-way traffic lanes and that a terminal moves along the left side of the major street. In the case of a minor street, we assume that it has a two-way traffic lane and that the terminal moves along the center of the lane in either direction. The probability of a terminal turning in a particular direction at a given corner is decided based on the Manhattan model for city area propagation.

To replicate an actual environment, the existence of buildings in places other than the major streets and the side streets is considered. In our simulation model, when one terminal starts to communicate, it first calculates the propagation loss between adjacent terminals based on their positions. If the propagation loss between terminals is less than 70dBm, these two terminals enable communication. The wireless ad hoc network is configured with such communication-enabled terminals. To calculate the propagation loss, we first make the line-of-sight judgment by considering the presence of buildings. If two terminals are in the line-of-sight, the propagation loss is derived by the formula of free-space propagation loss. If they are not in the line-of-sight, the propagation loss is derived by formula (1)-(3) below, which is the extension formula of free-space propagation loss taking into account the effect of diffraction. We set the maximum number of diffractions at n = 3. The line-of-sight judgment is done in two dimensions (directions of a horizontal plane), and the diffraction in a vertical direction is not considered.

$$L_{dB}^{(n)} = 20 \log\left(\frac{4\pi d_n}{\lambda}\right) \tag{1}$$

$$\begin{cases} k_j = k_{j-1} + d_{j-1} \cdot q_{j-1}, k_0 = 1 \\ d_j = k_j \cdot s_{j-1} + d_{j-1}, \quad d_0 = 0 \end{cases} \tag{2}$$

$$q_j(\theta_j) = \left(\theta_j \cdot \frac{q_{90}}{90}\right)^\nu, \ q_{90} = 0.5, \ \nu = 1.5 \tag{3}$$

We applied these scenarios and models to the network simulator OPNET ver. 11 and performed simulations.

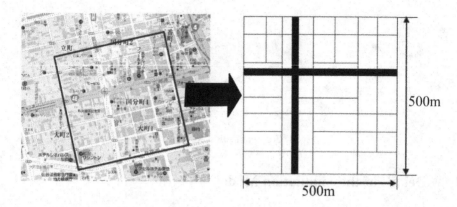

Fig. 2. Real city model

4   Simulation Result of Two-Way Communication Scenario

Table 1 lists the parameters used for the simulation of the two-way communication scenario. The number of terminals is set to 100. Each terminal randomly decides a destination terminal and starts to communicate. The speed of each terminal is set to a random value of 2 m/sec or less, which assumes the usual walking speed. The transmission data rate is 4096, 16384, and 32768 bits/sec. Data is sent with Constant Bit Rate (CBR) at intervals of 0.25 sec and 1.0 sec. The value of the Active Route Timeout (ART) in AODV is set to 0.25, 0.5, 1.0, 1.5, and 2.0 sec.

Table 1. Parameters for the two-way communication scenario

Simulation Time	900 sec.
WLAN Protocol	802.11 g / 11 Mbps
Routing Protocol	AODV
Transmission Power	10 mW

Variations in the number of routing packets affected by changing the ART in AODV and data transmission intervals were analyzed. Figure 3 shows an example of the number of the routing packets versus ART in the case of a data transmission rate of 32768 bits/sec and a maximum speed of the terminals of 0 m/sec or 2 m/sec. It is obvious that when the ART becomes longer than the packet transmission interval, the number of routing packets decreases. It is observed that the quantity of routing packets similarly decreases in proportion to the data transmission interval when even the amount of data and the maximum speed of the terminal are changed.

The data arrival rate in relation to the amount of data was analyzed. Figure 4 shows an example of the data arrival rate in relation to the ART when the terminal speed is 0 m/sec (meaning all terminals are fixed), the data transmission rate is 4096 or 32768 bits/sec and the data transmission interval is 0.25 sec or 1.0 sec. At a rate of 4096 bits/sec, a higher data arrival percentage is obtained with a data transmission interval of 1.0 sec compared to 0.25 sec. However, when the rate is 32768 bits/sec, the data arrival percentage is higher in the case of a 0.25-sec interval than a 1.0-sec interval.

Figures 5 and 6 show the same results as Figure 4 except for the difference in the maximum speed of the terminal, 1 m/sec or 2 m/sec, respectively. By comparing Figures 4, 5 and 6, it is clear that the data arrival rate for a maximum terminal speed of 1 m/sec or 2 m/sec is lower than for a speed of 0 m/sec. This is due to packet loss caused by terminal movement.

When the data rate is 32768 bits/sec and the maximum terminal speed is either 1 m/sec or 2 m/sec, the data arrival rate with a transmission interval of 0.25 sec is not necessarily higher than with a 1.0 sec interval. However, when the transmission rate is 32768 bits/sec, the difference between intervals of 0.25 sec and 1.0 sec is greater than when the transmission rate is 4096 bits/sec.

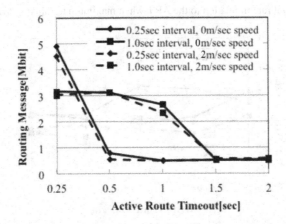

Fig. 3. Number of the routing packets per ART when the data transmission rate is 32768 bits/sec

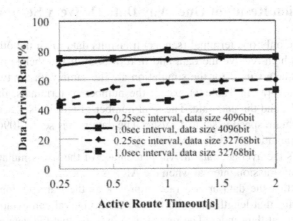

Fig. 4. Data arrival rate in relation to the ART when terminal speed is 0 m/sec

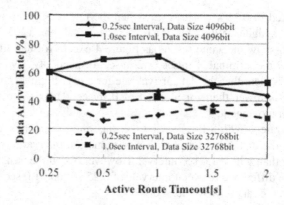

Fig. 5. Data arrival rate in relation to the ART when maximum terminal speed is 1 m/sec

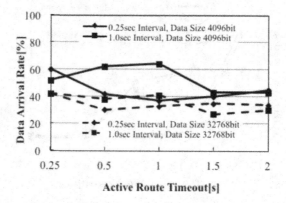

Fig. 6. Data arrival rate in relation to the ART when maximum terminal speed is 2 m/sec

5   Simulation Result of One-Way Data Delivery Scenario

In this simulation, only one terminal (sender) transmits data to all the other terminals in the network, which receive the data and in turn relay it to other terminals if it is needed. The parameters used for the simulation are the same with the two-way communication scenario (as in Table 1) except the number of terminals, the maximum speed of terminals, and the data rate. The total number of terminals is set to either 50 or 100. The maximum speed is set to 1 m/sec. The data rate is set to 4096 bit/sec. We conducted five simulations in this scenario.

Figure 7 shows the average data arrival percentage of the five simulations in relation to the data transmission interval when the ART is 3.0 sec.

It was shown that the data arrival rate improves as the transmission interval increases. This means that lengthening the transmission interval can avoid the congestion of routing data at the sender. The results also indicate that the data arrival rate is improved by increasing the number of terminals.

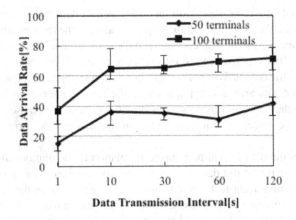

Fig. 7. Data arrival rate in relation to transmission interval when there are 50 or 100 terminals

Table 2 shows an example of the data arrival rate when the ART is changed from 3.0 sec to 0.5 sec. The data arrival rate is improved an average of about 5% by changing the ART. Table 3 shows an example of the average data arrival rate by changing the method of data transmission. We used two methods. One is simultaneous transmission, in which the sender transmits data from source to all terminals simultaneously. The other is partitioned transmission, in which the sender transmits data to ten terminals at a time and repeats it at intervals of a few seconds. The ART is set to 3.0 sec. It is clear that a high data arrival rate was not obtained even with partitioned transmission. However, the number of routing packets in the case of partitioned transmission is smaller than with simultaneous transmission. By decreasing the number of routing packet transmissions, power consumption is reduced. This is effective in saving power, and efficient communication is the expected result.

Table 2. Data arrival rate obtained by changing the ART in the one-way data delivery scenario

		1st	2nd	3rd	4th	5th	Average
Data Arrival Rate[%]	ART 3.0 s	73.1	73.8	67.9	62.1	68.4	69.1
	ART 0.5 s	79.3	73.7	76.2	68.1	81.4	75.7

Table 3. Avarage data arrival rate and average number of routing packets

	Simultaneous	Partitioned
Data Arrival Rate [%]	69.1	65.0
Routing Packet [Mbit]	517	350

6   Simulation Result of Browsing Scenario

In this simulation, only one terminal acts as an http server and all the other terminals in the network acts as http clients and sends requests to the http server. The parameters used for the simulation are the same with the one-way data delivery scenario except the number of terminals, the data size and the request interval. The total number of terminals is set to 101 (one server and 100 clients). The data size from server to clients is set to 4kbyte, 8kbyte, or 16kbyte. The request interval is set to 10, 30, or 60sec.

Figure 8 shows the data arrival percentage in relation to the data request interval. It was shown that the data arrival rate improves as the request interval increases. It also indicates that the data arrival rate is worsened as the data size increases. However, it can be said that the effect of request interval on the network performance is larger than the data size.

Figure 9 shows the data arrival percentage in relation to the number of clients (100 to 300). It was shown that the data arrival rate is worsened as the number of clients increase. It is very important to keep data arrival rate high even in the case when the number of clients increase. When the number of clients increases, both number of hops from client to server and the number of routing packets increase. So, we propose to change AODV parameters (TTL increment, TTL threshold, and Net diameter) to restrain the number of hops. As in the table 4, AODV parameters are changed from default value to Rev. A or Rev. B.

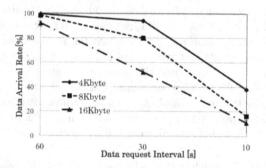

Fig. 8. Data arrival rate in relation to data request interval

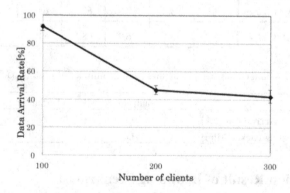

Fig. 9. Data arrival rate in relation to number of clients

Table 4. The value of AODV parameters

	TTL increment	TTL threshold	Net diameter
Default value	2	7	35
Rev. A	1	6	35
Rev. B	1	6	10

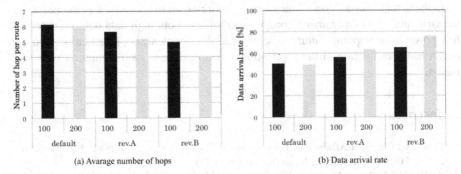

(a) Avarage number of hops　　　　　　　　　(b) Data arrival rate

Fig. 10. Average number of hops and data arrival percentage when the AODV parameters are changed (total number of clients is 100 or 200)

Figure 10 shows the average number of hops and the data arrival percentage when the AODV parameters are changed as the table 4 when the total number of clients is either 100 or 200. It was shown that the network performance is improved by decreasing TTL increment, TTL threshold, and Net Diameter.

7   Conclusion

We evaluated the performance of a wireless ad hoc network for constructing a network that provides the means of communication in a time of disaster.

We designed three communication scenarios and examined the effects of changing the network parameters on the data arrival rate and the number of routing packets in these scenarios.

In the case of the two-way communication scenario, we concluded that setting the ART longer than the data packet transmission interval can reduce the number of routing packets.

In addition, it is clear that in the case of a relatively large transmission rate that shortening the data packet transmission interval decreases packet loss.

More efficient communication can be expected by setting the appropriate setting of ART and the data packet transmission interval according to the data transmission rate and the network topology.

The one-way data delivery scenario clarified that the data arrival rate is improved by lengthening the transmission interval. It is also shown that the data arrival rate is improved by increasing the number of terminals. It is possible to communicate efficiently by partitioning the data transmission from the sender.

In the case of the browsing scenario, it is shown that the data arrival rate improves as the transmission interval increase as in the case of the one-way data delivery scenario. However, the data arrival rate decreases as the number of terminal increases because the number of routing hops and the number of routing packets are increased. AODV parameters are changed to improve the data arrival rate even the number of terminal increases. By choosing these parameters properly, it is shown that the number of routing hops is suppressed and the data arrival rate can be kept relatively high.

In the actual disaster communications, it is important to choose the communication scenario and AODV parameters properly to achieve both high data delivery rate and low power consumption. Future tasks include development, implementation, and the performance evaluation of the application corresponding to such communication scenarios.

References

1. Ministry of Internal Affairs and Telecommunications of Japan: 2011 White Paper Information and Communications in Japan (September 2011)
2. ARIB IMT-2000 Study Committee: Evaluation Methodology for IMT- 2000 Radio Transmission Technologies (Version. 1.1), pp. 35–37 (September 1998)
3. Gyoda, K., et al.: Performance Evaluation of Wireless Ad Hoc Network for Disaster Communication. Journal of the National Institute of Information and Communications Technology 58(1/2), 107–129 (2011)
4. Berg, J.-E.: A Recursive Method for Street Microcell Path Loss Calculations. In: Proc. PIMRC 1995, vol. 1, pp. 140–143 (September 1995)
5. OPNET Technologies, http://www.opnet.com

Improving Management of Medical Equipment

Yu Hao, Yida Gong, and Young Mi (Christina) Choi

Georgia Institute of Technology, USA
{yhao33,yidagong,christina.choi}@gatech.edu

Abstract. The wide array of devices used in critical care areas of hospitals creates difficulties in keeping order. Disorganized equipment in these areas can lead to numerous issues including lower task efficiency for health care workers, potential safety hazards and infection control issues. An equipment mounting rail and adapter system is one of the best tools available to help manage and organize critical equipment. Current rail systems perform well in many respects yet but there are still a number of areas that may be improved. Improved interfaces for attaching and positioning equipment are needed to enhance safety and improve ease of use. As equipment rail systems are widely used backward compatibility is important to allow health care facilities to deploy enhanced equipment management systems while still leveraging their investment in current hardware. This will aid effectively and efficiently managing the deployment of new technologies in these settings.

This paper discusses the process undertaken to design and test a new mounting rail for medical equipment aimed at improving the device organization and workflow in critical care areas. The project was sponsored by an equipment management manufacturer, so initial requirements were gathered through meetings with product experts as well as the sales and marketing director. This step helped to ensure that current market conditions and realistic business objectives were considered. Further requirements were gathered through on site observations and interviews. This included observations at the cardiac intensive care unit at Egleston Children's Healthcare of Atlanta in order to gather data on the using environment, to observe users in their natural work environment, and then to follow up the observations with one-on-one interviews to bring further clarity to observed issues. A participatory design process was utilized to engage stakeholders at various stages of the design process in order to identify potential design issues and continually evaluate the usability of the evolving concept.

These were followed by end user usability testing and analysis. The new rail system under development was show improvements in control, secure and flexibility, which will take more care on user experience. The usability evaluation was measured by effectiveness and satisfaction of the design, namely their impact on task efficiency, the impact on infection control and ergonomics of use. The final result showed the design almost meet the requirement, though some features need to be further improved.

Keywords: user experience, rail&adapter, usability, healthcare, medical equipment mounting system.

A. Marcus (Ed.): DUXU/HCII 2013, Part III, LNCS 8014, pp. 75–84, 2013.
© Springer-Verlag Berlin Heidelberg 2013

1   Introduction

There is currently much attention on hospital management and organization in the industries of both design as well as macroeconomics. This attention is not only because of the very nature of hospitals: the curing of diseases and the desire to prolong lives, but also because of the increasing demands brought on by technological improvements and innovations. Clinical engineering professionals need to continually review and improve their management strategies in order to keep up with improvements in equipment technology, as well as with increasing expectations of health care organizations [1].

Fig. 1. Disorganization of equipment in a clinical care environment

Clinical care areas can become unorganized, as shown in Figure 1. There are a lot of devices that need to be used in one room for completing multiple tasks simultaneously or within a given period of time. The issue can be compounded as the need to move patients often arises during clinical care. Disorganized equipment in these areas can lead to numerous issues including lower task efficiency for health care workers, potential safety hazards and infection control issues. An important question is what system provides the best tool to manage and organize equipment in these environments. There are many companies which manufacture organizational railing systems which are wall mounted with the goal of making nurses', doctors' and patients' live much easier and less overwhelming while in the hospital environment.

Current rail systems perform well in many respects yet but there are still a number of areas that may be improved. One major shortcoming, according to marketing research, is that the rail system cannot deal with some scenarios, though it is flexible to manage the disordered equipment with the system. For example, they may require specific tools to lock and there is no adapter profile for vertical pole, etc. New designs must also better meet the ergonomic requirements for the many different tasks that are performed in dynamic care environments. New devices must be able to keep pace with the iteration of clinical care and developments of new technology.

Hospitals are places many patients are gathered who bring with them a variety of different bacteria and viruses. As patients can come in contact with new infections in this environment, cleaning in hospitals is critical. Adverse outcomes or illness among patients or health care workers can occur from medical device use due to inadvertent exposures to environmental pathogens, improper ventilation and distribution of airborne exposure. Thus, the ability to sterilize, reliably clean, and maintain the integrity of medical devices is a critical design feature [2].

2   Prototype Development through User Input

The most salient feature of the medical equipment innovation process appears to be the fact that the end user of the equipment often plays an important role in its initial invention and subsequent development [3]. Stakeholders such as manufacturers also participate in the design iteration phases [4].

This project is based on a graduate course project sponsored by an equipment management manufacturer. Many of the manufacturer's users are existing customers. A primary goal was to create a new design that support the existing installed base and allow sales growth through differentiation. The ideal scenario would include the new adapter fitting on the existing profile rail, and the old adapter fitting on the new rail.

In order to gather data on the usage environment and gather end user feedback, observations and interviews were conducted at the cardiac intensive care unit at Egleston Children's Healthcare of Atlanta. Apart from the ease of use, the nurses desired a solution that would work in both vertical and horizontal and horizontal orientations without the need to remove the adapter from the equipment. Vertical systems are needed to work better in small spaces. It is preferable that equipment can be removed. Nothing but hand sanitizer was mounted on the wall because of the need of portability, so a movable and portable adapter is desired.

Based on the users input from the observation and interviews, design requirements were concluded as following.

— Special requirements for hospital environment- Anti-microbial and safety:
  In this controlled environment, the rail system has to meet the demand of sanitation. It should easy to clean, like rails and adaptors must not have areas that cannot be easily cleaned such as small crevices and hard to reach areas. All surfaces must lend themselves to a thorough cleaning. Some items required permanent stability. These items must be secure to ensure stability. Falling equipment raises costs and injury. And the rail and adapter system themselves should not be a hazard. Materials used must be non flammable and avoid sharp edges.
— Ease of use:
  The use environment contains many different devices, and the users' activities within it are very complex. The adapter and rail system must therefore be as simple to use as possible. Installation must be timely as to not impede other hospital activities. Easy use helps ensure a correct installation every time. The adapter must also avoid the need to use tools to lock it on to the rail.
— Vertical and Horizontal mounting:
  The ability to be mounted both vertically and horizontally is necessary for creating systems that can be adapted to any patient environment. It provides configuration flexibility and allows hospitals to manipulate space as patient demand changes.

— Appearance and affordability:
  The device should have an aesthetic appearance that gives the user a comfortable feeling. Also, the perceived and actual properties of it should demonstrate the right conceptual model of how it could be used. These requirements contribute to satisfaction of use.

According to the design requirements, a first iteration prototype was made, and being evaluated by users at Dekalb Medical at Atlanta. The vertical pole design was found useful, especially the rotation from vertical and horizontal which helped reduce nurses' effort a great deal. Height adjustability was also found to be a helpful feature. This gives users the flexibility to adjust the height of the height of the device to best facilitate their work. The vertical pole adapter can be used to hold temporary items such as alcohol sponges so that the nurses do not need to worry much about find somewhere to store or throw them. The initial feedback also suggested ways to expand usage of the vertical pole adapter. In order to achieve compatibility, there is a slot on the rotatable square, so the current adapter can be mounted on this vertical pole adapter. Sometimes the device mounted on the vertical pole is very heavy, which requires that the vertical pole adapter lock firmly so that the device is secure and stable. The clamp structure must be carefully determined and tested. For a general adapter, it was suggested that the pull stick should not seem too weak that easily broken.

Fig. 2. Initial/revised vertical pole adapter

3 Method

Eight healthcare workers were recruited to participate in a usability evaluation of a new rail adapter product. The participants had never used similar management tools before, so an introduction of the use of medical equipment management solutions was given. The new prototype adapter product is shown in Figure 3. The general adapter can be mounted and lock on the rail or the pole adapter without using any tools, the only thing need to do is aim at the slot and buckle up it onto the rail or the pole adapter. When release it off, the user just pull the stick and the adapter could be easily demounted. For the operation of the pole adapter, if users need to change the direction between horizontal and vertical, they just need to pull the rail out, rotate it, and then push it back to lock. Participants completed the following three simulation tasks which demonstrated the main feature of the new design:

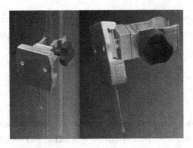

Fig. 3. The newly designed rail adapter

1. Mount and unmount: Hold the medical equipment, find out ways to mount it on the rail and find out ways to demount it.
2. Adjust the height on the vertical pole: hold the medical equipment, find out ways to mount it on the vertical pole, and adjust the height on the vertical pole and try to fix it.
3. Rotate from horizontal to vertical: mount the rail on the vertical pole adapter in horizontal, mount equipment on the rail and find out ways to rotate it from horizontal to vertical.

An evaluation survey designed to measure users' level of satisfaction and effectiveness was completed immediately after the tasks were completed. It consisted of 12 Likert items related to effectiveness and satisfaction. The items categorized by ease of use, time of use, function and complexity, effectiveness, appearance, conceptual understanding, safety and infection control and overall satisfaction. Each survey item had five possible answers (1 = strongly disagree, 2 = somewhat disagree, 3 = neither agree nor disagree, 4 = somewhat agree, 5 = strongly agree).

Five of the survey items were related to the satisfaction of the device, and seven of the items were related to satisfaction. An effectiveness score and a satisfaction score were obtained by adding the scores for the related items. A total usability score was obtained by totaling all 12 of the Likert items. The survey used can be found on the appendix.

An additional non-Likert item was stated at the end of the survey. This item was aimed at evaluating the overall opinion of the device immediately after its use. The item was as follows: Please place an X by the statement that most closely matches your overall opinion of the system.

- The product design is very good. I like almost everything about it.
- The product design is mostly good. There are only a few things about it that I do not like.
- The product design is average. There are about as many things that I like as dislike.
- The product design is mostly poor. There are only a few things about it that I like.
- The product design is very poor. I do not like anything about it.

The answers to this question were scored from 1 (the worst answer) to 5 (the best answer).

The averages of all responses for each task were used to describe the performance of this product in different tasks. The average of all responses for each of the three tasks is used to show comprehensive and overall performance of the product.

4   Results

The evaluation survey was tested before use to make sure that questions were understandable. A total of 24 healthcare workers performed the evaluation and

Table 1. Average scores of three different tasks

#		Task 1	Task 2	Task 3
1	Overall, I am satisfied with the ease of completing the tasks in this scenario	4.5	4.375	4.625
2	Overall, I am satisfied with the amount of time it took to complete the tasks in this scenario	4.75	3.375	4.875
3	It was easy to understand how to operate the product	3.25	4.75	4
4	Using the device to complete the task felt safe.	3.875	4.25	3.625
5	I would be satisfied if I had to use this system frequently.	4.125	4.125	4.25
6	I found the system unnecessarily complex.	1.5	1.625	1.25
7	I could easily complete the task with the system	4.5	4.375	4.5
8	I found the various functions in this system were well integrated.	4.125	4.25	4.625
9	I would imagine that most people would learn to use this system very quickly	3.625	3.875	4.25
10	Aesthetically, I like the overall look of the system.	4.375	4.125	4.375
11	Compared with other methods or products to aid with managing the medical equipment, the actual functionality of this system is better	4.125	4.375	4.25
12	The product is easy to clean which reduces the risk of infection	3.375	3.875	4.125
overall	The product design is very good/mostly good/average/mostly poor/very poor.	4.125	4.25	4.375

completed surveys. Table 1 displays average scores of three simulation tasks that participants completed with the rail system.

The data was categorized into 7 groups to evaluate 7 different features of this system. Questions #1, #5, #7 were used to describe ease of use. Question #8 and #11 were grouped together to evaluate the functionality. For safety and infection control issue, question #4 and #12 were given to users to evaluate. The aim of question #3 and #9 was to estimate whether it was a good conceptual model. Questions #2, #6, #10 were used to estimate the feeling of time of use, complexity and appearance. Figure 4 shows the results from the survey. For easy to use, time of use (efficiency), better function and aesthetics, most participants chose agree or strongly agree, and a few of them chose neither agree or disagree. For good conceptual model, safe and no infection issue, a lot of responses were agree or strongly agree, and some of responses were neither agree or disagree. For complexity, none of the participants thought the system was unnecessarily complex. Overall, most participants thought the product design was mostly good; some of them chose the statement that the product design is very good; two responses were the product design was average.

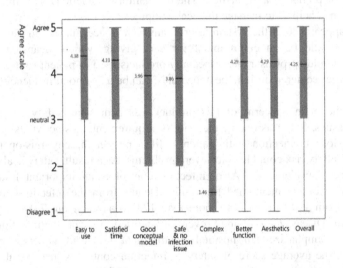

Fig. 4. Survey results based on various evaluation categories.

5   Discussion

The survey seemed to indicate that users basically are satisfied with the using product, as they were agreed with that the product design is mostly good.

— Participants thought it was easy to use this rail system. On one hand, for question #1, #5 and #7, the average scores of three tasks are all above 4.00. On the other hand, the average score for the complexity of the product is very low. Based on the feedback from healthcare workers, the disorder in patient room can disturb them and increase the workload, and sometimes may lead serious problems. They do need a management system to deal with medical equipment, particularly in a patient room which has a large number of equipment or in a scenario where nurses need to move equipment frequently. Functional management system which is easy enough to use allow for the possibility that controlling the disorder to provide a better and more efficient environment.

— Overall, users are satisfied with the time to complete the tasks. The average score for the second task is relatively low, but the other two are very high. Based on nurses' feedback, it is crucial to complete some tasks, like attach or detach equipment, very quickly, especially when it is an emergency. In other scenarios, nurses may need to repeat some tasks several times a day. Using this product should reduce the time of these tasks rather than increasing it, otherwise, it will be unnecessarily trouble.

— For average scores of functions, they are all above 4.00. Most of responses believed the various functions in this system were well integrated. Besides, the average scores of question #11 (comparison between this product and other methods or products) are satisfied. The evaluation of functions indicates that this rail system is helpful to manage medical equipment.

— For the appearance of the system, users found it was acceptable and satisfied. The hospital should be an environment for care giving, which means products in hospital should be pleasurable, especially products used in patient room. From the point of user centered design, the appearance can be a key point influencing the use process.

— One of the main concerns of this product was addressing safety and infection control issues. Safety is one of the priority requirements. As activities in hospital have a close connection with patient's life and health, any mis-operation or potential safety risk could lead to severe problems. As a result, safety is always one of the top considerations. Also, infection control is an important issue which healthcare workers mentioned frequently. Deaths from the infections more than doubled from 1999 to 2007, to more than 17,000 a year from 7,000 a year, the Centers for Disease Control and Prevention reported. It means the infection control has to be emphasized in hospital environment to avoid unnecessary death. However, the average score of safety & infection control is just passable. Some responses were the product was not safe enough for a specific task, and some responses were the product was not easy enough to sterilize.

The goal of this survey was to evaluate the effectiveness and satisfaction of the new rail system. The results of ease of use, time of use, appearance and functionality are basically favorable. However, some problems needed to be improved also showed in the results:

— First, only one task got an average score more than 4.00 for question #3, and a few responses collected revealed that user did not agree with that it was easy to understand how to operate the product. Second, question #9 had similar responses. The average scores were relatively low and there were a few disagree responses. Based on that, a conclusion was drawn that the design did not have a powerful conceptual model. Norman [5] mentioned that there are two gulfs between user goals and physical system, which are gulf of execution and gulf of evaluation. For gulf of execution, Norman means that the product should have good affordance to imply user to avoid confusion and mis-operation. To achieve a better performance, the product should have more clues of how to use. The clues may be specific shapes, colors or icons to indicate the operation.

— Users gave some feedback according to safety and infection control issues: 1) the pull stick on the adaptor may be a potential danger if it is broken because of unintentional behavior; 2) the pull stick may have infection control problem, so does the vertical pole adaptor. As mentioned above, both safety and infection control is crucial issues in hospital environment. Consequently, the pull stick is about to be replaced by a metal chain to avoid being broken and control infection. It is also considered that either widens the gap for easy cleaning or minimizes the gap for infection control.

6   Conclusion

Overall, the results of the survey meet the preset goals. However, there were some trade off may influence the accuracy of the result. First, there are a lot of tasks for this rail system. There may be large differences in the performance of the new adapter when attaching different types of equipment. The participants were all from the same organization so they may have similar experiences and opinions which prevents the generalizability of the results. Second, the prototype used in the survey was a prototype embodying most of the intended functionality but was not a final product. There is a large gap between prototype and final product with regards to the weight, feel, audible feedback, appearance, etc. The gap could lead to a less accurate user experience. For example, users may have better experience of the appearance with the final product and the sound feedback can make user feel more safe and easy to use. The most important difference is the functionality difference which may influence the evaluation of ease of use and functionality. Third, the rail system was evaluated in a simulation environment. Users did not actually use the system during their daily activities. Instead of that, they were asked to imagine the scenario, so there is a possibility that they overlooked or did not experience some potential problems.

The overall effectiveness and satisfaction of the device almost met the expected requirements. Scores were high for ease of use, efficiency, function and appearance. However, the evaluation of conceptual model, safe and infection control were not satisfactory. To improve these scores for the vertical pole adapter, adjusts to the shape, color and instructions (such as added icons) may be added to more clearly indicate proper use. To improve infection control the existing gaps must be widened to facilitate easy cleaning or reduced to eliminate the need. The general adapter might be improved by changing the stick into a chain.

References

1. Wang, B., Furst, E., Cohen, T., Keil, O.R., Ridgway, M., Stiefel, R.: Medical Equipment Management Strategies. Biomedical Instrumentation & Technology 40(3), 233–237 (2006)
2. Weinger, M.B., Wiklund, M.E., Gardner-Bonneau, D.J.: Handbook of human factors in medical device design. CRC Press (2010)
3. Hippel, E.V.: The dominant role of users in the scientific instrumentation innovation process. Research Policy 5, 212–239 (1976)
4. Biemans, W.G.: User and third-party involvement in developing medical equipment innovations. Technovation 11(3), 163–182 (1991)
5. Norman, D.A.: The design of everyday things. Technology & Engineering (1990)

Safety of Natural Disasters

Lamiaa F. Ibrahim[1,2], Reem Albatati[1], Samah Batawil[1], Rudainah Shilli[1],
Mai Bakeer[1], and Tasneem Abo Al Laban[1]

[1] Faculty of Computing and Information Technology, King Abdulaziz University
[2] Institute of Statistical Studies and Research, Cairo University
lfibrahim@kau.edu.sa

Abstract. Recently, Jeddah has witnessed catastrophic events that have caused the environment pollution, detention of people in one area and the inability of people to go to other safe places. For instance, flood has caused the sinking and destruction of homes and the private properties. Also, the existence of excavation works at Jeddah streets has been the main reason for the traffic disruption and the occurrence of many traffic accidents. All these incidents have been happened because these instructions have not been given to all individuals whereas the guidance and advising means were limited to the SMS. The occurrence of such events could be prevented in case that there is a consciousness program and if the civil protection forces play its significant role in these hard times. The goal of this work which will be available for free download, will deliver real-time disaster and road constructions information and notification to users such as fires, floods, constructions. It also receives warnings and tips on how to react before, during and after the disaster, direct to mobile phones. The use of GPS technology through this application could allow location-specific information to be fed to the citizens providing them with the nearest safe location and the shortest path to get there. Moreover, it will receive Google map updates for any newly added information. In time of a trouble, the user can benefit from the knowledge-based system feature that will give him a feedback on what action the user should take upon a specific situation. The knowledge-based system was building through interview with the Experts domains. All these features will improve access to the needed information at the needed time.

Keywords: safety, Natural disasters, smartphone, Knowledge-based system.

1 Introduction

Recently, Jeddah has witnessed catastrophic events that have caused the environment pollution, detention of people in one area and the inability of people to go to other safe places. For instance, flood has caused the sinking and destruction of homes and the private properties. Also, the existence of excavation works at Jeddah streets has been the main reason for the traffic disruption and the occurrence of many traffic accidents. All these incidents have been happened because these instructions have not been given to all individuals whereas the guidance and advising means were limited

A. Marcus (Ed.): DUXU/HCII 2013, Part III, LNCS 8014, pp. 85–94, 2013.

to the SMS. The occurrence of such events could be prevented in case that there is a consciousness program and if the civil defence forces play its significant role in these hard times.

The growing use of smartphones devices equipped with GPS and sensors has resulted in new types of spatial computing applications. Such technologies have enabled service providers to offer location-based and context-aware services to users that are always connected and interacting with various systems and information sources [1]. Using sensing applications is a recent IBM project on intelligent transportation is one example of a context-aware service. "Here, researchers aimed to help computers avoid congestion and enable transportation agencies to better understand, predict, and manage traffic flow"[2]. The project collects traffic data from various sensors on toll booths, roads, intersections, and bridges and combines it with location-based data from users' smartphones to learn their mobility patterns. Based on their favoured routes, participating users automatically received traffic information and alerts on their phones, resulting in reduced traffic congestion and accidents.

Another interesting application domain is that of mobile commerce [3] in which businesses can provide location-based and context-aware services to customers. For example, merchants can provide offers to customers based on customers' location (provided by location services), interests and preferences (extracted from their social media profiles or Facebook "likes"), and availability (inferred from their online activity, such as check-ins). Here, we look at disaster management as an application domain. In particular, we illustrate how citizens' participatory sensing coupled with social media can enable effective and timely information sharing for situational awareness and informed decision making. The combination of spatial computing and social media within the context of disaster management raises some unique and interesting challenges. Many application can found [4-21] showing the important of such technologies to solve days problems.

In section. 2 discusses related work. In section 3, the DSRG package is introduced. The paper conclusion is presented in section 4.

2   Related Work

Gaia GPS (for Haitian Disaster Relief): The app can be used to download maps and satellite imagery of the earthquake area, including up to date overlays of disaster sites, hospitals, and other relevant waypoints. The map data is provided by Digital Globe, GeoEye, openStreetMap and the maps are hosted by the New York Library. OpenStreetMap map images hosted by the Dutch OpenStreetMap community, courtesy of Oxilion. The app also provides other features that might be relevant to disaster relief efforts:

- Recording of GPS tracks, waypoints and geo tagged photos.
- Import / export GPX tracks and photos.
- Guidance to waypoints and along tracks [22].

ubAlert – Disaster Alert Network: This app gives you all the information you need when it comes to disasters, incidents and hazards happening across the world. With data

Collected from both verified sources and users like you, you will instantly have access to everything you need to know about an event. Alerts contain basic event details, impact statistics and maps.

Features include:

- Interactive map.
- Sort events by severity, popularity and location.
- Reports an event and submit a photo.
- Save alerts to your "watch" list for quick viewing.
- Adjust text size [23].

Disaster Alert: This app will detect and announce to all people at the same region about all kinds of natural disaster before a while from the time when it's occur, as the source of their information is the PDC organization Pacific Disaster Centre. Work as global disaster info on an interactive user map. It's grantee the publicity of all kinds of disaster.

Features:

- View Active Hazards on an interactive map or in the Alert list.
- Search for location (quick zoom).
- Choose background map.
- Get "more info" for most Active disaster.
- Receive automatic updates every five minutes.
- Choose a preferred time zone [24].

3   Implementation of DSRG Disaster Smart Road Guidance

This section will introduce to you the tools, technologies and languages used to develop smart road guidance DSRG package.

Eb2a free Hosting:The modern Internet community is moving towards social networks and clouds, there is still some space for traditional free web hosting that enables to publish a *custom web page*, or *custom blog*, or other *"manually" build website* on the web at absolutely no cost[25]. An Eb2a free hosting site gives the quality hosting and user friendly tools a user needs to start building and hosting their websites.

Types of panels used by eb2a[25]:

CPanel (Vista panel): The most preferred hosting control panel on the net today.

Fantastico: Installs complex scripts like forums and website templates in a few clicks.

Htaccess: Our Free Hosting is now Supporting the htaccess features.

Eb2a features and offers[25]:

Eb2a servers don't add fix ads on pages. They are configured for compatibility with PHP/MySQL scripts. It uses the latest versions of PHP, MySQL and Apache Web Server.The software is regularly updated to ensure optimal security and compatibility. It ensures Instant activation on free hosting accounts means users can sign up and within seconds the website is ready to use. Also, it includes some very handy features in the control panel, one feature which is enjoyed by customers is the automatic installer.another feature is that The self-named server does exactly what it says, users can choose from a large list of popular scripts such as message boards, gallerys, wikis etc. The script is installed into your webspace in seconds, saving long upload times and bandwidth. All current free hosting accounts get 5500MB Space and 200GB Bandwidth. In addition, the users' account will also have PHP and 50 MySQL Databases.

Eclipse SDK platform:

When we create a new Android project we will deal with three key items in the project's root directory[26]:

AndroidManifest.xml: It is an XML file describing the application being built and what components activities, services, etc that is being supplied by that application.

Category: Gives additional information about the action to execute. For example, CATEGORY_LAUNCHER means it should appear in the Launcher as a top-level application[27].

A launcher icon: is a graphic that represents your application. Launcher icons are used by Launcher applications and appear on the user's Home screen. Launcher icons can also be used to represent shortcuts into your application (for example, a contact shortcut icon that opens detail information for a contact)[28].

src/: It contains all source code file (.java file) of android application.

res/: Resources are to store all external contents that used in android applications. These are external elements that you want to include and reference within your application, like images, icons, audio, video, text strings, layouts, themes, etc. Static files that are packaged along with your application, either in their original form or, occasionally, in a preprocessed form. Some of the sub-directories you will find or create under res/ Contains several sub-directories for app resources. Here are just a few:

res/drawable-hdpi/ for images ,pictures (png, jpeg etc) e.g. .icon.png. Directory for drawable objects (such as bitmaps) that are designed for high-density (hdpi) screens. Other drawable directories contain assets designed for other screen densities.

res/layout/ for XML(User Interface) that UI layout used in Project or view window of an application.(E.g. main.xml).

res/menu/ for a common user interface component in many types of applications. To provide a familiar and consistent user experience, you should use the Menu APIs to present user actions and other options in your activities.

res/values/ Directory for other various XML files that contain a collection of resources, such as definitions, Arrays, colors, dimensions, strings, and styles.(E.g. strings.xml).

res/xml/ for other general-purpose XML files you wish to ship.

Google map API: MapView objects are views that display Maps tiles downloaded from the Google Maps service. To ensure that applications use Maps data in an appropriate manner, the Google Maps service requires application developers to register with the service, agreeing to the Terms of Service and supplying an MD5 fingerprint of the certificate(s) that they will use to sign applications. For each registered certificate fingerprint, the service then provides the developer with a Google Maps Android API v1 Key — an alphanumeric string that uniquely identifies the certificate and developer registered with the service [29]. Knowledge-based System: A knowledge-based is an information repository that provides a means for information to be collected, organized, shared, searched and utilized. It can be either machine-readable or intended for human use [30]. Figure 1 shows Components for DSRG Application.

Implementation Process:

As shown in Figure 2, there is no directly interacting between the server and the android application. Instead, the communication between them is through the database.

When developing DSRG package, our goal was to provide early warnings of all hazards to create effective response actions and dramatically reduce their effects on our lives and property. So, our plan was to create a mobile application that directs individuals in times of crises. We started the application building process by analyzing the users' needs in such circumstances. Then we designed the application according to their requirements and providing them with the needed efficient information. After facing a lot of problems, we successfully implemented DSRG application that operates on android mobile phones. Finally we tested it on a sample of people and we successfully met the objectives of our work. In conclusion, the rapid growth in the use of Smartphone – which offer internet access and a variety of internet-based applications – is changing the way we live our lives especially in a life threatening situations where critical instant information and support are needed from trustworthy resources. The GPS was played a vital role for the end user as it helps him to pinpoint the location while the GIS was helped him to get any significant information or advice related to how to evacuate from a dangerous place relying on the current site as provided by the administrator or the alternative road in case of road repair. In addition, this package contains up to date climate prediction. Also, the user can benefit from the knowledge-based system feature that will give him a feedback on what action the user should take upon a specific situation. Figure 3 shows Android application structure.

Server:

Create Database using PHP My Admin on server.

Create our website pages: We built a website containing 4 pages using HTML, PHP and CSS languages.

Home page:

Show the map that contains all events that is still happening.

Login: a link that navigate the admin to the login page.

Add event: a button from which admin can access event page.

Send tips: a button from which admin can access tips page.

Figure 4 shows Home Page and Figure 5 shows Map Screenshot.

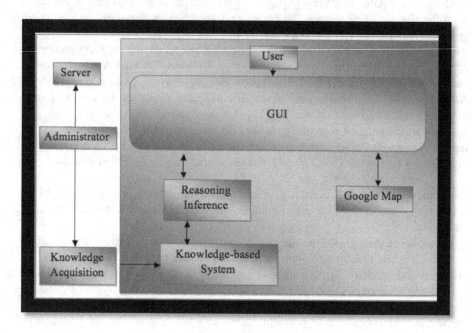

Fig. 1. Components for DSRG Application

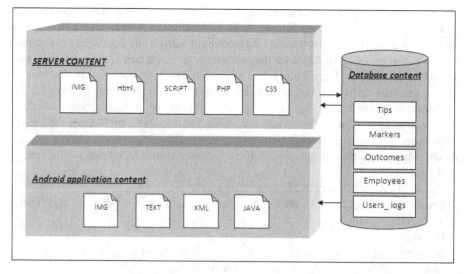

Fig. 2. Server and Android application content

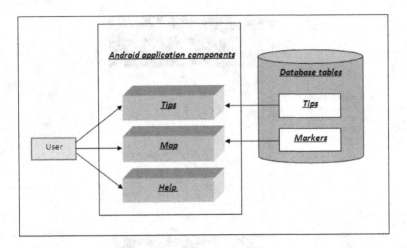

Fig. 3. Android application structure

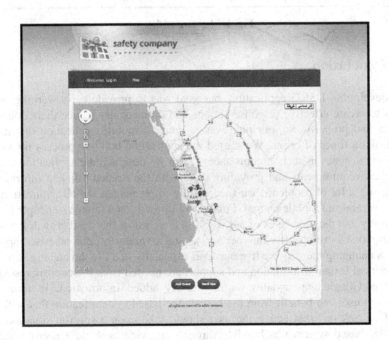

Fig. 4. Home Page

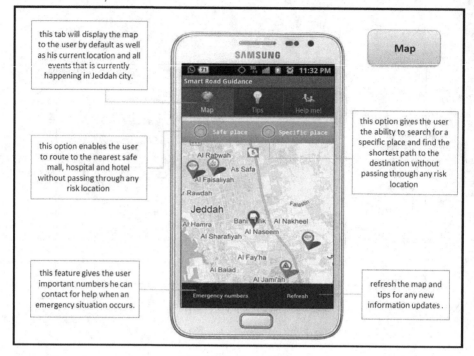

this tab will display the map to the user by default as well as his current location and all events that is currently happening in Jeddah city.

this option enables the user to route to the nearest safe mall, hospital and hotel without passing through any risk location

this feature gives the user important numbers he can contact for help when an emergency situation occurs.

this option gives the user the ability to search for a specific place and find the shortest path to the destination without passing through any risk location

refresh the map and tips for any new information updates.

Fig. 5. Map Screenshot

4   Conclusion

When developing DSRG application, our goal was to provide early warnings of all hazards to create effective response actions and dramatically reduce their effects on our lives and property. So, our plan was to create a mobile application that directs individuals in times of crises. We started the application building process by analyzing the users' needs in such circumstances. Then we designed the application according to their requirements and providing them with the needed efficient information. After facing a lot of problems, we successfully implemented DSRG application that operates on android mobile phones. Finally, we tested it on a sample of people and we successfully met the objectives of our work. In conclusion, the rapid growth in the use of Smartphone – which offer internet access and a variety of internet-based applications – is changing the way we live our lives especially in a life threatening situations where critical instant information and support are needed from trustworthy resources. It received Google map updates for any newly added information. In time of a trouble, the user can benefit from the knowledge-based system feature that will give him a feedback on what action the user should take upon a specific situation. The knowledge-based system was building through interview with the Experts domains. All these features improved access to the needed information at the needed time.

References

1. IBM, Caltrans, and UC Berkeley Aim to Help Commuters Avoid Congested Roadways Before their Trip Begins, press release, IBM (April 13, 2011), http://www-03.ibm.com/press/us/en/pressrelease/34261.wss
2. Youssef, M., Atluri, V., Adam, N.: Preserving Mobile Customer Privacy: An Access Control System for Moving Objects and Customer Profiles. In: Proc. 6th Int'l Conf. Mobile Data Management (MDM 2005), pp. 67–76. ACM, 2005
3. More Americans Using Social Media and Technology in Emergencies, Public Affairs Desk, Am. Red Cross (August 24, 2011), http://tinyurl.com/9bylh55
4. Adam, N., et al.: Social Media Alert and Response to Threats to Citizens (SMART-C). In: Proc. 8th IEEE Int'l Conf. Collaborative Computing: Networking, Applications, and Worksharing (ColCom 2012) (2012) (to be published)
5. Zhou, B., Pei, J., Luk, W.: A Brief Survey on Anonymization Techniques for Privacy Preserving Publishing of Social Network Data. SIGKDD Explorations Newsletter 10(2) (2008)
6. Aggarwal, C., Yu, P.S.: A General Survey of Privacy-Preserving Data Mining Models and Algorithms. Privacy-Preserving Data Mining 34, 11–52 (2008)
7. Dwork, C.: Differential privacy. In: Bugliesi, M., Preneel, B., Sassone, V., Wegener, I. (eds.) ICALP 2006. LNCS, vol. 4052, pp. 1–12. Springer, Heidelberg (2006)
8. Wang, C., et al.: Privacy-Preserving Public Auditing for Data Storage Security in Cloud Computing. In: IEEE Conf. Computer Communications (INFOCOM 2010), pp. 525–533. IEEE (2010)
9. Zhang, X., et al.: Formal Model and Policy Specification of Usage Control. ACM Trans. Information and Systems Security 8(4), 351–387 (2005)
10. Wickramasuriya, J., et al.: Privacy Protecting Data Collection in Media Spaces. In: Proc. 12th Ann. ACM Int'l Conf. Multimedia (MULTIMEDIA 2004), pp. 48–55. ACM (2004)
11. Golle, P., McSherry, F., Mironov, I.: Data Collection with Self-Enforcing Privacy. In: Proc. 13th ACM Conf. Computer and Communications Security (CCS 2006), pp. 69–78. ACM (2006)
12. Li, N., et al.: Privacy Preservation in Wireless Sensor Networks: A State-of-the- Art Survey. Ad Hoc Networks 7(8), 1501–1514 (2009)
13. Chen, R., et al.: Differentially Private Transit Data Publication: A Case Study on the Montreal Transportation System. In: Proc. 18th ACM SIGKDD Int'l Conf. Knowledge Discovery and Data Mining (KDD 2012), pp. 213–221. ACM (2012)
14. Shin, H., Vaidya, J., Atluri, V.: A Profile Anonymization Model for Location-Based Services. J. Computer Security 19(5), 795–833 (2011)
15. Hoh, B., et al.: Preserving Privacy in GPS Traces via Uncertainty-Aware Path Cloaking. In: Proc. 14th ACM Conf. Computer and Communications Security (CCS 2007), pp. 161–171. ACM (2007)
16. Jadliwala, M., Bilogrevic, I., Hubaux, J.-P.: Optimizing Mixing in Pervasive Networks: A Graph-Theoretic Perspective. In: Atluri, V., Diaz, C. (eds.) ESORICS 2011. LNCS, vol. 6879, pp. 548–567. Springer, Heidelberg (2011)
17. From GPS and Virtual Globes to Spatial Computing—2020: The Next Transformative Technology. US Nat'l Science Foundation/Computing Community Consortium workshop proposal (September 2012)
18. Adam, N., et al.: Approach for Discovering and Handling Crisis in a Service-Oriented Environment. In: Proc. Intelligence and Security Informatics (ISI 2007), pp. 16–24. IEEE (2007)

19. Christensen, J.: Using RESTful Web Services and Cloud Computing to Create Next-Generation Mobile Applications. In: Companion to the 24th Ann. ACM SIGPLAN Conf. Object-Oriented Programming, Systems, Languages, and Applications, pp. 627–634. ACM (2009)

20. Artail, H., Fawaz, K., Ghandour, A.: A Proxy-Based Architecture for Dynamic Discov-ery and Invocation of Web Services from Mobile Devices. IEEE Trans. Services Compu-ting 5(1), 99–115 (2012)

21. García-Macías, J., et al.: Browsing the Internet of Things with Sentient Visors. Comput-er 44(5), 46–52 (2011)

22. Gaia GPS,
    `https://play.google.com/store/apps/details?id=com.trailbehin`
    `d.android.gaiagps.pro&feature=search_result#?t=W251bGwsMSwxL`
    `DEsImNvbS50cmFpbGJlaGluZC5hbmRyb21kLmdhaWFncHMucHJvIl0`

23. ubAlert- Disaster Alert Network,
    `http://itunes.apple.com/us/app/ubalert-disaster-alert-`
    `network/id455647397?mt=8`

24. Disaster Alert,
    `https://play.google.com/store/apps/`
    `details?id=disasterAlert.PDC`

25. EB2A Internet Services (2006), `https://www.eb2a.com/en/`

26. Patil, S.: Android Project structure (December 2009),
    `http://www.mobisoftinfotech.com/blog/`
    `android/android-project-structure/`

27. Intent Structure (December 2012),
    `http://developer.android.com/reference/`
    `android/content/Intent.html`

28. Launcher Icons (December 2012),
    `http://developer.android.com/guide/practices/`
    `ui_guidelines/icon_design_launcher.html`

29. Obtaining a Google Maps Android v1 API Key (December 2012),
    `https://developers.google.com/maps/`
    `documentation/android/v1/mapkey?hl=ar-SA`

30. Knowledge base (December 2012),
    `http://en.wikipedia.org/wiki/Knowledge_base`

Interaction Design
Using a Child Behavior-Geometry Database

Hiroyuki Kakara[1,2], Yoshifumi Nishida[1], and Hiroshi Mizoguchi[1,2]

[1] Digital Human Research Center, National Institute of Advanced Industrial Science
and Technology, 2-3-26 Aomi, Koto-ku, Tokyo 135-0064, Japan
[2] Department of Mechanical Engineering, Faculty of Science and Technology, Tokyo
University of Science, 2641 Yamazaki, Noda-shi, Chiba 278-8510, Japan

Abstract. Unintentional injuries, that is, injuries due to accidents, account for a large share of the cause of death in children. Some accidents
can be prevented by designing products that are based on an understanding of the interaction between children and the object. Improving
products to prevent injuries requires a system that helps product designers predict the behavior that the object induces in children. In this paper,
we developed a behavior-geometry database that consists of 1) data on
children's behavior with common objects, 2) for various objects, data
from 3D shape models for which the feature vectors are calculated by a
3D discrete Fourier transform, and 3) two kinds of models for using a
3D shape-feature vector to predict the induced behavior, the barycentric
behavior model and the multiple linear regression model. We also developed the following behavior-symmetry-search functions that use the
database: a) a shape-similarity search, b) an induced-behavior search,
which is a function for predicting the behaviors induced by an object's
3D shape, and c) a behavior-symmetry search, which is a function for
finding objects that induce behaviors similar to those induced by the
shape of a target object. The third function is useful for finding shapes
that are similar in terms of inducing child behavior. In this study, we
evaluated the effectiveness of the implemented system using data from
275 accidents and 3D shape data from 45 objects.

Keywords: Injury prevention, interaction design, safety, 3D object retrieval.

1 Introduction

Unintentional injuries, that is, injuries due to accidents, account for a large share
of the cause of death in children. According to the National Vital Statistics
Reports 2012[1], in 2009 unintentional injuries accounted for more than 30%
of the deaths of children aged 1-14 years, as shown in Fig. 1. This trend is a
serious problem worldwide, and the number of unintentional injuries needs to be
reduced.

The number of unintentional injuries can be reduced by designing products
that are based on an understanding of the interaction between the child and
the shape of the objects. In the field of product safety, technology is strongly

A. Marcus (Ed.): DUXU/HCII 2013, Part III, LNCS 8014, pp. 95–104, 2013.

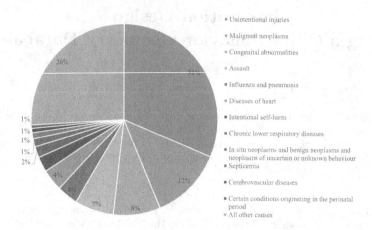

Fig. 1. Cause of Death, 1-14 years old (Source: National Vital Statistics Reports 2012)

needed that can predict a child's behavior with common objects. Childrenfs unforeseen interaction with an object often leads to accidents (e.g., climbing on an air conditioner compressor unit and then falling from a balcony). Product designers must consider the actual use of the target object and design products that do not induce children to engage in high-risk behaviors.

There are some systems that enable product designers to search actual accident data associated with an object. For example, an object-feature-based searching system has been developed[3]. This system enables users to retrieve data on actual accidents that were caused by not only the same category of object as the target object, but also objects in other categories that have features similar to those of the target object. With this system, users can predict behaviors even if there is no accident data associated with the target object. However, conventional systems support only a text-based search, namely, they can only search by literal information, making it impossible to determine behaviors and accidents induced by the shape of a target object.

We live in the real 3D world. Therefore, it is essentially important to consider 3D shape information. We therefore need to be able to search a shape-feature-based system in addition to a text-based system. Recently, technology for 3D shape processing has been developed, and many algorithms are available[2]. This technology allows us to develop a new system for supporting the design of safe products. If a shape-feature-based system becomes available, we will be able to predict the behaviors that may be induced by a 3D shape by associating the 3D shape of the object with behavior data. Without such a system, we overlook data on accidents that are associated with objects belonging to a different category or objects having different features, and are thus unable to take measures to prevent those accidents. Furthermore, we believe that this system allows a new approach to behavior science or interaction science by using accident information to reveal scientific knowledge about the relationship between an object's shape and the behaviors that are induced.

The objective of this study is to develop a database that allows users to predict the behaviors that can be induced by a object's shape (shape-to-behavior prediction), and to develop a method for retrieving shapes that can induce behaviors similar to the behaviors induced by the shape of a target object. This shape-to-shape prediction function is useful for understanding the shape features of objects that induce similar behaviors in children. We will refer to this database as the "behavior-geometry database."

2   Development of the Behavior-Geometry Database

The behavior-geometry database consists of 1) children's behavior with common objects, 2) data for an object's 3D shape model and its shape-feature vectors, and 3) two kinds of models for predicting the induced behavior by using the 3D shape-feature vector, the barycentric behavior model and the multiple linear regression model. Figure 2 shows a conceptual diagram of the behavior-geometry database.

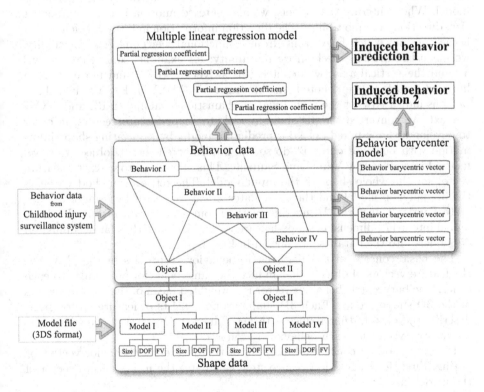

Fig. 2. Conceptual Diagram of Behavior-Geometry Database

2.1   Accumulation of Child Behavior Data

We extracted data on children's behavior and related objects from the Accident Database of the Injury Surveillance System[4,5] developed by the National Institute of Advanced Industrial Science and Technology. The database includes text that describes information such as the accident situation, any related objects, the place, and a summary of each accident. The behavior data consists of the behaviors before and during the accidents. Since we needed to collect behaviors that can trigger accidents, we used the database instead of conducting experiments to observe behavior. We have accumulated data on the behavior related to 275 accidents involving tables or chairs.

2.2   Implementation of 3D Object Retrieval Technology and Behavior Prediction Model

We used 3D model data to register the 3D shape of each kind of object. Also, for each kind of object, such as a dining table or a highchair, we collected more than two models in order to reduce the noise due to the artificial selection of the model. When entering the models, we also entered information on the model's size, direction, and movability. The direction information indicated which aspect is face up and which faces front, from a functional viewpoint. For movability, we mean the model's mechanistic movability; for example, some chairs swivel around the vertical axis (we denoted this swivel by "RZ") and move across a horizontal surface (we denoted this movement by "DXY"). For a swivel chair, we thus indicated that the model had mechanistic movability in RZ and DXY.

Next, we converted the 3D shape models to shape-feature vectors, in order to develop a shape-based behavior prediction model by associating shape information with behavior data. To do so, we implemented the 3D object retrieval method introduced by Vranić and Saupe[6]. This allowed us to extract a feature vector for the whole shape of the input model. The retrieval method voxelizes the 3D polygon model and then calculates a feature vector by using a 3D discrete Fourier transform. Using this method, our system converts a 3D shape model into a 172-dimension shape-feature vector. We have thus far accumulated 45 models into the database, as shown in Fig. 3.

The basic concept of the barycentric behavior vector lies in the idea that the feature vectors of objects that induce the same behavior are similar to each other. The barycentric behavior vector is a weighted mean of the feature vectors of the 3D shape groups. Each 3D shape group consists of feature vectors that describe the objects that induce a target behavior. Our system calculates the barycentric vector for each behavior, as follows.

Figure 4 shows a conceptual diagram of the barycentric behavior vector for sitting. First, for each object, the system calculates the mean feature vector of the models as

$$\mathbb{F}_{i,mean} = \frac{1}{M_i} \sum_{j=1}^{M_i} \mathbb{F}_{i,j}, \tag{1}$$

Object name	Number
Dining chair	4
Table (<400 [mm])	4
Table (400-700 [mm])	4
Table (700-1000 [mm])	10
Table (>1000 [mm])	3
High chair	3
Bench	3
Low chair	3
Swivel chair	3
School chair	3
Folding chair	2
Bench with backrest	3

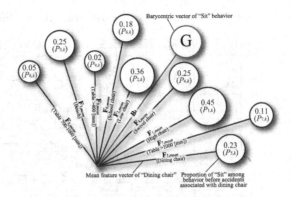

Fig. 3. Number of Models for Each Object

Fig. 4. Conceptual Diagram of Barycentric Behavior Vector

where $\mathbb{F}_{i,j}$ indicates the feature vector of the model$_j$ that describes object$_i$, and M_i indicates the total number of models that describe object$_i$. Next, the system calculates the barycentric vector of behavior$_k$ as

$$\mathbb{B}_k = \sum_{i=1}^{O} P_{i,k} \cdot \mathbb{F}_{i,mean}, \qquad (2)$$

where O indicates the total number of object categories accumulated in the database, and $P_{i,k}$ (the occurrence proportion) indicates the proportion of the occurrence of behavior$_k$ among all behaviors associated with the object$_i$. Thus, there exists the following relation:

$$\sum_{k=1}^{K} P_{i,k} = 1.0, \qquad (3)$$

where K indicates the total number of behavior categories.

Behavior Prediction Model using Multiple Linear Regression Analysis. We also developed another prediction model using the multiple linear regression analysis. Our system creates cross tables for each behavior, as shown in Table 1. In Table 1, for example, Object (ID=6) is a swivel chair, and since it has movability in DXY and RZ, they both equal 1. We removed the 172nd element of the feature vectors because all vectors had the same value. The rightmost column indicates the occurrence proportion of the behavior of standing on the object. For example, the value "0.223" in the top cell of the red area indicates that in 22.3% of the accidents related to Object (ID=1), standing on the object was the behavior that preceded the accident. We created a linear regression model for each behavior by using the cross table and the following variables:

Table 1. Example of the FV-Behavior Table (standing on the object)

Object ID	Model ID	Model size			Movability		Feature vector (FV)						Behavior
		x	y	z	DXY	RZ	1	2	3	...	170	171	Stand on
1	1-1	50.1	46.9	88.5	0	0	4.39E-03	2.74E-03	1.13E-02	...	4.42E-02	3.77E-02	0.223
	1-2	55.9	44.3	95.4	0	0	2.65E-03	1.54E-03	9.20E-03	...	2.25E-02	3.21E-02	0.223
	1-3	40.3	46.5	95.8	0	0	2.80E-03	5.79E-03	6.43E-03	...	1.52E-02	3.15E-02	0.223
2	2-1	142.8	81.6	59.5	0	0	1.85E-04	5.61E-04	1.38E-03	...	5.85E-02	6.25E-02	0.216
	2-2	100.0	100.0	45.6	0	0	1.13E-03	1.02E-03	2.70E-03	...	6.45E-02	6.62E-02	0.216
	2-3	120.0	120.0	63.1	0	0	1.46E-03	5.16E-04	2.99E-03	...	5.60E-02	4.49E-02	0.216
3	3-1	155.3	81.6	71.6	0	0	4.33E-04	2.91E-04	1.53E-03	...	5.89E-02	6.24E-02	0.093
	3-2	160.0	90.0	73.0	0	0	4.55E-04	8.34E-04	9.37E-04	...	5.83E-02	6.34E-02	0.093
	3-3	149.8	79.8	75.0	0	0	1.13E-03	7.95E-04	4.34E-03	...	4.37E-02	5.06E-02	0.093
4	4-1	110.0	92.1	37.7	0	0	5.84E-04	1.60E-03	2.49E-03	...	4.42E-02	5.97E-02	0.116
	4-2	101.8	101.8	38.2	0	0	2.87E-03	2.83E-03	2.96E-03	...	6.13E-02	6.51E-02	0.116
	4-3	148.4	86.9	40.0	0	0	6.07E-04	6.31E-04	6.00E-04	...	5.80E-02	6.53E-02	0.116
5	5-1	42.6	44.8	45.0	0	0	2.13E-03	8.08E-04	2.70E-03	...	1.25E-02	2.24E-02	0.375
	5-2	55.4	39.1	52.9	0	0	2.20E-05	1.10E-04	3.16E-04	...	1.97E-02	4.19E-02	0.375
	5-3	41.8	41.8	67.4	0	0	6.74E-04	1.56E-03	3.20E-03	...	2.61E-02	3.15E-02	0.375
6	6-1	60.5	61.0	93.0	1	1	1.79E-03	8.45E-04	2.08E-03	...	2.53E-02	2.30E-02	0.000
	6-2	66.5	61.0	120.4	1	1	1.50E-03	4.36E-03	5.14E-04	...	1.33E-02	2.16E-02	0.000
	6-3	62.1	61.0	114.4	1	1	2.18E-03	2.04E-03	3.71E-03	...	2.63E-02	1.92E-02	0.000
7	7-1	65.0	98.6	75.0	0	0	2.35E-03	2.68E-03	6.37E-03	...	1.82E-02	4.36E-02	0.500
	7-2	64.6	100.6	75.0	0	0	1.66E-04	9.41E-04	3.06E-03	...	2.49E-02	4.22E-02	0.500
	7-3	59.1	87.4	75.0	0	0	1.03E-03	1.31E-03	2.02E-03	...	2.07E-02	3.44E-02	0.500
8	8-1	67.3	67.3	110.0	0	0	8.73E-03	3.30E-03	1.25E-02	...	5.38E-02	3.65E-02	0.333
	8-2	64.6	64.6	110.0	0	0	5.16E-03	8.80E-03	9.99E-03	...	4.68E-02	4.19E-02	0.333
	8-3	79.7	79.3	110.0	0	0	1.16E-03	1.98E-03	4.92E-03	...	3.56E-02	3.66E-02	0.333

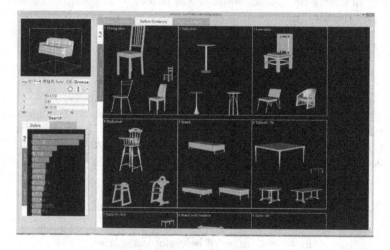

Fig. 5. Browser for the Behavior-Geometry Function

- Objective variable: the occurrence proportion of each behavior (red area in Table 1).
- Explanatory variables: the models' shape-feature vectors, size, and movability.

3 Development of the Behavior-Symmetry Search System

We developed a browser for the child behavior-geometry database and implemented the behavior-symmetry search functions in the browser. By behavior symmetry, we mean that an object induces the same or similar behavior as that induced by another object. The unique characteristic of our system lies in the fact that the system allows us not only to retrieve objects that are similar in terms of shape but also to retrieve behavior-symmetric objects. To operate our system, the user enters a query model that provides information, including the shape and the actual size. The system then produces a feature vector of the 3D shape model, which allows the user to conduct a behavior-symmetry search. This consists of 1) a shape-similarity search, 2) an induced-behavior search, and 3) a behavior-symmetry search that ranks the similarity.

3.1   Shape-Similarity Search

The system uses the inner product to calculate the similarity (S') between the feature vector of the 3D shape query and the feature vectors of the accumulated 3D shape models. Then, the system calculates the similarity $S = f(d_{max}) \cdot S'$ in order to consider information on both size and shape. $f(d_{max})$ expresses the similarity of the size and is defined as

$$f(d_{max}) = \exp\left(-\frac{d_{max}^2}{2\sigma^2}\right),\tag{4}$$

where d_{max} indicates the maximum value of the differences between models in the lengths of each side (x,y,z) of a bounding box, and σ is a controlling parameter. If the sizes of the bounding boxes are the same, $f(d_{max})$ becomes 1.0. σ is given. We selected $\sigma = 13.97$.

3.2   Induced-Behavior Search

In the case of using the barycentric model, for each behavior, the system uses the inner product to calculate the similarity between the feature vector of the 3D shape query and the barycentric behavior vectors. They are then sorted to create a ranking of the behaviors that can be induced by the object's shape query. When using the multiple linear regression model, the system calculates the occurrence probability of each behavior by using the model and the entered information (feature vector, size, movability). Figure 6 shows an example of an induced-behavior search result for the case where the user entered the dining chair model shown in Fig. 7 as a 3D shape query, and the system conducted a search using the multiple linear regression model. This search function enables product designers to predict the behaviors that will be induced by a target object based on its shape, instead of taking an intuitive approach or using literal accident information.

3.3   Behavior-Symmetry Search

Each object accumulated in the behavior-geometry database has ranking information for the occurrence proportion for each behavior. This ranking has the same format as the induced-behavior prediction. Thus we treated those rankings

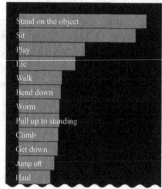
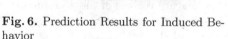

Fig. 6. Prediction Results for Induced Behavior

Fig. 7. 3D Model of Dining Chair

as vectors and used the inner product to calculate their similarity. In this way, we can calculate which object is more similar, in the sense of inducing behavior, to a shape given as a query. Figure 8 shows an example of the behavior-symmetry search result when using the dining chair shown in Fig. 7 as a shape query. The behavior-symmetry search function enables users to retrieve shapes that can induce behaviors similar to those induced by a query, even if the shapes are quite different.

Fig. 8. Example of Behavior-Symmetry Search Result

4 Behavior-Symmetry Search System Performance Evaluation

We evaluated the induced-behavior search by using the sofa models shown in Fig. 9. First, we prepared data on the behaviors related to sofas using the Accident Database that we used to accumulate the behavior data in Sect. 2.1. Next, we input 3D shape models of sofas and retrieved an induced-behavior ranking. We then calculated the following two measures to evaluate the induced behavior search performance: 1) f-measure and 2) average precision.

Fig. 9. Sofa Models

The F-measure is the weighted harmonic mean of precision and recall:

$$F - measure = \frac{2 \cdot precision \cdot recall}{(precision + recall)}. \tag{5}$$

The F-measure considers both precision and recall, and its best value is 1, while the worst value is 0. The average precision can consider the order of the resultant ranking by calculating the precision at each position:

$$precision(k) = \frac{1}{k} \sum_{i=0}^{k} r_i, \tag{6}$$

where k is the position in the ranking, and r_i equals one if the behavior at rank k is relevant, and is otherwise zero. Then average precision is calculated as

$$average \, precision = \frac{\sum_{k=1}^{N} r_k \cdot precision(k)}{number \, of \, relevant \, data}, \tag{7}$$

where N indicates the total number of data points that were retrieved.

Table 2 shows the result of the evaluation. We confirmed that a search using the multiple linear regression model performed better than the barycentric behavior model, and our system has a high retrieval performance.

Table 2. Result of Induced-Behavior Search Performance Evaluation

Prediction model	Model	F-measure	Average precision
Multiple linear regression model	Sofa model 1	0.688	0.78
	Sofa model 2	0.750	0.80
	Sofa model 3	0.688	0.79
	Average	0.708	0.79
Behavior barycenter model	Sofa model 1	0.500	0.69
	Sofa model 2	0.438	0.43
	Sofa model 3	0.625	0.80
	Average	0.521	0.64

5 Conclusion

In this study, we developed a child behavior-geometry database. The database consists of 1) 275 records of children's behavior with common objects, 2) for various objects, 3D shape model data and shape-feature vectors calculated by the 3D discrete Fourier transform, and 3) two kinds of behavior predicting models. We developed the barycentric behavior model and the multiple linear regression model as the prediction model. We implemented the behavior-symmetry search function in the database browser. This function allows a user to predict how a child may interact with an object, based on the 3D shape of the object, and to find objects that can induce similar behavior.

In the future, in cooperation with hospitals and fire departments, we will continue to accumulate both 3D shape data for objects related to childhood accidents and data on the interactions of children with those objects. Improving the shape-feature calculating method to process interaction with common objects more correctly is also an important area of future work.

References

1. Heron, M.: Deaths: Leading Causes for 2009. National Vital Statistics Reports 61(7), 17 (2012)
2. Dugelay, J.L., Baskurt, A., Daoudi, M.: 3D Object Processing. John Wiley & Sons Ltd, England (2008)
3. Nomori, K., Nishida, Y., Motomura, Y., Yamanaka, T., Komatsubara, A.: A Method of Evidence-Based Risk Assessment through Modeling Infant Behavior and Injury. In: Proceedings of The 3rd International Conference on Applied Human Factors and Ergonomics (AHFE), pp. 17–20 (2010)
4. Tsuboi, T., Nishida, Y., Mochimaru, M., Kouchi, M., Mizoguchi, H.: Bodygraphic Information System. In: Proceedings of The 9th World Conference on Injury Prevention and Safety Promotion, p. 79 (2008)
5. Tsuboi, T., Nishida, Y., Motomura, Y., Mochimaru, M., Kouchi, M., Yamanaka, T., Mizoguchi, H.: Bodygraphic Information System: Application to Injury Surveillance. In: 2008 International Conference on Modeling, Simulation and Visualization Methods (MSV 2008) (2008)
6. Vranić, D.V., Saupe, D.: 3D Shape Descriptor Based on 3D Fourier Transform. In: Proceedings of the EURASIP Conference on Digital Signal Processing for Multimedia Communications and Services, pp. 271–274 (2001)

Classifying Energy-Related Events Using Electromagnetic Field Signatures

Anand S. Kulkarni and Karla Conn Welch

University of Louisville, Department of Electrical and Computer Engineering, 448 Lutz Hall, Louisville, KY 40292, USA
{askulk02,karla.welch}@louisville.edu

Abstract. We propose a system that uses a set of mobile sensors, which fit on a keychain or ID/ access badge, for real-time feedback on a user's energy consumption. The work presented here is the first phase of the project where we demonstrate the feasibility of recognizing electrical activity in an uninstrumented space (e.g., home or office) with a simple sensor. We present a sensor which can eventually be made small enough to be able to install on a keychain or ID badge to be carried around during daily activities. The current phase of the project focuses on comparing the electromagnetic fields of several common appliances to determine unique signatures. In the next phase of this project, using our mobile sensors we can attribute energy-related events to an individual occupant over multiple locations and time.

Keywords: Energy consumption, EMF signatures, Decision Trees.

1   Introduction

Increasing demand of energy across the world has raised concerns about environmental impacts and limited availability of fuel. The United States Energy Information Administration (EIA) predicts world energy consumption will grow by 53 percent between 2008 and 2035 [1]. There is an immediate need to address the problem of depleting fuel and increasing pollution associated with electricity generation; energy consumption feedback is one of the remedies to address this problem. Research has shown that if consumers receive accurate and timely feedback about their energy usage, they can reduce their energy consumption by 20% [2-4].

The energy-related behaviors of every individual occupant in a building determine the aggregate energy consumption of a building. We believe that energy conservation can be achieved if we provide occupant-specific energy usage feedback. To provide individualized energy usage feedback it is necessary to gather more information about how each occupant is using energy. However, there is a dearth of gathered information in this research area [5], and what methods are useful for gathering this necessary information still remains an unresolved research question. A variety of products are available in the market that provide instantaneous feedback about energy usage but do not provide individualized energy usage [6]. Previous work in the area of

A. Marcus (Ed.): DUXU/HCII 2013, Part III, LNCS 8014, pp. 105–111, 2013.

electrical activity detection includes when Patel et al. [7] designed a system, tested in six different homes, which is plugged into an ordinary wall outlet to detect the transient noise generated by appliances and used that information to determine energy-related events. Although this approach is accurate, it cannot be used when calculating individual energy usage since it cannot identify which occupant initialized the energy-related event. Patel et al.'s system and our proposed system have similar aims, but our methods have distinct differences with distinguishable advantages in terms of mobility and ability to determine individualized energy usage. We believe influencing energy consumption must be addressed at the individual level to gain a significant and lasting impact. Therefore, a system that can attribute energy related events to an individual occupant over multiple locations and time may better address energy consumption concerns.

We propose a wireless system, which fits on a keychain or ID/ access badge. This compact wireless system moves with the user and can sense changes in illumination and power spikes indicating the user has turned an electrical equipment on and off, and that the user requires additional resources for heating, cooling, and ventilation. The system shares data with mobile phone sensors and intelligent sensors installed in the building for a detailed picture of individual energy use. The proposed system will alleviate the measurement problem by automating assessment and boosting efficiency by providing real-time feedback to users.

The work presented here is the first phase of the project where we demonstrate the feasibility of recognizing electrical activity in an un-instrumented living space with a simple sensor. The sensor perceives the entire spectrum of electromagnetic field (EMF). Electrical current developed in the antenna due to EMF is converted to a voltage. These data are fed into an algorithm to classify energy-related events.

2   Background

EMFs are invisible lines of force, which is the combination of an electric field and a magnetic field and exists wherever electricity is produced or used. Power supplied to home appliances generates extremely low frequency EMFs (e.g., 60 Hz in the U.S.). The motor, transformers, or any other electrical component of appliances generate EMFs with a variety of frequencies. For example, a hair dryer's heating coil radiates EMF at the frequency of 60 Hz, while the motor of the blower radiates EMF which is in the kHz range. The transformers in a computer may radiate EMF in kHz range, while the processor chip might emit EMF in the range of GHz. Each appliance has unique characteristics of EMF radiation, i.e., unique amplitude and frequency of radiation, which our algorithm uses for identification.

3   Experimental Setup

We collected scans of data using an EMF sensor (Figure 1), specifically the time series of EMF magnitude for individual appliances. A feature vector is generated by converting time series data to frequency domain and extracting features from it.

Five electronic devices (i.e., appliances and lighting) were scanned for their EMF signatures. Compact fluorescent lamps (CFL), incandescent bulb, fluorescent lamp, hair dryer, and small refrigerator were selected based on their common use as part of daily activities. Large appliances, such as a dishwasher or clothes dryer, will be examined in later studies but were not included in this initial pilot study of EMF signatures.

A photo capturing a typical data collection scene is shown in Figure 2. All readings were taken from approximately one foot away from the device. National Instrument's USB 6361 data acquisition system with sampling speed of 2 Mega samples per second was used for acquiring and saving data on a PC for later analysis. From the EMF data collected, FFT plots have been generated for each appliance examined.

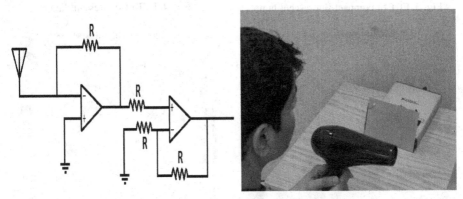

Fig. 1. Schematic of EMF sensor   **Fig. 2.** Experimental setup for data collection

4   Results

The plots in Figures 3-7 show the Fast Fourier Transform (FFT) of a one-second scan of each device, representing 2Msamples of data. We reduced this high-dimensional space to lower-dimensional space by building a histogram from the FFT plot for each device. Each bin of the histograms represents the mean of summed amplitudes of EMF for a range of frequencies. Frequency range of 0-1 MHz was divided into four sections. Each section was again divided into uniform subsections with widths of each subsection depending upon the importance of amplitude in particular frequency ranges. For example, 0-2kHz frequency range was divided into 100 sections of 20Hz each to create the first 100 bins of a histogram. The frequency range of 2-10kHz was divided into sections of 400Hz each. Further, frequency range of 10-100kHz was divided into sections of 10kHz each, and the range 100kHz-1MHz was divided into sections of 25kHz each. This procedure generated an array of 160 numbers, where each number represents mean of amplitude of EMF for a certain range of frequency. Figure 8 shows the histogram from the fluorescent lamp's EMF scan.

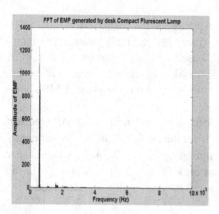

Fig. 3. FFT of compact fluorescent lamp

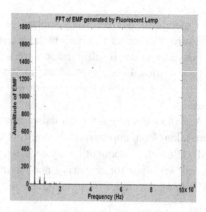

Fig. 4. FFT of fluorescent lamp

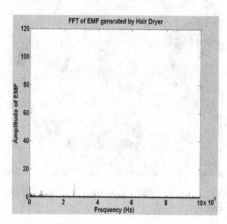

Fig. 5. FFT of hair dryer

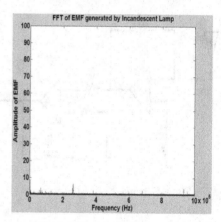

Fig. 6. FFT of incandescent lamp

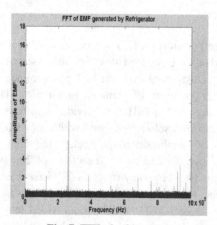

Fig. 7. FFT of refrigerator

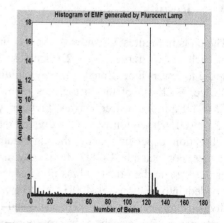

Fig. 8. Histogram of FFT for fluorescent lamp

The resultant histograms of each appliance were examined to empirically determine features that could classify each device, focusing on features that would provide a maximum value unique for each appliance as well as determining any thresholds that could be varied to discern different appliances. For example, the CFL used for this study emits significant EMF with frequencies in the range of 50-60kHz and 100-110kHz. Therefore, if bins number 125 and 130 are summed as one of the features, that feature separates the data well for an algorithm to identify the CFL; because bin 125 represents mean of amplitude of frequencies in the range of 50-60kHz and bin 130 represents mean of frequencies in the range of 100-125kHz, which produced high amplitudes of EMF when scanning the CFL. Similarly, signatures of each device were identified, and a feature was created from it. The features are listed in Table 1. The classification process manifests its substantial usefulness in that the features can be extracted from an unknown scan of EMF data and used to identify the type of appliance, which can be linked to its energy consumption. The raw data from an unknown scan can be processed for its FFT, from which a histogram is calculated and the features extracted. Furthermore, the features of an unknown scan can be sent as input into a Decision Trees (DT) algorithm to return the type of device. Therefore, an algorithm can provide feedback about what appliances are being used in a space based on EMF data mapped to EMF signatures of known devices.

Table 1. Listed are the features extracted from the histogram plots calculated from the data in this initial work

Feature no.	Feature
1	Sum of bins 125 and 130
2	Sum of bins 123 and 126
3	Mean of bins 10, 21, and 22
4	Sum of bins 25 and 28
5	Variance of bins 21 to 160

A comparison of EMF scans of the same appliance but taken at different times showed no marked difference. This consistency was as expected; since, for example, a device that emits a sizable amplitude of EMF at 90Hz and miniscule EMF at 110Hz is not expected to emit a sudden change in EMF data (e.g., give off a large 110Hz response and small 90Hz response at a later time) unless the electrical components of the device changed. Insomuch as the scans were sufficiently consistent, one scan from each appliance was used to build the DT structure for classifying the different appliances based on EMF data. The DT model (illustrated in Figure 9) was able to classify all five of the appliances studied in this pilot work based on example data from the features shown in Table 1. For example, feature 1 is very indicative of the CFL; if feature 1 is the largest value in an unknown EMF scan, the DT will return that the device being scanned is a CFL. This outcome makes sense in that feature 1 is made of bin 125 and bin 130 from the histograms. Bin 125's span includes 50-60kHz, and bin 130 includes 100-125kHz – both of which produced high amplitudes based on FFT's of the CFL's EMF scan. The remaining features differentiate the appliances such that the DT model can correctly return as output the type of device if given an unknown scan of one of the studied appliances as input. This initial work is in the proof-of-concept phase. Additional work is planned to (1) examine a large set of appliances, (2) test different techniques, such as exhaustive searches or correlation calculations, for identifying discerning features that differentiate the data and return high accuracy rates for classification, and (3) scan environments with multiple EMFs to classify multiple appliances simultaneously.

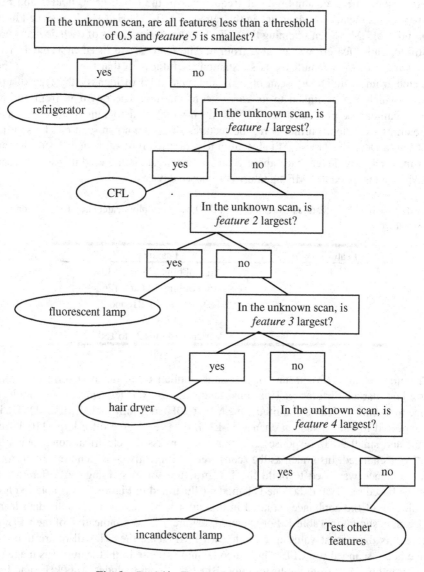

Fig. 9. Decision Tree model for this initial work

5   Discussion

This proof-of-concept phase of the research is promising; however, there are a few limitations to our current approach. The set of appliances used for this study was small and empirical selection of features might become complicated with increase in number of devices and when a combination of appliances working simultaneously is considered. In this study we maintained equal distance between every appliance and the sensor, which might not be true in practical use. We plan to work on optimizing the feature extraction process using a robust statistical method. Also, we plan to compare multiple machine learning algorithms like Neural Networks and Support Vector Machines against our current Decision Trees approach, to recognize the complex patterns of EMF signatures and infer on/off events of each appliance along with combinations of multiple on/off events.

Our future work is two-fold. First, we will design additional sensors to assist EMF signatures detected by the device described here, to make inferences about energy usage of individual users in a shared environment. Second, we plan to conduct user studies on perceptions of effective energy visualization. Feedback from these studies will inform us on how to provide users with useful information regarding their energy consumption. The visualization schemes will be incorporated into smart phone apps as feedback to users, to promote conservation on a real-time basis. Such a system must be able to detect when and how much energy is being used so that energy consumption can be monitored over time, given as information to a user, and used to calculate any change in consumption, preferably a reduction.

References

1. International Energy Outlook. U.S. Energy Information Administration (2011)
2. Darby, S.: The effectiveness of feedback on energy consumption: A review for DEFRA of the literature on metering, billing and direct displays. Environmental Change Institute (2006)
3. Seligman, C., Darley, J.M.: Feedback as a means of decreasing residential energy consumption. Journal of Applied Psychology 62(4), 363–368 (1977)
4. Rosenwald, M.S.: For Hybrid Drivers, Every Trip is a Race for Fuel Efficiency. Washington Post (2008)
5. Kavgic, M., Mavrogianni, A., Mumovic, D., Summerfield, A., Stevanovic, Z., Djurovic-Petrovic, M.: A review of bottom-up building stock models for energy consumption in the residential sector. Building and Environment 45, 1683–1697 (2010)
6. Kulkarni, A.S., Welch, K.C., Harnett, C.K.: A review of electricity monitoring and feedback systems. In: Proceedings of IEEE Southeast Conference, pp. 321–326 (2011), doi:978-1-61284-738-2/11
7. Patel, S.N., Robertson, T., Kientz, J.A., Reynolds, M.S., Abowd, G.D.: At the flick of a switch: Detecting and classifying unique electrical events on the residential power line (Nominated for the best paper award). In: Krumm, J., Abowd, G.D., Seneviratne, A., Strang, T. (eds.) UbiComp 2007. LNCS, vol. 4717, pp. 271–288. Springer, Heidelberg (2007)

Department of Homeland Security Websites Uncoupled: An Evaluation of Online Counterterrorism and Security Information across Agencies

Anna L. Langhorne

University of Dayton, Department of Communication
300 College Park, Dayton, Ohio 45469-1410
Alanghorne1@udayton.edu

Abstract. The purpose of this paper is to describe the content focus and hyperlink structure of the Department of Homeland Security (DHS) websites. This exploratory research is the first phase of a long-term effort to assess the degree to which information provided by DHS websites reflects the communication and information requirements of U.S. citizens. The present study uses content analysis and web link analysis methodologies to examine nine primary DHS websites. The findings reveal there are differences among the primary DHS agency websites in the use of hyperlinks and the coverage of national security topics.

Keywords: Department of Homeland Security, national security, content analysis, hyperlink analysis, information sharing, usability, communication, cyber security.

1 Introduction

With heightened concerns about terrorism, the current national security landscape requires that U.S. Federal agencies communicate efficiently, effectively, and accurately with agency stakeholders. Consequently, the World Wide Web (WWW) is one of many mediums available for facilitating government-citizen communication. The WWW enables government agencies to provide personalized e-governance services to citizens [1]. Moreover, citizens require information about policies, procedures, and current issues related to counterterrorism and national security in order to assist the government in vigilance and to preserve personal safety. Because ICT has the potential to improve government transparency through relevant and timely information distribution [2], government websites are salient mechanisms for communicating with citizens.

The U.S. government's interest in using the WWW is demonstrated by its estimated 11,013 Federal websites [3]. The Federal government recognizes that successful agency websites have the potential to create "a more citizen centered government" [4]. Furthermore, Federal agencies are required to improve customer service and

A. Marcus (Ed.): DUXU/HCII 2013, Part III, LNCS 8014, pp. 112–119, 2013.

efficiently manage their websites by addressing information dissemination mandates such as information quality, objectivity, utility, and integrity [5].

The purpose of this exploratory study is to determine the nature and extent of terrorism, counterterrorism and national security information presented on the Department of Homeland Security (DHS) websites. The DHS, an agency tasked with preserving the nation's security, safety, and resiliency, has approximately thirty-six Federal websites under its purview. DHS websites are intended to satisfy critical citizen information needs, especially during high-uncertainty situations. However, it is unclear whether 1) DHS-generated website content is designed to meet citizen national security information needs and 2) It conforms to government information usability standards [6].

Past studies have focused on important issues: Cyber warfare and security [7], terrorist network identification [8, 9], agency information sharing [10], interoperability [11], and information assurance [12]. And with regard to U.S. government websites, the literature has focused considerably on usability and accessibility assessments of websites [13, 14, 15, 16].

There is a dearth of literature, however, characterizing the content of government websites. Furthermore, no studies were found that evaluated the DHS website semantic structures from usability, communication, and hyperlink structure perspectives.

In the present study, content analysis, a quantitative method for systematically studying the characteristics of communication content, is applied to a sample of DHS websites. The objectives are: 1) Identify the occurrence frequency of citizen-focused national security information presented via DHS agency websites, 2) Identify information inconsistencies in the web content across DHS websites, and 3) Articulate the hyperlink structure of the DHS websites in reference to each other.

2   Methodology

2.1   Sample

A sample of nine websites was selected from an estimated population of thirty-six DHS websites (See Table 1). The sample selection was based on the DHS' designation of the following websites as primary: www.dhs.gov, www.fema.gov, www.fletc.gov, ww.ice.gov, www.secretservice.gov, www.tsa.gov, www.uscg.mil, www.uscis.gov, and www.cbp.gov [17]. All nine sampled DHS websites were analyzed for patterns across content themes and the agency-to-agency hyperlink structure within the context of citizen-focus and agency purpose.

2.2   Content Analysis

A content-analysis methodology was used to examine the sample of nine primary DHS websites. The data comprised web page content, which incorporated all file formats (e.g., .pdf and .doc), on the primary DHS agencies' websites. The data collection was performed in February 2013. The content was analyzed using a coding scheme that was created to classify national security issues from a citizen perspective. The coding scheme centered on four primary categories: Communication, proactive measures, threats/incidents, and post-incident response. Google Advanced Search was used to conduct queries of each website for each national security topic listed in the coding scheme in Table 2.

Table 1. DHS website sample

DHS agency	Daily	Abbreviation	Agency purpose
U.S. Department of Homeland Security	www.dhs.gov	DHS	To ensure U.S. homeland is safe, secure, and resilient against terrorism and other hazards
Federal Emergency Management Agency	www.fema.gov	FEMA	Support U.S. citizens and first responders to prepare for, protect against, respond to, recover from, and mitigate all hazards
Federal Law Enforcement Training Center	www.fletc.gov	FLETC	Interagency law enforcement training for 91 Federal agencies
U.S. Immigration & Customs Enforcement	www.ice.gov	ICE	Homeland security and public safety through criminal and civil enforcement of border control, customs, trade, and immigration laws
U.S. Secret Service	www.secretservice.gov	SS	Protects national and visiting foreign leaders, and conducts criminal investigations
Transportation Security Administration	www.tsa.gov	TSA	Maintains security of the traveling public and sets transportation security standards
U.S. Coast Guard	www.uscg.mil	USCG	Maritime military enforcement along rivers, ports, littoral regions and on high seas
U.S. Citizenship and Immigration Services	www.uscis.gov	USCIS	Provide accurate and useful information, grant immigration and citizenship benefits, promote citizenship awareness and understanding, and protect the immigration system
U.S. Customs & Border Protection	www.cbp.gov	CBP	Safeguard the U.S. borders and homeland and protect the American public against terrorism

2.3   Web Link Analysis

Web link analysis is a network analysis method used to articulate the structure among web nodes that associate with each other via hyperlinks. This study applies an approach used to evaluate the web link structure of the web space occupied by the American Library & Information Science field [18]. Essentially, the hyperlink data between sites are mined and analyzed for directional patterns.

The data consisted of hyperlinks identified from the primary agencies' websites under the umbrella of the Department of Homeland Security. The in- and out-link data were gathered from the nine websites using Google Advanced Search. Google Advanced Search was designed to collect such hyperlinks to external domains. The data collection was performed in February 2013.

Table 2. DHS coding scheme

National security topic categories	
Communication	Emergency procedures
	Warning system
	Progress reporting
	Emergency information
	Citizen hotline
	Crime reporting
	Safety information
Readiness	Action plan
	Disaster preparedness
	Emergency preparedness
	Emergency plan
	Emergency kit
	Safety plan
	Workplace plan
Threat/ incident	Pandemic
	Fire
	Crime victim
	Terrorist weapon types (e.g., chemical, biological)
Post-incident response	Returning home
	Help survivors
	Emergency assistance
	Casualty

3   Results and Discussion

The national security topics addressed by the primary DHS websites showed some commonalities. As shown in Table 3, topics of focus across many DHS websites included emergency procedures, emergency information, safety information, emergency preparedness, and emergency assistance. Because DHS agencies are tasked with protecting the nation and its citizens, it follows that considerable web content would relate to emergency communication, readiness, and response. However, many agency websites completely neglected or weakly provided content in numerous categories.

Table 3. DHS content analysis results

National security topics		DHS	FEMA	FLETC	ICE	SS	TSA	USCG	CIS	CBP
Communication	Emergency procedures	1090	2980	330	418	35	479	2390	0	389
	Warning sys	568	20300	61	251	16	239	955	0	310
	Progress report	975	2010	25	236	951	108	1220	0	279
	Emergency informa-tion	3420	56400	514	977	61	1430	6220	0	2510
	Citizen hotline	114	329	2	97	10	6	68	0	94
	Crime reporting	815	283	24	500	52	33	402	0	170
	Safety info	2120	21400	751	2510	79	667	6920	0	1960
Readiness	Action plan	1710	3940	56	424	44	278	3320	0	577
	Disaster prepared-ness	942	2180	5	20	2	39	416	0	19
	Emergency prepared-ness	1300	38700	277	38	14	102	752	0	45
	Emergency plan	2490	83000	325	506	43	359	4300	0	544
	Emergency kit	140	19800	5	238	0	69	341	0	72
	Safety plan	1380	2030	458	851	59	231	3410	0	410
	Workplace plan	388	2030	20	94	20	78	812	0	108
Threat/ incident	Pandemic	339	533	0	7	1	6	11	0	9
	Fire	1440	140000	255	562	33	74	6360	0	930
	Crime victim	334	89	95	250	35	8	191	0	49
	Terrorist weapon types	1520	1560	0	1	0	3	5	0	0
Post-incident response	Returning home	210	906	32	247	6	33	739	0	305
	Help sur-vivors	238	10200	0	13	2	7	855	0	18
	Emergency assistance	1170	28700	146	361	34	171	1960	0	493
	Casualty	157	1460	1	11	2	3	2970	0	64

Primary examples are the U.S. Secret Service (SS) and the U.S. Citizenship and Immigration Services (CIS). The SS exhibited minimal content in every category, except progress report. Although this may mirror its reputation for covertness, it fails to comport with the Federal government's conception of an open digital government. Similarly, the CIS website failed to exhibit content in every category. The complete absence of information is a concern especially for new citizens or those in the process of becoming citizens, who may lack knowledge about other government agency websites. Notable content deficits existed for TSA in the areas of citizen hotline, crime reporting, and terrorist weapon types. Again, when considered within the context of a citizen focus, many agencies failed to empower citizens; DHS websites frequently exhibited gaps in relevant information.

In addition to the differences found in DHS website content, there was variance among the DHS website hyperlinks. Given the Federal directive to improve information sharing, it is interesting to note the vast differences in hyperlinking among the primary DHS websites (See Table 4). The DHS website accounts for 48.64% of the links to www.dhs.gov from other primary DHS websites and 26.56% of the links to primary DHS websites. Because DHS is the parent agency for the other primary DHS agencies, it follows that DHS would possess the greatest number of in- and out-links. Contrastingly, www.fletc.gov, the website of a training facility/school, exhibited marginal in- and out-links accounting for less than 1% in both cases. Because FLETC's relevance to the general public is limited, the low hyper linkage to other DHS websites is not a concern. The remaining agencies, however, may improve citizen service by increasing linkages to related content at relevant agency websites. It is anticipated that strategic hyperlinking will facilitate information sharing among citizens.

Table 4. Descriptive statistics of Department of Homeland Security websites' in- and out-link asymmetric matrix data

Organization website	(A) In-links from other DHS sites		(B) Out-links to other DHS sites		(C) Total (A + B)	
	Frequency	Ratio	Frequency	Ratio	Frequency	Ratio
DHS	1412	48.64%	771	26.56%	2183	37.6%
FEMA	382	13.16%	686	23.63%	1068	18.39%
FLETC	24	.83%	6	.2%	30	.52%
ICE	231	7.96%	113	3.89%	344	5.9%
SS	28	.97%	10	.34%	38	.65%
TSA	257	8.85%	128	4.41%	385	6.63%
USCG	131	4.51%	303	10.44%	434	7.48%
CIS	249	8.58%	765	26.35%	1014	17.46%
CBP	189	6.51%	121	4.17%	310	5.34%
TOTAL	2903		2903		5806	

4   Future Research and Limitations

This study provided an initial assessment of the content subject matter of primary DHS websites and the agency-to-agency hyperlink structure. The magnitude of the DHS websites presented a feasibility issue. It was difficult, if not impossible, to assess with certainty all of the citizen-focused website content. In future project stages, the researcher will address this issue and will code the content after sorting by file format (e.g., .pdf, .ps, .dwf, .kml, .kmz, .xls, .ppt, .doc, .rtf, and .swf). In the present study, the site architecture and sheer volume of website pages demanded reliance on automated search tools. Although such tools were effective, some error was likely produced due to a tool's inability to capture the qualitative dimension of information. Furthermore, it was beyond the scope of the current project to confirm whether or not the content location and type as citizen-focused were consistent. Future research will investigate this issue. Additionally, it would be informative to evaluate the primary agency-to-agency hyperlink structure within the context of citizen-focused topic areas to determine whether interagency connections appropriately support citizen-focused communication of information. Finally, a questionnaire will be developed 1) to identify salient topics which remain absent from the DHS websites and 2) to assess citizen perceptions of the utility of the information.

5   Conclusion

This study analyzed the semantic structure of national security information presented via DHS agency websites, identified information patterns in the web content, and described the hyperlink structure of agency-to-agency directed links. Based on the results of the aforementioned analyses, the national security topics addressed by the primary DHS websites shared commonalities in the content themes, but also fundamental differences. Furthermore, as indicated by the preliminary results of the hyperlink analysis, a refocusing of the content and structure toward citizen users may be warranted to achieve improved information sharing with the public.

References

1. Pieterson, W., Ebbers, W., van Dijk, J.: Personalization in the Public Sector: An Inventory of Organizational and User Obstacles Towards Personalization of Electronic Services in the Public Sector. Government Information Quarterly 24(1), 148–164 (2007)
2. Kim, P., Halligan, J., Cho, N., Oh, C., Eikenberry, A.: Toward Participatory and Transparent Governance: Report on the Sixth Global Forum on Reinventing Government. Public Administration Review 65(6), 646–654 (2005)
3. Gov Reform Task Force. State of the Federal Web Report (Report), 60 (December 16, 2011) (retrieved January 3, 2012)
4. Johnson, C.: Policies for Federal Agency Public Websites. M-05-04 Memorandum for the Heads of Executive Departments and Agencies (December 17, 2004)

5. Gordon, D., Kundra, V.: Improving the Accessibility of Government Information. Memorandum for Chief Acquisition Officers, Chief Information Officers (July 19, 2010)
6. Executive Order 13571; OMB Circular A-130
7. Ahmad, R., Yunos, Z., Sahib, S.: Understanding Cyber Terrorism: The Grounded Theory Method Applied. In: 2012 International Conference on IEEE Cyber Security, Cyber Warfare and Digital Forensic (CyberSec), pp. 323–328 (2012)
8. Sageman, M.: Understanding Terror Networks. University of Pennsylvania Press (2011)
9. Perliger, A., Pedahzur, A.: Social Network Analysis in the Study of Terrorism and Political Violence. PS: Political Science and Politics 44(1), 45 (2011)
10. Relyea, H.: Homeland Security and Information Sharing: Federal Policy considerations. Government Information Quarterly 21(4), 420–438 (2004)
11. Headayetullah, M., Pradhan, G.: Interoperability, Trust Based Information Sharing Protocol And Security: Digital Government Key Issues. International Journal of Computer Science & Information Technology 2(3), 72–91 (2010)
12. Bellomo, S., Woody, C.: DoD Information Assurance and Agile: Challenges and Recommendations Gathered Through Interviews with Agile Program Managers and DoD Accreditation Reviewers. Software Engineering Institute (2012)
13. Youngblood, N., Mackiewicz, J.: A Usability Analysis of Municipal Government Website Home Pages In Alabama, Government Information Quarterly (2012)
14. Baker, D.: Advancing e-government performance in the United States through enhanced usability benchmarks. Government Information Quarterly 26(1), 82–88 (2009)
15. West, D.M.: State and Federal Electronic Government in the United States. The Brookings Institution, Washington, DC (2008)
16. Olalere, A., Lazar, J.: Accessibility of U.S. Federal Government Home Pages: Section 508 Compliance and Site Accessibility Statements. Government Information Quarterly 28(3), 303–309 (2011)
17. http://www.dhs.gov/dhs-website-directory
18. Joo, S.: A Web Link Structure of the American Library & Information Science Field: A Pilot Study (2010)

Development of an Unconventional Unmanned Coaxial Rotorcraft: GremLion*

Feng Lin, Kevin Z.Y. Ang, Fei Wang, Ben M. Chen, Tong Heng Lee, Beiqing Yang,
Miaobo Dong, Xiangxu Dong, Jinqiang Cui, Swee King Phang, Biao Wang,
Delin Luo, Shiyu Zhao, Mingfeng Yin, Kun Li, Kemao Peng, and Guowei Cai

UAV Research Group, National University of Singapore, Singapore 117576

Abstract. In this paper, we present an unmanned system design methodology for a fully functional unmanned rotorcraft system: GremLion, developed with all necessary avionics and a ground control station. It has been employed to participate in the 2012 UAVForge competition. The proposed design methodology consists of hardware construction, software development, dynamic modeling and flight control, as well as mission algorithms. The test results have been presented in this paper to verify the proposed design methodology.

1 Introduction

In the last two decades, unmanned systems aroused great interests world wide [1, 2], especially advanced micro unmanned aerial vehicle (UAV) systems capable of vertical take-off and landing, beyond line of sight observations, autonomous obstacle avoidance in cluttered environments and much more [3, 4, 5, 6]. These capabilities could provide researchers, rescuers, and other users a new and valuable tool.

To boost the progress in urban UAV development, in year 2012, the Defense Advanced Research Projects Agency (DARPA) and Space and Naval Warfare Systems Center Atlantic (SSC Atlantic) collaboratively launched an initiative called the UAVForge competition to design, build and manufacture advanced micro unmanned air vehicle systems.

To participate in the UAVForge competition, the NUS UAV research group started to design and develop an unmanned coaxial rotorcraft: GremLion, together with necessary avionics and a ground control station. Here, we propose the design methodology which enabled us to efficiently develop the GremLion system comprising of the rotorcraft, avionics, software system, ground control station, flight control system and mission system.

2 UAVForge Competition

In the UAVForge competition, the mission of each team is to outfit a fictional Task Force with an unmanned remotely operated micro air vehicle system. The entire air vehicle

* This research is funded by DSO National Laboratories, Singapore.

A. Marcus (Ed.): DUXU/HCII 2013, Part III, LNCS 8014, pp. 120–129, 2013.

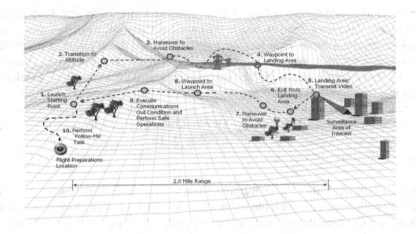

Fig. 1. UAVForge Competition Course

system must fit within a rucksack and a single person traveling by foot must be able to carry and operate the vehicle without assistance.

The job of the Task Force is to conduct observations of suspicious activities occurring within the vicinity of two nondescript buildings in an urban area. Due to the security in the region, all operations must be conducted beyond line of sight so as not to compromise your presence. If the UAV system is detected, the mission will be jeopardized. The total observation time required may be up to three hours of pictures and/or video to document the surveyed area. Once key observations have been made, the team must quickly retreat to their designated rendezvous location. Fig. 1 outlines the overall course of the competition.

3   The Coaxial Helicopter

GremLion, shown in Fig. 2, features a coaxial design driven by two contra-rotating rotors that can compensate the torque due to aerodynamic drag. Coaxial rotor designs

Table 1. Main specifications of GremLion

Specifications	GremLion
Upper rotor span	798 mm
Lower rotor span	895 mm
Upper rotor speed	1900 rpm
Lower rotor speed	1700 rpm
No-load weight	2.4 kg
Maximum takeoff weight	5.1 kg
Power source	LiPo battery
Flight endurance	15 mins

Fig. 2. GremLion

allow for a more stable, more maneuverable, quieter and safer helicopter due to inclusion of a coaxial main rotor and exclusion of a tail rotor. Coaxial rotor design also means a smaller footprint. Coaxial rotor helicopters also provide a better power to weight ratio than traditional helicopters, produce greater lift and are also much more efficient. Therefore, this platform is suited for the size requirement of the competition, which can be kept in a rucksack. Its key specifications are listed in Table 1.

To reduce the mechanical complexity of conventional dual-swash plate designs, a novel actuation system has been employed in GremLion with a single swash plate linked to the lower rotor system, which is shown in Fig. 3. The operating principle of such a actuation system is presented as follows:

a. **Heave Channel**: Unlike the conventional single rotor helicopters which utilize the collective pitch of their rotor blades to adjust the lift force, GremLion's collective pitches are fixed and thrust variation is accomplished by changing the rotor spinning speed simultaneously.

b. **Yaw Channel**: The yaw motion (head turning) is produced by the difference of spinning speed between the top and bottom rotors. In order to stabilize the heading of the rotorcraft, a hardware rate gyro is installed to finely adjust the spinning speed of the two rotors so that yaw dynamics becomes much more damped.

c. **Lateral and Longitudinal Channels**: To have lateral and longitudinal motions, the bottom rotor cyclic pitch is actively controlled by three servos. This is done through a swash plate mechanism which acts as a link between the servos and the bottom rotor cyclic pitch. The aileron and elevator inputs cooperate with the roll and pitch rate feedback controller to stabilize the angular rate of roll and pitch motion.

d. **Mechanical Stability Augmentation**: The top rotor is not actively linked to any servos, but it is passively controlled via a mechanical stabilizer bar. This slows down the whole platform's response to the rapid changes in the cyclic pitch of the bottom rotor.

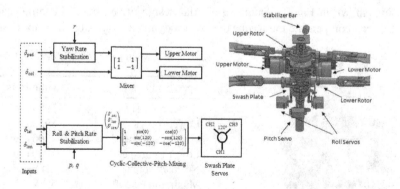

Fig. 3. Operating principle of the actuation system

4   Avionic System

The avionic system has been developed to realize fully autonomous flight. The following key components have been selected, which are the most suitable commercial off-the-shelf (COTS) products to date.

1. **Navigation Sensors.** IG-500N is currently the world smallest GPS enhanced attitude and heading reference system (AHRS) embedded with extended Kalman filter (EKF). It includes a MEMS-based inertial measurement unit (IMU), a GPS receiver and a pressure sensor. It is able to provide precise and drift-free 3D orientation and position even in aggressive maneuvers, updated at 100 Hz.
2. **Onboard Computer.** The onboard processor is the brain of the whole avionic system. It collects measurement data from various sensors, does filtering and fusion, executes flight control laws, and output control signals to carry out the desired control actions. In addition, it is also responsible for communicating with the GCS for real-time inspection and command issuing, as well as logging in-flight data for after-flight analysis. We have chosen two Gumstix Overo Fire embedded computers for flight control, navigation and vision processing purposes respectively. It has Wi-Fi functionality despite its small size and weight. In order to improve its real-time performance, the original Linux operating system provided by the manufacturer is replaced by the QNX Neutrino Real Time Operating System (RTOS).
3. **Servo Controller.** The UAV100 is an 8 channel radio control (RC) PPM servo controller and 8 channel PPM servo receiver that is designed to allow ground personnel to take over the control of the UAV at the flick of a switch to prevent a catastrophic failure from a malfunction in the flight computer.
4. **Communication.** The communication unit includes a pair of Microhard wireless data transceivers. This pair of transceivers establish communication between the onboard system and the ground station. They are configured to operate in point-to-point mode and works in the 2.400 to 2.4835GHz range.

System integration is not a trivial task in small-scale UAV development. We proposed a simple and uniform design approach, which is independent of the hardware components used and can be easily adopted to construct any small-scale UAVs [1]. Based on this method, essential mechanical parts and all related avionic components have been assembled onto the vehicle. The integrated components resulted in the final integrated platform which is shown in Fig. 2. This platform have been extensively used in test flights for model identification and verification.

5   Onboard Software and Ground Control Station

Based on the developed hardware system, a framework of a UAV software system is proposed which consists of two main components: onboard system and ground control system.

The UAV onboard system has six main modules: simulation model, sensing (sensor data acquisition and processing), flight control (automatic navigation and control), wireless communications (vehicle-vehicle and vehicle-ground communications).

The sensor data acquisition, navigation and control and UAV dynamics construct the control loop. Specifically, a UAV model is built in the onboard to realize hardware-in-the-loop simulation. Besides, the vehicle-vehicle communication is applied for cooperative data exchange to feed to the cooperative control module to realize UAV team cooperative control, such as formation flight control. In addition, the flight status data of each UAV is transmitted back to ground station via the vehicle-ground station communication. While the user can send commands to each UAV with this communication link. Sensors come into play apart from the traditional inertial navigation system (INS) with GPS, ultrasonic sensor can be used for landing where precise height measurement is necessary. Currently, with the development of image processing, the onboard camera becomes a more important role in target detection, tracking and many other applications. For detailed information of software development for UAVs, please refer to [7].

The GCS is composed of background tasks and foreground tasks. The background layer has mainly two tasks, receiving flight status from and sending commands to multiple UAVs, both of which interact with the UAV onboard communication task. The receiving thread accepts all the data from the fleet of UAVs and identify each status data via the telegraph packet header. Consequently, the corresponding multiple display is executed, and the cooperative way points of the paths are demonstrated. Similarly, the upload link can broadcast the commands to all UAVs, or alternatively send commands to a specific UAV, both via the sending task. The global status data from UAVs are dynamically updated from the background layer. The foreground task composes of information monitoring and task management, where the information monitoring module consists of various user-friendly views. A document class implementation in MFC is deployed to realize the communication between the background tasks and foreground tasks. The document class performs the flight data storage (up to 2000 updates), data processing (rotation computation in 3D view), command interpreting and packaging, and etc.

Specifically, based on our previous development for single UAVs, we incorporate the Google Maps view to better demonstrate the cooperative behaviors of the fleet of multiple UAVs. We captured several maps from Google Earth where we will conduct outdoor flight test and recorded the GPS data on the corners of the map. In the flight test, the GPS signal from the onboard system will be updated on the global shared data, and the cooperative paths of multiple UAVs are displayed on the Google Map way point view. For indoor flight tests, since the GPS signal is not available, we can manually set the position information to simulate this functionality in the way point view.

6 Dynamics Modeling

In order to systematically design a flight control law for the GremLion platform with good performance, an accurate mathematical model reflecting the flight dynamics of the air vehicle needs to be derived. To obtain this model, two approaches can be considered. One is called the first-principle modeling method which focuses on direct mathematical formulation of the system based on the law of physics, while the other one is called the system identification method which numerically estimates the parameters of a system with sufficient in-flight data. Although both approaches have shown their individual successes in literature, using either of them alone is not good enough to generate a model with good fidelity for the full envelope of UAV flight. Therefore, for the modeling of GremLion, the above two methods will be used in a complementary way.

Quite a few assumptions based on the facts of near-hovering condition has been made to reduce the model complexity. First of all, linear acceleration, linear velocity, angular rates, and roll pitch angles are all near zero when hovering, thus terms involving the second order of these variables can be dropped off when deriving mathematical expressions. Second, we assume very fast response of servos and motors (i.e. the response time from control inputs to the change of servo positions or change of speed of motors is much faster than the UAV dynamics). Third, although the coaxial helicopter flies with the top and bottom rotors pitching cyclically at different angles, it is reasonable to look at the two rotors as a whole system and model them as a single imaginary rotor with the so-called resultant longitudinal and lateral angles expressed as a_s and b_s. With this assumption, the model can be simplified to a large extent, yet maintaining good fidelity when the helicopter does not do aggressive maneuvering.

A reasonable linear model of GremLion flying at the near-hover condition with the coupling terms can be represented in the following state-space form:

$$\dot{x} = A_{id}x + B_{id}u \tag{1}$$

where $x = x_{act} - x_{trim}$ is the difference between the actual state variables and their trimmed values, and similarly, $u = u_{act} - u_{trim}$, which are respectively given as

$$x = [u,\ v,\ p,\ q,\ \phi,\ \theta,\ a_s,\ b_s,\ w,\ r]^{\mathrm{T}}$$
$$u = [\delta_{lat},\ \delta_{lon},\ \delta_{col},\ \delta_{ped}]^{\mathrm{T}}$$

Where $[u,\ v,\ w]^{\mathrm{T}}$ are the body-axis velocity in x, y and z directions, $[p,\ q,\ r]^{\mathrm{T}}$ are the angular velocity in x, y and z axes, $[a_s,\ b_s]^{\mathrm{T}}$ are the equivalent longitudinal and lateral flapping angles of the top and bottom rotors together. $[\delta_{lat},\ \delta_{lon}, \delta_{col}, \delta_{ped}]^{\mathrm{T}}$ are the inputs to the system (aileron, elevator, throttle, rudder). And A_{id} and B_{id} matrices are derived in the near hovering condition by the identification of the unknown model parameters which could be obtained by doing manual flight tests and giving frequency sweeping signals (sinusoidal signals with various frequencies) to the four input channels.

7   Navigation and Control

In flight control engineering, a natural stratification of the full-order dynamic model of a helicopter is based on motion types, i.e. rotational motion and translational motion. In general, the dynamics of rotational motion is much faster than that of the translational motion. Thus, the controlled object can be divided into two parts and the overall control system can be formulated in a dual-loop structure. In this way, inner-loop and outer-loop controllers can be designed separately.

The main task of the inner-loop controller is to stabilize the attitude and heading of GremLion in all flight conditions. H_{∞} technique is preferred for robust stability. For the outer loop, the controlled object covers only the translational motion. The main task is to steer the UAV to fly with reference to a series of given locations. A robust and perfect tracking (RPT) approach is implemented for the outer-loop since time factor is important. It should be noted that both control laws are designed using the asymptotic time-scale and eigenstructure assignment (ATEA) method, which is fully developed for MIMO LTI systems by Chen et al. [8]. It makes the design process very systematic and effective. To give an overall view, the dual-loop control structure is shown in Fig. 4.

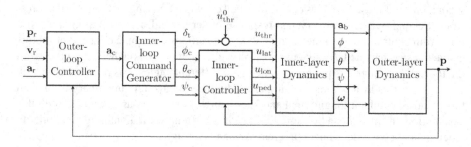

Fig. 4. Dual-loop Structure of Flight Control System

7.1   Inner-Loop Control Design

The inner-layer dynamics is a 8th-order MIMO system with three control inputs, namely u_{lat}, u_{lon}, and u_{ped}. The uninvolved fourth input, u_{thr}, is reserved for control of vertical motion and needs be set at its trimming value (denoted as u_{thr}^0) at this stage. For the measurement part, IMU gives ϕ, θ, ψ, p, q, and r. The other two state variables (i.e. the flapping angles b_s, a_s) have to be estimated by an observer. Therefore, the linearized inner-layer controlled object can be formulated from Eqn. 1 as

$$\begin{cases} \dot{\mathbf{x}} = A_{\text{in}}\mathbf{x} + B_{\text{in}}\mathbf{u} + E_{\text{in}}\mathbf{w} \\ \mathbf{y} = C_{\text{in},1}\mathbf{x} + D_{\text{in},11}\mathbf{u} + D_{\text{in},1}\mathbf{w} \\ \mathbf{z} = C_{\text{in},2}\mathbf{x} + D_{\text{in},2}\mathbf{u} + D_{\text{in},22}\mathbf{w} \end{cases} \tag{2}$$

where $\mathbf{x} = [\phi\ \theta\ \psi\ p\ q\ r\ b_s\ a_s]^{\text{T}}$ is the inner-loop state variables. $\mathbf{y} = [\phi\ \theta\ \psi\ p\ q\ r]^{\text{T}}$ is the measured output vector, $\mathbf{z} = [\phi\ \theta\ \psi]^{\text{T}}$ is the controlled output vector, and all variables are the deviations from their trimming values. Note that the direct feed through matrices $D_{\text{in},11}$ and $D_{\text{in},2}$ are both zero. No external disturbance is considered for this part of model at the current stage, so the disturbance input matrix E_{in} and the feed through matrices $D_{\text{in},1}$, $D_{\text{in},22}$ are all empty. They are reserved in the expression for integrity so that external disturbances such as wind gusts can be considered in future. The controlled subsystem characterized by quadruple (A_{in}, B_{in}, $C_{\text{in},2}$, $D_{\text{in},2}$) is both observable and controllable. By transforming the quadruple into the special coordinate basis (SCB) form [8], we find that the subsystem is invertible and of minimum phase. Hence, we can design an H_∞ controller via the ATEA method using state feedback to obtain robust stability. Matrix F_{i} is the state feedback gain, Matrix G_{i} is the corresponding reference feed forward gain to make sure the ratio between output and reference is unity.

7.2 Outer-Loop Control Design

The outer-loop control can then be designed separately and based on the dynamic model GremLion's translational motion only, provided that the outer loop is slow enough as compared to the inner loop. Furthermore, the outer-loop control signals are all defined in the North-East-Down (NED) frame and for all three directions, the dynamics are approximately formulated as double integrators. So,

$$\begin{cases} \dot{\mathbf{x}} = A_{\mathrm{out}}\mathbf{x} + B_{\mathrm{out}}\mathbf{u} + E_{\mathrm{out}}\mathbf{w} \\ \mathbf{y} = C_{\mathrm{out},1}\mathbf{x} \\ \mathbf{z} = C_{\mathrm{out},2}\mathbf{x} \end{cases} \tag{3}$$

where,

$$\mathbf{x} = [x\ y\ z\ u\ v\ w]^{\mathrm{T}}\ ,\ \mathbf{y} = [x\ y\ z\ u\ v\ w]^{\mathrm{T}}\ ,\ \mathbf{z} = [x\ y\ z]^{\mathrm{T}}\ ,\ \mathbf{u} = [ac_x\ ac_y\ ac_z]^{\mathrm{T}}$$

Since the translational motion in these three directions are largely decoupled (inner-loop should have decoupled them if designed correctly), the RPT control laws for these three channels can be designed separately. Since they are all standard 2nd order systems, by choosing an appropriate natural frequency and damping ratio, they should be able to achieve desired performance. Of course, minor tuning is needed after trial flight tests have been carried out.

7.3 Inner-Loop Command Generator

We have designed the inner-loop and the outer-loop controllers separately to avoid the non-minimum phase problem and to relieve task complexity. To preserve the overall system stability, the closed outer loop should be slower than the closed inner loop. In this case, the closed inner loop can be seen as a static gain when combining with the outer loop. We approximated an inner-loop command generator from the outer-loop controller output $\mathbf{a}_{\mathrm{c}}$,

$$[\delta_{\mathrm{t}}\ \phi_{\mathrm{c}}\ \theta_{\mathrm{c}}]^{\mathrm{T}} = G_{\mathrm{c}}\mathbf{a}_{\mathrm{c}} = G_{\mathrm{a}}^{-1}\mathbf{a}_{\mathrm{c}} \tag{4}$$

Notice that G_{a} must be non-singular otherwise $\mathbf{a}_{\mathrm{b}}$ cannot be manipulated by the control inputs u_{thr}, u_{lat}, u_{lon}. Flight tests show that this inner-loop command generator G_{c} is feasible.

7.4 Flight Results

One of the flight test results in the UAVForge competition has been shown in Fig. 4, which consists of several key flight modes, e.g. hovering, ascending, forward flight, etc. This test result verified the proposed flight control design and onboard avionics. The detailed path generation is as follows.

The proposed control law was sufficiently stable and GremLion should be able to finish the required 2 mile flight. Unfortunately, the electronic speed controller (ESC) overheated when GremLion began its forward flight. The ESCs cut off temporarily and started functioning after a short moment. The consequence was disastrous as the platform could not stand such a big and sudden disturbance. The top and bottom rotors

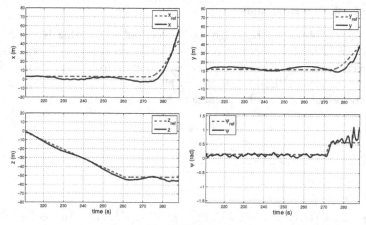

Fig. 5. Flight results

struck each other and followed by loss of lift. GremLion crashed into the trees and our attempt was suspended. Nonetheless, the on-board recorded data had been saved and transferred to PC and Fig. 5 show various signals just before the crash.

8   Vision-Based Obstacle Detection and Avoidance

In order to perform autonomous navigation in unknown outdoor environments, the UAV should have the capability to detect and avoid obstacles, e.g. trees, electrical cables, buildings, etc., in its flight path. We propose a depth-based obstacle detection algorithm using vision sensing. We chose to use vision sensors because monocular cameras are light-weight and low priced and can provide rich information of the environment. Our obstacle detection method is based on 3D vision techniques, more specifically, optical flow. Optical flow can provide the velocity of features on the images.

The main steps in our algorithm are feature extraction, feature matching, and depth estimation. The purpose to achieve feature extraction and matching is to obtain the feature position on the image, and to calculate the feature velocity on the image. The idea behind our depth estimation is based on structure from motion. More precisely, if the state (i.e., position, velocity and attitude) of the UAV can be measured, e.g., by GPS and inertial sensors, and the image of a 3D point can be matched between two images, then the 3D position of the 3D point can be determined. In our work, since we are more interested in the distance between the obstacles and the UAV, we focus on how to estimate the depth of the feature points since we can obtain the state of the UAV using GPS and inertial sensors. If the depth of certain parts of the scene is less than a prescribed threshold, then that part will be classified as an obstacle and obstacle avoidance procedures will be activated.

9   Vision-Based Target Tracking

The UAVForge competition requires UAVs to perform a series of advance behaviors and one of them is to execute the "Follow Me" task, which requires the vehicle to autonomously follow the ground operator from the Starting Point back to the designated Flight Preparation Area and maintain a safe altitude.

The strategy used to solve the above problem statement is to implement mono-camera target tracking of the required vehicle. As the target mentioned in the above statement is that of a vehicle traveling at about 15-30 mph, it is necessary to firstly mark the target that is required to be tracked. It is achieved by using a mono-camera sensor to capture an image of the target vehicle and drawing a rectangular target box around the required target. Next, the selected target box is extracted from the image and training of the target is implemented using the Continuously Adaptive Mean-SHIFT(CAMSHIFT) algorithm. Assuming that the mono-camera sensor on the GremLion UAV is stable, the movement of the target could be tracked by observing the new object center calculated from the algorithm. The GremLion UAV is then controlled to maintain the tracked object in the center of the image captured from the camera.

10   Conclusion and Future Work

In this paper, the development and implementation of GremLion has been presented. The flight test results of the GremLion in the UAVForge competition have been presented too. Further experiment and research work is required to obtain a reliable and accurate dynamic model of GremLion in full envelope condition. That is also important for the automatic control law design. In addition, we have implemented the vision-based algorithms on the onboard vision computer, including obstacle avoidance and target tracking. These algorithms will be tested in further experiments, though we did not test them in the competition.

References

[1] Cai, G., Chen, B.M., Lee, T.H.: Unmanned Rotorcraft Systems, 1st edn. Springer, New York (2011)

[2] Cai, G.W., Lin, F., Chen, B.M., Lee, T.H.: Development of fully functional miniature un-manned rotorcraft systems. To be presented at the 29 Chinese Control Conference, Beijing, China (2010)

[3] Sarris, Z., Atlas, S.: Survey of UAV applications in civil markets. In: Proceedings of the 9th Mediterranean Conference on Control and Automation, Dubrovnik, Croatia, vol. WA2-A (2001)

[4] Enderle, B.: Commercial Applications of UAV's in Japanese Agriculture. In: Proceedings of the AIAA 1st UAV Conference, Portsmouth, Virginia (2002) AIAA-2002-3400

[5] Ludington, B., Johnson, E., Vachtsevanos, G.: Augmenting UAV autonomy. IEEE Robotics & Automation Magazine 13, 63–71 (2006)

[6] Campbell, M.E., Whitacre, W.W.: Cooperative tracking using vision measurements on seascan UAVs. IEEE Transactions on Control Systems Technology 15, 613–626 (2007)

[7] Dong, X., Chen, B.M., Cai, G., Lin, H., Lee, T.H.: A comprehensive real-time software system for flight coordination and cooperative control of multiple unmanned aerial vehicles. International Journal of Robotics and Automation 26(1), 49–63 (2011)

[8] Chen, B.M.: Robust and H_∞ Control. Springer, London (2000)

Heuristic Evaluation of iCalamityGuide Application

Aaron Marcus[1], Scott Abromowitz[1], and Maysoon F. Abulkhair[2]

[1] Aaron Marcus & Associates, Inc. (AM+A), 1196 Euclid Avenue, Suite 1F,
Berkeley, CA, 94708 USA
[2] Faculty of Computing and Info. Technology, King Abdulaziz University,
Jeddah, Saudi Arabia
Aaron.Marcus@AMandA.com, scott@abromo.com
mabualkhair@kau.edu.sa

Abstract. Researchers at King Abdulaziz University are developing an application intended to assist people during natural and man-made disasters. The iCalamityGuide presents two distinct user experiences based upon a user's credentials. This paper reports on a heuristic evaluation of the application and suggests revisions that combine the two experiences when they are the same and differentiate them when they are different.

Keywords: calamity, design, development, evaluation, experiece, heuristic, interface, mobile, Saudi Arabia, safety, university, user.

1 Introduction

Researchers at King Abdulaziz University (KAU) are developing an application intended to assist people during natural and man-made disasters. The iCalamityGuide presents two distinct user experiences based upon a user's credentials. This paper reports on a heuristic evaluation of the application and suggests revisions that combine the two experiences when they are the same and differentiate them when they are different. AM+A conducted a heuristic evaluation of the iCalamityGuide (iCG) during June through August 2012. The materials for the evaluation included the iCalamityGuide iOS application and some competitor products. This evaluation applied AM+A's heuristics to the above materials and drew from the expertise of the evaluator. AM+A analyzed the entirety of the iCalamityGuide application. The findings have been organized into the information architecture of the iCG. The iCalamityGuide presents two distinct user experiences based on a user's credentials. This paper combines/differentiates the two experiences when they are the same/different

Methodology. A heuristic evaluation is a systematic inspection of a user-interface design regarding usability issues, as well as usefulness and appeal, according to pre-established categories of issues and criteria. The objective of a heuristic evaluation is to find design issues so that they can be resolved as part of an iterative user-centered design process. A list of these usability principles, "AM+A Heuristics," is included in the Appendix. each observation, the severity of the issue is stated/depicted, and the relevant heuristic labels are provided that refer to the Heuristics appearing in the Appendix.

A. Marcus (Ed.): DUXU/HCII 2013, Part III, LNCS 8014, pp. 130–139, 2013.
© Springer-Verlag Berlin Heidelberg 2013

2   Initial Set Up

System Set-up. iCG's initial installation did not afford several options that reassure the user that she/he is capable of undoing a particular action. According to one of Shneiderman's "Eight Golden Rules" of user-interface design, there should be an easy reversal of action if a user wishes to log out of her/his account or change her/his password. Nielsen's Heuristics further emphasize the importance of consistency and standards by stating that an application must incorporate efficient and clearer wording to ensure that a user is not confused in regard to using an application such as logging into the system. Current initial installation set a poor tone for users/customers in proceeding with use of the app. Throughout the process, it was unclear what happened if users mistype their passwords or usernames when creating an account for iCalamity-Guide. For example, users first opening iCalamityGuide were given insufficient guidance during the set-up of iCG regarding what happens if users forget their account names and/or passwords. It would be more effective for the overall experience to state why users must create an account to utilize the application. Explaining to users why they must create an account is especially important for visitors to King Abdulaziz University (KAU) because visitors might be cautious about signing-up for an account out of fear of an invasion of privacy. One should explain to potential users the importance of allowing iCG to identify their location while using the iCG (*e.g.*, the app could save their lives).

Heuristic: **Severity level:** 4
User   control   and   freed▆▆ ▆▆ ▆▆ ▆▆
Fitt's Law
Give feedback

Initial uncertainty in regard to user credentials: It was unclear to users what happens once they register to use the iCG because the system currently does not alert users of successful account creation. A confirmation via email or an in-app notification would be a good feedback mechanism. This approach reassures users with a visible system status that an outcome, registration for the iCG, has occurred. In addition, it was unclear what happens if a person has multiple devices. A simple sentence such as, "Please sign-in with your University username and password," would be sufficient to avoid any user confusion.

Heuristic: **Severity level:** 3
User   control   and   freedom   ▆▆ ▆▆ ▆▆ ☐
Feedback
Support easy reversal of action

Basic Functionality: Education, Workflow, Language, Navigation: iCG is a powerful tool that offers two distinct experiences, the individual user and the security controler, based on a user's credentials. These tools can be vital in a situation in which the environment can be dangerous, such as a flooding or an incident of violence, such as riots or protests.

Information about Features: For individual users of iCG, not the security controllers, once they are registered to use the application they are presented with a map view and a number of functions. The system then presents each building with a color scheme predefined by KAU. Although the color scheme is not random, to visitors visiting KAU, the colors may appear confusing and random, because of a lack of consistency. We suggested following a set of standards in regard to building safety, such as red for danger, yellow/orange for caution, and green for safety. KAU's building color scheme can be confusing to not only campus visitors, but also students, faculty, and staff who are familiar with the color scheme. In times of crisis, there is a possible chance that people will react differently to and/or forget KAU's predefined building colors. Once more, in the toolbar section for the first view of a user screen, it was unclear what functionality the Twitter logo performs. Users might confuse the sign as a means of launching the Twitter application or Website. A possible solution would be to incorporate the iOS built-in sharing features, because iOS 5+ has this functionality already built-in to its operating systems. This approach also allows those who use other services such as Facebook or email to do so within the menu displayed of available sharing services. Nevertheless, if one desires to limit the app's functionality to only Twitter, we suggested following the Twitter guidelines for using the Twitter logo. The current design does not fit with its guidelines, because the design utilizes the old logo and modifies the logo with a speech bubble.

Heuristic: **Severity level:** 3
Information legibility and density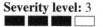
Consistency and standards
Match between system and real world
Help and documentation

Recommendations:

• Provide users with clear, short descriptions of services and their benefits right up front. Text used to describe features of the application should be present in a tutorial.
• Standardize one a set of three colors to signify: Danger, Caution, and Safe.

Heuristic: **Severity level:** 4
Visible interfaces/WYSIWYG
Direct manipulation/See and point
Consistency and standards

Notifying Users of Calamity: The push notification to alert users of an emergency could be enhanced, because the notification does not provide much context about the type of emergency that is present. The notification also does not inform users if they are affected by the situation.

Heuristic:
Consistency and standards

Severity level: 2

Recommendation:

- A clearer description should be utilized.

Content: Clarity of Language and Detection of Users: The general language of the application was clear given the limited abilities of the application's purpose. A more effective means to detect users (to locate them and to display them) is necessary for enhanced usability. To detect the application's users in the location-pin mode can become quite cumbersome and ineffective, because the screen layout will appear quite cluttered and, consequently, the system can become difficult to use. Often, it is more effective to use a list similar to the app's safe building list. We suggested that one consider adding the number of people in the building next to the building's title. This suggested enhancement is visible in the redesigned Security Screen shown below. Another addition would be to include a number overlays over each building that depicts the number of people inside the building, if this design approach does not add significant clutter and/or does not obscure other visual details.

Heuristic:
Consistency and standards
Recognition rather than recall

Severity level: 3

Key Words: Users look for information by scanning for keywords. If the terminology users expect to see is not present/used, they may have difficulty finding the information they are seeking. For example, users who want to find an important evacuation route may not initially know where to look in the zoomed-out map view. The color of buildings (*e.g.,* green, blue, red) leads to confusion about how to differentiate among buildings. The Guide Me button seemed too ambiguous, because users might infer its functionality is as a user-guide about how to use the application or a guide around campus. Better terminology is necessary to alleviate any potential confusion.

Recommendation:

- Consider how users think about tasks, and specifically what words or phrases make most sense to users. Validate these words and phrases in user tests.

Heuristic:
Consistency   and   standards
Information legibility and density
Match between system and real world

Severity level: 3

To enhance usability, consider the iOS Human Interface Guidelines: In iOS applications, only navigation buttons appear in the navigation bar; therefore, the KAU buttons should change locations to the toolbar, because functions are typically located in this area. If, however, one wishes to keep the KAU buttons in the navigation bar, consider centering them because the function is not a navigational function, as is visible in the iOS YouTube and App Store apps. We also suggested that iCG use initial capital letters for the titles of buttons in either the navigation bar or the toolbar, because of better consistency and readability.

Error Handling: The error message warning should use better terminology, and should reword terms, instead of using computer "jargon." For instance, when security personnel decide to change a building's status to safe and the security person selects only one building, not two, the error message could state:

"Selection Error - Please select a current safe building followed by a new safe building."
Recommendations:

- Review specific High Level Findings recommendations, below.
- When conducting user tests, examine both users' abilities to figure out how to install and use the system as well as ease-of-use of the system once they've learned their way around the system. Particular findings about the initial learning curve will provide invaluable feedback.

Heuristic: **Severity level:** 3
Consistency and standards
Help and documentation

3   Application Management

Manage Accounts: Deleting Accounts: Currently, no visible option/ability is present for users who wish to be removed or logged-out from the system. This absence prevents users from successfully feeling that they are in control by not being able to delete their accounts.

Recommendations:

- Allow users the ability to disassociate their accounts with the iCG application.
- Allow users to logout of the application.

Heuristic: **Severity level:** 3
User control and freedom

Changing a Building's Status: Currently, it is confusing for security personnel who wish to change the status of a building from unsafe to safe. The current setup is difficult to discern if a person is changing building #420-6 or changing building #420 from being safe to building #6 becoming safe. In addition, there is no quick way to change the status of several buildings from either safe to unsafe, or vice-versa.

Recommendations:

• Consider the implantation of our proposed screen redesign

Heuristic: **Severity level:** 3
Modelessness   ▬ ▬ ▬ ☐

4   Competitive Analysis

AM+A performed a competitive analysis of three mobile applications in order to offer direction and comparison for redesigning the iCG user interface. A competitive analysis can be helpful in informing and critiquing design decisions. Comments on these three mobile applications follow:

4.1   Deloitte's Bamboo (http://bamboo4bcm.com)

The application is targeted at businesses that wish to replace paper-based disaster-management protocols with an electronic/interactive system.

Positive: Enables users to see location of fellow colleagues; Follows Shneiderman's Eight Golden Rules of User-Interface Design

Negative: Generally designed for offices in a single building; Uses location-pins for finding colleagues, which can become cumbersome because the screen becomes cluttered; Provides no toolbar for easy navigation

4.2   MyDisasterDroid (http://www.scribd.com/doc/94311333/Android)

MyDisasterDroid is a calamity application designed by two professors in the Philippines. The application determines the optimal route to safety based on users' current locations and the location of safe areas.

Positive: Prioritization of closer location for rescuers; Prioritizing location with lots of people in need

Negative: No user awareness; User interface is unintuitive; Neither able to see the location of users nor able to designate safe and dangerous buildings

4.3   Meridian App (http://www.meridianapps.com)

The Meridian application is marketed for hospital, malls, and other large building complexes. The purpose of the application is to guide users from one point within a building to another point within the same building with easy-to-understand directions and visual cues. The product does not rely on a GPS signal, but instead on users' abilities to follow steps until they reach their destinations.

Positive: Logically designed user interface with legible words and warnings; Allows for direct manipulation
Negative: Not designed for a multi-building campus

5   Screen Redesigns

Based on the above analysis, AM+A also provided, beyond a typical heuristic analysis, the following screen redesigns that incorporated the comments in the above evaluation and suggested possible functionality improvements to screen layout, color, typography, and navigation.

Non-Security User Screens

Fig. 1. This screen illustrates a rewording of a screen to enhance usability of a pop-up notification. The screen also introduces a legend or key above the tab bar for glanceable reference.

Fig. 2. This screen is another iteration of screen; however, this version places the legend inside of the tab bar to conserve screen real estate.

Fig. 3. This screen is an additional iteration; however, the key in this version is only visible if a user selects the "I"/Info button.

Security Personnel Screens

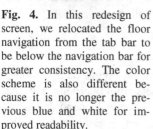

Fig. 4. In this redesign of screen, we relocated the floor navigation from the tab bar to be below the navigation bar for greater consistency. The color scheme is also different because it is no longer the previous blue and white for improved readability.

Fig. 5. In this redesign, we made the selection more logical for personnel who are changing a building to becoming safe. We separated the two columns so users do not confuse the two options and incorporate an arrow to direct users to the next selection for easy recognition.

Fig. 6. In this redesign, we reworded the statement under building name if a building is safe or not by simply stating "Safe, Caution, or Danger." We incorporate the number of people in the building for easy reference. Personnel can also select the right blue arrow button to see a list of people located in the selected building.

6   Conclusions

This heuristic evaluation identified areas for improvement in a good application's user-interface design. In the future, detailed user testing could determine which of the redesign suggestions would provide the most powerful enhancements of the application to make it more usable, useful, and appealing.

Acknowledgements. Thanks go to the IT Dept. KAU, development team students: Hajer Assiri, Reham Fiesal, Somaia Alyoubi, Marwah Samarkandi, Noura Alsaba'an, and Oraib Abdullah.

Appendix: AM+A's Heuristics

AM+A's heuristics used in this report are adapted from many sources including the following:

- Graphic Design for Electronic Documents and User Interfaces, by Aaron Marcus (Addison-Wesley, 1992).
- The original list authored by Jakob Nielsen, in Usability Inspection Methods (1994 Nielsen, Mack).
- The classic Human Interface Guidelines (Apple, 1992). These deal more with the quality of modern user interfaces in general, rather than specifically with usability concerns.
- Principles of clear information visualization and graphic excellence in The Visual Display of Quantitative Information, Envisioning Information, and Visual Explanations, by Edward Tufte (Graphics Press).
- Tog on Interface, by Bruce Tognazzini (Addison Wesley, 1992).
- Designing the User Interface: Strategies for Effective Human-Computer Interaction, by Ben Shneiderman (Addison-Wesley Computing, 2009).
- iOS Human Interface Guidelines (Apple, 2012)

Aesthetic integrity and minimalist design: Dialogs should not contain irrelevant or rarely needed information. Every extra unit of information in a dialog competes with the relevant units of information and diminishes their relative visibility. Information should be well organized and consistent with principles of visual design. Avoid information overload.

Consistency and standards: Users shouldn't ask if different words/situations/actions mean the same thing. Follow platform conventions.

Direct manipulation/See and point: Users should be able to see on the screen what they're doing and should be able to point at what they see. This forms a paradigm of noun (object) then verb (action). When the user performs operations on the object, the impact of those operations on the object is immediately visible.

Error prevention: Even better than good error messages: careful design that prevents problems from occurring in the first place.

Feedback / Visible system status: The system should always keep users informed about what is going on, through appropriate feedback within reasonable time. Provide confirmations when the outcome of an action is not visibly apparent.

Fitt's Law: The time to acquire a target is a function of the distance to and size of the target.

Flexibility and efficiency of use: Accelerators—unseen by the novice user—may often speed up the interaction for the expert user such that the system can cater to both inexperienced and experienced users. Allow users to tailor frequent actions.

Help and documentation: Even though it is better if the system can be used without documentation, it may be necessary to provide help and documentation. Any such information should be easy to search, be focused on the user's task, list concrete steps to be carried out, and be concise.

Help users recognize, diagnose, and recover from errors: Error messages should use plain language, indicate the problem, and constructively suggest a solution.

Information legibility and density: Maximize the amount of data to the amount of ink or pixels used. Eliminate any decorations on charts and graphs that do not actually convey information, such as 3-dimensional embellishments. Less is More is the rule in information design as every pixel used that does not contribute to information, dilutes it.

Match between system and real world: The system should speak the users' language, with words, phrases and concepts familiar to the user, rather than system-oriented terms. Follow real-world conventions, making information appear in a natural and logical order. Accommodate the ways in which users are accustomed to working.

Modelessness: Try to create modeless features that allow people to do whatever they want whenever they want to. Avoid using modes because they typically restrict the operations that users can perform. Modelessness gives users more control over what he or she can do and allow the user to maintain context of the work.

Perceived stability: In order to cope with computer-based complexity, people need stable reference points. To give users a conceptual stability, the user interface should provide a clear, finite set of objects and actions.

Recognition rather than recall: Make objects, actions, and options visible. Users shouldn't need to remember information from one part of the dialog to another. Instructions system use should be visible or easily retrievable whenever appropriate.

User control and freedom: Allow the user, not the computer to initiate and control actions. Users often choose system functions by mistake and will need a clearly marked "emergency exit" to leave the unwanted state without having to go through an extended dialog. Support undo and redo.

Visible interfaces/WYSIWYG: Don't hide features in applications by using abstract commands. People should be able to see what they need when needed. Most users can't and won't build elaborate mental maps and will become lost or tired if expected to do so. Clearly convey key information without making users dig or click to find it.

Severity Ratings: The severity of a usability problem is a combination of three factors:

1. The frequency with which the problem occurs: Is it common or rare?
2. The impact of the problem if it occurs: Will it be easy or difficult for the users to overcome?
3. The persistence of the problem: One-time problem that users can overcome once they know about it or will users repeatedly be bothered by the problem?

One needs to assess market impact of the problem because certain usability problems can have a devastating effect on the product's popularity even if they are "objectively" quite easy to overcome. Even though severity has several components, it is common to combine all aspects of severity in a single severity rating as an overall assessment of each usability problem in order to facilitate prioritizing and decision-making. The severity ratings used in this report are described below:

Severity level 1   Cosmetic problem only; need not be fixed unless extra time is available on project.

Severity level 2   Minor usability problem—could impair users' productivity and ability to learn.

Severity level 3   Major usability problem; important to fix; high priority; impacts users' productivity and increases likelihood of errors.

Severity level 4   Usability catastrophe; imperative to fix this before product can be released.

The Driving Machine: Mobile UX Design That Combines Information Design with Persuasion Design

Aaron Marcus and Scott Abromowitz

Aaron Marcus and Associates, Inc.,
1196 Euclid Avenue, Suite 1F, Berkeley, CA, 94708 USA
Aaron.Marcus@AMandA.com, scott@abromo.com

Abstract. Travel and tourism is a booming sector of the 21st century world economy. Vehicles are becoming smarter and using advanced graphical displays. The Driving Machine seeks to provide an innovative vehicle dashboard that combines information design and persuasion design to change the driver's behavior, promoting safety and fuel efficiency, or sustainability.

Keywords: dashboard, design, development, experience, incentives, information, interface, mobile, persuasion, safety, social networks, sustainability, user, vehicle.

1   Introduction

A 21st-century global vehicle dashboard-design challenge is to take advantage of technology to increase safety and conserve energy. The context is this: advances in technology increase driving distractions, and global warming increases our desire to reduce our carbon footprint. In particular, the Green movement has helped to increase people's awareness of sustainability issues and propelled development of innovative products to help decrease our ecological footprint.

The Driving Machine seeks to increase safe driving-behavior and fuel-efficient driving by offering information, overviews, social networking, just-in-time knowledge, and incentives, including gamification, that can help to reduce, even prevent, vehicular accidents and promote more fuel-efficient driving. The question then shifts to how best to motivate, persuade, educate, and lead people to adopt safe-driving behavior and reduce their energy consumption. For our project we researched and analyzed powerful ways to improve safe and green behavior by persuading and motivating people to become more alert drivers and to reduce their energy consumption through a vehicle dashboard application we call the "Driving Machine."

Dashboards and automotive-related applications are available to increase people's awareness of safety and the environment, but such technologies often do not focus on innovative data visualization, and they may lack persuasive effectiveness to encourage drivers to continue good driving behavior. Communicating one's carbon footprint, driving skills, and alertness, helps build awareness and identity, but does not result automatically in effecting behavioral changes. The question then becomes: How can we better motivate, persuade, educate, and lead people to become safer and

A. Marcus (Ed.): DUXU/HCII 2013, Part III, LNCS 8014, pp. 140–149, 2013.

more efficient drivers? Aaron Marcus and Associates, Inc. (AM+A) has embarked on the conceptual design of a mobile-phone/tablet-based product, the Driving Machine, intended to address this situation.

The author's firm previously designed and tested similar concept prototypes that seek to change people's behavior: the Green Machine application in 2009, oriented to persuading home consumers to make energy-conservation behavior-changes; the Health Machine application in 2010, oriented to avoiding obesity and diabetes through behavior changes regarding nutrition and exercise; and the Money Machine in 2011, targeted to baby boomers and oriented to assisting them to manage their wealth more effectively. The Driving Machine uses similar principles of combining information design/visualization with persuasion design. The Driving Machine's objective is to combine information design and visualization with persuasion design to help users achieve their goals of driving more safely and efficiently by persuading users to adapt their driving behavior, for example to follow traffic laws better and adopt carpooling behavior. AM+A intends to apply user-centered design along with persuasive techniques to make the Driving Machine highly usable and to increase the likelihood of success in adopting new driving behavior. This white paper and an accompanying presentation explain the development of the Driving Machine's user interface, information design, information visualization, and persuasion design.

2   Initial Discussion

As the amount of computing technology continues to increase in our cars and trucks, careful consideration must be given to dashboard design to ensure the safety and reliability of drivers, passengers, and vehicles. Increasingly states are passing laws that limit drivers' abilities to operate mobile phones or to read/send text messages while driving. Recent research illustrates that even such laws may not go far enough, as cited by Paul Green (see Bibliography). Paul Green describes how driving and using a cell phone, regardless of having hands free or not, places drivers at greater risk of causing accidents than drivers who only talk to passengers inside their vehicles. The reason talking on the phone is a greater danger than talking to passengers is because passengers are more aware of current driving situations than people being communicated with on the phone. One study by Redelmeier and Tibshirani cite, as stated by Green, that using a cell phone increases the likelihood of a crash by up to 4.3 times versus those not using a cell phone while driving. Estimates for distraction-related crashes in the United States typically come from a sample of about 5,000 police-reported crashes called the Crashworthiness Data System (CDS) [Green, 2003]. To overcome future problems that new technologies might have on driving, the National Highway Traffic Administration (NHTASA) proposed a set of guidelines to test the impact of a specific task on driving performance and safety. If a task is deemed too distracting to a driver's focus based on the Visual-Manual NHTASA Driver Distraction Guidelines for In-Vehicle Electronic Devices, NHTASA encourages automobile manufactures to prevent a driver's from being able to perform the interfering task [National Highway Traffic Safety Administration, 2012].

AM+A previously has done research for BMW (2002) in a report titled "Future HMI Directions," in which AM+A thoroughly researched a driver-centered approach to HMI (Human-Machine Interaction). Although the report is over ten years old, the human factor issues are still highly relevant today as evidenced in Green's research and the NHTASA report. In addition to safety, designing a system that encourages being environmentally conscious is an important attribute of our research. While fuel prices and the threat of global warming continue to rise, carpooling in the United States is at a very low 11% [Johnson, Jones, & Silverman, 2010]. Services such as Zimride seek to counter the low rate of carpooling by creating a social network where people can be drivers and passengers in carpools. Zimride also offers Lyft, which helps those who would normally travel alone in a taxi request on-demand ridesharing. Honda Motors developed its Ecological Drive Assist System to encourage efficient driving by supporting behavior change, in offering visual feedback via an ambient green or blue color, and also by gamifying driving behavior through the design of virtual leaves for more sustainable driving [Honda Motors, 2008].

Our research shows that an innovative approach to vehicle dashboard design must account for the following: design for safety where a driver easily should be able to take a second glance at a display cluster and then refocus his/her attention on the road. Next, a display cluster must not increase the level of complexity that a driver encounters. For example, a focus on helpful rather than powerful features is important to ensure a reduction of complexity. A graphical user interface should not focus on visual complexity with an overabundance of graphics; rather, it must use graphics only if it enhances dynamic content that would otherwise be less visible. The user interface should not constrain the user to conform to a particular layout, but instead allow him/her to customize the available information present in the digital dashboard. Lastly, the dashboard development must follow a user-centered design process. The user-centered user-experience design (UCUXD) approach links the process of developing software, hardware, and user-interface (UI) to the people who will use a product/service. UCUXD processes focus on users throughout the development of a product or service. The UCUXD process comprises these tasks, which sometimes occur iteratively: planning, research, analysis, design, implementation, evaluation, and documentation. AM+A carried out these tasks in the development of the Driving Machine concept design, except for implementing working versions.

3   Personas and Use Scenarios

To better understand the demographics and to focus on creation of user-centered designs, our company incorporates the use of personas (user profiles). Personas are characterizations of primary user types and are intended to capture essentials of their demographics, contexts of use, behaviors, and motivations/objectives, and their impact on design solutions.. For the Driving Machine personas, we identified three target markets: young drivers, early adopters, and elderly drivers and defined appropriate personas, male and female, aged 17-73, from several racial/ethnic groups (see full description in the AM+A White paper [Marcus, 2013]). We wrote their descriptions, vehicle-related objectives, contexts, behaviors, and design implications. We wrote use scenarios for each person and a general use persona. Use scenarios are a UI development technique that emphasizes user-centered stories about product/service use. The following general use scenario topics were drawn from three personas because we anticipated that these would be representative of the others.

Carbon Footprint Monitoring

- Receive up-to-date articles, advice, and tips regarding monitoring current and past driving behavior.
- Set customizable alerts for driving, whether positive or negative
- Receive unsafe alerts
- Establish and maintain objectives (*e.g.,* "I want to reduce my carbon footprint")
- Establish and maintain goals (*e.g.,* specify number of people you want to drive in a carpool). See the ramifications of this goal on current and past trends.
- Visualize and monitor the carbon footprint

Carpooling

- Share current location with people near by
- Alert driver of any potential passengers
- Visualize and monitor the number of and location of carpool passengers

Social Media

- Post green/efficient driving achievements on the users' own walls and possibly their friends' walls, similar to a merit-badge system
- Connect with insurance agent by automatically sending them status reports on your driving behavior
- Share tips and strategies with specific friends or family
- Import personal information from social media sites (*e.g.,* race, sex, age). Users not connected to a social media site can add their information manually through the Driving Machine
- Resolve any urgent ethical issues

Gamification

- Set and use pre-existing achievements to help reduce insurance premiums
- Compare estimated fuel economy to actual fuel economy
- Earn badges for being a driver in a carpool or on-demand carpool
- Purchase carbon offsets by carpooling
- Reward posting gas prices with gas reward cards
- Develop an "economy of tipsterism," likes and dislikes, bribes and no bribes, objective *vs.* biased opinion, *etc.*

4   Competitive Analysis

Before undertaking conceptual and perceptual (visual) screen designs of the Driving Machine, AM+A first studied six dashboard user interfaces. Through screen comparison-analysis and analysis of recent articles about trends in vehicle dashboard design, AM+A derived a synopsis of each dashboard's features, which contributed to improvements of initial ideas for the Driving Machine's detailed functions, data, information architecture (metaphors, mental model, and navigation) and look-and-feel (appearance and interaction). We considered the following products:

— **Audi A8 dashboard:** Audi's A8 dashboard incorporates a traditional instrument cluster with a large LCD between gauges. The system uses the Internet to grab fuel prices and find points of interest via Audi connect.
— **Cadillac User Experience:** The Cadillac User Experience (CUE) incorporates an LCD display in lieu of a traditional analog instrument cluster to allow for greater user customization. The CUE unifies Cadillac's infotainment and telematics systems for a more uniform user experience.
— **Ford SmartGauge with EcoGuide:** The EcoGuide is a system that coaches a driver how to maximize his/her fuel economy by incentivizing driving behavior. A key component of coaching behavior change is Efficiency Leaves, which grows leaves by driving efficiently or shrinks leaves by driving less efficiently.
— **Honda Ecological Drive Assist System:** Honda's Ecological Drive Assist System incorporates three functions for greater fuel economy: an ambient color meter, a continuously variable transmission, and a scoring function. Together these three components seek to use persuasive techniques to encourage drivers to drive more environmentally friendly. The System's scoring function is visible via the ability to grow leaves depending on a driver's driving efficiency.
— **Johnson Controls Multilayer Instrument Cluster:** Johnson Controls' prototype dashboard user-interface seeks to utilize spatial techniques to allow for prioritizing driving data such as speed and assistance information depending on the driving conditions.
— **1.6 Nissan Leaf Dashboard:** The Nissan Leaf Dashboard is a two-tier dash that separates driving diagnostics such as current speed and battery range. Nissan's system seeks to influence driving behavior by using persuasive techniques through which a driver is able to grow leaves depending on how efficient he or she drives.

From our investigations of dashboard and automotive-related applications, including those cited above, AM+A concluded that usable, useful, and appealing vehicle user-interface (UI) design must include incentives to lead to behavior change. Safe and sustainable driving behavior is possible by providing incentives such as a games, and just-in-time systematic instructions to motivate people to change their behavior. The proposed Driving Machine needs to combine persuasion theory, provide better incentives, and motivate users' to achieve short-term and long-term behavior change towards a Driving Machine everyday user. Our Driving Machine concept assumes that the primary vehicle dashboard is one of approximately six screens that might be available in a vehicle, three in the front and three in the rear behind the front seats.

The Driving Machine should be non-obtrusive, but encouraging to use. Well-designed games will serve as an additional appealing incentive to teach, *i.e.*, to train the driver. Drivers should be able to receive badges for accomplishing certain tasks. The Driving Machine should allow users to share their experience with friends, family members and the world, primarily through Facebook and Twitter. The Driving Machine should also allow drivers to communicate their experiences with insurance companies to allow drivers to receive reduced rates, and with family/friends.

Based on these concepts and available research documents, we have proposed and are developing conceptual designs of the multiple functions of the Driving Machine. Subsequent evaluation will provide feedback by which we can improve the metaphors, mental model, navigation, interaction, and appearance of all functions and data in the Driving Machine's user interface. The resultant improved user experience will move the Driving Machine closer to a commercially viable product/service. In particular, we believe a well-designed Driving Machine will be more usable, useful, and appealing to memory-conscious users, especially those experiencing long and short-term memory loss. Another objective is to provide a dashboard experience that can reliably persuade people to become safer and energy-conscious drivers.

5   Persuasion Theory

According to Fogg's persuasion theory [Fogg, B. J., and Eckles,D., 2007] to create behavioral change through the Driving Machine, we have defined four key processes, each of which affects the application:

- Increase frequency of reporting driving behavior to social networks
- Motivate changing some driving habits: talking on the phone, texting while driving, follow traffic laws, and driving over the speed limit
- Teach how to drive efficiently (*e.g.*, green, use less fuel)
- Persuade drivers to carpool

We drew on Maslow's A Theory of Human Motivation [Maslow, 1943], which he based on his analysis of fundamental human needs. We adapted these to the Driving Machine context:

- The safety and security need is met by the possibility to visualize the amount of food expense saved
- The belonging and love need is expressed through friends, family, and social sharings and support

- The esteem need can be satisfied by social comparisons that display weight control and exercise improvements, as well as by self-challenges that display goal accomplishment processes.
- The self-actualization need is fulfilled by being able to visualize the improvement progress of the health mattered indexes and mood, and also by predicting the change of the users' future health scenarios.

6   Information Architecture

AM+A believes that effective Machine design that combines information and persuasion requires these essential components:

- Dashboards: How am I doing now?
- Overview: What is my path, structure/process?
- Focus on social networks
- Focus on just-in-time knowledge: Tips and advice
- Incentives: Games, awards, rewards, competitions, stores

Based on the above, AM+A designed the information architecture shown in Fig. 1.

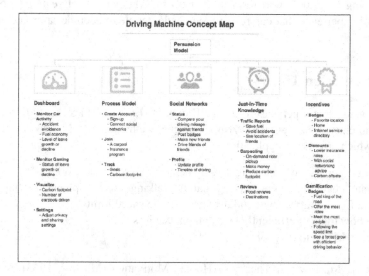

Fig. 1. Diagram of the Driving Machine information architecture

7   Screen Designs

AM+A designed key tablet screens shown in Figures 2-11.

Fig. 2. Dashboard **shows all default information.** An automobile logo and original equipment manufacturer (OEM) logo are at top/bottom. The inner rectangle shows (clockwise from top left) external temperature (78 °ext), time (10:00 am), internal temperature (65 °int), miles to empty (225 mte), compass (SW), and miles per gallon (17 mpg). In the center, the current speed appears as large numbers (70 mph) with the speed limit in smaller numbers above (65 mph).

Fig. 3. Figure 3: Dashboard shows all industry-standard indicators that could appear (e.g., low gas, emergency brake engaged, maintenance required)

Fig. 4. Dashboard with the left-turn signal

Fig. 5. Dashboard **with left-turn collision signal.** The red bar indicates the car is close to colliding with an obstacle on the left.

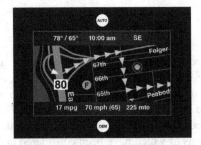

Fig. 6. An **alternative dashboard view, which emphasize navigation capabilities.** The dashboard showcases the same elements (clockwise from top left), external temperature/internal temperature (78°/65°), time (10:00 am), compass (SE), miles to empty (225 mte), current speed (speed limit) (70 mph (65)), miles per gallon (17 mpg).

Fig. 7. A **dashboard view with a themed background featuring the movie, "Avatar"** Users would be able to shift and select different themed backgrounds or "skins" depending on interest, pre-designed to ensure maximum legibility/readability. (Image Credit: Fair use of copyrighted material.)

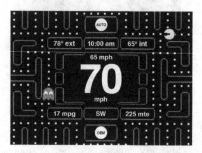

Fig. 8. A dashboard view with a themed background featuring the game, "Pacman." (Image Credit: AM+A design using Pac-Man-like image elements. Fair use of copyrighted materials.)

Fig. 9. A dashboard view with a themed background inspired by Swiss typographer, Wolfgang Weingart. The "sparkles" would turn red when the driver exceeds the posted speed limit.

Fig. 10. A dashboard with a themed background that indicates the eco-friendliness of a driver's behavior. The more eco-friendly the driving, the more trees will appear. (Image Credit: Tree image by Megan Chiou. Used with permission.)

Fig. 11. The dashboard indicates a driver's eco-friendliness. Red, yellow, or green outlines indicates the driver is/isn't making efforts to drive in ecofriendly.

8   Next Steps and Conclusions

Following the user-centered development process described above, AM+A plans to continue to improve the Driving Machine screen designs. AM+A aimed to incorporate information design and persuasion theory for behavior change into a mobile tablet application that would constitute an advanced vehicle dashboard. The approach has already been demonstrated successfully with a previous project, the Green Machine [Marcus and Jean, 2010], versions of which have been considered and used by SAP for enterprise software development [Marcus, Dumpert, and Wigham, 2011].

AM+A's long-term objective for the Driving Machine is to create a functional working prototype to test whether the application can actually persuade people who experience driving challenges to exercise greater vehicle control, increase safety, and reduce their carbon footprint.

Acknowledgements. The authors thank Ms. Megan Chiou, AM+A Designer/Analyst, for her significant assistance to design images for this paper.

References

1. Audi A8. Audi of America (2012), http://models.audiusa.com/a8 (retrieved August 10, 2012)
2. Berman, B.: EV Expert Says Nissan LEAF's Dashboard Lacks Most Important Number. PluginCars.com. (December 21, 2010), http://www.plugincars.com/ev-expert-says-nissan-leaf-dashboard-lacks-most-important-number-106590.html (retrieved August 10, 2012)
3. Cialdini, R.: The Science of Persuasion. Sci. American 284, 76–81 (2001)
4. Fogg, B.J., Eckles, D.: Mobile persuasion: 20 perspectives on the future of behavior change. Persuasive Technology Lab, Stanford University, Palo Alto, CA (2007)
5. Ford's Smartgauge With Ecoguide Coaches Drivers to Maximize Fuel Efficiency on New Fusion Hybrid | Ford Motor Company Newsroom (October 28, 2008), http://media.ford.com/article_display.cfm?article_id=29300 (retrieved August 10, 2012)
6. Green, P.: The human-computer interaction handbook. In: Jacko, J.A., Sears, A. (eds.), pp. 844–860. L. Erlbaum Associates Inc., Hillsdale (2003), http://dl.acm.org/citation.cfm?id=772072.772126 (retrieved)
7. Honda Motors. Honda Develops Ecological Drive Assist System for Enhanced Real World Fuel Economy: Implementation on All-New Insight Dedicated Hybrid in Spring 2009 (Press Release) (2008), http://world.honda.com/news/2008/4081120Ecological-Drive-Assist-System/ (retrieved)
8. Johnson, T., Jones, S., Silverman, A.: Programs hope to reverse skid in car pooling - USATODAY.com. (August 5, 2010), http://www.usatoday.com/news/nation/2010-08-04-carpooling-down_N.html (retrieved August 9, 2012)
9. Marcus, A., Chen, E., Brown, K., Ball, L.: BMW: Future HMI Directions. Aaron Marcus and Associates, Inc. (2002)
10. Marcus, A., Dumpert, J., Wigham, L.: User-Experience for Personal Sustainability Software: Determining Design Philosophy and Principles. In: Marcus, A. (ed.) HCII 2011 and DUXU 2011, Part I. LNCS, vol. 6769, pp. 172–177. Springer, Heidelberg (2011), http://www.springerlink.com/content/f81m37795r3743v7/abstract/
11. Marcus, A., Jean, J.: Going Green at Home: The Green Machine. Info. Design Jour. 17(3), 233–343 (2010)
12. Maslow, A.H.: A theory of human motivation. Psychological Review 50, 370–396 (1943)
13. Multilayer Instrument Cluster, Johnson Controls Inc. (n.d.) (August 10, 2012), http://www.johnsoncontrols.com/content/us/en/about/our_company/featured_stories/multilayer_instrument.html
14. National Highway Traffic Safety Administration. Visual-Manual NHTSA Driver Distraction Guidelines for In-Vehicle Electronic Devices (2012)
15. Ziegler, C.: Cadillac CUE: driving is safer (and more dangerous) than ever. TheVerge (August 8, 2012), http://www.theverge.com/2012/8/6/3220366/cadillac-cue-safety

Human Error in Aviation: The Behavior of Pilots Facing the Modern Technology

Isnard Thomas Martins[1], Edgard Thomas Martins[2],
Marcelo Márcio Soares[2], and Lia Giraldo da Silva Augusto[3]

[1] Estácio de Sá University – Rio de Janeiro, RJ, Brazil
isnard@openlink.com.br
[2] Post graduate Programme in Design, Federal University of Pernambuco, Brazil
edgardpiloto@gmail.com, marcelo2@nlink.com.br
[3] Centro de Pesquisas Aggeu Magalhães – Recife, PE, Brazil
giraldo@cpqam.fiocruz.br

Abstract. All the official records of aircraft accidents investigated by official preventing and detecting agencies always has concluded that the human as guilty or as a major component in accidents, a rate close to eighty percent. One must consider that the pilot receives an artifact that started its manufacturing project a few years before being delivered into his hands. He is now responsible for keeping it in the air, safely, weighing 50,000 pounds or more and carrying five tonnes of highly flammable fuel and has about two hundred people aboard. This complex machine depends on the perfect working condition. Human beings are fallible and aviation history shows that these devices have and will continue presenting defects. Innserido this way for technical perfection and operating the aircraft, the pilot is invariably, in the end, is the one who is always within the artifact when it crashes and usually pay a high price: his life.

Keywords: Mental Health Pilots, modern technology in aviation.

1 Introduction

The flaws in the commitment of decision-making in emergency situations and the lack of perception related to all elements associated with a given situation in a short space of time indicate, often, lack of situational awareness. Automation always surprises the crews and often prevents them from understanding the extent of this technology that is very common in aircraft units with a high degree of automation. These facts are discussed in a subtle way by aircraft drivers who can not do it openly, as it might create an impression of professional self-worthlessness (self-deprecation). This leads to common questions like: What is happening now? What will be the next step of automated systems? This type of doubt would be inadmissible in older aircraft because the pilot of those machines works as an extension of the plane. This scenario contributes to emotional disorders and a growing hidden problem in the aeronautical field. These unexpected automation surprises reflect a complete misunderstanding or

A. Marcus (Ed.): DUXU/HCII 2013, Part III, LNCS 8014, pp. 150–159, 2013.
© Springer-Verlag Berlin Heidelberg 2013

even the misinformation of the users. It also reveals their inability and limitations to overcome these new situations that were not foreseen by the aircraft designers. Our studies showed a different scenario when the accident is correlated with systemic variables. It has identified the problems or errors that contribute to the fact that drivers are unable to act properly. These vectors, when they come together, may generate eventually a temporary incompetence of the pilot due to limited capacity or lack of training in the appropriateness of automation in aircraft or even, the worst alternative, due to a personal not visible and not detectable non-adaptation to automation. We must also consider in the analysis the inadequate training and many other reasons, so that we can put in right proportion the effective participation or culpability of the pilot in accidents. Our doctoral thesis presents statistical studies that allow us to assert that the emotional and cognitive overload are being increased with automation widely applied in the cockpits of modern aircraft, and also that these new projects do not go hand in hand with the desired cognitive and ergonomic principles

The emotional stability and physical health of workers on board aircraft are faced with the factors and conditions that enable professionals to carry out their activities and develop normally, despite the fact that these conditions may present themselves to professionals in adverse conditions [1]. The modern history of aviation with its great technological complexity has pilots as redundant components that integrate embedded controls in modern aircraft. This leads us to say that the value of the worker as a permanent social group in society does not receive, currently, the proper priority. In research on the health of the pilot, there are three major perspectives that have been investigated that influence his stability, as well as the mental and emotional development of the modern airline pilot [2]. The previous life of the individual directly tied to experience, age, genetic and physiological vectors, The social environment, cultural environment and formal education leading to the final result, manifested by the ability, personality, strength and character and The verifiable standards of quality and quantity of life desired, ambition and achievements and its effects.

The Digital technology advances, has changed the shape and size of instruments used for navigation and communication. This has changed the actions of pilots, especially in relation to emergency procedures. There are few studies that correlate the reduction of accidents with the cognitive and technological changes. The increased cognitive load relates to these changes and requires assessment. The benefits presented by new technologies do not erase the mental models built, with hard work, during times of initial training of the aircraft career pilots in flying schools.

The public must be heeded when an aircraft incident or accident becomes part of the news. In search of who or what to blame, the pilot is guilty and immediately appointed as the underlying factors that involve real evidence of the fact they are neglected. The reading of the Black-Boxes notes that 70% to 80% of accidents happen due to human error, or to a string of failures that were related to the human factor [3]. We can mention stress and the failure to fully understand the new procedures related to technological innovations linked to automation. Complex automation interfaces always promote a wide difference in philosophy and procedures for implementation of these types of aircraft, including aircraft that are different even manufactured by the same manufacturer. In this case, we frequently can identify inadequate training that contributes to the difficulty in understanding procedures by the crews. Accident investigations concluded that the ideal would be to include, in the pilot training, a psychological stage, giving to him the opportunity of self-knowledge, identifying possible "psychological breakdowns" that his biological machine can present that endangers the safety of flight. Would be given, thus, more humane and scientific support to the crew and to everyone else involved with the aerial activity, minimizing factors that cause incidents and accidents. Accident investigators concluded that the ideal situation for pilot training should include a psychological phase [4], giving him or her, the opportunity of self-knowledge, identifying possible "psychological breakdowns" that biological features can present and can endanger the safety of flight. It should be given, thus, more humane and scientific support to the crew and everyone else involved with the aerial activity, reducing factors that can cause incidents and accidents. Accidents do not just happen. They have complex causes that can take days, weeks or even years to develop [5]. However, when lack of attention and / or neglect take place resulting in a crash, we can be most certain there was a series of interactions between the user and the system that created the conditions for that to happen. We understand that human variability and system failures are an integral part of the main sources of human error, causing incidents and accidents. The great human effort required managing and performing actions with the interface as the task of monitoring, the precision in the application of command and maintaining a permanent mental model consistent with the innovations in automation make it vulnerable to many human situations where errors can occur.

The human variability in aviation is a possible component of human error and we can see the consequences of these errors leading to serious damage to aircraft and people. It is not easy, in new aviation, to convey the ability to read the instruments displays. This can conduct to the deficiency and the misunderstanding in monitoring and performing control tasks: lack of motivation, the fact that it is stressful and tiring, and generate failures in control (scope, format and activation), poor training and instructions that are wrong or ambiguous. The mind of the pilot is influenced by cognition and communication components during flight, especially if we observe all information processed and are very critical considering that one is constantly getting this information through their instruments. There is information about altitude, speed and position of one's aircraft and the operation of its hydraulic power systems. If any problem occurs, several lights will light up and warning sounds emerge increasing the volume and type of man-machine communication which can diminish the perception of detail in information that must be processed and administered by the pilot. All this information must be processed by one's brain at the same time as it decides the necessary action in a context of very limited time. There is a limit of information that the brain can deal with which is part of natural human limitation. It can lead to the unusual situation in which, although the mind is operating normally, the volume of data makes it operate in overload, which may lead to failures and mistakes if we consider this man as a biological machine.

All situations in which a planned sequence of mental or physical activities fails to achieve its desired outputs are considered as errors. Thus, it is necessary that steps be taken toward reducing the likelihood of occurrence of situations which could cause a problem. The flight safety depends on a significant amount of interpretations made by the pilot in the specific conditions in every moment of the flight. Accidents do not only occur due to pilot error, but also as a result of a poor design of the transmission of information from the external environment, equipment, their instruments, their signs, sounds and different messages. In these considerations, the human agent will always be subject to fatality, which is a factor that can not be neglected.

Because of human complexity, it is difficult to convince, in a generic way, people with merely causal explanations. Further analysis of the problem will always end with the identification of a human error, which was probably originated in the design phase, at the manufacturing stage, or given simply as a result of an "act of God". Aeronautical activities, designing human-machine systems becomes very necessary to characterize and classify human error. Human activities have always been confronted with the cognitive system. On the result of the causality of accidents, we must consider the human contribution to accidents, distinguishing between active failures and latent failures due to the immediate adverse effect of the system aspect. The main feature of this component is that it is present within the process of construction of an accident long before declaring the event like an accident, being introduced by higher hierarchical levels as designers, responsible for maintenance and personnel management. This statement is derived from the design philosophy that treats the defense in depth. In Fig. 1, based on the model "Swiss Cheese" [6]. a fail of defense of an accident may occur as a Swiss cheese with "holes", which mean "latent failures" that sometimes began the construction of an accident long before the event.

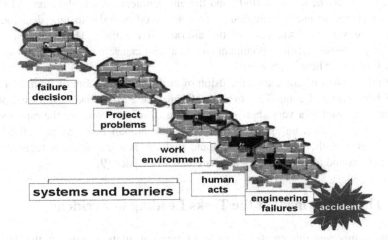

Fig. 1. Latent failures, based on the "Swiss Cheese Model" of Reason

We can always guarantee, with respect to organizational accidents, that the layers of defenses, that are the protective barriers, were constructed to prevent the occurrence of natural or man-made disasters. In certain circumstances, such failures (holes) can align themselves and then, the accident happens. An accident is a succession of failures. When these barriers are destroyed or are flawed or become vulnerable, the accident occurs. In this fact, that is called latent failure.

2   Fundamentation

The following factors are an integral part of cognitive activity in the pilot: fatigue, body rhythm and rest, sleep and its disorders, the circadian cycle and its changes, the G-force and acceleration of gravity, the physiological demands in high-altitude, night-time take-offs and the problem of false illusion of climbing. But, other physiological demands are placed by the aviators. It is suggested that specific studies must be made for each type of aircraft and workplace, with the aim of contributing to the reduction of incidents arising from causes so predictable, yet so little studied. We must also give priority to airmen scientists that have produced these studies in physiology and occupational medicine, since the literature is scarce about indicating the need for further work in this direction. Human cognition refers to mental processes involved in thinking and their use. It is a multidisciplinary area of interest includes cognitive psychology, psychobiology, philosophy, anthropology, linguistics and artificial intelligence as a means to better understand how people perceive, learn, remember and how people think, because will lead to a much broader understanding of human behavior. Cognition is not presented as an isolated entity, being composed of a number of other components, such as mental imagery, attention, consciousness, perception, memory, language, problem solving, creativity, decision making, reasoning, cognitive changes during development throughout life, human intelligence, artificial intelligence and various other aspects of human thought [7].

The procedures of flying an aircraft involve observation and reaction to events that take place inside the cabin of flight and the environment outside the aircraft [8]. The pilot is required to use information that is perceived in order to take decisions and actions to ensure the safe path of the aircraft all the time. Thus, full use of the cognitive processes becomes dominant so that a pilot can achieve full success with the task of flying the "heavier than air."

With the advent of automated inclusion of artifacts in the cabin of flight that assist the pilot in charge of controlling the aircraft, provide a great load of information that must be processed in a very short space of time, when we consider the rapidity with which changes occur, an approach that cover the human being as an individual is strongly need. Rather, the approach should include their cognition in relation to all these artifacts and other workers who share that workspace [9].

3   The Deployment of the Tasks Leading to Accidents

A strong component that creates stress and fatigue of pilots, referred to the design of protection, detection and effective handling of fire coming from electrical short circuit on board, is sometimes encountered as tragically happened on the Swissair Airlines flight 111, near Nova Scotia on September 2, 1998. The staff of the Federal Aviation Administration (FAA), responsible for human factors research and modern automated interfaces, reports a situation exacerbated by the widespread use an electrical product and a potentially dangerous wire on aircrafts, called "Kapton" [10].

If a person has to deal with an outbreak of fire, coming from an electrical source at home, the first thing he would do is disconnect the electrical power switch for the fuses. But this option is not available on aircraft like the Boeing B777 and new Airbus. The aviation industry is not adequately addressing the problem of electrical fire in flight and is trying to deal recklessly [11]. The high rate of procedural error associated with cognitive errors, in the automation age, suggests that the projects in aviation have ergonomic flaws. In addiction, is has been related that the current generation of jet transport aircraft, used on airlines, like the Airbus A320, A330, A340, Boeing B777, MD11 and the new A380, that are virtually "not flyable" without electricity. We can mention an older generation, such as the Douglas DC9 and the Boeing 737.

Another factor in pushing the pilots that causes emotional fatigue and stress is the reduction of the cockpit crew to just two. The next generation of large transport planes four engines (600 passengers) shows a relatively complex operation and has only two humans in the cockpit. The flight operation is performed by these two pilots, including emergency procedures, which should be monitored or re-checked. This is only possible in a three-crew cockpit or cockpit of a very simple operation. According to the FAA, the only cockpit with two pilots that meets these criteria is the cabin of the old DC9-30 and the MD11 series. The current generation of aircraft from Boeing and Airbus do not fit these criteria, particularly with respect to engine fire during the flight and in-flight electrical fire.

The science of combining humans with machines requires close attention to the interfaces that will put these components (human-machine) working properly. The deep study of humans shows their ability to instinctively assess and treat a situation in a dynamic scenario. A good ergonomic design project recognizes that humans are fallible and not very suitable for monitoring tasks. A properly designed machine (such as a computer) can be excellent in monitoring tasks. This work of monitoring and the increasing the amount of information invariably creates a cognitive and emotional overload and can result in fatigue and stress.

According to a group of ergonomic studies from FAA [12] in the United States this scenario is hardly considered by the management of aviation companies and, more seriously the manufacturers, gradually, introduce further informations on the displays of Glass cockpits. These new projects always determine some physiological, emotional and cognitive impact on the pilots.

The accident records of official institutes such as the NTSB (National Transportation Safety Bureau, USA) and CENIPA (Central Research and Prevention of Accidents, Brazil) show that some difficulties in the operation, maintenance or training aircraft, which could affect flight safety are not being rapidly and systematically passed on to crews worldwide. These professionals of aviation may also not be unaware of the particular circumstances involved in relevant accidents and incidents, which makes the dissemination of experiences very precarious.

One of the myths about the impact of automation on human performance: "while investment in automation increases, less investment is needed in human skill".   In fact, many experiments showed that the progressive automation creates new demands for knowledge, and greater, skills in humans. Investigations of the FAA [13], announced that aviation companies have reported institutional problems existing in the nature and the complexity of automated flight platforms. This results in additional knowledge requirements for pilots on how to work subsystems and automated methods differently. Studies showed the industry of aviation introduced the complexities of automated platforms flight inducing pilots to develop mental models about overly simplified or erroneous system operation. This applies, particularly, on the logic of the transition from manual operation mode to operation in automatic mode (NTSB, 2011). The process of performing normal training teaches only how to control the automated systems in normal but do not teach entirely how to manage different situations that the pilots will eventually be able to find. This is a very serious situation that can proved through many aviation investigation reports that registered the pilots not knowing what to do, after some computers decisions taken, in emergences situations [14]. VARIG (Brazilian Air lines), for example, until recently, had no Boeing 777 simulators where pilots could simulate the emergence loss of automated systems what should be done, at list, twice a month, following the example of Singapore Airlines. According to FAA [15], investigations showed incidents where pilots have had trouble to perform, successfully, a particular level of automation. The pilots, in some of these situations, took long delays in trying to accomplish the task through automation, rather than trying to, alternatively, find other means to accomplish their flight management objectives. Under these circumstances, that the new system is more vulnerable to sustaining the performance and the confidence. This is shaking the binomial Human-Automation compounded with a progression of confusion and misunderstanding. The qualification program presumes it is important for crews to be prepared to deal with normal situations, to deal with success and with the probable. The history of aviation shows and teaches that a specific emergency situation, if it has not happen, will certainly happen.

4   Future Work to Make an Assessment in Systemic Performance on Pilots

Evaluating performance errors, and crew training qualifications, procedures, operations, and regulations, allows them to understand the components that contribute to errors. At first sight, the errors of the pilots can easily be identified, and it can be postulated that many of these errors are predictable and are induced by one or more factors related to the project, training, procedures, policies, or the job. The most difficult task is centered on these errors and promoting a corrective action before the occurrence of a potentially dangerous situation. The FAA team, which deals with human factors [16], believes it is necessary to improve the ability of aircraft manufacturers and aviation companies in detecting and eliminating the features of a project, that create predictable errors. The regulations and criteria for approval today do not include the detailed project evaluation from a flight deck in order to contribute in reducing pilot errors and performance problems that lead to human errors and accidents. Neither the appropriate criteria nor the methods or tools exist for designers or for those responsible for regulations to use them to conduct such assessments.

Changes must be made in the criteria, standards, methods, processes and tools used in the design and certification. Accidents like the crash of the Airbus A320 of the AirInter (a France aviation company) near Strasbourg provide evidence of deficiencies in the project.

This accident highlights the weaknesses in several areas, particularly when the potential for seemingly minor features has a significant role in an accident. In this example, inadvertently setting an improper vertical speed may have been an important factor in the accident because of the similarities in the flight path angle and the vertical speed in the way as are registered in the FCU (Flight Control Unit).

This issue was raised during the approval process of certification and it was believed that the warnings of the flight mode and the PFD (Primary Flight Display-display basic flight information) would compensate for any confusion caused by exposure of the FCU, and that pilots would use appropriate procedures to monitor the path of the vertical plane, away from land, and energy state. This assessment was incorrect. Under current standards, assessments of cognitive load of pilots to develop potential errors and their consequences are not evaluated. Besides, the FAA seeks to analyze the errors of pilots, a means of identifying and removing preventively future design errors that lead to problems and their consequences. This posture is essential for future evaluations of jobs in aircraft crews. Identify projects that could lead to pilot error, prematurely, in the stages of manufacture and certification process will allow corrective actions in stages that have viable cost to correct or modify with lower impact on the production schedule. Additionally, looking at the human side, this reduces unnecessary loss of life.

5   Conclusion

We developed a study focusing on the guilt of pilots in accidents when preparing our thesis. In fact, the official records of aircraft accidents blame the participation of the pilots like a large contributive factor in these events. Modifying this scenario is very difficult in the short term, but we can see as the results of our study, which the root causes of human participation, the possibility of changing this situation. The cognitive factor has high participation in the origins of the problems (42% of all accidents found on our search). If we consider other factors, such as lack of usability applied to the ergonomics products, the choice of inappropriate materials and poor design, for example, this percentage is even higher.

Time is a factor to consider. This generates a substantial change in the statistical findings of contributive factors and culpability on accidents. The last consideration on this process, as relevant and true, somewhat later, must be visible solutions. In aviation, these processes came very slowly, because everything is wildly tested and involves many people and institutions. The criteria adopted by the official organizations responsible for investigation in aviation accidents do not provide alternatives that allow a clearer view of the problems that are consequence of cognitive or other problems that have originate from ergonomic factors. We must also consider that some of these criteria cause the possibility of bringing impotence of the pilot to act on certain circumstances. The immediate result is a streamlining of the culpability in the accident that invariably falls on the human factor as a single cause or a contributing factor. Many errors are classified as only "pilot incapacitation" or "navigational error". Our research shows that there is a misunderstanding and a need to distinguish disability and pilot incapacitation (because of inadequate training) or even navigational error.

Our thesis has produced a comprehensive list of accidents and a database that allows extracting the ergonomic, systemic and emotional factors that contribute to aircraft accidents. These records do not correlate nor fall into stereotypes or patterns. These patterns are structured by the system itself as the accident records are being deployed. We developed a computer system to build a way for managing a database called the Aviation Accident Database. The data collected for implementing the database were from the main international entities for registration and prevention of aircraft accidents as the NTSB (USA), CAA (Canada), ZAA (New Zealand) and CENIPA (Brazil). This system analyses each accident and determines the direction and the convergence of its group focused, instantly deployed according to their characteristics, assigning it as a default, if the conditions already exist prior to grouping. Otherwise, the system starts formatting a new profile of an accident [18].

This feature allows the system to determine a second type of group, reporting details of the accident, which could help point to evidence of origin of the errors. Especially for those accidents that have relation with a cognitive vector. Our study showed different scenarios when the accidents are correlated with multiple variables. This possibility, of course, is due to the ability of Aviation DataBase system, which allows the referred type of analysis. It is necessary to identify accurately the problems or errors that contribute to the pilots making it impossible to act properly. These problems could point, eventually, to an temporary incompetence of the pilot due to limited capacity or lack of training appropriateness of automation in aircraft. We must also consider many other reasons that can alleviate the effective participation or culpability of the pilot. Addressing these problems to a systemic view expands the frontiers of research and prevention of aircraft accidents.

This system has the purpose of correlating a large number of variables. In this case, the data collected converges to the casualties of accidents involving aircraft, and so, can greatly aid the realization of scientific cognitive studies or applications on training aviation schools or even in aviation companies [19]. This large database could be used in the prevention of aircraft accidents allowing reaching other conclusions that would result in equally important ways to improve air safety and save lives.

References

1. Henriqson, E.: Coordination as a Distributed Cognitive Phenomena Situated in Aircraft Cockpits- Aviation in Focus. A Coordenação Como Um Fenômeno Cognitivo Distribuído e Situado em Cockpits de Aeronaves, vol. 12, pp. 58–76. UFRGS, Porto Alegre (2010)
2. Dekker, S.: Illusions of explanation- A critical essay on error classification. The International Journal of Aviation Psychology 13, 95–106 (2003)

3. FAA- Federal Aviation Administration, DOT/FAA/AM-10/13, Office of Aerospace Medicine, Causes of General Aviation Accidents and Incidents: Analysis Using NASA Aviation. Safety Reporting System Data. U.S. Department of Transportation Press, Washington, DC (September 2010)
4. Dekker, S.: Illusions of explanation- A critical essay on error classification. The International Journal of Aviation Psychology 13, 95–106 (2003)
5. Reason, J.: Human Error, 2nd edn., pp. 92–93. University Press, Cambridge (1990)
6. Reason, J.: Human Error, 2nd edn., pp. 103–107. University Press, Cambridge (1990)
7. Sternberg, R.: Cognitive psychology. Ed Artmed, Porto Alegre (2000)
8. Green, R.G., Frenbard, M.: Human Factors for Pilots. Technical Aldershot, Avebury (1993)
9. FAA- Federal Aviation Administration, DOT/FAA/AM-10/13, Office of Aerospace Medicine, Causes of General Aviation Accidents and Incidents: Analysis Using NASA Aviation. Safety Reporting System Data. U.S. Department of Transportation Press, Washington, DC (September 2010)
10. FAA- Federal Aviation Administration- FAA, The Interface Between Flightcrews and Modern Flight Deck Systems. Federal Aviation, Administration Human Factors Team Report, pp. 34–35 (May 2005)
11. FAA- Federal Aviation Administration, Human Error Analysis of Asrts Reports: Altitude Deviations in Advanced Technology Aircraft. Federal Aviation Administration, Human Factors Team Report (1992, 1996, 2002)
12. NTSB- National Transportation Safety Board, Airline Service Quality Performance- User Manual- ASQP, pp. 75–77. Bureau of Transportation Statistics, U.S. Department of Transportation Press, Washington, DC (October 2011)
13. FAA- Federal Aviation Administration- FAA, Human Error Analysis of Accidents Report. Federal Aviation Administration- Human Factors Team Report, pp. 201–206 (2010)
14. NTSB-National Transportation Safety Board, C.F.R.- 234 Airline Service Quality Performance Reports, pp. 45–61. Bureau of Transportation Statistics, Research and Innovative Technology Administration (RITA), U.S. Department of Transportation Press, Washington, DC (October 2011)
15. FAA- Federal Aviation Administration- FAA, Human Error Analysis of Accidents Report. Federal Aviation Administration- Human Factors Team Report, pp. 201–206 (2010)
16. Dekker, S.: Illusions of explanation- A critical essay on error classification. The International Journal of Aviation Psychology 13, 95–106 (2003)
17. Reason, J.: Human Error, 2nd edn., pp. 92–93. University Press, Cambridge (1990)
18. Martins, E.: Ergonomics in Aviation: A critical study of the causal responsibility of pilots in accidents. Ergonomia na Aviação: Um estudo crítico da responsabilidade dos pilotos na causalidade dos acidentes, Msc. Monography, Universidade Federal Pernam-buco, Pernambuco, Brasil, pp. 285–298 (March 2007)
19. Martins, E.: Study of the implications for health and work in the operationalization and the aeronaut embedded in modern aircraft in the man-machines interactive process complex. Estudo das implicações na saúde e na operacionalização e no trabalho do aeronauta embarcado em modernas aeronaves no processo interativo homem-máquinas complexas, thesis, Centro de Pesquisas Aggeu Magalhães, Fundação Oswaldo Cruz, Pernambuco, Brasil, pp. 567–612 (August 2010)

Breaking Technological Paradigms – Sustainable Design in Air Transport Multi-mission

Edgard Thomas Martins[1], Isnard Thomas Martins[2], and Marcelo Márcio Soares[1]

[1] Post graduate Programme in Design, Federal University of Pernambuco, Brazil
edgardpiloto@gmail.com, marcelo2@nlink.com.br
[2] Estácio de Sá University – Rio de Janeiro, RJ, Brazil
isnard@openlink.com.br

Abstract. Since the successful experiences of the human being for flying since the late nineteenth century, the Air Transport has established itself like a technological presence. The aerostat has been treated as the "ship-to-air" and has been more adaptable to transport of passengers and cargo, even after the appearance of heavier-than-air. In expanding of road systems, the option for airship resurges like the best option. The Blimp-Hybrid-Multimission is the great solution as the best and single complement than all other types. In 1982 an airplane for 200 passengers costs U.S. $25 million, while the Airship should cost half or less, with the same load capacity. The price of oil derivatives are vectors that push the world for employment-intensive transport almost extinct in the last century. Favorable weather and conditions, in many places of the world, allow uninterrupted operation almost all the year with economic advantages and high rate of return on investments.

Keywords: Product design, product development process, sustainability.

1 Introduction

An aircraft remains in the air due to the resultant vector of four components: traction, weight, air resistance (drag). This fourth component represents finally the substantial consumption of fuel because the airplane just flies mainly for neutralizing the weight vector using the air movement over the wings. We can alleviate the effort of this component with the aid of nature's elements, which are gases lighter than the air that significantly reduce fuel consumption due to the traction of the motors that were primarily intended for directional control. But this has a price unquestionable: the loss of speed. The format of this type of aircraft needs to accommodate large amounts of gases. The aerodynamic design is very different from aircraft we are used to seeing in the skies. Until recently, balloons and blimps had been restricted to recreational use, some applications such as advertising, monitoring, filming and controlling with meteorological balloons. The energy crisis elects the airship as an alternative clean, affordable, meeting the demands of geophysical space and using the potential of the nature in most of the world, supported by best practices in sustainable environment.

A. Marcus (Ed.): DUXU/HCII 2013, Part III, LNCS 8014, pp. 160–168, 2013.

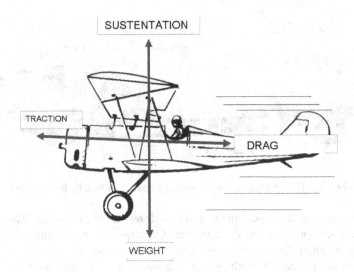

Fig. 1. - Vectors operating in aerodynamic movement of the aircraft (figure assembled by the authors)

This airship is a vehicle that moves supported by a gas lighter than the air and that may be equipped with motors for propulsion. These four components: traction, weight, air resistance are represented on fig.1.

It is also equipped with control mechanisms provided with a large autonomy and exceptional comfort to users, free of noises, with very low vibration and good visibility. The blimp has the ability to navigate by day (on a flight VFR - Visual Flight Rules) and at night, under instruments flight rules - VFR or IFR, or supported by instruments that allow Flight Rules Flight Rules in which means the set of regulations and procedures that are applied to piloting aircraft when flight conditions do not ensure that the pilot can see and avoid obstacles or other air traffic. We see in fig. 2, the traditional composition of one blimp. This design, combined with aerodynamic controls surfaces and propeller, allows that modern airships change the altitude and fly more efficiently and at a lower cost than others based traditional aircraft flying systems. It may have greater load capacity than the largest existing helicopter and dispenses complex and expensive port infrastructure, water or land berth. They use a temporary basis while significantly reducing operating costs. The airship makes use of modern internal compartments of gas that can be sucked from he outside in order to increase the total weight and the efficacy of the airship and for decrease the pressure of gas for lifting.

This nave suffers low electromagnetic interference as a result of its structure that is constructed of composite material. These are different from traditional metals and are combinations of different materials in the composition or form which retain their identity in the final composite material and do not dissolve and do not merge them-selves completely into another, although they act together. The concrete is an example

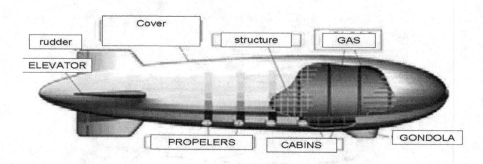

Fig. 2. - The structure of a traditional blimp (Assembled by the authors)

of a composite structure where the materials still retain their identities. The steel carries tension, compression on the concrete. On airplanes, composite structures are combinations where the tissue is embedded in resin, but still retains its identity. Among the advantages of airships, we emphasize greater mobility than any land transportation, aircraft or ship

2   Fundamentation

The lift phenomenon by gas supports this proposal. Hydrogen, helium, methane, ammonia and hot air are all capable of lift the artefact. Due to the principles of the buoyancy of the sustaining that these gases create, they are much less dense than the surrounding air While the denser air is pulled downward by gravity to lift the less dense gas tends to be separated from denser. As the air is being pulled to Earth by gravity, there is no place for the less dense gas to go, but up.

Hydrogen is the first element of the periodic table and is also the lightest element in the universe and more abundant. In the early days of aviation lighter than air, hydrogen was very commonly used. But hydrogen is highly explosive and when in the presence of oxygen, contributed to some spectacular disasters, including the explosion of the Hindenburg. Hydrogen was used because it could be produced in abundance by a variety of different chemical processes and low cost. The Helium gas is more commonly used today and it is the gas filling party balloons and allows you to talk with a high pitch when inhaled. It is the second element of the periodic table and also the second lightest and most abundant in the universe after hydrogen. Helium is very stable and is more affordable today than it was in the time of old age blimps.

LTA (Lighter Than Air) or blimps were used from the very beginning of the last century until 1960. During World War I, were built about 100 aircraft (Ranging from the smallest: 100 cubic feet and not rigid up to the largest: 2.5 million cubic feet and rigid). In 1933, the Zeppelin Corporation Company has fabricated two rigid airships, Akron and Macon to the Navy of the United States of America. These were the largest aircraft built at that time. Four of the largest airship ever built not rigid (ZPG-3W), were also completed in 1960 by Goodyear. Rigid airships are constructed of a lightweight structure with an outer fabric treated tissue [1]. The gas used is contained in several independent compartments. In contrast, the not rigid airship is a simple envelope (hull) typically made from a coated fabric filled with a gas. Various air compartments within the hull are used to maintain constant pressure ballast and provide for air circulation as needed [2].

3   The Potential Properties of the Modern Airships

According to a recent study by NASA - National Aeronautics and Space Administration [3], studies based on the Goodyear Aerospace Corporation, report that 26 percent reduction in the empty airplane weight may be obtained from LTA (light than air) modern artifacts, and they could be achieved using modern plastic and metal materials. The weight-loaded / empty-weight can be reduced from 40% to about 50%. The amount of loading will depend on the quantity of fuel loads and depends on the requirements of the mission [4]. Such technological advances can substantially improve the payload of modern airships. Fig. 3 shows a drawing representing what could be an airship Hybrid Multimission.

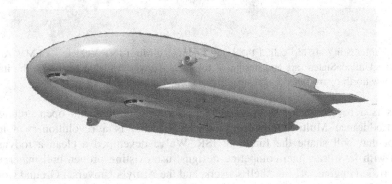

Fig. 3. - The Hybrid Airship Multimission - (assembly by authors, based on the general drawings of the moderns LTA- *LIGHT THAN AIR*)

The conventional propulsion system (propeller) improves the cruising speed and the performance of operations in the terminal. It may be provided with multiple units of rotor that could provide precision to develop lifting capacity supporting up to 20-150 tons [5]. This design has the characteristics advocated by development centers of the modern LTA (LIGHT THAN AIR). The conventional system of propulsion (propeller) improves the cruising speed and the performance of operations in the terminal. It could be provided with multiple units of rotor that reverts itself on precision and develops the lifting capacity supporting 20-150 tons [6].

This artifact will be the size of a football field with a fuel consumption of an medium airplane. Since this type of aircraft could operate in remote and unprepared locations it would be followed by a substantial reduction of costs that current alternatives with loads compared with existing methods of air transportation or any other.

4   The Applications Effective of this Flying Machine

The Army of the United States is developing a modern unmanned airship for surveillance and reconnaissance with this purposes and it is inserted in the program called Long Endurance Multi- INT Vehicle - LEMV) as shown in fig. 4. The first tests of LEMV will be done soon. This will be hybrid airship buoyancy with propulsion and aerodynamic means to facilitate the landing and takeoff. It should take a load of more than 1 ton flying at 20,000 feet (7000 meters) and could remain in the air for up to three weeks.

Fig. 4. - Interesting airship called the Long Endurance Multi-INT Vehicle - LEMV Army - from the United States (art and design of the U.S. Army, available for use with citation) http://www.northropgrumman.com/Capabilities/LEMV/Pages/default.aspx

This is a revolutionary weapon system. Northrop Grumman's open architected Long Endurance Multi Intelligence Vehicle (LEMV) is a revolutionary aviation concept that will shape the future of ISR. We've developed a clean aerodynamic design with less drag than competing designs, use existing proven hull materials, a type certified engine, off-the-shelf sensors, and the Army's Universal Ground Control Station with 100% interoperability with DCGS-A. We integrate ISR payloads most efficiently through our Murphy Bay on the vehicle centerline. Every design tradeoff was made with an unyielding commitment to schedule. Our open architecture and business model invites third parties to get onboard the aircraft with limited interference, weapon system, balanced by its elegant simplicity. It may be optionally piloted. In this option, may have the reach of 2,500 miles. The payload of the transportable LEMV is 2 tons. The maximum speed is 80 miles per hour with a speed of 20 miles / hour in cruise flight regime. Flying at 10,000 feet (three thousand meters) altitude where even this is not required pressurization or oxygen for pilots and passengers (soldiers).

5   Discussion

Developing countries also have this deficiency but struggle with limited resources to deploy it. The airship is a suitable solution for the environment to be much faster to deploy. In Brazil, given its size and the needs of transportation systems compatible in

Fig. 5. - Legal Amazon (*Amazônia Legal* - in northern of the Brazil

Amazonia (Jungle complex and system covering almost all Amazon State and Para State) with the current state of development and growth, the airship fits like a great solution. It is the only means of transport able to interconnect and complement each other [7]. The Amazon Area is sown in fig. 5 . Almost 50% of Brazil area.

The current situation in the third world or even in the jungle is put into focus. Due to the extremely high costs of implementation and expansion of land transportation (consisting of ecological parameters increasingly stringent) it is required the rehabilitation of road networks and the exponential growth of new interconnection by bus use priority needs a political / social / commercial model and should be changed to diversify more consistently with the geo-economic scenario. When we stopped for attend the needs of reconstruction and expansion of the national highway system, the option for the airship could be, in many cases, the solution with extensive logistical advantage, operational and economic. Developed countries about 2.5% of its Gross Domestic Product (GDP), apply in their transportation infrastructure to move forward in their development as far, they need a modern transportation system

In Brazil, for the purposes of government and economy, the Amazon is bounded by an area called "Legal Amazon". It is also called the Amazon biome in Brazil, holds 49.29% of the territory and covers three (North, Northeast and Center-West) of the five regional divisions of the country, the largest terrestrial biome in the country. An area of six million hectares in the center of its watershed, including the Jau National Park, was considered by the United Nations Educational, Scientific and Cultural Organization in 2000 (with extension in 2003), a World Heritage Site.

6   Aplications

This airship offers possibilities to fulfill missions of search and rescue, aerial surveillance, river patrol and maritime support to isolated nucleus in the form of a social and civic action, and especially transportation for personnel and materials with great efficiency and ease, compared with other vehicle of transportation by air, land and sea, which must operate together as intermodal system.

6.1 Our Experience in Rio de Janeiro in 2002

The following news was released on 09.02.2002 at 20h14 at a newspaper called Folha Online: "Airship begins patrolling the Rio de Janeiro on Thursday" The Secretariat of Public Security of Rio de Janeiro successfully conducted an experiment with the patrol by an airship. The program "An Eye in the Sky" monitored throughout the city, especially the 380 spots mapped by the Department of Safety. The airship was used in the Bosnian (fig. 6) war and flew in Rio de Janeiro, 16 hours per day. There were obtained high quality images both day and night using cameras with special high resolution. Furthermore, was equipped with transmission devices for microwave imaging and sensing infrared radiation, which were recorded and sent messages in real time. The images captured were immediately sent to a central communications that worked in the building Security Secretariat, in the city center.

Fig. 6. - A blimp that performs a silent air patrol mission in Rio de Janeiro in 2002. Images captured during the surveillance in the flying by the brothers Edgard and Isnard Thomas Martins.

6.2 The Airships-Hybrids-Mutimission in Amazon and in Edges of Far Frontiers

Many experiments have occurred worldwide for the return of the airship. The Hybrid-Airships-Mutimission Amazon is one of these proposals. The transport airship may be another medium used near future on worldwide. And your success will be directly proportional to the rising cost of fuel used by increasingly heavy and highly polluting on traditional airplanes. The design of this vehicle is crying out to happen. Fig. 7 presents an art for this proposal of this interesting airship [8].

According to the Brazilian Army, the project "AIRSHIPS OF THE AMAZON", is a airship inflated with helium gas (not flammable) that allows great autonomy and economy suffering low electromagnetic interference, it is safer environmentally

Fig. 7. - The Future Hybrid Airship Multimission DHM CD-300 (Heavyweight, 300-ton) of EB and MB. (Author's adaptation of the specifications of an aircraft of this nature)

friendly, offers exceptional comfort to users, will be free of noise with very low vibration and good visibility, this factor makes it capable of day and night navigation, including flying by instruments.

The Brazilian Army has been preparing since 1990 for the definitive introduction of transport vehicle and the military structure today has already is equipped and is supporting operations of airships in the Amazon, covering military units in several locations in the states of the north of Amazonia. Only military logistical aspect of its operation, blimps are designed, on the one hand, the transport of equipment and products needed for the construction and operation of engineering works, small communities, air bases, naval and military squads, and on the other hand, the transport of vehicles, vessels, aircraft, troops, and services (surveillance and patrol) safety and security of our extensive borders.

A simulation of the Army indicated that his biggest task will be to meet and interconnect the different units and operations: Army, Navy and Air Force in the Amazon integrating Organic Forces operating in liaison with networks serving both the Infantry Platoons jungle Brazilian Army and the Navy patrol vessels, giving to them the logistics synergy that no other medium or intermodal has reached considering the inhospitable and difficult jungle access. The history shows [9] that the technological studies of "lighter than air" has always been involved with the socio-political-historical in Brazil, in the Army since 18th century and in the civil area, with Alberto Santos Dumont when we saw the maneuverability of the airship, to circumvent the Eiffel Tower in Paris in the year 1901.

The Brazilian Amazon is, in territorial terms, the largest regional share of Brazil's territory, forming a biome of about 3.7 million km2, while containing the widest surface freshwater reserve in the world, with 175,000 m3/sec Only the Amazon River pouring into the Atlantic (20% of all rivers in the world), and harboring their greatest biodiversity, with many components still unknown by technical sectors involved, with 1/3 of the tropical forests of the globe where illegal logging is currently around 80% of world production. The Amazon region, because of its importance for social and environmental sustainability, has areas with very significant legal restrictions, observing the following distribution: 20% of the total corresponds to indigenous areas, 7.6% use areas and sustainable development, 4% strictly protected areas. According to Pinto "has not been possible until now perform a real control of these areas, even worse for those who are not legally protected" [10]. This large area of our territory

168 E.T. Martins, I.T. Martins, and M.M. Soares

has some legal protection (about 32% of the total area of the region, ie the order of 1 million km2) but it houses a huge biodiversity. The news lead us to assume that the rest of its territory there are threats to species survival and sustainable development of the regional flora and fauna rich. We can register an example where the primates, of the 94 species identified until today, 71 live in the above areas and 23 in areas that are not legally protected.

References

1. Craig, B.: Computer Blimp: A Technical History Environmental monitoring using airships. Technology News, Military Institute of Engineering, Brazil, vol. 239 (Dez 2007)
2. Powers, J.: The Intelligent Surveillance Blimp, Military Institute of Engineering Brazil (2006) (unpublished)
3. NASA- National Aeronautics and Space Administration, Modern Flight Deck Systems- Human Factors Team Report, Fla, USA (2010)
4. Machado, J.L.: Blimps/Airships - "Back to the Future". Technology News, Military Institute of Engineering (Military Institute of Engineering), Brazil (2009)
5. Escher, R.: Airship and Blimp Resources (2003),
   http://www.hotairship.com/index.html
   (acessed in June 21, 2011, autorized by citation)
6. Machado, J.L.: Blimps/Airships - "Back to the Future". Technology News, Military Institute of Engineering (Military Institute of Engineering), Brazil (2009)
7. Machado, J.L.: Blimps/Airships - "Back to the Future". Technology News, Military Institute of Engineering (Military Institute of Engineering), Brazil (2009)
8. Barahona, A.J.: Environmental monitoring using Airships. Technology News, Military Institute of Engineering (Military Institute of Engineering), Brazil (2010)
9. Felippes, M.A.: Monograph The Transportation Battalion in the Amazon. Board of Transportation. Military Engineering Institute (1995), Project Airships to Amazon, Article, Military Institute of Engineering (1990)
10. Pinto, E.M.: Available resources and Futures Airships Future Brazilian-army (2009),
    http://www.defesabr.com/exércitobrasileiro/
    exército_dirigiveis_futuro.htm (accessed June 26, 2011)

Ergonomics Aspects in Operators of the Electric Power Control and Operation Centers

Miguel Melo[1], Luiz Bueno Silva[1], Ana Almeida[1], and Francisco Rebelo[2]

[1] Federal University of Paraiba, Cidade universitária, 58051-970, Joao Pessoa-PB, Brazil
{mobcmelo,bueno,secmestrado}@ct.ufpb.br
[2] Faculdade de Motricidade Humana, Universidade Técnica de Lisboa, Estrada da Costa,
1499-002, Cruz-Quebrada, Portugal
frebelo@fmh.utl.pt

Abstract. The activity of the operator of the electrical power control centers is the prevention of incidents and errors that disrupt the operation of the electrical system. They have to do it by mobilizing knowledge and reasoning for which they have received training, which from the point of view of the existing rules are adequate. However, there are some factors that need to be improved, because there are still accidents and incidents, caused manly caused by fatigue, lack of concentration or due to inadequacy of human Computer Interface. This article aims to analyses ergonomics aspects and human factors in the electric power control centers and contribute with a methodology of studies including the topics of Human; Machine; Interface IHM; and critical factors.

Keywords: IHM in Electric Power Control Centers, Workload in Operators, Fatigue.

1 Introduction

With technological advancement the operator in Electric Power Control and Operation Centers tasks and are more complex and automated [1, 2, 3]. Similarly to the systems developed for other industries, the automation in electric power sector resulted in more sophisticated equipment and demanding more attention from operators, who now control and operate a growing body of equipment. This results in increased the cognitive load and hence fatigue and environments more conducive to error [4]. Electrical systems can be categorized as critical systems, where failures can result in significant economic loss, physical harm or threats to human life.

The activity of the operator of the electrical power control centers are the prevention of incidents and errors that disrupt the operation of the electrical system, or when it is no longer possible, the process of trying to return to normal, which is called recovery. There are some factors that need to be improved, because there are still accidents and incidents, caused manly caused by fatigue, lack of concentration or due to inadequacy of Human Computer Interface (HCI) [5]. His activities are extremely complex with numerous variables and the technician has a high degree of uncertainty.

A. Marcus (Ed.): DUXU/HCII 2013, Part III, LNCS 8014, pp. 169–178, 2013.

It is essential to make decisions and process information continuously, with a frequent request mental due to the necessity of maintaining attention, memory and reasoning request.

Among the factors involved in the decision-making capacity can be cited: the postural requirements, existing facilities, the status of ongoing attention that the task requires, fatigue, health, the difficulty in interpreting the information, the issue of shifts work [6,7].It is also emphasized environmental conditions such as noise, temperature and lighting inadequate. Also influencing the response of operators, there are also those related to media like visual signals and verbal information and human-machine interface [8] and workload NASA - TLX [9].

This article aims to analyses ergonomics aspects and human factors in the Electric Power Control Centers and contribute with a methodology of studies including the topics:1-Human (Operators: Work Characteristic, Experience, Life Quality, Personal Data); 2-Computer (Control Centers: Work Organizational, Organizational Culture, Work per shift; attention, Information Safety); 3-Interface IHM: (Tasks, Monitoring, Supervision, Planning, Operation, Equipments, Monitors, Computers, Panels Supervisory System); 4-Critical Factors: (Amount of information, Information Quality, Workload Fatigue, Work Environmental Factors, Noise, Lighting, Thermal Comfort).

2   Electric Power Control Centers

The electricity sector is characterized by a set of processes, tools and equipment, focused on generation, transmission and distribution of electricity [10]. The electric power goes a long way to reach the end consumer as in figure 1, where is produced in the power plant, goes through a voltage substation and it is transported over long transmission lines to areas where there is need for consumption. Here goes through another substation, this time, step-down voltage being delivered to end users through distribution systems [11]. The monitoring system is in electrical power control centers. There are used techniques distance automated commands that allow decisions together in one place [12].

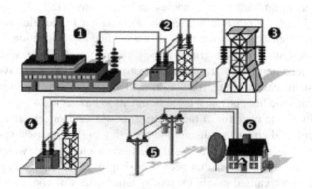

Fig. 1. Transmission and Distribution of Electricity-source [11]

Fig. 2. Typical Electric Power Control and Operation Cnter

2.1 The Operators: The Work and Tasks

The work carried out by operators in control centers occurs through monitoring screens, communication systems and specific programs (specific software) designed to meet the needs of this type of activity [13]. His routines involves receiving information gathered from the previous turn in an application, check the functionality of other applications and planned interventions for hours.

In case of failure, it is essential that the control centers operators act to make the process returns to normal. Generally, in these situations, the amount of information received is very large and generated from various sources. It is a fact that during the period of a contingency, even under stress, the operator needs to analyze and interpret this information list of failures quickly and safely, separating the important from those that are secondary, preventing further damage. Therefore, it is up to the operator to decide whether or not reconnection of equipment, and may be at risk of causing accidents due to misinterpretation of events or flagged by the notices of deficiency [14, 15].

The tasks of operators in control centers are associated with hazardous processes and systems. Implies supervision systems where some critical events occur infrequently and regularity, but requiring monitoring and decision making continuously.

The main tasks of operators are to execute: monitoring the substation equipment; power measurement; substations equipment and transmission line protection; protection supervision; automatic restart; location of line fault; power remote controls; overload on transformers; control voltage; reactive flow; selective cutting loads; alarms in general; Print reports; Interface with the Distribution Operation Centers (DOCs);

2.2 Interface in the Electric Power Control Centers

The interface of the human-operator with the control rooms (Computer) occurs through several monitoring stations. The screens of the computer must be positioned to facilitate the handling of operators, both for normal operations and for preventing accidents. One of the factors that can influence the decision-making is the difficulty of interpreting the information provided by the system. Due to the large amount of information available to the operator, there is a decrease in the ability of maneuvering and understanding of the tasks to be performed. A fundamental problem in this type of system is that agents (human or machine) must understand what the other is doing. If the operator believes that the system is in a way, but is actually in other conditions, situations can arise very dangerous [16].

The number of alarms is high when changes occur in electrical systems, which means that the operator has difficulty in determining the causes of these disorders and to determine the actions to be performed. People in controlling such systems must often pay attention to a large amount of information from a variety of sources in order to acquire knowledge of the situation in question. They must be able to identify at all times the state of the system to power on a contingency informed decisions.

One of the major studies that should be performed for about HMI- Human-machine interface is the cognitive ergonomics. These studies contribute to research on Human-machine interface as well as decision-making at work [17]. These studies have the following objectives [18]: 1-Decrease the time needed to accomplish tasks; 2- Reduce the number of errors; 3- Reduce learning time; 4- Improving people's satisfaction with a system.

May [19] says the complexity of Human-machine interface (HMI) in Operation Centers and Control for the following reasons: 1-Greater integration and increase the size of the national and regional networks; 2-Increased level of automation involving distributed measurements and automatic decisions; 3- Increased complexity of coordination arising from the implementation of optimal power flow, market-based

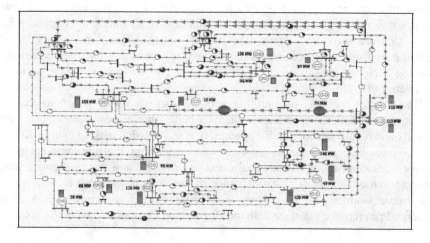

Fig. 3. – Unifilar Diagram of Load Flow displayed on a screen in the control room of the electric power center, source: [20]

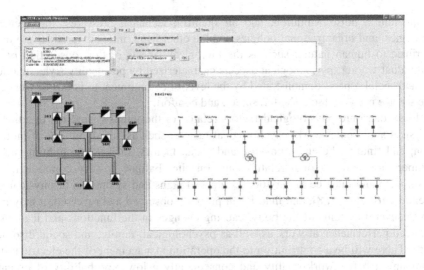

Fig. 4. – Unfiled diagram of substation equipment displayed on a screen in the room of the electric power control center

electricity; 4- Increased demand for power grids resilient in the form of permanent " micro-networks" or "islanded" that can help protect networks from higher voltage instabilities.

Besides the supervisory panels shown in Figure 2, each operator has three to four monitors with screens and information about the electric power system. These information generally has been shown using a display interface with figure two dimensional (2D) according to Figures 3 and 4.

3   Workload and Fatigue in Operators of the Electric Power Control Centers

The mental burden is placed as a hypothetical construct, induced by performance of a task and causing a decrease in the mental activity of other tasks. The aspects of fatigue were analyzed by Ilda [21], who noted that a balance between the demands at work and the ability of workers is needed. This balance can be supported by ergonomics research conducted in the workplace, because ergonomics aims to study the interactions of people and technology, as well as organization and environment to cooperate in an integrated way for the safety, comfort, welfare, and efficiency of human activities.

Many research about work fatigue and workload were analyzed last years [22, 23, 24] classified the main determinants of fatigue in internal and external variables. The following external variables are those that act more explicitly on the subject: Availability of time, equipment, instruments, and securities, for the physical environment (temperature, noise, vibration, and air quality); technical pressures; management; strategies; and organizational policies. On the other hand, internal variables are those intrinsic to human nature, such as the biological aspects of the constitution of the individual worker; psychological aspects characterized by personality style, emotional, and social aspects demonstrated by the level of commitment to issues of work and the service needs of food, shelter, safety, and comfort.

First, there are physiological factors related to the intensity and the duration of physical and mental work; psychological factors, such as boredom, lack of motivation; and finally, the environmental and social factors, such as the lighting, noise, temperature, and personal relationships on site. Fatigue is very common in the workplace and must be understood as a set of signs and symptoms of physical and mental attributes [4, 8], and that, if not properly observed and reversed, it may pass on to several systems of the body, causing changes in the functions and leading to reduced performance at work as well as psychological, family, and social disorders [25]. There will be a contribution to the operation management of the electric utility company a better work quality and consequently a lower probability of operator error.

3.1   Workload Evaluation: Ergonomics Aspects

There are several methods for the evaluation of cognitive and workload. One is the National Aeronautics and Space Administration Task Load Index known as the NASA-TLX (NASA, 2008), developed by the NASA Ames Research Center in 1986, after 3 years of studies involving over 40 laboratories research and flight simulations. This method works with physiological indicators associated with subjective methods in situations simulated in the laboratory or in real situations and operational work, taking great advantage of being applicable to various operators and activities without the need of change in its structure.

It is a multidimensional assessment procedure that gives an overall score of the workload based on a weighted average of the scores obtained in the six factors of NASA-TLX scale. These six factors are as follows: levels of achievement, effort and frustration, which have strong influence from the characteristics of individual operators, and the requirements of mental, physical, and time factors that are determined by the work situation [9].

With regard to satisfaction with the performance of the staff, the level of effort with respect to how much one has to work physically and mentally to achieve a good performance, as well as the level of frustration, there are factors that inhibit the performance of work, such as insecurity, irritation, lack of stimulation, and setbacks are important. On the other hand, the mental requirement involves mental activity needed to complete the work, and the physical requirement corresponds to physical activity required for the performance of work requirement and time on the level of pressure needed to achieve the same as shown in the Table 1.

Table 1. Factors considered in the NASA-TLX Instrument

Factors	Low Limit	High Limit
Mental Demand	Tasks considered easy, simple, goals achieved without difficulties	Tasks difficult, complex, requiring much mental effort to achieve the goal
Physical Requirement	Light, slow, easily accomplished tasks	Heavy, quick, strong, and lively tasks
Temporal Requirement	Slow and relaxed pace, with low pressure to the termination of activities	Fast and furious pace, with lots of pressure for completing the activities
Level of Effort	You feel very happy and are praised when it reaches the goals	You become no satisfied and almost no one notices your work
Level of Achievement	For the task to be performed successfully, surface concentration, muscle strength light weight, and simple reasoning are required (lack of skills)	Deep concentration, muscle strength, intense, complex reasoning, and great skill are needed
Level of Frustration	You feel safe, happy, and relaxed when you run the task	You feel insecure, discouraged, angry, and bothered with the task

4   Proposed Methodology

The proposed methodology for analyzing human factors and ergonomics, and human-machine interface in the electric power control centers would have the following steps

4.1   Steps of the Methodology

- Step I – Work Situation Characterization

— Human operator (experience, professional activities, age, style and life quality, personal and biomechanical data, anthropometrics).
— Organizational (organizational culture, work per shift; commitment labour; labour requirement, attention and concentration, information safety, automation);
— Environmental (temperature, noise, level luminance, lay out, position of monitors, supervisory panels, furniture especially chairs operators).

- Step II–Activity analysis by systematic visual observations of the work

— -Postural activities
— -Workers strategies to accomplish the task
— -Communications (with the other workers and devices)

- Step III–Worker Perceptions

— -Utilization of collected through questionnaires: (cognitive aspects, mental workload, types of tasks, difficulty of execution, emergency switching). These questionnaires using the methods described above with emphasis on methods NASA-TLX.
— -Interviews with a selected group. It is recommended that the interview be quick with answers structured to provide a better understanding of the factors involved between the work situation and the ergonomic aspects.
— -Data collection for the study with the interview: (software type, colors, symbols, size of the graphics system; modeling of equipment, types of screens, web design and other data).

- Step IV – Data Analyses and Identification of Critical Factors

— -Statistical analysis of data from questionnaires basic and the results of the interview. A correlation study should always be conducted to identify possible associations between the data and the variables collected in the studies.

- Step V – Proposed Solutions

— -Proposed solutions:

5　　Results and Conclusions

The activities of the operator are extremely complex with numerous variables and the technician has a high degree of uncertainty. His tasks are associated with hazardous processes and systems. Implies supervision systems where some critical events occur infrequently and regularity, but requiring monitoring and decision making continuously. The Human-machine interface (HMI) are specialized by the many reasons like a greater integration and increase the size of the national and regional networks and increased level of automation involving distributed measurements and automatic decisions;

With this methodology there will be a contribution to analysis of human factors of the operators of the Electric Power Control Centers. This new procedure will improve the few existing procedures with an innovative character and include other topics in cognitive ergonomics and Interface Human-Machine.

There will be a contribution to the strategic planning of electric power companies providing data for a better match of activities of the operators of the electric power control centers, contributing to a reduction in operating errors.

Acknowledgements. This paper was developed in the scope of a Research Project financed by Brazilian Agency CNPq (Conselho Nacional de Desenvolvimento Científico Tecnológico).

References

1. Ku, C.-H., Smith, M.J.: Organisational Factors and Scheduling in Locomotive Engineers and Conductors: Effects on fatigue, health and social well-being. Applied Ergonomics 41, 62–71 (2010)
2. Marmaras, N., Kontogiannis, T.: Cognitive Task. In: Salnend, G. (ed.) Handbook of Industrial Engineering. John Wiley & Sons, New York (2001)
3. Cañas, J.J., Quesada, J.F., Antoli, A., Fajardo, I.: Cognitive flexibility and adaptability to environmental changes in dynamic complex problem solving tasks. Ergonomics, 482–501 (2003)
4. Murata, A., Uetake, A., Takasawa, Y.: Evaluation of Mental Fatigue using Feature Parameter Extracted from Event-related Potential. International Journal of Industrial Ergonomics 35(8), 761–770 (2005)
5. Salles, P.F.: The Contribution of Cognitive Ergonomics in the Analysis of Activities of the Operator Control Room. UFSC, Florianopolis (2008)
6. Akerstedt, T.: LANDSTRÖM, Ulf. Work place countermeasures of night shift fatigue. International Journal of Industrial Ergonomics 21(3-4), 167–178 (1998)
7. Baulk, S.D., Fletcher, A., Kandelaars, K.J., Dawson, D., Roach, G.D.: A field study of sleep and fatigue in a regular rotating 12-h shift system. Applied Ergonomics 40(4), 694–698 (2009)
8. Meijman, T.F.: Mental Fatigue and the Efficiency of Information Processing in relation to Work times. International Journal of Industrial Ergonomics 20(1), 31–38 (1997)
9. Nasa, (2008), TLX Disponible in:
   http://humansystems.arc.nasa.gov/groups/TLX/computer.php
10. Oliveira, A.M.B.: Avaliação da Fadiga em Operadores de Salas de Controles de Subestações Elétricas. (MSc Dissertation in Production Engineering), Federal University of Paraíba (2008)
11. Oleskovicz, M.: Power Quality; Basic Fundamentals. São Paulo University, São Paulo (2004)
12. Santos, V., Zamberlan, M.C.: Ergonomics Design of Control Rooms. Fundacion Mapfre, São Paulo (1992) (in Portuguese)
13. Almeida, F.R., Kappel, G.B., Gomes, J.O.: Ergonomic Analyses of Work Cognitive in Control Centers COSR-SE. ENEGEP 2007 (2007) (in Portuguese), Disponible in:
    http://www.abepro.org.br/biblioteca/
    ENEGEP2007_TR670485_9258.pdf (acess in: Setember 2012)
14. Leao, F.B.: Metodologia para Análise e Interpretação de Alarmes em Tempo Real de Sistemas de Distribuição de Energia Elétrica. (PhD Thesis Electrical Engineering), Universidade Estadual Paulista, São Paulo (2011)
15. Menezes, et al.: Processamento de Alarmes do Sistema da CPFL. Congreso Latinoamericano de Distribucion Electrica. Mar del Plata, Argentina (2008)
16. Gatto, L.B.S.: Realidade Virtual Aplicada na Avaliação Ergonômica de Salas de Controle de Plantas Nucleares. (MSc Dissertation in Reactor Engineering), Instituto de Engenharia Nuclear, Rio de Janeiro (2012)
17. Vidal, M.C., Carvalho, P.V.: Cognitive Ergonomics. Virtual Cientifica, Rio de Janeiro (2008) (in Portuguese)
18. Cañas, J.J.: Cognitive Ergonomics in Interface Development Evaluation. Journal of Universal Computer Science 14(16), 2630–2649 (2008)

19. May, M.: Human Supervisory Control of Electric Power Transmission. LearningLab DTU, Technical University of Denmark Anker Engelundsvej 1, DK-2800, Denmark. EAM-08. European Annual Conference on Human Decision-Making and Manual Control, June 11-13, Delft University of Technology (2008)
20. Wiegmann, D.A., Overbye, T.J., Hoppe, S.M., Essenberg, G.R., Sun, Y.: Human factors aspects of three-dimensional visualization of power system information. IEEE Power Engineering Society General Meeting (2006)
21. Iida, I.: Ergonomics – Project and Production, 2nd edn. Edgard Blucher Ltda, São Paulo (2005) (in Portuguese)
22. Grandjean, E., Kroemer, K.H.E.: Manual de Ergonomia: adaptando o trabalho ao homem. 5ª Edição, Bookman, Porto Alegre (2005)
23. Rebelo, F., Rodrigues, A., Santos, R.: Can Anti-fatigue Industrial Mat Efficient. In: Proceedings of the International Ergonomics Association and The 7th Joint Conference of Ergonomics Society of Korea/Japan Ergonomics Society Ergonomics in the Digital Age, Seul (2003)
24. Melo, M., Masculo, F., Silva, L. B., Vitório, D.: Ergonomics Aspects and Mental Workload of Operators of Electric Power Control Centers: Case Studies in Northeast Brazil. In: International Symposium on Occupational Safety and Hygiene, Guimarães, Proceedings SHO 2012. Minho University, Guimarães (2012)
25. Limongi, A., Rodrigues, A.: Stress and Work. Atlas, São Paulo (2002) (in Portuguese)

HALO the Winning Entry to the DARPA UAVForge Challenge 2012

Stephen D. Prior[1], Siu-Tsen Shen[2], Mehmet Ali Erbil[1],
Mantas Brazinskas[1], and Witold Mielniczek[1]

[1] Faculty of Engineering and the Environment, University of Southampton,
Highfield Campus, Southampton SO17 1BJ, United Kingdom
s.d.prior@soton.ac.uk
[2] Department of Multimedia Design, National Formosa University,
64 Wen-Hua Rd, Hu-Wei 63208, Taiwan
stshen@nfu.edu.tw

Abstract. The DARPA UAVForge challenge was designed to bring together a diverse group of UAV enthusiasts to develop the next generation, low cost, small unmanned air system (SUAS) for perch and stare operations in a military context. The challenge combined a web-based collaboration site with a live competitive fly-off event held at Fort Stewart, Georgia, USA in May 2012. UAVForge was a Defense Advanced Research Projects Agency (DARPA) and Space and Naval Warfare Systems Center, Atlantic (SSC Atlantic) initiative to leverage the exchange of ideas among an international community united. More than 140 teams and 3,500 registered citizen scientists from 153 countries participated in this year long event. From several selection rounds, a core of nine teams competed in the fly-off event and in June 2012 Team HALO from the UK was declared the winner scoring 47.7 points out of a maximum possible 60 points, with their co-axial tri-rotor Y6 design.

Keywords: DARPA, UAVForge, SUAS, Crowd Sourcing, NLOS.

1 Introduction

In July 2011, DARPA together with SSC Atlantic jointly announced a crowd sourcing competition to develop the next generation, low cost, Small Unmanned Air System (SUAS) for use in a perch and stare military scenario. The target unit cost per system would ideally be less than US$10k.

The concept was for a man-portable, Vertical Take-Off and Landing (VTOL) SUAS to have the capability to be carried into a forward operating base from where it would be launched by a single operator on a mission to reconnoiter a target some 3.2 km away in a Non Line Of Sight (NLOS) location, which consisted of an urban terrain environment, namely the Colmar UTS at Fort Stewart, Georgia, USA.

The challenge began with Milestone 1, a 1 min 'Concept Video Submission' stage which had the effect of stimulating debate and encouraging team formation.

A. Marcus (Ed.): DUXU/HCII 2013, Part III, LNCS 8014, pp. 179–188, 2013.
© Springer-Verlag Berlin Heidelberg 2013

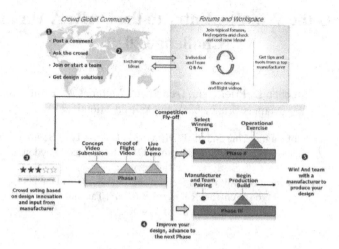

Fig. 1. DARPA's Crowd Sourcing Model [2]

Teams consisted of individuals, companies, universities, as well as groups of enthusiasts brought together either by the challenge or already working on Open Source UAV projects [1].

As stated on the UAVForge website:

"This challenge is guided by crowd sourcing. UAVForge provides you with the virtual environment and tools necessary to collaborate independent of geographic location, education, profession, or experience. Individuals, ad hoc teams or any other formative organizations are encouraged to submit innovative ideas, designs, algorithms, materials, etc. where other members of the crowd can respond, vote, comment and contribute." [2]

By the deadline of November 2011, forty-eight submissions had been received. These consisted of rotary-winged as well as fixed-winged hybrids, tail sitters, ducted-fans, etc. There was even a suggestion to attach a camera to an eagle and train it to fly the mission. By far the most prevalent solution was a conventional quadrotor design in an 'X' or '+' configuration. Registered users had the opportunity to post comments, ask questions and ultimately score each design out of five stars. The top scoring team (4.128) at this point was MAAV - A team from the University of Michigan with sponsorship from Northrop Grumman. The HALO team's submission was ranked 24th with a score of 2.4.

The next phase, Milestone 2, was a 1 min 'Proof of Flight' video. By the submission date in January 2012, twenty-two teams had entered. The necessity to actually prove that something could be built and could fly whittled down the entries by over 50%. The clear favorite at this point was the GremLion team (3.148) from the National University of Singapore with their co-axial rotorcraft, moving up from second place in the previous round. At this juncture, the HALO team was also on the move, ranked 8th with a score of 2.611 with our detachable arm Y6 design.

The final phase (Milestone 3) before the fly-off, was a 'Live Fly Demo' whereby each team had to operate their UAVs to perform a series of set tasks whilst connected via Skype to the organizers in the US. Twenty teams entered this phase by the March 2012 deadline and the leader at this point was the Dhaksha team (4.487) from MIT India with their range of quadrotors and hexrotors. Interestingly, after using a filtered crowd rating system, the icarusLabs team from MIT in the USA came out top with a score of 3.59. Team HALO was in fifth place with a score of 3.02.

Analysis of these systems shows that there were: 10% Single Rotor, 10% Tandem Rotor/Co-Axial, 35% Quadrotor, 10% Quadrotor (Tail sitter), 10% Hybrid Rotor/Fixed Wing, 20% Hexrotor/Y6, 5% Octorotor.

After further deliberation by an independent governmental judging panel based in the US, the top twelve teams going to the fly-off were announced:

Table 1. Final Fly-off Selection

Team Name	Country	UAV Type
AeroQuad	Intl.[†]	Y6
ATMOS	The Netherlands	Tail sitter 4Rotors
DHAKSHA	India	Octorotor
Extractor X	Singapore	Tail sitter 4Rotors
GremLion	Singapore	Co-axial
HALO	UK	Y6
icarusLabs	USA	Hybrid Ducted-Fan
Navy EOD	USA	Quadrotor
Phase Analytic	USA	Quadrotor
SQ-4 Recon	UK	Quadrotor
SwiftSight	USA	Quadrotor
WIDrone	Italy	Quadrotor

†The AeroQuad team was based in the US, but had an international mix of team members based around their online community of UAV enthusiasts.

As can be seen in Table 1 above, Quadrotors still dominated the field in the final fly-off selection. The members of the HALO team also participated in the SQ-4 Recon team and were therefore the only representatives from the UK and the only team to have two teams in the final selection. However, before the fly-off took place, three teams pulled out, citing commercial interests (WIDrone, SQ-4 Recon) or system failure (icarusLabs).

2   Milestone 4 - The Fly-Off Event

2.1   Target Location

The venue chosen for the fly-off event was the Colmar Urban warfare Training Site (UTS) at Fort Stewart, Georgia, USA. This was an old U.S. Army base constructed

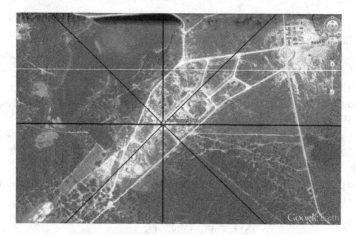

Fig. 2. Google Earth Map of the Colmar Urban Warfare Training Site

during WWII and home to the 3rd Infantry Division. The base covers an area of 1,100 km^2 and contains the recently built Colmar (UTS). Colmar consists of a number of buildings arranged in a typical town complex arrangement as shown in Figure 2.

2.2   Mission Scenario

The mission scenario was to outfit a fictional Task Force with an unmanned remotely operated micro air vehicle system. The entire air vehicle system must fit within a rucksack and a single person travelling by foot must be able to carry and operate the vehicle without assistance. The job of the Task Force is to conduct observations of suspicious activities occurring within the vicinity of two nondescript buildings in an urban area. Due to security in the region, all operations must be conducted beyond line of sight so as not to compromise your presence. If the UAV system is detected the mission will be jeopardized. The total observation time may require up to three hours of pictures and/or video to document the facts. Once key observations have been made, the team must quickly retreat to their designated rendezvous location. It is possible the vehicle will be handed off to another member of the Task Force to ensure mission success.

   Due to the nature of the task and the variety of the proposed solutions put forward, it was clear from the start that the perch and stare task could be achieved in a number of different ways. The UAVForge website stated that:

"Once the vehicle has flown to the predefined search area, the vehicle needs to identify a vantage point from which to conduct observations. This task can be accomplished by any means which includes landing, adhering, hanging, and/or hovering above or under a physical structure." [2]

Clearly there was a degree of ambiguity in the rules, which was designed to cater for an unknown type of UAV which could have been deployed, i.e. a blimp or a balloon.

2.3   Technical Performance Requirements

- The complete air vehicle system must fit in a rucksack carried by a single person.
- The air vehicle must take off vertically from a starting location, fly out to an observation location, perform observations, return to an ending location that is different from the starting position, and land vertically.
- The air vehicle must be able to operate successfully in winds up to 6.7 m/s.
- At the observations area, the air vehicle system must be able to identify persons or activities of interest up to 30 m away.
- The air vehicle system must send real time video or pictures from its observation area back to the operator (a distance up to 3.2 km).
- The vehicle design must consider noise reduction features to make it as quiet as possible so as not to attract undue attention.
- The air vehicle user interface and vehicle controls should be simple and intuitive.

2.4   Scoring

The scoring for the fly-off event was sub-divided into three elements:

- Baseline Objectives   (30 points)
- Advanced Behaviors   (140 points)
- Manufacturability   (30 points)

Therefore the maximum possible score was 200 points. Each of the Baseline Objectives was pass-fail, and all of the baseline objectives must have been completed in order to be eligible to earn points for advanced behaviors. Teams were given the opportunity to conduct the Advanced Behaviors assessment before or after attempting the Baseline Objectives.

The manufacturability assessment was conducted by Northwest UAV (experienced UAV manufacturers) contracted in by DARPA. The teams had to submit a detailed Bill of Materials (BOM) which included pricing information, as well as upload CAD files for all manufactured components.

3   The Halo Small UAS

Our entry to the competition took the form of a Y6, co-axial tri-rotor design. The concept for this was originally developed for the MoD Grand Challenge Event in 2008 [3]. The Y6 configuration has six rotors: two co-axial rotors, situated at three locations, as can be seen below.

Fig. 3. HALO UAV Landed on the Target Location at the Colmar UTS

3.1   HALO UAS Specification

- Mass: 2.5 kg
- Endurance: 32 min+ (hover)
- Range: 6 km (max)
- Props: 16 inch Carbon Fibre
- GPS Waypoint Control via Tablet Computer
- 50 Waypoints/Point of Interest
- Flight Controller : WK-M (900 MHz or 2.4 GHz)
- Autonomous Take-off and Landing
- GPS Hold, Altitude Hold and Return to Home
- Fail safes – Low Battery, Loss of Communications, etc
- 11,000 mAh Li-Po (4S) Battery
- 1280 MHz, 2.5 W Video TX
- Detachable Arms
- Detachable Legs
- Two Switchable Micro Cameras (one gimbaled)
- Ability to Land on Flat Ground or on a Roof Apex

The complete HALO UAS is self-contained within a single back packable flight case which contains the UAV, two LiPo batteries, tablet computer, tripod, aerials, video RX, 7 inch preview screen, FPV goggles and operators seat. The total system mass is approximately 15 kg. The system set-up takes less than five minutes and with an optimum flight velocity of 10 m/s the UAV has an operational range of approximately 6 km (max), the limiting factor being the capacity of the current generation of LiPo batteries (Specific Energy = 197.3 Wh/kg).

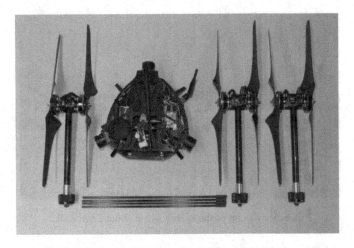

Fig. 4. HALO UAV Showing Detachable Elements

HALO was designed to have two micro cameras, one forward facing on a gimbal and one fixed at the center pointing directly downwards. The operator can switch between the two views at any time during the mission. The downwards facing camera is particularly useful for landing.

For the UAVForge mission scenario the concept was to attempt a perch landing on the church which would provide an excellent viewpoint over the target area.

4   Problem Areas

All of the teams that attempted the Baseline Objective over the 10 day fly-off period at Fort Stewart encountered problems with data communications. The NLOS environment was not conducive to good RF communications. Even though this was anticipated, it still represented a considerable problem. When combined with possible interference (whether intentional or unintentional from other military users) this made the challenge that much more demanding.

Analysis of the terrain elevation profile using Google Earth (Figure 6) provides some answers as to why this was such a difficult task (the launch site is on the LHS and the target, at the center of the Colmar UTS, is on the RHS at 3.2 km).

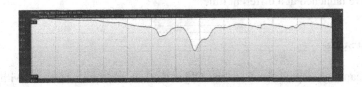

Fig. 5. Google Earth Elevation Profile at the Colmar UTS

Fig. 6. Viewpoint of the launch site at about 23 m AGL

When combined with the dense, 30 m high woodland which surrounded the Colmar UTS and the launch site, it was incredibly difficult to approach any landing location with good communications (data and/or video).

Each team tried to overcome this situation in different ways, some increased the output power (up to 7 Watts) without much luck and some teams decided to increase the height of their antennae using tripods or helium balloons, sometimes combined with directional Yagi antennae.

The HALO team, like all the others, experienced this issue during its first two flights. Whereas we could reach the target using GPS waypoints, every time that we reduced the altitude we lost the video downlink. This would occur at around 50 m AGL. Our initial response to this was to increase the height of our Yagi antenna (13 dBi) by placing it together with the receiver in a tree about 23 m AGL. This definitely helped with the range; however, communications over the target were still not reliable enough to attempt a landing. On the last but one day, we tested a higher power 1280 MHz video transmitter moving from 1.5 to 2.5 Watts. This setup gave us good video link all the way down to roof top height during a range test with HALO flying over Colmar under manual control and the GCS situated at the launch site.

On the final day we were ready to attempt a landing on the church when we lost GPS signal on route to the target. This caused us to have an uncontrollable landing in trees which caused major damage which was not repairable in the field. Subsequent analysis using satellite predictor software [4] showed that at the exact time of the accident (08:20-08:30) we were experiencing a very weak GPS signal (only 3 satellites) caused by a constellation dropout. Had we know about this software tool prior to the event, we would have launched at a different time.

5   Results

Several teams attempted the Baseline Objectives on multiple occasions with partial success. However the HALO team was the only team to score some points under every scoring category. The final results of the challenge were announced on the UAVForge website in late June 2012.

Table 2. Final rank and Scoring

Rank	Team	Final Score
1	HALO	47.7
2	AeroQuad	39.1
3	ATMOS	37.3
4	SwiftSight	37.3
5	Navy EOD	36.5
6	Extractor X	32.0
7	DHAKSHA	31.5
8	Phase Analytic	30.5
9	GremLion	19.2

DARPA stated that as no team had successfully completed the Baseline Objective there would be no award of the US$100k prize and no follow on operational exercise or production of up to 15 units for trials with military units.

It is important to note that the above score is out of 60 points and relates only to the first and third scoring elements. If we were to include the Advanced Behaviors scoring elements then our score would be an estimated 150/200 points.

6   Conclusion

When the UAVForge event was first announced, Wired magazine called this challenge "Beyond the Beyond", which is an apt descriptor for this difficult endeavor.

Some have labeled this event a failure, since none of the teams successfully passed the Baseline Objective. However, one has to remember that all of the entries were experimental aircraft, built by enthusiasts, in their own time and largely out of their own money. People have criticized the inability of any of the systems to perch and stare at the target. However, all of these systems cost less than US$10k, many less than $5k.

It is understood that the AeroVironment Shrike quadrotor (estimated cost US$150k each) was tested over the same course prior to the fly-off event and that it too had problems with data communications and could not perch and stare for the required time. The Shrike was developed over four years, funded by DARPA to the tune of US$4.6 million [5], if this system struggled with the course, it was perhaps no surprise that less resourced systems, costing a fraction of this, also struggled.

If success is measured by how many DIY UAV enthusiasts there are out there, and how far such systems have come over the last decade, then UAVForge was a resounding success. The Y6 configuration (ranked 1st and 2nd) has proved itself an ideal platform for such tasks. Further developments will include active directional antennae, digital video links and improved battery technologies.

Acknowledgement. The authors would like to thank DARPA and SSC Atlantic for hosting the challenge, which spurred on innovations in this exciting area of unmanned systems research.

References

1. Carancho, T.: AeroQuad – The Open Source Quadcopter/Multicopter, http://aeroquad.com/forum.php (accessed January 19, 2013)
2. UAVForge – Crowdsourcing for UAV Innovation, http://www.uavforge.net/uavhtml (accessed February 20, 2013)
3. Prior, S.D., Karamanoglu, M., Odedra, S., Foran, T., Erbil, M.A.: Development of a Co-Axial Tri-Rotor UAV. In: 24th Bristol International Unmanned Air Vehicle Systems Conference, University of Bristol, March 30 -April 1, pp. 15.1–15.16 (2009)
4. Navcom Technology, Satellite Predictor Tool, http://www.navcomtech.com/Support/Tools/satellitepredictor/main.cfm (accessed July 15, 2012)
5. AeroVironment Inc., News and Events, AeroVironment Receives $4.6 Million in DARPA Funding to Develop Stealthy, Persistent, Perch and Stare UAS Based on Wasp (August 20, 2008), http://www.avinc.com/resources/press_release/aerovironment_receives_4.6_million_in_darpa_funding (accessed December 20, 2012)

Main Usability Issues in Using Virtual Environments for Older Population Warning Studies

Lara Reis[1,2], Emília Duarte[3], and Francisco Rebelo[1,2]

[1] Laboratório de Ergonomia, Faculdade de Motricidade Humana, Universidade Técnica de Lisboa, Estrada da Costa, 1499-002 Cruz-Quebrada, Dafundo, Portugal
[2] CIPER, Interdisciplinary Center for the Study of Human Performance, Universidade Técnica de Lisboa, Estrada da Costa, 1499-002 Cruz-Quebrada, Dafundo, Portugal
{laramaiareis,frebelo}@fmh.utl.pt
[3] Unidcom, IADE – Creative University, Av. D. Carlos I, 4, 1200-649 Lisboa, Portugal
emilia.duarte@iade.pt

Abstract. Over the last decades, Virtual Reality (VR) technology has emerged as a promising tool for numerous human performance assessments. Together with the expansion of such systems, several Virtual Environment (VE) usability criteria have been developed to ensure their optimal production and efficiency. However, the current status of such measures for warning research is scarce; and most importantly, design guidelines for defining VEs for middle-aged and older adult interactions with warnings are even more rare. In order to create effective and inclusive VEs for older age groups, warning researchers must be informed of the main age-related perceptual and cognitive changes that may hinder the experience, as well as should determine which of the usability issues are most important for a particular VE system. This paper provides a theoretical framework which seeks to highlight the main subject matters that embrace the design, implementation and evaluation of VE studies for older population warning research.

Keywords: Virtual Reality, Virtual Environments, Usability, Warnings, Agiing, Inclusive Design.

1 Introduction

This paper presents a discussion about the key usability issues in using Virtual Reality-based (VR) technologies and Virtual Environments (VEs) for studies involving older populations (i.e., 55 to 65 years old) and warnings. An overview of the most important factors that should be taken into consideration when carrying out such studies is provided. Such theoretical framework was developed within the scope of a project which proposes to: 1) highlight the use and effectiveness of technology-based warnings as inclusive solutions for compensating and/or assisting age-related deficits; as well as 2) promote VEs as feasible research tools for enhancing the field of warning research and inclusive design.

A. Marcus (Ed.): DUXU/HCII 2013, Part III, LNCS 8014, pp. 189–198, 2013.

The nature of the study is justified by the fact that due to the economical, medical and technological revolutions, the workforce population is rapidly aging. In western societies, the older generation is growing faster than the total population. According to demographic estimates, the older population aged 60+ is expected to increase by more than 50% in the next four decades, rising from 264 million in 2009, to 416 million in 2050 [1]. Based on such facts, safety for older workers has become a growing topic of societal concern, since inadequately and/or poorly designed working environments and warnings, conjointly with age-related changes (which characterize old age and thus turn older age groups more prone to accidents, as well as injury), can degrade the quality of life [2]. Safety warnings play a vital role in work contexts: they alert and inform people of potential hazards [3]. In recent studies, technology-based warnings have been highlighted as a potential solution for overcoming age-related deficits and communicating safety messages to older populations [4]. Conversely, research regarding the effectiveness of such warnings is limited by several methodological, economical and ethical constraints. Contemporary technological advances, however, have highlighted the use of VR as a viable tool to surpass these limitations and to undergo such studies [5]. The advantages of using such technology encompass the ability to create low cost experimental and interactive VEs in which compliance in hazardously simulated situations can be safely assessed.

Although the applications of VEs in various scientific domains are considerable, in the field of safety communications, VE usability knowledge is scarce and very much in its infancy. The current body of VE warning research raises some concerns when generalizing and applying their principles to real-world users, since the majority of the performed studies used younger adult populations (mainly university students) and/or specific target groups (e.g., participants with various degrees of cognitive and/or health disabilities/disorders) as research subjects. Furthermore, the few existent studies, which used older age groups and VEs, highlight important performance differences when compared to younger adults [6]. However, seldom of them provide usability criteria and inclusive VE design guidelines.

In this context, this paper primarily aims to discuss: 1) the main age-related perceptual and cognitive changes that may jeopardize the processing of warnings and technology; 2) the theoretical framework which serves to guide the utilization of VE studies with older generations; and 3) VE study examples which have used older participants and the implications of their findings for warning research.

2   Age-Related Changes

With aging, the ability to notice, encode, comprehend and comply with a warning and/or technology is adversely affected by age-related deficits. These include declines in the visual, auditory and cognitive capacities [7, 8, 9]. Visual modality impairments consist of: diminished visual acuity (e.g., presbyopia, myopia); greater glare sensitivity; reduced ability to perceive colors; decreased contrast sensitivity; and temporal resolution deterioration. Auditory deficits embrace difficulties in distinguishing between high frequencies, as well as different tones, voices and/or speech sounds in noisy backgrounds. Tactile changes include declines in the capacity to accurately judge force (e.g., over-or-under gripping) [9, 10].

Cognitive deficits are associated to: diminished reaction times and decision-making in emergency situations; increased attentional distraction; decreased visual search; and difficulties in comprehending and drawing textual, language, or pictorial inferences. Since interactions require the use of different types of memory, research has shown, for example: declines in working memory increase with complex tasks and procedures; semantic memory grows and remains intact throughout the years; and decreases in prospective memory, especially in what concerns time-based tasks [9].

In sum, 'old age' encompasses a number of age-related changes, and as a result, may hinder an older individual's overall safety. In order to design effective and inclusive warnings and/or VE solutions, as well as improve older population performances, researchers must be informed of these limitations.

3   Virtual Reality and Virtual Environments

Over the last two decades, VR as a cutting-edge technology has emerged as a potential tool in many research areas, such as engineering, architecture, design, medicine, education, rehabilitation, aviation, among others [11]. When compared to conventional field and laboratory studies, Rizzo and Kim [12] claim that the advantages of using such technology include: enhanced ecological validity; control and consistency of experimental conditions, which supports repetitive and hierarchical delivery; real-time performance feedback; self-guided and independent exploration; interface modification contingent on user's impairments; safe testing and training, as well as "error-free learning" environment; gaming factors to enhance motivation; low-cost functional VEs that can be easily created, duplicated and distributed; among others.

The most common definitions of VR describe it as a sophisticated interface (i.e., a real-time visual, auditory and touch/haptic feedback computer-based system) that generates VEs in which users visualize, navigate, manipulate, as well as interact with 'objects' and 'people' which have locations and orientations in a three-dimensional (3D) space. Such VEs are used to 'transport/carry' a user to an artificially simulated world/reality in which he/she is not physically present, but to some extent, has the feeling of actually 'being there', i.e., is psychologically involved. A basic VR system consists of several input and output devices. These include: 1) graphics software to produce 3D VEs; 2) stereoscopic displays to visualize the VEs; 3) motion tracking systems to register head/hand/body movements/actions and orientations/displacements inside the VEs; 4) sound/audio technology, to enable realistic VEs; 5) interaction devices to navigate, manipulate, and explore the VEs; and 6) haptic feedback mechanisms to provide force, tactile and proprioceptive/vestibular data during interaction inside the VE. With the advanced development of various complex technologies, different types of VR systems have become commercially available, thereby giving rise to several types of human performance research. Together with the expansion of such systems and assessments, several usability principles and evaluation methods have emerged to ensure the optimal creation, effectiveness and satisfaction of VEs [e.g.,12, 13, 14, 15].

3.1   Key VE Usability Issues

A review of the literature [e.g., 12, 13, 15, 16] concerning the definition of the main VE usability taxonomies identifies two distinct, yet correlated, types of analyses, namely: 1) a VE system characteristics evaluation, which is concerned with the physical, technological and/or constructional components of the experience, i.e., software, hardware and overall interaction techniques and devices; and 2) a VE user characteristics evaluation, which encompasses the users' behavioral and subjective experiences, i.e., his/her physiological, psychological and psychosocial responses. Both of these experiences vary in light of the technology used, as well as the users' and tasks' characteristics. In order for VEs to be efficiently developed, a number of basic theoretical and pragmatic issues need to be considered. Firstly, when conducting such studies, researchers should adopt the UCD approach to ensure that the users are proficiently part of the iterative design cycle, and that all aspects of their VE interaction are carefully accounted for [16]. Together with such an approach, the following key VE usability criteria, associated with the two types of VE experiences, should be considered.

VE System Characteristics. According to usability research, when maximizing effective VE systems for older populations, key and intrinsically linked features such as interaction and multimodal system output should be carefully accounted for. In other words, researchers must incorporate and merge: on the one hand, an understanding of the system's technicalities (interaction techniques and devices); and on the other hand, the older users' capacities (perceptual, cognitive and motor skills) and how these may influence such a system.

Interaction. Also referred to as interactivity, is provided both by and to the user (i.e., motion inputs) and the VR system (i.e., multimodal outputs); this is, the system's ability to detect the user's performance and to instantaneously modify, as well as update the VE in response to the actions performed. Bowman et al. [14] classified three categories of interaction, namely: 1) travel, i.e., the user's displacement and change in viewpoint as he/she moves from one place to another inside the VE; 2) object selection, i.e., when the user targets virtual objects within the VE; and 3) manipulation, i.e., the modification of a virtual object's position and/or orientation. Therefore, usability measures associated with this feature are concerned with task performances such as: 1) wayfinding, i.e., locating and orienting oneself in the VE; 2) navigation, i.e., moving from one location to another in the VE; and 3) object or target selection and manipulation, i.e., the reposition and/or reorientation of target virtual objects. When designing effective VEs for older population warning studies, researchers must be aware that age-related deficits may affect such task performances, and as a result, should identify which of these limitations hinder their processing, as well as the adequate usability methods. The following questions, for example, should be addressed: does an older user understand how he/she can navigate inside the VE and interact with its virtual objects?, how challenging is it for an older user to move from point A to point B?, does the VE include appropriate visual and navigational cues to assist the older users' spatial knowledge?, are the chosen interaction techniques and devices difficult to manipulate or intrusive?, etc.

Multimodal system output. This feature consists of the various sensorial and perceptual inputs/outputs that affect the users' overall interaction. It includes all types of devices used to present information about the VE to the users. Usability criteria associated with this system for older population performance assessments are concerned with design constraints related to human sensory perception, namely: 1) visual outputs, i.e., the technical and non-technical cues which include, but are not limited to, stereoscopic support, spatial resolution, field-of-view (FOV), optical flow, update/refresh rates, depth perception, etc.; 2) auditory outputs, i.e., cues which provide aural (localization and sonification) feedback resulting from the user's own actions, others' actions, and/or the environment, e.g., speech recognition, 3D auditory localization, synthetic speech, etc.; and 3) haptic outputs, i.e., cues which provide force or touch sensations, e.g., kinesthetic (which is felt by moving or forcing muscles and/or joints) and/or tactile (received through skin contact) information. Knowing that with aging, an older individual's visual, auditory and cognitive abilities may be impaired, the subsequent usability issues, for example, should be considered: is the perceptual information conveyed by the VE readily seen, heard, understood and/or felt by the older user?, does the type of visual/auditory/haptic output influence the older user's overall perception of the VE?, are the traditional and general output specifications appropriate for an older user?, etc.

VE User Characteristics. According to usability criteria associated to this type of analysis, when designing effective VE systems for older populations, the following vital and innately connected user characteristics should be considered: engagement, as well as health and safety. This is, researchers must identify and accommodate the older age groups' unique physiological and psychological abilities so as to promote a captivating VE experience, while ensuring their well-being and safety.

Engagement. This refers to the user's psychological state of being actively, absorbingly and/or emotionally occupied/involved with the VE experience, i.e., the individual's capacity/ability to perceive/believe that they are inside and a part of the VE, even when he/she knows to be physically situated in another. Stanney et al. [13] suggest that this feeling of involvement is associated to factors such as: the user's motivation to comply and interact with the VE; and the VE system's ability to update the user's actions in real-time. In other words, it is both user driven (i.e., the individual's feeling of presence) and system driven (i.e., the interface's immersive function). Presence is associated to the psychological and subjective 'feeling' or 'idea' of 'being inside' a VE. Immersion is defined as the extent to which the user feels 'isolated' from the real world during the simulation. In order for an older user to feel present and immersed in a VE, various sensory channels (in particular the visual and auditory senses) should be stimulated. According to Gutiérrez et al. [17], such stimulation depends on the physical configuration of the system; they defined three types of systems: 1) fully immersive, using stereoscopic or non-stereoscopic head-mounted displays (HMDs), sometimes referred to as VR glasses; 2) semi-immersive, such as stereoscopic or non-stereoscopic CAVEs (i.e., multiple screen projection systems); and 3) non-immersive, which includes standard desktop-based interfaces (e.g., LCD displays) and stereophonic acoustic systems (e.g., 3D surround sound). The main difference between these three systems depends on how much the user is isolated (i.e., can see, hear or touch) from the real-world surroundings, i.e., the degree to which the interface can or cannot 'transport' a person, at a mental and sensorial level, to a 'second reality'. When designing effective VEs for older population warning studies, researchers must, once again, be aware that these psychological and subjective states may be impaired by a number of age-related changes, and therefore should address, for example, the subsequent usability issues: does the older user feel actively motivated, involved, immersed and present during the simulation?, is the type of display disturbing, distracting or intrusive?, etc.

Health and safety. This refers to the main and most crucial ethical principle of ensuring the older participants' well-being and safety during the simulation. If VE systems dismiss/ignore the human/user element of the study, such simulations can result in discomfort, sickness, harm or even injury. Such negative impacts are generally referred to as Virtual Reality Induced Symptoms and Effects (VRISE) [18].

VRISE, as defined by Cobb et al. [19], includes the variety of symptoms which occur both during (referred to as side-effects) and post (i.e., after-effects) VE simulation/exposure. The most common sign of such effects is cyber-sickness (CS). Such sickness symptoms generally fall under three categories: 1) nausea, which includes increased salivation, sweating, vomiting, burping, among others; 2) disorientation, for example, difficulty in focusing, dizziness, vertigo, etc.; and 3) ocular motor disturbances, which embraces fatigue, headaches, eyestrain, blurred vision, difficulty in focusing gaze, among others. Occurrences of such VRISE may be influenced by several factors such as: technological aspects (e.g., display delay, type of display); system design issues (e.g., level of navigational control and speed, type of interaction technique and device; visual scene complexity; exposure duration); and individual differences (e.g., age, gender, sickness susceptibility). Therefore, when designing effective and inclusive VEs for warning studies, researchers must certify that the older users are comfortable while interacting with the VE system, since pain or distress during the experience may ride over all of the other sensations, and thus, invalidate its findings. Consequently, the following health and safety questions, for example, should be addressed: do certain displays and devices cause some side/after-effects among the older participants?, if so, is it related to the different levels of immersion or FOV specifications?, do the older users experience high levels of discomfort, fatigue, or nausea during the VE simulation?, do orientation and coordination after-effects persist for long periods of time after the older users have been exposed to the VE?, etc.

In conclusion, both VE system and VE user characteristics influence each other reciprocally. As a result, in order to maximize any type of VE interaction with warnings, VE and warning researchers must identify which of the usability criteria, discussed above, are most important for a particular VE experiment, i.e., the significance of each of the guideline categories will depend on the goals established for the problem matter under study.

3.2   Examples of Older Population VE Studies

Although the use of VEs for warning research and inclusive design is in its early stages, a few current studies have successfully used VEs and older age groups, while others report some usability difficulties. Therefore, in light of the paper's objective, this section provides a brief outline of a couple of these studies and discusses the main implications of their findings for warning research.

In what concerns task performances such as target selection and evaluation, Pacheco et al. [20] successfully used a VE for the selection and assessment of chromatic environments for interior design studies. Using a sample of twenty older adults with ages ranging from 60 to 85 years old, and a basic VR system (i.e., a motion tracker, joystick, HMD, wireless headphones and graphics station), the study procedure compared two types of display mediums (i.e., a paper-based illustration versus a VE) in which the participants were asked to evaluate four VEs with four different ambient colors. Study variables included level of realism, interaction, sense of presence, chromatic fidelity and overall engagement. The attained results revealed no statistical differences regarding color selection, nor in the subjective evaluation of the setting, between the two types of displays; the authors state that such a result may indicate that both display mediums were evaluated equally, i.e., the VE presented a high level of chromatic fidelity. Nevertheless, important discrepancies were found for all variables, thereby denoting that the VE display was more effective. In conclusion, the authors enclose that VEs can be used to conduct studies with older adults for interior design research and report no usability problems or simulator sickness.

In another study, Moffat et al. [21] used a VE to assess spatial memory and navigation during a wayfinding task. Making use of a sample of 133 participants (123 older participants and 10 students) with ages ranging from 22 to 91 years old, and a standard desktop VR system (i.e., a graphic interface, computer and joystick), the study procedure evaluated age differences regarding navigational behavior when carrying out a route/maze learning task, as well as compared such results to other traditional measures of cognitive aging. After a training period, subjects were engaged in a VE spatial learning task in which they had to navigate through a series of interconnected hallways, some of which lead to dead ends and others to goal points.

The attained results determined that the older participants' overall performance was impaired when compared to the younger participants, i.e., they took longer to solve trials, traveled longer distances, and therefore, made more spatial memory errors. Moreover, 10% of the participants experienced some degree of VRISE; the majority of them were older adult females (mean age = 76.3 years). Nevertheless, such a fact did not comprise the validity of the study. Consequently, the authors conclude that the use of VEs in assessing spatial navigation of older age groups provides researchers with a promising and effective tool to comprehend age differences in route/place learning, as well as in the use of landmarks/cues.

In light of such outcomes, the authors recommend the subsequent guidelines for future research on older population interaction: 1) VE tasks which rely on completion time as a dependent measure should assess differences in what concerns computer experience and psychomotor processing speeds; and 2) in order to obtain a complete perception of older user navigation, it is important to quantify their VE performance and then correlate such findings with additional cognitive measures.

In a different study, Liu [22] evaluated which factors contribute to cyber-sickness (CS), during and after navigating a VE on a TFT-LCD (i.e., thin film transistor liquid crystal display), as well as verified the efficacy of a fuzzy cyber-sickness-warning system (i.e., a neuro-fuzzy technology which incorporates fuzzy logic reasoning and neural network learning) to detect the occurrence of such symptoms and determine their level of severity, as well as reduce their impact on the older adults' overall performance. Using a sample of 32 older adults, with ages ranging from 66 to 73 years, as well as a simple VR system (i.e., a TFT-LCD display, HMD, standard PC mouse and keyboard, as well as graphics software), the study procedure was two-fold: 1) in the first experiment, the authors compared differences between navigation rotating speeds, scene inclination angles and exposure durations, and two types of user navigation (i.e., in which the participant passively watches the VE's scenes move by themselves versus actively viewing and changing their viewpoint inside the VE), while participants were asked to search a classroom scene and confirm objects on a check box list; and 2) in the second phase, the participants were subjected to two stages, i.e., firstly, participants actively and independently navigated the VE without being exposed to an alarm system; secondly, they were exposed to the fuzzy warning system when levels of CS were detected. Therefore, in second phase the authors compared the differences between both performances.

The author's findings, regarding the first experiment, indicate that increases in navigational rotating speeds resulted in higher SSQ scores overall, particularly when the participants passively watched as the VE oscillated. However, the same was not verified when angle inclinations were amplified. As for the second experiment, the results attained clearly indicate that the warning system was successful in identifying CS symptoms and reducing their impact on the older adults' performance. According to the authors, such a system produced better results in the active condition, than in the 'no system' condition. In conclusion, the authors enclose that although some levels of CS can occur during long VE exposures, VEs can be used to conduct studies with older adults and that the CS-warning system proves to be a useful tool in detecting VRISE. Taking into consideration such outcomes, the authors recommend the subsequent guidelines for future research on older population interaction: 1) systems which are developed to manage and predict VRISE should include the time/duration in which the participants are exposed to the VE; 2) in order to ensure no CS aftereffects, researchers should not expose participants to the same VE within the same week of the experiment, i.e., they should let participants rest for a two week interval; and 3) active VE tasks, in which users have greater control over their navigation, produce lower levels of CS.

4   Conclusion

This paper presents a theoretical framework of the main usability issues that should be taken into consideration when conducting studies with older age groups, warnings and

VEs. As the studies outlined in this paper demonstrate, VEs provide researchers with the means to assess a number of older population performances. When compared to traditional research methods, the potential benefits of such tools, particularly for the purpose of studying middle-aged and older adult warning interaction, are manifold: the ability to create low cost experimental, interactive and quasi-real scenarios (i.e., in which hazardously simulated situations can be studied in a safely manner) with an enhanced control, as well as ecological validity over the experimental conditions. Since 'old age' embraces several age-related changes (i.e., declines in the visual, auditory and cognitive abilities) that can potentially impact interactions with warnings and technology, a number of usability criteria must be considered. This paper, although not comprehensive, provides a summary of the main theoretical framework which supports such issues. In short, these include important aspects of the VE system (i.e., interaction techniques and devices) and user (i.e., engagement, as well as health and safety concerns) characteristics. In light of our research project which proposes to highlight the use of technology-based warnings for compensating and/or assisting age-related deficits, future work will be dedicated to the definition of effective and inclusive VE criteria measures for warning interaction studies. Given the lack of such usability standards for this area of research, our project seeks to design and implement a number of VE systems, and subsequently evaluate the impact of using different interaction techniques and devices, as well as levels of engagement have on older population performances. Since such an analysis has not yet been conducted, we hope to create a body of work which will promote VEs as feasible research tools for enhancing the field of warning research and inclusive design.

Acknowledgements. A PhD scholarship (SFRH/BD/79622/2011) granted to Lara Reis, from FCT: Fundação para a Ciência e Tecnologia (the Portuguese Science Foundation), supported this study. Such a study was developed within the scope of a Research Project (PTDC/PSI-PCO/100148/2008), also financed by FCT.

References

1. DESA – Department of Economic & Social Affairs: Population Division: World Population Prospects, The 2008 Revision Executive Summary (2008), http://www.un.org/esa/population/publications/wpp2008/wpp2008_highlights.pdf
2. Mayhorn, C.B., Nichols, T.A., Rogers, W.A., Fisk, A.D.: Hazards in the Home: Using Older Adults' Perceptions to Inform Warning Design. Injury Control and Safety Promotion 11(4), 211–218 (2004)
3. Conzola, V.C., Wogalter, M.S.: A Communication-Human Information Processing (C-HIP) Approach to Warning Effectiveness in the Workplace. Journal of Risk Research 4(4), 309–322 (2001)
4. Wogalter, M.S., Mayhorn, C.B.: Providing Cognitive Support with Technology-based Warning Systems. Ergonomics 48(5), 522–533 (2005)
5. Duarte, E., Rebelo, F., Wogalter, M.S.: Virtual Reality and its Potential for Evaluating Warning Compliance. Human Factors and Ergonomics in Manufacturing & Service Industries 20(6), 526–537 (2010)

6. Cobb, S.V.G., Sharkey, P.M.: A Decade of Research and Development in Disability, Virtual Reality and Associated Technologies: Promise or Practice? In: Proceedings of the 6th International Conference on Disability, pp. 3–16. Virtual Reality and Associated Technologies, Esbjerg (2006)

7. Rogers, W.A., Rousseau, G.K., Lamson, N.: Maximizing the Effectiveness of the Warning Process: Understanding the Variables that Interact with Age. In: Park, D.C., Morrell, R.W., Shifren, K. (eds.) Processing of Medical Information in Aging Patients: Cognitive and Human Factors Perspectives, pp. 267–290. Erlbaum, Mahwah (1999)

8. Czaja, S.: The Impact of Aging on Access to Technology. ACM SIGACCESS Accessibility and Computing 83, 7–11 (2005)

9. Mayhorn, C.B., Podany, K.I.: Warnings and Aging: Describing the Receiver Characteristics of Older Adults. In: Wogalter, M.S. (ed.) Handbook of Warnings, pp. 355–361. Lawrence Erlbaum Associates, Mahwah (2006)

10. McLaughlin, A.C., Mayhorn, C.B.: Designing Effective Risk Communications for Older Adults. Safety Sci. (2012),
    `http://dx.doi.org/10.1016/j.ssci.2012.05.002`

11. Rizzo, A.A., Kim, G.J.: A SWOT Analysis of the Field of Virtual Reality Rehabilitation and Therapy. Presence 14(2), 119–146 (2005)

12. Hix, D., Gabbard, J.L.: Usability Engineering of Virtual Environments. In: Stanney, K. (ed.) Handbook of Virtual Environments: Design, Implementation and Applications, pp. 681–699. Lawrence Erlbaum Associates, Mahwah (2002)

13. Stanney, K.M., Mollaghasemi, M., Reeves, L., Breaux, R., Graeber, D.A.: Usability Engineering of Virtual Environments (VEs): Identifying Multiple Criteria that Drive Effective VE System Design. International Journal of Human-Computer Studies 58, 447–481 (2003)

14. Bowman, D.A., Johnson, D.B., Hodges, L.F.: Testbed Evaluation of Virtual Environment Interaction Techniques. Presence: Teleoperators and Virtual Environments 10(1), 75–95 (2001)

15. Wilson, J.R.: Virtual Environments Applications and Applied Ergonomics. Applied Ergonomics 30, 3–9 (1999)

16. Gabbard, J.L., Hix, D., Swan II, J.E.: User-Centered Design and Evaluation of Virtual Environments. IEEE Computer Graphics and Application 19(6), 51–59 (1999)

17. Gutiérrez, M.A., Vexo, F., Thalmann, D.: Stepping into Virtual Reality. Springer, Lausanne (2008)

18. Nichols, S., Patel, H.: Health and Safety Implications of Virtual Reality: a Review of Empirical Evidence. Applied Ergonomics 33, 251–271 (2002)

19. Cobb, S.V.G., Nichols, S., Ramsey, A., Wilson, J.R.: Virtual Reality-Induced Symptoms and Effects (VRISE). Presence: Teleoperators and Virtual Environments 8, 169–186 (1999)

20. Pacheco, C., Duarte, E., Rebelo, F., Teles, J.: Using Virtual Reality in the Design of Indoor Environments: Selection and Evaluation of Wall Colors by a Group of Elderly. In: Kaber, D.B., Boy, G. (eds.) Advances in Cognitive Ergonomics. Advances in Human Factors and Ergonomics Series, pp. 784–792. CRC Press/Taylor & Francis, Ltd., Boca Raton, Florida (2011)

21. Moffat, S.D., Zonderman, A.B., Resnick, S.M.: Age Differences in Spatial Memory in a Virtual Environment Navigation Task. Neurobiology of Aging 22, 787–796 (2001)

22. Liu, C.-L.: A Neuro-Fuzzy Warning System for Combating Cybersickness in the Elderly caused by the Virtual Environment on a TFT-LCD. Applied Ergonomics 40(3), 316-324

Merging Two Worlds Together

Alex Schieder

8/270 Campbell Parade
Bondi, Sydney NSW, 2026
Australia
schieder.alex@gmail.com

Abstract. Nowadays campaigns are not running anymore just below or above the line. To create meaningful experiences for customers we need to get them involved and connect to them in a physical and digital way. Customers need to interact with brands and create content for them, which will be spread out on different platforms. We created a campaign for the Surf Life Saving Club in Australia to connect to their customers on an out door event where customers can compete with the Surf Life Savers. The collected data/content was spread out on different digital platforms to create an ongoing interaction between the brand and their customers and to create their own branded story.

Keywords: Design, User experience, Human Interface Design, Digital Design, Out Door, Installation, Integrated Campaign, Brand story, Simplicity, Social Media, Smartphone, Tablet, Touchscreen, Case Study.

1 Introduction

The general mentality of traditional marketing doesn't work in this new world, and the best digital solutions acknowledge the reality of how people use technology as part of their everyday lives.

The more we understand the reality of this cultural shift, the better equipped we are to influence behavior, but more importantly connect on a relevant and meaningful level.

We know that devices are converging at an astounding rate. Smartphones have transformed from text based communication tools to multimedia hubs, tablets from a niche idea to transformative mass technology, and TV, games and media players from internet connection points to the gateway to new worlds of digital content.

The concept of a destination platform is quick becoming dated, with the more complex and integrated design of social media and content as fluid concepts that extend across multiple paid, owned and earned platforms. The idea of being a content contributor to the digital community, rather than a digital destination owner is more fitting with the drop-in, drop-out mentality of digital behavior.

However only focusing on digital doesn't work either. We need to connect the costumer in an online digital environment and bring them on a journey where the brand connects to them in a physical way as well. Giving costumers an opportunity to get

A. Marcus (Ed.): DUXU/HCII 2013, Part III, LNCS 8014, pp. 199–204, 2013.

face to face with the brand. Creating content or a contribution to a brand and allow them to go viral and share their stories, achievements on online platforms. This can be an outdoor installation, events etc., where the brand connects with their costumers and collects data, stories and feelings to create an ongoing movement between events and their digital platforms.

Customers become contributors and feel being part of a brand and a movement which guaranties awareness, engagement and followers in the brands future. And a physical and digital connected content approach ensures that every user's interaction with a brand will forge a closer, layered and more intimate brand connection.

Relationships are everything. In our digitally immersed world, brands need more than ever to deliver experiences that are intrinsically real. Brands need to create moments of impact, connections that are lasting and relationships that matter.

2   Surf Life Saving

In the year 2012 I've got invited to attend to a workshop in the Facebook office in Sydney. Goal of this workshop was to come up with a campaign idea and a few creative executions for a charity organization in only 6 hours. That was a very tight timeframe and we came up with a decent idea with good potential, it only needs to be well conceived. I've spent more time on the idea and worked out a full campaign.

The charity organization for which we had to come up with a campaign was the Surf Lifesaving Club in Australia, NSW.

Surf Life Saving is Australia's major water safety, drowning prevention and rescue authority. The SLS creates a safe environment on Australia's beaches and coastline through patrols, education and training, public safety campaigns and the promotion of health and fitness. They comprise key aspects of voluntary lifeguard services and competitive surf sport.

With 158,806 members and 310 affiliated surf life saving clubs, Surf Life Saving is the largest volunteer movement of its kind in Australia. Surf Life Saving is a not-for-profit movement that exists only through community donations, fundraising and corporate sponsorship. Their movement prides itself on offering friendship, education, experience and in doing so gives back to the community.

SLS Vision
To save lives, create great Australians and build better communities.

SLS Mission
To provide a safe beach and aquatic environment throughout Australia.

SLS Driving Forces
To save lives in the water.

To promote a healthy, inclusive, clean, family lifestyle.

3   The Brief

Surf Life Saving is very well known in Australia and gets a lot of acknowledgement. They have several websites, one national page and each club/state has his own website to promote and to give costumers access to their upcoming events, classes or simply to sign up to become a proud member of the SLS Australia. They are present on diverse social platforms like Facebook, Twitter and YouTube and send out monthly Newsletter to manage their customer relationship.

The Surf Life Saving club also organizes events, classes and goes into schools to improve their relationship with kids or to teach them and share information.

This sounds already really good and gives the impression Surf Life Saving has a good community and outreach. But if we look at the market potential there is still a lot to do. Australia has 22.915.906 inhabitants. SLS is well known along the coast and because they help people in cities and towns in the interior of the country they got there a lot of supporters as well. Nevertheless the Surf Life Saving Club only has 16.330 fans on Facebook and just 1.492 followers on Twitter. In comparison with the total population it's not enough.

For this reason Surf Life Saving was looking for a campaign which integrates social media. The main focus was on Facebook. They wanted to increase awareness and get more people to sign up to become a member or to just join the club. And it was important to them to turn one's attention as well on bringing more kids into the club.

The campaign also should get people to engage with the Life Savers and to get them involved with the club, and to bring the customers down to their actual workplace – the beach. Because health and fitness plays an important role for a Life Saver they want to get a movement going so that people go more outside and live a healthier life.

4   Insight

As we know, people in Australia live according the motto "Life is a beach". They spend hours on the beach relaxing and to get some sun, drinking beers on the beach with their mates and to go surfing at their beautiful coast. But as well for a lot of them the beach is a ideal place to work out and exercise to be in good shape. People do boxing on the beach or cardio sessions. Long story short Australia is a beach nation.

5   Solution

So the solution was easy. We need to create an idea which connects with Australians on the beach. It needs to be entertaining and fun. It needs to tell a story which they are willed then to share on social platforms. The costumers need to have an outcome of the campaign, that makes it worth to continuously come back to the brand so a closer relationship can grow and a interaction with the brand takes place.

6   The Idea

In my understanding a meaningful and well thought through campaign plays in different territories and uses physical and digital areas. And that's exactly what we need to achieve the Surf Live Savings goals. From the SLS perspective it won't work to engage with people and get them out and down to the beach if we only base the campaign on a digital plane or on Facebook. To interact with the customers we need to offer them an experience, which happens right at their workplace on the beach. We need to send them on a journey where the costumer enjoys a fun physical activity and are then tempt to share this activity with their family and mates in an online environment. The campaign needs to be powerful with lasting memories of the customers.

So we came up with the idea to organize an outdoor event a competition. People can go down on the beach and challenge a Life Saver in different disciplines like swimming, paddle, run-ning etc. The challenges are quite hard. It's not as easy as we would think because Surf Life Savers are very fit. They are well trained and that makes the challenge even more interesting and harder. People need to be in good shape if they want to be able to win. But as we know Australians are really competitive and love a good sporting challenge.

The whole competition will look like a smaller version of the famous "Iron Man Triathlon" and will be hold on different locations like Sydney, Brisbane, Gold Coast, Melbourne, Cairns. At the begging the focus will be only on the area New South Sales.

Kids can as well take part of the competition and compete with other kids. Their competitions won't be as hard as the adults ones.

6.1   The Campaign Name

A Life Saver in his learning stage is also called "Nipper". For Nippers, the beach is the classroom just as it will be on the race day for the competitors. The nippers of today are the future of surf lifesaving tomorrow and we want our customers to become a Nipper or a Live Saver tomorrow. So it was standing to reason for us that we need somehow to incorporate that name into the Campaign Name. The result was a wordplay for the campaign name: **"Fitter than a Nipper"**. Can you beat the Nipper?

6.2   How We Spread the Word

The competition will be sharable on Facebook, Instagram and on their landing page. To do so, we are going to set up a profile for each participant.

On the beach there will be a stand where users can log in via a tablet. That links them direct to their profile where they can find all their statistics and photos. Through out the whole competition we are going to take photos and upload them straight to Instagram, Facebook and the landing page. There will be a scoreboard to keep the competition going, so people can compare themselves with friends and can challenge them as well. It's necessary to keep the people engaged and a reason to come back to their profiles and check what's happening around them.

In this way we are using social media platforms to create awareness of the Surf Life Saver Club and that will increase their fan base. And as well customers are "learning by doing". Even if it is a fun event, people can see what it needs to become a Life Saver. The get in close contact with them and can talk to them face to face.

As well on the stands we will hand out forms, so people can sign up straight away to the club and we offer more information on screens and brochures. This gives as well time to ask questions to the Club Members.

The campaign will be promoted through TVC's on YouTube, Facebook and the Landing Page and as well banner ads on websites or ads on Facebook. Ones the costumer get's to our Facebook Page they get informed about upcoming events, where the next Competition will be and can set up their profile. Another user journey will be if people join the competition on the beach. Customers can there sign up as well and then follow the results online. And keep engaging with the brand.

The outcome of this event is, that the brand will be able to create interesting and fun content for their social platforms and share this with their people. They keep engaging with their target audience and give people a closer look into their work environment.

This will go on for years and can grow to a big national event. The campaign also should get people to engage with the Life Savers and to get them involved with the club, and to bring the customers down to their actual work-place – the beach. Because health and fitness plays an important role for a Life Saver they want to get a movement going so that people go more outside and live a healthier life.

7   Style Guide

Out going from the Surf Life Saving brand Guide Lines we added a fresh, sporty look and feel to the campaign. We changed Surf Life Saving to a sporty brand. It reflects the beach and sport culture of a "Nipper". The voice inspired to be a Surf Life Saver, to challenge people in a positive way and add fan factor to a serious service. The imagery we use in our communications is vital in portraying this emotions. The imagery sets the tone for what the campaign stands for, how people feel and how they will respond to the campaign. The imagery we shot reflects the core of a Life Saver, the core of the competition. Born of the Surf Life Saving logo we implemented the colors red, blue and yellow to the campaign and we used big bold fonts to convey the emotions of the competition.

Because we are aware of the usage of smart phones and tablets these days, and because we are using tablets on the stands to connect with the audience we made the design responsive, to provide an optimal viewing experience and easy reading on every device. All the content can be reached on all different devices, whereby we turn one's attention on smartphones and make this design very user friendly and easy to read.

8   Design Process

Inspired from big brands like Nike, Adidas, Burton, etc. we knew in which direction we have to lead. After analyzing those brands we were ready to start with a campaign Logo. A few mock-ups and after several color, font and composition analysis and trials we finally got to our Logo, which created the base for the campaign style.

The following steps were scribbles and turned than into wireframes. The final designs were still based on the final wireframes, because we planned it step by step and quite well. All the wireframes and design changes were well thought over so that it was easier for the designer and the creative still leant to the style guide we came up with earlier in the brainstorming.

The design is supported really well by the campaign idea and gave a new sporty, fresh look and fell to the brand Surf Live Saving.

Are Emergency Egress Signs Strong Enough to Overlap the Influence of the Environmental Variables?

Elisângela Vilar[1,2], Francisco Rebelo[1,2], Paulo Noriega[1,2], Luís Teixeira[1,2], Emília Duarte[2], and Ernesto Filgueiras[3]

[1] Interdisciplinary Centre for the Study of Human Performance (CIPER),
[2] Technical University of Lisbon, Ergonomics Laboratory, Estrada da Costa 1499-002, Cruz Quebrada - Dafundo, Portugal
elipessoa@gmail.com, {frebelo,pnoriega,lmteixeira}@fmh.utl.pt
[3] Unidcom, IADE – Creative University, Av. D. Carlos I, 4, 1200-649 Lisboa, Portugal
emilia.duarte@iade.pt
[4] Beira Interior University – Communication and Arts Department, Rua Marquês d'Ávila e Bolama 6200-001 Covilhã, Portugal
ernestovf@gmail.com

Abstract. This paper aims to explore the strength of environmental variables (i.e., corridor width and brightness), in directing people to indoor locations during emergency situations. The existence of contradictory information was manipulated by inserting posted signs pointing to the opposite direction to the one suggested by the environmental variables. A Virtual Reality-based methodology was used to collect participants' directional choices. Sixty-four participants had to find a specific room as quickly as possible in a virtual hotel in which they navigated through 12 corridor intersections (two-forced-choices). Two experimental conditions were considered (i.e., Signs and No-signs conditions) according to the exit signs availability. Results indicated that for the first decision point in an emergency situation with signs, 65.6% of the participants preferred to follow the wider corridor instead of the exit sign direction. Percentages of choices favoring the path opposite to that posted by the sign decreased along the escape route suggesting that with the repeated exposure to an exit sign people increased their compliance with it.

Keywords: wayfinding, route-choice, virtual reality, emergency egress, corridor width and brightness, signage.

1 Introduction

With buildings becoming increasingly larger and more complex, the needs of the occupants in terms of accessibility and safety have also significantly increased. Buildings use is now so diversified that sometimes facilities combine the functionalities of a variety of structures such as airports, hotels, shopping center areas, public transportation terminals, apartments, and offices. Additionally, emergency situations and wayfinding generally are not the main focus for developing such

A. Marcus (Ed.): DUXU/HCII 2013, Part III, LNCS 8014, pp. 205–214, 2013.
© Springer-Verlag Berlin Heidelberg 2013

facilities, and many times, such as in interventions in historical buildings, renovations and changes in buildings use, critical situations may appear. These critical situations could be related to ambiguous situations that arise with the placement of exit signs when they are posted in opposition to the paths that are the most used by the buildings' visitors. Thus, a large concentration of people, with different degrees of familiarity with the building, motivations, and anxieties, has to be able to satisfy their needs in a network of paths leading to different destinations, even when they face doubtful situations created by the incongruence between the architecture and the signage system. Wayfinding within complex buildings can become problematic under normal circumstance but can literally be life threatening during emergency situations, such as fires or terrorist attacks or natural disasters.

Thus, to study these critical situations in which signage points to a direction and people may be attracted to the opposite one by some environmental variables, such as corridor width and brightness, is an important issue to consider when investigating individual behavior during emergency situations. In this sense, with this study we seek to answer a main question: Could the environmental variables influence/disturb the effectiveness of directional signage in an emergency situation?

This current study was made as a continuation of a previous one [1], which had as objective to verify the influence of environmental variables in directing people while in an emergency situation. Results from this study shown that in T-shaped intersections, people prefer to follow by wider and brighter corridors and that brightness is a stronger factor of attraction than width in directing people's movement. In this way, corridors width and brightness can be considered environmental affordances (i.e., implicit information) that somehow inform users about which path to choose. However, according to Tang, Wu and Lin [2], this relationship between explicit (i.e., signage) and implicit (i.e., environmental affordances) directional information is not yet completely understood and should be useful to environmental designers and safety planners by informing them about people's undesired behavior.

Considering these issues, the current study aims to explore the strength of environmental variables (i.e., corridor width and brightness) in directing people during natural movement indoors in an emergency situation (i.e., a fire in a hotel building) and when in the presence of contradictory information (i.e., exit signs pointing to the opposite direction of the environmental variables). Two experimental conditions were considered according the presence/absence of exit signs (sign vs. no-signs conditions). To conduct the study, a virtual building was designed and a Virtual Reality (VR)-based methodology was used to facilitate the manipulation and control of the variables, as well as to allow the exposition of participants to a stressful emergency situation without submitting them to a real hazard. The use of VR to study behavior during emergency situations has been studied by Gamberini and colleagues [3]. These authors used VR to examine how people respond during a fire in a public library by manipulating variables such fire intensity and the initial distance to the emergency egress. Their results suggest that users seemed to recognize a dangerous situation within the context of a simulation and readily produced adaptive responses, thereby indicating that VR is a suitable venue for emergency simulations.

2   Methodology

Considering the main research question (i.e., could the environmental variables influence/disturb the effectiveness of exit signs in an emergency situation?) the main hypothesis for this study was that the environmental variables (i.e., corridors width and brightness) can influence the effectiveness of the exit signs. To test this, an experiment using VR was carried out considering the result attained in a previous study [i.e., 1].

2.1   Design of the Experiment

The influence of corridor width and brightness in directing the participants towards an intended direction was tested in two experimental conditions resulting from one factor, the signage presence (i.e., Signs and No-signs conditions). The study used a between-subjects design. The dependent variable is the percentage of choices favoring an predicted direction in twelve corridor intersections. This predicted direction is based on the results attained by Vilar and colleagues [1] considering the location of the variables, considered as attractors (Table 1).

The experimental conditions were:

- No-signs – without any emergency exit signs and in which people were directed only through the environmental variables (i.e., corridors width and brightness), considered as attractors, and;
- Signs – with emergency exit signs pointing to the exit direction, and contrary to the one with the environmental variable (attractor).

2.2   Participants

Sixty-four university students were randomly assigned to the two groups (i.e., Signs and No-signs) as follows. Each group had thirty-two participants equally distributed in to gender. For both groups, thirty participants declared themselves, through a questionnaire, to be right-handed and two declared themselves to be left-handed. For the Signs condition, participants were aged between 18 and 31 years old (mean age = 22.31 years, SD = 3.44), and for the No-Signs condition, they were aged between 18 and 35 years old (mean age = 21.88 years, SD=3.62).

All participants had normal sight or wore corrective lenses and no color vision deficiencies were detected. They also reported no physical or mental conditions that would prevent them from participating in a VR simulation.

2.3   The Scenario (Context and Virtual Environment - VE)

This experiment used a virtual hotel building as interaction environment. For the design of this virtual hotel, there were used twelve corridors intersection previously selected from Vilar and colleagues [1], which can be seen on Figure 1.

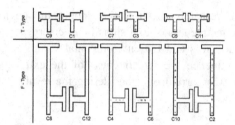

Fig. 1. The twelve "T-type" and "F-type" corridor intersections selected from the study of Vilar and colleagues [1]

Table 1. - Percentages of choice for the twelve most chosen corridor intersections from Vilar and colleagues [1] used as the basis for the design of the virtual building and signs placement.

Corridor intersection	Variable (attractor)	Direction	% of choices towards the attractor
C1	Width	Right	72.05
C2	Brightness	Front	75.83
C3	Brightness and width	Left	87.87
C4	Brightness and width	Right	89.58
C5	Brightness	Left	81.67
C6	Brightness and width	Left	91.25
C7	Brightness and width	Right	89.58
C8	Width	Right	63.75
C9	Width	Left	72.92
C10	Brightness	Front	78.33
C11	Brightness	Right	83.68
C12	Width	Left	57.50

These twelve corridors were those with the highest percentage of choices favoring one of the two alternative corridors. They represent the choice points through which all participants have to pass and to make a directional choice. The percentages of choices for each direction attained in Vilar and colleagues [1] can be seen on Table 1.

These intersections were mixed and then randomly divided into three groups of four corridors each that comprise three sections of the building floor plan. Each section was designed to have the same travel distance, regardless of participants' directional choice at each choice point. Figure 2 shows the top view of the entire VE.

The scenario was generated based on requirements operationalized during systematic meetings involving experts in Ergonomics, Architecture, Psychology, Design and Computer Engineering. Requirements were mainly related to the context, the building's design aspects, the wayfinding tasks that participants have to perform, the navigational aspects and the strategies to enhance the sense of presence and involvement.

For the present experiment, the cover story created was that the participant had to give a lecture in an important conference at a hotel and conference center, however he/she is late yet still has to talk to the receptionist to complete his/her conference registration and to know the location where the presentation will be made. When the participant reaches the second floor where the presentation is to occur, he/she is informed that a fire has been detected on the premises. Figure 3 shows the fire locations within the building.

It was used a controlled navigation strategy in which the corridors already passed by the participant were closed by doors during the wayfinding tasks accomplishment and by fire and smoke in the emergency situation. Thus, for each choice point, when participants chose one of the two alternative corridors, the corridor of the path that was not chosen was closed by a door (or fire), forcing them to continue along their initial selected path. At the beginning of each section, there was a room which was used to deliver the wayfinding task via virtual characters and to calculate the partici-pants' partial performance.

In experimental conditions where posted signs were available (i.e., Signs Condi-tion), exit signs were inserted in the second floor (i.e., emergency situation) of the virtual building. The signs were always positioned to point to the directions opposite to those that were considered the most probable choice (see Table 1) according to the results of the study conducted by Vilar and colleagues [1].

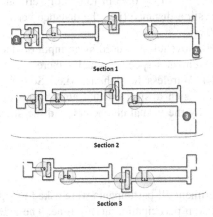

Fig. 2. Top view of the floor plan with the three sections and with the location of the 12 se-lected corridor intersections. Numbers 1, 2 and 3 show where the wayfinding instructions were delivered to the participants.

Fig. 3. Examples of fire with smoke in the second floor of the VE during the emergency situation

Exit signs are symbol-based and consistent with the International Organization for Standardization's 3864-1 [4] standard. ISO standard exit signs are required by law to illustrate an arrow and running figure in a doorway. Figure 4 shows examples of the exit signs placed in the VE.

Fig. 4. Left image shows the ISO type exit sign, and the right image shows an example of the placement of the exit signs in the second floor

2.4   Experimental Settings

The VE was projected onto a screen using a stereoscopic projector (i.e., Lightspeed DepthQ 3D) and visualized by the participants through active shutter glasses (i.e., MacNaughton Inc.'s APG6000). The projected image size was 1.72 m (59.7° of horizontal field-of-view - FOV) by 0.95 m (35.2° of vertical FOV) with an aspect ratio of 16:9. The observation distance (i.e., the distance between the observers' eyes and the screen) was 1.50 m.

A Logitech®Attack™ 3 joystick was used as an input device to collect the participants' answers. The movement's speed gradually increased from stop (0 m/s) to a maximum speed (3 m/s). Wireless headphones (i.e., Sony® MDR-RF800RK), allowed the participants to listen to instrumental ambient music, the wayfinding task instructions given orally by the virtual characters, and the sounds of a fire siren and fire.

2.5   Procedure

Before starting the experiment all participants were asked to sign a consent form and advised that they could stop participation at any time. The average duration of each experimental session was approximately 30 minutes, divided into a training session and an experimental session. Participants were told that the objective of the experiment was to evaluate new software for VR simulation, so they ought to fulfill some tasks as accurately and as quickly as possible. Participants were unaware of the real objective of the experiment.

The experiment began with the training session which had as main objectives: i) to familiarize participants with the simulation setup; ii) to allow them to practice the use of navigation and visualization devices, to bring their virtual movements closer to their realistic/natural actions; iii) to homogenize differences in the participant's performance using joystick; and iv) to make a preliminary check for symptoms of simulator sickness. Participants were encouraged to explore freely and navigate into the

VE, as quickly and efficiently as they could, without time restrictions. The researcher monitored participants' control of the navigation device by verifying their accuracy in executing some tasks, such as circumnavigating a pillar placed in the middle of a room without bumping into this element and walking through a zigzag corridor without touching the walls. Only after verifying some of these equipment-related skills did the researcher permit the participant to start the experimental session.

At the beginning of the experimental session the cover story was given to the participants: "You were invited to give a lecture in an important conference at a hotel and conference center. The conference staff told you that you must talk with the receptionists to complete your registration at the conference and to know in which room your lecture will be. As the city has a lot of traffic, you are late for your presentation. Please, complete your registration and find your lecture room as soon as possible". Participants were also told that they should behave as they would in a real-life situation. No dialogue between the participant and the researcher was allowed after the simulation started.

The interaction started in the ground floor of a hotel and convention center where participants received three wayfinding tasks (i.e., find three different locations in the building) from virtual characters present in the VE. The last task sent the participants to the second floor of the building via an elevator. Once they exited the elevator, a fire alarm sounded and they were prevented from further elevator use. Thus, participants were faced with finding an emergency egress point by navigating through the second floor in order to escape from the fire. Only the data regarding to the emergency situation, after participants reach the second floor was considered for this paper.

If the participants reached a time limit of 20 minutes inside the simulation, the experimental session was stopped to prevent eye fatigue, or simulation sickness, or both. Simulator sickness was mainly evaluated through participants' verbalizations.

At the end of the experimental test, a post task questionnaire was used to collect demographic information such as age, gender, occupation and dominant hand. Participants were also asked to answer, in seven-point scale format, questions related to their perceived hazard and overall involvement during the interaction with the simulation.

3   Results and Discussion

Results are related to the choices favoring a predicted direction influenced by corridor width and brightness in two experimental conditions: No-Sign, and Signs. Participants' route performance preferences in terms of the percentage of choice were recorded for the entire route (12 corridor intersections). Table 2 summarizes the results obtained. The results are presented according to the corridors disposition on the building's plan. The statistical significance level was set at 5%.

3.1   Environmental Variables: No-Signs Condition

Data related to the No-Signs condition shows that for eight of the twelve intersections studied, most of the participants preferred to follow the predicted direction (i.e., suggested by the environmental variables). The influence of the front corridor was more noticeable, suggesting that participants might have used wayfinding strategies such as the "Least-angle strategy" [e.g., 5, 6-8], and/or the "direction strategy" [9]. This influence can be observed for corridor intersections C4, C6 and C12 (percentages of choices favoring the predicted direction when the front corridor was an available alternative can be seen on Table 2). An unexpected result was also found for intersection C9. In this particular case, participants found the choice point after crossing a room diagonally such that turning right could represent an effect of direction strategy. The decision in this choice point might have been influenced only by a differentiation between corridor widths (right was narrower than left), and it is possible that the environmental variable in this case was not strong enough to superimpose a wayfinding strategy. Also, participants might have been aware of proximal temporal and spatial cues (e.g., the fire direction) that could have influenced their decisions.

Table 2. – Results considering the predicted directions, participants' route performance and percentages of choices favoring the predicted direction for the experimental conditions: No-Signs and Signs. Corridors were arranged according to their disposition on the building's plan.

Corridor	Variable (predicted attractor)*	Predicted Direction*	No-Signs	Signs
			% choice towards predicted direction	% choice towards predicted direction
C1	Width	Right	78.10	65.60
C2	Brightness	Front	81.30	31.20
C3	Brightness and width	Left	90.60	28.10
C4	Brightness and width	Right	31.30	6.20
C5	Brightness	Left	78.10	12.50
C6	Brightness and width	Left	43.80	15.60
C7	Brightness and width	Right	78.10	21.90
C8	Width	Right	56.30	15.60
C9	Width	Left	37.5	6.20
C10	Brightness	Front	68.80	6.20
C11	Brightness	Right	71.90	6.20
C12	Width	Left	28.10	6.20
Participants Route Performance (%)			61.98	18.49
SD			14.03	21.66

*Predicted results were attained from Vilar and colleagues [1] study.

3.2   Environmental Variables vs. Exit Signs: Signs Condition

Data from the Signs condition shows that percentages of choices favoring the predicted direction decreased along the egress route. The highest percentages were achieved in the first three intersections. It is important to note that for the first intersection (C1), 65.6 % of choices favored the predicted corridor (opposite to the way posted by the sign). To explain this trend, it is possible that people did not see the exit sign and they were attracted by the widest corridor, or they deliberately chose to follow the widest corridor ignoring the exit sign. Second and third corridor intersections (i.e., C2 and C3) also presented a considerable percentage of choices favoring the predicted direction. These results are in line with those found by Tang, Wu and Lin [2]. Data from this study do not allow us to determine the causality of the observed route selection behavior, but it is evident that the exit sign in this case was not strong enough to produce a desired safety behavior (comply with the exit sign).

3.3   Post-task Questionnaire

The post-task questionnaire involved questions related to the perceived level of hazard and overall involvement during the interaction with the simulation. Two specific questions of interest were asked: (1) "How would you rate the hazard level on the ground floor (from reception desk, where you received directions to the elevator)? (2) "How would you rate the hazard level on the second floor (when you exited the elevator until you reached the exit door)? Participants responded using a 7-point rating scale (1 – very low; 7 – very high).

When asked to classify the perceived hazard level on the ground floor (i.e., everyday situation), eleven participants classified it as Medium (N = 64, Mdn = 4, IQR = 2). However, when asked about the second floor (i.e., emergency egress), eleven classified it as very high (N = 64, Mdn = 6, IQR = 2). The Wilcoxon Matched-Pairs Signed-Ranks Test was performed and results showed statistically significant differences between the declared perceived hazard level in both floors (T = 91.50, z = -5.131, p < .001, one-tailed, N = 64). This finding allowed us to perform a manipulation check because it was confirmed that participants perceived differences between the two situations created, and that the elements (such as flame and smoke, sounds of the emergency alarm and the crackle of wood) inserted into the VE increased their hazard perception in the emergency egress situation.

4   Conclusion

The purpose of this research was to investigate the influence of environmental variables (i.e., corridor width and brightness) in disturbing the behavioral compliance with emergency egress signage when an ambiguous situation concerning wayfinding information is provided. The impact of conflicting information was assessed by creating conditions where signage was present or absent.

The main findings of this study suggest that during emergency egress, participants preferred wider and brighter corridors in a left/right decision, and the front corridor (when it was available), even when it was darker and narrower. In the presence of competing information from exit signs, decisions that favored these environmental variables decreased along the route.

When emergency exit signs are available, results indicated that for the first decision point presented to the participants (i.e., corridor C1), they preferred to follow the wider corridor instead of the direction posted on the exit sign. Percentages of choices where people followed the predicted direction decreased along the escape route suggesting that, with the repeated exposure to an exit sign people increased their compliance with it. Considering only the three first decisions, almost 42% failed the direction posted on the exit sign. A decision to follow the direction opposite of the path to the emergency egress could foreseeably make people walk greater distances and spend more time than necessary to escape from a hazardous situation and could potentially increase the likelihood of injury or death.

Given the main findings from this work, the ISO-type exit signs (static and usually found "running man" sign) for the studied conditions, presented themselves as poor in directing people to a safe place. Other types of signs should be explored. Technology-based signs could be used to increase people's perception about the exit sign even during the first exposure and in situations where conflicting information is present. Technology-based signs could be personalized and more salient than the usual exit signs, they could persuade people to avoid obstructed paths, alert them to the presence of a sign, or even personally conduct users through an egress route by calling their names thereby decreasing the loss of time during pre-movement and movement phases.

Acknowledgements. A PhD scholarship from Portuguese Science Foundation (FCT) supported this study (SFRH/BD/38927/2007), which was developed in the scope of a Research Project financed by FCT (PTDC/PSI- PCO/100148/2008).

References

1. Vilar, E., Rebelo, F., Noriega, P., Teles, J., Mayhorn, C.: The influence of environmental features on route selection in an emergency situation. Applied Ergonomics 44(4), 618–627 (2013)
2. Tang, C.-H., Wu, W.-T., Lin, C.-Y.: Using virtual reality to determine how emergency signs facilitate way-finding. Applied Ergonomics 40(4), 722–730 (2009)
3. Gamberini, L., Cottone, P., Spagnolli, A., Varotto, D., Mantovani, G.: Responding to a fire emergency in a virtual environment: different patterns of action for different situations. Ergonomics 46(8), 842–858 (2003)
4. International Organization for Standardization (ISO): Graphical Symbols - Safety Colors and Safety Signs. Part 1: Design Principles for safety Signs in Workplaces and Public Areas. ISO 3864-1. International Organization for Standardization, Geneva (2002)
5. Hochmair, H., Frank, A.U.: Influence of estimation errors on wayfinding-decisions in unknown street networks - analyzing the least-angle strategy. Spatial Cognition and Computation 2(4), 283–313 (2000)
6. Hochmair, H.H., Karlsson, V.: Investigation of Preference Between the Least-Angle Strategy and the Initial Segment Strategy for Route Selection in Unknown Environments. In: Freksa, C., Knauff, M., Krieg-Brückner, B., Nebel, B., Barkowsky, T. (eds.) Spatial Cognition IV. LNCS (LNAI), vol. 3343, pp. 79–97. Springer, Heidelberg (2005)
7. Conroy-Dalton, R.: The Secret Is To Follow Your Nose: Route path selection and angularity. Environment and Behavior 35(1), 107–131 (2003)
8. Conroy, R.: Spatial navigation in immersive virtual environments. Doctoral dissertation. University of London, London (2001)
9. Hölscher, C., Meilinger, T., Vrachliotis, G., Brösamle, M., Knauff, M.: Up the down staircase: Wayfinding strategies in multi-level buildings. Journal of Environmental Psychology 26(4), 284–299 (2006)

Calculation of Areas of Permanence in Public Spaces, According to Solar Radiation Simulated Conditions

Julie A. Waldron* and Jorge H. Salazar

PVG Arquitectos Ltda., Medellín, Colombia
{juliewaldron,jorgesalazar}@pvgarquitectos.com

Abstract. Permanence of people in public spaces is conditioned to several environmental factors, such as solar insolation. This specific factor is of particular interest in tropical countries, since it determines the comfort levels of people staying in public places for a length of time.

This paper contains the analysis of people´s *Areas of Permanence* in public spaces, taking into account solar radiation. The solar radiation data was obtained through simulations developed with a LISP routine named Torres 15.0 [1] executed in AutoCAD, which registers the number of hours that each point is affected by direct solar radiation.

Resulting solar data were transformed to data of *Areas of Permanence* by creating *Tolerance Ranges* to sun exposure. The ranges were divided into five types of areas: *Long* and *Short Permanence, Pause, Slow* and *Fast Traffic*. These areas correspond to the time that people are willing to tolerate sun in different activities.

The objective of this analysis is to collect data of environmental influence on the human body and its response, allowing the creation of principles for enhanced design.

Keywords: Public Spaces, Solar Insolation, Areas of Permanence, Tolerance Ranges.

1 Introduction

Colombia is located in the world's tropical zone. In this zone, environmental factors such as insolation and temperature remain stable during the year, due to the lack of extreme seasonal variability.

These steady conditions given by the particular geographical zone encourage the continuous use of outdoor spaces. Therefore, it is of particular interest within urban design to maximize the various functions served by the available public spaces. Consequently, it is important then to provide open air areas that can be used for leisure or for work, to exercise or simply to rest [2]. The previous should provide sound foundations on which to build adequate guidelines of urban design [3].

---

* Corresponding author.

A. Marcus (Ed.): DUXU/HCII 2013, Part III, LNCS 8014, pp. 215–223, 2013.
© Springer-Verlag Berlin Heidelberg 2013

Within this context, the use of public spaces is highly conditioned by the availability of solar radiation. The time of permanence of a person in a specific part of the public space, *i.e. a bench*, is directly related to the amount of solar radiation falling on that bench. As a result, the furniture and areas designed for *Long Permanence* in the public spaces should provide certain amount of sheltering from direct solar radiation, in order to guarantee activities to remain in those spaces.

Nowadays, solar radiation simulation is available from different software routines. These programmes allow the identification of the impact of solar radiation over surfaces, calculating the solar exposure in a determined period of time [4]. In this research, data from Torres 15.0 LISP routine was used in order to classify and analyse the results [1].

The solar phenomenon is an important area of research: the sun is part of the influential environmental factors that modify the behavior of people under different activities [5]. The software tools used in this research, allowed the development of accurate calculations based on solar exposure, making it possible to convert Solar Radiation Areas into *Areas of Permanence* of people in certain spaces, taking into account the *Tolerance Ranges*. This paper presents the analysis of such results, classifying and evaluating the data obtained from insolation values, in order to predict the areas of public spaces where people will be more likely to stay for different periods of time.

2   Methodology

2.1   Insolation Simulation

The impact of solar radiation upon the built environment can be accurately predicted through simulation software. These results are mainly used to provide guidance on how to improve energy consumption and reduce carbon emissions [4].

Torres 15.0 is a LISP routine executed in AutoCAD® [6], this software tool simulates the average hours of direct solar radiation exposure of a certain point in a given period of time, within a 3D building model [1].

The routine is designed to register the solar impact in a grid of dots spread over the evaluated zone. Each dot changes its position in the Z axis, every time it receives direct solar radiation. Figure 1 shows a theoretical example of the evaluation process performed in Torres 15.0 to obtain solar radiation results.

This simulation was developed with the Latitude of Bogota - Colombia 4.35N. It was configured to evaluate a solar year and to collect data every 15 days, every half hour, from 7:00 h to 17:00 h.

The image above (Fig. 1) shows an evaluation of solar radiation over a building and its surroundings where are located various trees. The grid observed in the model corresponds to several dots with a numeric value that represents the amount of solar exposure received in the simulation.

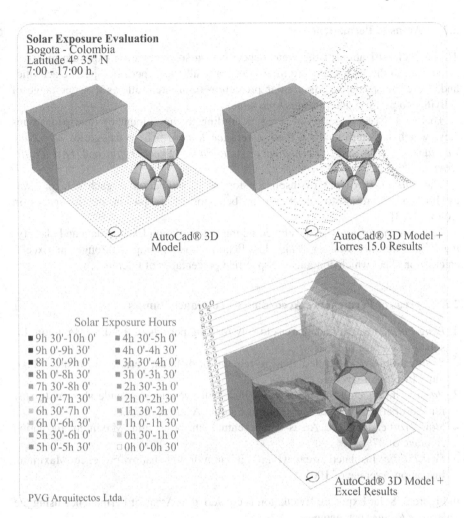

Fig. 1. Solar Exposure Evaluation applied to a theoretical case of a building and a group of trees located in Bogota – Colombia. The upper images indicate the process in 3D modeling and the bottom image contains the mapped results. The colour scale indicates the average of solar exposure hours, where the red areas are the maximum insolation and grey colours contain the areas with the minimum exposure.

After the simulation has finished, the resulting data was processed through an Excel® [7] Sheet, to reassign the interpretation of the values, which will no longer indicate solar exposure but permanence of people in the space, mapping it into a graph and assigning different colours for the resulting areas. The bottom image in Figure 1 contains an overlapped view of the Excel® results and the 3D model. The different colours represent the average of solar exposure received, red being the maximum exposure to solar radiation and grey being the least: 10 hours and 1 hour a day per year respectively.

2.2   Areas of Permanence

This is a classification of the areas depending on solar radiation exposure received. According to the solar exposure time, every area allows to perform specific activities and, therefore, postures. More solar protection in an area, allows a wider range of activities to perform and postures to assume.

There are five categories of areas, according to the amount of time pedestrians stay, which is determined by their *Tolerance Ranges.* These categories are: *Long Permanence Area, Short Permanence Area, Pause, Slow Traffic* and *Fast Traffic Area.*

The *Tolerance Ranges* of insolation for the classification in each category was established according to observational behavior of people in public spaces in Colombia [3].

The data conversion was developed taking the insolation Excel® data and classifying it in *Tolerance Ranges.* This classification was developed through an Excel® calculation sheet which contains the specified percentages of tolerance.

2.3   Areas of Permanence According to Tolerance Ranges

1. *Long Permanence:* Shaded areas to stay for long periods of the day. Maximum Insolation Average of 25%.
2. *Short Permanence:* Shaded areas to remain for different periods of the day. Maximum Insolation Average of 50%.
3. *Pause:* Unprotected Shaded Areas which will eventually provide shadow to stay for short periods of time. Maximum Insolation Average of 75%.
4. *Slow Traffic:* Insolated Areas with eventual sun protection. Maximum Insolation Average of 87%.
5. *Fast Traffic:* Insolated Areas with a minimum or null shadow presence. Maximum Insolation Average of 100%.

In Figure 2, Solar Exposure Evaluation is converted to Areas of Permanence using the *Tolerance Ranges* percentages.

2.4   Body Postures and Activities

The categories mentioned above were defined to predict human behaviour and postures according to solar availability in the *Areas of Permanence.*

Taking into account solar radiation data and *Tolerance Ranges,* a list of Body Postures was built classifying them by their movement or stillness. The postures are conditioned by the activities, furniture and environmental conditions, because of: physiological necessities, objects/space options and comfort perception in terms of temperature.

Figure 3 describes the standard positions of the body from movement to stillness. These positions are categorised according to the *Tolerance Ranges* and the demand of sun protection, to determine which postures are more likely to be used in every zone.

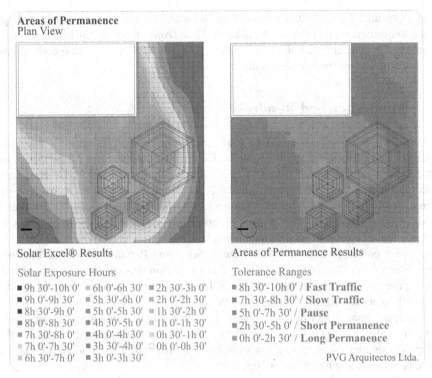

Fig. 2. Areas *of Permanence*. The left image corresponds to the insolation evaluation from plan view; the colour scale indicates the average of solar exposure during the year. The right figure corresponds to the insolation data converted to *Areas of Permanence*; the colour scale indicates the *Tolerance Rages*.

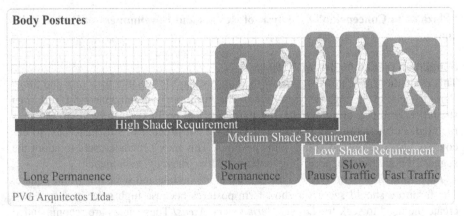

Fig. 3. Standard Postures adopted in public spaces with colours in accordance to the *Tolerance Ranges*. From the left to the right side of the figure, the postures are: Lay, Sitting, Lotus, Sitting Standard, Ischiatic Support, Standing Standard, Walking and Jogging. The mentioned body positions are a simplified group of postures which includes suspended positions and movement positions.

The postures *Lay Position* to *Standing Standard Positions* corresponds to High Shade Requirement area, *Sitting Standard* to *Slow Traffic Positions* as Medium Shade Requirement area and *Standing Standard* to *Jogging Postures* corresponds to the minimum or null sun protection requirement area.

3   Application and Results

The method described was used to evaluate "Plaza de la Concepción", the main square of the Historical City of Mompox, Colombia. Mompox is a Municipality located in Bolívar, Colombia, with 31°C average temperature [8] and 9° 14´ N of Latitude. The purpose of PVG Arquitectos was to assess the design to recover of the square, performed in 2012 by the Architecture Office OPUS Oficina de Proyectos Urbanos from Colombia. The project proposal integrated the analysis of Areas of Permanence according to solar radiation availability.

Figure 4 corresponds to the plan view of Solar and Permanence results obtained from "Plaza de la Concepción" analysis. The simulation was executed in two periods to compare early morning with midday results. The selected periods were: from 6:00 hrs to 10:00 hrs and from 10:00 hrs to 14:00 hrs.

The upper images of Figure 4 contain the sun exposure evaluation. It can be observed that the areas near buildings and vegetation are always protected against solar radiation, contrary to what happens with the areas located at the middle, that is, far from the surrounding buildings or vegetation.

At the bottom of Figure 4, there is an analysis of *Areas of Permanence*, performed with insolation exposure results. The shades resulting from the evaluation showed a possible path to connect the buildings that may be extended by artificial means. This strategy will also promote remaining activities in this area.

"Plaza de la Concepción" / Analysis of Results and Development of Design Principles.

Simulation from 6:00 hrs. *to 10:00 hrs*.
This evaluation indicates that almost the entire square is suitable for *Long* and *Short Permanence*, excluding the west zone. The furniture recommended for this area should serve for meeting and staying purposes, and be flexible to be re-arranged as required. Furthermore, floor surfaces should be constructed in soft materials, to encourage lay position and sitting lotus postures. This may persuade users to adopt the suggested body posture, according to the respective *Area of Permanence*.

Pause and *Slow Traffic Areas* are located at the middle and west side of the square. The furniture should serve for short term postures because high solar exposure will create the need to seek for *Longer Permanence Areas*. These areas are recommended for transitory activities, such as waiting for somebody. On the other hand, the furniture should have low thermal conductivity in order to prevent high temperature gained by the surfaces, which will be exposed to direct solar radiation.

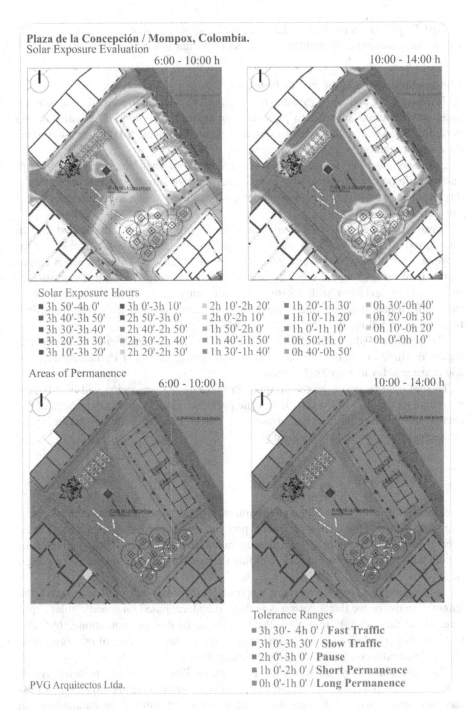

Plaza de la Concepción / Mompox, Colombia.
Solar Exposure Evaluation

6:00 - 10:00 h   10:00 - 14:00 h

Solar Exposure Hours
- 3h 50'-4h 0'   ■ 3h 0'-3h 10'   ■ 2h 10'-2h 20'   ■ 1h 20'-1h 30'   ■ 0h 30'-0h 40'
- 3h 40'-3h 50'   ■ 2h 50'-3h 0'   ■ 2h 0'-2h 10'   ■ 1h 10'-1h 20'   ■ 0h 20'-0h 30'
- 3h 30'-3h 40'   ■ 2h 40'-2h 50'   ■ 1h 50'-2h 0'   ■ 1h 0'-1h 10'   ■ 0h 10'-0h 20'
- 3h 20'-3h 30'   ■ 2h 30'-2h 40'   ■ 1h 40'-1h 50'   ■ 0h 50'-1h 0'   ■ 0h 0'-0h 10'
- 3h 10'-3h 20'   ■ 2h 20'-2h 30'   ■ 1h 30'-1h 40'   ■ 0h 40'-0h 50'

Areas of Permanence

6:00 - 10:00 h   10:00 - 14:00 h

Tolerance Ranges
- 3h 30'- 4h 0' / **Fast Traffic**
- 3h 0'-3h 30' / **Slow Traffic**
- 2h 0'-3h 0' / **Pause**
- 1h 0'-2h 0' / **Short Permanence**
- 0h 0'-1h 0' / **Long Permanence**

PVG Arquitectos Ltda.

Fig. 4. Solar Exposure and *Areas of Permanence* Evaluation applied to "Plaza de la Concepción" Mompox – Colombia

Fast Traffic Areas are located far from the facades. The size of this area shrinks in the morning and grows at midday, increasing or decreasing the remaining areas.

Midday Simulation 10:00 hrs. *to 14:00 hrs.*
At Midday, *Long* and *Short Permanence Areas* were reduced to a small zone near the buildings and trees. In order to promote long permanence outdoor activities in this period of the day, it is necessary to provide shading devices or tall vegetation to reduce solar radiation exposure.

Long and *Short Permanence Areas* were reduced to a small zone near the buildings and trees. In order to promote long permanence outdoor activities in this period of the day, it is necessary to provide shading devices or tall vegetation to reduce solar radiation exposure.

However, according to the simulation, *Fast Traffic* category is the largest area in this period of the day, which means that at midday the place is suitable for in-movement activities. In this circumstances, the materials used for the urban equipment, should meet specific qualities of colour and finishing. For instance, traffic activities require surfaces with friction and uniformity in order to avoid slipping or stumbling of pedestrians. It is also necessary to prevent the glare caused by the reflection of the sun falling on bright or glossy surfaces.

The benches used as urban furniture belong to different permanence areas depending on the time of the day: in the mornings to *Pause* and *Short Permanence Areas*, and in the midday to *Fast Traffic Area*.

To sum up, the use of the public space in Plaza de la Concepcion will be different according to the hour of the day. Under the previous considerations, the design of the square and its furniture should consider a schedule of uses of the public space throughout the year, and across the day.

4   Conclusions

Technical evaluation tools of the environment, such as solar radiation software simulators can enhance the design of spaces, particularly if appropriate analysis is developed by converting environmental data to human behavior data. This prediction of human behavior is a powerful tool to define the possible uses of spaces at the design stage of the project.

Defining the *Tolerance Ranges* is important, since they are used to measure the length of permanence that a person is willing to endure, based on specific solar exposure. These ranges apply to a particular location since they are conditioned by: relative humidity, rainfall, sunshine hours, physiological characteristics of user (age, gender, origin, health conditions, clothing, amongst other).

There are unexplored paths regarding *Tolerance Ranges* as a tool to define *Areas of Permanence* in a space, which must be objects of further investigations. It is necessary to define *Tolerance Ranges* according to solar exposure of the human body in different environmental conditions.

The main aim of this research has been to acknowledge the sun as a significant factor in the design process of outdoor spaces, moreover if it takes into account the human factors.

Acknowledgements. PVG Arquitectos Ltda. is the organization responsible of promoting and supporting these field of research. MSc. Arch. Ader Augusto García and MSc. Arch. Alexander Gonzalez guided the process of construction of these theories. Arch. Juliana Sanchez developed the graphical products of this paper and supported the total production from her experience.
Dr. Juan Jose Salazar and MSc. Eng. Diana C. Waldron were the patient and active reviewers of this production.

References

1. Salazar Trujillo, J.H.: Sombra con elementos verticales. Diseño de las Agrupaciones de las torres de luz en la Plaza de Cisneros. Medellín, Colombia. In: Construido IENeVLAdCNA (ed.) Sombra con elementos verticales Diseño de las Agrupaciones de las torres de luz en la Plaza de Cisneros Medellín, Colombiaed, Ouro Preto, Brasil, p. 10 (2007)
2. Francis, J., Wood, L.J., Knuiman, M., Giles-Corti, B.: Quality or quantity? Exploring the relationship between Public Open Space attributes and mental health in Perth. Western Australia. Social Science & Medicine 74, 8 (2012)
3. Salazar Trujillo, J.H.: Uso y apropiación de los espacios públicos, p. 107. Universidad Nacional de Colombia, Sede Medellín, Medellín, Colombia (2010)
4. Haese, G.: Analysis of the influences of solar radiation and facade glazing areas on the thermal performance of multi-family buildings. Building and Environmental Engineeringed, p. 170. Technical University of Bialystok, Bielastok (2010)
5. Metje, N., Sterling, M., Baker, C.J.: Pedestrian comfort using clothing values and body temperatures. Journal of Wind Engineering and Industrial Aerodynamics 96, 24 (2008)
6. Autodesk. AutoCAD. AutoCAD 2011 (2011)
7. Microsoft. Microsoft Excel (2010)
8. Comunicaciones MdTdlIyl. Santa Cruz de Mompós (2012)

Part II

Designing for Smart and Ambient Devices

Design Methodology for Body Tracking Based Applications - A Kinect Case Study

Felipe Breyer, Bernardo Reis, Luis Arthur Vasconcelos, Aline Cavalcanti,
João Marcelo Teixeira, and Judith Kelner

Virtual Reality and Multimedia Research Group, Computer Science Center,
Federal University of Pernambuco, Recife, Pernambuco, Brazil
{fbb3,bfrs,lalv,asc3,jmxnt,jk}@cin.ufpe.br

Abstract. Along with the popularization of new body tracking technologies such as Microsoft Kinect, and the increasing individual initiatives in order to design solutions for such platforms, it is necessary to improve and to adapt all the framework of methods and processes for developing new applications for this context. Just like that, this paper proposes a direction towards the formalization of an agile methodology for developing new applications on the background of body interaction, suitable for modest innovation projects with short schedules and small teams. To achieve that, we executed an experiment during a graduate course in Informatics, due to its similarities to the start-up context. The participating students followed a four-step methodology comprehending the stages of requirements identification, ideas generation, prototyping, and evaluation. The experiment outcomes are described in a way to enlighten the methodology techniques. As a conclusion, the students provided an extremely positive feedback regarding the adoption of the proposed methodology during the development of body interaction applications.

Keywords: Design methodology, body tracking, interaction applications.

1 Introduction

When it comes to small innovation projects, a quick development process suitable for each project's needs is essential in order to increase the odds of success. In such circumstances, it is common to have small development teams supported by one main idea and with short initial knowledge due to the use of recent technologies. Since these initiatives present high levels of uncertainty, a business model based on short development cycles and regular deliveries is desirable, once it is easier for the stakeholders to keep track. Summarizing, apart from the scarce human-resources and short schedule issues, innovation projects are also highly susceptible to severe budget limitations [12].

Regarding the interaction design context, these small initiatives generally make use of innovative platforms such as the Microsoft Kinect body tracking system in order to develop new applications. In addition to the great number of built-in features and

A. Marcus (Ed.): DUXU/HCII 2013, Part III, LNCS 8014, pp. 227–236, 2013.

sensors, this technology might be considered the first low-cost body tracking system, which provided designers and developers the opportunity to create a multitude of body interaction applications.

Distinct interaction approaches demand different functioning that must be considered when developing for this background. Errors in gesture recognition are highly likely to lead to frustration, requiring more robust solutions, and for reaching a high quality system, extensive testing is mandatory. On the other hand, prolonged usage of body tracking applications can overwhelm the tester, especially for the development team, causing too many interruptions during the implementation stage. These nuances bring new challenges in the development process, which are not equally found when developing for other devices.

In such way, this paper suggests an agile methodology for developing new applications in the context of body interaction, which is suitable for small innovation projects with short schedules and low budget. Accordingly, a methodological model for this reality should not hold back on documentation activities, but to aim at building functional disposable prototypes iteratively. It helps to keep regular productivity and the team members focused on validating the application concept.

2   Related Work

It is noticeable that a large majority of research about non-conventional body interaction applications are focused on developing software and describing the experiment for its validation. For instance, [9] presents important directions in order to formalize a methodology for the development and evaluation of interactive television applications (iTV), although his work did not formalize any recommendation yet.

In [14] is presented a solution to deal with the drawbacks of computer-mediated communication when compared to aspects of face-to-face communication like gestures and expressions. However, it is not one of its objectives to propose any design methodology or guidelines for developing similar applications.

Finally, [4] designed the MOWGLI system, in which the user interacts remotely and multimodally with large screen applications in real time. An ad hoc interface development methodology is presented and properly detailed, which, however, does not afford flexibility and does not focus on applications' development.

In such way, even though the interaction design field has in its theoretical body enough relevant studies towards the improvement of user interaction through movement and gesture, still few are the researches that propose general guidelines for the development of applications for this background. More critically, there is a lack of methodological uniformity that could direct the design of new body interaction systems.

Therefore, it is important to perform researches that aim to identify models in order to guide and facilitate other individual initiatives of development of new interfaces and applications for this field.

3   The Development Context

As it was commented previously, the start-up perspective presents some characteristics that demand many adjustments regarding its development process. Hence, a methodology suitable for this reality should emphasize agility along the procedure, especially in regard of testing activities.

At the same time, even though Microsoft Kinect may be considered a device of easy acquisition, small teams with limited resources may find restrictive the need of purchasing several Kinects for programming tasks. Aiming to keep up with rapid prototyping cycles means to abstract the Kinect presence so programing and testing tasks must be fast.

Projects for Kinect may have both serious or entertainment characteristics, thus the proposed methodology should be flexible enough to guide the development for either situation. Due to the early prototypes' stage, methods to be incorporated in such a framework should let final users free to criticize the system as well as to allow rapid compilation of testing results.

Once the scenario described above is understood, it was possible to establish similarities with another context: classes in the academy, for both situations imply learning, preparing and presenting results in a short period. Considering this time issue, it was established that the final working prototype should be developed within a four-month deadline, which is the common period of a course during a student's graduation. The methodology was executed in a Computer Science course throughout the beginning of its professional cycle, in a way that all the students had already finished the basic theoretical cycle, at the same time that they did not have enough practical experience.

4   The Proposed Methodology

The proposed methodology in this work is inspired in the lifecycle model for interaction design presented by [11], which comprehends four iterative main stages: identify needs and establish requirements, design or redesign, build an interactive version, and evaluate it. For each stage a specific method was chosen as discussed and presented next.

4.1   Competitor Analysis

Among several possible methods for exploring the problem, the analysis of similar products or competitors presents multiple benefits: it has easy execution once it can be performed using the internet; it simultaneously provides the description of how existing products compete among themselves as well as how they would compete with the one under development; it identifies and evaluate innovation opportunities, and also establishes goals for the new product in order to improve its competitiveness. Once enough data about products were collected, a parametric analysis should be structured in order to organize the information. This analysis aims to compare the product under development with existing ones, based on relevant parameters for the project. These parameters can be categorized as quantitative, qualitative or for classification [2].

The positive aspects of using the competitor analysis guaranteed the choice of this the technique for execution in the initial step of the proposed methodology. This procedure, more than selecting products, detail their characteristics through a parametric analysis, and it should result on a summary containing all requisites and guidelines for designing the new product based on its similar.

4.2   Lessons Learned and Brainstorm

To understand design as a process of generating solutions means comprehending the synthesis stage as the core of it. In spite of some methodological models presented in the literature do not specify techniques for generating alternatives or reference it in the framework, every model has a mandatory stage of creation. Commonly, if tools are specified for this step, the brainstorm technique is very likely to be mentioned.

The brainstorm procedure is straightforward: team members suggest ideas spontaneously as they come to their minds, as inconsistent and random as they like to be. The ideas are said out loud while someone writes them down on a flipchart or board. The technique's objective is to produce the bigger load of possible ideas, whereas quality is not the focus at this stage [6].

Although it has its mechanics well defined, the brainstorm can take different executions according to the stages that precede it. The amount of previous information about the problem – or even the lack of it – may severely influence the idea generation in many ways. It may cause ideas to be either properly feasible or entirely unreal, for instance.

For the proposed methodology, the brainstorm was executed right after the problem exploration step. This way, it had as inspiration source the document of lessons learned conceived at the end of the competitor analysis, which was also useful to define constraints. Generation of ideas happened in groups with related stimuli and forced association, according to the classification proposed by [13].

The selection of the alternatives created, however, was later performed as an independent process of simple voting and involved all groups.

4.3   Design of Prototypes with the Kina Toolkit

The authors in [5] defend the use of prototypes for various purposes, such as for identifying inconsistencies on project requisites or clarifying the evaluation of critical and complex parts of the system. In order to guarantee coherence among its functions, an application must be frequently tested along the entire programming stage.

Due to the complexity of the data produced by all the Kinect sensors – color image, depth map, skeleton pose and sound stream – deterministic tests are almost unfeasible, considering that for each testing cycle the programmer should provide the same input into the system. While programmers could be able to do so, it would quickly become an exhausting activity. Finally, the Kinect SDK still requires its hardware to be continually connected to the computer in order to execute the system while programming, and as it was commented previously, the need of several devices for programming is likely to discourage the investment in such technology by a small design team.

From the analysis of the issues discussed above as regards the development of body tracking applications, it was proposed the Kina toolkit with the objective of aiding and improving the creation of this kind of software. The Kina Toolkit is a group of tools that enhance the development process of applications that use the Microsoft Kinect SDK and makes the development not fully conditional to the existence of a sensor. Moreover, by providing playback capabilities together with an online movement database, it reduces the physical effort found while performing testing activities [10].

4.4   Questionnaire for Evaluation

Among several usability evaluation methods, [8] considers the questionnaires as indirect methods because they do not precisely evaluate the interface, but rather the users' opinion about it. Therefore, questionnaires are usually handled as post-evaluation methods in shape of quantitative forms presented to users once they have already interacted with the system. [15] point out as a positive aspect of this method the convenience of collecting data from users quickly as well as the fast tabulation and extraction of statistical information. It is common to make use of scales when preparing questionnaires, like a semantic differential scale or Likert. The latter was chosen for providing an easier way to formulate sentences to inspect specific issues, while semantic differential scales usually require more effort in order to employ the right terms for a very specific context.

The proposed questionnaire presented alternate positive and negative questions as suggested by [3]. According to the author, it demands more attention of the respondents and avoids a possible biased behavior. The final version of the questionnaire presented fourteen statements in order to evaluate user experience aspects. They were:

- I quickly understood what to do to interact with the system;
- I repeated the same movement several times consecutively;
- Movements are easy to be performed;
- It took me a while to perform the right movements in order to achieve a true interaction;
- The system recognized my movements properly;
- I felt tired after using the system;
- The proposed interaction with the system seemed more suitable than using traditional devices;
- I was too concerned about hitting close objects while using the system;
- the feedback for my movements were clear and quite satisfying;
- The feedback for my movements were delayed;
- I unintentionally activated features;
- I would feel uncomfortable to interact with the system in public;

- The interaction is compatible with the real world task, and
- It was not satisfying to use the system with interaction based on movements.

These statements comprehend, among other characteristics, user satisfaction, usability aspects and intuitiveness, as well as the learning curve. Users' physical welfare is also a constant concern when designing gesture-based applications, so it was analyzed fatigue and repetitive strain. Some other statements refer to the user's environment, regarding both spatial and social aspects. Another distinguished characteristic analyzed is the system robustness to gesture recognition, in order to avoid false positives and false negatives, since both situations are extremely likely to lead to frustration. These statements also respect some guidelines present in [7] published by Microsoft.

5   Methodology Results

5.1   Competitor Analysis

As commented previously, the first stage of the procedure was to perform a competitors' analysis, which was executed with an online collaborative tool. This way, students could insert the results of their investigation and observe contributions from other groups at the same time. This feature avoided equal data from different groups, guaranteeing a greater variety of analyzed applications. For each application, the following metadata were applied:

- title: it identifies the application among the others and allows fast searching;
- short description: application purpose, nature (entertainment, education, etc.), components and distinguishing features;
- positive and negative aspects: detailed review (the most relevant information is here), and
- images, videos and web links: all additional information.

A total of twenty applications were listed, among commercial, academic, and for productive or entertainment purposes. A brief example of entries of the final catalog is shown next. Only textual content is presented here due to page limitations.

Title: NAVI – Navigational Aids for the Visually Impaired – A student project in the course Blended Interaction [16].
Description: NAVI is a project developed by students with the objective of improving the navigation of visually impaired people. It makes use of a Kinect, a vibrotactile belt and ARToolKit makers.
Positive aspects: the NAVI system brings together on the same project powerful Kinect features, combined with the augmented reality provided by the ARToolKit. It gives tactile feedback by vibrating on users' waist, which supports orientation tasks when walking on a wide and populated environment.

> Negative aspects: high cost in order to buy the entire system. The need to carry a wooden box attached to a backpack with a notebook, as well as the implications of wearing a Kinect on the user's head, may be considered bad ergonomic aspects.

5.2   Lessons Learned and Brainstorm

The second step started with a session of lessons learned, in which the participants presented their observation based on the previously acquired experiences from the competitor analysis technique. All students should compose a brief list of concepts in order to be employed as a related stimulus for a later stage, in which creative techniques could take place. This list also leveled everyone's knowledge about the main issues on developing body tracking interaction systems. At the end of it, the list of lessons learned was composed by nine topics as following:

- a multi-user system is more likely to be more entertaining;
- a system may undergo some delay depending on its complexity;
- the extended use of gestures inevitably tires players;
- the system must provide constant feedback to its users;
- to perform the same movements is boring; movements must constantly change;
- an application must have easy tasks;
- gesture-based applications demand considerable floor space;
- Kinect-like systems have a restricted tracking area; lateral movements should be avoided, and
- speech recognition features are generally underutilized by the analyzed applications.

Given that this research was performed along with Computer Science graduate students, it is necessary to emphasize that while the topics of the lessons learned list may seem obvious to an expert at a first sight, the formalization and sedimentation of the knowledge are fundamental for the creative process [1].

After finished the session of lessons learned, the students were asked to form groups and to start the creative process. This way, the class was divided into three groups (two with three members and one with four members), but all of them took part of the brainstorm session and cooperated among groups in order to define three scopes for all teams. As a result for this step, three main concepts were conceived and should be developed as described in the next session.

5.3   Prototyping with the Kina Toolkit

The BugClapper (Figure 1A) is a game in which the players must kill flying mosquitos by clapping their hands to achieve higher scores. Each match has a predetermined duration, although it can be extended by killing lots of mosquitos. The Kinect is used to capture users' movement and keep track of their hands, mapped into the virtual world as two white gloves. Power-ups were used as means to diversify the interaction movements, like the power of an insecticide, which requires the user to pretend to be holding a spray can.

The Functional Training project consists of a system capable of supporting users in functional training tasks (Figure 1B). This activity, first applied in rehabilitation, is based on performing fundamental movements and staying in specific positions for a given period in order to improve one's physical conditioning. The posture they should keep was classified according to three difficulty levels. Each level demand different physical preparation considering: balance, strength, flexibility, resistance, motor coordination and speed. The Kinect identifies if a posture is correct or not and informs the player. The system also has a general performance evaluation system that rates users from zero to ten according to the time spent on right positions.

The Paint.iNEct (Figure 1C) is a digital painting system that presents as a main characteristic the fact that users can paint with their body and use any part of it as a brush. It features the possibility of painting several different patterns on the screen, as well as an eraser and color pick tools. Another option given was to choose the distance to the painting screen. To do so, users should perform specific gestures that could not be misunderstood by the tracking system, avoiding possible false positives.

Fig. 1. BugClapper (A), Functional Training (B) Paint.iNEct (C)

5.4   Questionnaire for Evaluation

The three groups evaluated their applications with twenty subjects each. The prepared questionnaire was used in this phase, in which each subject should place his/her level of agreement according to each statement on a five-point Likert scale. Since it was known the applications had distinct purposes, it was defined an expectation control regarding the possible answers. For example, one of the final solutions was supposed to aid users while they executed physical exercises, thus if inquired about "feeling tired after using the system", to strongly agree with that would be considered a positive feedback. On the other hand, as for the Paint.iNEct application, which was designed for productive purposes, the expected answer to the same topic should be the opposite, which means that feeling too tired is obviously bad.

In order to analyze the questionnaires' information, it was taken the mean of each statement and this value was compared to the previously defined expectations for each group, as it can be observed in Figure 2. The evaluation can be observed by comparing both curves: the expected one, as an optimal outcome, and the real result, presented by the mean curve.

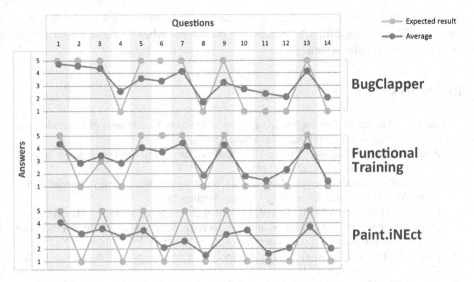

Fig. 2. Evaluation results for each application

6   Conclusions and Future Work

Even though more case studies are needed to validate this methodology, it presented a very satisfactory level of adequacy considering the proposed scenario. According to the participant students, the competitor analysis had a key role in order to formalize their knowledge and to specify the scope for body tracking systems as a possibility for interaction. Likewise, the concatenated session of lessons learned and brainstorm received excellent feedback.

The ease-of-use and convenience provided by the Kina Toolkit during the prototyping steps and functional tests was emphasized as a positive aspect, especially regarding the gain in time in programming tasks and the effort reduction when performing tests. Another advantage was mentioned, which is the possibility of easy interchanging for the execution of the prototype either in the Kinect or connected to a computer.

The questionnaire for evaluation has also shown itself very appropriate to this experiment due to the fast data tabulation and interpretation. Moreover, it rapidly suggested what to improve on each prototype precisely.

Overall, all students agreed that the adoption of a collaborative and structured design process during the development of body interaction applications with short schedule was imperative as a way of building their body of knowledge. Finally, the solution each group conceived achieved its objective of validating the application concepts that were initially proposed.

Future works indicate the need of more iterations aiming to verify the outcomes of using this methodology in more complex and longer projects. Considering the developed applications, a few flaws must be solved regarding its use. The BugClapper game presented some issues affecting the action recognition when users clap their hands, while for Paint.iNEct, users reported difficulties when trying to find a proper distance from the paint screen.

References

1. Adair, J.: The Art of Creative Thinking - How to Develop Your Powers of Innovation and Creativity. Kogan Page Limited, Philadelphia (2007)
2. Baxter, M.: Product Design: Practical Methods for the Systematic Development of New Products. CRC Press, Cheltenham (1995)
3. Brace, I.: Questionnaire Design - How to Plan, Structure and Write Survey Material for Effective Market Research. Kogan Page Limited, Sterling (2004)
4. Carbini, S., Delphin-Poulat, L., Perron, L., Viallet, J.E.: From a Wizard of Oz experiment to a real time speech and gesture multimodal interface. Special issue of Signal Processing on Multimodal Human-Computer Interfaces, vol. 86, pp. 3559–3577. Elsevier (2012)
5. Dustin, E.: Effective Software Testing: 50 Specific Ways to Improve Your Testing. Addison-Wesley, Boston (2003)
6. Jay, R.: The Ultimate Book of Business Creativity: 50 Great Thinking Tools for Transforming Your Business. Capstone Publishing Limited, Mankato (2000)
7. Microsoft Corporation. Human Interface Guidelines - Kinect for Windows v1.5.0 (2012), Disponível em: http://go.microsoft.com/fwlink/?LinkID=247735 (acessado em: June 2012)
8. Nielsen, J.: Usability Engeneering. Academic Press, Cambridge (1993)
9. Pirker, M.: Enhancing and Evaluating the User Experience of Interactive TV Systems and their Interaction Techniques. In: EuroITV 2011 – Adjunct Proceedings, pp. 43–46. ACM Press (2011)
10. Reis, B., Teixeira, J.M.X.N., Breyer, F.B., Vasconcelos, L.A.L., Cavalcanti, A., Ferreira, A., Kelner, J.: Increasing Kinect Application Development Productivity by an Enhanced Hardware Abstraction. In: Proceedings of Engineering Interactive Computing Systems, Copenhagen (2012)
11. Sharp, H., Rogers, Y., Preece, J.: Interaction Design. John Wiley & Sons, West Sussex (2007)
12. Sorli, M., Stokic, D.: Innovating in Product/Process Development - Gaining Pace in New Product Development. Springer, New York (2009)
13. VanGundy, A.B.: Getting to innovation: how asking the right questions generates the great ideas your company needs. AMACOM, New York (2007)
14. Walkowski, S., Dörner, R., Lievonen, M., Rosenberg, D.: Using a game controller for relaying deictic gestures in computer-mediated communication. International Journal of Human-Computer Studies 69(6), 362–374 (2011)
15. Zazelenchuk, T., Singer, C., Gonzales, A.: User Centered Design Methods (2002), Disponível em: http://www.indiana.edu/~usable/presentations/ucd_methods.pdf (acessado em: Abr 2012)
16. Zöllner, M., Huber, S.: NAVI – Navigational Aids for the Visually Impaired – A student project in the course Blended Interaction (2011), Disponível em: http://hci.uni-konstanz.de/blog/2011/03/15/navi/ (acessado em: Abr 2012)

Empowering Electronic Divas through Beauty Technology

Katia Fabiola Canepa Vega and Hugo Fuks

Department of Informatics, PUC-Rio
{kvega,hugo}@inf.puc-rio.br

Abstract. The evolution of Wearable Computers is making it possible for wearers to move and interact freely with the world with nearly invisible technology embedded into clothing. Our aim is to create technology that is not just in clothing but on the skin surface as removable and hidden electronics. In this paper, we introduce the term 'Beauty technology' as an emerging field in Wearable Computing that hides electronic components within beauty products. This work outlines the technology used to hide electronic components in eyelashes, make-up, tattoos and nails, and it presents examples of the use of Beauty Technology in everyday beauty products.

Keywords: Wearable Computers, Beauty Technology.

1 Introduction

Wearables add more than physical, social and psychological variables. The accessibility, reliability and miniaturization of technology gives the opportunity to embed sensors and actuators into wearables to increase the possibilities of interacting with the world. Nowadays we cannot think of Wearable Computers just as an exploration of the capabilities of devices into clothing but also about breaking through barriers of technology to make them useful to us in a way never imagined.

Our 'Electronic Divas' could keep secrets, amplify our stimulus, reveal their personality and activate the world. They shake their secret nails and doors are opened. They wink with their special make-up and objects are levitated. They play music on imaginary instruments with their fancy nails. Beauty Technology was embedded into their enhanced products to amplify their capabilities, sense the world and highlight their personalities.

This paper introduces the term Beauty Technology and discusses the materials and processes used for developing the first prototypes. It also presents some examples of the use of beauty technologies in everyday beauty products.

We used conductive makeup that connects sensors and actuators by the use of conductive materials that stick to the skin as well-defined eyeliners and eyebrows. Removable tattoos were used as aesthetics lights on the body skin and for enacting with the world by skin capacitance sensitivity. We also used black false eyelashes that were chemically metalized to react to blinking. As an example, Blinklifier is presented as a communication interface to amplify blinking and create expressions

A. Marcus (Ed.): DUXU/HCII 2013, Part III, LNCS 8014, pp. 237–245, 2013.

commanded by the user. Superhero is another example of the conductive false eye-lashes used to levitate objects just by blinking. Beauty Technology Nails embed RFID tags into false nails in order to preserve privacy and give special permissions to the wearer and also to create personalized gestures and musical instruments. These nails could contain embedded magnets for amplifying the wearers' capabilities by giving the sense of reading magnetic fields but also give them access to different objects with magnetic switches.

2 Related Work

Wearable Computing had changed the way individuals interact with computers, in-tertwining natural capabilities of the human body with processing apparatus [1]. But most of this technology had been designed just for clothing or accessories, it is still flat and rigid, and circuits visibly appear through the wearables. There are some ef-forts for crossing the border in designing other kinds of wearable technology, mainly for healthcare, fitness and medicine.

Wearable electrochemical sensors are a new sensing paradigm developed for healthcare [2]. Advances in this technology when integrated into clothing could be considered as non-invasive but they cannot easily be attached and adapted to the body for extracting data [3]. Temporary Transfer Tattoo [4] are electrodes that were printed directly on the epidermis realized by dispersing carbon fiber segments within the tat-too ink and having more than 12 hours of continuous wear without degradation. These electrodes could be designed in artistic tattoo patterns, but still a true integration with wearable computers and an attractive way of hidden sensors is expected.

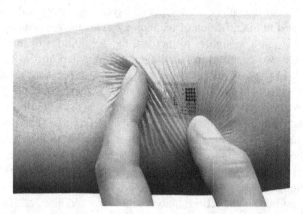

Fig. 1. MC10 Inc.'s flexible electronic sensors are about the size of a postage stamp [5]

Mc10 is proposing smart sensing stickers for medicine, therapy and healthcare in a bandage-like device [6]. They printed electronic mesh into a flexible and thin plastic that is malleable and adaptable to the human skin as a removable tattoo in order to obtain signals from the heart, muscle, body temperature and motion, signals from the brain, and even hydration levels. Figure 1 shows an example of this technology [5].

Mc10 stickers containing different sensors, wireless communication and a thin-film battery inside are expected, however, this technology is still in development and while the circuits are designed in an attractive shape they are still shown.

Even though the privacy and health issues are still evolving, wearers nevertheless seize opportunities to experiment with the sensation of being injected with tiny electronic devices – not just for health management, but also looking for new experiences and fashion, like tattoo implants for using the skin as a display [7] and chipping humans with RFID tags implants for tracking people's comings and goings [8, 9]. In the Arts field, there are some efforts too in including LEDs next to the eyes connected by thin wires. They can simulate larger eyes [10] or act as eye shadow lights when the eyes are closed [11].

The work presented in this paper differentiates from the aforementioned work for using wearable computers in a different field where electronic components are not visible, are removable, enhance wearers' personalities and are embedded into everyday products as beauty products.

3   Beauty Technology

Technologies for sensing information in personal spaces like blinking, pulse rates and respiration monitoring have being increasingly progressed in recent years. In parallel technologies for communicating with smart spaces, smart objects, wearable devices, virtual worlds and social networks have also been developed. These technologies empower human capabilities and the use of wearable computers became a key component for interacting in that world. With this evolutionary technology and our aim of hidden embedded electronics in everyday life objects, we visualized 'Electronic Divas', individuals empowered with 'Beauty Technology', enhanced techno sensual objects that could sense and enact in the world.

'Beauty technology' are wearable devices that act as removable and hidden electronics attached to body surfaces enabling wearers to interact with the digital world without interfering in everyday activities. In particular, the term includes electronics embedded into beauty products. Common beauty products are easy to attach and remove, are designed ergonomically for human bodies, are widely available and their main goal is to enhance physical appearance. This work adapted beauty products and embedded electronics for increasing the possibilities for wearers to interact with the world.

Wearable computers sense the wearer's personal space and the space that they interact with. They could be used for the wearer to understand himself, as a reflective tool to stimulate and modify positive or negatively his behaviors thereby becoming a feedback loop [12]. Beauty Technology could also sense the personal space, keep personal data and act as a feedback loop tool. For example, blinking exposes psychological and physical states: a low blinking rate is indicative of a bored or uninterested state [13]. One can easily envisage the benefits of a natural and unobtrusive makeup that understands this blinking rate, returns this information to the wearer enabling her to modify her posture and behavior.

False eyelashes, false nails, conductive makeup and capacitance tattoos are some examples of beauty products that were adapted with electronic components in order to create actuators that communicate with the wearer, other objects and the virtual world. For example, instead of using a staff card for opening the office door, a special finger movement with RFID TechNails could identify employees and grant them access.

Beauty technology gives wearers the opportunity to experiment in the customization of these techno-sensual objects, highlighting their personalities and even more, keeping the mystery of hidden technology, changing its appearance each day. They could play changing the makeup color and eyeliner intensity, nail polish and decoration but the functionality is kept.

Unlike other facial expression wearables, beauty technology products do not make use of video cameras, electromyogram or galvanic skin response. They minimize the use of intrusive devices on the face, giving the wearer the possibility of motion and without distracting the wearer's attention away from their daily life activities.

4 Technology

We used everyday beauty products and attached circuits or electronic components, or transform them in order to create this Beauty Technology. This technology will be used for develop different wearables and interact with other smart objects. This section presents our first prototypes in Beauty Technology.

4.1 Conductive Makeup

Conductive makeup connects sensors, actuators and their connections in an attractive way that the wearer's observers would not notice the hidden circuit. Our first step [14] for using conductive eyeliner was using conductive ink [15]. We faced the issue that though the ink we were using is a safe material to have around the body, it is not specifically approved for use on the skin. Even more, for using it as eyeliner as this product is soluble to water, the humidity of the eyes and skin could cause issues for the wearer. Thus, we move to create some stickers that look like makeup, they are conductive and easy to remove from skin. We used a thin conductive fabric tape and cut it in a makeup shape and covered it with different common makeup inks for giving it the appearance of normal makeup.

4.2 Black False Eyelashes

In order to avoid using any electronic device on the wearer's face, skin conductive material was applied as black eyeliner to connect conductive false eyelashes to the wearable device. These eyelashes were chemically metalized in order to maintain the natural black color of the eyelashes. Figure 2 shows one of the phases of the electrochemical process.

The chemical process was carried out in 2 phases: Activation and Electrolysis. During the first phase, the false eyelashes, being plastic non-conducting surfaces, require that activation to enable them to be used in an electrochemical process. The first activate was made using Hydrogen and Tin Chloride and then a silver nitrate

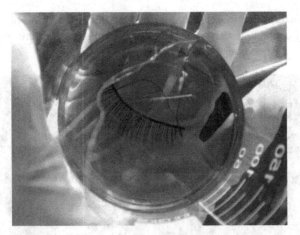

Fig. 2. Chemical process for metalizing false eyelashes

solution was added in the second activate, setting up the eyelashes as catalysts of electron transfer reactions and ready for metalizing. The electrolysis phase deposits a layer of nickel on our actived eyelashes to plate them. It made use of copper for making the eyelashes electrically conductive and black nickel for the natural black effect of the eyelashes.

4.3   Beauty Technology Nails

Beauty Technology Nails are false plastic or acrylic nails that embedded RFID tags, small magnets or conductive polish that enables the wearer to interact with their own wearables and other objects in the environment. RFID glass capsule tags were embedded into false nails so a RFID reader could understand each tag and different application could be created with the combination of the fingers movement and timing next to the reader like special gestures and musical instruments. Magnets were embedded into a nail to amplify the wearers' capabilities by giving the sense of reading magnetic fields but also give them access to different objects with magnetic switches in smart objects and smartphones.

5   Projects

In this section, three Beauty Technology projects are presented. Blinklifier and Superhero projects use black false eyelashes and conductive eyeliner for amplifying blinking and for enacting world objects respectively. TechNails embedded RFID tags into false nails.

5.1   Blinklifier

Blinklifier [14] is a wearable computer that amplifies human blinking and minimizes the use of intrusive devices on the face such as heavy glasses and electromyography.

It follows the natural eye muscles' contractions, extending that motion into a visible light array that changes pattern depending on the blinking gesture. Figure 3 shows Blinklifier pattern when both eyes are closed.

Fig. 3. Blinklifier, a wearable device that amplifies human blinking [14]

5.2   Superheroes

TEI 2013 Design Challenge [16] students were challenged to celebrate TEI creativity with a game or performance. Superhero project was presented. It made used of conductive makeup and black false eyelashes that the wearer could levitate objects with blinking. Eyelashes worked like switches that were connected to a circuit that sends signals via a Zigbee radio to a nearby Superhero Handbag. This bag contained the Zigbee receiver radio for understanding the Superhero blinking. Accordingly, animated images were displayed (POW, Bam, Zap) or infrared commands, decoded from a remote controller's protocol, were reproduced in order to make an object fly. Figure 4 shows the superhero levitating the object by blinking the right eye.

Fig. 4. Superhero blinks for levitating objects

Fig. 5. RFID tags hide into gel nails. Abrete Sesamo project.

5.3   Abrete Sesamo

This project was inspired in the Ali Baba story [17] that a cave that has a treasure just could be opened with the words "iftah ya simsim" (commonly written as "Open Sesame" in English and "Ábrete Sésamo" in Spanish). In our project, a secret combination of finger movements could open the door. RFID glass capsule tags were inserted into gel nails and they were hidden with nail polish and decorative crystals as it is shown in Figure 5. A RFID reader gets the combination and transmits to the microprocessador that controls the door. If the combination is correct, the door is unlocked.

6   Conclusion and Future Work

This paper introduces the term 'Beauty Technology' as an emerging field in Wearable Computers. We propose the use of products on the skin surface that hides electronics, are easy to attach and remove, are ergonomic to the human body and highlight the wearer's personality.

The first technologies developed for Beauty Technology are conductive makeup for connecting sensors and actuators in the face skin, black false eyelashes that were chemically metalized for acting as switches for understanding blinking and false nails (plastic, acrylic and gel) that hide components like RFID glass capsule tags, magnets and conductive materials.

Blinklifier, Superhero and Abrete Sesamo were presented as examples that made use of Beauty Technology. Blinklifier uses false eyelashes and conductive eyeliner for understanding blinking and amplifying the blinking to an artistic head dress that has a microprocessador and a LED matrix that change the lights depending on the wearer's blinking. Superhero uses also false eyelashes and conductive eyeliner for understand the wearer's blinking and change the environment like shift the images displayed and even, levitate an object. Abrete Sesamo is a Beauty Technology project that unlocks the door when a secret combination of fingers move is read from the wearer's nails that have RFID tags embedded.

Future work will include the evaluation of materials for creating new Beauty Technologies like a colorful conductive eye shadow that is flexible and adaptable to the eyelid. A Beauty Technology Framework that could be customized to use these products with smart objects, smartphones and virtual world protocols will be developed.

Acknowledgments. Katia Vega is a PhD research candidate with grant funding by CNPq-Bazil. Hugo Fuks is the recipient of an individual grant by CNPq (302230/2008-4). This work was partially financed by UBILIFE FAPERJ/ADT1-190.116/2010,FAPERJ/INC&T (E-26/170028/2008) and CNPq/INCT (557.128/2009-9). The authors acknowledge EQA Lab for the collaboration in the development of the black false eyelashes. Blinklifier was developed in collaboration with Prof. Patricia Flanagan of the Academy of Visual Arts, Hong Kong Baptist University. Blinklifier photo by Dicky Ma.

References

1. Mann, S.: Humanistic intelligence/humanistic computing: 'wearcomp' as a new framework for intelligent signal processing. Proc. IEEE 86(11), 2123–2151 (2008)
2. Windmiller, J.R., Wang, J.: Wearable Electrochemical Sensors and Biosensors: A Review. Electroanalysis 25, 29–46 (2013)
3. William, J.T., Mark, J.B., Anthony, J.K., Stephen, P.M.: Acceptability of a Wearable Vital Sign Detection System. In: Proceedings of the Human Factors and Ergonomics Society Annual Meeting, vol. 51, pp. 1006–1010 (2007)
4. Windmiller, J.R., Wang, J.: Wearable Electrochemical Sensors and Biosensors: A Review. Electroanalysis 25, 29–46 (2013)
5. Schlatka, B.: Breaking Free. Future Materials Magazine (October 2012)
6. Mc10: http://www.mc10inc.com/company-information/technology
7. Bitarello, B., Fuks, H., Queiroz, J.: New technologies for dynamic tattoo art. In: Proceedings of the Fifth International Conference on Tangible, Embedded and Embodied Interaction, TEI 2011, Funchal, Portugal (2011)
8. Rotter, P., Daskala, B., Compano, R.: RFID implants: Opportunities and and challenges for identifying people. IEEE Technology and Society Magazine 27(2), 24–32 (2008)
9. Foster, K.R., Jaeger, J.: RFID Inside. IEEE Spectrum 44(3), 24–29 (2007)
10. Park, S.: http://soomipark.com/main/?portfolio=led-eyelash
11. Ding, L.: http://dlulin.com/projects/digital-eyeshadow/
12. Mann, S.: Wearable computing: toward humanistic intelligence. IEEE Intelligent Systems 16(3), 10–15 (2001)
13. Russell, J., Fernandez-Dols, J.: The Psychology of Facial Expression. Cambridge University Press (1997)
14. Flanagan, P.J., Vega, K., Fuks, H.: Blinklifier: The power of feedback loops for amplifying expressions through bodily worn objects. In: Proceedings of the 10th Asia Pacific Conference on Computer Human Interaction (APCHI 2012), Matsue, vol. 2, pp. 641–642 (2012)
15. Bare Conductive: http://www.bareconductive.com
16. TEI 13: http://www.tei-conf.org/13/dc
17. Burton, R.F.: Supplemental Nights to the Book of the Thousand Nights and a Night with Notes Anthropological and Explanatory, vol. 3, fasc. 2, p. 369(n.)

An Empirical Study of the Characteristics of Interactive Projection Systems in Multi-media Exhibits

Ting-Han Chen[1] and Shiau-Yuan Du[2]

[1] XXtraLab DESIGN Co., Taipei, Taiwan
daniel@xxtralab.tw
[2] Interaction Design Association Taiwan
grace@ixda.org.tw

Abstract. This paper defines and summarizes the characteristics of interactive projection systems based on an empirical study of the authors' past design works. The characteristics are analyzed and reflected in several application examples, with implications for future study suggested at the end of the paper.

Keywords: Interactive projection, interactive material, interactive exhibit, projection material, tangible interface.

1 Introduction

Following advances in display and interactive technologies, over the last two decades projectors combined with different sensors or camera equipment have been widely used as an interface technology in multi-media exhibits. Research shows that interactive materials such as these projectors can play a critical role in the success of the design of a museum exhibition or exposition [1]. For design practitioners—especially in the fields of interaction, interior, or architectural design—the use of projectors with sensor technology is often applied as a type of design material [2].

Though interactive projections systems are commonly found in museums and expositions where they are used as design material, a more detailed look into such systems has so far been lacking. In order to better help define what is meant by interactive projection systems this paper summarizes their various characteristics into nine categories: Physical and Digital Duality, Tangibility, Size Flexibility, Form Variety, Distance, Reflection, Environmental Effect, Shadow Intervention, and Lamp Expiration. Definitions are based on an empirical study of the authors' previous multi-media exhibits and are given in hopes that they will help future practitioners better form design strategies and also aid further studies and applications in the field.

2 Relevant Work

The history of the projector can be traced back to the 17th century when magic lanterns were first being popularized in Europe [8]. But it was not until the 1980s as

A. Marcus (Ed.): DUXU/HCII 2013, Part III, LNCS 8014, pp. 246–254, 2013.

the projector begun to be widely used in both schools and businesses that its potential to facilitate human communication and interaction became apparent [9].

Working in the field of Human-Computer Interaction, Hiroshi Isshi at the MIT Media Lab proposed the concept of Tangible Bits [3] that employs digital projection combined with physical material to achieve tangible and intuitive human-computer interactive experiences. Such a mixed reality method embodies digital information into physical materials through a projector-camera system framework, thus offering visitors a novel type of interface material. This method has become a common approach for interaction design researchers when implementing interactive technologies in their pursuit of the vision of Ubiquitous Computing [4]. Technically similar, IBM's Everywhere Display Project uses an omni-directional motor that rotates a projector to project interactive screens everywhere inside a room as an approach to turn any surface into interactive material [5]. Although it's arguable that the interactive projector was not specifically created for design purposes, it has nevertheless found a home as a design material in interior and architectural design, interactive installations design, new media art, and exhibit design to name just a few fields. Many interaction design practices applying projection techniques have been carried out in the design of interactive exhibits, resulting in various interactive exhibit technologies, which are commercially affordable [6].

3   An Empirical Study Based on Design Practices

The goal of this paper is not to define the technical specifications of interactive projection systems, but to clarify why and how it is seen as a design material. It must also be noted that the framework proposed in this paper is limited to present-day projector technology and practices and, thus, should be modified in later research stages.

As a practice-based research, this paper uses the constructive design method [7]. It carries out an empirical study of the projects undertaken between 2007 to 2012 by the authors, during which digital projection systems in combination with different sensing methods and sensor technology were used to create various types of interactive design installations. In the authors' nearly six years of practice, digital projection as an interactive material, has been used to create interactional and communicational spaces in the context of museum exhibitions, commercial spaces, and public art settings. Based on these experiences and perspectives derived from related works, the characteristics of an interactive projection system are summarized below.

4   Characteristics of Interactive Projection System

We define an interactive projection system as a creating a projection image that overlays onto a physical object to create a new 'sensation' for that object, while enabling visitors to interact with said object via touch, movement, or mechanical controls. The interactive projection system encompasses several characteristics.

4.1   Digital and Physical Duality

Interactive projection systems encompass both digitality and physicality. Digital projection (digitality) can be projected onto any physical surface (physicality) to become tangible, while physical surfaces can be turned into dynamic digital material when projected on by digital images.

4.2   Tangibility

A projection is visible, but not tangible. It, however, creates a sense of tangibility when projected onto differently textured surfaces, collocating with physical materials in a cohesive framework. By projecting onto different physical materials such as acrylics, wood, water, paper, etc, different sensory effects are created. A projection also creates different tactile responses when combined with different textures.

4.3   Size Flexibility

The size of an interactive projection system can be varied by adjusting projection distance, or by merging different projections into a single, large one. It can be as large as a building facade, or as small as a hand-held device. It can also be made to fit the different shapes and forms of physical materials through the overlay of black masks in front of the projector lens, or through corresponding virtual masks in the software.

4.4   Form Variety

A projection can be projected onto any 2D or 3D physical object, wrapping it with a luminous projection material. Projection distortions occur when projecting onto uneven surfaces, or with projection angles that are not 90 degrees to the projected surface. This can be fixed by reversing the projection image using software or different projection lenses. This will enable the projection to be correctly overlaid on an uneven surface.

4.5   Distance

State-of-the-art projectors require a certain distance to project a certain size of projection. The distance between the projector and the projection image will decide the size and the quality of the projection. The longer the distance and the larger the projection size, the lower the resolution and the lighter the image. Conversely, the shorter the distance and the smaller the projection size, the higher the resolution and the more vivid the image.

4.6   Reflection

A projection can be redirected towards different directions and imaged onto different places via mirror reflection with different angles. This method is often used to overcome physical space constraints by shortening the projection distance using multiple mirror reflections.

4.7   Environmental Effects

The brightness, contrast, and clarity of the projection image will differ under different ambient lighting conditions. In general, the darker the environment, the clearer the projection image, and vice versa.

4.8   Shadow Intervention

Any visible object that appears inside the scope of projection will cause a shadow on the projection image. The location of the shadow is based on the position and projection angle of the projector.

4.9   Lamp Expiration

The life of a projector lamp will come to an end after a certain time (in most cases, 1.5 to 2 years). Performance in the form of color, contrast, and brightness may also decline with time. Nevertheless, with regard to the time span for an average exhibition, the current working life of a projector lamp is seen as being acceptable.

5   Application Examples

The various characteristics of interactive projection systems discussed above have been in implemented in different forms among the authors' many multi-media exhibit designs. When used as a visual communication tool, or as material for interaction, projection systems are excellent at creating engaging experiences and enticing visitors to learn more about the exhibit content. This section will provide some examples of the application of projector systems.

5.1   A Ballad Grinding Project

This project was one of the several installations designed for Hakka Expo 2010. It aimed at bringing fun via a traditional grinding action in Hakka, a category of Taiwanese traditional culture. The installation plays Hakka ballad and projects virtual flowers on the bowl while the user grinds the projection of moving lyrics inside the bowl via a pestle (Figure 1).

Fig. 1. Ballad Grinding project. Visitors interact with the virtual flower projection in the bowl via a physical pestle.

This project attempted to enhance the impressions received by the audience by enabling them to play with a virtual projection via a physical pestle. The main characteristics of the interactive projection system for this project are summarized below in Table 1.

Table 1. Projection system characteristics as seen in Ballad Grinding project

Characteristics	Design strategy
Digital & Physical Duality	The virtual flowers and lyrics as digitality; the physical bowl and pestle as physicality.
Tangibility	Visitors grind virtual flowers via a physical pestle as a method of tangible interaction.
Size Flexibility	The projection is cropped to fit the size and shape of the bowl.
Form Variety	The projection is projected onto the bowl's concave surface.
Distance	The projector is hung 2 meter above the bowl.
Reflection	The projection is projected directly without reflection.
Environmental Effect	The installation is set up in a dark room for best image performance.
Shadow Intervention	The projector angle is adjusted to decrease shadow intervention.
Lamp Expiration	The lamp is checked regularly upon starting up the system.

5.2   A Multi-touch Wall Project

This multi-touch wall was part of the Zhonggang Ditch Pavilion. It was a 14-meter wide glass interactive projection that enabled multiple users to interact with the digital information presented through touch (Figure 2). Traditionally, descriptive information in exhibits is given as text and graphics on standard 2D boards. Interactive projection interfaces alter this method of communication by making text and graphics dynamic and interactive.

By altering the traditional communicative forms of an exhibition board, this multi-touch wall was an attempt to entice visitors to learn more about content of the exhibition by virtue of the interactive process. The characteristics of this interactive projection system are shown in Table 2.

Table 2. Projection system characteristics as seen in the Multi-touch Wall project

Characteristics	Design strategy
Digital & Physical Duality	The digital text and graphics are the digital, and the physical glass-made multi-touch wall is the physical.
Tangibility	Visitors can directly interact with the digital information projected on the wall through touch.
Size Flexibility	The projection is the result of the merging of 6 projectors onto a 14-meter wide surface.
Form Variety	The 14-meter wide projection surface is composed of 6 large pieces of glass; each piece shifts 5 degrees to form an overall curve.
Distance	The projector is set 1 meter behind the glass wall projecting an image onto a mirror that is then reflected back to the glass wall. This lengthens the projection distance to 3 meters.
Reflection	In order to fit the projectors in the space behind the glass wall, they are set to project towards the opposite direction to a mirror, with the images then reflected back to the glass wall.
Environmental Effect	Interior lighting containing infrared is used to avoid interference with multi-touch image tracking. The ambient light conditions are also controlled to maximize image clarity and vividness.
Shadow Intervention	To maximize the performance and quality of the multi-touch image tracking, the system uses rear projection to avoid any possible shadows in front of the glass wall.
Lamp Expiration	A blending machine is used to synchronize the quality of the image performance for the 6 projectors used, and the lamp is checked regularly upon starting the system.

Fig. 2. A glass 14-meter wide interactive projection multi-touch wall

5.3   An Interactive Entrance Project

This project was located at the entrance of the Zhonggang Ditch Pavilion. It was designed as a multi-projection environment that used interactive walls and floors to immerse visitors in an engaging spatial experience (Figure 3). Projected creatures and fauna (e.g. fishes, fireflies, flowers, and grass) react to the position and movement of visitors by detecting shadow changes.

Fig. 3. An interactive walls and floor projection that react to visitors' movements and positions by detecting shadow changes

Table 3. Projection system characteristics as seen in the Interactive Entrance project

Characteristics	Design strategy
Digital & Physical Duality	The digital creatures as digitality, and the physical environment (e.g. the surrounding walls and the floor) as physicality.
Tangibility	The users can interact with the projected creatures on the surrounding walls and the floor by physical movements such as waving their hands or moving to different areas of the space.
Size Flexibility	The projection merges 2 wall projections and 1 floor projection using a blended boundary. The blended boundary blurs the edges of the projection and makes the size of the floor projection frameless.
Form Variety	Strips of cloth hang on the wall to create a curve with a sense of layers. This, along with the frameless floor projection, creates a sensual space into which visitors can immerse themselves.
Distance	The wall projectors are set 3 meters away from the wall and the floor projector is set 3 meters above the floor.
Reflection	The projector is set on the middle of ceiling and directly projects images toward the walls and the floor without reflection.
Environmental Effect	Ambient light conditions are controlled to allow best image clarity and vividness.
Shadow Intervention	Visitors can use their shadow caused by the projection to interact with digital creatures on the surrounding walls and floor.
Lamp Expiration	The lamp is checked regularly upon starting up the system.

This project attempted to create engaging experiences by immersing visitors in an interactive environment. The main characteristics of this interactive projection system are shown in Table 3.

6   Discussion

For designers, the above characteristics of an interactive projection system can be used as a checklist to check the feasibility of an interactive projection design in its early design stages. It can also be used to inspire novel interactive projection applications.

The examples shown in the previous sections are different applications of these characteristics aimed at creating vivid impressions and engaging experiences for visitors, as well as enticing them to learn more about exhibit content. The authors believe that interactive projection systems can also be applied in various contexts to achieve different interfacial or communicative purposes, such as fostering social interactions, as noted in [6].

Compared to other display systems such as OLED, LED, or HDTV, projection systems are flexible in size and alterable in their tactile texture. They can be used either outdoors or indoors, and can communicate different sensations or create different interactive experiences when paired with other physical materials and sensor components. Although the authors can't say for certain whether the projection system will remain their main approach for interactive exhibit design; however, this approach has empowered the authors, as both curators and designers, to think of alternative and unique ways to design interfaces for the display of exhibit contents.

Today, with the advancements in projection technology, using interactive projection systems can be a technically and economically affordable way to create multi-media exhibits, especially since integrating interactive media into exhibits has become a standard in the design of exhibitions today. Therefore the question is not whether projections are a suitable system of design, but how we can develop appropriate designs and effective applications that employ the characteristics of such interactive systems, instead of using projections solely as a screen interface.

7   Conclusion and Future Work

It is arguable that projections as a material for interactive exhibits have some technical limitations, such as projector lamp life and a higher threshold for implementation and maintenance. And though projectors still have technical and usability issues that need to be resolved, and interactive projection systems are still not seen as the standard in design mediums, designers, researchers, and new media artists have been using projection systems in exhibits for decades. The application examples discussed in this paper have shown different ways in which these systems can be achieved through proper design.

This paper summarizes the characteristics of an interactive projection system based on the empirical studies of the authors' own interactive exhibit design practice. These characteristics can be seen as the operational parameters when designing different human-computer interactive surfaces, spaces, and visual or environmental narratives within multi-media exhibits. With such parameters in hand, the authors hope that others will find it easier to uncover new application methods and development strategies in the future. Another possible future direction perhaps can be to investigate qualitatively the sensory experience of different materials when combined with projection systems and observe how this match affects the emotive and cognitive understanding of the information being presented.

References

1. Stevenson, J.: The long-term impact of interactive exhibits. International Journal of Science Education 13(5) (1991)
2. Brownell, B.: Transmaterial: A Catalog of Materials That Redefine our Physical Environment. Princeton Architectural Press (2005) ISBN-13: 978-1568985633
3. Ishii, H., Ullmer, B.: Tangible bits: towards seamless interfaces between people, bits and atoms. In: CHI 1997 Proceedings of the ACM SIGCHI Conference on Human Factors in Computing Systems, pp. 234–241 (1997)
4. Weiser, M., Brown, J.S.: Designing Calm Technology. PowerGrid Journal 1(1) (1996)
5. Pinhanez, C.: Augmented Reality with Projected Interactive Displays. In: Proc. of International Symposium on Virtual and Augmented Architecture (VAA 2001), Dublin, Ireland (2001)
6. Snibbe, S.S., Raffle, H.: Social Immersive Media: Pursuing Best Practices for Multi-user Interactive Camera/Projector Exhibits. In: Proceedings of CHI 2009, pp. 1447–1456 (2009)
7. Koskinen, I., Zimmerman, J., Binder, T., Redstrom, J., Wensveen, S.: Design Research through Practice: From the Lab, Field, and Showroom. Elsevier (2011) ISBN-13: 978-0123855039
8. Vermeir, K.: The Magic of the Magic Lantern (1660-1700): On Analogical Demonstration and the Visualization of the Invisible. British Journal for the History of Science 38(2), 127–159 (2005)
9. History of the Development of Projectors, http://global.epson.com/innovation/projection_technology/history

Evaluation of Effects of Textures Attached to Mobile Devices on Pointing Accuracy

Yoshitomo Fukatsu, Tatsuhito Oe, Yuki Kuno,
Buntarou Shizuki, and Jiro Tanaka

University of Tsukuba, Japan
{fukatsu,tatsuhito,kuno,shizuki,jiro}@iplab.cs.tsukuba.ac.jp

Abstract. When a user holds a mobile device that has a touch screen, his/her fingers and palm touch the back of the device. For this reason, we think that input accuracy can be improved by attaching textures on the back of the device. We selected ways to attach textures and then evaluated pointing accuracy with each texture. In the results, the texture attached to the center of the device achieved the best results of accuracy.

Keywords: eyes-free interaction, single-handed interaction, touch screen.

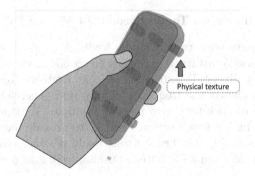

Fig. 1. Mobile device with physical texture attached on the back

1 Introduction

Many mobile devices have touch screens for input. However, poor tactile feedback from those touch screens requires user's visual attention when touching GUI elements [1]. Therefore, eyes-free input on touch screens is difficult.

Despite this difficulty, there are some situations where users do want to use their mobile devices in eyes-free [2]. For example, users must reply to messages they receive while talking with others, whereas such overtly use of mobile devices is socially inappropriate.

A. Marcus (Ed.): DUXU/HCII 2013, Part III, LNCS 8014, pp. 255–263, 2013.

In this research, our aim is to improve eyes-free and single-handed input accuracy on mobile devices. We focus on single-handed input because the vast majority of users want single-handed interaction with mobile devices [3,4].

To this end, our idea is to attach textures to the back of the devices. These are touched by users' fingers and palm (Figure 1), thus giving tactile feedback to users. Therefore, input accuracy could be improved in the same way as raised dots or bars on home position keys of ASCII keyboards. Moreover, since a texture can be implemented as a phone case, the implementation would be very simple and low cost.

To explore how the pointing accuracy is improved by the textures attached to the back of mobile devices, we first prepared mobile devices with no texture and three kinds of textures. Then, we evaluated pointing accuracy by a user study.

The findings of this research is that on the mobile device with touch screens used in this study, which is generally used, if one bead is attached to the center of the mobile device's back, users can point the screen accurately in eyes-free under the condition where the screen is divided into a 3 × 3 grid.

2   Related Work

Our research builds on the following two areas of prior work: tactile feedback on touch screens of mobile devices and eyes-free input in a mobile environment.

2.1   Tactile Feedback on Touch Screens of Mobile Devices

Some researchers have tried to add tactile feedback to touch screens of mobile devices. Active Click [5] attached actuators to mobile devices to provide click-feeling to users. Similarly, TouchEngine [6] and Ambient Touch [7] attached actuators that can change the frequency of vibration. Therefore, they can provide various types of click-feeling to users. Fukumoto [8] attached transparent urethane soft-gel films to touch screen's surface to provide button-pushing feeling to users. Yu et al. [9] attached buttons made of conductive rubber to the edges of touch screens to provide button-pushing feeling to users and to reduce finger occlusion.

These researches attached physical textures to mobile devices to provide the feeling of operation to users. In contrast, we attached physical textures to mobile devices to improve users' input accuracy.

2.2   Eyes-Free Input in a Mobile Environment

Some researchers have proposed eyes-free input systems in a mobile environment. PocketTouch [10] enables eyes-free multi-touch input with a capacitive touchscreen on the back of a smartphone detecting finger-strokes through fabric, allowing users to input without taking the device out of their pocket. However, PocketTouch requires auxiliary hardware. Imaginary Phone [11] enables users to operate mobile devices in eyes-free by gesturing on their palm in the same way as gesture on the mobile devices. By leveraging spatial memory of their mobile devices, users can operate mobile devices even in eyes-free. In this system, users can utilize existing input methods they normally use. However, Imaginary Phone also requires auxiliary hardware. Jain et al. [12] proposed a bezel-based text input system with high accuracy in eyes-free. However, users must learn a new input method.

In contrast, our approach is only to attach textures to the back of the devices. Therefore, it does not cost much and is widely applicable to existing input methods.

3   Evaluation

We conducted a user study to evaluate pointing accuracy using mobile devices in four cases with different textures.

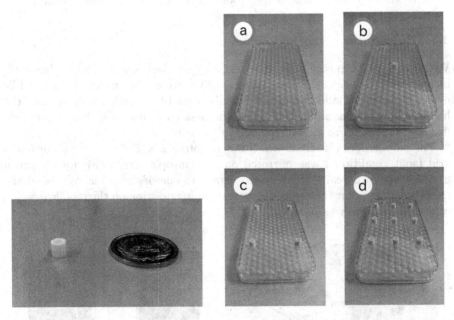

Fig. 2. White cylindrical bead

Fig. 3. Texture conditions: a) non-texture, b) center texture, c) corners texture, and d) latticed texture

3.1   Participants

12 participants (11 male and 1 female) ranging in age from 21 to 24 ($mean = 22.3$, $SD = 0.94$) took part in the experiment as a volunteer. They had used mobile

devices with touch screens from 0 to 36 months ($mean = 17.8$, $SD = 11.6$). All participants were right-handed.

3.2   Apparatus

We attached white cylindrical beads shown in Figure 2 (5 mm in diameter and 5 mm in height) to mobile device case (Apple iPhone 4S, which a 3.5-inch screen). We prepared the following four kinds of mobile device's cases, each of which has a different texture condition:

Non-texture (Figure 3a)
   We attached nothing to the mobile device case.
Center texture (Figure 3b)
   We attached one bead to the center of the mobile device case.
Corners texture (Figure 3c)
   We attached four beads to the corners of the mobile device case.
Latticed texture (Figure 3d)
   We attached nine beads to the mobile device case in a latticed pattern.

3.3   Procedure

We located a laptop computer on a desk (Apple MacBook Pro, which has a 13-inch screen). We asked the participants to sit down on a chair and hold a mobile device with single hand (Figure 4). We also asked the participants to place the hand holding the mobile device under the desk so as not to look at the mobile device's screen and to look at the laptop's screen.

The mobile device's screen which is split into a 2 × 2, 3 × 3, 4 × 4, or 5 × 5 grid (split conditions) was mirrored on the laptop's screen (Figure 5), and a gray rectangle (hereafter target) was shown in one of the grids. We asked the participants to point (i.e., tap) the corresponding position on the mobile device's screen as accurately as possible.

Fig. 4. Experiment environment   **Fig. 5.** Example of target shown on laptop

Figure 6 shows the relationship between split conditions and texture conditions. In this figure, shows a texture of center texture condition, shows textures of corners texture condition, and shows latticed texture condition. Under the split condition and texture condition, the participants carried out the task in accordance to the following procedure:

1. The participant taps any position of the mobile device's screen, a task starts, and a target is shown on the laptop by mirroring as shown in Figure 5.
2. The participant points the corresponding position on the mobile device's screen.
3. Regardless of the success or failure of the pointing, a beep is played to promote the participant to perform the next trial, and the next target is shown. (Split condition and target position were changed in a randomized order.)
4. The participant takes a break after 100 trials (25 trials × 4 split condition = 100 trials).

Each participant carried out this task four times in each texture condition (presentation order of the four texture conditions was counterbalanced) and completed all four tasks in approximately 30 minutes.

After completing the task, each participant answered a questionnaire about his/her impressions of the four texture conditions.

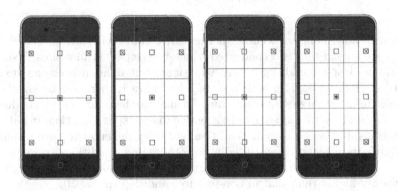

Fig. 6. Relationship between split conditions and texture conditions

3.4 Questionnaire

Participants said which of the four texture conditions were easiest and hardest to input and gave a reason for both choices.

4 Results

4.1 Results of Measurement

Figure 7 shows pointing accuracy per texture condition. One-way repeated measures ANOVA shows no significant difference among texture conditions. Post-hoc analysis with Bonferroni correction shows marginally significant difference between non-texture condition and center texture condition (p = .089).

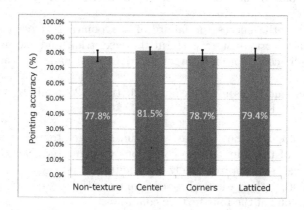

Fig. 7. Pointing accuracy per texture condition

Figure 8 shows pointing accuracy per texture condition in each split condition. In each split condition, we conducted a one-way repeated measures ANOVA. In the 3 × 3 split condition, there was significant difference among texture conditions ($F_{3,33}$ = 4.964 p = .006 < .05). In contrast, there was no significant difference in other three split conditions. To analyze these further, we conducted a post-hoc analysis with Bonferroni correction in each split condition. In pairwise comparisons, in the 3 × 3 split condition, accuracy in center texture condition was significantly higher than those in the other three conditions (p < .05). In the 4 × 4 split condition, accuracy in latticed texture condition was marginally significantly higher than that in non-texture condition (p = .050).

4.2 Results of Questionnaire

As shown in Table 1, center texture condition received the most votes for "easiest to input" (5 participants). Non-texture condition received the most votes for "hardest to input" (7 participants). Latticed texture condition was the only one to receive votes for both "easiest to input" (3 participants) and "hardest to input" (5 participants).

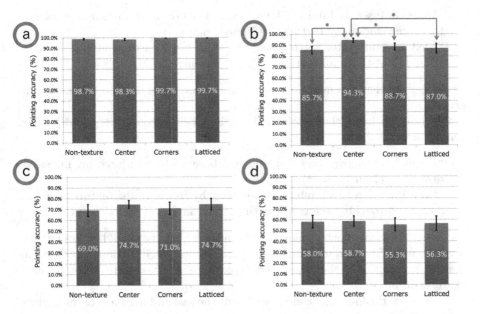

Fig. 8. Pointing accuracy per texture condition: split condition is a) 2 × 2, b) 3 × 3, c) 4 × 4, d) 5 × 5

Table 1. Results of questionnaire [participants]

	Texture condition			
	Non-texture	Center texture	Corners texture	Latticed texture
Easiest to input	0	5	4	3
Hardest to input	7	0	0	5

5 Discussion

In this experiment, the best results of accuracy in three split conditions (3 × 3, 4 × 4, 5 × 5) were achieved in center texture condition. In addition, in the questionnaire, center texture condition received the most votes for "easiest to input" (5 participants).

In the 2 × 2 split condition, pointing accuracy was above 98% in every texture condition. This suggests that even in eyes-free users can accurately touch buttons whose layout is like that in the 2 × 2 split condition.

In the 3 × 3 split condition, pointing accuracy was 94.3% in center texture condition. In addition, accuracy in center texture condition was significantly higher than those in the other three texture conditions. This suggests that even in eyes-free users can accurately touch buttons whose layout is like that in the 3 × 3 split condition by using a texture attached to the center of device as a clue.

In the questionnaire, there were the following comments about latticed condition, which we had assumed would be the most accurate before this experiment:

- "I was confused and did not know which texture to touch as a clue because there were too many textures." (2 participants)
- "I felt uncomfortable when touching textures." (2 participants)
- "I could not touch all textures." (1 participant)

This suggests that too many textures can confuse users and stop accuracy improving.

On the other hand, there were the following positive comments about latticed condition:

- "It was easy to grip the mobile devices because I could hitch my fingers to textures." (1 participant)
- "I think I could touch intended positions by touching the texture with one finger and touching the target with another finger." (1 participant)

As shown these comments, some participants felt that they could utilize latticed textures well. In the questionnaire, 3 participants voted latticed condition as "easiest to input". On the other hand, 5 participants voted latticed condition as "hardest to input".

There were the following comments about the size and hardness of the texture in the questionnaire:

- "I would like to try a softer texture." (1 participant)
- "I am curious about the results in using textures of various hardnesses." (1 participant)
- "The texture was too large to use normally" (1 participant)

In this experiment, we used large and hard textures to emphasize the influence of the textures. We need to reconsider the form, size, and hardness of texture in accordance with the comments.

6   Conclusion and Future Work

We evaluated eyes-free and single-handed pointing accuracy by using mobile devices that had different textures attached. Specifically, we prepared four kinds of mobile device cases that had different texture conditions (non-texture, center texture, corners texture, and latticed texture). By using the mobile devices with the four kinds of cases, we evaluated eyes-free and single-handed pointing accuracy under four kinds of split conditions (2×2, 3×3, 4×4, and 5×5). As a result, we found that in the 2×2 split condition, pointing accuracy was above 98% in every texture condition. This suggests that even in eyes-free users can accurately touch buttons whose layout is like that in the 2×2 split condition. In addition, we found that in the 3×3 split condition, the texture attached to the center of the device resulted in 94.3% pointing accuracy, which is significantly higher than those for the other three kinds of textures. This suggests that even in eyes-free users can accurately touch buttons whose layout is like that in the 3×3 split condition by using the texture attached to the center of the device.

On the other hand, in a questionnaire, some participants said that they were confused when there were too many textures. This might decrease accuracy. For the future, we plan to evaluate textures of various forms, sizes, and hardnesses. Specifically, we plan to evaluate some softer textures. In addition, we plan to evaluate the learning effects of textures.

References

1. Yatani, K., Truong, K.N.: Semfeel: a user interface with semantic tactile feedback for mobile touch-screen devices. In: Proceedings of the 22nd Annual ACM Symposium on User Interface Software and Technology, UIST 2009, pp. 111–120. ACM, New York (2009)
2. Yi, B., Cao, X., Fjeld, M., Zhao, S.: Exploring user motivations for eyes-free interaction on mobile devices. In: Proceedings of the 2012 ACM Annual Conference on Human Factors in Computing Systems, CHI 2012, pp. 2789–2792. ACM, New York (2012)
3. Karlson, A.K., Bederson, B.B.: Understanding single-handed mobile device interaction. Technical report, Department of Computer Science, University of Maryland (2006)
4. Parhi, P., Karlson, A.K., Bederson, B.B.: Target size study for one-handed thumb use on small touchscreen devices. In: Proceedings of the 8th Conference on Human-Computer Interaction with Mobile Devices and Services, MobileHCI 2006, pp. 203–210. ACM, New York (2006)
5. Fukumoto, M., Sugimura, T.: Active click: tactile feedback for touch panels. In: CHI 2001 Extended Abstracts on Human Factors in Computing Systems, CHI EA 2001, pp. 121–122. ACM, New York (2001)
6. Poupyrev, I., Rekimoto, J., Maruyama, S.: Touchengine: a tactile display for handheld devices. In: CHI 2002 Extended Abstracts on Human Factors in Computing Systems, CHI EA 2002, pp. 644–645. ACM, New York (2002)
7. Poupyrev, I., Maruyama, S., Rekimoto, J.: Ambient touch: designing tactile interfaces for handheld devices. In: Proceedings of the 15th Annual ACM Symposium on User Interface Software and Technology, UIST 2002, pp. 51–60. ACM, New York (2002)
8. Fukumoto, M.: Puyosheet and puyodots: simple techniques for adding "button-push" feeling to touch panels. In: CHI 2009 Extended Abstracts on Human Factors in Computing Systems, CHI EA 2009, pp. 3925–3930. ACM, New York (2009)
9. Yu, N.H., Tsai, S.S., Hsiao, I.C., Tsai, D.J., Lee, M.H., Chen, M.Y., Hung, Y.P.: Clip-on gadgets: expanding multi-touch interaction area with unpowered tactile controls. In: Proceedings of the 24th Annual ACM Symposium on User Interface Software and Technology, UIST 2011, pp. 367–372. ACM, New York (2011)
10. Saponas, T.S., Harrison, C., Benko, H.: Pockettouch: through-fabric capacitive touch input. In: Proceedings of the 24th Annual ACM Symposium on User Interface Software and Technology, UIST 2011, pp. 303–308. ACM, New York (2011)
11. Gustafson, S., Holz, C., Baudisch, P.: Imaginary phone: learning imaginary interfaces by transferring spatial memory from a familiar device. In: Proceedings of the 24th Annual ACM Symposium on User Interface Software and Technology, UIST 2011, pp. 283–292. ACM, New York (2011)
12. Jain, M., Balakrishnan, R.: User learning and performance with bezel menus. In: Proceedings of the 2012 ACM Annual Conference on Human Factors in Computing Systems, CHI 2012, pp. 2221–2230. ACM, New York (2012)

A Proposal for Optimization Method of Vibration Pattern of Mobile Device with Interactive Genetic Algorithm

Makoto Fukumoto and Takafumi Ienaga

Fukuoka Institute of Technology
fukumoto@fit.ac.jp

Abstract. The vibration patterns are often used in mobile devices such as cellular phone, tablet computer and smartphone, etc. However, these vibration patterns are ready-made patterns. Most of the users do NOT use vibration pattern suited to each user's preference and objectives to use. Interactive Evolutionary Computation (IEC) was known as effective method to create contents suited to each user, and IEC was applied for creating various media contents. This study proposes an Interactive Genetic Algorithm (IGA) creating vibration pattern. Although some previous IEC studies have tried to optimize media content related to sense of touch, an IEC method optimizing vibration pattern of mobile device have not been proposed. The proposed method will dedicate to use of the vibration pattern by improving its ability of notice and/or by enhancing its suitableness in preference.

Keywords: Interactive Evolutionary Computation, Preference, Vibration Pattern, Genetic Algorithm.

1 Introduction

Recently, we use various types of media contents in various situations. We enjoy these media contents, furthermore, some of them dedicate to change atmosphere. To utilize the media contents, it is ideal that each of the users obtain the media contents suited to each user's preference. However, it is still difficult to obtain the media contents, because preference of the users is very different and complex.

Interactive Evolutionary Computation (IEC) was known as an effective method to create contents suited to each user, and IEC was applied for creating various media contents [1]. Most of IEC applications were related to sense of sight such as image, movie, and graphics [1, 2]. Music and sound were next candidates of IEC applications. In recent years, with helps of development of information technology, the area of IEC applications were spread to various fields related to other human senses such as taste [3], smell [4], and touch [5, 6].

This study focuses our attention on the creation of vibration pattern. The vibration patterns are often used in mobile devices such as cellular phone, tablet computer and smartphone, etc. However, these vibration patterns are ready-made patterns: Most of

A. Marcus (Ed.): DUXU/HCII 2013, Part III, LNCS 8014, pp. 264–269, 2013.

the users do NOT use vibration pattern suited to each user's preference and objectives to use.

This study proposes an IEC creating vibration pattern suited to each user. Although some previous IEC studies have tried to optimize media content related to sense of touch [5, 6], an IEC method optimizing vibration pattern of mobile device have not been proposed. The proposed method will dedicate to use of the vibration pattern by improving its ability of notice and/or by enhancing its suitableness in preference. Furthermore, this study investigates the efficacy of the proposed IEC method through experiment.

2 Proposed Method: IEC for Vibration Pattern

Evolutionary Computation (EC) is used for optimizing several variables suited to certain problem. In other words, EC searches best combination of several variables for the problem. IEC is an interactive type of EC by using human as a function of problem.

Generally, vibration pattern used in cellular phone is composed of on- and off- vibrations. In the proposed method, individual (solution candidate) in IEC is designed as combination of successive several time lengths of vibration and non-vibration (Fig. 1). In this example, number of variables (dimension) of the optimization problem is six. The strengths of the vibrations were set in equal.

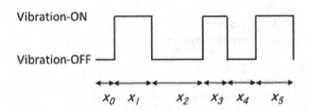

Fig. 1. Correspondence between vibration pattern and values in GA individual

3 Experiment

To investigate the efficacy of the proposed method, two types of experiment was conducted with a vibration device based on the proposed method. In the first experiment optimizing vibration pattern, vibration patterns were created based on the proposed method. To have precise comparison between initial (randomized) vibration pattern and optimized vibration patterns, representative vibration patterns were directly compared in the re-evaluating experiment (Fig. 2).

3.1 Experiment 1: Optimization of Vibration Pattern

To create the vibration patterns based on the proposed method, creating experiment was conducted. In the creating experiment, the vibration pattern was presented by the system based on the proposed method. Nineteen males participated in the experiment as the subjects. The subjects evaluated the vibration patterns created from the system continuously in 7-point scale (1: Extremely dislike – 7: Extremely like).

Genetic Algorithm (GA) [7, 8], the most popular evolutionary algorithm, was employed as evolutionary algorithm in the system. Interactive type of GA is called as Interactive Genetic Algorithm (IGA). An IGA system with a mock-up of cellular phone based on the proposed method was constructed. The vibration pattern was composed of six time lengths of on and off vibrations (Fig. 1). Set of GA parameters were as follows:

> Generation: 10
> Number of individuals: 8
> Selection: Roulette shuffle selection
> Crossover: 1-point crossover, 90%
> Mutation: 5%

3.2 Experiment 2: Re-evaluation of Optimized Vibration Patterns

The same nineteen subjects participated in the experiment 2, the re-evaluating experiment. The re-evaluating experiment was conducted after the experiment 1 at least on day. The subjects evaluated only four vibration patterns: these four patterns were representative patterns picked up from the experiment 1: best pattern in each of the 1st, 4th, 7th, and 10th generations. The subjects evaluated these four vibration patterns in 7-point scale as same as the experiment 1.

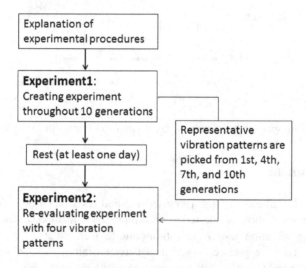

Fig. 2. Experimental Procedure

4   Experimental Results

Fig. 3 shows progress of fitness values in the experiment 1. Once progress of maximum and mean fitness values were obtained in each of the subjects, average of them were calculated.

The lowest fitness values were observed in the 1st generation in both of maximum and mean. Through the fluctuated state, the maximum and mean fitness value reached to the highest in the 10th generation, respectively. The difference of the highest and the lowest fitness in average fitness was smaller than 1 point.

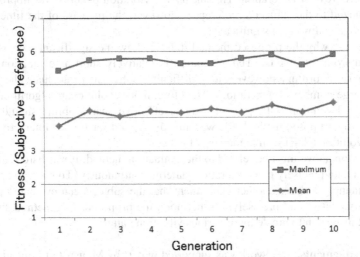

Fig. 3. Progress of maximum and average fitness values in the creating experiment

Fig. 4 shows progress of average fitness values and its standard deviation in the experiment 2, re-evaluating experiment. The lowest fitness value was observed in the 1st generation. The fitness value obviously increased from the 1st generation to the 4th generation. However, the increase stopped and the fitness value keeps it level to the 10th generation.

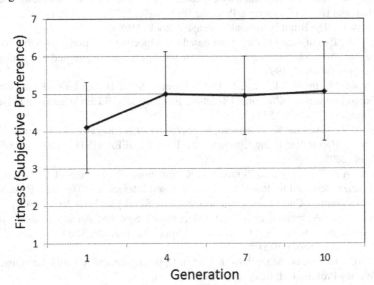

Fig. 4. Progress of average fitness value and its standard deviation in the re-evaluating experiment

5   Discussion and Conclusion

The results of the experiments showed the increase of the fitness value in accordance with the progress of generation. This means the vibration patterns was improved and was optimized to the subject's preference. However, the increase of the fitness value was not large and was not significant.

The reason why the proposed method did not show the significant increase might be caused from set of IGA. Ten generation is relatively short as evaluation time in evolutionary algorithm, however, it is difficult for human to evaluate the patterns through large number of generations. Therefore, other evolutionary algorithm such as Differential Evolution (DE) [10, 11] having effective search ability should be employed in the proposed method. DE was already applied for IEC as Interactive Differential Evolution (IDE) with human user [4, 12].

The reason above must be related to the evaluation method. It was hard for the subject to evaluate precisely many vibration patterns continuously. To solve the problem, we are planning to have another experiment that the subjects can evaluate the vibration patterns easily and precisely. Furthermore, the proposed IGA method should be improved its design to create more various vibration patterns.

Acknowledgements. This work was supported in part by Ministry of Education, Culture, Sports, Science and Technology, Grant-in-Aid for Young Scientists (B) and Grant from Computer Science Laboratory, Fukuoka Institute of Technology.

References

1. Takagi, H.: Interactive Evolutionary Computation: Fusion of the Capabilities of EC Optimization and Human Evaluation. Proc. the IEEE 89(9), 1275–1296 (2001)
2. Dawkins, R.: The Blind Watchmaker. Penguin Books (1986)
3. Herdy, M.: Evolutionary optimization based on subjective selection – evolving blends of coffee. In: Proc. 5th European Congress on Intelligent Techniques and Soft Computing, Aachen, pp. 640–644 (1997)
4. Fukumoto, M., Inoue, M., Imai, J.: User's Favorite Scent Design Using Paired Comparison-based Interactive Differential Evolution. In: Proc. 2010 IEEE Congress on Evlutionary Computation, pp. 4519–4524 (2010)
5. Nishino, H., Takekata, K., Sakamoto, M., Salzman, B.A., Kagawa, T., Utsumiya, K.: An IEC-Based Haptic Rendering Optimizer. In: Proc. the IEEE WSTST 2005, pp. 653–662. Springer (2005)
6. Dharma, A.A.G., Takagi, H., Tomimatsu, K.: Emotional Expressions of Vibrotactile Haptic Message Designed by Paired Comparison-based Interactive Differential Evolution. In: Proc. Evolutionary Computation Symposium 2011, S4-01 (2011) (in Japanese)
7. Holland, J.H.: Adaptation in Natural and Artificial Systems: An Introductory Analysis with Applications to Biology, Control and Artificial Intelligence. The University of Michigan Press, Ann Arbor (1975)
8. Goldberg, D.: Genetic Algorithms in Search, Optimization and Machine Learning. Addison-Wesley Professional, Reading (1989)

9. Osgood, C.E., Suci, G.J., Tannenbaum, P.: The measurement of meaning. University of Illinois Press (1957)
10. Storn, R., Price, K.V.: Differential evolution–A simple and efficient adaptive scheme for global optimization over continuous spaces. Institute of Company Secretaries of India, Chennai, Tamil Nadu. Tech. Report TR-95-012 (1995)
11. Price, K.V., Storn, R., Lampinen, J.: Differential Evolution–A Practical Approach to Global Optimization. Springer, Berlin (2005)
12. Takagi, H., Pallez, D.: Paired Comparison-based Interactive Differential Evolution. In: Proc. World Congress on Nature and Biologically Inspired Computing, Coimbatore, pp. 375–380 (2009)

NUI-Based Floor Navigation — A Case Study

Ulrich Furbach and Markus Maron

Department of Computer Science, Artificial Intelligence Research Group
University of Koblenz-Landau, Universitätsstr. 1, 56070 Koblenz
{uli,maron}@uni-koblenz.de

Abstract. In this paper, we describe a nui-based application using a Microsoft Kinect. The system displays a digital representation of a university building, where users can navigate virtually through contact-less gestures. Users can step up and couple their hand with a virtual mouse cursor to navigate through the program such that hand movements to the right lead to cursor movements to the right for example. We present an evaluation of the system, which is based on a 100' day operation by logging 2.000 user sessions.

1 Introduction

Natural user interfaces is a well researched topic over the past years. Gestures play a central role for contact and non-contact interfaces as well. In particular, the huge success of smart phones fosters a lot of innovative development.

However, there is also the need for contact-less gestures, e.g. within an operating room or behind a shop front window[11]. The number of smart ideas and applications of contact-less gestures have exploded since the availability of the Microsoft Kinect[6]; a piece of hardware which is cheap, and the OpenNI Framework[10] easy to programand easy to embed into complex systems.

We describe the design and evaluation of a system for NUI-based floor navigation within a campus building. Users can navigate virtually through contactless gestures. They can step up and couple their hand with a virtual mouse cursor to navigate through the program such that hand movements to the right lead to cursor movements to the right for example. The system is part of a campus-wide information system, which is used to display various kind of information[1].

Located in the entrance area of a newly constructed building users unfamiliar with this should find their way around quickly. Therefore, the goal was to develop an innovative interactive application, which empowers their users to acquire detailed information on floor levels and individual rooms, such as names of employees and contact data. Fulfilling the HCI design constraint "Come as you are" [14] , the application allows users to navigate through the building just with the help of gestures without any additional requirements needed, moving a virtual hand over a floor map displayed on an up-right widescreen TV mounted in a brushed iron frame fixed to a wall (cf. Figure 1). Using gestures instead of

---

[1] http://www.wizai.com/index.php/loesungen/campusnews

A. Marcus (Ed.): DUXU/HCII 2013, Part III, LNCS 8014, pp. 270–279, 2013.

Fig. 1. Wall-mounted gesture control floor navigation system

a touchscreen makes the content on the screen accessible for everyone, also for small or handicapped people.

In the context of public displays to motivate and focusing the attention [3][4][5][8] of the passers-by to the display are well discussed topics. In our case there are three main challenges:

- *Users do not play a game.* The user who stops in front of the floor plan wants to solve a specific task, namely looking for a room or a person. They are generally not willing to spend time to learn or to experience something new.
- There is *no chance to teach* the user or to make them read a manual before using the device.
- There are *no commonly accepted gestures* for controlling a screen - we have to assume no prior user experience.

Specially the last point turned out to offer a real challenge for the design of the gesture interface. Many users find themselves rather helpless with regard to the system. During the design phase of the system we did some experiments in order to find the most appropriate gestures. After installing the system, we collected data about the usage in log files along with videos of the users's behavior. We will offer an evaluation of the first few months of the application in a public building on campus.

2 Related Work

The scene in Steven Spielberg's *Minority Report* science fiction movie is well-known where Tom Cruise uses gesture control to manipulate images. This was unimaginable in 2002, but now 10 years later it is a reality. Samsung has just released a new Smart TV with voice and gesture control. In the field of natural user interfaces a lot of research has been conducted not least since Microsoft released the Kinect: A cheap and robust sensor and a SDK for developing. More than 100.000 individuals downloaded the SDK in the first six weeks. Using a display with gesture control instead of a touchscreen offers the chance to install an interactive display behind a shop front window for presenting their goods or just analyzing the user behavior.[11] Besides doing research and using it within home entertainment, the usage of the Kinect can be useful in several scenarios where input with controller or touch are not useful. In the medical field it is used to manipulate medical images without having to touch a controller[1], reducing the chance of hand contamination in operating theatres[7][15]. For using it in such a critical environment it is important that the handling is as simple as possible. But finding simple and intuitive gestures is not trivial. *"Poke it or press it*, everybody had a very different idea of what that actually meant." [2]

3   The Application

The system is located in the entrance area of a newly constructed university building. Users unfamiliar with the new building should find their way around quickly. Therefore, the goal was to develop an innovative interactive application, which empowers their users to acquire detailed information on floor levels and individual rooms, such as names of employees and contact data. The application allows users to navigate through the building with the help of gestures, moving a virtual hand over a floor map displayed on an upright widescreen TV fixed to a wall. Using gestures instead of a touchscreen enables the usage of the entire display for everyone, also for small or handicapped people.

The floor plan of the entire building, including all rooms, was to be coherently displayed in an application and run permanently on a mini linux computer. The navigation through rooms and floors is enabled by gesture controls. The following gestures were to be implemented: Wave, push and swipe. Each of these are then associated with actions to enable navigation as shown in the following table.

In order to allow the selection of certain rooms, the user's hand should be coupled to a virtual mouse cursor on the screen so that objects can be selected

Table 1. Defined gestures and their calling actions. *Push is realized by holding the hand 4 sec. above the clickable element. (cf. Figure 3)

gesture	action
Wave	Activate
Swipe_Left, Swipe_Right	Switch_Person
Swipe_Up	Switch_Floor_UP
Swipe_Down	Switch_Floor_Down
Push*	Entered_Room, Left_Room, Floorbox_Pushed, HelpButton_Pushed

on the screen similarly to the way objects are selected with a normal mouse on a computer. An object should be selected by an appropriate gesture. Depending on the selected object, different information can be displayed. For lecture halls, this information contains the name of the current lecture being held, the person holding the lecture, and the subsequent lecture. For offices, this information includes the employee's name, his/her contact information, an avatar or photograph, and a QR-Code with condensed information of that person. The necessary contact data for all employees and lectures can be updated every night and saved in a database.

Implementation. The system development was separated into two parts. The floor plan application and the development of the gesture recognition and control of the application. The entire program is written in C++ with the help of the OpenFrameworks toolkit.

All necessary employee and lecture information for the floor plan part is retrieved from a database so that only up-to-date information is displayed.

For the gesture recognition, the SensorKinect driver by Primesense[12] was used in combination with OpenNI (Open Natural Interaction)[10], a framework which provides several different APIs for natural interaction devices. Additionally, NITE (Natural InTEration) was used. This framework also provides APIs for interaction between humans and machines. By combining these three technologies it is possible to read and analyze Kinect data. OpenNI provides functionality so that new data from the Kinect can be analyzed and gestures identified.

Fig. 2. Video help for session activation. Translated into English: "Hand–control: Wave. Please two meters distance."

Gesture design. As mentioned in the introduction, there are three main characteristics of this application. During the design of a prototype we had to address all three of them:

- *Users do not play a game.* A user stops in front of the screen in order to get information quickly. At this moment they do not know that the screen can be controlled by gestures. This is in the field of public displays a very common problem[9]. In order to clarify this, we run during the standby phase permantely a movie in the lower part of the screen (cf. Figure 1), which shows a hand waving permanently together with the written info, that this is the way to activate mouse-control manually (cf. Figure 2). After the user's hand is recognized and tracked, the user can move the curser. This turns out to work nicely, however many users put down their hand after activation instead of controlling the curser. They simply expect another action from the system.

Fig. 3. Mousehoover feedback for clicking actions

– *No chance to teach the user.* In a first approach during the development of the system we offered our test users wiping and pushing gestures. However, it turned out to be rather difficult to offer these gestures. We learned that users do not read any further help which is displayed on screen. Moreover, they immediately try to use individual gestures. Recognizing and scaling these gestures appears to be too difficult for a practical application. Therefore, we decided to use a rather traditional approach, clicking is implemented by mouse-hovering, depicted in Figure 3.
– *No commonly accepted gestures.* During the experimental phase of the system design we learned that an average user has a lot of problems in using gestures for navigation if there is no instruction. We will discuss this point in the following evaluation.

4   Evaluation

In this section we describe the evalution based on collected data within 145 days about the usage in log files along with 2,245 videos of the users's behavior. These data gave us a insight in the behaviour and the emotions of the user interacting with a NUI-based control. The video analysis brought out that man and female users are dealing in different ways with that nui-based floor control. Besides some interesting gender aspects we observed group dynamics as well.

4.1   Usage of the System

Figure 4 shows the distribution of the usage during the last months. The number of sessions and actions decreased during the semester and reached their minimum in the semester break. Afterwards, both figures started to increase again. The number of actions per session is nearly constant about 6 (see Figure 5).

This development during the last 5 months proves the acceptance of the system as a daily routine. We will investigate this in more detail in the following.

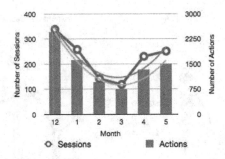

Fig. 4. Usage during the time period: shows the number of sessions and the number of actions per month

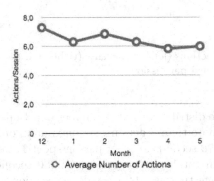

Fig. 5. Average number of actions per session during the time period

4.2 Sessions, Actions and Events

Overall, since the rollout till now (14th of May) a total of 2.065 sessions have been started. On closer inspection, we have detected that 165 sessions have been opened unintentionally by people standing close to the system while talking to another person gesturing with their hands. Additional, 368 sessions have been recorded which contain no opening action. This means that during these sessions the person in front of the system tried to activate the control but did not succeed. Additional, 469 sessions have been successfully opened but the interacting person did not recognize the announcement on the display. If we adjust the logs and reduce these failure sessions we count 1.202 successfully opened sessions with 7.833 actions and 4.751 events. Unfortunately, we count 3.083 actions which did not lead to an event.

Figure 6 depicts the distribution of actions. The most performed action was *Floorbox_Pushed* and, interestingly, the HelpButton was pushed only 19 times, even though it is placed very visibly.

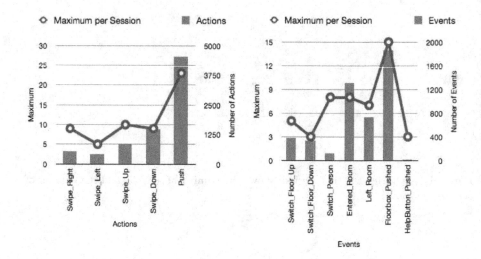

Fig. 6. Total number of actions (left) and events (right) and the maximum number of each action/event performed per session

Figure 7 presents the distribution of the number of actions per session. 60% of all people performed more than 5 actions. At maximum, one person performed 34 interactions within 79 seconds another person spent 181 seconds while doing 18 interaction steps. In total, all users spent 36.380 seconds accordingly 10h 6min. The average usage time is 30.2 seconds per session and 4.6 seconds per action.

Figure 8 shows that most of the users spent more than 10 seconds within a session. This is not because of the unfamiliarity with the user interface, as shown in the following evaluation of the recorded videos.

4.3   Observing the Users

The videos, we recorded for a more careful semantical evaluation, show that many users performed exaggerated motions in front of the system at the beginning of a session, but after a short while they learned how to control the system.

Indeed, learning-by-doing is the most important factor in the shift from novice to experienced user.

We analyzed the videos of 188 sessions during a period of 17 days. In these sessions we counted 176 different people standing in front of our camera, 88 people interacted with the application (Figure 9). In 129 sessions the interacting person was accompanied by other people. The maximum was a group of 5.

The video analysis also showed some gender aspects. 33 of the interacting people were female and 55 male. Males performed more actions and harder than

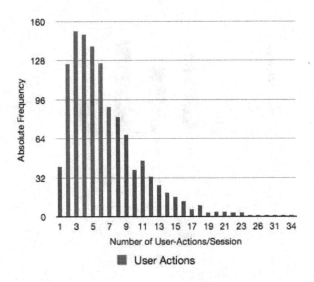

Fig. 7. Distribution of number of actions per session

females. The maximum amount of actions was 16 performed by a male (11 female) and the average amount of actions per session was 7.7 by males (5.0 female).

Most of the interacting persons showed positive emotion. 85 percent of the females and 78 percent of the males left the place with a smile on their face.

5   Lessons Learnt

The development and the evaluation of the system reported in this paper started as a student project. In the beginning a lot of experiments have been done in order to find easy and precise gestures for the specific task of a floor navigation system. During this initial phase it turned out that this is by far not trivial. For example, we thought that waving is a good and simple gesture to activate the application control. But we had to learn that people wave hands in their own way and a lot of them did not achieve to take control of the application. From this experience we came to the solution to show the activating waving-gesture in an introduction video, which is shown whenever the screen is not in use.

When we finally mounted the system on a wall in the entry area of the building, we learnt a lot about changing lighting in the building in the course of an entire day and about its influence on the performance of the system. Also, the area in which the Kinect should identify users and react to their actions has to be determined by numerous experiments. Then we started the evaluation phase in which we collected the data which was evaluated in the previous section.

The main points from this evaluation are

– Since there is no chance for such a system to train users, it is important that learning can be done during a single session. The number of actions necessary

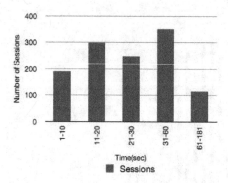

Fig. 8. Duration time user spent

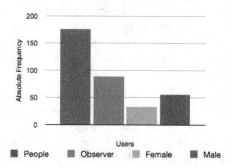

Fig. 9. Distribution of interacting people

to perform an event is usually decreasing during a single session, which clearly indicates that the user learnt to control the system more efficiently.
– Our evaluation during several months proves that such NUI-based systems are ready to be used in real-life applications under realistic and natural conditions.
– The video analysis of a smaller sample gave us additional insight into the behavior of users. Although this analysis is of course rather limited, because it is based on interpretations of the assessor, it can be used very well as a kind of formative empirical evaluation.

For us it was fun to develop the application and for most of the people using it, it is was fun too [13]. A more detailed description and evaluation we will give in an other paper.

Acknowledgments. We thank the University of Koblenz for giving us the opportunity to install the system and thus having the chance to use thousands of users for this research.

References

1. Gallo, L., Placitelli, A.P., Ciampi, M.: Controller-free exploration of medical image data: Experiencing the Kinect. In: CBMS, pp. 1–6. IEEE (2011)
2. Goth, G.: Brave NUI world. Commun. ACM 54, 14–16 (2011), http://doi.acm.org/10.1145/2043174.2043181
3. Huang, E.M., Koster, A., Borchers, J.: Overcoming assumptions and uncovering practices: When does the public really look at public displays? In: Indulska, J., Patterson, D.J., Rodden, T., Ott, M. (eds.) PERVASIVE 2008. LNCS, vol. 5013, pp. 228–243. Springer, Heidelberg (2008), http://dx.doi.org/10.1007/978-3-540-79576-6_14
4. Jacucci, G., Morrison, A., Richard, G.T., Kleimola, J., Peltonen, P., Parisi, L., Laitinen, T.: Worlds of information: designing for engagement at a public multitouch display. In: Mynatt, E.D., Schoner, D., Fitzpatrick, G., Hudson, S.E., Edwards, W.K., Rodden, T. (eds.) CHI, pp. 2267–2276. ACM (2010)
5. Michelis, D.: Interaktive Großbildschirme im öffentlichen Raum: Nutzungsmotive und Gestaltungsregeln. Gabler Edition Wissenschaft, Gabler Verlag (2009), http://books.google.de/books?id=Q9UkyR--HEOC
6. Microsoft Kinect, www.xbox.com/en-US/kinect (last accessed on February 26, 2013)
7. Moretti, S.: Doctors use Xbox Kinect in cancer surgery (March 2011), http://tinyurl.com/4ym6866 (last accessed on February 26, 2013)
8. Müller, J., Walter, R., Bailly, G., Nischt, M., Alt, F.: Looking glass: a field study on noticing interactivity of a shop window. In: Proceedings of the SIGCHI Conference on Human Factors in Computing Systems, CHI 2012, pp. 297–306. ACM, New York (2012), http://doi.acm.org/10.1145/2207676.2207718
9. Müller, J., Walter, R., Bailly, G., Nischt, M., Alt, F.: Looking glass: a field study on noticing interactivity of a shop window. In: Konstan, J.A., Chi, E.H., Höök, K. (eds.) CHI, pp. 297–306. ACM (2012)
10. OpenNI - The standard framwork for 3D sensing, www.openni.org (last accessed on February 26, 2013)
11. Peltonen, P., Kurvinen, E., Salovaara, A., Jacucci, G., Ilmonen, T., Evans, J., Oulasvirta, A., Saarikko, P.: It's mine, don't touch!: interactions at a large multitouch display in a city centre. In: Proceedings of the Twenty-Sixth Annual SIGCHI Conference on Human Factors in Computing Systems, CHI 2008, pp. 1285–1294. ACM, New York (2008), http://doi.acm.org/10.1145/1357054.1357255
12. PrimeSensor™ Reference Design, http://www.souvr.com/Soft/UploadSoft/201005/2010050617295050.pdf (last accessed on February 26, 2013)
13. Shneiderman, B.: Designing for fun: how can we design user interfaces to be more fun? Interactions 11(5), 48–50 (2004)
14. Triesch, J., von der Malsburg, C.: Robotic gesture recognition. In: Wachsmuth, I., Fröhlich, M. (eds.) GW 1997. LNCS (LNAI), vol. 1371, pp. 233–244. Springer, Heidelberg (1998)
15. Wall, J.: Kinect and Medical Imaging, www.youtube.com/watch?v=U67ESHV8f_4 (last accessed on February 26, 2013)

Capturing Nursing Interactions from Mobile Sensor Data and In-Room Sensors

Sozo Inoue[1], Kousuke Hayashida[1], Masato Nakamura[1],
Yasunobu Nohara[2], and Naoki Nakashima[2]

[1] Kyushu Institute of Technology, 1-1 Sensuicho, Tobata-ku,
Kitakyushu, 804-8550, Japan
sozo@mns.kyutech.ac.jp
http://sozolab.jp
[2] Kyushu University Hospital, 3-1-1, Maidashi, Higashi-ku,
Fukuoka, 812-8582, Japan
{nnaoki,y-nohara}@info.med.kyushu-u.ac.jp

Abstract. In this paper, we show two approaches for capturing nursing interactions in a hospital: 1) finding nursing intervals from mobile sensors with accelerometers and audio on nurses, and 2) recognizing nurses' entrance to a patient's room from in-room sensors of bed, loudness, and illuminance sensors. For 1), we firstly detect the nurses' entrance to the patient's room by walking detection from accelerometers and noise level on mobile sensors, and detect the interval of interaction between nurses and the patient. For 2), we recognize the nurse's entrance to the patient's room with in-room sensors, using separate algorithms between day and night. We developed the algorithms using the sensor data collected in a cardiovascular center in a real hospital for one year. It could be a important baseline technique to find valuable intervals from long and big data of sensors.

Keywords: Activity Recognition, Annotation, Speech Interval Estimation, Nursing Activity.

1 Introduction

In this research, we aim at capturing nursing interactions with patients from mobile accelerometers attached to each nurse. Capturing nursing is important, since 1) it helps understanding what/when/how interactions should be performed for better health results of the patients, and 2) it can be utilized to improve the skills of nurses. If we have evidences of interactions and the health result, we can analyze the correlations between them, and find the key factors for better interaction.

However, very few data sets for such purpose have been published and shared among the research community so far, either because of the immaturity of sensing/network/storage technology, or because of the privacy risk.

In our one-year trial in a cardiovascular center in a hospital, we have collected 7,400 hours of mobile sensor data in total from nurses after one-year trial in a hospital[1]. We asked nurses to bring smart devices (iPod touches), which records

A. Marcus (Ed.): DUXU/HCII 2013, Part III, LNCS 8014, pp. 280–289, 2013.

sounds and accelerations, into their breast pockets with a roughly fixed direction. They also attached small 2 accelerometer devices on their right wrists and the back waists. Moreover, each of them attached a semi-passive RFID tag in the breast pocket to recognize entrees and exists from the patientsf rooms.

We also asked to 70 hospitalized patients who have been applied PCI (Percutaneous Coronary Intervention) or CABG (Coronary Artery Bypass Graft), and have consented to the experiment, to provide vital sensor data such as monitoring cardiogram, bed sensor to measure heart rate and breath, accelerometer, environmental sensors, and also medical information which were recorded in the electronic clinical pathways and indirectly in patients' sensor data.

In this paper, we show two approaches for capturing nursing interactions: 1) finding nursing intervals from mobile sensors with accelerometers and audio on nurses, and 2) recognizing nurses' entrance to a patient's room from in-room sensors of bed, loudness, and illuminance sensors. For 1), we firstly detect the nurses' entrance to the patient's room by walking detection from accelerometers and noise level on mobile sensors, and detect the interval of interaction between nurses and the patient. For 2), we recognize the nurse's entrance to the patient's room with in-room sensors, using separate algorithms between day and night.

Although this is the first step to analyze and mine the nursing interactions leading to clinical pathways, it could be an alternative to install costly RFID readers to all rooms, and could be an important baseline technique to find valuable intervals from long and big data of sensors.

2 Background

In our one-year trial in a cardiovascular center in a hospital, we have collected large-scale mobile sensor data from nurses and patients, along with the medical records of the patients[1](See Fig.1). We asked nurses to bring mobile devices (iPod touches), which records audio and accelerations, into their breast pockets with a roughly fixed direction. They also attached small 2 accelerometer devices on their right wrists and the back waists. Moreover, each of them attached a semi-passive RFID tag in the breast pocket to recognize entrees and exists from the patients' rooms. To realize them, RFID readers are installed on the entrance of each of the patients' rooms. As a result, we have collected total 7,400 hours of real nursing activities and 4,600 hours of RFID data.

We also asked 70 hospitalized patients who have been applied PCI (Percutaneous Coronary Intervention) or CABG (Coronary Artery Bypass Graft), and have consented to the experiment, to provide vital sensor data such as monitoring cardiogram, bed sensor to measure heart-rate/breath/body-movement, accelerometer, in-room sensors, and also medical information which were recorded in the electronic clinical pathways and indirectly in patients' sensor data.

We used a bed sensor system in which a thin, air-sealed cushion is placed under the bed mattress of the patient[3]. The system measures heartbeat, respiration and body movement of the patient non-invasively by detecting the changes of air pressure of the cushion caused by their vital signs. Finally, we have collected total 2,500 hours of bed sensors.

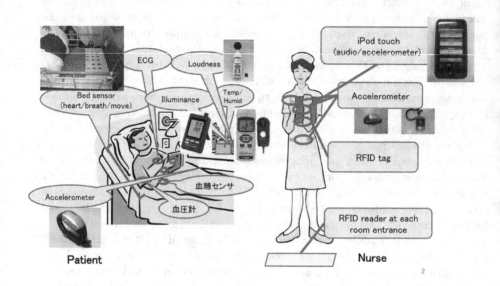

Fig. 1. Illustration of sensor installation

We also installed three in-room data loggers at the patients' room, and recorded four types of data: temperature/humidity, illuminance and loudness. Temperature and humidity are recorded every 5 seconds and the others are recorded every second. As a result, we have collected 5,600 hours of in-room sensors' data.

In the experiment, we have a requirement to know the nursing activity interval to know what kind of care are done to each patient. We can focus on the intervals when the nurses are in the patients' rooms, so the RFID system is thought to be useful. However, RFID system is not always available, since the readers and antennas should be placed many places, such as every entrance of the patients' rooms. Therefore, it is welcomed if we can know when nurses stayed in patient rooms without using RFID, but with mobile sensors or other in-room sensors.

3   Related Work

In the literature, some work utilizes accelerometer and audio data to recognize human context. Lukowicz et al.[5] recognizes activities in a wood shop using body-worn multiple microphones and accelerometers. Lester et al.[6] shows the performance of activity recognition for 8 activity classes using accelerometers, audio, and barometric pressure sensor in a single device. Choudhury et al.[7] developed to implement them on a mobile embedded system. In the device, audio is down-sampled as not to be able for humans to harm privacy of the owner.

One of the differences of our work from above is that these work assume simple activity classes to recognize such as, "walk", "stair up", but our research aims at recognizing more complex and more number of nursing interactions. For complex and more number of interactions, the recognition accuracy will be worse. Therefore, we need more effort to refine larger-scale dataset as well as sophisticated machine learning that can be used in higher dimensions with larger-scale training data.

4   Nursing Interval Detection from Nurses' Mobile Sensors

In this section, we describe the method to find the interval which corresponds to nursing activities, introduced in the workshop paper[2]. This method uses three-axis acceleration data and audio data that are collected by the devices attached to the breast pockets. Upon the collected activity data, we use two characteristics in order to efficiently locate the intervals where nurses performed medical activities.

One is the characteristic that a nurse certainly speaks to a patient when s/he performs medical practice to a patient. Nurses always talk to the patients what to do for medical practice. Therefore, if we can find an interval where nurses are talking, we can guess that the interval of medical activities is being performed.

The other is that a nurse walks for a specific while when s/he moves into a patient 's room. If we can detect the walking of nurses to move into the patient's room from 3-axis accelerometer, we can segment the time to either of being inside or outside the room. In addition, we can estimate if s/he is in the patient's room by examining the noise level from the audio data after a walking period.

In order to utilize the above characteristics, we adopt mobile sensors which record three-axis acceleration and audio data. With the data collected by the devices, we apply walking detection method for the accelerometer, speech interval estimation for audio data, and location estimation for the environmental noise level of the audio data. We can find the duration of walk from three-axis acceleration data by walking detection, location estimation from the environmental noise level of the audio data after walking periods, and the durations where a nurse talks from audio data by speech interval estimation.

Walking Detection. In order to detect the walk of nurses, we recognize the walk of nurses using the technology of activity recognition. We calculate the feature vectors to train an activity recognition model from the three-axis acceleration data. Feature vectors are calculated with the time window of 2 seconds being shifted by 0.5 seconds. A feature vector consists of the variance and the entropy of the intensity: the square root of the sum of squares of the three-axis values of acceleration data. The recognition model is trained by Support Vector Machine (SVM) with linear kernel. To smooth continuous walking, the duration of less than 15 seconds between detected walks are also assumed as walk.

Location Estimation. We can estimate if s/he is in the patient's room by the environmental noise level from the audio data. If the audio is recorded in 16-quantization bit rate, the amplitude bandwidth is from -32768 to +32767. From our experience, environmental noises of our target were found to be from -1500 to 1500. Therefore, at first, we remove the intervals of amplitudes outer than -1500 from 1500, which contains human voices and metal sounds. After that, we estimate the location by the median amplitude value of 30 seconds after the end of walking period.

Speech Interval Estimation. To find the nurses' speech interval, we estimate the speech interval by seeking fundamental frequency of the audio data. The fundamental frequency is one of the speech features used in speech recognition, and it represents the height of the voice. Calculation of the fundamental frequency is performed by the cepstrum method[4]. Although the cepstrum technique is weak for noises, there are advantages that the fundamental frequency can be correctly acquirable in any languages.

In this study, using the Cepstrum method, fundamental frequency is calculated with the time window of 0.04 seconds being shifted by 0.02 seconds. By obtaining the time window with high peak quefrency, we can obtain the spoken interval.

4.1 Experiments

We have conducted the experiments using real nursing data to evaluate the proposed method. The used data is activity data of one day of a nurse.

Walking Detection In order to evaluate the walking detection, each of the training and test data with annotation for 300 seconds were prepared from a day of a nurse. Two kinds of annotations, "walk" and "others", are attached to the data. The data contained 100 seconds of "walk", and 200 seconds of "others". Recognition model was created by the modelusing the training data, and was evaluated by the test data. Tab. 1 shows the recognition result before smoothing. From the table, the whole recognition rate is 93.6%.

Table 1. Confusion matrix of the number of time windows for walking detection

→ Ground truth	Walk	Others
Walk	52	18
Others	19	492

4.2 Location Estimation

We picked up 43 data points from 4 audio data, and investigated the environmental noise level, which is put together in Fig. 2. In Fig. 2, the left box is the distribution of the median environmental noises in the patient's room, and the right is in other places. Since the inter-quartile ranges (IQRs) do not overlap each other, we can estimate that we can differentiate the location at more than 75%. If we take priority on the recall rate, we can achieve at least 87.5%.

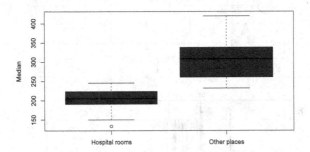

Fig. 2. Distribution of median environmental noise levels of 43 data points of 30 seconds after a walking period. The left is in the patient's room and the right is in other places.

Speech Interval Estimation. We evaluated the speech interval estimationusing audio data of 300 seconds. The audio data was prepared from a day of a nurse.

Table 2. Confusion matrix of the durations for speech interval detection.

→ Ground truth	Nurse	Patient	Noise	Silence
Speech	27.62[s]	7.65[s]	0.14[s]	0.76[s]
None-speech	0.83[s]	2.6[s]	13.72[s]	246.68[s]
Total	28.45[s]	10.25[s]	13.86[s]	247.44[s]

The confusion matrix which counts of the results are shown in Tab. 2. For comparison, the ground truths are classified as the nurses' speeches, patients' speeches, noises, and the silent intervals, whereas the proposed method only estimates speech or non-speech. The silent intervals of the ground truths were determined by whether the amplitude is greater than a specific threshold value, which resulted in that negligible small voices were included in the silence class. From the table, the method recognizes the speech intervals with the accuracy of 98.6%. However, the recognized speech includes patients' speeches. If we evaluate the rate of recognizing nurses' speeches only, it becomes 96.9%, which is still a higher recognition rate.

Integration. We integrated the three method described above, and applied to 300 seconds which are obtained from a day of a nurse.

Fig. 3 shows the results of the speech interval estimation and walking detection. The above figure of the figure is the result of walking detection, in which three walking periods are detected. After applying location estimation method to the three intervals of 30 seconds after walking, only the first one of after 65.5 second was estimated to be in a patient's room. Then, applying speech interval estimation to that interval, the total time of speech interval were found to be 24 seconds.

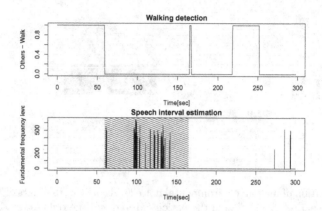

Fig. 3. Result of integrated process. The upper is the result of walking detection, and the lower is the speech interval estimation. After applying 3 parts of 30 seconds after walking period detected by the upper part, the first 30 seconds were detected as in the patient's room, which could be applied by the speech interval estimation of the lower part.

5   Nursing Interval Detection from In-Room Sensors

In this section, we try to analyze the in-room sensor data, and detect the intervals when a nurse enters the room only from these in-room sensors. In the previous study[1], we found that the candidate sensors which have correlations with nursing intervals are 1) bed sensors, 2) loudness sensors, and 3) illuminometer. Therefore, we focus on these sensors in this section.

In this section, we target on recognizing nurse's entrance to a patient's room and intervals where the nurses are absent from the room. This is the first step of the nursing interval detection from in-door sensors, and if it is accurate, we can step further to add recognition of nurse exits, and apply for any time using time window method.

5.1   Method

Dataset. To prepare the dataset for target classes for nurses' entrance and absence, we picked up 100 durations from each sensor data, in which

- (*ENTER*) 50 of them include the RFID event of a nurse's entrance, and
- (*ABSENT*) the rest 50 are between the events of nurse's exit and entrance, which could be estimated that there are no nurses in the room.

Moreover, since we found that the sensor data behave differently between day and night, each of the 50 durations are divided into:

- (*day*) 25 durations of between 8:00 and 18:00 of a day, and
- (*night*) 25 durations of between 18:00 of a day and 8:00 of the next day.

Features. For each duration of each sensor in the dataset, we extract the feature vectors. The idea for recognizing ENTER and ABSENT is that the sensor values will change in the former case, but not in the latter case. Therefore, we take the difference between statistic values of several while after and before a target time, considering a margin. For a duration, a feature vector (v_1, v_2) consists of:

$$v_1 = ||E(t + 10, t + 40) - E(t - 40, t - 10)||$$

$$v_2 = ||V(t + 10, t + 40) - V(t - 40, t - 10)||$$

where $||x||$ is the absolute value of x, $E(a, b)$ is the mean of the sensor values of a duration $[a, b]$, and $V(a, b)$ is the variance of them. Moreover, we set different t for ENTER and ABSENT: the time (sec) of the RFID event of a nurse's entrance for ENTER, and the the center time (sec) of the duration for ABSENT.

This means that we take the difference of statistic values of 30 seconds after and before the target time, including a margin of ± 20 seconds.

Recognition. To recognize the entrances of nurses, we train the feature vectors with SVM with radial kernel. We applied 5-fold cross validation to evaluate the accuracy, in which the feature vectors of the dataset are randomly divided in to 5 groups, and each of them is treated as a test data, while the others are as training data.

As we mentioned, we found that the feature values are different between day and night from the preliminary study. Therefore, we compared the 3 cases of using all feature vectors together, those of daytime only, and those of nighttime only.

Moreover, we tried several combinations of sensors from bed sensors, illuminance sensors, and loudness sensors, for the sake of finding better combination of input variables for recognition.

5.2   Result

Fig. 4 is the accuracy of recognition for nurses' entrances and absence, for several combinations of day/night and those of sensors which have conducted best accuracies among our trials. In Fig. 4, (a) is with all dataset, (b) is only with daytime, and (c) is only with nighttime. Each of them shows both of with all sensors (bed, loudness, and illuminance) and without illuminance sensors.

From Fig. 4, we can see that (a) which use all the dataset, is almost worse than the corresponding ones which use only daytime or nighttime dataset, except for (c) right. From this, we can conclude that the features behaves differently between daytime and nighttime, and we should firstly distinguish the recognition algorithms of day and night.

Moreover, from Fig. 4, we can see that, for the daytime, (b) is the same if we omit illuminance sensors, and illuminance sensors improves the accuracy for the nighttime. This means that the illuminance sensors do not necessarily play effective role for recognition at daytime, but do at nighttime. Therefore, we can

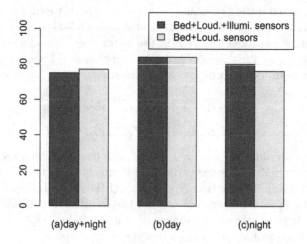

Fig. 4. Accuracies of entrance recognition

conclude that the best and smaller combinations of sensors is bed sensors and loudness sensors at daytime, and is plus illuminance sensors at nighttime.

Based on the consideration above, we show the confusion matrix of the recognition for the best cases, which are (b) right and (c) left, in Tab. 3, respectively.

From Tab. 3(a), the recall rate of entrance recognition at daytime is 72.0%, and the precision rate is precision 94.7%. Those at night time is 87.5% and 77.9% from Tab 3(b), respectively.

Table 3. Confusion matrix for entrance recognition

(a) Daytime without illuminance sensors
Accuracy: 84.0%

Ground truth→	ENTER	ABSENT
ENTER	18	1
ABSENT	7	24

(b) Nighttime with all sensors
Accuracy: 80.0%

Ground truth→	ENTER	ABSENT
ENTER	21	6
ABSENT	4	19

6   Conclusion

In this paper, we described two approaches for capturing nursing interactions: 1) finding nursing intervals from mobile sensors with accelerometers and audio on nurses, and 2) recognizing nurses' entrance to a patient's room from in-room sensors of bed, loudness, and illuminance sensors. For 1), we firstly detect the nurses' entrance to the patient's room by walking detection from accelerometers and noise level on mobile sensors, and detect the interval of interaction between nurses and the patient by Cepstrum method. For 2), we recognize the nurse's entrance to the patient's room with in-room sensors, using separate algorithms between day and night.

Although this is the first step to analyze and mine the nursing interactions leading to clinical pathways, it could be an alternative to install costly RFID readers to all rooms, and could be an important baseline technique to find valuable intervals from long and big data of sensors. The future step should be applying the proposed methods to the longer period, and evaluate the accuracy combining the approaches.

Acknowledgements. This work is supported by Grant-in-Aid for Young Scientists (A) (21680009) of JSPS and Funding Program for World-Leading Innovative R&D on Science and Technology (FIRST). The authors would like to thank their support. We also appreciate the cooperation for experiment by the staff of Saiseikai Kumamoto Hospital, Japan.

References

1. Nohara, Y., Inoue, S., Nakashima, N., Ueda, N., Kitsuregawa, M.: Large-scale Sensor Dataset in a Hospital. In: International Workshop on Pattern Recognition for Healthcare Analytics, Tsukuba, Japan, November 11, 4 p. (2012)
2. Nakamura, M., Inoue, S., Nohara, Y., Nakashima, N.: Finding Nursing in the Room from Accelerometers and Audio on Mobile Sensors. In: IUI Workshop on Location Awareness for Mixed and Dual Reality (LAMDa), Santa Monica, USA, March 19 (to appear, 2013)
3. Watanabe, K., et al.: Noninvasive measurement of heartbeat, respiration, snoring and body movements of a subject in bed via a pneumatic method. IEEE Transactions on Biomedical Engineering 52(12), 2100–2107 (2005)
4. Bogert, B.P., Healy, M.J.R., Tukey, J.W.: The Frequency Analysis of Time Series for Echoes: Cepstrum, Pseudo-auto Covariance, Cross-cepstrum, and Shaft Racking. In: Rosenblatt, M. (ed.) Proceedings of the Symposium on Time Series Analysis, ch. 15, pp. 209–243. Wiley, New York (1963)
5. Lukowicz, P., Ward, J.A., Junker, H., Stäger, M., Tröster, G., Atrash, A., Starner, T.: Recognizing Workshop Activity Using Body Worn Microphones and Accelerometers. In: Ferscha, A., Mattern, F. (eds.) PERVASIVE 2004. LNCS, vol. 3001, pp. 18–32. Springer, Heidelberg (2004)
6. Lester, J., Choudhury, T., Borriello, G.: A Practical Approach to Recognizing Physical Activities. In: Fishkin, K.P., Schiele, B., Nixon, P., Quigley, A. (eds.) PERVASIVE 2006. LNCS, vol. 3968, pp. 1–16. Springer, Heidelberg (2006)
7. Choudhury, T., et al.: The Mobile Sensing Platform: An Embedded Activity Recognition System. IEEE Pervasive Computing Magazine 7(2), 32–41 (2008)

Creating Instantly Disappearing Prints Using Thermochromic Paint and Thermal Printer in an Interactive Art Installation

Miu-Ling Lam

School of Creative Media, City University of Hong Kong
miu.lam@cityu.edu.hk

Abstract. This paper outlines the techniques used in an interactive art installation, called *Time Axis*, created by the author. The installation invites viewers to take a portrait of themselves in front of a wall-mounted device that is embedded with a camera and thermal printers. The image captured by the camera will be printed on paper by the thermal printers. One of the thermal printers is loaded with some custom-made thermochromic paper that changes color reversibly when temperature is changed. Images printed on the thermochromic paper will disappear due to heat loss to surroundings after a few seconds of being printed out. Thus, the participants will witness the silhouettes of their portraits appearing and dissipating on paper instantly. The mechanical noise generated by the printers is manipulated by a digital resonator and sent through a pair of headphones to be listened by the participants to intensify their experience.

Keywords: Thermochromism, thermal printer, temporary image, ephemeral, fading, interactive art, installation.

1   Introduction

1.1   Interactive Visual Art Installations: Digital vs. Analogue

Interactive art is a genre of art that involves the participation of viewers that makes dynamic changes to the contents of the artwork. The exploration of the participants and the dialogue between the audience and the system creates meanings to the artwork. In many interactive visual art installations, due to the nature and requirement of dynamic visual contents, the presentation technology is usually based on digital media, such as computer screen, projection and head-mounted display. A vast range of augmented reality works use projection mapping technique and modern mobile computing devices.

On the contrary, creating visual interactivity using ordinary, physical object, such as a piece of paper or wood, without digital media and mechanical actuation of the object is traditionally challenging for artists and designers. Today, media artists create artworks that left the screen and lie in more direct, tangible physical phenomena [1]. They study the sciences of materials to explore new possibilities for art making and

A. Marcus (Ed.): DUXU/HCII 2013, Part III, LNCS 8014, pp. 290–295, 2013.
© Springer-Verlag Berlin Heidelberg 2013

design. Creating interactivity on ordinary, analogue objects can bring these everyday objects to life and manifest highly compelling and spectacular aesthetic due to human's strong desire and enjoyment for magical experience.

1.2   Chromism: Approaches to Achieve Visual Interactivity on Ordinary Physical Objects

Chromism is a process that changes the color of a compound reversibly. In recent decades, wide ranges of chemical materials that can give chromic (color-changing) phenomena have become commercially available and commonly used in consumer products. Chromism is usually induced by external stimuli, such as irradiation and heat, which alter the electron density of substances and give rise to a change in electron states of molecules. Two major types of chromism are thermochromism and photochromism. Thermochromism is the most common chromism. It refers to the property of substances to change color reversibly when temperature is changed. It is utilized by the work *Time Axis* to be presented in this paper. Photochromism is induced by light irradiation. This phenomenon is based on the isomerization between two different molecular structures, light-induced formation of color centers in crystals, precipitation of metal particles in a glass, or other mechanisms. We will discuss some artistic projects that have exploited thermochromism or photochromism techniques to achieve color-change on physical objects.

1.3   Related Works

There are a number of interesting works recently appear in the art scene that have employed chromism techniques. *Thermochromic Clock* (2011) by Che-Wei Wang and Taylor Levy (CW&T) [2] is a 4-digit 7-segment timepiece, where each segment in the display is made with nichrome wire and then covered by a thick layer of black thermochromic paint. Time is displayed by applying voltage to the nichrome wire. As the wire sustains an electric current, it heats up the surrounding thermochromic paint, causing it to become transparent.

Apart from thermochromic paint, many artworks have been created with photochromic paint/ink to produce temporary visual effects on physical objects. There are a number of interactive art installations that exploit phosphorescent (glow-in-the-dark) paint or materials excited by sequenced light. An audio-visual installation *Fade Out* (2010) by Daito Manabe and Motoi Ishibashi [3] uses an infrared camera to capture a portrait of a viewer in dark. It then uses a laser projector to project a ray of laser beam that moves on a screen painted with phosphorescence paint to render the captured portrait pixel by pixel. The trace of the laser beam leaves the screen a glowing image of the portrait that fades away in around 30 seconds.

Temporary Printing Machine (2011) by rAndom International [4] also uses photochromism technique to depict viewers in a transient light portrait. As the viewer stands in front of an empty canvas that is coated with a layer of light-sensitive material, his/her image is slowly revealed by an array of sequenced light source moving slowly accross the canvas. The portrait gradually fades away and leaves the canvas empty again.

The Book That Can't Wait (2012) is a literary book created by publishing house Eterna Cadencia in collaboration with creative agency draftFCB, for an anthology of new Latin American authors. The book is printed in light-sensitive ink that begins to disappear when the book is opened and expose to light and air for the first time. The ink will completely disappears within two to four months of opening the package, urging purchasers to actually completely read the book shortly after they buy it.

2   Time Axis

2.1   Artistic Concept - Capturing the Permanence and Evanescence of a Moment

The title of the art installation presented in this paper is Time Axis. It evokes the viewers to think about what time is while seeing the installation. Time has long been a subject of study across many different disciplines. However, it is extremely difficult to define time in a non-controversial manner. Moreover, most people in the world have never thought about what time is. This art piece evokes the consciousness of the concept of time through an unfamiliar experience - taking self-portraits and watching them vanish on paper instantaneously. Photography is a process of capturing an instance of dynamic events as a permanent visual at that moment: turning fleeting matters to permanent. Still images are time-invariant, whilst still images that fade away are time-variant: turning permanent matters to evanescent. More interestingly, the evanescence of the event captured by the image is different from that of the ephemeral image itself.

2.2   Coating Thermochromic Paint on Paper Rolls

Thermochromic paper that changes color reversibly with temperature is not commercially available. We need to custom-made our own thermochromic paper with thermochromic materials, which usually come in paint or powder form. In this project, the thermochromic paper has to be in form of a roll of receipt paper or thermal paper so as to fit into a thermal printer. Thus, for convenience, we coat the thermochromic materials on regular thermal paper. The thickness and resulting texture of the thermochromic paint is crucial, because thick and frictional paint on paper can easily adhere to the print head of thermal printer and cause paper jam. The thermochromic paint used in Time Axis is prepared by mixing thermochromic powder in white gesso and water. The thermochromic powder is purchased from [5]. It is called thermal-dust. It comes in many different colors, while black color is picked in this project. The thermal-dust loses it color (turns white) at 30°C or warmer. As the dust cools, it returns to its original color. Gesso is used as the paint base rather than acrylic or other common painting media, as it has been tested to give the smoothest discharge of paper from the thermal printer. We carefully applied a thin, even coat of thermochromic paint mixture with a sponge brush on a roll of thermal paper (Fig. 1), and let the paint dry in hot air. The thermochromic paper is then rolled up and loaded into thermal printer. The thermochromic paper is reusable due to the reversibility of color change.

Fig. 1. Custom thermochromic paper made with a thin coat of thermochromic paint on thermal paper

2.3   Thermal Printer, Arduino and Processing

Thermal printers are a fast, cheap and reliable way to create mini paper documents. The thermal printer used in this project is manufactured by Cashino Electronic Technology in China. It became very popular among the maker community after being introduced by a famous electronic online store Sparkfun in their New Product Post in March of 2011. The most interesting feature of this low cost thermal printer lies in its communication protocol. It reads TTL serial, thus can read print data conveniently from an Arduino [6] microcontroller.

We have created a sketch in Processing [7] to capture image from a USB camera. The image is converted to binary image based on a threshold that depends on the space's light intensity. We have added some LED strips at the back of the wooden enclosure of the device to ensure enough amount of light illuminating on the viewer's face. The binary image is then sent through an Arduino to the thermal printer byte by byte. Upon receiving the packets of image data, the thermal printer's print head will heat up the thermal paper and thermochromic paper on corresponding pixels.

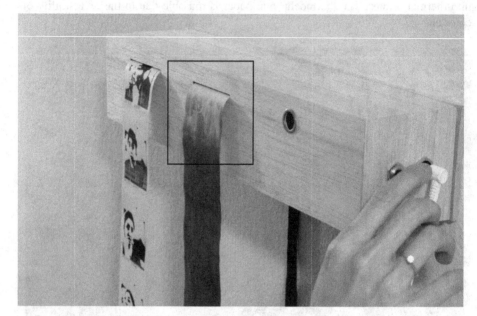

Fig. 2. Image printed on thermochromic paper slowly fades out

Fig. 3. Installation view of *Time Axis*

2.4   The Time Axes

At the bottom of each image of portrait, there is a time stamp to indicate the time and date when the portrait is taken. Thus, on the white thermal paper, there exists a time axis along the strip of paper pointing in upward direction. For the black thermochromic paper, the image is dissipating slowly. We can interpret that there is an imaginary time axis in on the thermochromic paper that remarks the time-variant nature of the image.

2.5   Sound

There is a notable mechanical noise produced by the thermal printers during the printing process. We have embedded a microphone in the device and put it next to the thermal printers to capture the noise. The sound is then fed to the computer and processed using software Ableton Live to generate real-time resonance effect. This intensified sound is heard by the participant through a pair of headphones and creates an immersive audio environment that mimics the condition of meditation.

3   Concluding Remarks

The disappearing image on paper can be referred to the concept of trace suggested by French philosopher Jacques Derrida [8][9]. Trace is not strictly defined, but is usually explained as the absence of presence. In *Time Axis*, the black thermochromic paper leaves a trace of portrait in the viewer's memory, which will never appear on the paper again.

References

1. Klanten, R., Ehmann, S., Hanschke, V.: A Touch of Code: Interactive Installations and Experiences. Die Gestalten Verlag (2011)
2. Thermochrmic Clock by CW&T http://cwandt.com/#thermochromic-clock
3. Manabe, D., Ishibashi, M.: Fade Out,
   http://www.daito.ws/en/work/uvlaserfadeout.html
4. rAndom International, http://random-international.com/
5. Solar Color Dust, http://www.solarcolordust.com/
6. Arduino, http://arduino.cc/
7. Processing, http://processing.org/
8. Derrida, J.: Writing and difference. University of Chicago Press (1980)
9. Derrida, J.: Of grammatology. Johns Hopkins University Press (1998)

Fashioning Embodied Interfaces:
Open Wearables Crafting

Valérie Lamontagne

Concordia University, Design & Computation Arts, 1515 St. Catherine St. West, Montreal,
Quebec, Canada H3G 2W1
valerie@3lectromode.com

Abstract. This paper investigates the role of the designer in the "opening" of
culture in fashion and technology. In particular it explores the convergence of
"open practices" in vanguard technologies and fabrication processes found in
the history of Modernist fashion, as well as recent popular uses of technology,
and engineering, and more specifically wearables design practices.

Keywords: Wearables, fashion, open design, embodiment, interface culture,
textiles, prototyping, performance.

1   Introduction

Two narratives that contextualize the relationship between open culture, technology,
and the history of fashion are proposed in this paper.

The first narrative is rooted in turn-of-the-century Paris, where the concept and role
of the fashion designer was birthed in tandem with unheralded innovations in the
manufacturing industry. This transformation changed and challenged our relationship
with garments, the changes stemming from shifts in clothing's cultural capital and the
processes associated with their production.

The second narrative stream explores the expanding landscape of current hybrid
techno-artistic practices of wearables design and production—a field combining
technical know-how from various fields, including engineering, textile innovation,
fashion production and sartorial expression. The common thread tying these stories
together is found in the increased access to materials, technologies and skill-practices
since the modern era. Access to materials, tools, and information figure prominently in
the drama of how fashion and technology came to be "opened up" through open design
practices.

2   Fashion and Engineering

Fashion and engineering, as practiced-based disciplines, have more in common than
is initially visible. To begin with, both are practices rooted in research and iteration
that participate in a continuum of evolution and constant transformation. The products
of fashion and technology are transient, trend-driven, technology-based and
irrevocably "of the moment."

A. Marcus (Ed.): DUXU/HCII 2013, Part III, LNCS 8014, pp. 296–305, 2013.
© Springer-Verlag Berlin Heidelberg 2013

Fashion and technology are also both children of the modern era. Technology and fashion as we know it emerged at the turn of the century as a result of rapid change in material and industrial innovations, social and economic events, and mass-market transportation networks [1; 2].

As cultural products, fashion and technology define and materially embody the times during which they are designed and used. As cultural artifacts, they are beacons of our desires, projected fantasies, hopes and beliefs. Fashion and technology crystallize the contemporary in an ever-unfolding and insatiable process of production. I will also argue that, perhaps due to their fleeting and evanescent nature, the survival and constant re-invention of fashion and technology is deeply entwined with open culture practices in which the sharing of information, techniques and processes are key.

2.1 Modernism, Sewing and Fashion: Poiret

Before 1900, there were no real fashion designers. There were garment makers or seamstresses who gained a reputation by executing the sartorial visions of their clients, making to-order garments based on general stylistic trends or rank [1; 2]. However, they did not consider themselves artists or creative individuals. All this changed in Paris at the early turn of the century, when couturiers such as Paul Poiret marketed and crafted identities as "artists," as opposed to mere "makers." It was Poiret who, in 1904, pronounced himself a fashion "designer," claiming the position of style arbitrator [3; 4; 5]. Having worked at the House of Worth (1990-1004), Poiret was the first to align his craft with artistic practices such as Modern painting and sculpture that were coming to the fore in Paris and Europe at the time. In this climate of economic affluence, rapid social change and artistic dynamism, Poiret cast himself as a fashion innovator, gaining international influence and markets across Europe and America [3]. Within his active career (1903-1929), Poiret was dubbed "The King of Fashion" and "Le Magnifique." He was prolifically active in fashion, perfume, film and theatre costumes, and fashion training schools, as well as the international trunk shows that brought him to America numerous times. At peak of his influence, Poiret's styles and opinions made numerous news headlines and transformed the ways in which his clients and society at large viewed fashion's role in society [4].

2.2 Paris and Fashion

Not coincidentally, the upgrading of the garment "maker" to that of a "designer" and "artist" arrived at a time of great technological and material transformation that affected the social and tangible make-up of everyday life [6; 7]. At the turn of the century, numerous technological changes transformed the social sphere, including the proliferation of transportation channels—from trains and automobiles to steam-powered ships—that facilitated the exchange of ideas, styles and social groups across a larger geographic area. Also in this time period, city architecture was completely transformed. Baron Georges-Eugène Haussmann re-tooled the Parisian cityscape, adding wide boulevards, street lights and clean, safe paved streets and alleys; these developments changed the way that the city was used and by whom. The modern city's infrastructure of boulevards, civic parks and interior shopping arcades encouraged greater urban mobility, especially among the women who could now walk though the city safely, without social stigma.

These changes in transportation and urban design—along with an increase in economic prosperity and leisure time on the part of a growing middle class—contributed to the increased importance of personal sartorial expression, as well as the exploration of fashion innovation and variety [1; 8]. The modern era built a need for individuals to be seen as being personally expressive, combined with a desire to display newly acquired wealth, social standing and stylistic "savoir faire." During this same modernist era were cemented the legacies of today's major Parisian couture houses. Many now-ubiquitous couture labels had humble beginnings as "makers." These artisans and craft-focused ateliers later evolved into significant style arbiters and international economic powerhouses. Louis Vuitton, for example, was known as a luggage maker who dabbled in doll clothes up until the mid-twentieth century. Coco Chanel, the revolutionary designer who introduced "poor" materials and sportswear cuts to fashion, worked primarily as a seamstress until the First World War. However, is was Poiret who daringly embarked on a journey of making fashion fashionable for its own sake. Influenced by the bohemian scene of artists living in Paris at that time, Poiret is known for having done away with corsets and embraced Oriental themes and textiles; he was also influential in introducing the public to works of contemporary artists such as Raoul Dufy, featured in the couturier's textile designs, party invitations and set designs for fashion shows. In fact, Poiret is one of the inventors of today's runway performance. Heavily inspired by theatre work, he mounted theatrical showcases of his fashion designs on custom stages in his couture house as well as department stores such as Gimbels in New York City [3].

2.3   Trademarks and Logos

By all accounts, Poiret was very media savvy for his era. He took every opportunity to promote his name and brand. When he discovered that his designs were being forged in America and at home, he became president of La Chambre Syndicale de la Couture, laying the groundwork to protect intellectual property design in fashion. Many other growing couture houses were also becoming more and more invested in protecting their brand. This legalistic push to protect the integrity of creative elements, until then unseen in the garment industry, led to the creation of logo copyrights as seen today. To this day it is logos and trademarks that are prominently protected, much more than the aesthetic cut or style of a garment or accessory, though there have been recent cases to the contrary, such as Christian Louboutin trying to protect his famous red under heel.

2.4   Pattern-Making and Distribution

The rise of the "designer" occurs, interestingly, in parallel with both the proliferation of home sewing machines and an increased access to products such as textiles

Fig. 1. Paul Poiret advertisement 1912

imported from various parts of the world, giving everyday "makers" an opportunity to craft their own design [9]. This meant an increase in makers, as well as access to the tools to make things at a higher level of quality and customization. Therefore, it wasn't only the logos by Poiret (and other designers) that were being copied. In fact, professional seamstresses and store manufacturers were reproducing entire styles and patterns—sometimes as legal and "official" copies. For Poiret and his contemporaries, a more radical approach had to be taken to protect the "intellectual property" of their designs and their status as "designers." The pirating of patterns occurred especially in America where Parisian styles were all the rage, and Poiret was considered the City of Light's reigning monarch. In an effort to stave off imitators, Poiret created one of the first official designer "patterns," sold and "authenticated" as an original "Paul Poiret" design. Although it was intended to protect the integrity of the designer, what Poiret had in fact inaugurated was the democratization of fashion as seen in designer patterns today from Vogue to McCalls. Instead of authenticating his products through their origins (made in his Paris atelier) or their logo, these patterns placed value on the design of the product, rather than the product itself. The design as opposed to the origin of making was most valued. Poiret can also be credited, via his proliferation of patterns, as the first populist DIY promoter of fashion, though he may not have thought of it this way.

3   Open Design and Wearables

The exciting ramifications of such a shift in thinking about fashion creativity, from a finished object to one which may be executed and potentially customized by others, inspired the values also at the heart of the avant-garde open design culture blossoming today. Design kits and DIY templates executed by individuals factor in and inevitably celebrate the vagrancies of different styles of interpretation, material choices, tool-exploration and end results. Fashion patterns, along with numerous kits from multiple industries, became popularized at the start of the 20th century. One could order kits, instructions and materials to build such things from homes to radios, from socks to furniture. These original templates form the core of open culture thinking today, a revival of pre-post industrialism and craft engagement as described by Sennet [10]. According to Andersen and Gershenfeld, we are presently facing a new kind of post-industrial revolution of "making," enabling individuals to enter the chain of production on a small and personal scale [11; 12].

Wearables, the result of the admixture of fashion and electronics, are closely aligned with the growing movement of open design practices and access to technology. Wearables has greatly benefited from a belief that the field has the potential to amalgamate contributions from many individuals and practices coming from the fields of engineering, electro-mechanical industries, textiles and fashion field. As well, the field of wearables and fashion-tech would not be where it is today without immense contributions by people working in electronics, craft, hobbyist and other forms of admixtures of tech-design experimentation that are increasingly open-sourced and available via networks such as the Web. In this section I want to highlight how current innovation in wearables is a natural evolution of open design practices stemming from innovation and re-thinking in modern fashion, art and technological popularization.

3.1   Materials

The field of wearables would not be where it is today without the belief that artists and designers had something to contribute to technology. Coined in 1991 by Steve Mann at MIT, "wearables" as fashion tech has principally been a door through which the material experimentation of electronics could be elaborated in design contexts, often related to the body, as this is the site of technological exploration for wearables. Books such as "Physical Computing" by Tom Igoe from New York University's Interactive Telecommunications Program revolutionized the language of electronics, making it accessible to a whole new set of actors with art backgrounds and hacker mentalities [13]. In Canada, robotics pioneer Norm White at OCAD schooled computational innovators such as David Rokeby, forever changing the landscape of media arts practices from users of tools (such as video cameras) to makers of tools (such as circuits and programming languages).

Closer to the field of wearables, Leah Buechley developed the LilyPad Arduino platform, the first instance of adapting electronics for wearables. From an engineering perspective, Arduino is like a cake mix for arts electronics, bringing all essential ingredients together and simplifying the language. Since then, other companies such as Adafruit's Flora, Aniomagic and SparkFun have expanded the repertoire and accessibility of materials and technologies offered to users, making it even easier to customize electronics effects. Furthermore, "prêt-à-faire" (ready to make) DIY practices in fashion—incorporating the new production technologies of digital textile printers, 3D printing, and laser cut patterns—are being seen all over the runways, heralding a new way of conceiving of how to dress the body. In less than 10 years, we have seen the material landscape of wearable technologies not only expand but become dynamically accessible, affordable, and full of potential for creative "designerly" (as opposed to thinking that only engineering matters) results.

3.2   Access = Knowledge + Tools

Open design practices flourish with access to knowledge and tools—this means placing not only materials and tools within easy reach, but the practices, methods and knowledge that give ready hands access to creative solutions. There are two prominent areas of access: the first is through publishing, formerly the Diderot's Encyclopédie, now encountered in the everyday as how-to manuals, guide-books, and increasingly the Internet with its wealth of photo and video tutorials. Books such as Sabine Seymour's "Fashionable Technology" and "Functional Aesthetics," Syuzi Pakchyan's "FashioningTech," the collaborative "Open Softwear," and Otto von Busch's hacking couture guidebook "Becoming Fashion-able" have proven important in bringing wearables to an audience of novices. Furthermore, sites such as Instructables and Craft, FashioningTech, and Etsy feature a wide range of technology, craft-based tutorials and ideas for materials, methods, providing inspiration and a community to share it with.

Other websites such as Thingiverse share files for the emerging practices of 3D printing and other forms of machine-tooled and 3-dimensional object making. Tangible meeting and working sites and fabrication laboratories (or FabLabs), such as ProtoSpace (Utrecht, Netherlands) and Open Design City (Berlin) as well as labs such as V2_ (Rotterdam) have made a significant change in the availability of access to machines such as 3D printers and laser cutters, as well as bringing individuals into contact with a community of technical and computational experts. Of course, festivals, fairs and events such as MakerFaire, SIGGRAPH, SXSW, Transmediale, FutureEverything and ISEA provide great opportunities to share knowledge and skills and meet the actors involved in the global shift of sharing design expertise. In short, the design, art and technical world is producing an increasing number of nodes of information, sharing, encounters, testing, advice and hands-on material making.

3.3   Social Adaptation = Made 4 U

Another area of interest is how remote and online platforms are proposing ways for designers and consumers to collaborate in creating open designs. Using as a template the pattern adjustments and choices of textiles or embellishments that sewing patterns provide, online and rapid prototyping technologies offer new opportunities for social adaptations. Customization and user-input platforms invite experts and novices alike to reproduce, modify, improve, customize, and be inspired by the work of others. This type of network and platform fosters co-creation, and "personal design nodes" where the shape and making of design can be seamlessly personalized and adapted to use or aesthetic preference, It is both about the personal and the collective in as much as it solicits input from individuals for their needs and desires while also keeping the practice and knowledge open-ended enough for collective contributions and specializations over time.

Products such as the user-generated, nature-inspired jewelry by Nervous System and Shapeways propose new and exciting design collaborations where the results unfold unexpectedly. From within fashion, companies such as Unitestyles propose platforms to customize their designs, while the über-rarefied Maison Martin Margiela has been inviting users since 2004 to adapt unfinished designs to their liking and post them online. Finally, computational couture mavens such as May Huang propose 3D algorithmic designs, which are also user-generated. These online platforms offer a way in which the consumer may become part of the design process—an invitation which can at times be daunting, yet exciting. Even in the event of a design failure, the consumer can better appreciate the importance of design and the power of networked and rapid prototyping technologies in making ideas tangible. These kinds of open access platforms have been thoroughly explored and documented at Amsterdam's Open Design Lab of the Waag Society where designers are encouraged to create "open" design for commerce [14].

3.4   Unzipping Wearable Fashion

Open design materials, knowledge and tools, as previously mentioned, have democratized and 'unzipped' wearables practice. Increasingly fashion-tech is making use of an increasing complex array of engineering and computational skills, sartorial knowhow and material experimentation, making the design studio more akin to a laboratory producing new aesthetics and technologies to transform the body. What were previously craft or technical-only niche groups are becoming increasingly mainstream—yet independent—hybrid tech-fashion design studios. The factory is no longer over "there" but rather down the street, or in our living rooms. Access to high-tech tools and experts is 'industrializing' the practice of small scale designers, giving them more options to professionalize their craft through access to custom circuits, 3D printing, laser cutting, etc. These technical networks, both local and networked, help shape the hybridization of the wearables field by giving designers access to specialized knowledge and tools, resulting in the expansion of their material repertoire and craft expressiveness.

Increasingly, fashion is playing an important role in communicating who we are— from the personal to the global—as it did at the turn of the 20th century [15]. Fashion designers are regularly pushing the material envelope of what our sartorial choices can say about us. Contemporary designers such as Dutch Pauline van Dongen have collaborated with 3D printing companies like Freedom of Creation to create 3D printed shoes, while Iris van Herpen, also Dutch, has created entire garments out of 3D printing technologies. Anouk Wipprecht has collaborated with wearable art labs such as V2_ to develop interactive garments that paint themselves, become transparent or are made of a cloud of smoke. These garment designs, though speculative for the moment, are forging a new material vision of what our garments can be and how they might convey who we are in a dynamic technological fashion world.

Meanwhile, other aspects of wearables are forging emerging tangible interfaces for technologies to be embedded in garments in a very concrete way. Diffus, a Danish design studio, has paired with Swiss lace company Forster-Rhoner to develop working prototypes in wearables that piggyback on century old know-how in lace making. Together they have fabricated solar-powered embroidered handbags that combine embellishment with functionality. Moon Berlin, a Berlin fashion label

Fig. 2. Pauline van Dongen, Morphogenesis Shoe, 2011

exploiting light in their designs, have collaborated with the Fraunhofer IZM, an internationally reputable institution for the testing of technologies, to incorporate state-of-the-art stretchable circuits into their bespoke designs. All of these wearable designers are tapping into expertise and tools that are distributed on an increasingly collaborative scale. This is in part due to the many technical (garment, design, textile, electronics) types of expertise needed to create aesthetically and technically successful wearables. These are just a few of the examples of design and tech industries coming together to explore the potential of wearables. Often the collaborations are open exchanges, birthed out of necessity, stemming from this increasingly high-tech, hybrid, networked cottage/professional industry in which fashion innovation and electronics developments converge in professional yet highly craft-focused fashion-technology collaborations. Though the overlaps in knowledge fields of wearables at times come from divergent technical/artistic fields and economies, there is a desire for "sharing becoming a default standard," as noted in the Creative Common's recent anthology of interviews *The Power of Open*. This is a revolutionary moment for wearables and 3D objects—similar to the paradigm shift that occurred in the 2D world of desktop publishing in 1985—which we should embrace, share, contribute to and protect via Open Design philosophies and practices.

4   3lectromode

4.1   DIY Kits

I want to take this opportunity to speak about my own involvement in open design, via the 3lectromode platform. 3lectromode has a vision to innovate in the field of wearables by combining technology with customizable prêt-a-porter fashion. As a small group of practitioners working in the field of fashion and technology, we aim to inspire a future where wearables are democratized and aestheticized. We are interested in developing accessible wearables combining DIY technology with current fashion research and aesthetics. We are fascinated with the potential for technology to create new modalities of interaction between the body and its environment, and are interested in the expressive potential of technology to transform the experience derived from garment use from the poetic to the practical.

Fig. 3. 3lectromode, "Future Matter" 2012

4.2   Prêt-à-Porter Tech

Key to 3lectromode's design ethos is the desire to create a library of open sourced fashion designs which can be easily assembled as kits by anyone with an interest in wearables, electronics or fashion. The kits come complete with the printed garment, the necessary electronics and instructions, taking the guesswork out of electronics assembly while allowing the user to create a customized and fashionable design. Designs are printed on textile printers on which also include the layout of electronic schematics and sewing directions. The methods for assembling the electronic components of the wearable are integrated into the design and can be visually followed, much like a paint-by-numbers picture, without having to refer to a manual. Each piece is uniquely designed, and comes with customizable options for different print patterns, colours, models and sizes, giving the user-end designer the agency to creating his or her own iteration. Computational variations are also included to modify the LilyPad Arduino program. So far, 3lectromode designs have focused on integration of LEDs with various sensors, using the LilyPad Arduino platform for electronic components and programming. 3lectromode's kits are the perfect entry point into wearable technology because of their graphic visualization of electronics assembly methods, while also creating uniquely stylish and fashionable garments. In the process of testing out this open design platform, we at 3lectromode have been interested in integrating feedback from the user-end designers and welcoming collaborations on the sharing of techniques, designs and applications. Ultimately, while maintaining a stylistic curatorial vision true to 3lectromode, we are interested in seeing how people might hack and interpret our work in an open design fashion.

3lectromode as a platform was created for selfish reasons—to create wearables that one could wear in the everyday that have a higher design value component than some of the one-off (and admittedly fashion-starved) productions made in a crafting context. It's really the meeting of the sewing pattern and DIY circuit-design used to create recipes for making fashion that is at the heart of 3lectromode. Our designs are somewhere between a prototype for wearables and a way of having engineers discover fashion, or fashionistas discover engineering. 3lectromode articulates itself as a kind of bridge between fashion and technology.

Acknowledgments. I would like to thank Christopher L. Salter, Joanna Berzowska, Patrick H. Harrop, Anouk Wipprecht, and Isabelle Campeau for their participation in sharing ideas and expertise as well as acting as idea bouncing boards.

References

1. Entwistle, J.: The Fashioned Body: Fashion, Dress and Modern Social Theory. Polity, Cambridge (2000)
2. Lipovetsky, G.: The Empire of Fashion: Dressing Modern Democracy (Porter, C., trans.). Princeton University Press, Princeton & Oxford (1994)
3. Troy, N.J.: Couture Culture: A Study in Modern Art & Fashion. The MIT Press, Cambridge & London (2003)
4. White, P.: Poiret. Studio Vista, London (1985)
5. Wilson, E.: Adorned in Dreams: Fashion and Modernity. Virago, London (1985)
6. Berman, M.: All That Is Solid Melts Into Air. Penguin, London (1988)
7. Kern, S.: The Culture of Time and Space: 1880-1919. Harvard University Press, Cambridge & London (1991)
8. Lehmann, U.: Tigersprung: Fashion in Modernity. The MIT Press, Cambridge & London (2000)
9. Breward, C., Evans, C. (eds.): Fashion and Modernity. Berg, Oxford & New York (2005)
10. Sennet, R.: The Craftsman. Yale University Press, New Haven & London (2008)
11. Andersen, C.: Makers: The New Industrial Revolution. McClelland & Stewart, Toronto (2012)
12. Gershenfeld, N.: FAB: The Coming Revolution on Your Desktop—from Personal Computers to Personal Fabrication. Basic Books, New York (2005)
13. Igoe, T., O'Sullivan, D.: Physical Computing: Sensing and Controlling the Physical World with Computers. Thomson Course Technology, Boston (2004)
14. Able, B.V., Evers, L., Klaassen, R., Troxler, P. (eds.): Open Design Now. Waag Society, Amsterdam (2011)
15. Barnard, M.: Fashion as Communication. Routledge, London & New York (2002)

InTouch: Crossing Social Interaction with Perception

Rung-Huei Liang, Wei-Ming Chung, Hsin-Liu Kao, and Tsen-Ying Lin

Department of Industrial and Commercial Design,
National Taiwan University of Science and Technology, Taipei, Taiwan
liang@mail.ntust.edu.tw

Abstract. With visual feedback serving as a major output of current social interaction through Internet, we aim to explore how alternative sensory outputs can enrich the experience of mediated social interaction. Thoughtfully making design choices, we deliver an artifact called InTouch to address the qualities we are interested in. InTouch consists of four sections in a wooden box surfaced with elastic Lycra. Each section stands for a communication link with a friend. By pressing a link, an individual can express her consideration for a friend. When pressed, the color changes from blue to red, while raising the temperature on a friends' device. The temperature of each link is provided from a thermoelectric cooler (TEC), turning hot or cold based on the input electrical current. One movement triggers two senses, namely touch and vision, forming perceptual-crossings as perceiving while being perceived. In addition to the description of the system, we discuss the motivation and concept behind design, present a pilot test and point out directions for future work.

Keywords: Perceptual crossing, social interaction, tangible interaction design.

1   Introduction

There is an increasing amount of smart electronic devices enabling social interaction in our everyday life; we simply slide icons over screen to manipulate social information on the touch-based interface. However, the UI designer of Apple, Bret Victor [9], points out that those technology-oriented interfaces do not provide sensuous feedback, nor can they allow us to perceive inherent properties of objects. Namely, capabilities of human sensors shouldn't be ignored since everything we experience in this world, including social interaction, is perceived with sensory details: sight, sound, smell, taste, and touch..

Moreover, how we interact with devices and how devices and users mutually inform play important roles in the process of experiencing interaction. An awful user experience could make users feel frustrated if we can't provide a good dialogue in the form of awareness of others' condition or awareness of others being aware of us. Taking a terrible experience of entering through an automatic door for example, we don't have any idea why the automatic door keeps closed. Broken? Didn't sense me? Out of service? Black-out?

With these concerns, under what situation can we recreate an embodied experience to mediate social interaction through an artifact with more sensory perceptions

A. Marcus (Ed.): DUXU/HCII 2013, Part III, LNCS 8014, pp. 306–315, 2013.
© Springer-Verlag Berlin Heidelberg 2013

Fig. 1. Scenario of using InTouch

involved? Also, how can we make perception perceivable between artifacts and people across the Internet (Figure 1)?

2   Literture Review

French phenomenologist Maurice Merleau-Ponty investigates perception in his book, Phenomenology of Perception [10], and defines phenomenology as the study of essences, especially regarding the essence of consciousness and of perception. He argues that the whole world is a field for perception, to which we can assign meaning through human consciousness. We can't separate ourselves from our perception, which is a reciprocal interplay between the perceiver and the perceived of this world. Phenomenology of perception highlights the nature of embodiment when we perceive the world through our bodies and articulates that we are essentially embodied subjects.

Of special interest to us is the term "perceptual crossing" emerging in recent studies of embodied interaction while the semantics of it however differs in different contents. Da Jaegher [2] reports that two people encountering from the opposite direction might step towards the same side for couple times and just can't walk past each other. This is how we form dynamically mutual coordination and ceaselessly adjust our movement influenced by others in the real word. We perceive while being perceived by others making dual perception at the same time, forming perceptual crossing [1]. Related experiments or projects in terms the notion of "perceptual crossing" include the following three examples.

First, Deckers et al. [3] delivered an interesting experiment to make an artifact capable of perceiving self-presence (perceive the body-image), to further, perceiving perceptive action (perceive other perceiving me), and finally, perceiving of expressivity (perceive others' mind). Second, Friendly Vending Machine (master graduation project by Guus Baggermans, 2009) [4], which behaves in coordination with customers' movements delivers an idea of human-computer interaction through perceptual crossing. Third, being adapted to medical therapy for autistic kids, a human-robot interaction through perceptual crossing is easier to bring the kids to the crowd [4].

In short, the uses of the notion of perceptual crossing are manifold. It could refer to the situation that one perceives while being perceived as well as while knowing that she is perceived. Crossing could also indicate that a single perception encompasses two or more different sensory perceptions with intended semantics respectively. Instead of being analytical to the definition, we take a perspective of generative logic based on the inspiration of the notion of perceptual crossing and deliver design outcomes to better voice ourselves. This paper aims at designing an embodied everyday artifact informed by the notion of perceptual crossing.

In order to expose more experience value, researchers adopt ambiguity as a resource for design [6]. Thus, it allows users to find their own usage and meaning instead of constraining how to use and how to work. The inconsistence that we deliberately use encourages interpretative space and imaginative privilege. In contrast to the center of technology practice, which concerns functionality, efficiency, optimality, and task focus, the intriguing design we proposed is a domestic future. We argue that, our artifact is not designed to improve intended function simply, instead, to create more space of interpretation.

Ludic design [5] aims to articulate an alternative thinking that technology should not only provide a clear, and quest oriented solution to a specific problem. Human beings are joyful, poetic, and spiritual rewarding creatures; they expect unknown thing in life world, and have their own interpretation of product usage. That is, ludic design intends to elicit the real essence of people. Ludic design is neither entertainment nor gaming. Entertainments are concerned with creating a stimulus and user oriented context, and gaming pursues user racing and competition where users are anxious about winning. Instead, Ludic design which focuses on a self-motivated form of play can initiate human kind's curiosity of all things and their pleasant nature.

To sum up, this paper's position is to research through designing [11] an aesthetic experience embodied in our everyday practice to allow ludic and ambiguous social interaction over Internet with richness of human sensors, which guide every conscious action by perceptual crossing through an artifact. The next section will discuss the process of design choice in detail, including perception, functionality, materiality, and making of form. Then we provide a prototype with sensing color and temperature properties and describe the experience of participants who lived with our artifacts over few days. Through elicited accounts from observing phenomena and semi-structure interviews, researchers illustrate what kind of social interaction we present and what kind of knowledge we learn from this design with a clear summary.

3   Design Process

3.1   Extended Perception

InTouch is inspired by the notion of McLuhan's famous book, Understanding Media: the Extensions of Man [9], which suggests that a medium, affects the society not by the content delivered through it but by the characteristics of the medium itself.

We wonder how "extensions of man" can be implemented in our daily practices across Internet connection, creating "an environment by its mere presence" as McLuhan states. If we see the Internet and the corresponding embodied artifacts as innovative media, how the concept of "the medium is the message" can be understood through embodied interaction with these media? Therefore, rather than appealing to visual cognition of UI such as semiology on the screen, we explore the extensions of man through the nature sensors of our body.

People construct this world by building on their sensation while sensing texture, lighting, odor, tasting, and sound. Our nature sensor is so exquisite and filled with abundant emotional value. We question that finger-slide-on-screen is not the only interface to connect people.   Our sensation can be regarded as an interface bringing out deeper and realistic tangible feedback to a user directly. The Cryoscope is an example that outputs this idea: a haptic weather forecasting device that fetches the weather data from the Internet and a user can feel tomorrow's temperature by simply touching the cube [10]. More than functional purpose of Cryoscope, our intention is to create a new ambient interface that is implicit and expresses the new aesthetic experience embedded to our everyday life. For this goal, we open up the richness of different sensors and bring in the concept of perceptual crossing. Finally, we come up with this artifact: InTouch.

3.2   Function of InTouch

What we seek in interactive functionality of our design is a simple and intuitive mapping between a gesture and its coupling feedback. Therefore, we attempt to address this issue by answering the following questions. How can one movement (input) trigger two sensations (outputs)? How can these two sensations come across between two people with two devices?

Moreover, we intend to make people stay in touch with InTouch, which is a social network system that an individual can express her consideration for friends by pressing a link. When pressed, the color gradually changes from blue to red on InTouch, while raising the temperature on friends' device from 4 degree minus Fahrenheit (-20 c) to 113 degree Fahrenheit (45c), and vice versa. The more frequency an individual pokes, the redder the link turns to, and the higher temperature friend's InTouch is raised. It's an interesting way to mediate interaction through two artifacts than typing text via smart electronic devices.

In this case, unlike other traditional devices, which only perform one-way I/O function, InTouch addresses a new issue: an interface could enable two-way transmission. In each of links, InTouch allows an individual to sense two sensations at one time, sensing color (sense of vision) and temperature (sense of touch) triggered by another one, while being sensed by temperature in friends' devices. Therefore, an individual can express her concerns and receive others' at the same time in a single movement, forming a crossing of perception between two friends. We intend to stimulate participant's curiosity to explore the meaning of such a functional mapping of input and output. During the process of making design choices, a poetic expression that definitely made us go toward a clear destination came up: Can you imagine a red link feeling cold (Figure 2)? Besides the simplicity of movement, gesture, and function, we investigate materials ranging from physical form to digital material. Making an alternative usage beyond its intended function hidden behind the computer, we employ a thermoelectric cooler as our technical implementation choice.

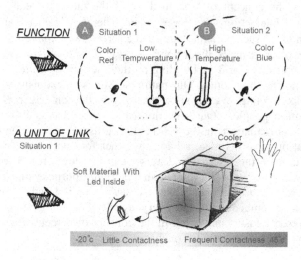

Fig. 2. Conceptual sketch of function of InTouch

3.3   Material and Form

Getting rid of solid ice-cold high-tech appearance, we try to make InTouch more domestic as a part of home furniture. InTouch is a social device contains four sections in a wooden frame. Each of the section stands for a communication link with a friend. Its window-like form plays a communicative role to allow our users at home to manage their social network in the real world. About the material choice, InTouch embeds a tactile surface: elastic Lycra. This flexible material enables people to physically poke and feel the response through the temperature and morph of surface. InTouch delivers a social aesthetic interaction through integrated material such as soft fabric instead of conventional interfaces like plastic or metal. Unlike other 2D interfaces, InTouch has a wooden-framed 3D surface unfolding possibility in making forms within the interface. We consider the material choice to make people feel more like at home (Figure 3).

Fig. 3. Form and material choice of InTouch

3.4   Multidisciplinary Cooperation

Our multidisciplinary team iteratively discussed, widely explored in our design process, and learned to collaborate with different mindset of multiple disciplines. Designers focused on the materiality and form-making of our artifact simultaneously. They made decisions about how to construct a daily practice with domestic style and aesthetic quality. On the other hand, engineers addressed its feasibility and innovative usage of technology to provide various opportunities to its functionality. Both of them concerned establishing an embodied interaction that performs a perceptual crossing in terms of perceiving while being perceived.

4   Prototyping

The InTouch system consists of the following components, as in Figure 4:

- Input button: There is an input button beneath the lycra cloth of each compartment in InTouch. By pressing the button, a user can express consideration to a friend.
- LED lights: The LED lights change color from blue to red in a compartment based on how often the user presses it to deliver cares for a friend.
- Thermal-Electric Cooler (TEG): The TEG provides tactile feedback in the form of heat. By feeling if a compartment is warm or cold, a user can know how much a friend cares for her.
- Arduino: An Arduino Uno microcontroller board is placed in each compartment. It acts as the Central Processing Unit (CPU), i.e.: processes the incoming signals and provides tactile and color feedback based on each signal.
- Networking: A networking component transfers signals between two InTouch through the Internet.

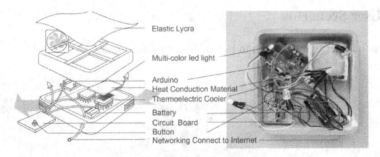

Fig. 4. Components of InTouch

4.1   Thermal-Electric Cooler (TEC)

As discussed in previous sections, we have placed a 3cm x 3cm Thermal-Electric Cooler (TEC), i.e., a Peltier heat pump device, inside each InTouch compartment. With the consumption of electrical energy, the TEC transfers heat from one side of the device to the other. This results in one side being cooled and the other side being heated. The direction of heat transfer is based on the direction of the current. The temperature range of the TEC used in this work is from -20°C to 45°C. TECs were originally used in computer cooling to remove the waste heat produced by computer components. We exploit the flexible and configurable temperature characteristic of the TEC to provide a wide range of temperature feedback to users.

4.2   Signal Processing and Sensory Feedback

The main part of our system is the signal processing which triggers tactile and color feedback. When a user presses the input button, signals are transferred to the Arduino board. The Arduino board then sends corresponding color signals to the LED lights on the users' InTouch and heat signals to the respective friend's TEC. The flow model of the prototype is described in Figure 5.

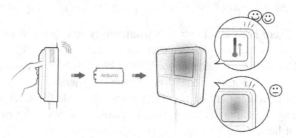

Fig. 5. InTouch flow model

If the Arduino does not receive signals over a period of time, it will send output signal to lower the temperature of the TEC and change the LED light from red to blue.

5   User Scenarios

Users can interact with InTouch in two main scenarios (Figure 6.).

Fig. 6. Interaction with InTouch in two main scenarios

- Send your considerations: When a user thinks of a friend, he/she can press the compartment on the wooden box to send considerations. This will trigger the user's InTouch component to turn red, which is a metaphor for how much the user cares about the friend. On the other hand, the respective friend's InTouch component will turn hot.
- Feel the heat: A user can feel the temperature of her InTouch component. The temperature indicates how often a friend sends her considerations through InTouch.

6   User Evaluation

The InTouch system was demonstrated and played by 5 students coming from design and 5 from computer science backgrounds, respectively. For each play session, we briefly introduced the system and then let users interact with the system. All players found the system to be "fun" and "very interesting". The system was able to engage users to explore for an enough span of time to report their accounts.

We found the tactile and color feedback of InTouch to be the most intriguing aspects of the system. User A1 said: "...if I keep on pressing it, it gets hotter visually, but actually the temperature is so cold...this is so contradicting...like I care a lot for her, but she doesn't feel the same for me." A Chinese proverb "placing one's hot face on another's cool behind" was mentioned to describe this experience. The device also triggered another user to think more about a friend; user A3 reported: "It feels so hot, he thinks a lot about me. I should really press this more often." The perceptual crossing phenomenon also generated feedback; user A4 described: "Temperature is passive, you need to touch it to feel the heat...this makes me want to touch it more often." That is, the implicit characteristic of temperature triggered users to interact with the device more often. The use of the TEC also raised discussion. User A4, a student from the computer science department expressed: "The TEC is a device for cooling down CPUs...it is very interesting to see it used for other purposes...such as interaction design."

7   Discussion

The observation of InTouch in daily use and in-depth interview with participants gave us some lessons. These can be summarized as follows:

- The ambiguity of InTouch allows users to explore its ludic value

The inconsistence of sensing color and temperature inspires participant's engagement, and the ambiguity of social connection provokes their curiosity. Unlike the traditional GUIs (Graphical User Interfaces) that are designed to fix specific problems through modeling what people behave accurately, the tangible interaction focuses on what situated activities people are engaged and what's going on around ambiguous features. The embodiment of our artifact encourages participant to keep in touch with his/her friends with perception of touch.

• The perceptual crossing evokes implicit social meanings

InTouch allows multiple users to sense temperature triggered by each other in a remotes side. As a result, the perceptual crossing engages people to expect responding more than ordinary functions of social network. It is not an explicit signal that alerts someone concerning you or messaging you, but implicitly informs you through self-motivated touch. It is expected in the future that the moment of coincidentally two-way sensing will create more experience of serendipity.

• Users find their own appropriation over time

We don't cater to user's need; otherwise, our design is a catalyst to provoke the communication of participants and their social groups. Users would explore alternative ways to use. Furthermore, it might allow user to share the using experience with their friends and create a conversation in social groups. The purpose of our design is to raise topics for provoking users' point of view instead to force target users to persuade.

We argue that, human beings interact with each other in various ways and the reaction of everyone is very different, in other words, it would be meaningless to constrain or measure the behavior of human kinds. On the contrary, we see the interaction as an embodied phenomenon that could inspire future innovation. Therefore, the intentionality of InTouch is not a physical form only but a participative situation manifesting artifact in the domestic context. Furthermore, our design instantiates a form of interaction that is embodied, open, and ambiguous.

8   Conclusion and Future Work

From our empirical user study, we have found that users concerned how many friends they can interact with through the system. User A7 wondered, "So I only get to choose four friends? This is weird. Can I change these four people? Or to make it even more fun, can it randomly select for me?" Certain users found the four compartments within a wooden box to be limited; user A5 commented: "this is an emotional design, nice, I like how it is covered with fabric, but the form is sort of limited...the wooden box limits my interaction." There were also suggestions to increase the sense of coincidence; user A9 explained: "if my friend happens to be using this at the exact same time as I do, will anything happen? How about making a sound or something? This would be a nice surprise to know my friend's presence." Serendipity in terms of human senses was also discussed; user A10 described: "can the system stimulate more senses in a random sort of way? I would like it to be even more complicated and unpredictable." To embody InTouch into everyday lives, user A10 asked, "Can it become even more intimately integrated into our lives? Or on the other way, just make it an obvious art installation." In conclusion, through the designing and prototyping of InTouch, we have explored how the inspiring notion of perceptual crossing can be crafted into embodied experience as well as how the Thermal-Electric Cooler can be alternatively used to lead to advancement in terms of technology.

Moreover, this paper stresses a design artifact as outcome that can transfer the world from visual feedback as a major output of networked social interaction to a preferred future where all sensory outputs can become significant feedback ready for meaning-making in terms of social interaction. How this work adopts and uses technology as material for crafting embodied experience has made a solid contribution, which can also be leveraged by the interaction design community.

References

1. Auvray, M., Lenay, C., Stewart, J.: Perceptual interactions in a minimalist virtual environment. New Ideas in Psychology 27(1), 32–47 (2009)
2. De Jaegher, H.: Social understanding through direct perception? Yes, by interacting. Consciousness and Cognition 18(2), 535–542 (2009)
3. Deckers, E., Wensveen, S., Ahn, R., Overbeeke, K.: Designing for Perceptual Crossing to Improve User Involvement. In: Proceedings of the SIGCHI Conference on Human Factors in Computing Systems, pp. 1929–1938. ACM Press, New York (2011)
4. Godshaw, R.: Feel tomorrow's air temperature today (2012), http://robb.cc/Cryoscope
5. Gaver, W.: Designing for Homo Ludens. i3 Magazine, 2–5 (June 2002)
6. Gaver, W., Beaver, J., Benford, S.: Ambiguity as a resource for design. In: Proceedings of the SIGCHI Conference on Human Factors in Computing Systems, pp. 233–240. ACM Press, New York (2003)
7. Marti, P.: Perceiving while being perceived. International Journal of Design 4(2), 27–38 (2010)
8. McLuhan, M.: Understanding Media: The Extensions of Man. Signet, New York (1964)
9. Merleau-Ponty, M.: Phenomenology of Perception (Original: Phénoménologie de la perception 1945). (Tiemersma, D., Vlasblom, R.) Boom (1945)
10. Victor, B.: A Brief Pant on the Future of Interaction Design (2011), http://worrydream.com/ABriefRantOnTheFutureOfInteractionDesign
11. Zimmerman, J., Forlizzi, J., Evenson, S.: Research through design as a method for interaction design research in HCI. In: Proceedings of the SIGCHI Conference on Human Factors in Computing Systems, pp. 493–502. ACM Press, New York (2007)

A Pilot Study of the Intuitiveness
of Smartphone Camera Interface for Elderly Users

Hyunju Shin, DaeSung Ahn, and Junghyun Han

College of Information and Communications, Korea University, Seoul, Korea
juliedp@korea.ac.kr

Abstract. We propose a ZUI (zoomable user interface)-based smartphone inter-face for elderly users. The proposed interface extends the application design space to provide an overview that allocates space to each function of the appli-cation according to its importance. According to the feedback of interviewees, an overview augmented by text-based guidance facilitated their understanding of the application.

Keywords: Design philosophy of HCI and UX, Zoomable User Interface.

1 Introduction

Figure 1 shows the information structure on a smartphone. A number of applications are installed, and each application has its own information space. The small smart-phone screen causes space fragmentation. Users should build their own virtual infor-mation hierarchy to help them understand the applications available on their device. In addition, as more functions are added to these applications, the information struc-ture becomes more complicated and memorizing it becomes harder.

Another problem related to smartphones is an overabundance of icons. The early smartphone user interface was almost the same as that of a desktop PC. A text-based

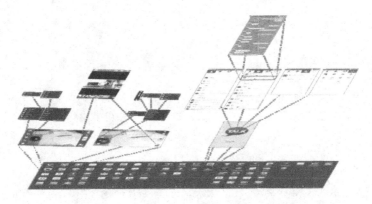

Fig. 1. Information structure on smartphone

A. Marcus (Ed.): DUXU/HCII 2013, Part III, LNCS 8014, pp. 316–323, 2013.
© Springer-Verlag Berlin Heidelberg 2013

hierarchical menu was a common interface, and a stylus pen was therefore essential for selecting text commands presented in small fonts. As the finger touch interface became more popular, menu sizes increased, thus making touch-based selections possible. As a result, implicit icons have become a common design paradigm on smartphones. These issues may create further complications and difficulties for users, especially the elderly.

2   Related Work

There are several studies on the usability of handheld computers for elderly users, who generally experience a higher level of disorientation when navigating a menu on a handheld computer. This is one of the most serious problems of handheld computers [1-2]. Zhou et al. [3] discussed two ways to achieve simplicity: **reducing functionality** and **improving the design** of individual functions. Some studies insisted that handheld computers for elderly users should provide only limited functionality [4-5]. However, many studies disagree that limited functionality is beneficial. In Ziefle et al. [6], the tradeoff between readability and orientation demands was investigated experimentally. Two factors, font size and the size of preview, were varied. The results showed that large font and preview sizes contributed to optimal navigation performance. Further, if the two factors were mutually exclusive, preview was more important than font size.

Kurniawan et al. [7] reported that older women wanted menus to be simplified by being presented in list form. Textual menus arranged in a list are preferred to icon-based menus arranged in columns and rows. Ziefle et al. [8] provided contextual information so that users would not forget the position of and route to an item in the menu. The study designed two mobile phone menu navigation aids for elderly users: **category aid** and **tree aid**. **Category aid** showed the name of the current category as well as a list of its contents. The **tree aid** was identical to the former except that it also showed the parents and parent–parents of the current category, and it indented the subcategories to emphasize the hierarchical structure. The results showed that tree aid was more useful than category aid for both younger and older users.

3   Camera Interface Design

In our study on improving the usability while maintaining the functionality of a smartphone interface, we adopted the user interface of Android applications as our reference model.

The more smart features are installed in the camera, the more icons will appear on the smartphone camera interface. Let us consider the sample camera application shown in Fig. 2(a), which has eight top-level commands represented by icons. Some of these commands have second-level commands, which are displayed on a pop-up menu (Fig. 2(b)).

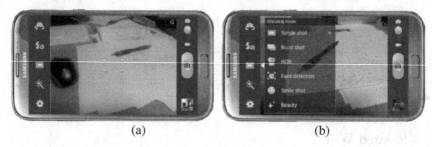

(a)   (b)

Fig. 2. An example of smartphone camera interface

To reduce the number of icons, we design the user interface based on an expanded space. The size of the area allocated to each function differs depending on its importance.

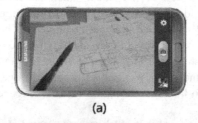

(a)

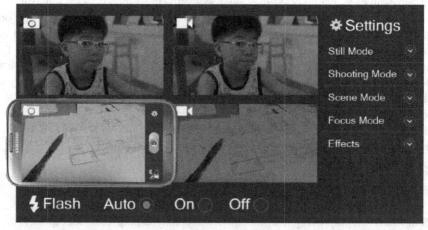

Fig. 3. Expanded screen space. (a) Default view; (b) Overview screen of an expanded space

Figure 3 shows the redesigned interface implementing the zoomable concept. The default view (Fig. 3(a)) is very simple. It uses only three icons for the "Shutter button," "Gallery preview," and "Settings" commands, which are essential camera features. Figure 3(b) shows the expanded space of the camera interface. At any time, users can zoom out to maneuver to the overview screen (Fig. 3 (a)). Every visual element on the overview screen can be recognized.

If users want to use supplementary functions, they need to return to the overview screen (Fig. 4(a)). To provide interactive manuals, the proposed interface uses semantic zooming. The green circle in Fig. 4(a)) indicates that the user has selected "Shooting mode" from the "Settings" menu. Figure 4(b) shows an animated transition effect. Figure 4(c) shows an expanded space providing interactive manuals for each shooting mode. When we return to the overview screen, the manuals collapse. Using an expand-and-collapse method, we can maintain the context (outline) of the camera interface. Just as desktop applications have a "Help (F1)" menu on their toolbar, the "Settings view" (Fig. 4(c)) provides a manual for each command.

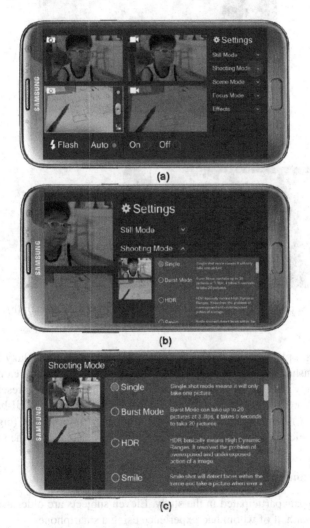

Fig. 4. Space navigation from the overview screen to detailed views. (a) Overview screen; (b) Animated transition; (c) Settings view

4   Pilot User Study

The main hypotheses we sought to test in this study are as follows:

• Elderly users may have difficulty using an icon-based interface.
• Elderly users may prefer a zoomable interface to an icon-based interface.
• Younger and older users have different preferences.

Fig. 5. Icon-based camera interface

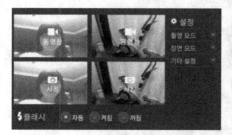 

Fig. 6. ZUI-based camera interface: (a) Overview screen (zoom-out mode); (b) Shooting view (zoom-in mode)

The hardware platform used in the experiment was Samsung Galaxy S3. Figure 5 shows a screenshot of our reference camera interface for the default camera application on a Galaxy S3. The reference interface uses eight icons to represent eight top-level menus. We call this an icon-based interface. The proposed ZUI-based camera interface (Fig. 6) contains exactly the same amount of information (eight top-level menus) as the reference interface, but the menus are not displayed at the same time.

4.1   Design and Procedure

Seventeen subjects participated in the study. Eleven subjects are older users (over the age of 50), about half of whom had experience using a smartphone.

The first task given to the subjects was to explain or guess the meaning of each menu item of an icon-based interface without executing any functions. We then explained how to use the two camera interfaces, and the subjects tried to use them for about 10 to 20 minutes. The amount of time required to complete the task differed according to the user's smartphone experience.

The second task was to execute the proposed command (menu) list.

- Turn on the flash;
- Set shooting mode to "Smile";
- Take a picture using the rear camera;
- Record video using front side camera.

The completion times for the two interfaces were recorded. The list below is a subset of the tasks that the participants were asked to complete. When the experiments were completed, the subjects were asked about their preference for each camera interface.

4.2   Experimental Results

While younger users understood more than three of the six icons, most elderly users could not explain or guess the meaning of even one icon. Younger users also could not understand the meaning of certain icons. However, all the younger users answered that they still tried to use unfamiliar icons, whereas most elderly users said that they did not. We speculated that the reasons why elderly users do not try to use unfamiliar features are that they have no interest in new features or they cannot recall how to use such features even after having used them previously. However, the interview results are significantly different from our speculations. The most dominant response was fear. Although they may want to use many useful functions, they are unwilling to press an unfamiliar icon for fear of breaking the device or being charged a fee. This means that it is difficult for elderly users to learn how to use new applications or features by themselves.

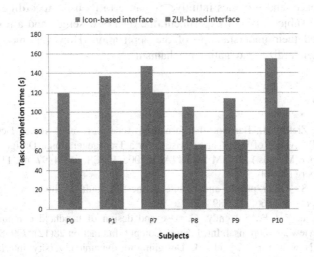

Fig. 7. Configuration and photo-taking completion times of elderly users

Figure 7 shows a comparison of the completion times of the tasks on the icon-based interface and the zoomable interface of elderly users. While the completion times for the two camera interfaces of younger users did not show a significant difference, all the elderly users spent more time completing the tasks on the icon-based camera interface than on the zoomable interface. Many spent a long time finding the presented configuration menu when using the icon-based interface because they were unable to remember the meaning of the icons. The younger participants most often cited that fact that they were already familiar with the icon-based interface as the reason why they found the ZUI-based was not an improvement on the icon-based interface. Moreover, the icons can function as shortcuts for younger users. However, the icon-based interface did not outperform the ZUI-based interface.

5   Conclusion and Future Work

We designed a ZUI-based camera interface for elderly users. The zoomable overview screen emphasizes the main functionality and provides a text-based menu instead of supplementary icons. As a result, the number of icons on the interface is small enough to allow them to be memorized. To verify the usability of the proposed interface, we conducted an interview with eleven elderly users. Most preferred the zoomable camera interface to an icon-based interface. The results of our experiment using six elderly users with smartphone experience and the younger users as our subjects also showed that their task completion time was reduced when the proposed zoomable interface was used. The dominant reason for this reduction is that icons cannot provide elderly users with a shortcut, and their unfamiliarity simply made the elderly users afraid of using them.

The proposed interface can simplify an application information structure using a continuous space, and provides intuitive guidance to its use. According to the feedback from the subjects of our experiment, the overview screen and a text-based manual facilitated their understanding of the application. However, more research is required on standardized navigation mechanisms.

References

1. Arning, K., Ziefle, M.: Barriers of Information Access in Small Screen Device Applications: The Relevance of User Characteristics for a Transgenerational Design. In: Stephanidis, C., Pieper, M. (eds.) ERCIM Ws UI4ALL 2006. LNCS, vol. 4397, pp. 117–136. Springer, Heidelberg (2007)
2. Kurniawan, S.: Older people and mobile phones: A multi-method investigation. Int. J. Hum.-Comput. Stud. 66(12), 889–901 (2008)
3. Zhou, J., Rau, P.-L.P., Salvendy, G.: Use and design of handheld computers for older adults: A review and appraisal. Int. J. Hum. Comput. Interaction 28(12), 799–826 (2012)
4. Gregor, P., Newell, A.F., Zajicek, M.: Designing for dynamic diversity: interfaces for older people. In: Fifth Annual ACM Conference on Assistive Technologies. Solutions for aging, pp. 151–156 (2002)

5. Kang, N.E., Yoon, W.C.: Age- and experience-related user behavior differences in the use of complicated electronic devices. Int. J. Hum. Comput. Stud. 66(6), 425–437 (2008)
6. Ziee, M.: Information presentation in small screen devices: The trade-off between visual density and menu foresight. Applied Ergonomics 41(6), 719–730 (2010)
7. Kurniawan, S.: An exploratory study of how older women use mobile phones. In: Dourish, P., Friday, A. (eds.) UbiComp 2006. LNCS, vol. 4206, pp. 105–122. Springer, Heidelberg (2006)
8. Ziee, M., Bay, S.: How to overcome disorientation in mobile phone menus: a comparison of two different types of navigation aids. Hum. Comput. Interact. 21(4), 393–433 (2006)

Part III

Designing for Virtual and Augmented Environments

Sharing Kinetic Interactions for Mobile Devices

Bashar Altakrouri[1,2], Darren Carlson[1], and Andreas Schrader[1]

[1] Ambient Computing Group, Institute of Telematics
University of Luebeck, Luebeck, Germany
{altakrouri,carlson,schrader}@itm.uni-luebeck.de
https://www.itm.uni-luebeck.de/
[2] Graduate School for Computing in Medicine and Life Sciences,
University of Luebeck

Abstract. Infrastructure for sharing, adapting and deploying interaction techniques remains an enduring challenge for real-world pervasive computing ecosystems (ambient spaces). In this paper, we address this challenge by introducing the concept of *Interaction Plugins*, which enables interaction techniques to be constructed as shareable units of functionality and dynamically deployed into a variety of ambient spaces during runtime. To this end, this paper will discuss two important issues in detail: community-based creation of interaction plugins and runtime deployment of interaction plugins. The paper also features a mobile-based implementation of this approach based on the Dynamix context framework.

Keywords: Ambient Assisted Living, Natural Interactions, Kinetic Interactions, Sharing Interactions.

1 Introduction

Interaction possibilities in many environments are rapidly increasing due to the emergence of interconnected mobile devices, smart objects, and seamlessly integrated context-aware services. Natural Interfaces (NI) is one of the most frequent solutions being proposed to support the flow of (inter-)action patterns in these hybrid environments. NI techniques enable human users to interact with the physical space using familiar physical body interactions and intermediaries [19]. This is clearly visible through broad adoption of natural interaction techniques as a primary source of interaction within ambient spaces, leading to a rapid increase in the number of techniques proposed by research and commercial efforts. Pioneering work on NI have been reported in HCI literature, ranging from scratch-based interactions [8], accelerometer-based interactions [18], sensor-based interactions [18], ambient gestures [10], etc. Hence, methods for sharing interaction techniques are becoming more important then ever for the successful adoption and distribution of NI. In this paper, we will focus on kinetic-based interactions, which are characterized by motion and movement activities [2].

Modelling, designing, and managing context information are significant problems facing application developers, particularly in the area of mobile computing.

A. Marcus (Ed.): DUXU/HCII 2013, Part III, LNCS 8014, pp. 327–336, 2013.

In [6] and [21], the authors point out that those problems are mainly caused by the absence of appropriate support for rich context types, approach extensibility, and easy-to-use context frameworks. In the literature, a variety of approaches have been proposed for solving those problems through specialized middleware [16], context servers [7], and environmental instrumentation [14]; however, such approaches fail to scale in wide-area mobile scenarios [6] [3].

In response to the increasing availability of commodity sensor data such as orientation and accelerometer information; geo-location; proximity; light levels; camera and microphone streams; etc [12]; we are seeing increasing interest in mobile context frameworks capable of providing abstractions for sensing; context modeling and representation; service discovery and binding; etc [4]. Such context information can be very useful to mobile applications, which can use it to fluidly adapt to the user's changing environment and context of use [12].

As an interesting milestone, dynamic component integration, which has been thoroughly investigated in ubiquitous and pervasive computing research, has been recently successfully applied in mobile environments. This approach enables software components to be discovered, downloaded and integrated on-demand as a means of adapting an application's behavior and enhancing its features [17]. For example, the Context-Aware Machine learning Framework for Android (CAMF) promotes plug-in-based adaptation on Android by introducing processing widgets as discrete abstractions used to hide machine learning complexities [20]. The Funf Open Sensing Framework[1] promotes statically-linked context modeling plug-ins integration. One of the first projects to support dynamic component integration on Android using OSGi container was the Mobile USers In Ubiquitous Computing Environments (MUSIC) system [5]. More recently, the Dynamix framework [4] was introduced as an open plug-and-play context framework for Android. It supports automatic discovery and integration of context sensing and acting plugins at runtime; 3rd party context plug-in support; and custom context representations based on Plain Old Java Objects (POJOs), which enables the creation of arbitrarily complex context events objects that are easy to parse and use.

In HCI research, Pruvost et al. [15] call for interaction environments to be open and dynamic, due to the complexity of interaction contexts. They argue for highly adaptable user interfaces that preserve utility and usability across contexts. In their described adaptation vision, they have presented the concept of Off-the-shelf Interaction Objects, which are pre-implemented bundles of code, intended to be reused and composed at runtime to provide the necessary adaptation required for the interaction technique. While their vision is focused on the structural adaptation of user interfaces and the adaptation of a running dialogue, our work is more concerned with the sharing aspects of natural interactions, especially kinetic interactions. The Gestureworks Core[2], which is limited to multitouch interactions, is one of the earliest multitouch gesture authoring solution for touch-enabled devices on a variety of platforms such as

---

[1] http://funf.org, visited on February 21th 2013.

[2] http://gestureworks.com, visited on February 23th 2013.

Flash; C++; Java; .NET; Python; and Unity. Based on the Gesture Markup Language (GML), the solution comes with a rich library of pre-built gestures and allows for new custom gestures and gesture sequences to be built by designers. The OpenNI is an open source SDK[3] used for the development of 3D sensing applications and middleware libraries. One of the main aims of this framework is to enhance the NI techniques development community; make it possible for developers to share ideas problems; share code with each other; and address the complete development lifecycle by a standard 3D sensing framework.

2   Approach

Despite rapid innovation in NI techniques, it is well understood that user interface adaptation and adoption in ambient spaces remain challenging problems [15], due to issues related to heterogeneity and distributivity; dynamic media mobility; and user mobility. In this paper, we argue that kinetic interactions are currently hindered due to the lack of:

- Systematic consideration of the increasing diversity of user populations in ambient spaces. In particular, existing approaches fail to address users with varying intrinsic sensorimotor capabilities and fail to comply with the general trend of designing for the whole body in motion.
- Effective means for documenting, adapting and deploying interaction techniques. Interaction techniques are currently hard-wired into applications, leaving few possibilities for the integration of new NI techniques at runtime. Consequently, the task of sharing interactions becomes unrealistic in many scenarios.

To address these hindrances, this paper presents the concept of **Interaction Plugins (IP)** as a novel approach for sharing kinetic-based NI techniques in ambient spaces. In our previous work [2], an IP is defined as *"an executable component in ambient interactive systems that encapsulates a single natural interaction technique with a set of interaction tasks as input and delivers higher level interaction primitives to applications based on specific interaction semantics"*. To the best of our knowledge, there is no research specifically targeted at community-based creation and sharing of encapsulated natural interaction techniques. Hence, we have defined our own structured approach based on three main design characteristics: matching users and NI physical context; precise and extensible NI descriptions (human and machine readable); and flexible deployment of NI plugins at runtime.

In this section, we will discuss two main design choices in our approach that foster the three aforementioned characteristics: 1.) Anthropometric driven matching and presentation of Interaction Plugins; and, 2.) On-demand wiring of interaction resources.

---

[3] http://www.openni.org, visited on February 23th 2013.

2.1   Anthropometric Driven Matching and Presentation of Interaction Plugins

NI techniques are inherently affected by a wide range of physical impairments and disabilities such as limited range of motion, tremors, impaired balance, gait, etc. These might occur only temporarily as a result of previous body exercises and contextual restrictions, but are particularly challenging for the senior citizens and elderly adults, due to the notable effect of ageing in one's physical and motor abilities [11][13]. In this work, we opted for an anthropometric approach for describing, discovering and presenting Interaction Plugins. As such, we've extended work from Labanotation (Kinetography) [9], which is one of the most powerful systems for describing physical movements for dance choreography, physical therapy, and drama. We defined a complimentary Labanotation XML representation, which is used to analyze, describe, document, and preserve a plugin's required physical movements, enabling plug-ins to reason about all physical movements required for a given interaction scenario. Our plugin discovery mechanisms utilize this information to optimize the selection of suitable Interaction Plugins for a given scenario and user.

Our investigation revealed three essential building blocks (information components) for anthropometric driven IP. First, we utilize a movement information component represented by a profile that is used to describe the essential physical movement required by the interaction from the user and interaction capture point of view. For example, for a balance interaction technique, this profile precisely describes the body balance, position and posture required by the interaction. The flexibility of Labanotation allows interaction developers to set the abstraction details of the movement to reflect essential and important aspects of the interaction technique. Interaction developers may also describe the detailed micro-aspects of the movement, which may lead to a complex but precise movement description. In addition, they may describe the movement on a macro level while leaving a lot of movement details out.

The ability profile is the second information component needed in our design. This component defines the physical abilities that are required for an appropriate execution of NI. It is composed from two building blocks: major physical activities vital for the interaction, such as holding, standing, balancing, lifting, walking, etc; and physical disabilities that may impact the quality execution of the interaction. Both aspects are evaluated through an impact score for each, which defines their importance and impact to the quality of interaction execution. We argue that movement and ability profiles are essential for designing interactions "for all" instead of focusing on a limited population percentile and to avoid inaccessible interfaces.

The third component in our model is the interaction profile that includes the main interaction semantics, including the interaction primitives such as pointing, selecting, dragging, etc. This is important in ambient spaces because it provides an indication of the main use of the interaction technique and its offerings. This profile is also used by the application when subscribing to available interaction plugins that provide the same type of interaction primitives.

2.2   On-Demand Wiring of Interaction Resources

Interaction sharing can only be realized with a comprehensive approach for on-demand discovery, selection and integration of interaction modules at runtime. Support for runtime provisioning of suitable Interaction Plug-ins should be based on the user's capabilities and a plugin's required physical movements. Figure 1 illustrates a conceptual view of Interaction Plug-ins deployment on mobile devices. IP are discovered, loaded into devices on demand, activated seamlessly, and exposed to interactive applications through an easy subscription mechanism.

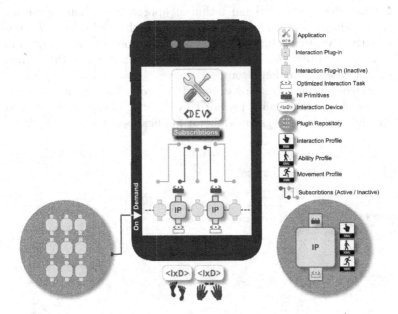

Fig. 1. Interaction Plug-ins Deployment - Conceptual Overview

Interaction Plug-ins are hosted by a plug-in repository, where they can be requested and downloaded on-demand by applications. IPs expose their offered interaction capabilities though interaction primitives (e.g., pointing or selection) through which interactive applications can subscribe to the plug-in. After deployment, the IP resides in the user's mobile device in an inactive state. This state is changed to active once a subscription is received by the plug-in, in order to allow plug-ins to only occupy the needed interaction and computation resources. This allows to attend to certain amount of plug-ins at a time, leading to save resources and computation power on the device. During runtime, interaction events are fired and delivered to the application. In our current model, applications can be informed about which plug-in to subscribe to and activate based on the physical abilities and qualities required by an application in a particular user context.

3   Sharing IP Based on the Dynamix Framework

In our previous work on Ambient Dynamix (our plug-and-play context framework for Android) [4], we described our comprehensive approach for on-demand discovery and runtime integration of context sensing and acting capabilities in wide-area mobile contexts. In this work, we leverage Dynamix as a mechanism for sharing natural interactions on mobile devices, due to its unique capabilities and flexibility, especially related to dynamic discovery and deployment of suitable context plugins during runtime.

Figure 2 illustrates our underlying technical approach for sharing natural interactions as IPs based on the Dynamix framework on the Android platform. In this approach, the Dynamix framework runs as a background service (Dynamix Service) and is situated between Dynamix enabled applications and the device's hardware (in our case interaction resources).

Dynamix-enabled applications are standard Android applications with extra context modeling functionality provided by a local Dynamix Service. We developed an Interaction Manager module for applications, which controls the

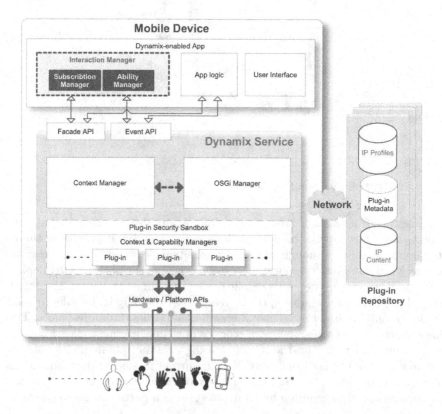

Fig. 2. Interaction Plugins Realisation Using Dynamix (Based on [4])

activation of the available interaction plugins based on the ability, movement, and interaction profiles. The Interaction Manager and the application logic communicate with Dynamix service through its Facade API, which enables apps to request and control context modeling support; and its Event API, which enables apps to receive framework notifications and context events.

Interaction plugins are tailored OSGi-based Bundles, which are loaded into the Dynamix embedded OSGi container at runtime. Once loaded and activated, the plug-in sends interaction encoded events to subscribed applications (as interaction primitive events) using POJOs. An Internet-based plugin repository hosts IP Bundle files, the IP profiles, and (optionally) additional related plugins. In addition to context sensing tasks, the IPs hosted by Dynamix can be queried by the application's Interaction Manager to access the information encoded in the available IP profiles. Currently, the Dynamix Service provides all plug-in discovery services, plug-in filtering based on the interaction requirements (interaction primitives required), and plug-in installation support. Filtering and activating the available interaction plugins are currently handled by the Interaction Manager; however, in future work we will introduce highly configurable plugin selection and activation functionality as a core extension of the Dynamix architecture.

4   Provisioning Interaction Plug-ins

The provisioning of an Interaction Plug-in is triggered once the interaction technique passes the usual design and implementation phases and satisfies the function and utility defined by an interaction developer (i.e., designer, developer, or team). The interaction developer should then define the interaction's movement profile, based on an acceptable level of movement description using Labanotation; define the interaction's ability profile, based on the most important physical qualities that impact the interaction; assign the interaction semantics, based on the envisioned utility and user study of the technique; wrap the interaction's internal logic as a Dynamix plug-in; and place the IP in an accessible repository. Interactive application developers can then easily create Android-based on the Dynamix framework and available IPs (according to the required semantics).

For illustration, Spin&Swing [1] is a spatial interaction technique that leverages the user's orientation for browsing temporal data on mobile phones. The movement profile defines the user's 360° medial rotation with the mobile held with right hand facing the front of the body. The ability profile defines important physical qualities for this interaction such as body balance, normal grip, and absence of hand trembling (the later quality has low importance, hence is given a low score). Moreover, the interaction profile defines selection as the main interaction primitive. Finally, the Spin&Swing IP wraps the core orientation-to-selection mapping based on the technique's original logic.

5 Discussion and Implications

In this paper, we have argued that flexible sharing techniques represent an essential cornerstone for adapting interactions to ambient spaces. Such techniques are increasingly vital due to the advancement of interaction technology; innovative interaction design; and large-scale adoption of natural interactions and applications. Without standardized means of describing and sharing interactions, the HCI community will suffer from a number of key problems, such as:

- a lack of proper documentation and preservation of novel interactions;
- unrealistic chances for collaborative interaction development and enhancement;
- continued inaccessibility of novel interaction techniques; and
- overly complicated real-world deployment of interaction techniques.

For the successful sharing of NI, interaction developers and designers should carefully consider the targeted user group and try to maximise the usability of the interaction based on the user's physical skills and abilities. The analysis of such information should be defined and encoded in the interaction's ability profile, which is used to help applications discover, select and activate associated plugins at runtime. The complexity and details of this profile can be left to the designer; however, describing the movement profile is a challenging task due to the flexibility and details of movement description provided by the movement annotation language (Labanotation in our case). The community should strive to find the right balance between abstraction and detail.

6 Conclusion

Ongoing research across various HCI disciplines has resulted in the development of a broad range of novel interaction techniques that emphasize the simultaneous use of multiple body parts during interactions with the surrounding environment. Unfortunately, these emerging interaction techniques often remain unavailable to real-world ambient computing systems due to a lack of wide-area deployment infrastructure. In this paper, we address this challenge by introducing the concept of *Interaction Plugins* as a means of sharing, adapting and deploying interaction techniques on-demand during runtime. We also describe the details of our approach for community-based plug-in creation and runtime plug-in deployment.

Acknowledgement. This work was partially supported by the Graduate School for Computing in Medicine and Life Sciences funded by Germany's Excellence Initiative [DFG GSC 235/1].

References

[1] Altakrouri, B., Kawsar, F., Kortuem, G.: Spin&swing: Spatial interaction with orientation aware devices. In: The Eighth International Conference on Pervasive Computing, Pervasive 2010, Demo Section, May 17-20 (2010), http://www.pervasive2010.org/demos.html

[2] Altakrouri, B., Schrader, A.: Towards dynamic natural interaction ensembles. In: Devina Ramduny-Ellis, A.D., Gill, S. (eds.) Fourth International Workshop on Physicality (Physicality 2012) co-located with British HCI 2012 Conference, Birmingham, UK (September 2012)

[3] Blackstock, M., Lea, R., Krasic, C.: Toward wide area interaction with ubiquitous computing environments. In: Havinga, P., Lijding, M., Meratnia, N., Wegdam, M. (eds.) EuroSSC 2006. LNCS, vol. 4272, pp. 113–127. Springer, Heidelberg (2006), http://dx.doi.org/10.1007/11907503_9

[4] Carlson, D., Schrader, A.: Dynamix: An open plug-and-play context framework for android. In: Proceedings of the 3rd International Conference on the Internet of Things, IoT 2012 (2012)

[5] Consortium, I.M.: Òist-music: Context-aware self-adaptive platform for mobile applications (2010), http://ist-music.berlios.de

[6] Davies, N., Gellersen, H.W.: Beyond prototypes: challenges in deploying ubiquitous systems. IEEE Pervasive Computing 1(1), 26–35 (2002)

[7] Endres, C., Butz, A., MacWilliams, A.: A survey of software infrastructures and frameworks for ubiquitous computing. Mob. Inf. Syst. 1(1), 41–80 (2005), http://dl.acm.org/citation.cfm?id=1233803.1233806

[8] Gary Halajian, J.W.: Gesture recognition based on scratch inputs. Tech. rep., Cornell University (April 26, 2009), eCE 4760

[9] Hutchinson, A.: Labanotation The System of Analyzing and Recording Movement, 4th edn. Routledge, NewYork and London (2005)

[10] Karam, M., Hare, J., Lewis, P., Schraefel, M.: Ambient gestures. Tech. rep., Intelligence, Agents, Multimedia Group, University of Southampton (2006)

[11] Mahmud, M., Kurniawan, H.: Involving psychometric tests for input device evaluation with older people. In: Proceedings of the 17th Australia Conference on Computer-Human Interaction: Citizens Online: Considerations for Today and the Future, OZCHI 2005, Computer-Human Interaction Special Interest Group (CHISIG) of Australia, Narrabundah, Australia, pp. 1–10 (2005), http://portal.acm.org/citation.cfm?id=1108368.1108399

[12] Niemelä, E., Latvakoski, J.: Survey of requirements and solutions for ubiquitous software. In: Proceedings of the 3rd International Conference on Mobile and Ubiquitous Multimedia, MUM 2004, pp. 71–78. ACM, New York (2004), http://doi.acm.org/10.1145/1052380.1052391

[13] Piper, A.M., Campbell, R., Hollan, J.D.: Exploring the accessibility and appeal of surface computing for older adult health care support. In: Proceedings of the 28th International Conference on Human Factors in Computing Systems, CHI 2010, pp. 907–916. ACM, New York (2010), http://doi.acm.org/10.1145/1753326.1753461

[14] Priyantha, N.B., Chakraborty, A., Balakrishnan, H.: The cricket location-support system. In: Proceedings of the 6th Annual International Conference on Mobile Computing and Networking, MobiCom 2000, pp. 32–43. ACM, New York (2000), http://doi.acm.org/10.1145/345910.345917

[15] Pruvost, G., Heinroth, T., Bellik, Y., Minker, W.: User Interaction Adaptation within Ambient Environments, ch. 5, Next Generation Intelligent Environments: Ambient Adaptive Systems edn., pp. 153–194. Springer, Boston (2011)

[16] Román, M., Hess, C., Cerqueira, R., Ranganathan, A., Campbell, R.H., Nahrstedt, K.: Gaia: a middleware platform for active spaces. SIGMOBILE Mob. Comput. Commun. Rev. 6(4), 65–67 (2002), http://doi.acm.org/10.1145/643550.643558

[17] Schrader, A., Carlson, D.V., Busch, D.: Modular framework support for context-aware mobile cinema. Personal Ubiquitous Comput. 12(4), 299–306 (2008), http://dx.doi.org/10.1007/s00779-007-0151-6

[18] Scoditti, A., Blanch, R., Coutaz, J.: A novel taxonomy for gestural interaction techniques based on accelerometers. In: The 15th International Conference on Intelligent User Interfaces, IUI 2011, pp. 63–72. ACM, New York (2011), http://doi.acm.org/10.1145/1943403.1943414

[19] Wachs, J.P., Kölsch, M., Stern, H., Edan, Y.: Vision-based hand-gesture applications. Commun. ACM 54, 60–71 (2011), http://doi.acm.org/10.1145/1897816.1897838

[20] Wang, A.I., Ahmad, Q.K.: Camf - context-aware machine learning framework for android. In: Rey, M.D. (ed.) Iasted International Conference on Software Engineering and Applications, SEA 2010, CA, USA, November 8-10 (2010)

[21] Want, R., Pering, T.: System challenges for ubiquitous pervasive computing. In: The 27th International Conference on Software Engineering, ICSE 2005, pp. 9–14 (May 2005)

Virtual Reality Immersion:
An Important Tool for Diagnostic Analysis
and Rehabilitation of People with Disabilities

Helda O. Barros, Marcelo Márcio Soares, Epitácio L. Rolim Filho,
Walter Correia, and Fábio Campos

Post-graduate program in Design, Universidade Federal de Pernambuco,
Recife, Pernambuco, Brazil
helda_barros@yahoo.com.br, marcelo2@nlink.com.br,
rolimfilho@uol.com.br, ergonomia@terra.com.br,
fc2005@gmail.com

Abstract. This paper sets out the case for the importance of using virtual reality immersion for diagnostic analysis and rehabilitating people with disabilities. To do so, a review of the literature was undertaken by examining articles published between 2000 and 2012. The results show that browsing in virtual immersion environments simulates real-world situations, with the advantage that this enables there to be full control over the variables analyzed and consequently over the health aspects involved. Furthermore, when using multisensory channels, the human-task-system interface tools enable there to be simultaneous treatment of multiple morbidities, which characterizes there having been an important advance made in the functional independence of people with disabilities.

Keywords: virtual reality, people with disabilities, rehabilitation.

1 Introduction

Virtual reality uses an interactive environment, created by software and hardware, so as to give users sensations similar to those in the real world. Virtual environments can be used in any creative process, ranging from the presentation of ideas to the final phase of conceiving projects. [15]

Virtual reality is a way of transporting the subject to a virtual environment in which he/she is not physically inserted, but which generates this sensation [19].

The use of multisensory devices, browsing in three-dimensional spaces, immersion in the context of the application and interaction in real time extend the senses previously linked to simply viewing, listening and manipulating to touching, feeling pressure, and even smelling, and this leads to migrating to the concept of learning-knowing-feeling-communicating [4].

In addition, Ergonomics considers technical indicators related to usability, applicability and utility as constructs that are essential to users regarding the interface as comfortable and mindful of their well being [19].

A. Marcus (Ed.): DUXU/HCII 2013, Part III, LNCS 8014, pp. 337–344, 2013.

This result will be achieved only when users are involved in the cycle of assessing, diagnosing, designing and validating their physical environment, whether in the design of products, of environments or of urban space. A process of User-Centered Design will promote better knowledge of subjects, their needs, expectations and abilities, and thus achieve what projects set out to do [19].

When projects serve specific populations, not only in the social sphere, but by including the user in the perspective of the disability, the creation process attains its most important contribution: this characterizes design as a tool that promotes good health.

Thus, the design process goes beyond the goals of efficiency, effectiveness and satisfaction and achieves a new construct: functionality, which the World Health Organization considers is a variable which is essential for defining the state of health itself.

Within this context, this paper seeks to set out the advantages of using virtual reality in the process of rehabilitating people with disabilities, and stresses the efficiency and effectiveness of the gain in functional independence by users who have been submitted to virtual immersion environments.

1.1   Rehabilitation in the Virtual Environment

Currently, virtual reality is being used in several areas of rehabilitation. Tools have been developed for training de-ambulation in patients with Parkinson's disease in order to facilitate a gait pattern. Virtual environments have been used for children with cerebral palsy to improve spatial perception and the operation of motorized wheelchairs. And likewise in the post-operative period of surgeries of the hand and in the rehabilitation of stroke patients [8].

This technology offers the ability to create an environment in which the intensity of the training can be systematically manipulated and individualized, thereby seeking motor learning that is appropriate for each patient by means of semi-automated programs [7].

The objective of the characteristics of hardware and software, and the complexity of the task requested are to provide users with a significant experience in the context of the researcher's therapeutic goals. These include the opportunity for active learning, which encourages and motivates the participant, the ability to measure behavior objectively into a challenge, the security of maintaining control over the experiment and the ability to measure results [5].

The multisensory resources of virtual reality can promote behavioral changes, improve neural plasticity in children and encourage learning and performance [4].

The human forms of apprehension are multimodal and, as regards the constructivist assumptions of learning, this means putting the user at the center of the process, thus giving him/her the tools necessary for experimentation-decision [12].

Learning is an individual and complex process, which is underpinned by the individuals' experiences and by his/her consequent global view of the world [14, 21]. As it is related to the development of the skills of observation, analysis, planning, decision, implementation and evaluation, VR is seen to be a powerful feature, since it prompts visualization, interaction and real-time responses [17].

Thus, considering the prognosis and the very evolution of the disease, sensory-motor cognitive learning is founded on pathological bases, and influences the subject's mental models with, in and about the world, thus exacerbating his/her motor and cognitive disabilities and making the planning and carrying out of activities and skills difficult [2.7, 24]

The formation of mental models is therefore based on sensorimotor engrams[1] influenced by the physiological changes caused by the disease [18, 23]. Experiments are undergone in abnormal pathological bases which alter the proprioceptive responses of arthresthesia and kinesthesia, and cause considerable postural orientation and balance deficits [16, 20, 22].

In this context, virtual reality immersion, by activating the cognitive processes needed for browsing and interpreting the environments, will promote the automation of daily activities, thus causing permanent changes in subjects' mental models. This is because immersion is characterized by the user's perception of his/her being inserted into a real environment, while being directly linked to the settings of the virtual environment and the sensations of seeing, hearing, touching and feeling that the virtual one causes. [19]

The central nervous system is not able to distinguish between the sensory-motor experiences and relational experiences that occur in the real world and in virtual environments. During immersion, learning overcomes the limit of the cognitive mind supported by sensory-motor corporeality, thus permitting a full analysis of the subject in an environment of controlled variables [20, 22].

The researcher can then define the plans of sensory-motor action and mental-relational action thus controlling a new process of self-awareness and promoting the alteration of the postural engrams within the pathology itself.

1.2   Immersion in Virtual Environments

The concepts of immersion, presence, interaction and involvement are fundamental in order to understand subjects' physical and psychological experiences in virtual environments [19].

Immersion provokes the sensation of living in the real world in users when they are browsing in the virtual environment. On the other hand a feeling of being present is linked to the psychological aspects involved, this being verified in the sensations provoked - visual and auditory ones – in the subject's relationship with the virtual interface [19].

The involvement depends on the concentration of the individual on the virtual environment and on the isolation from the real world, being a better fit for immersion.

Finally, the interaction is about the connection between the user and the virtual environment, and evaluates the efficiency and effectiveness of the communication of this system [10].

---

[1] Engram is a permanent feature in the cerebral cortex, resulting in learning, training or experience in which the interneuronal synaptic become broader, more secreting neurotransmitters and richer in postsynaptic receptors.

Immersion VR, the object of this research, depends on artifacts that will allow the sensation of living in a real world to be experienced.

The sensation is so real that sensory conflicts may even cause uncomfortable symptoms after immersion in virtual environments. In this context, fatigue, eyestrain, dizziness, ataxia, visual flashbacks, disorientation and imbalance stand out [6, 9].

The resources used in immersion VR are: audio-visual devices, which help the sensation of movement and location; tactile interfaces, which produce sensations of shape, warmth and texture; and kinesthetic response, which requires the use of force, in addition to perceptions of pressure and vibration. [12]

1.3   Use of Haptic Devices and Their Importance for the Virtual Environment

Virtual reality and tactile technologies have emerged as promising tools to support the diagnosis of patients and interventions in the rehabilitation process [1].

Besides virtual reality systems, which provide virtual environments in 3-D within which the user can browse, haptic devices improve the user's interactivity and task performance.

Haptic, a term which was derived from the Greek verb "Haptesthai" which means "touch", adds the sense of touch and feedback of forcevin human-computer interaction.

Haptic devices enable the user to manipulate objects in virtual environments in a natural and effective way and can provide information on matters such as the rigidity, texture and weight of objects [11].

In rehabilitation, the objective is to help people with disabilities to improve their functional independence, by recovering their strength and range of movements. By helping patients improve their motor skills, thereby compensating for the permanent loss of function, patients can achieve a better quality of life.

Due to the feedback of force, tactile devices are indispensable tools in virtual rehabilitation because they help to measure performance and adjust the basis of exercises for each patient [25].

This potential for evaluating the patient's performance by measuring different parameters, which cannot be evaluated in traditional rehabilitation, may be of benefit to patients and professional therapists.

2   Methodology

The study consists of a review of the literature which fits into the presentation of papers in the category of theory.

First of all, 107 papers were pre-selected by conducting a search that used keywords. The search placed emphasis on the areas of Ergonomics and Health - namely: Applied Ergonomics, Ergonomics, Human Factors and Ergonomics and International Journal of Industrial Ergonomics, and on the databases of IEEE, Scielo, Pubmed and Medline.

In addition to journals, the research also included the annual IEEE International Conferences on Virtual Reality held between 2009 and 2012.

After analysis, only 25 publications were used to draw up this article. The selection of articles was based on their appropriateness to the research context and the impact factor and the periodicity of the journals.

3 Discussion

The virtual environment offers opportunities to manipulate therapeutically relevant variables and to work on the performance of motor and cognitive skills during immersion. The rehabilitation of each deficiency will depend on the movements required, the number of repetitions, the length of the experiment, the speed of presentation of the stimulus and of the complexity of browsing the environment itself, while always observing the time required to perform the task [6] .

The main advantages of virtual rehabilitation are repetition, feedback on performance and motivation. Moreover, recent studies with stroke patients [5, 7, 8] have proved that VR can contribute positively to the neural organization and recovery of functional motor skills.

The largest effect of immersion is the perception of presence in the virtual environment. The sense of reality enables a larger number of neural units to be recruited, thus constituting in addition to the motor stimulus, an important item of cognitive training.

On the other hand, the greatest difficulty lies in the very design of the virtual environment. First of all, users' needs and functional limitations must be listed, based on the User-Centered Design method, which includes a prospective clinical study of a representative sample. Later, the design should limit the deficiencies that will be addressed, and list the main inabilities and the correlated symptoms and clinical signs for each disability, thus determining the interfaces to be used in the virtual environment.

In order to construct the virtual environment, the resources used in immersion are: audio-visual devices, which help the sensation of movement and location; tactile interfaces, which produce sensations of shape, warmth and texture; and the kinesthetic response, which requires the use of strength, besides the perceptions of pressure and vibration.

It is important to emphasize that, within the concept of Inclusive Design, the virtual environment of rehabilitation should cover the broad spectrum of disabilities. This concept is essential for the rehabilitation of multiple functional variables. However, this makes the design of the virtual environment even more complex.

The use of virtual reality as a tool for diagnostic analysis and rehabilitation is undoubtedly a trend. However, studies are still scarce and their sample sizes small. Moreover, there is no reference standard [13].

So that a discussion of different research studies may be reliable, the following variables need to be considered: sample size, age range, gender and ethnic characteristics, type of disability and length of sequel. This is because the same functional limitation can be caused by different deficiencies.

4   Conclusion

Making use of virtual reality enables real-world situations to be simulated, thereby giving the researcher total control over the variables analyzed and enabling the health aspects involved to be controlled.

The simultaneous control of variables is of the utmost importance in the systemic treatment of the disease, as it allows patients with multiple disabilities to be rehabilitated.

When designs serve specific populations, not only in the social sphere, but include the user from the perspective of disability, the process of creation reaches its most important contribution: this characterizes design as a tool that promotes good health.

Thus, the design process extrapolates the objectives of efficiency, effectiveness and satisfaction and achieves a new construct: functionality, considered by the World Health Organization (WHO) as a variable that is indispensible for defining the state of health itself.

In this context, virtual reality immersion, by activating the cognitive processes needed for browsing and interpreting the environment, will promote the automation of everyday activities, thus bringing about permanent changes in the subjects' mental models.

During immersion, learning overcomes the limit of the cognitive mind supported by sensory-motor corporeality, thus allowing full analysis of the subject in an environment of controlled variables.

The researcher can then define the action plans for sensory-motor action and for mental-relational action, thereby controlling a new process of self-awareness and promoting the alteration of the postural engrams within the pathology itself.

What is therefore concluded is the importance of the design process in maintaining good health and fostering functional independence, its being a decisive part of rehabilitating and reintegrating people with disabilities.

References

1. Alamri, Eid, M., Iglesias, Shirmohammadi, Saddik, A.E.: Haptic Virtual Rehabilitation Exercises for Poststroke Diagnosis. IEEE Transactions on Instrumentation and Measurement 57(9) (September 2008)
2. Alamri, Cha, El Saddik: AR-REHAB: An Augmented Reality Framework for Poststroke-Patient Rehabilitation. IEEE Transactions on Instrumentation and Measurement (May 2010)
3. Antley, Slater: The Effect on Lower Spine Muscle Activation of Walking on a Narrow Beam in Virtual Reality. IEEE Transactions on Visualization and Computer Graphics 17(2) (February 2011)
4. Bohil, Alicea, Biocca: Virtual reality in neuroscience research and therapy. Nature Neuroscience 12 (December 2011)
5. Cameirão, Bermúdez, Duarte, Verschure: Virtual reality based rehabilitation speeds up functional recovery of the upper extremities after stroke: A randomized controlled pilot

study in the acute phase of stroke using the Rehabilitation Gaming System. Restorative Neurology and Neuroscience 29, 287–298 (2011)

6. Chen, Jeng, Fung, Doong, Chuang: Psychological Benefits of Virtual Reality for Patients in Rehabilitation Therapy. Journal of Sport Rehabilitation 18, 258–268 (2009)

7. Connelly, Jia, Toro, Stoykov, Kenyon, Kamper: A Pneumatic Glove and Immersive Virtual Reality Environment for Hand Rehabilitative Training After Stroke. IEEE Transactions on Neural Systems and Rehabilitation Engineering 18(5) (October 2010)

8. Crosbie, Lennon, McGoldrick, McNeill, McDonough: Virtual reality in the rehabilitation of the arm after hemiplegic stroke: a randomized controlled pilot study. Clinical Rehabilitation 26(9), 798–806 (2012)

9. Jack, D., Boian, R., Merians, A.S., Tremaine, M., Burdea, G.C., Adamovich, S.V., Recce, M., Poizner, H.: Virtual Reality-Enhanced Stroke Rehabilitation. IEEE Transactions on Neural Systems and Rehabilitation Engineering 9(3) (September 2001)

10. Sharan, D., Ajeesh, Rameshkumar, Mathankumar, Jospin Paulina, Manjula: Virtual reality based therapy for post operative rehabilitation of children with cerebral palsy. Work 41, 3612–3615 (2012)

11. Diodato, Mraz, Baker, Graham: A Haptic Force Feedback Device for Virtual Reality-fMRI Experiments. IEEE Transactions on Neural Systems and Rehabilitation Engineering 15(4) (December 2007)

12. Galvin, Levac: Facilitating clinical decision-making about the use of virtual reality within paediatric motor rehabilitation: Describing and classifying virtual reality systems. Developmental Neurorehabilitation 14(2), 112–122 (2011)

13. Gyia, Sims, Porter, Marshall, Case: Representing older and disabled people in virtual user trials: data collection methods. Applied Ergonomics 35, 443–451 (2004)

14. Harmatz: Entering a new treatment age for mucopolysaccharidosis VI disease: a search for better markers of disease progression and response to treatment. Journal de Pediatria 84(2) (2008)

15. Kaber, Li, Clamann, Lee: Investigating Human Performance in a Virtual Reality Haptic Simulator as Influenced by Fidelity and System Latency. IEEE Transactions on Systems, Man, and Cybernetics—Part A: Systems and Humans 42(6) (November 2012)

16. Lange, Teive, Troiano, Bitencourt, Funke, Setubal, Zanis Neto, Medeiros, Werneck, Pasquini, Bonfim: Bone marrow transplantation in patients with storage diseases. Arq Neuropsiquiatr. 64(1), 1–4 (2006)

17. Ma, Hwang, Fang, Kuo, Wang, Leong, Wang: Effects of virtual reality training on functional reaching movements in people with Parkinson's disease: a randomized controlled pilot trial. Clinical Rehabilitation 25(10), 892–902 (2011)

18. Pinto, Scheartz, Puga, Vieira, Munoz, Giuliani: Prospective study of 11 Brazilian patients with mucopolysaccharidosis II. J. Pediatr. 82(4), 273–278 (2006)

19. Rebelo, Duarte, Noriega, Soares: Virtual reality in consumer product design: methods and applications. In: Karwowski, W., Soares, M.M., Stanton, N. (eds.) Human Factors and Ergonomics in Consumer Product Design, ch. 24, pp. 381–404. CRC Press, Boca Raton (2010)

20. Resnik, Etter, Klinger, Kambe: Using virtual reality environment to facilitate training with advanced upper-limb prosthesis. Journal of Rehabilitation Research & Development 48(6) (2011)

21. Thorne, Javadpour, Hughes, Wraith, Cowie: Craniovertebral abnormalities in type VI mucopolysaccharidosis (Maroteaux-Lamy Syndrome). Neurosugery 48(4), 849–853 (2011)

22. Ueki, Kawasaki, Ito, Nishimoto, Abe, Aoki, Ishigure, Ojika, Mouri: Development of a Hand-Assist Robot With Multi-Degrees-of-Freedom for Rehabilitation Therapy. IEEE/ASME Transactions on Mechatronics 17(1) (February 2012)
23. Viana, Lima, Cavaleiro, Alves, Souza, Feio, Leistner-Segal, Schwartz, Giugliani, Silva: Mucopolysaccharidoses in northern Brazil: Target Mutation screening and urinary glycosaminoglycan excretion in patients undergoing enzyme replacement therapy. Genetics and Molecular Biology 34(3), 410–415 (2011)
24. Vougioukas, Berlis, Kopp, Korinthenberg, Spreer, Velthoven: Neurosurgical interventions in children with Maroteaux-Lamy Syndrome. Pediatric Neurosugery 35(1) (2001)
25. Zhou, Malric, Shirmohammadi: A New Hand-Measurement Method to Simplify Calibration in CyberGlove-Based Virtual Rehabilitation. IEEE Transactions on Instrumentation and Measurement 59(10) (October 2010)

Virtual Reality Applied to the Study of the Interaction between the User and the Built Space: A Literature Review

Alexana Vilar Soares Calado, Marcelo Márcio Soares,
Fabio Campos, and Walter Correia

Centre for Arts and Communication, Graduate Program in Ergonomics, Federal University of Pernambuco, Av. Moraes Rego, of University City Sn 50670-420 - Recife, PE, Brazil
{alexanavilar,fc2005}@gmail.com, marcelo2@nlink.com.br,
ergonomia@terra.com.br

Abstract. This article examines from a theoretical academic research, concepts, definitions and elements that consist the universe of virtual reality (VR) and Augmented Reality (AR), with the goal of applying them to spaces constructed both by professionals specialized in developing environments, as many by its users.

Keywords: Architecture, Interior Design, Virtual Reality, Augmented Reality.

1 Introduction

The representation of an architectural or interior design has always faced limitations from the instrumental available for their achievement. The idea of sharing is essential in designing the project. Despite the spread of computers in professional architects routine, designers and engineers, still show little explored new techniques of representation and visualization as virtual reality (VR) and augmented reality (AR). These new tools may represent a major advance in understandability of built spaces as they allow professionals to troubleshoot before its completion and the user experience it in a way never experienced. This article aims to develop a theoretical review prepared for the development of research in the field of virtual reality (VR) and augmented reality (AR).

For this, a literature review including definitions and established applications for virtual reality (VR) and augmented reality (AR) was performed. Additionally, we conduct an analysis on these concepts and verified the needs and ways of applying these new technologies in day-to-day lives.

Virtual reality (VR) is an "advanced user interface" to access applications running on the computer, providing viewing, handling and user interaction in real time and in three-dimensional computer generated environments (6). According Kirner and Tori (5) a virtual environment can be designed to simulate a real environment as much as an imaginary environment, the degree of interaction will be greater or lesser depending on the class of systems (virtual reality immersive, non-immersive, augmented reality, telepresence) .

A. Marcus (Ed.): DUXU/HCII 2013, Part III, LNCS 8014, pp. 345–351, 2013.

As Rebelo Duarte, Soares and Noriega (12) in the field of architecture, RV has been applied to allow interaction (through manipulation) in virtual spaces, indoors or outdoors, with different levels of realism. In these spaces, the users move freely and, in some cases, make changes, such as changes in the environment, the placement of furniture, and lighting.

Because it operates without the need to use special equipment, augmented reality has been considered a real possibility of becoming the next generation of popular interface and can be used indoors and outdoors, and is therefore more comprehensive and universal (6) . In this context the architectural and interior design can take hold of these tools to simulate real space designed in virtual reality, allowing the space to be built and interior design, be it institutional, industrial, commercial or residential, can be evaluated on their demands ergonomic, aesthetic and cognitive before one wall will be raised, avoiding operating expenses with the implementation of the project prior to its implementation, allowing the user experiences the property and its surroundings with refined details, and may even evaluate issues such as natural ventilation, insulation, lighting, acoustic-term condition, functionality, layout, etc.. The potential of Virtual Reality and Augmented Reality proved to be adequate to study aspects such as safety, comfort and usability of the built environment.

2   Methodology

The methodology used in this study was characterized by the theoretical analysis developed for academic research, which were scored several authors who speak about the issue at hand. Thus the theoretical basis was based on study and analysis of the current landscape of digital technology, considering the new technologies introduced in the sector, the role of architect and designer in the preparation of architectural and interior design, research physical needs and cognitive user / customer focus of the work of architects and designers, the aesthetic that permeates the world of design, beyond considerations of ergonomics, usability and comfort.

For the selection of quota review of the material, it was considered issues related to the digital technologies of Virtual Reality and Augmented Reality, its application to architecture, design and urban planning and aspects of the interaction of the cognitive system. Were consulted in this research journal articles, books and / or book chapters, communication events (anal) and electronic texts.

3   Virtual Reality and Augmented Reality

A filmmaker was in charge of, in 1955, the design of the first application of virtual reality, an engineer, in 1970, the construction of the first virtual reality helmet and a professional multidisciplinary, in the 1980s, the proposal of the term has come to consolidate as virtual reality (5)

Since its inception virtual reality is a research area that relies on a multitude of other areas, and can be applied in other plethora of them.

According to Soares and Zuffo (13) one of the biggest barriers in virtual reality (VR) is the computational requirements for the generation and display of multi-realistic images in real time, requiring research and development in computing systems and graphics processing high Performance.

Even with current levels of quality, computer-generated worlds are not yet indistinguishable from reality, the development of technology and the reduction of price for the equipment needed to conduct studies based on RV, tend to increase the number of searches using their means (11).

The applications of virtual reality (VR) can be seen under a rather broad, ranging from a single person, using a single computer, to many users using a distributed system, according to Kubo et al (2004) Distributed Virtual Environments (ADL) have a high potential for application. They are characterized as virtual environments (AV) interactive, where users geographically dispersed aim at cooperation and sharing of computational resources in real time, allowing the exchange of information enhanced by a sense of shared spaces, users have the illusion they are located in the same place, in the sense of presence, each participant becomes a "virtual person", called AVATAR, in this environment, each participant can view other AVATARS located in the same space.

The AVATARS or "virtual humans" are also used when any activity that involves the interaction of human beings with a physical world in risky tasks when requested, avoiding security problems and physical limitations, as in replacement of real people in ergonomic tests computer-based vehicle projects.

To ensure the user's immersion in order to make it interact with the virtual environment, technology input and output data associated with virtual reality (VR) seek to stimulate efficiently as many senses as possible and with maximum capture fidelity the various movements of the user, such as the movements of the hands, head, eyes.

Through the device response technique, the user is encouraged to feel heat when approaching a fire in the virtual world, driven by the presence of semiconductors, receivers and heat sources. Another trick used to print more realism to virtual world platforms are mobile, considered a response device physics because they provide sensation of movement.

In virtual reality (VR) interface acts as the body: is it relates to hardware and software, interacts with worlds, design, programs and bits, is attributed to him that are the degrees of interaction and thereby the relations of immersion environment. The more the body is integrated into the greater its potential for immersion (6).

A multisensory interaction of the body with the environment takes place via devices attached to the body (helmets, gloves, clothing, sensors, chips) and physical environments (rooms, CAVEs) (Figure 01).

Fig. 1. Virtual Reality Devices. Source: eletronicos.hsw.uol.com.br.

By the 90s, there is the emergence of the use of augmented reality technology which allows to overlay virtual objects and environments with the physical environment, through some technological device, enriching the real environment with virtual objects, running in real time. The application of augmented reality has become more accessible in the early 2000s, with the convergence of computer vision techniques, software and devices with better cost benefit (6). The RA has the advantage of allowing the use of tangible actions (7) and multimodal operations involving voice, gestures, touch, etc.., Facilitating the work of the user without the need for training.

Azuma (2) defines an augmented virtual reality system (RA) as the one that has the following characteristics: combines real and virtual objects in a real environment; operates interactively and in real time and records (aligns) real and virtual objects with each others. Since RA is, by definition, strongly directed to the presentation and manipulation of virtual objects, environments lend themselves naturally to the sharing of these objects.

4   Virtual Reality and Augmented Reality Applied to Architecture and Urban Planning

As stated by Stanney and Zyda (13), a virtual environment can represent a "truth" that people can be educated, trained, observed, entertained and inspired. He immerses users in a world that stimulates multiple senses and can be used to provide experiences that often can not be experienced in the real world.

According to Wang (14), Li (9) virtual reality technology can be widely used in urban planning from the production model of a large urban scale, contributing to the research design and planning of the urban environment. Using virtual reality technology can evaluate all kinds of planning and design in the real environment, investigate environmental impacts, to subsequently enter the problem and assess the reasonableness of the program.

For the authors, this technology creates conditions for the practice of many viable options, a condition not as expensive and time consuming as the actual construction of the building. Thus, virtual reality can not only improve the scientific nature of urban planning or urban ecological construction, how to reduce the cost of urban development, and also reduce the time available for this purpose. Public managers, technicians in urban policy and planning, construction managers and the public play different roles in urban planning, and benefit from the RV that provides the ideal bridge for cooperation.

According to Neto (3) the application of technology in virtual reality (VR) and 3D computer graphics in the areas of architecture, civil engineering design and is treated by many authors as one of the most important applications of VR, researchers say, in Nowadays, VR technologies and computer aided design, are almost as important for professional architectural and engineering as for developers of electronic games, according to the author, this technology proves extremely efficient, not only in product marketing, but also in the design stage, volumes of studies and solutions to implementation problems.

Another aspect pointed in relation to virtual reality is the ability to reduce the number of physical prototypes substituting them for virtual prototypes (VP) which have the advantage of reducing the cost and time to develop new solutions (12).

Notably, the entertainment business and marketing has a greater uptake of these technologies in their daily applications, however, have begun to appear examples of the use of virtual reality (VR) and Augmented Reality (AR) in the project areas (4).

A number of applications of augmented reality in architecture and urbanism has been cataloged, they are among the projects layout, apartment renovations, construction (systems that assist the project), urbanism, in landscaping and restoration, such as The system for urban planning ARTHUR, who developed an interface to project group around a table, this is a collaborative project where users make decisions together (1).

With the help of software such as RAMSIS (Humam Solution) and JACK (Siemems), it is possible to predict whether certain structures will cause discomfort and pain in employees, it is also possible for administrators to anticipate the implementation of the new plant in different scenarios (land sizes, different locations and geological features) before opening the new company (1).

Li (9) notes that the architects for the location of the building is one of the most important aspects. The use of virtual reality technology can provide a comprehensive assessment of the environment, so that customers and agents can raise awareness of construction. Through analysis of relevant environmental parameters, one can predict the ambient space, comfort, pollution, noise indicators, etc..

The creative potential of digital media together to advances in manufacturing already applied in the automotive, aerospace and marine, are opening up new dimensions for architectural and interior design.

5   Virtual Reality, Augmented Reality, Cognition and Interaction

To Leston (8) companies have used the RV in fields such as design automation, sales and marketing, planning and maintenance, training and simulation, design and data visualization. However, any time there are new applications in various areas of human knowledge and quite diverse, depending on the existing demand and creative capacity of people. In many cases the virtual reality is changing the way people interact with complex systems, providing better performance and reducing costs.

Ayman, Clayden and Higgins (10) stated that recent studies have shown that digital virtual environments has the potential to replicate some interactive qualities of the "real world", this statement motivates us to direct our gaze to the issue, believing that digital technologies can contribute immensely to creating hardware and software, developed in partnership with professionals from various interrelated areas, also including the active participation of the potential consumer, aiming to design tools that will meet the demands of the market.

The design of interaction techniques will pursue three main objectives: performance, usability and usefulness. Performance relates to how well activities are being performed by the user and the system, in cooperation, in addition to efficiency, accuracy and depth. Usability is the ease to inform the system about user interactions, as well as the ease of use and learning, and user comfort. Utility shows that the interaction helps the user achieve their goals, and can focus on the task (10).

6   Final Thoughts

After reviewing the references discussed some theoretical aspects were highlighted.

Every day hundreds of thousands of architects, engineers and designers around the world design spaces that will house people from all backgrounds and cultures, which have different desires and needs, and seek to make their dream come true of acquiring the property that possibly will call home this reality that is repeated daily can be aided by the possibilities of computer graphics and features that increase every day. Subscribe to this development is a challenge faced by professionals, educators and students in a developing country.

Climate change, population densities, many variables and many current problems can be treated from the use of new forms of design, with the aid of digital tools that provide a preview of the issue through simulation and analysis, for the act of projecting this mode design means greater comprehensibility of the problem more quickly and in the same solution. As an architect, working in the market for over 20 years and researcher in the field of ergonomics, I realize how the lack of information generated in a timely manner can harm the development of the project at any stage.

As part of the project design of architecture and interior design, considering the ergonomic viewpoint, the user must be the starting point for the development of the project, however to satisfy consumers needs to be considered beyond their needs and desires , capabilities and limitations, the technical specifications of the materials used in their own project design and implementation. It is believed possible that with the introduction of new techniques of representation and visualization as virtual reality (VR) and Augmented Reality (AR), with the use of specific software projects Architecture and interior design will have increased its interaction with the client and the professional.

From the analysis of the theoretical study, questions arose referenced in the use of digital tools for the development of architectural design and interior design projects, such as the operating cost for software adoption in the design and development of the project, its compatibility with gains and solutions, facilitating the relationship of software to aid the investigative process demands ergonomic, technical and aesthetic derived from the project; relative to earnings caused by the interaction between complementary projects, as well as analysis of the expectations formed by the users / customers and users / professionals regarding the use of the tool.

Thus, this research concludes that the proposition of applying virtual reality (VR) and Augmented Reality (AR) in the field of Architecture and Interior Design, specifically in improving the process of developing a project with emphasis on the concepts of ergonomics will deliver real gains to this equation. Furthermore, we intend to add visualization processes images from the experiences in the physical as well as the relationship of the body in an environment, in order to expand to the degree of sensory and cognitive ergonomic studies, providing the user a greater interaction

References

1. Amim, R.R.: Realidade Aumentada aplicada a Arquitetura e Urbanismo. Dissertação em mestrado em Engenharia Civil, UFRJ (2007)
2. Azuma, R., et al.: Recent advances in Augmented Reality. IEEE Computer Graphics and Applications 21(6), 34–47 (2001)
3. Espinheira Neto, R.A.: Arquitetura digital: A realidade virtual, suas aplicações e possibilidades. Dissertação de mestrado. UFRJ, Rio de Janeiro (2004)
4. Kirner, C., Kirner, T.G.: A data visualization virtual environment supported by augmented reality. In: Proceedings of XXIX IEEE International Conference on Systems, Man and Cybernetics, Taipei, Tawan, pp. 97–102 (2006)
5. Kirner, C., Tori, R.: Realidade Virtual: conceitos e tendências – Pré-simpósio SVR 2004, Editora Mania do livro, São Paulo (2004)
6. Kirner, C., Siscouto, R.: Realidade virtual e aumentada: Conceitos, projetos e aplicações. In: IX Symposium on Virtual and Augmented Reality, Petrópolis, RJ (2007)
7. Kawashima, T., et al.: Magic Paddle: A Tangible Augmented Reality Interface for Object Manipulation. In: Proc. of ISMR 2001, pp. 194–195 (2001)
8. Leston, S.: Virtual Reality: The It perspective. Computer Bulletin, 12–13 (1996)
9. Li, Yu: Virtual Reality in Urban Planning. Hei Longjiang Techknowlege Information (2007)
10. Mahmoud, A.H., Clayde, A., Higgins, C.A.: Comparative Study of Environmental Cognition in a Real Environment and its VRML Simulation (Virtual Reality Modelling Language), pp. 1106–1109. IEEE (2009)
11. Raubal, M., Egenhofer, M.: Comparing the complexity of wayfinding tools in built environments. Environment & Planning B 25(6), 895–913 (1998)
12. Rebelo, F., Duarte, E., Noriega, P., Soares, M.M.: Virtual reality in consumer product design: methods and applications. In: Karwowski, W., Soares, M.M., Stanton, N. (eds.) Human Factors and Ergonomics in Consumer Product Design, ch. 24, pp. 381–404. CRC Press, Boca Raton (2010)
13. Soares, L.P., Zuffo, M.K.: JINX: an browser for VR immersive simulation based on clusters of commodity computers. In: Proceedings of the Ninth International Conference on 3D Web Technology, Monterey–CA-EUA (2004)
14. Stanney, K.M., Zyda, M.: Virtual Environments in the 21st Century. In: Stanney, K.M. (ed.) Handbook of Virtual Environments: Design, Implementation, and Applications, pp. 1–14. Lawrence Erlbaum Associates, Mahwah (2002)

Gestural, Emergent and Expressive: Three Research Themes for Haptic Interaction

Jared Donovan, Gavin Sade, and Jennifer Seevinck

Creative Industries Faculty, Queensland University of Technology, Brisbane Australia
{j.donovan,g.sade,jennifer.seevinck}@qut.edu.au

Abstract. Drawing on three case studies of work in the fields of participatory design, interaction design and electronic arts, we reflect on the implications of these studies for haptic interface research. We propose three themes: *gestural*; *emergent*; and *expressive*; as signposts for a program of research into haptic interaction that could point the way towards novel approaches to haptic interaction and move us from optic to haptic ways of seeing.

Keywords: Haptic interaction, gesture, emergent interaction, expressive interaction, passive haptics, ways of seeing.

1   Introduction

Research in the field of haptic interaction has been dominated by a representational approach, which emphasises haptic fidelity and focuses on the simulation of real-world, physical objects and materials. Although this approach has obvious practical utility, it excludes consideration of potentially fruitful alternative approaches to haptic interaction, which have so far received less attention. Working from our combined backgrounds in participatory design, interaction design and electronic arts, we see potential in an alternative and less literal approach to haptic interface design - one which emphasises haptic interactions' gestural, emergent and expressive qualities.

The aim of the paper is therefore to expand the bounds of haptic interaction design. More specifically we aim to identify some broad research themes for exploring non-representational haptic interfaces, interaction designs and research. These insights stem from the authors' previous work and are generated through the use of Reflective Practice methods (e.g. [1]) in addition to theoretical research.

The paper is broadly structured in two parts. In the first part, outlines our approach to the subject of haptic interaction design which is grounded in a broad reading of literature relating to perception and sensory experience – drawing from HCI, philosophy and media studies. The second part of the paper consists of three case studies on interactive systems created by each of the authors. These highlight the themes of gestural, emergent and expressive interaction as fertile areas for exploration in relation to haptic interfaces. Each of the interactive systems, through practitioner reflection and case study analysis, reveals a theme. These themes combine with the theoretical insights gained through the literature survey to point towards a less conventional,

A. Marcus (Ed.): DUXU/HCII 2013, Part III, LNCS 8014, pp. 352–361, 2013.

non-representational haptic design and research agenda. We believe that such a research agenda has the potential to expand the domain of haptic design and research, to lead to new knowledge and approaches for addressing problems within Interaction Design - ranging from the exploration of complex data sets through to affective interaction, embodiment, and applications in health.

2   Background

Haptic perception involves the somatosensory system that a complex array of sensory receptors associated with our embodied tactile experience of objects and the world – essentially the human perceptual abilities of extroception and proprioception. While haptic rendering in engineering and the sciences typically distinguishes between active haptics and passive haptics. The difference is one of response – where force feedback is provided to the user, the system is active and where there is no force feedback provided in real-time, the system is considered passive. The significance of the passive haptic system is its potential to leverage everyday passive objects and their affordances. This is a driving force behind the Tangible Computing field of research [2]. Such definitions provide a clear outline of the haptic sensory modality and the ways it can be studied in a quantitative manner, and employed in the development of functional haptic interfaces. However, through the literature in the field of haptic interface design and research haptic interfaces are commonly combined with 3D simulations of space and objects. To help us understand this relationship between haptic and visual perception, and the preference for combining haptic interfaces with 3D representations of the real world and objects we begin by looking at the etymology of the term haptic. Haptic originates from the greek *haptesthai*, to fasten onto, to touch [3]. This provides a point of departure for approaching haptic, that our touch fastens us in the world, as opposed to sight that situates us within a continuous space as distinct subjects. Touch, and our hands, draw us into the world.

Outside of HCI and human factors, philosophers and theorists have addressed the subject of haptic perception from a cultural, phenomological and social perspective. From McLuhan's [4], [5] understanding of electronic media as tactile to Deluze and Guattari's notions of smooth and striated space [6], to more recent work looking at the haptic visuality and tactility of film [7], [8] to the design of haptic interface technologies and computer space [9] and haptic interfaces from a cultural, ethic and social perspective [10]. This body of work provides valuable cues to how to develop a haptic research agenda, without falling to what Hansen describes as an ocular centric paradigm [11].

Of specific interest in this paper is the distinction made between haptic and optic ways of seeing, and understanding space. This distinction, which has it origins in the work of visual arts theorist Reigl involves understanding the way image and space are represented and perceived in visual media forms, from painting to film to computer games, by different cultures and societies [9]. The distinctions between haptic and optic ways of seeing are grounded in the relationships between culture, subjectivity and perception, and the representation of objects in space. Put simply, optic space organises objects within in a unified spatial continuum (e.g. perspective) and establishes a viewing distance between the viewer and objects, as such the viewer can situate themselves as viewing subjects. By contrast haptic space focuses on the surface, concerned with tactility and texture rather than illusionary depth [7]. Haptic visuality considers the experience of seeing as an immersion in colour, light and movement – to feel the work with the eyes, to be drawn too close. This is well summed up by Cézenne when he describes immersion in the visual filed and how this translates into artistic techniques [12].

It is Deleuze, however who discusses the way haptic space is a space in which neither the hand nor the eye are subordinate [13]. While haptic interfaces remain coupled to 3D simulations of optic space and objects, there remains a subordination of the hand to the eye. It is this sense relationship that we see as central to developing an approach to both research into haptic interaction and the design of haptic interfaces.

This desire to draw us into the virtual world, through the combination of 3D computer graphics and haptic interfaces echoes the 1990s dream of immersive virtual reality – a vision which has not come to pass as imagined by its originators. Instead the digital world has become integrated into the 'real' world in a more seamful, mixed manner, and has lead to theories of embodiment [14], emergence [15], aesthetics [16], [17] and somaesthetics in interaction design [18].

3   Cases

Following we present three case studies, which highlight the themes of gestural, emergent and expressive interaction as fertile areas for exploration in relation to haptic interfaces.

The gestural case study describes research into the use of gestural interaction in the context of a skilled workplace - dentistry. Through extended field studies and a participatory design process, gestures were investigated as a possible means of interacting with computer systems. This work highlighted important qualities of gestural interaction for interface design, which are also highly relevant for work in the area of haptic interfaces. Especially relevant is the finding that gestural interactions can usefully be conceived as skilled movements encompassing both movements we would conventionally consider gestures (communicative hand movements) as well as the skilled haptic tool-manipulation movements of dentists as they work.

The emergent case study concerns the interactive artwork +-NOW, which has a tangible user interface. During participant interaction with the work, emergent behaviours were found to occur. The discussion reflects on the role of materials, their affordances and the design of the haptic interface in effecting these surprisingly new, participant behaviours. The discussion draws on theories of emergence, game design and perception. it also includes excerpts of participant interaction with the artwork to exemplify the emergence.

Finally, the expressive case study draws on work from the context of electronic arts to reflect on the expressive possibilities of haptic interaction. This case draws on the interactive artwork *Pulse Guantlets*, which explores the evocative, poetic and playful aspects of interaction. The discussion centers on how attention to aesthetic qualities of interaction can create more meaningful, memorable and impactful contexts for experience around issues related to inter-personal relations.

3.1 Gestural

The first of our case studies was taken from a design research project, which investigated the design of a gestural interface for use in the context of the dental surgery. What emerged from this study was a broad and inclusive view of gesture as skilled embodied movements (Fig. 1). Any movement of the body can be considered a gesture. Gestures can be produced for a variety of purposes, including for the purpose of expressing meaning to another or oneself, to explore meaning or gain information from the world, and to manipulate objects effect material changes in the world. Gestures should be understood as socially and environmentally situated [19].

Fig. 1. An inclusive view of gestures as skilled movements

This framework presents a quite radical understanding of gesture compared to the view that has previously been taken in gesture interface research, which typically considers only the leftmost end of the continuum above – gestures made to express meaning to another or oneself [20]. Although this conventional focus of gesture interface research has the attraction that it lines up with an everyday understanding of gesture as *communicative* movements, it is limiting for framing a theoretical understanding of gestural activity for Human Computer Interaction, because it cuts off consideration of other kinds of gestural movements that might be usefully employed in interaction design and diminishes the possibility of creating connections between gestural interaction and other fields, such as haptic interaction, which are also fundamentally concerned with human capacities for skilled (gestural) movement.

Furthermore, considering gestures as *only* communicative movements is challenged by findings from empirical studies of existing contexts of use. As part of the case study, a detailed analysis of video recordings of dental practitioners at work was carried out in order to understand the kinds of gestural interactions that occur there. As one would expect, this study clearly showed that gestures are employed in supporting communication between the dentist and patient, especially where the dentist had to explain concepts from dentistry. However, the study also revealed the role that gestures play coordinating the activities of dentists, patients and dental assistants as they go about their work. These coordinative gestures presented a continuum of gestural interactions from more directly communicative in purpose through to gestures that were intimately tied to the use and manipulation of physical instruments and materials in the dental examination [19].

These findings accord with insights from other studies of human gesture, which point to deep links between gestures and: sensorimotor-experience, cognition and learning [21], [22]; tool-use and manipulation [23], [24]; and the coordination of situated human interaction [25], [26]. It is simply not the case that there is a clearly separable boundary between different purposes of skilled movement. Rather, skilled movements *are* skilled by virtue of the fact that practitioners are able to enfold multiple modes of embodied activity into situated fields of interaction [25].

In terms of design, this view suggested the concept of a 'gestural dental instrument' (Fig. 2), which was an augmented dental instrument capable of detecting movements acting on it which the dentist could use during a dental examination to interact with a computer interface. From the perspective of gesture interface design, this design concept points to the possibility of designing input devices that allow a

range of kinds of gestural interaction, from more communicatively focused on physical manipulation, or meaning making gestures. It also suggests questions for haptic interface research around how haptic input and feedback could be coupled with a broad range of gestural interactions, and what possibilities this would raise for the design of haptic interfaces.

Fig. 2. Prototype of a 'gestural instrument' for use in a dental examination

3.2 Emergent

The interactive art system *+-NOW* (plus minus now) [27] uses sand as a continuous, tangible interface. The audience can interact with this passively haptic medium to create two types of imagery – the colourful augmented reality image that is projected directly onto the fine, white beach sand; and the monochromatic image that is rear projected onto a wall screen. Gestures in the sand effect 'layers' of imagery in re-

sponse, like visual echoes that mimic the shape, direction and speed of a mark in the sand with repeated renderings (see below). These 'visual echoes' of gestures add up in opacity to create areas of increased brightness on the wall image, enabling the interpretation of new shapes. At the same time the image persists and one can interact with a history of one's gestures. In this way the work facilitates "...layering and moving across time" [27].

Fig. 3. The interactive art system *+-Now*, 2008

During its three month installation at Beta_Space in the Sydney Powerhouse Museum, a qualitative evaluation of the public's experience and interaction with the work was conducted [28], [29]. Findings from this study have reframed this author's (and artist's) understanding of haptic interaction, particularly as it relates to those non-traditional human computer interactions that are not focused on supporting clearly defined goals and behaviours.

Audience behaviours while interacting with the work were a particular focus of the study. Following the Constructivist viewpoint of perception it is possible to look at these people's behaviours in terms of the environment that they occurred in, and in particular, at the materials that they interacted with [30], [31]. Thus the affordances of the sand are a key influencer in the behaviours observed. Not surprisingly then it was found that a number of participants 'made marks' in the sand or created drawings. Given the temporal quality of the work – the fact that the image persists after the gesture and can layer – it also meant that it was possible for people to animate. (See the example of one person's interactive animation of a heartbeat, shown above). Given that sand affords drawing and mark making, the interactive animation behavior is not surprising. Other less predictable and relatively novel behaviors were also observed. These *emergent* behaviors include 'stir look feel' and 'follow lights'. The first involved stirring the sand then looking at the imagery to wait and see what might appear. The second behavior involved making clearings in the sand and then touching them as coloured light would appear in them (for more detail see [32]). Both of these game-like behaviors rely integrally on the affordances of the interface – whether to stir up this continuous, analogue material or to make small holes in it, mounding it around the sides. These participant behavior that emerged are largely due to the nature of the sand interface – and how people perceive it.

Emergent behaviors are not a new concept in gameplay. Emergent games are one of two kinds, as described by theorist Juul [15]. This is the open-ended game that facilitates new and surprising outcomes and is different with every re-play. The other is the progressive game where for example a player meets a sequence of challenges. Bluffing in the game of poker is an example of an emergent behaviour. It is not explicitly defined in the rules of Poker. Other research into emergence literature, perception and haptics have combined with the evaluations of participant interaction with +-*NOW* to reframe this author's view of haptics. The insight gleaned is to consider the affordances and other material attributes of the haptic, tangible interface as analogous to rules in a game, given that both influence and determine the participant's behavior. This shift in design perspective locates haptics at the forefront of the design process for creating emergent interactions. Such design work can be further informed by a framework of emergence in interaction [28]. This framework is based on theoretical research. It provides further scope in the creation and evaluation of haptic interactions that are creative, surprisingly new, unpredictable and emergent – in short, non-traditional HCI.

3.3 Expressive

To feel another person's pulse is an intimate and physical interaction. The work *Pulse Gauntlets* – created by Gavin Sade, Priscilla Bracks and Dean Brough – employs near field communications[1] to extend the tangible reach of the human heart beat, so another person can feel our heart beat at a distance. The work is an initial experiment in near field haptic interaction, and was initial created for presentation at the *Haptic Interface* Exhibition[2] in Hong Kong in late 2012. The focus of the work was to explore the quality of interactions resulting from feeling another persons pulse.

---

[1] In this work we use XBee Series 1 Radio Frequency transmitter receivers from Digi.
[2] http://hapticinterface.hkbu.edu.hk/

The work takes the form of two feathered white gauntlets, to be worn on the forearm. Each of the gauntlets contain a pulse sensor, XBee radio frequency transmitter receiver, a pink LED and a small vibration motor. The pulse of the wearer is recorded and transmitted to the other gauntlet where it is transformed into haptic feedback, in the form of a short pulse of the vibration motor, which makes direct contact with the skin. The length and intensity of the vibration were aesthetic variables manipulated to achieve a desired feeling of a "heartbeat", without the vibration being either an annoying buzz or unperceivable.

Fig. 4. Pulse Gauntlet - showing final visual form, with feathers, white leather and pink LED

The pair of *Pulse Gauntlets* are the first stage of a more ambitious project that will involve a larger number of similar gauntlets, all broadcasting pulse of the respective wearers. The aim of making this larger haptic interactive system is to explore interaction within larger groups, and development of new use cases through observing emergent behaviors of wearers.

The *Pulse Gauntlets* are the result of a practice-led approach – which means the practice of making in the studio came before the formulation any specific research question. As opposed to a typical engineering or HCI approach, practice-led research is emergent in nature, with both questions and new knowledge emerging through practice. In this respect the *Pulse Gauntlets* need to be seen as the result of creative practice, as opposed to being a goal directed research. Aesthetic decisions, choice of materials and even conceptual connections all arose from interplay of making and thinking about making which occurs within the studio, and reflection upon the outcomes. In this setting the aesthetic qualities and resolution of the final objects were an important focus of the practice, and as such the gauntlets are more than a technically function prototype produced as a research instrument. Instead the gauntlets can be considered a finished creative outcome that embodies some of our thinking about haptic interaction, which can only be experienced through actually wearing one of the gauntlets.

The physical materials from which the gauntlets are fabricated play an important role in the passive haptic experience of the work. This careful concern for aesthetics and the textural quality of material is an aspect that is sometimes missing in research focused on active haptic systems. The textural and physical qualities of the leather and ostrich feather play an important part in the final haptic experience of the pulse gauntlets – and form part of a carefully crafted visual aesthetic, which is a pastiche of minimal science fiction and flamboyant glam rock. The feel - touch - of the leather and the encompassing gauntlet draw attention to the forearm, the physical size and extent of the feathers alters the way the arm is normally held in relationship to the body, and similarly alters and draws attention to the arms' movements through space.

From the experience of the gauntlets in the studio to the reception of the work at *Haptic InterFace* Exhibition in Hong Kong in late 2012, several key observations have suggested future directions for research into haptic interaction. Most notable is the way the direct haptic exchange of heart beat between two people was responded to by wearers, and then the way this haptic interaction changes the wearers experience of each other over longer periods of time. In the studio the artists wore the gauntlets in varying stages of completion and for longer periods of time than at *Haptic InterFace*. In this setting changes in pulse rate were observed by each person, and often in respect to the nature of interpersonal interactions or tone of conversations. For example, on several occasions wearers noted an increasing pulse rate during a more stressful conversation, and the observation of the increased heart rate altered the interactions in ways that would not have otherwise occurred. Over longer periods of use the wearers would walk around the studio and in and out of the XBee modules' communications range. The wireless range of the XBee modules was beyond direct line of sight, but did not cover the whole studio. As a result the wearers became aware of proximity, by way of haptic feedback of the other persons heartbeat, often well before seeing each other. Thus developing a tactile bond beyond physical touch or sight.

It is the extension of the intimate feeling of another persons heartbeat which has been the focus of most interesting comments from people wearing the work. During the presentation of the work at *Haptic InterFace* many people wearing the gauntlets were uncomfortable about feeling another persons pulse in such an intimate way - especially when the over person was a stranger. This was often the case many interactions involved the artist (Gavin) wearing one of the gauntlets and a visitor to the exhibition wearing the other. If the heartbeat was not felt in a haptic manner this response was be reduced or did not occur – i.e. before the gauntlet was put on the heartbeat could be seen visibly by way of a LED.

In discussion about the design at *Haptic InterFace* the most surprising comment was that people about to put on a gauntlet needed to be informed people of the function of the gauntlets, and that there needed to be permission gained before they put the gauntlets on. While there were didactic materials, many people put the gauntlet on prior to knowing its actual function. The apparent need to inform and gain permission for what was initially thought a rather unproblematic concept was surprising. This raises several possible explanations for what is it about the tangible feeling of stranger's pulse that is concerning, or off-putting. Perhaps the form of the gauntlet was a factor – as it wraps around and encloses the majority of the forearm. Or maybe the direct feeling of another heartbeat while seeing the person at a distance introduces an experiential tension, or disconnection – as it is an experience that one cannot have without technological mediation. Also, as an experience it is grounded in one of a few social interactions typically medical or intimate in nature.

4   Discussion and Conclusions

This paper grew out of a series of discussions between the authors as researchers interested in the field of haptic interaction wondering what our previous research might have to offer the field of haptics research. As such, it has not been our aim to present a comprehensive research program for haptic interaction – but rather to express what we see as our own possibilities for contributing to the field. We have presented this as three themes – drawn from our previous research – of *gestural, emergent* and *expressive*. In order to focus what we see as the core ideas of these three thematic areas we have developed a series of questions related to haptic interactions in each theme.

Table 1. Guiding questions for themes

Theme	Guiding quesionts
Gestural	• How do the interactions connect with a continuum of skilled gestural movements?
	• Do the interactions support the coordination of work or maintenance of shared understanding between interactants?
	• Do the interactions allow people to explore and make sense of the world?
Emergent	• How do haptic interactions evolve and emerge over time?
	• How are interactions layered within the interface?
	• How are interactions supported by the affordances of the interface?
Expressive	• What are the social and cultural significances of the interface?
	• How does the interface unsettle or reframe ordinary ways of experiencing?
	• How does the interface make use of aesthetic and expressive dimensions?

The case studies also show the importance of **passive haptic** systems and suggest that this may be a valuable path for further investigation. In that work has to date not paid as much attention to the design of the tangible materials and the way this influences experience interaction and communication, and is in itself culturally loaded. While there has been some work in this area of tangible interaction there is more work to be done in developing an understanding (useful interaction design knowledge) of the role haptics play in gestural, emergent and expressive applications.

Similarly there is work to be done to develop a useful way of describing the parameters or variable that influence haptic interface design and how these can be manipulated to achieve specific design outcomes. Of interest would be developing a framework which shows **how haptic qualities align with established qualities of interaction**, for example those presented by Löwgren and Stolterman [33]. Such knowledge would allow interaction designers develop tangible interaction design concepts which bridge the digital material divide.

References

1. Schön, D.A.: The Reflective Practitioner: How Professionals Think in Action. Basic Books, New York (1983)
2. Ishii, H., Ullmer, B.: Tangible bits: towards seamless interfaces between people, bits and atoms. In: SIGCHI Conference on Human Factors and Computing Systems, Atlanta, Georgia, United States, pp. 234–241 (1997)
3. Oxford English Dictionary, "'haptic, adj. (and n.)'",
   http://www.oed.com/view/Entry/84082
4. McLuhan, M.: Understanding media: The extensions of man. McGraw-Hill, NY (1964)
5. McLuhan, M., Fiore, Q.: The medium is the massage. Random House, New York (1967)
6. Deleuze, G., Guattari, P.F.: A Thousand Plateaus: Capitalism and Schizophrenia. University of Minnesota Press (1987)
7. Marks, L.U.: The Skin of the Film: Experimental Cinema and Intercultural Experience. University of Rochester. Department of Art and Art History (1996)
8. Marks, L.U.: Haptic Visuality: Touching with the Eyes. Framework, The Finnish Art Review (2), 79–82 (2004)
9. Manovich, L.: The Language of New Media. MIT Press (2001)

10. Boothroyd, D.: Touch, Time and Technics Levinas and the Ethics of Haptic Communications. Theory Culture Society 26(2-3), 330–345 (2009)

11. Hansen, M.B.N.: New Philosophy for New Media. MIT Press (2004)

12. Gasquet, J., Cézanne, P.: Joachim Gasquet's Cézanne: A Memoir with Conversations. Thames & Hudson (1991)

13. Smith, D.: Deleuze on Bacon: Three Conceptual Trajectories in the Logic of Sensation. In: Francis Bacon: The Logic of Sensation. University of Minnesota Press (2003)

14. Dourish, P.: Where the Action is: The Foundations of Embodied Interaction. MIT Press, Cambridge (2001)

15. Juul, J.: The Open and the Closed: Games of emergence and games of progression. In: Computer Game and Digital Cultures Conf. Proc., Tampere, Finland, pp. 323–329 (2002)

16. Fishwick, P.A.: Aesthetic Computing. In: Soegaard, M., Dam, R.F. (eds.) The Encyclopedia of Human-Computer Interaction, 2nd edn. The Interaction Design Foundation, Aarhus (2013)

17. Löwgren, J.: Pliability as an Experiential Quality: Exploring the Aesthetics of Interaction Design. Artifact 1(2), 85–95 (2007)

18. Shusterman, R.: Somaesthetics Thinking Through the Body and Designing for Interactive Experience. In: Soegaard, M., Dam, R.F. (eds.) The Encyclopedia of Human-Computer Interaction, 2nd edn. The Interaction Design Foundation, Aarhus (2013)

19. Donovan, J.: Framing Movements for Gesture Interface Design. PhD Dissertation, The University of Queensland, Queensland (2011)

20. Donovan, J., Brereton, M.: Movements in Gesture Interfaces. In: Proc. of the Workshop: Approaches to Movement-Based Interaction, Aarhus, Denmark, pp. 6–10 (2005)

21. Roth, W.-M., Lawless, D.V.: How does the body get into the mind? Human Studies 25, 333–358 (2002)

22. Goldin-Meadow, S.: Hearing Gesture: How Our Hands Help Us Think. Belknap Press (2005)

23. Ingold, T.: Walking the plank: meditations on a process of skill. In: Dakers, J.R. (ed.) Defining Technological Literacy: Towards an Epistemological Framework, pp. 65–80. Palgrave Macmillan (2006)

24. Streeck, J.: A body and its gestures. Gesture 2(1), 19–45 (2002)

25. Goodwin, C.: Action and embodiment within situated human interaction. Journal of Pragmatics 32(10), 1489–1522 (2000)

26. Hindmarsh, J., Pilnick, A.: The Tacit Order of Teamwork: Collaboration and Embodied Conduct in Anesthesia. The Sociological Quarterly 43(2), 139–164 (2002)

27. Seevinck, J.: +-now. Powerhouse Museum, Sydney (2008)

28. Seevinck, J.: Emergence in Interactive Art. Ph.D., University of Technology, Sydney, Australia (2011)

29. Seevinck, J., Edmonds, E.: Emergence and the art system 'plus minus now'. Design Studies 29(6), 541–555 (2008)

30. Gibson, J.J.: The Theory of Affordances. In: Perceiving, Acting, and Knowing: Toward an Ecological Psychology, vol. ix, pp. 127–143. Lawrence Erlbaum, Oxford (1977)

31. Gibson, J.J.: The ecological approach to visual perception. Routledge (1986)

32. Seevinck, J., Edmonds, E.A., Candy, L.: Emergent participant interaction. In: Proceedings of the 24th Australian Computer-Human Interaction Conference, New York, NY, USA, pp. 540–549 (2012)

33. Löwgren, J., Stolterman, E.: Thoughtful Interaction Design: A Design Perspective on Information Technology. MIT Press (2004)

Sense of Presence in a VR-Based Study
on Behavioral Compliance with Warnings

Emília Duarte[1], Francisco Rebelo[2,4], Luís Teixeira[2,4],
Elisângela Vilar[2,4], Júlia Teles[3,4], and Paulo Noriega[2,4]

[1] Unidcom, IADE – Creative University. Av. D. Carlos I, 4, 1200-649 Lisbon, Portugal
emilia.duarte@iade.pt
[2] Ergonomics Laboratory, Faculdade de Motricidade Humana, Universidade Técnica de Lisboa
{frebelo,lteixeira,elivilar,pnoriega}@fmh.utl.pt
[3] Mathematics Unit, Faculdade de Motricidade Humana, Universidade Técnica de Lisboa
jteles@fmh.utl.pt
[4] CIPER – Interdisciplinary Center for the Study of Human Performance, Universidade Técnica
de Lisboa, Estrada da Costa, 1499-002 Cruz-Quebrada, Dafundo, Portugal

Abstract. Recent researches suggest that Virtual Reality (VR) is amongst the
best tools for examining behavioral compliance with warnings, therefore overcoming some ethical and methodological constrains that have been limiting this
type of research. Yet, such evaluation using VR requires both usable and engaging virtual environments (VEs). This study examines the sense of presence experienced by the participants after having been immersed in a VE designed for
evaluating the effect of sign type (static vs. dynamic) on compliance. The VR
simulation tested here allowed participants to perform a realistic work-related
task and an emergency egress, during which they were supposed to interact with
warnings and exit signs. A neutral condition (i.e., no/minimal signs) was used
as a control condition. Subjective and objective data were gathered from two
sources, respectively, i.e., a post-hoc questionnaire administered to the participants, and a video analysis of the participants' interaction behavior during the
VR simulation. Results reveal high levels of presence across the three experimental conditions.

Keywords: Virtual Reality, Presence, Behavioral Compliance, Warnings.

1 Introduction

Behavioral compliance with warnings generally requires that people take some sort of
action. Thus, evaluating compliance involves observing what people do, i.e., if individuals carry out the warning-directed behavior. Although behavior is considered one
of the most important measures of warning effectiveness, it is usually quite difficult to
conduct behavioral tests [1]. The reasons include, among others: ethical and safety
concerns (research participants cannot be intentionally exposed to real hazards), rarity
and unpredictability of the hazardous events, difficulty of creating scenarios that
mimic real-life situations which appear to be risky yet are safe, and the costs in terms

A. Marcus (Ed.): DUXU/HCII 2013, Part III, LNCS 8014, pp. 362–371, 2013.
© Springer-Verlag Berlin Heidelberg 2013

of time and money to conduct such type of research. However, nowadays, the traditional way of conducting research on compliance with warnings is changing thanks to recent advances in technology and computer graphics. Consequently, Virtual Reality (VR) has been suggested as a promising tool to overcome such limitations [2]. Yet, such evaluation using VR requires both usable and engaging Virtual Environments (VEs) which enable users to feel as if they are there (sense of presence). Presence can be defined either as the sense of being there, in a mediated environment (e.g., VE), even when one is physically present in another [3, 4] or as a "perceptual illusion of nonmediation" [5], that is, when the person fails to acknowledge the existence of the display medium. Also, VEs that prompt a high degree of presence are usually considered as more enjoyable by participants, which can result in more effective VEs [6].

In this context, in this paper we present the results from an experiment that aimed to investigate participants' sense of presence by examining their interaction behavior and subjective perceptions in a two-part VR simulation (i.e., work-related situation and emergency egress), with tasks involving navigation, visual search, activation/deactivation of devices (i.e., compliance with warnings) and escaping from a fire. We specifically compare the users' responses, for the same tasks, across three experimental conditions resulting from manipulations made to the warnings and signs (i.e., static printed vs. dynamic multimodal) and a no/minimal-sign control condition. This study, which was part of a larger study about behavioral compliance with warnings [7], is grounded on the idea that VEs are a promising option for research on compliance with warnings.

To determine the extent to which the users felt they were present in the VE, we examined two types of measures commonly used for evaluating presence [8]: behavioral measures and subjective measures. Behavioral measures refer to interaction, that is, actions or postural responses in reaction to the events in the VE, such as startled reactions in reaction to an explosion or attempts to use firefighting equipment to extinguish the subsequent fire. Interaction is acknowledged, by several authors [e.g., 9, 10, 11], as one of the key reasons of presence in VEs. The interaction is closely related to functionality, concept that is considered to be more important for the ecological validity of the VE than its appearance [12]. Subjective measures refer to factors thought to underline the sense of presence. According to Insko [8], these factors can be grouped into four categories: control, sensory, distraction and realism. Usually these reported perceptions are gathered through post-immersion questionnaires. There are several well-established questionnaires for measuring presence, which usually have participants rating their experience on several questions across a numerical scale; e.g., Witmer-Singer [3], Slater-Usoh-Steed [13], ITC-SOPI [14].

2   Method

2.1   Apparatus

The study was conducted using the ErgoVR system [15], created by the Ergonomics Unit of the Technical University of Lisbon (http://www.fmh.utl.pt/ergovr/). For this study, the ErgoVR was an immersive VR system. The participants could see the VE through a Sony® PLM-S700E HMD, with 800 × 600 pixels resolution, at 32 bits, a FOV of 30°H, 22.5°V and 38°D, and an egocentric viewpoint, as well as were able to interact with the VE using a joystick. Two magnetic motion trackers from Ascension-Tech®, model Flock of Birds, were used for monitoring head and left hand movements. Wireless Sony® stereo headphones, model MDR-RF800RK, allowed participants to hear the sounds present in the VE. Figure 1 depicts the experimental setup. For a more comprehensive description of the software and hardware used see Duarte et al. [16].

Fig. 1. Positioning of the participant and the apparatus

2.2   Participants

A total of 100 university students participated in the study. A group of 10 participants (10%) were "experimental deaths", i.e., they underwent the procedure as a whole, or only part of it, but were excluded from the final sample due to simulator sickness or data corruption. Therefore, the study's sample consisted of 90 individuals, 45 males and 45 females, aged 18 to 35 years old (mean age = 21.3, SD = 3.2 years). They had normal sight or corrective lenses, as well as no color vision deficiencies. Participants were randomly assigned to conditions. Each condition contained 30 participants, equally distributed by gender.

2.3   Virtual Environment and Scenario

A virtual company's facilities, with four main rooms (i.e., meeting room, laboratory, cafeteria and warehouse) and six T-shaped escape routes, was developed for a simulating an end-of-day safety inspection routine task (experimental scenario) that was suddenly disturbed by an explosion, followed by a fire. Screen shots of the VE are depicted in Figure 2. Both parts of the simulation (routine and emergency) required participants to carry out safety related actions (i.e., press buttons to activate/deactivate safety-related devices and select egress routes). Posted warnings and signs gave the safety-related information. In the no-warning/sign condition, text-only labels positioned below the buttons identified the safety devices. In Figure 3, the foreseen sequence of tasks that the participants were asked to fulfill is depicted and marked on the VE floor plan. For a more comprehensive description of the VE used see Duarte et al. [16].

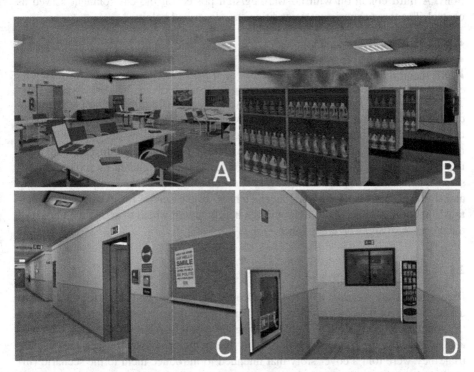

Fig. 2. Screen shots of the VE (A – Inside the Laboratory; B – Inside the Warehouse with fire and smoke after the explosion; C – Outside the Cafeteria showing the siren warning (ST) and button; D – At one of the T-shaped intersections showing the exit sign on top of the window).

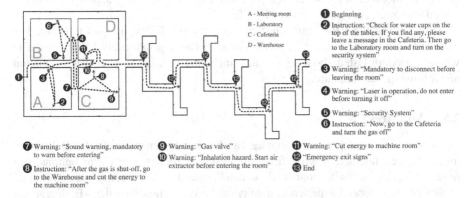

Fig. 3. Floor plan of the VE, showing the participants' foreseen sequence and the location of the instructions, warnings and signs

2.4   Design

This study used a between-subjects design. One experimental factor was manipulated: warning/sign type (i.e., static and dynamic), resulting into two experimental conditions. A third condition with no warning/sign posted on the environment served as control. The three experimental conditions are described below.

- ST (static warnings/signs);
- DY (dynamic warnings/signs);
- NE (neutral, no/minimal-sign).

The warnings and signs differ on modality and state according to the experimental condition. Regarding modality, the static warnings/signs were only visual, whereas the dynamic warnings/signs were multimodal (visual plus auditory), backlit, augmented with five flashing lights and supplemented by a tone. Regarding state, dynamic warning/signs had two states, activated or deactivated, triggered by proximity sensors (invisible triggers). For the control condition (NE) the VE had no posted warning and signs (except for the buttons' labels, which were essential for identifying the buttons' functions). This condition provides a baseline with which to assess the impact of the presence of signs on compliance.

2.5   Procedure

Participants were welcomed by the researcher and, after briefed about the study, were asked to sign an informed consent form. They were also advised that they could stop the simulation at any time without suffering any consequences or prejudice. The procedure started with a practice period. After the participants had finished the practice trial, they were told a cover story that intended to introduce them to the scenario (including the task). Participants were unaware of the real objective of the research. The task was to explore each room, according to the given instructions, and look for safety-related devices that should have been connected or disconnected during the night. At a given moment in the simulation (i.e., when they entered the warehouse) an unexpected explosion occurred, followed by a fire.

At the end of the VR simulation, they were given a follow-up questionnaire. The experimental session, in the VE, was intended to last approximately 15 minutes. The whole procedure lasted about 45 minutes, including training session, VR simulation and follow-up questionnaire.

2.6   Measures

For this study, the dependent variables can be grouped in two sets: (a) Behavioral measures, i.e., interaction with: fire extinguisher cylinders, fire alarm buttons, fire hose reels, electric switchboards, door handles; and (b) Subjective measures, i.e., quality of the sensorial experience, quality of the interaction with the VE, distraction factors, realism level, and notion of time.

The researcher collected data regarding participants' behavior through a free video analysis, while a multipart questionnaire, with 7 point Likert-type items, was used to measure participants' perceptions. Some items in the questionnaire were adapted from the Witmer and Singer Presence Questionnaire [3], and others were created in this study. All the items were communicated in Portuguese. English translations are given in this paper (see Table 1).

Table 1. Presence questionnaire items

Item	Score
1. How would you classify the overall level of sensory stimulation experienced during the simulation (e.g., involvement of your senses in the virtual experience)?	QSE
2. To what extent did the visual stimuli make you feel "inside" the VE?	QSE
3. To what extent did the auditory stimuli make you feel "inside" the VE?	QSE
4. To what extent could you identify the sounds present in the VE?	QSE
5. To what extent could you locate the sounds in the VE?	QSE
6. To what extent could you visually explore the VE?	QSE
7. To what degree was it easy to dislocate through the VE, by using the joystick (e.g., how easy was it for you to get to a certain point in the VE)?	QI
8. To what degree could you control your displacement by using the joystick (e.g., how accurately could you position/stop yourself at the desired place)?	QI
9. How quickly did you manage to adapt to the displacement, by using the joystick?	QI
10. At the end of the simulation, how do you classify your displacement performance in the VE, by using the joystick?	QI
11. To what degree was the looking behavior, offered by the system, natural (e.g., when you wanted to see something, in the VE, you moved your head in that direction)?	QI
12. To what degree could you control the looking behavior (e.g., the capacity to direct your head, with precision, to a certain direction)?	QI
13. To what degree was the execution of the virtual hand movements natural (e.g., when you wanted to touch the buttons, in the VE, did you move your hand in that direction)?	QI
14. To what degree did you have control over the movements of the virtual hand (e.g., the ability to operate, accurately, the buttons in the VE)?	QI
15. To what extent were you conscious of the HMD's presence during simulation?	DF
16. To what extent did the form of navigation (joystick) cause distraction in the performance of the required tasks?	DF
17. To what extent did the quality of the image displayed of the VE affect the performance of the required tasks?	DF
18. To what extent, during the simulation, were you aware of what was happening around you, in the real world (e.g., be aware of sounds from the real world)?	DF
19. To what degree is the simulation, you have just experienced, real?	RL
20. To what extent do you consider your experience in the VE to be different from your experience in the real world?	RL
21. Were you involved in the simulation to the extent that you lost track of time?	NT

Note: QSE = Quality of Sensorial Experience; QI = Quality of Interaction; DF = Distraction Factors; RL = Realism Level; NT = Notion of time; ENJ = Enjoyment.

3   Results

3.1   Behavioral Measures

Descriptive statistics for the behavioral measures across experimental conditions, as well as grouped altogether, are depicted in Table 2.

Table 2. Descriptive statistics (percentage and frequency of interactions) for behavioral measures across the three experimental conditions (30 in each condition) and total ($N = 90$)

| Interaction with: | Experimental conditions | | | |
	ST	DY	NE	Total
Fire extinguisher cylinders	57% (17)	43% (13)	53% (16)	51% (46)
Fire alarm buttons	67% (20)	57% (17)	73% (22)	66% (59)
Door handles	63% (19)	23% (7)	93% (28)	60% (54)
Fire hose reels	3% (1)	7% (2)	17% (5)	9 % (8)
Electric switchboards	3% (1)	3% (1)	0% (0)	2% (2)

To ascertain whether there were significant differences in interaction behaviors between the three experimental conditions, Pearson chi-square tests for homogeneity were conducted. No significant differences between the three experimental conditions were found on the participants' interaction behavior with fire extinguisher cylinders ($\chi^2(2, N = 90) = 1.156, p = .646$), fire alarm buttons ($\chi^2(2, N = 90) = 1.870, p = .433$), fire hose reels ($\chi^2(2, N = 90) = 3.567, p = .263$), and electric switchboards ($\chi^2(2, N = 90) = 1.023, p = 1.000$). Besides such differences, as demonstrated in Table 2, very few participants tried to interact with fire hose reels and electric switchboards, unlike the fire extinguisher cylinders and fire alarm buttons. Significant differences were found only on the participants' interaction behavior with door handles ($\chi^2(2, N = 90) = 30.833, p < .001$); $\phi_C = .585$, high effect). In what concerns the interaction with door handles, the NE condition exhibit higher percentages, and the DY condition present lower percentages of interactions, when compared with the ST condition.

3.2   Subjective Measures

The questions posed to the participants were thought to assess their perceptions regarding the major factors that contribute to the sense of presence. Descriptive statistics for the subjective measures, by each group of questions, across experimental conditions and in total are depicted in Table 3.

Table 3. Descriptive statistics, median (Mdn) and interquartile range (IQR), for the subjective measures of presence and enjoyment, across the three experimental conditions and altogether.

	Experimental conditions			Total
	ST	DY	NE	
QSE	5.08 (1.17)	5.50 (0.92)	5.50 (0.88)	5.33 (1.00)
QI	4.56 (1.09)	4.88 (0.91)	5.13 (1.31)	4.88 (1.25)
DF*	2.63 (1.63)	3.00 (1.13)	2.75 (2.00)	2.75 (1.75)
RL	3.88 (1.56)	3.50 (1.75)	3.88 (2.06)	3.75 (1.75)
NT	4.00 (3.00)	5.00 (2.50)	4.50 (2.25)	4.00 (3.00)

* Lower values are better

Overall, as indicated by the total values in Table 3, the median values of presence in the VE ranged from 3.75 to 5.33, according to a 7-point Likert scale with 7 indicating the highest level of presence.

To ascertain whether there were significant differences, among the three experimental conditions, in the participants' perceptions, Kruskal-Wallis tests were conducted. Results revealed statistically significant differences among the experimental conditions only for the participants' perceptions about the sensorial experience ($\chi^2_{KW}(2, N = 90) = 6.60$, $p = .037$). Nonparametric post-hoc multiple comparisons (Fisher's LSD method performed on ranks) showed that there were only marginally significant differences between ST and DY ($p = .055$), and ST and NE ($p = .073$). The boxplots for the quality of the sensorial experience by experimental condition, presented in Figure 4, illustrate these differences.

No statistically significant differences were found regarding the quality of the interaction ($\chi^2_{KW}(2, N = 90) = 3.86$, $p = .145$), distraction factors ($\chi^2_{KW}(2, N = 90) = .814$, $p = .666$), realism level ($\chi^2_{KW}(2, N = 90) = 1.55$, $p = .460$) and notion of time ($\chi^2_{KW}(2, N = 90) = .76$, $p = .683$).

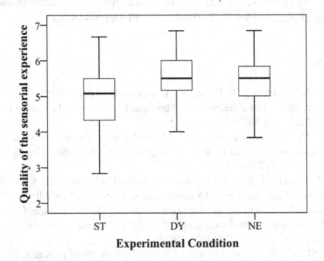

Fig. 4. Boxplots for Quality of the sensorial experience by experimental condition

4　Conclusions

The main contribution of this paper is to evaluate participants' sense of presence in a VE conceived for research on compliance with warnings. We have assessed presence by measuring both subjective and behavioral measures of presence. High levels of presence were considered important for our research on compliance with warnings, due to their potential influence on the study's ecological validity. Furthermore, consistency on the values of presence across the three experimental conditions was critical for the study because of its possible influence on the participants' behavior.

Overall, our data indicates that participants experienced a medium-high sense of presence across all the experimental conditions, as supported by both subjective and behavioral measures. In what concerns subjective measures, significant differences between the three experimental conditions were found only for the quality of the sensorial experience. To some extent this is an expected finding, since the VEs strongly differed visually, according to the manipulations made to the displayed warnings and signs.

We conclude that this VE was able to produce relatively high levels of presence that were consistent across the experimental conditions. Thus, it can be stated that VR did in fact allow the reproduction of a work-related task, and an emergency egress, while ensuring an engaging experience. Therefore, we conclude that there are positive indications about the use of VEs for research on behavioral compliance with warnings.

A second stage of this validation procedure is going on and involves studying participants' perceptions collected after exposed to other experimental conditions, as well as the examination of other variables such as previous experience with computer systems, gender, and degree of enjoyment.

Acknowledgements. A PhD scholarship from Portuguese Science Foundation (FCT) supported this study (SFRH/BD/21662/2005), which was developed in the scope of a Research Project financed by FCT (PTDC/PSI- PCO/100148/2008).

References

1. Kalsher, M.J., Williams, K.J.: Behavioral Compliance: Theory, Methodology, and Results. In: Wogalter, M.S. (ed.) Handbook of Warnings, pp. 313–332. Lawrence Erlbaum Associates, Inc., Mahwah (2006)
2. Duarte, E., Rebelo, F., Wogalter, M.S.: Virtual reality and its potential for evaluating warning compliance. Human Factors and Ergonomics in Manufacturing & Service Industries 20(6), 526–537 (2010)
3. Witmer, B., Singer, M.: Measuring presence in virtual environments: A presence questionnaire. Presence: Teleoperators and Virtual Environments 7(3), 225–240 (1998)
4. Ijsselsteijn, W.A., de Ridder, H., Freeman, J., Avons, S.E.: Presence: Concept, determinants and measurement. In: Proceedings of the SPIE, Human Vision and Electronic Imaging V, San Jose, USA, pp. 3959–3976 (2000)
5. Lombard, M., Ditton, T.: At the heart of It all: The concept of presence. Journal of Computer-Mediated Communication 3(2) (1997)

6. Sadowski, W.J., Stanney, K.M.: Presence in Virtual Environments. In: Stanney, K.M. (ed.) Handbook of Virtual Environments. Design, Implementation, and Implications, pp. 791–806. Lawrence Erlbaum Associates (2002)
7. Duarte, E., Rebelo, F., Teles, J., Wogalter, M.S.: Behavioral compliance in virtual reality: Effects of warning type. In: Kaber, D.B., Boy, G. (eds.) Advances in Cognitive Ergonomics. Advances in Human Factors and Ergonomics Series, pp. 812–821. CRC Press, Boca Raton (2010)
8. Insko, B.F.: Measuring presence: Subjective, behavioral and physiological methods. In: Riva, G., Davide, F., Ijsselsteign, W.A. (eds.) Being There: Concepts, Effects and Measurements of User Presence in Synthetic Environments, pp. 109–120. IOS Press, Amsterdam (2003)
9. Draper, J.V., Kaber, D.B., Usher, J.M.: Telepresence. Human Factors 40(3), 354–375 (1998)
10. Steuer, J.: Defining Virtual Reality: Dimensions Determining Telepresence. Journal of Communication 42(2), 73–93 (1992)
11. Burdea, G., Coiffet, P.: Virtual reality technology, 2nd edn. John Wiley & Sons, Inc., Hoboken (2003)
12. Flach, J.M., Holden, J.G.: The Reality of Experience: Gibson's Way. Presence: Teleoperators & Virtual Environments 7(1), 90–95 (1998)
13. Usoh, M., Catena, E., Arman, S., Slater, M.: Using presence questionnaires in reality. Presence: Teleoperators and Virtual Environments Archive 9(5), 497–503 (2000)
14. Lessiter, J., Freeman, J., Keogh, E., Davidoff, J.: A cross-media presence questionnaire: The ITC-sense of presence inventory. Presence: Teleoperators and Virtual Environments 10(3), 282–297 (2001)
15. Teixeira, L., Rebelo, F., Filgueiras, E.: Human interaction data acquisition software for virtual reality: A user-centered design approach. In: Kaber, D.B., Boy, G. (eds.) Advances in Cognitive Ergonomics, pp. 793–801. CRC Press, Boca Raton (2010)
16. Duarte, E., Rebelo, F.S., Teles, J., Wogalter, M.S.: Behavioral compliance for dynamic versus static signs in an immersive virtual environment. Applied Ergonomics (forthcoming)

Interactive Shopping Experience through Immersive Store Environments

Kunal Mankodiya, Rolando Martins, Jonathan Francis,
Elmer Garduno, Rajeev Gandhi, and Priya Narasimhan

Department of Electrical & Computer Engineering,
Carnegie Mellon University, 5000 Forbes Ave, Pittsburgh, PA, USA
{kunalm,rolandomartins,jmfrancis}@cmu.edu,
elmerg@andrew.cmu.edu, rgandhi@ece.cmu.edu, priya@cs.cmu.edu

Abstract. In the era of high competition with E-commerce and online shops, brick-and-mortar retail industry seeks new opportunities to enhance shopping experience through engaging technologies. Even though retailers are applying their omnichannel strategies to attract more shoppers through technology-driven solutions including websites, mobile apps, and so forth, we find that these technologies are somewhat basic and do not represent the "disruptive" innovations. Along with these current technologies, retailers should leverage their store physical real estate, and transform it into immersive store environments (ISEs) that allow shoppers to navigate in 3D store aisles through rich media interface ported onto networked devices. Therefore, we propose our own study of what ISE use-cases are most desirable by customers and retailers in such contexts; we describe the implementation of our cloud-based interactive shopping interface for ISE, before discussing the promising results of its deployment in a "real-world" store.

Keywords: AndyVision, retail technology, human-computer interaction, immersive shopping.

1 Introduction

Today's retail industry is experiencing a dramatic shift, as the market is facing fierce competition with online shops. Retailers are grappling with finding new ways to meet high expectations of modern connected shoppers, and to enhance their shopping experience. According to a recent comprehensive survey on US retailers in 2012 [1], 40% of them believe that the 'inability to find the desired product' is the primary contribution to their shoppers' dissatisfaction in their stores, and therefore, 75% of these retailers agree to develop a more engaging shopping experience that will be essential to their business over the next 5 years. Shoppers now crave more engaging, convenient, efficient and informative shopping experience that provides benefits beyond online shopping.

In response to the rise of the online shops, brick-and-mortar retailers are fighting back aggressively with their omnichannel strategies, in which they attract

A. Marcus (Ed.): DUXU/HCII 2013, Part III, LNCS 8014, pp. 372–382, 2013.

consumers by keeping them informed about discounts, offers, deals, etc. through mobile phones and websites [2]. However, retailers have yet to turn their store real estate into a tool of digital visual merchandizing and to offer shoppers immersive experience of store environments. Indeed, the idea of immersive experience for exploration or information gathering is not unknown to consumers today; in fact, this has become part of their daily lives. Such immersive environments as city-streets [3], international museums [4], deep-ocean exploration [5], and even Mars [6] are among those that are freely available. Similarly, immersive store environments (ISEs) would allow shoppers to virtually navigate the store aisles, to browse products, and to engage with ad-hoc promotional media–directly from their smartphones, tablets, or the in-store digital signage devices. ISEs will become crucial for retailers omnichannel strategies, allowing them to service their customers with cutting edge interactive tools. Retailers may generate augmented multimedia such as product pricing, discounts and offers, related-product recommendations, and user feedback–all dynamically–expanding their upsell strategies in the process.

In this research initiative, we present a design, implementation, and deployment of the cloud-based shopping interface framework for immersive store environment that can be ported to personal computing devices as well as larger networked displays, such as retail kiosks and television (see Fig. 1). This ISE is a part of the multi-faceted research project, 'AndyVision–the Future of Retail' and has been piloted at the Carnegie Mellon University (CMU) Store in Pittsburgh, PA, USA [7]. We have also conducted a user interface study, wherein real shoppers have interacted with our ISE on an in-store digital signage, equipped with touchscreen capabilities. The target use-case for the ISE implementation is to promote store's bestselling merchandises (bestsellers), to help shoppers locate the items, and to present multi-media marketing through this fully-immersive rich media interface.

Fig. 1. Examples of the devices ported with our immersive store environment

2   Related Work

Immersive environments virtually surround individuals such that they psychologically perceive themselves to be enveloped by an environment providing continuous visual stimuli, and feel their presence at the remote environment [8]. Experiencing immersion into a different world has been around in the form of storytelling, paintings, sculptures, carvings, and so forth for ages. Moviemap, the term defined as virtual travel through pre-recorded spaces, was first produced using a camera car and presented on an interactive touchscreen-based system at MIT in 1970s [9]. There have been several subsequent moviemap projects that demonstrated the potential of immersive environments in the field of media arts [10]. Today, the 3D visualization and exploration of real-world spaces on the computer screen is very much a product of panorama photography and its applications in the field of computing and human computer interactions. The process of generating immersive environments for real-world scenes involves collections of multi-point panoramas and their deformation into spherical, cubical cylindrical planes in order to fit the visualization model [11].

One such example, that facilitates interactions for immersive outdoor environments, is Googles "Street View" feature within the Google Maps framework [3]. Now, efforts are being made to bring the Street View technology to the indoor environments [12], via the Google Art Project [4] that used multi-point panoramas of indoor spaces and then presented them for navigation inside prominent international museums through the user's web-browser. Representation or visualization of the real-world immersive environments, when accompanied by 2D planar maps, eases the process of navigation by enhancing the spatial knowledge acquisition [13] [14].

Our AndyVision team has designed and implemented an immersive store environment that is particularly unique within the world of retail technology. In addition to immersive environment, we purposely used the map interface to establish correspondence between icons on the map and the objects on the real-world environments, and to assist shoppers to better orient themselves in the store with these reference points on the map. Our pilot deployment in the real physical store attempted to produce an interactive and immersive experience for shoppers and to furnish them with augmented information of the merchandises. We also aimed to capture shopper-signage interactions and provide the store staff with the analytics that can help them plan their visual merchandizing fitting to the changing seasons.

3 System Framework

With the increasing number of available computing platforms, namely through the massive adoption of mobile devices, it is important to have a portable and scalable solution that is able to run across these heterogeneous environments. As shown in Fig. 2, the user-end for this solution is based on a web application that uses JQuery, a heavy-duty general-purpose javascript framework, and Seadragon, a deep zoom viewing library that provides support for high-resolution panoramic photos. This web application can be configured to run on any internet-accessed personal computing device with a screen e.g., smartphones, laptops, retail digital signage kiosk.

3.1   Cloud-Computing Back-End

As its cloud-computing back-end, our approach leverages the Google Application Engine (GAE), a Platform-as-a-Service (PaaS) cloud-computing framework that offers hosting for web applications within a comprehensive development environment. We currently use the python web runtime environment–more specifically, Django and webapp2–and the DataStore and MemCached services.

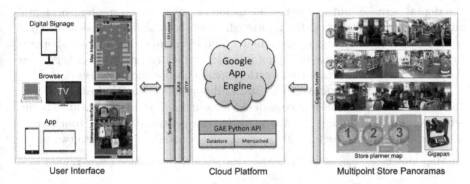

User Interface   Cloud Platform   Multipoint Store Panoramas

Fig. 2. A framework of the immersive and interactive shopping interface

In order to meet our design goals, we have defined the following interface in our back-end:

LoadItems loads the information of all items to be used in the immersive application.
SendFeedback operation used to send the feedback about the application.
GetBestsellers retrieves the list of bestsellers items.
LogClick operation used to log the click on a particular item.
Analytics used for loading the analytics UI for retailers.
LoadClicks retrieves the list of logged clicks, which is used by the analytics to create the statistical graphs.

3.2   Immersive Store Environment Construction

Gigapan, a robotic camera mount, was used to capture panoramas from various vantage points within the CMU store and to construct the ISE. In our current deployment, we used n=2 distinct panoramas, where n is scalable and can be increased to meet the desired specification goals. Taking the panoramas was a manual process, in which our team visited the store with a camera kit, and identified the best spots in the store for the panorama captures, based on clearance from retail structures in the field of view. After being taken, the high-resolution images were uploaded to the Gigapan server and later accessed by our GAE back-end. Our web application interface provided the functionalities of browsing and navigating the store by utilizing these multi-point panoramas in the form of a 3D model.

4 Interface Design

Interactive displays are becoming more common in the retail sector, and provide real-time information with personalized service to the shoppers on their fingertips. The CMU store was specifically interested in promoting their bestsellers on the digital signage, but did not want to follow conventional method of digital advertisement e.g., merchandise multimedia slideshow, scrolling flash screen and so forth. Instead, they wanted us to find a unique way of servicing their shoppers by designing an interactive shopping interface, which can not only engage their shoppers, but also facilitate them with merchandise location services.

A digital signage–Touch&GO Digital Lollipop 46P (Micro Industries, USA), 46" touchscreen monitor–was considered for our interface deployment. The interface design was required to adapt to portrait orientation of the touchscreen with the resolution of 1080x1920. The interface is mainly divided into two parts:

(i) **Map interface**, a 2D planar map view that provides merchandise coarse-grained locations.

(ii) **Immersive interface** provides merchandise fine-grain locations in 3D store environment.

4.1 Bestselling Merchandise Selection

Our team collaborated with the store staff to identify their bestsellers by statistically evaluating their POS data over the prior 5-month period; we finalized twelve bestsellers that fall into three categories (see Table 1): (i) male gender-specific items, (ii) female gender-specific items, and (iii) unique unisex gifts. Apart from POS data, other selection criteria include merchandise visibility in the store display, stocks in their backroom, and the latest trends among the student shoppers. The bestsellers were coded with their unique identification numbers in our framework database for data collection and analysis.

Table 1. The selected bestsellers and their category distributions

Categories	Qty	Merchandise (database serial no.)
Men	4	T-shirt(1), long sleeve t-shirt(2), hoodie(3), Sweat pant(4)
Women	4	Polo t-shirt(5), t-shirt(6), hoodie(7), pant(8)
Gifts	4	Hat(9), mug(10), t-shirt(11), sweat shirt(12)

4.2 Panorama Overlays

We collected the necessary info and related multimedia for the bestsellers from the store, such as: merchandise name, price, features, and high-resolution merchandise pictures. They also provided us the locations of these bestsellers on a

Fig. 3. Locations of the bestsellers in the store panoramas

2D store planar map; hence, we identified them in the previously-collected store panoramas. As shown in Fig. 3, the bestsellers were tagged with '+' icons, visible in two of the store panoramas. Product description overlay windows, containing merchandise specific information and images, were produced and used as augmented information for the bestsellers.

4.3 Map Interface

As shown in Fig. 4, the 2-dimension store planar map interface displays the locations of the bestsellers with merchandise icons and also allows shoppers to narrow down their search by choosing one of the category button icons in the side menu bar. When a category button is engaged, their corresponding products icons are highlighted in the map-view. As it is conventional of layout map views, whether digital or not, our interface also shows the "you-are-here" icon, which helps users to orient themselves within the store relative to the signage device. We placed a feedback form to capture the shoppers response to this interactive technology. The feedback form consisted of four questions as well as a QR code for promoting our research on the social networking web.

4.4 Immersive Interface

So far, the shoppers were provided the coarse-grain locations of the bestsellers on the planar map. The immersive interface shown in Fig. 5, as its name indicates, lets the shoppers immerse them into the real 3D environment and see the fine-grain locations of the bestsellers. The immersive interface appears on the screen, when a shopper engages with any bestseller icons on the map interface. Shoppers can navigate within this environment by swiping their fingers left/right and up/down. For novice shoppers, we have superimposed arrow icons for easing the navigation process. The panel icons offer zoom-in and zoom-out functionality, while also allowing shoppers to quickly return to the map interface at any time. '+' icons, also superimposed on top of the 3D plane on the item it indicates, unveils the augmented information of the bestsellers when tapped. Touching

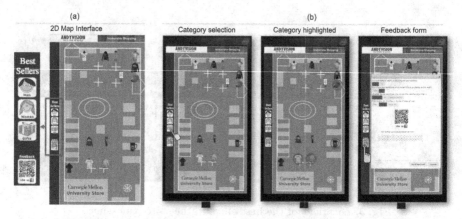

Fig. 4. (a) 2D map Interface showing categories of the bestsellers, and (b) Interface interaction steps on the map interface

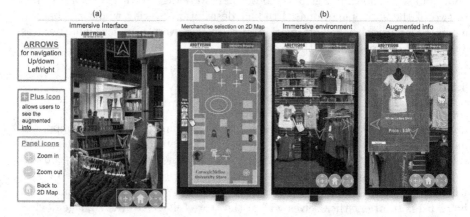

Fig. 5. (a) Immersive interface with descriptions of each element, and (b) Interface interaction steps from map interface to the augmented information of the bestseller on the immersive interface.

open areas within the product description overlays themselves will dismiss them, allowing for further store exploration.

5   Signage Deployment and In-Store Pilot

The digital signage displaying our shopping interface was deployed in the CMU store, targeting the university's commencement season in May 2012. During these periods, the store experiences dramatically increased sales and customer interaction from students and their families, relative to comparatively less active, non-event periods. The store staff identified a physical location for the signage inside the store, where the interface could receive the most visibility to the shopping crowd.

At this time, the immersive interface shown in Fig. 6 was displayed on the signage and contained a 2D map as an overlay with the functionality of viewing the store from three different 3D in-store vantage points. To promote this research, the store also generated a special discount on particular items, which could be claimed by scanning the QR barcodes on the corresponding items augmented product description overlays. The merchandises for promotion were randomly picked by the store. Although, during these initial trials, we did not collect any interaction data, lessons learned from this experience helped us to generate a more intuitive shopping interface for the seasons to come. The approach of subsequent high-volume events–Thanksgiving, students/faculty/staff special discount days, Christmas vacation, and the start of the 2013 semester–motivated us to target our interface for collecting shopper-signage interaction data.

Fig. 6. Images of the interactive signage deployed at the Carnegie Mellon University store and the previous version of the shopping interface

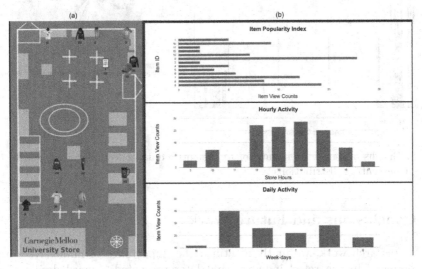

Fig. 7. AndyVision retailer's interface showing the signage activity analytics: a) activity flags corresponding to the items on the map and b) graphs showing shopper-signage overall activity

6   Data Collection of Shopper-Signage Interactions

From the day one of our deployment in the store, we logged each and every interaction of the shoppers on the signage. Our log file included the item-id and the time and date of item view counts. Via our cloud backend scripts, we continually accessed the log file in order to dynamically construct the interface for retail operations (see Fig. 7) that displayed the shoppers' activity in the form of retail-oriented analytics, such as an item's popularity score, based on overall activity, and an item's view-counts per hour and day. The part of interface also showed the overall activity on the stores 2D map along side of the merchandise.

As shown in Fig. 8, there was healthy shopper-signage interaction at the end of the fall 2012 semester. A sudden burst of activity during this period was anticipated, since the students, who were returning to their homes for Winter Break, rushed to the store to shop gifts for themselves or their relatives. Accordingly, we also observed a long inactive period for signage activity during Christmas and New Year break; signage activity resumed as the spring semester 2013 began. Percentage distribution of the activity across the bestsellers contained a good insight of merchandise popularity. The bestsellers falling within the 'Men' category received the highest item view counts.

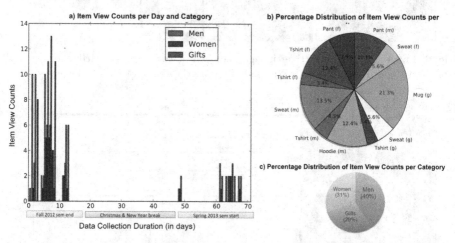

Fig. 8. Graphs of item view counts for a) the entire data collection period, and b) & c) their percentage distributions

7   Conclusions and Future Work

In this research work, we firstly identified the importance of immersive store environments in the retail industry, and later presented a novel design of a cloud-based interactive shopping interface embedded with our ISE implementation. Our shopping interface, which was piloted through interactive signage at the CMU store, allowed the shoppers to locate the stores best-selling items on the signage without any store-staff intervention. Moreover, the interface also facilitated an immersive shopping experience via 3D environment navigation. The AndyVision ISE interface not only enabled shoppers to virtually walk through the store, but also allowed them to visualize the augmented product description overlays featuring additional merchandise information. Our pilot at the CMU store that captured shopper-signage interaction activity revealed that ISE is an attractive element to shoppers and offers a new channel of visual merchandizing for the retailers.

Our ISE is currently generated manually through multi-point panorama capture, when the store changes its layout. In the future, AndyVision will provide a robot-centric solution to automate the process of ISE construction and store layout mapping [7]. Our on-going effort in this research work is to make our ISE accessible via web browsers and mobile devices, and to expand the coverage area.

Acknowledgements. This work is partially supported by Intel Corporation under the Intel Science and Technology Center - Embedded Computing (ISTC-EC). We are very thankful to Ryan Wolfe, Angela Tumolo Neira, and the Carnegie Mellon University Store staff for their collaboration and efforts in making this research work successful.

References

1. Whitepaper, Motorola Solutions Survey: Retailers Need to "Tech-Up" (June 2012)
2. Whitepaper, Motorola Solutions: How Brick-and-Mortar Retailers Can Win The Omnichannel Battle (2012)
3. The Google Street View, http://maps.google.com/intl/en/help/maps/streetview (accessed on February 22, 2013)
4. Google Art Project, http://www.googleartproject.com (accessed on February 22, 2013)
5. Virtual World: Deep Sea - National Geographic, http://animals.nationalgeographic.com/animals/crittercam-virtual-world-antarctica (accessed on February 22, 2013)
6. WorldWide Telescope, http://www.worldwidetelescope.org/Home.aspx (accessed on February 22, 2013)
7. Mankodiya, K., Gandhi, R., Narasimhan, P.: Challenges and Opportunities for Embedded Computing in Retail Environments. In: Martins, F., Lopes, L., Paulino, H. (eds.) S-CUBE 2012. LNICST, vol. 102, pp. 121–136. Springer, Heidelberg (2012)
8. Witmer, B.G., Singer, J.M.: Measuring presence in virtual environments: A presence questionnaire. Presence: Teleoperators and Virtual Environments 7, 225–240 (1998)
9. Mohl, R.: Cognitive Space in the Interactive Movie Map: An Investigation of Spatial Learning in Virtual Environments, PhD dissertation, Education and Media Technology, M.I.T. (1981)

10. Naimark, M.: A 3D Moviemap and a 3D Panorama. In: SPIE Proceedings, San Jose, vol. 3012 (1997)
11. Guarnaccia, M., Gambino, O., Pirrone, R., Ardizzone, E.: An Explorable Immersive Panorama. In: 2012 Sixth International Conference on Complex, Intelligent and Software Intensive Systems (CISIS), July 4-6, pp. 130–134 (2012)
12. Colbert, M., Bouguet, J., Beis, J., Childs, S., Filip, D., Vincent, L., Limy, J., Satkin, J.: Building Indoor Multi-Panorama Experiences at Scale. In: SIGGRAPH 2012, Los (2012)
13. Darken, R.P., Peterson, B.: Spatial Orientation, Wayfinding, and Representation. In: Stanney, K. (ed.) Handbook of Virtual Environment Technology (2001)
14. Zhang, X.: M2S maps: supporting real-world navigation with mobile VR. Virtual Real 11(2), 161–173 (2007)

Minimal Yet Integral – Designing a Gestural Interface

Martin Osen

Osen Design, Franz-Lehar-Straße 5,
4563 Micheldorf in Oberösterreich, Austria
martin@osen.at

Abstract. Minimalism and simplicity have become key success factors in the post-PC era. Touchscreens have superseded physical buttons as the dominant user interface of mobile devices. Some of the industry's most successful products tightly integrate hardware, software and services into one convenient solution. All this transformed the setting in which we are designing user experiences today. This paper describes the two-year development of a gestural user interface for a mobile app. Our design process can be broken down into five basic principles: Find a tangible metaphor, understand your hardware, care for your content, reduce it to the essence, and if you feel you can do better, iterate. Finally some yet unsolved issues are described that may impede the design of truly natural interfaces on a fundamental level.

Keywords: Design Philosophy, Minimalism, Mental Model Design, Metaphor Design, Gestural UI, Natural UI, Card-based UI, Smartphone, Tablet, Touchscreen, Casual Reading, Digital Publishing, Case Study.

1 Introduction: Beyond Flat Screens

A classic quote by Alan Kay suggests that people who are really serious about software should make their own hardware.[1] While that was certainly true in the early days of computing, surprisingly it seems even more relevant today. In my own experience as a designer, I frequently enjoyed projects the most where we could at least theoretically consider a holistic solution integrating software and hardware (e.g. IO Concept 2002 [1], Sony Spotlight Navigation 2004 [2], Sony Haptic Chameleon 2004 [3], Volkswagen Concept Study 2006). Recently, Alan Kay's quote has frequently been utilized in the context of big players pitching their vertical business models (e.g. Apple iPhone 2007, Amazon Kindle 2007, Microsoft Surface 2012).

As an interaction designer, the vast majority of my projects involves working on the software layer only. For obvious reasons, tinkering with the hardware is out of reach. It's simply not part of the job. Even in an ideal world it would not be: Time and money constraints aside it would probably not be desirable to reinvent smart phones over and over again every time an app developer is getting serious. I know plenty of interaction designers, software developers, startups and the like who are all really

---

[1] Alan Kay at a talk at Creative Think seminar, 20 July 1982.

A. Marcus (Ed.): DUXU/HCII 2013, Part III, LNCS 8014, pp. 383–392, 2013.
© Springer-Verlag Berlin Heidelberg 2013

serious about their software, and yet they usually have to design it for a given hardware, which is always limited and sometimes just plain bad.

So in that typically limited context, how can we still think out of the box, "beyond flat screens"? How can we create an integral result if we cannot control the whole experience?

First and foremost, we need to deeply understand the hardware we are designing for: Their limitations, but even more than that their particular qualities. This understanding is of course not limited to a technological point of view. Social, philosophical and artistic perspectives are just as important. In metaphysical terms, we have to understand not just the body of a technical object, but get a feeling of its soul. It's the same kind of deep understanding that leads a sculptor to an idea of the sculpture already extant inside a raw block of stone. [4] The creative process is then just to remove any excess material.

2   State of the Art: Direct User Interfaces

Touch based user interfaces of smartphones and tablets have considerably changed the public perception of a "computer". Even to the untrained eye it is obvious that simplification and minimalism are no longer side issues discussed in circles of design enthusiasts only. They have become a mainstream factor driving current innovation. Unlike only ten years ago, today simplicity is key to commercial success.

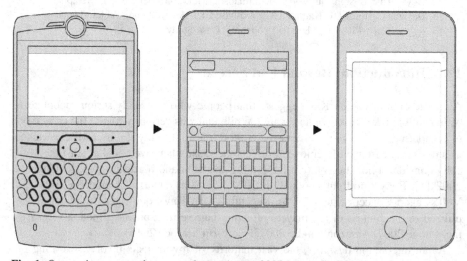

Fig. 1. On previous generation smartphones (e.g. a 2007 Motorola Q, left), casing, ornament and UI elements take up the greater part of the device's surface. In this example, only approx. 20% of it are left for actual presentation of content. The use of touchscreens (e.g. on an iPhone, center) can radically simplify the surface of a device and therefore free up space for content. However, depending on the amount of UI elements that are simulated on screen, the actual signal-to-noise ratio can be even worse. Direct, gestural interfaces (right) that depend less on visual chrome can – in some cases – reveal the true potential of current touch devices.

Touchscreens have replaced hardware buttons as the dominating user interface. In most cases though, the resulting clean and minimal look is only skin deep. The complexity of the user interface has simply moved to another layer: On screen we still interact with simulated buttons, knobs and switches. In terms of usability, a bad solution has arguably been replaced with one that's even worse.

One of the bigger challenges of the near future will be to replace those outdated, out of place paradigms by more natural, direct interaction with the content itself. The entire user experience has to deliver the simplicity that is promised by the minimalistic looks of current hardware.

Natural user interfaces are still in its infancy. Developing such interfaces today means taking part in a highly dynamic and evolutionary process. It should be clear that at the present state, failure and constant iteration are inevitable. The following chapter outlines selected problems that emerged during the two-year development of a gestural, direct user interface for a mobile application and discusses some of the short term and long term solutions we considered.

3   Case Study: CardSkid

CardSkid is a new digital-only publishing format that focuses on "casual reading", "casual learning" and "casual exploring". It enables publishers to quickly and efficiently build companion apps for their printed or digital books without any development effort. Content can be created, packaged and deployed using the newly developed standard CML (CardSkid Markup Language).

The end user gets a smartphone app that keeps the essence of a book in their pocket. Favorite quotes, lessons and key facts serve as teaser for a book that hasn't been explored yet. Once the book has been read, CardSkid keeps adding value by serving as an anchor to remember and further connect with the content.

A compelling user experience is crucial to the acceptance of such a publishing format.[2] The industry wide key topics of simplicity and minimalism lie at the very center of CardSkid's focus. It's all about distilling down to the essence. In essence, our design process can be described by five key principles:

3.1   Find a Tangible Metaphor

The metaphor of a deck of cards was the starting point for our design process. This was by far the single most important design decision. The card gave us something tangible, definite, rememberable. It transformed an abstract concept (a digital mobile publishing format for non-fiction literature) into something that could be easily grasped and discussed (a deck of cards in your pocket). From that moment on, every subsequent design decision followed a clear goal: The app should feel like a deck of cards in your hand. That's the soul of our product. Ideally, the user would not even be

---

[2] While this case study is mainly focusing on the user experience of the player app for iOS, this holds true for all steps of the CardSkid production chain.

aware of the interface or the hardware wrapped around our metaphor, and just be fully immersed in the content. [5]

While the card metaphor has been around since the early days of the GUI [6], we came to value it while fiddling about with real, physical cards. We learned that there is already a market for distributing analog content as cards. For some vertical markets like education, cards are a well-established form of distributing analog content, e.g. flashcards for learning foreign languages. There is ongoing research on how to bring such paradigms into the digital domain. [7]

Since we started development of CardSkid in September 2010, we kept noticing how several new or redesigned GUIs intended to simplify interaction by building on card metaphors: The product view in Amazon's mobile apps (2010), the card stack UI in HP's webOS (2011), or the Chomp-inspired redesign of Apple's App Store (2012), just to name a few. This reinforced our impression that we were on to something.

3.2   Understand Your Hardware

Together with the smartphone app we envisioned the prototype of a tablet app. The requirements for both user interfaces turned out to be completely different. The experience had to be true to the qualities of the respective form factor.

For creating the illusion of holding a real deck of cards, a touchscreen smartphone is the obvious choice, being roughly the same size and thickness. It also fits the bill of casual reading on the go: Take it out, shuffle through some cards, put it back.

On a tablet, due to its different ergonomics, it would have been impossible to recreate a similar feeling of holding a deck. While technically it was trivial to derive a tablet version by simply scaling up the UI to the bigger screen, it broke the whole metaphor, rendering the very foundation of the user experience meaningless. We came up with another paradigm instead: Whereas the smartphone should conceptually *be* a card (instead of *showing* one), the tablet is just that: A viewport to a threedimensional stage with cards floating in space. While the content *per se* always looks the same, the interaction paradigm adapts depending on its context.

Starting point of the tablet experience is again a deck of cards which is fanned out horizontally. A single card on the tablet corresponds in size approximately to a card on the smartphone. Different functionality (e.g. related to content acquisition, organization or annotation) is located in 3D space around the deck at the four cardinal directions. Rotating and tilting the viewport allows to zero in on a particular functional group while still keeping sight of the actual content. As for gestural control, various options have been considered. Basic on-screen swiping gestures to change the viewport appeared to be the most straight-forward solution. However, rotating and tilting the whole device might allow for an even more natural experience. Further user testing will examine whether the latter option also fares better in terms of usability.

3.3   Design Your Content First

It makes a huge difference if you deeply care about your content. In our case, we spent a great deal of the design process designing the look and feel of a card to get out of the content's way. We did this in part by deliberately defining what can not be done. For example, a card can not be scrolled. The boundaries of the screen limit the amount of content that can be shown. Design can be seen as a process of reducing options. What remains is the essence.

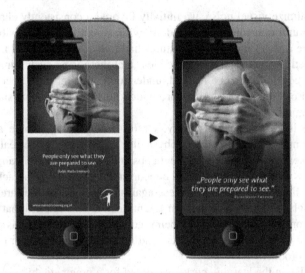

Fig. 2. Existing design, taken from printed cards (left) and minimalistic redesign optimized for on-screen and casual, mobile use cases (right)

What, in essence, defines a card? We determined three fundamental rules: A card has a defined size, capable of holding a limited amount of content, a card has a front and a back, and while self-contained, a card is in many cases part of a larger deck.

The main design challenge at this early stage was to digitally recreate as much as possible of an analog deck's user experience. For instance, how does it feel to shuffle cards? Which design parameters (e.g. shape, material, texture, physics, sound) are at hand to evoke that feeling? Most important, how can we ensure to keep the design honest, without reaching the point of adding visual noise and suffering from the negative effects of skeuomorphic design that are widely criticized? [8]

From day one of the design process, we explored our ideas on real content. Two authors allowed us to transform their printed cards into first digital prototypes.[3] Our starting point was a clean and minimalistic design which worked well for printed cards. However, for our purpose it still felt too heavy, cramped and distracting. In order to allow for a truly casual reading and learning experience, we favored an even

---

[3] Holzer, A.: "CoachingSet" and Ebertz, A.: "Re-Think!"

more minimalistic approach. What remained was pure visual information: Image, text, color. Using gradients and transparency, the design allows each element to take up maximum screen real estate while all elements can coexist in harmony. What is often referred to as "design" goes out of the way to an extent where the cards feel almost "undesigned".

3.4   The Content Is the Interface

In order to minimize visual noise, we initially favored a consistently chromeless user interface. A natural user interface should allow for direct interaction with the content itself. Therefore a set of multi-touch gestures had to be introduced and mapped to the required interaction outcomes. It became clear that there is no such thing as a natural gesture. Every gesture has to be learned, understood, remembered. Specification and standardization of "intuitive" gestures are widely unsolved problems standing in the way of truly natural user interfaces. [9]

Consistency is key to good usability. Unfortunately though, there are instances where any attempt to be consistent is physically impossible. In the realm of mobile computing, typically a number of different apps and services and, in many cases, even different devices and platforms are used concurrently. Even if we can achieve consistency within a single app, we are helpless against other entities that are inconsistent between themselves, be it incidentally or intentionally. This implies that we can only partially build on learned behavior by being consistent. At least at this current state, supporting the user in learning and understanding novel interaction paradigms is central to a usable product.

In order to flatten the learning curve, we opted for a pragmatic hybrid solution: We identified parts of the UI that benefit from novel gestural interaction, and other parts that gain efficiency by employing more established "standard" interaction.

Basic Navigation. Defining element on screen is always a card. A card displays key information on its front, and can be flipped over for additional content. Per default, cards of a deck are laid out horizontally and can be navigated through by performing horizontal swiping gestures. Groups of cards can be organized into stacks. Any card can be pushed up to reveal contextual actions located behind it.[4] Cards can generally be viewed zoomed in or zoomed out. It is of note that those views are non-modal, i.e. any interaction is available in either view. Either view serves a specific purpose: When zoomed in, no visual elements besides the card are visible. Nothing distracts from pure content ("content view"). When zoomed out, visual context like adjacent cards or icons representing core functionality comes into view, easing interaction especially for novice users ("navigation view").

---

[4] During development, parts of this particular interaction were replaced to be more consistent with standard iOS 6 behavior.

Fig. 3. Early 2012 prototype of CardSkid UI. The device in the center depicts a deck of cards zoomed out into an overview, providing additional visual cues for navigation. On the left screen, a card has been pushed up to reveal a list of contextual actions. On the right screen, a card is being flipped over to show additional content on its back.

Help. In a typical use case, we hardly have the opportunity to explain basic interaction techniques the way we did in the paragraph above. Still, if we rely on non-standardized interaction techniques and can not guarantee consistency with prior user experience, we have to educate the user in one way or another. The crucial question is when and how to provide instructions.

Basically, most current solutions can be subsumed under two strategies: Explain interaction before any issues can occur (often referred to as "tutorial") or provide selective support as needed after interaction came to a standstill (commonly referred to as "help"). In many cases, a combination of both strategies is used.

In a 2011 user study testing our prototype[5], the task of finding help was consistently challenging for users and therefore a suggested focus area for improvement going forward. We tried both aforementioned strategies, separate and combined, in total over a dozen different implementations. Our approaches included but were not limited to:

First, a tutorial explaining basic interaction at first start of the app. While a very common solution, the prominent position of the tutorial interfered with the user's urge to actually try the app and was often described as "pushy". In many cases, users skipped the tutorial entirely.

---

[5] In November and December 2011, a rapid iterative test of two versions of the CardSkid iPhone app was conducted in San Francisco. A total of nine users completed several exploratory tasks and six specific tasks and gave their feedback about the usability and overall experience of using the app.

Second, a separate stack of "tutorial cards". This allowed the user to progressively learn how to use the UI by actually using it ("learning by doing"): The initial card would explain how it could be flipped over, the back would then explain how to progress to the next card etc. While this approach might be beneficial to some types of applications, we found no coherent way of connecting all gestures into one story.

Third, we started with another common solution: A button that turns on a modal help overlay. While easily understood, a permanent help button adds visual noise and takes up valuable screen real estate even when not needed. We developed a visually cleaner (and non-modal) alternative where the help overlay would be displayed while performing a "swipe down and hold" gesture. An animated help icon served as visual indicator that was only shown when necessary, that is only when we interpreted user behavior as uncommon or "helpless" (e.g. a rapidly repeating gesture that has no interaction outcome).

Getting back to our minimalistic design philosophy, we dispensed with a dedicated help feature altogether. Instead we introduced visual interface elements where they would improve usability, e.g. a dog-ear visual indicating that a card has a back. Full-screen "content view" still shows barely any chrome that would detract attention from the content. At all times, the zoomed out "navigation view" provides a more self-explaining fallback option.

3.5   Think, Test, Fail, Iterate. Think Again

A fair amount of pragmatism helps to achieve workable results. We found ourselves constantly oscillating between theoretical, pure concepts and hands-on testing. This approach proved to be beneficial, since conceptually perfect solutions tend to dash against an imperfect reality. On the other hand many of the usability issues that manifested during user testing first looked like a matter of fine tuning but actually arose from unsolved conceptual issues. We identified two main areas where gestural user interfaces on current multi-touch hardware fall short on a fundamental level:

Problem of Threshold. Multi-touch hardware allows us to interact via "natural", analog gestures (e.g. a continuous swipe or rotation). However, many required interaction outcomes in software are still discrete and binary (e.g. opening a dialog or rotating the screen by 90 degrees). An interaction designer has to choose a threshold where a continuous gesture triggers a discrete result. Regardless of whether the dimension of the gesture is distance (e.g. how far to swipe), area (e.g. where to tap) or time (e.g. how long to hold), the threshold will generally be invisible and arbitrary to the user. Fine tuning of thresholds can ease usability issues, but will not solve them. Truly natural user interfaces require applications that are natural from the ground up. Pulling a natural interface over an inapt application can never be honest. Put another way, analog real-world metaphors may not apply well at all to abstract, "digital" topics.

Problem of Reversibility. In our tests users performed quite well in the task of navigating to a card at the lowest hierarchy level. Navigating back to where they left was in contrast found much more difficult. While the analogy of getting *into* a stack of cards by tapping it was easily understood and consistent with user's expectations, there was no clear idea how to reverse that operation.

Reversibility of operations is considered a defining factor of direct user interfaces. [10] While most of today's basic multi-touch gestures are easily reversible, there is one striking exception: The most common and maybe most "intuitive" gesture, a single tap, has no obvious counterpart. While multi-touch gestures are movements along the x/y-axis at the surface of the screen, a tap can conceptually be seen as a movement along the z-axis: Tapping *into* the screen typically goes a level *deeper* (e.g. open a stack of cards, or jump to the next level of a hierarchical list). A natural counterpart like "pulling out" of the screen would be desirable but is not feasible on current multi-touch hardware. Once we understood how this was in essence a hardware limitation, we accepted that we would not be able to solve this problem with a natural gesture. After months of hesitation, we finally introduced a back button.

4 Conclusion

Designing usable and satisfying user experiences today means to strive for concistency in a largely inconsistent environment. In this paper our design methodology is described by five key principles. In addition we identified two fundamental conceptual problems currently standing in the way of designing natural user interfaces for multi-touch hardware.

Acknowledgements. This paper is based on a project supported by the "Pre-Seed program" of the Austrian Wirtschaftsservice Gesellschaft (aws), "Academia plus Business" an initiative of the European Union and "Go-Silicon Valley" a program of the Austrian chamber of commerce. Without the deep appreciation for design driven development that both CardSkid founders David Schwingenschuh and Hannes Schmied brought into the project this paper would not have been worth writing. We further like to thank our content partners and study participants.

References

1. Osen, M.: Model of A Universal Interface For Mobile Communications. Micheldorf (2002)
2. Rapp, S., Michelitsch, G., Osen, M., Williams, J., Barbisch, M., Bohan, R., Valsan, Z., Emele, M.: Spotlight navigation: Interaction with a handheld projection device. In: International Conference on Pervasive Computing, Vienna (2004)
3. Michelitsch, G., Williams, J., Osen, M., Jimenez, B., Rapp, S.: Haptic chameleon: a new concept of shape-changing user interface controls with force feedback. In: CHI 2004 Extended Abstracts on Human Factors in Computing Systems, Vienna (2004)
4. Zöllner, F., Thoenes, C., Pöpper, T.: Michelangelo. Taschen, Cologne (2007)
5. Csíkszentmihályi, M.: Flow: The Psychology of Optimal Experience. Harper and Row, New York (1990)
6. Kahney, L.: HyperCard Forgotten, but Not Gone. Wired (August 14, 2002), http://www.wired.com/gadgets/mac/commentary/cultofmac/2002/08/54365

7. Edge, D., Fitchett, S., Whitney, M., Landay, J.: MemReflex: adaptive flashcards for mobile microlearning. In: 14th International Conference on Human-Computer Interaction, San Francisco (2012)
8. Poole, S.: Against Chrome: A Manifesto (2011), http://www.3quarksdaily.com/3quarksdaily/2011/02/against-chrome-a-manifesto.html
9. Ingram, A., Wang, X., Ribarsky, W.: Towards the establishment of a framework for intuitive multi-touch interaction design. In: International Working Conference on Advanced Visual Interfaces, Capri (2012)
10. Shneiderman, B.: Direct manipulation: A step beyond programming languages. In: Joint Conference on Easier and More Productive Use of Computer Systems. (Part II): Human Interface and the User Interface. ACM, New York (1981)

Efficient Information Representation Method for Driver-Centered AR-HUD System

Hyesun Park and Kyong-ho Kim

Electronics and Telecommunication Research Institute(ETRI),
Daejeon, Korea
{hspark78,kkh}@etri.re.kr

Abstract. Providing a suitable and efficient representation of a driver's perspective is a way to reduce traffic accidents. In this paper, we first introduce a driver-centered AR (augmented-reality) HUD (head-up-display) system that superimposes augmented virtual objects onto a real scene under all types of driving situations including unfavorable weather (such as rainy, foggy, overcast, and snowy) conditions. We next explain the scenario and method used in our comparative experiments on a method for improving both the cognitive usability and visibility of drivers. For this, we comparatively analyzed not only information display locations but also information representation for six information types using a driving simulator with thirty subjects. For the effects on safety, the situational driver awareness of safety-related road events was measured. To determine the differences in the visual cognitive workload placed upon drivers, we tracked their eye movements. The subjective workload of the participants was assessed using the RSME (Rating Scale Mental Effort).

Keywords: Efficient Information Providing Method, Information Representation, Information Display Location, Driver Centered System, AR(augmented reality), HUD(head up display), Vehicle Simulator, Cognitive Usability, Visibility, Subjective Workload.

1 Introduction

1.1 Motivation

Necessity for the development of AR-HUD for Driving Safety. Popular vehicle manufacturers around the world are currently commercializing HUD technologies as a part of their premium strategies. In 2001, the first HUD system was mounted into a GM Cadillac [1, 2]. Thereafter, HUD systems have been equipped mainly in advanced vehicles. BMW developed an LED-based HUD, which displays various information for driving safety such as the vehicle speed, driving direction, cruise control information, and a variety of warning messages [3,4]. However, all developed commercial HUDs do not provide by superimposing information between the real world and virtual 'safety driving information' like AR-HUD. Such HUD systems have a problem in terms of cognitive workload caused by a mismatch between virtual

A. Marcus (Ed.): DUXU/HCII 2013, Part III, LNCS 8014, pp. 393–400, 2013.

objects and the real scene. To solve this problem, GM has started the development of a full-windshield HUD system, which provides an augmented lane or road signs by superimposing virtual objects onto the real world seen through the windshield under conditions of poor nighttime visibility [5].

Importance of Information Type Provided. In an AR-HUD system, it is important to not only provide information suitable to the driver's field of vision, it is also very important to provide necessary information to the driver through an efficient information representation. To improve driving safety and minimize the driving workload, the information provided should be represented in such a way that it is more easily understood and imposing less cognitive load onto the driver. It is therefore necessary to classify the characteristics of the information given, and find a way to represent the information according to these characteristics. In addition, research needs to be conducted into both the amount of information that can minimize a driver's cognitive load and the types of representation that can minimize the driver's visual load.

1.2   Hypothesis and Goals

Hypothesis. The representation method used for each type of information differs depending on the characteristics of the information. Therefore, we need to research a type of representation that allows for a faster recognition that is easy to understand. Thus, we divided the provided augmented safety information in the AR-HUD system into six categories, and displayed the various representation methods to suit the characteristics. In this case, we comparatively analyzed the experimental results of the driving performance, information comprehension, and driving workload based on the measured driver cognitive reaction rate, simulator-based driving variables (steering angle, brake, etc.), and driving workload.

Goals. The goals we are trying to achieve in this work are as follows:

— How information representation in the AR-HUD affects driver performance.
— How information representation in the AR-HUD affects driver understanding.
— How information representation in the AR-HUD affects driver workload.

2   Driver-Centered AR (Augmented-Reality) HUD (Head-Up-Display) System

2.1   Overview

Figure 1 shows an overview of the proposed system, and figure 2 provides a system flowchart. The results in figure 1 show a detected lane, vehicle, and obstacle. The system is composed of five main modules: vehicle position estimation, 3D object recognition, view tracking of the driver, registration, and projection and display.

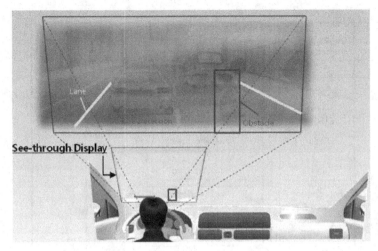

Fig. 1. System overview (unseen situations under unfavorable weather conditions)

2.2   Description of the Sub-module

Vehicle Position Estimation Module. This module estimates the 3D location of the vehicle using a GPS and an IMU. It then utilizes a 3D map DB from the 3D map extraction sub-module. We use a modified Kalman filter to increase the rate of correct information provided [6].

3D Object Recognition Module. This module detects ground-plane based obstacles from an input stereo image, and thereafter classifies the detected obstacles into pedestrians or cars using an HOG (Histogram of Oriented Gradients) based SVM (Support Vector Machine) [7,8], and provides their distances during daytime conditions. Otherwise, during the nighttime, it tracks obstacles out of visual range using a fusion between night-vision and radar technologies. This module then conducts a preprocessing procedure, such as edge detection and noise elimination, from the input image sequence.

Driver-view Tracking Module. This model detects the driver's head location, estimates the driver's gaze, and thereafter calculates the driver's viewpoint using a camera equipped on the display housing device. For this module, it is assumed that the driver's eyes are aimed in the same direction as their head.

Registration Module. This module matches the 3D objects generated according to the driver's perspective. To do so, this module receives 3D data integrated from the output of each module, which are transformed into coordinates of the real world as viewed by the driver.

Projection and Display Module. This module displays safety-warning and useful traffic information to the driver using a see-through HUD with an interactive design.

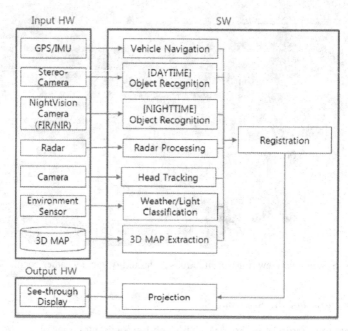

Fig. 2. System flowchart

3   Comparative Experimental Design of an Efficient Information Representation Method for the Proposed AR-HUD System

Experimental Design. We designed two objective experiments for the driving performance and cognitive usability, and one subjective assessment for driving satisfaction. The first experiment was conducted to determine the effects on the driving performance and cognitive usability, and was implemented using a high-fidelity driving simulator. The second experiment was conducted to find the effects on the driver's cognitive reaction when various types of information are provided. The subjective satisfaction of each driver was measured using a psychology-based traffic questionnaire.

Driving Simulator and Peripherals. A 3DOF motion-based, high-fidelity driving simulator was used in the experiment. The simulator provides force feedback and a rich 3D audio environment. Three channel displays for the front, left, and right screens provide a 130 deg. x 40 deg. full-scale field of view. The fully textured graphics were generated using SCANNeRTM software, which delivers a 60 Hz frame rate at a 1024*768 resolution. The software can simulate various kinds of traffic scenarios such as the motion of nearby vehicles and pedestrians, and changes in traffic signals. Various kinds of vehicle data including the location, motion, velocity, acceleration, RPM, braking, and steering were collected by vehicle sensors at a rate of 50 Hz. A face LAB4.6TM eye-tracking system was installed on the dashboard of the simulation vehicle to track the driver's head and eye movements. Figure 3 shows the experimental environment used.

Dependent Variables. During the experiments, vehicle data, eye-tracking data, and video data were collected. The vehicle data were collected from the simulator and include the velocity, steering-wheel angle, accelerator and brake angle, and vehicle position and motion. Eye-tracking data include the head position and orientation, gaze orientation, gazing region, fixation time, and PERCLOSE. For verification of the data, video images from the camera were recorded.

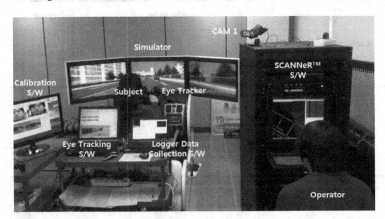

Fig. 3. Experimental Environment

Scenario and Procedure. Each of the thirty participants drove the in-vehicle simulator from start to destination for each information type provided in the AR-HUD system, the order of which was counter balanced. During the experiment, the subjects were encouraged to adhere to the following guidelines: observe the traffic signals, maintain the speed limit indicated by the road signs, and avoid collisions with other vehicles or pedestrians. The driving route for the experiment was planned based on a real road in a 3D graphic scene database. We designed a total of fifty events for four types of routes. Table 1 describes the information type and representation of the designed events.

Subjective Assessment. Using multiple-choice questionnaires and RSME (Rating Scale Mental Effort) [9], the subjective satisfaction and preference for the information provided, and the cognitive workload were measured.

Experimental Method for the Comparative Analysis. The representation of each type of information was determined based on the information attributes, driving situation, and driver characteristics. These predefined representations were divided into non-representations and 3D visualization, and were analyzed using a pairwise comparison between the two. Figure 4 shows the A-route, which is one of the four routes used. In figure 4, E and the number listed next to it are an event and its sequential occurrence, respectively. The route used in the experiments is built using a 3D map. This route includes both an 80 km/h roadway and a footpath. S and F are the starting and final driving points, respectively. To perform each event, all participants drove down the same path several different times. The arrow and number next to each event represent the driving orientation and driving order. Events with the same color share the same event type. Thus, E4, E9, E10, and E15 are the same event type, i.e., pedestrian warning information. In figure 4, the driving starting point is E1, and route A finishes at E16.

Table 1. Information Type and Representation of the Designed Events[1]

Information Type	Event No. (Route Type)	Representation	Attribute
Route	E1 (A-route)	only audio	Default
	E12 (A-route)		3D Visualization (short upper arrow)
Vehicle	E2 (A-route)		3D Visualization (rectangle)
	E5 (A-route)	Non-representation	Default
Pedestrian	E4 (C-route)	Non-representation	Default
	E5 (C-route)		3D Visualization (arrow at head position)
Lane Change	E5 (B-route)		3D Visualization (under arrow)
	E8 (B-route)	Non-representation	Default
POI (Point of Interest)	E3 (A-route)	Non-representation	Default
	E4 (A-route)		3D Visualization (rectangle)
.Traffic Sign	E6 (B-route)	Non-representation	Default
	E6.5 (B-route)		3D Visualization (rectangle)

---

[1] We described the events of the representative comparison-pairs for the representation according to the information type.

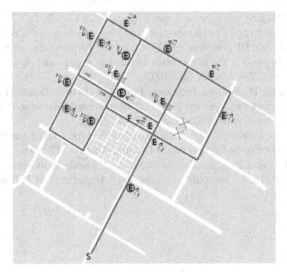

Fig. 4. Experimental Scenario

4   Conclusions and Future Directions

To provide traffic information to drivers using an efficient method, we defined an information representation by considering both the driving situation and the drivers themselves. To prove the suitability of the representation, we also described the experimental design. The results of this experiment will support the effectiveness and validity of the AR-HUD system in the future as an effective representation method based on driver characteristics under complex roads or unseen environments such as those occurring during unfavorable weather conditions. For this, we will further analyze three different methods according to the experimental design described in this paper. The first method is a paired t-test, which compares the differences between non-representation and 3D visualization. The next method is a graph analysis to determine the average distribution of the 30 subjects. Finally, a subjective preference and cognitive load will be measured through questionnaires.

Acknowledgments. This work was supported by the Industrial Strategic technology development program, Development of Driver-View based in-Vehicle AR Display System Technology Development(10040927), funded by the Ministry of Knowledge Economy (MKE, Korea).

References

1. General Motors, http://www.gm.com/
2. Cadillac-Motor Trend Blog,
   http://blogs.motortrend.com/manufacturer/cadillac/
3. BMW HUD (2009), http://Youtube.com

4. BMW_Blog (2011), http://www.bmwblog.com/2011/10/10/
   video-bmw-head-up-display-simulation-augmented-reality/
5. GM's full-windshield HUD technology (2010), http://Youtube.com
6. Brown, R.G., Hwang, P.Y.C.: Introduction to Random Signals and Applied Kalman Filtering, 2nd edn. John Wiley & Sons, Inc. (1992)
7. Xu, Y., Xu, L., Li, D., Wu, Y.: Pedestrian Detection Using Background Subtrac-tion Assisted Support Vector Machine. In: 2011 11th International Conference on Intelligent Systems Design and Applications (ISDA), pp. 837–842 (2011)
8. Boser, B., Guyon, I., Vapnik, V.: A training algorithm for optimal margin classifiers. In: Fifth Annual Workshop on Computational Learning Theory. ACM Press (1992)
9. Zijlstra, F.R.H., van Doorn, L.: The construction of a scale to measure subjective effort. Technical Report, Delft University of Technology, Department of Philosophy and Social Sciences (1985)

Towards Medical Cyber-Physical Systems: Multimodal Augmented Reality for Doctors and Knowledge Discovery about Patients

Daniel Sonntag[1], Sonja Zillner[2], Christian Schulz[1],
Markus Weber[1], and Takumi Toyama[1]

[1] German Research Center for AI (DFKI)
Stuhlsatzenhausweg 3, 66123 Saarbruecken, Germany
[2] Siemens AG, Corporate Technology, Otto-Hahn-Ring 6, 81739 Munich, Germany

Abstract. In the medical domain, which becomes more and more digital, every improvement in efficiency and effectiveness really counts. Doctors must be able to retrieve data easily and provide their input in the most convenient way. With new technologies towards medical cyber-physical systems, such as networked head-mounted displays (HMDs) and eye trackers, new interaction opportunities arise. With our medical demo in the context of a cancer screening programme, we are combining active speech based input, passive/active eye tracker user input, and HMD output (all devices are on-body and hands-free) in a convenient way for both the patient and the doctor.

1 Introduction

In ubiquitous computing, it can be said that most profound technologies are those that disappear by weaving themselves into the fabric of everyday (professional) life. It would be even better if we could carry and wear those technologies on our bodies which would make us rather independent of the location in which they are used. Recent display systems are available as head-mounted displays (HMDs) which provide new ubiquitous possibilities for interaction and real-time systems often referred to as cyber-physical systems [5]. In this paper, we present the design of our multiple device on-body augmented reality interaction system for doctors while examining cancer patients in the medical routine. The augmented reality system comprises a speech-based dialogue system, a head-mounted augmented reality see-through retina display (HMD), and a head-mounted eye-tracker. The interaction devices have been selected to augment and improve the expert work in a specific medical application context which shows its potential. In the sensitive domain of examining patients in a cancer screening programme we try to combine active and passive user input devices in the most convenient way for both the patient and the doctor. The resulting multimodal AR application has the potential to yield higher performance outcomes and provides a direct data acquisition control mechanism. It effectively leverages the doctor's capabilities of recalling the specific patient context by a virtual, context-based patient-specific "external brain" for the doctor

A. Marcus (Ed.): DUXU/HCII 2013, Part III, LNCS 8014, pp. 401–410, 2013.

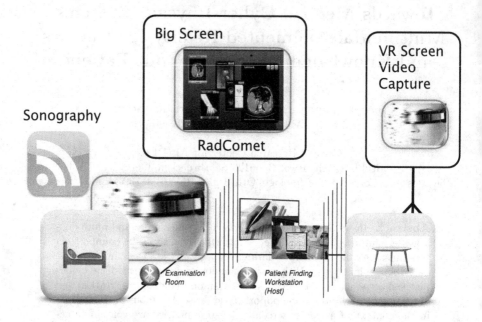

Fig. 1. Medical CPS application environment

which can remember patient faces. In addition, patient data can be displayed on the see-trough HMD—triggered by voice or automatic object/patient recognition. The architecture includes several state-of-the art input and output device strategies: natural speech, graphical head-mounted HCIs, and eye-gesture-based interaction. The prototype of the augmented reality application combines a medical healthcare related (industrial) usecase with multimodal realtime interaction (figure 1). In addition to the doctor's active input at the patient finding station, passive input can be captured from the mobile eye tracker during examination in combination with active speech input. Results can be presented on a big screen (RadComet) or the head mounted augmented reality HMD we will focus on (figure 2). In addition, the picture of the head-mounted camera can be displayed on a large virtual reality (VR) screen for other medical staff members getting access to the real-time video capture. This forms our medical CPS application environment.

2 Background

A cyber-physical system (CPS) is a system featuring a tight combination of the system's computational and physical elements. Potential CPS systems include intervention (e.g., collision avoidance); precision (e.g., robotic surgery); operation

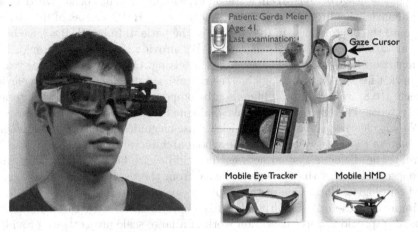

Fig. 2. Mounted eye tracker and HMD combination (left); doctor's view with HMD (right image: courtesy of Siemens AG)

in dangerous or inaccessible environments (e.g., search and rescue); augmented reality, and the augmentation of human capabilities (e.g., healthcare monitoring and decision support for doctors and patients). We bring together augmented reality and augmentation of human capabilities in the mobile medical context: mobile CPS, in which the physical system with a medical purpose has got inherent mobility. This is motivated by the rise in popularity of mobile interaction devices such as smartphones and tablets which has increased interest for CPS developers. As technologies have become small, mobile, and pervasive, the logical next step (beyond the rapid growth of smartphones or tablet PCs or surrounding computers) is the usage of mobile augmented reality and mobile decision support CPS, which will draw people's attention. For example, recent see-through HMD systems (cf. Brother AirScouter or Google Glasses) show massive potential for the future of augmented reality.

The argumentation is as follows: First, mobile eye-tracking glasses allow for mobile gaze-based user input (see figure 2, right: the gaze cursor's position helps to identity the patient's face). Second, semantic sensor data enrichment for HCI has a fundamental role to play (for example, a digital pen can capture the handwriting and interpret it according to a specific patient record [11]). Ideally, this represents the operation of monitoring and interpreting the data coming from mobile sensor in the light of background knowledge expressed in a logical way (ontologies, processes.) Third, background knowledge can describe how a specific medical process is structured, e.g., what are the next actions? What are the possible actions and the "impossible" actions? Which background knowledge provides a set of constraints for the interpretation of the signals for mobile medical CPS?

In [2], the usage of an HMD in ultrasound scanning task has been investigated. [15] enhanced the direct sight of the physician by an HMD overlay of the virtual data onto the doctors view in the context of the patient. In [4], HMDs have been used in various forms to assist surgeons. We provide the first see-through implementation in a multimodal speech-based setting. Over the last several years, the market for speech technology has seen significant developments [7]. In earlier projects [16,8] we integrated different sub-components into multimodal interaction systems. Thereby, hub-and-spoke dialogue frameworks played a major role [9]. We also learned some lessons which we use as guidelines in the development of *semantic* dialogue systems [6]; the whole architecture can be found in [10]. Thereby, the dialogue system acts as the middleware between the clients and the backend services that hide complexity from the user by presenting aggregated ontological data. One of the resulting speech system, RadSpeech [12], is the implementation of a multimodal dialogue system for structured radiology reports. In previous implementation work of a large-scale project[1], we provided a technical solution for the two challenges of speech-based multimodal system engineering and debugging functional modules in domain-specific applications [13]. The next step is the inclusion of a knowledge lifecyle in multimodal CPS.

3   Knowledge Lifecyle in Multimodal Medical CPS

Within multimodal medical CPS as information systems, we distinguish between data acquisition and data retrieval steps (figure 3). Data acquisition steps aim to capture relevant health data on the basis of a multi-modal user interaction, store the captured data in an integrated repository, and extract and semantically label meaningful information units. Due to the sensitiveness of medical data, the data acquisition process is completed by a quality control loop that ensures high quality as well as compliant and consistent data sets. Within the data retrieval step, the existing knowledge repository is accessed to retrieve context-relevant information. Again, by means of a dedicated multimodal user interaction dialogue, significant context data, such as the name of the patient can be identified. By transforming the extracted context information into query or filtering request, context-relevant results can be accessed and presented in an intelligent, context-dependent manner (in the HMD).

Described here as two distinguished activities, there is a strong interaction between the two depicted layers. For instance, information extraction can be a acquisition related off-line process. However, within a real-time retrieval application according to a CPS workflow, context data dependent (precision-oriented) information extraction is to be understood as a key element to CPS knowledge discovery. In the following, we will describe the impact and associated opportunities of the health data acquisition and retrieval steps in more detail.

---

[1] This work is part of THESEUS-RadSpeech (see www.dfki.de/RadSpeech/) to implement dialogue applications for medical use case scenarios. It has been supported by the German Federal Ministry of Economics and Technology (01MQ07016).

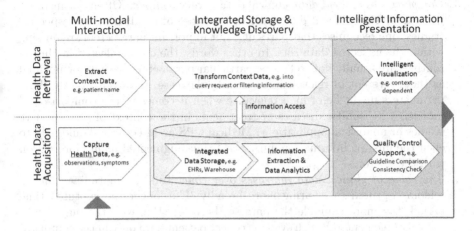

Fig. 3. Knowledge Lifecyle in Multimodal Medical CPS

3.1 Health Data Acquisition

The more clinicians know about the health condition of a patient, the better the treatment can be. For instance, comprehensive and high-quality health data of patients can be used to identify patterns within the longitudinal progress of patients health condition; the data can be used to identify silent signals indicating a rare disease or the data can be compared with the health data of related patient populations. However, in todays clinical practice, only a small percentage of patient health data is captured, stored, exchanged, and accessed in a seamless and intelligent manner [14]. The very limited quality as well as density of clinical data is due to several reasons:

1. *Missing IT-Infrastructure*: the overall clinical data acquisition process is often still paper-based and the seamless exchange of data is hindered by either missing or badly implemented interfaces. As of today, a large number of clinical experts share and exchange patient data by scanning and emailing or faxing paper-based documents.
2. *Lack of time*: clinicians do not have "extra time" which they could spend on comprehensive documentation tasks. Usually, the patient interaction—be it an operation or a patient visit—requires almost 100% of their attention. Documentation tasks are only accomplished if they are mandatory, which again is only the case for a very limited number of clinical tasks. The documentation task per se should not draw off the attention of the clinician and this can be achieved along the way without any interruption of the workflow. Speech recognition has been used for that purpose, and we try to extend it to the augmented reality realm.

3. *Complexity of clinical data*: clinical data is very complex. Often, for instance when analysing clinical data with the purpose of conducting retrospective studies, one recognises that particular but important parameters are missing within the collected data sets. In other words, the data collected in clinical routines are usually not complete; particular parameters are not documented as they were not of relevance for a particular case. However, exactly those parameters might be of high relevance when it comes to the comparison of patients with similar diseases or treatments in the context of retrospective studies or analytical applications. Medical CPS architectures should help to elicit the missing information during real-time augmented reality interaction with the doctor.

4. *The value of clinical data increases over time*: Today, longitudinal data is seldom captured for sharing more broadly. The longer the captured time period, the more valuable the data set becomes. However, the majority of todays implemented health systems collect patient data only in the context of a particular treatment episode. Although the documentation of longitudinal patient health data is very promising (in terms of seamless data access and analytics), as of today it is only accomplished for rare or severe diseases. In such cases, the data is maintained/stored within dedicated long-term disease registries, the data collection/acquisition processes are mainly accomplished manually (often on the basis of Phd-studies of doctors-in-training) and implemented as parallel tracks to the clinical routine processes. In other words, the return of investment of longitudinal clinical patient acquisition takes a long time to become measurable.

Comprehensive and high quality clinical data is of high value but it takes some effort to acquire. In the following, we will show how multimodal user interaction in CPS establishes the basis for a seamless health data acquisition process, as well as its intelligent processing and semantic visualisation, and demonstrate its potential to improve the overall quality as well as efficiency of health care delivery. In the long run, also on-body passive sensors should help us collect longitudinal data automatically to be re-injected into the automatic, semi-automatic, manual clinical decision process.

3.2   Health Data Retrieval

The medical application environment comprises of a patient finding workstation (to write digital medical patient reports) and a patient examination room (figure 1). When using our multimodal interaction system, the doctor has the ability to retrieve patient-related information about the patient during the examination and is able to input new data in a convenient way (speech activation with eye tracker) during the examination. When the eye of the doctor focusses on a patient face, recorded faces can be recognised. In addition, new patients can be added by a speech command "*Add new patient x*," while the face is being detected. The retrieval architecture includes virtual databases which can also gather information from web repositories.

First, we want to leverage the doctors capabilities to recall patients and inform himself about a specific patient record. For this purpose, we implemented the first online, head-mounted face learning system which uses a mobile eye-tracker. In the most elaborate interface mode, we allow for a real-time interactive face detection. The face detection scenario is as follows: in a cancer screening programme, which takes place every three months, we evaluated the doctor-patient relationship. As a matter of fact, the probability of being examined by the same doctor in the routine checks is about 10% (due to daily routine personal shift in full treatment hospitals in Germany). As a result, the verification of a patient at the beginning of an examination is a welcome feature for the doctors. In addition, it avoids the need for additional active user input, e.g., a voice command about opening a specific patients record, which can be done automatically. Further, the patient needs not to be interrogated about facts which can easily pop-up automatically in the HMD display.

Second, in the interactive experience with the doctor and the patient, the system should improve the performance of the human-computer interaction and the usability in the patient context. Once the patient is recognised, further speech commands such as show the last CT examination, or what was the last finding allow the doctor to display additional image and text based information in the HMD (privately) or on the big screen when patient should be actively involved in the reading process. Finally, additional annotations and remarks to the specific medical case can be added using speech during the examination without neglecting the patient in, for example, a sonography examination. For this purpose, we use the gaze position on the HMD in combination with an automatic speech recognizer (ASR) as part of the multimodal interaction structure. A little gaze to activate the ASR (and natural language understanding component, NLU) makes the daily routine much more effective and yields higher performance outcomes on the knowledge intensive medical examination and reporting tasks, because the doctor can use the speech system during the sonography examination in a robust way (push-to-talk through the activation), and the results a presented in the see-through HMD (figure 4).

The technical architecture, which includes active and passive input modes (a combination of state-of-the-art components), and a setting for online learning algorithms, is currently under development. Currently we use a simple nearest neighbour search method to recognise faces, but this can be extended to an approximate nearest neighbour method such as in [3] to become productive in a clinical environment. The idea of the "external brain" for doctors and other hospital staff receives a lot of attention according to our discussions with them. In addition, automatic detection of objects and faces provide a situation context which is very interesting from an academic point of view: which information is adequate in specific contexts to be displayed automatically (system-initiative). It provides avenues for future research in multimodal interaction systems and mobile web applications inside and outside the medical domain context. Two medical storyboards for augmented reality-based CPS interaction have been developed (figure 5).

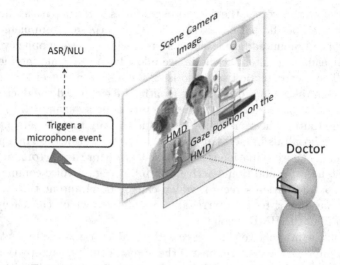

Fig. 4. Patient Examination Scenario where the doctor wears a head-mounted eye-tracker and an HMD

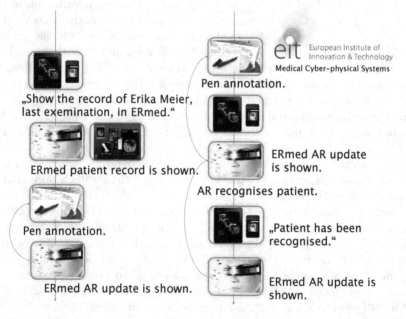

Fig. 5. Two medical storyboards for augmented reality-based CPS interaction

4 Conclusion

In the RadSpeech use case, we work on the direct industrial dissemination of a medical dialogue system prototype. Recently, structured reporting was introduced in radiology that allows radiologists to use predefined standardised forms for a limited but growing number of specific examinations. However, doctors feel restricted by these standardised forms and fear a decrease in focus on the medical the images [1,17] and the patients. As a result, the acceptance for structured reporting is still low among radiologists for example while referring physicians and hospital administrative staff are generally supportive of structured standardised reporting since it eases the communication with the radiologists and can be used more easily for further processing. In this paper, we extended our first Radspeech scenario (http://www.youtube.com/watch?v=uBiN119_wvg) to an augmented reality CPS application. The design of the CPS solution supports the daily routines very well, anticipating todays constraints in hospitals. Doctors are directly put in context and are relieved from manual data capture. It will be interesting to see in future usability studies to what depth doctors will actually apply the sophisticated and facilitated CPS interfaces.

Acknowledgements. This research has been supported by the THESEUS programme funded by the German Federal Ministry of Economics and Technology (01MQ07016). This work was partially supported by EIT ICT Labs and the Nuance Foundation. It is part of MedicalCPS http://www.dfki.de/MedicalCPS/ and DFKI's ERmed http://www.dfki.de/RadSpeech/ERmed projects.

References

1. Hall, F.M.: The radiology report of the future. Radiology 251(2), 313–316 (2009)
2. Havukumpu, J., Vähäkangas, P., Grönroos, E., Häkkinen, J.: Midwives experiences of using hmd in ultrasound scan. In: Mørch, A.I., Morgan, K., Bratteteig, T., Ghosh, G., Svanaes, D. (eds.) NordiCHI, pp. 369–372. ACM (2006)
3. Indyk, P., Motwani, R.: Approximate nearest neighbors: Towards removing the curse of dimensionality. In: Proceedings of the Thirtieth Annual ACM Symposium on the Theory of Computing, Dallas, Texas, USA, pp. 604–613 (1998)
4. Keller, K., State, A., Fuchs, H.: Head mounted displays for medical use. J. Display Technol. 4(4), 468–472 (2008)
5. Lee, E.A.: Cyber physical systems: Design challenges. Technical Report UCB/EECS-2008-8, EECS Department, University of California, Berkeley (January 2008)
6. Oviatt, S.: Ten myths of multimodal interaction. Communications of the ACM 42(11), 74–81 (1999)
7. Pieraccini, R., Huerta, J.: Where do we go from here? Research and commercial spoken dialog systems. In: Proceedings of the 6th SIGDdial Workshop on Discourse and Dialogue, pp. 1–10 (September 2005)
8. Reithinger, N., Fedeler, D., Kumar, A., Lauer, C., Pecourt, E., Romary, L.: MIAMM - A Multimodal Dialogue System Using Haptics. In: van Kuppevelt, J., Dybkjaer, L., Bernsen, N.O. (eds.) Advances in Natural Multimodal Dialogue Systems. Springer (2005)
9. Reithinger, N., Sonntag, D.: An integration framework for a mobile multimodal dialogue system accessing the Semantic Web. In: Proceedings of INTERSPEECH, Lisbon, Portugal, pp. 841–844 (2005)

10. Sonntag, D.: Ontologies and Adaptivity in Dialogue for Question Answering. AKA and IOS Press, Heidelberg (2010)

11. Sonntag, D., Liwicki, M., Weber, M.: Digital pen in mammography patient forms. In: Proceedings of the 13th International Conference on Multimodal Interfaces, pp. 303–306. ACM (November 2011)

12. Sonntag, D., Schulz, C., Reuschling, C., Galarraga, L.: Radspeech's mobile dialogue system for radiologists. In: Proceedings of the 2012 ACM International Conference on Intelligent User Interfaces, IUI 2012, pp. 317–318. ACM, New York (2012)

13. Sonntag, D., Sonnenberg, G., Nesselrath, R., Herzog, G.: Supporting a rapid dialogue engineering process. In: Proceedings of the First International Workshop On Spoken Dialogue Systems Technology, IWSDS (2009)

14. Sonntag, D., Wennerberg, P., Buitelaar, P., Zillner, S.: Pillars of Ontology Treatment in the Medical Domain. In: Cases on Semantic Interoperability for Information Systems Integration: Practices and Applications, pp. 162–186. Information Science Reference (2010)

15. Traub, J., Sielhorst, T.: Advanced display and visualization concepts for image guided surgery. Display Technology, ... (2008)

16. Wahlster, W.: SmartKom: Symmetric Multimodality in an Adaptive and Reusable Dialogue Shell. In: Krahl, R., Günther, D. (eds.) Proceedings of the Human Computer Interaction Status Conference 2003, pp. 47–62. DLR, Berlin (2003)

17. Weiss, D.L., Langlotz, C.: Structured reporting: Patient care enhancement or productivity nightmare? Radiology 249(3), 739–747 (2008)

Border Crosser

A Robot as Mediator between the Virtual and Real World

Anke Tallig, Wolfram Hardt, and Maximilian Eibl

Chemnitz University of Technology, Department of Computer Science, Chemnitz, Germany
{anke.tallig,wolfram.hardt,
maximilian.eibl}@informatik.tu-chemnitz.de

Abstract. Expositions are offering many information regarding the exhibits. These facts are normally presented in the form of charts and audio guides. For more and supplementary information some museums have robot guides or interactive touch tables. This paper describes a mixed device consisting of a robot guide and a touch table. This mobile robot connects the real exhibition environment and the virtual channel which contains all the interesting information. Therefore the Border Crosser itself is mixed reality device and produces and presents a mixed reality. It combines the advantages of real and virtual world. In this setting the Border Crosser also works as a mediator. A mediator which perceives the people, the environment and the possible interactions with the virtual channel. The robot is a friend, a host and a teacher. In this way the visit of an exhibition becomes to an adventure.

Keywords: Robot mediator, mixed reality, human-robot interaction, human-computer interaction.

1 Introduction

The Industrial Museum Chemnitz offers a variety of technical exhibition pieces, industrial machinery, a bowling alley, several cars and a lot of other technical equipment [1]. It's fun to stroll alongside other visitors and to learn more about the exhibits. During the visit a steam locomotive catches the eye. Many people stop and marvel about the size, a restrained touching is permitted. Standing there, admiring the machine, one thinks aloud: *Too bad I can not see the locomotive in action.* Other people think: *How does it look from the inside and how does a steam locomotive work? One would have to see the locomotive without cladding.* Someone starts to talk: In the past I drove such a locomotive … He describes what he remembered and tried not to forget any detail, so that the listener can imagine, because they can't have a look inside.

Additional information are normally acquired by mobile phones or other mobile devices. In this way the user, respectively the visitor of a museum, is isolated from the real environment. Between the perception of the real world and the sought-after information originates a gap.

A. Marcus (Ed.): DUXU/HCII 2013, Part III, LNCS 8014, pp. 411–418, 2013.
© Springer-Verlag Berlin Heidelberg 2013

But, how could one provide an insight into experiences, designs, technical processes etc. – all while promoting interpersonal communications in real?

The solution is a robotic Border Crosser! What is needed: Comprehensive information and clear description of technical processes. All these contents are provided by the virtual world. Additional to this points people need the awareness of the exhibits. They want a friend for communication and a teacher for learning more about the exhibits and technology which is inside the machinery. These tasks are provided by the real world.

For this kind of solution four elements are necessary (depicted in Fig.1):

- controlled robot (Border Crosser)
- virtual channel (virtual world)
- real environment (real world)
- interactive portal (interaction interface).

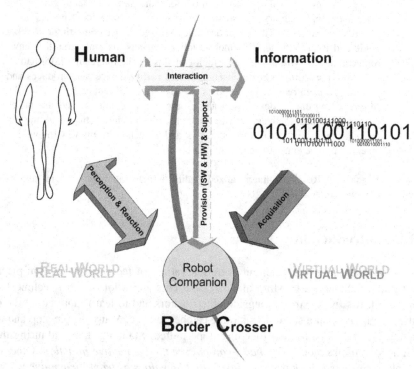

Fig. 1. Nexus of Robot Companion, Real and Virtual World

The interactive portal ancillary to the robot companion is essential for the human-computer interaction. It is the visual interacting interface produced and presented by the robot. This portal is a step into a mixed reality, but this is not a component of this paper.

The real environment is a public place, a special surrounding with many human beings. In this particular case the special surrounding is the museum. But of course all forms of surroundings are possible, for example airports, public buildings or other public places where a robot could interacts with people.

The virtual channel contains comprehensive information about the topic, in this case information about the exhibits.

The fourth element is the controlled robot itself. A mobile robot which navigates through the real environment while perceiving the human beings and acts as 'helping hand' in the real world. In addition the robot has a virtual 'helping hand' for the people who interact with the information of the virtual channel. As a mediator between the real and the virtual world it'll to the Border Crosser.

2   Border Crosser

Service robots in museums are tour guides [2, 3], entertainment devices [4], memento tinkerer [5] or as a combination of guide and information point [2, 6]. The Border Crosser is a combination of a museum's host and an interactive mediator. As a host the robot presents the exhibits which are in the museum. During the driveway it observes the humans and interacts with them. It is an entertaining friend in the real and a friendly tutor in the virtual world.

2.1   The Technical Device

The Border Crosser is designed without human appearance. The robot should not substitute a human being, it is a supplemental device. This is because the robot looks like a technical device with a sympathy factor. A technical achievement created by humans hands. People want a well functioned apparatus but no perfectionism. The humanity loathed perfectionism: If the service robot better then human, then it is not accepted [7]. In avoidance of confusion: the hard- and software of the robot is implemented so that the Border Crosser works flawlessly. But the programmed personality of the robot is conscious not perfect. It only seems that the robot is in trouble. Folly is a interesting thing for people

The robot is a small robot, the construction is described in [8]. The platform has a diameter of 370 millimetre and a height of 210 millimetre. Including the inner frame the height is 1200 millimetre, shown in fig. 2. The inner frame is used for the storage of the on-board computer, projector, sensors and the speaker. Due to its small size it makes attackable by human beings. Arrangements for its own security are necessary: perception by sensors and a apposite answer of Border Crosser. For the realisation the robot contains a lot of sensor, infrared sensors for the distance measurement and depth perception sensors for the localisation of approaching people.

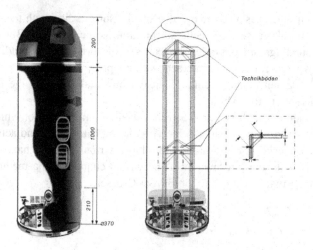

Fig. 2. Sketch of the Border Crosser

2.2   Safety and Human Perception

For the localisation of obstacles and human beings the robot possesses two safety distances. The first distance is the interaction circle, within this distance detected humans are ascertained as objects for interaction. The second distance represents the inner circle, within this distance detected humans are perceived as intruders.

Whenever a human being is detected in the inner circle the robot turns into the self protection mode. Depending on the current mode (cf. fig. 3) the options for the robot are: drive away, change the direction or initiate a communication with the intruder. The robot itself is a member of the environment and a member of the social situation and so the implementation of the precaution heeded the social situation. No technical warning signals or forbiddances are applied. The robot speaks with a not synthesised voice. With the help of voice records acts the robot whit a human voice and adverts of the security of the situation.

Furthermore the robot observes people in its immediate environment (interaction circle) for execution of possible human-robot interactions. With the variety of sensory perception the robot can perceives a single person or a group of people. Dependent on the posture of the human body the robot reacts with a corresponding action or an offering. For instance: A person who looks with a careful posture will be addressed with an encouraged invitation. People who appear like a "competent user" will be offered several possibilities. Combined with a face tracking system which detects elementary facial expressions the robot can establish a human-robot contact.

3   Mediator Between Virtual and Real World

The robot itself is a device between virtual and real world, a Border Crosser, a mixed-reality device. On the one hand the robot parts are real physical hardware. On the other hand it works only with the help of the virtual digital world [9].

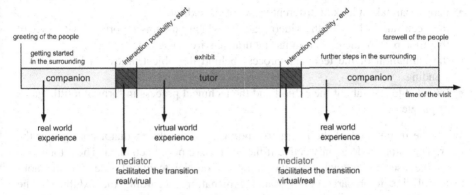

Fig. 3. Extract of a sequence of robot interactions

Which one is more suitable as a mediator between the two worlds while functioning as a mixed reality device?

The robot mediator facilitates the transition from real to virtual and vice versa, shown in fig. 3. The acquisition of additional information from the virtual channel is a process which dissociates the human being from the real world. People who acquire these additional information generally use a mobile phone. With theirs eyes on the mobile screen they lose the comprehension of their environment. For the prevention of the separation is the Border Crosser applied. The robot mediator directs the attention of the humans. It is a anchor into the real world and offers complementary information. The robot contains a programmed personality and acts with the whole body and a human voice.

Depending on transition from real to virtual or virtual to real the robot directs the attention towards the digital information or to the real environment.

3.1   Transition from Real to Virtual

At the transition from the real to the virtual world the attention changes from real world experience to the virtual world experience. After the robot mediator presents the exhibits in the real environment it points to the additional information provided by the virtual digital channel. Before people can interact with the interactive portal they get a introduction.

While the robot device make technical arrangements for the interactive portal which shows the additional information for example pictures, videos or technical details, the Border Crosser changes in the role of a mediator and prepares the humans for the next step.

Like a human host the robot talks about the exhibition: when the exhibition started, how many objects are included and, maybe, even a little small talk about the weather. When approaching the next exhibit the robot changes the method of the presentation. It comes to the description of the exhibit. The description ends with the normal dates, time and place of origin, who constructed it and where and so on. Now the Border Crosser as mediator gives the special note: Because they can't have a look inside the exhibit, we present the digital look inside. The human voice of the mediator explains what the people can do with the digital version. The mediator points to the possibilities:

- people can take a look at different views of the exhibit
- they can take a look at the video material which contains reports of witnesses of that time period, the exhibit in its "natural" environment etc.
- the animation of the technical process behind the object, allows a better understanding
- knowledge tests about the exhibit and the technical process in form of a little game or puzzle

When the installation of the interactive portal is ready, the mediator consigns at the tutor. The tutor-mode is only active if the interactive portal activated. The tutor-mode helps the user to interact with the computer on the technical side. On the non-technical side it prepares contents and explanations regarding the exhibit. In the course of the tutor-mode the Border Crosser perceives all around the surrounding. If the robot detects an intruder it activates the security measures. In all modes, showed in fig. 3, are the preventive measures enabled.

In additional to this activities the robot perceives people who look like an interested person or a group of interested people. At this monitoring it attempts to "win" the person or the group of people to do interaction with the other people.

3.2   Transition from Virtual to Real

The visitor of the museum terminated the interactive portal if she or he is finished with studying the content and ready for next exhibit. When the tutor-mode is terminated by the user, the Border Crosser, now mediator again, is reactivated.

Like the transition from real to virtual the mediator attempts to facilitate the transition from virtual to real. The human voice diverts the user's attention from the interactive portal towards the real environment. This happens with reference to the next interesting exhibit.

Every exhibition tour guide follows a assigned path through the exhibits, in a thematic or a temporal order. So the guide directs the attention of the visitors from one exhibit to the next. This is what the robot does. With the thematic or temporal order which connect the exhibits the robot put the attention in the real world on the next exhibit. In this way the robot directs the human attention on itself and by association on the exhibition environment. So at every exhibit the Border Crosser directs the attention away from virtual to real.

With the help of the Border Crosser the ratio of attention between the real environment and the virtual channel is in balance.

4   Discussion

As previously stated the robot possesses no human appearance. This decision is based on the fact that a robot is a tool for the visitors. Its main task is present additional information while acting as a helping hand to learn more about the items of the exhibition. It is not a replacement for a human tutor. But the question remains: Should this robot have a human-like appearance? Is such a human appearance better to facilitate a communication between the visitor and robot or isn't it?

Against the comment in [10], which means that humanlike appearance is connected to the willingness of communication, the decision for a non-human robot was: the nature of the industrial museum is presenting a lot of technical instruments and the Border Crosser is a technical instrument and its appearance is like a technical instrument. Technology is presented by technology. Because the robot is not an exhibit per se, it shall not divert from the exhibition. A human robot would change this situation so the robot is a part of the exhibition. This is unintended.

One main problem of this questioning remains: there is no human robot with the same technology and the same programme. A comparative evaluation appears to be impossible. Only with equal robots, one with human and one with non-human appearance, is a comparative evaluation possible. The study in [10] describes two different kinds of robots, with different skills. A really comprehensive evaluation is only possible with two robots with identical functions and different appearance. That is the situation, it must be accepted. With the evaluation of the acceptance of only the non-human robot is the question, which device is the better, not answered.

5   Conclusion

The described robot is a service robot for a public area. The public area is in this example an exhibition. In this exhibition area the robot acts as a Border Crosser between the real and the virtual world. It interacts with the visitors in the real exhibition environment and in the virtual digital world. For a better transition between the two worlds the robot acts as a mediator.

The robotic communication are implemented with different body movements and a human voice. In combination of those two features should increase the acceptance by human beings. Because not only the power of speech of the robot is important for a successful human-robot communication [10].

Both as a tool and as an assistant the robot helps to facilitate in the transition between real/virtual and virtual/real. In this way the perception of the visitors in the surrounding exhibition is necessary. It has to perceives the obstacles, exhibits and visitors and in this combination it can presents interaction possibilities. This function as assistant is the most encouragement by the participants. In [11] it is described that most of the questioned participants wanted an assistant robot in the future. This specific evaluation only considered the idea of a future robot assistant inside the home, an assistant in every situation of life appears to be a good idea, isn't it.

The mediation between the virtual and real world closes the gap between the experience in real environment and acquisition of additional information. With the steering of the human attention the people can perceive the exhibition environment better.

In this manner the exhibition visit becomes an adventure with both real perceptions and a lot of additional information about the exhibits.

References

1. Sächsisches Industriemuseum Chemnitz, http://
   www.saechsisches-industriemuseum.de/_html/www/
   chemnitz/home.htm (last access: February 11, 2013)
2. Thrun, S., et al.: Probabilistic Algorithms and the Interactive Museum Tour-Guide Robot Minerva. International Journal of Robotics Research 19(11), 972–999 (2000)
3. Burgard, W., et al.: The Interactive Museum Tour-Guide Robot. In: Proceedings of the Fifteenth National Conference on Artificial Intelligence (AAAI 1998), Madison, Wisconsin (1998)
4. Fraunhofer-Institut für Produktionstechnik und Automatisierung IPA,
   http://www.ipa.fraunhofer.de/
   Museumsroboter_Berlin.510.0.html (last access: February 06, 2013)
5. Technik Museum Speyer,
   http://speyer.technik-museum.de/de/de/robotershop
   (last access: February 08, 2013)
6. Faber, F., et al.: The Humanoid Museum Tour Guide Robotinho, http://
   www.informatik.uni-freiburg.de/~joho/publications/
   faber09roman.pdf (last access February: 08, 2013)
7. Weber, K.: Roboter und Künstliche Intelligenz in Science Fiction-Filmen: Vom Werkzeug zum Akteur. In: Fuhse, J.A. (ed.) Technik und Gesellschaft in der Science Fiction, Kultur und Technik Band 09. LIT Verlag, Berlin (2008)
8. Tallig, A.: Grenzgänger-Roboter als Mittler zwischen der virtuellen und realen sozialen Welt. Chemnitzer Informatik-Berichte, CSR-12-05, Chemnitz
9. Young, J., et al.: What is mixed reality, anyway? Considering the boundaries of mixed reality in the context of robots. In: Wang, X. (ed.) Mixed Reality and Human-Robot Interaction. Springer Science+Business Media (2011)
10. Savicic, A.: Gesprächsakzeptanz von Robotern, Am Beispiel von Actroid-DER2 und Leonardo. Grin Verlag, München (2010)
11. Dautenhahn, K., et al.: What is a Robot Companion – Friend, Assistant or Butler?
    https://uhra.herts.ac.uk/dspace/bitstream/2299/7119/
    1/901108.pdf (last access: February 06, 2013)

Strategy for the Development of a Walk-In-Place Interface for Virtual Reality

Luís Teixeira[1,2,*], Elisângela Vilar[1,2,4], Emília Duarte[1,3], Paulo Noriega[1,2], Francisco Rebelo[1,2], and Fernando Moreira da Silva[4]

[1] Ergonomics Laboratory - Faculdade de Motricidade Humana, Universidade Técnica de Lisboa, Estrada da Costa, 1499-002, Cruz Quebrada – Dafundo, Portugal
[2] CIPER – Interdisciplinary Center for the Study of Human Performance, Universidade Técnica de Lisboa, Cruz Quebrada-Dafundo, Portugal
{lmteixeira,elivilar,pnoriega,frebelo}@fmh.utl.pt
[3] Unidcom, IADE, Creative University, Av. D. Carlos I, 4, 1200-649 Lisbon, Portugal
emilia.duarte@iade.pt
[4] CIAUD - Research Centre in Architecture, Urban Planning and Design – FA – Technical University of Lisbon, Lisbon, Portugal
fms.fautl@gmail.com

Abstract. Many features of a Virtual Reality system can influence the immersion and the sense of presence. Navigation is one of those features, since proprioceptive and vestibular cues can have a positive impact on immersion and sense of presence. This is especially important for studies about human behavior, where behavioral responses should be as close as in the real world. Different types of interfaces are been developed to be more natural and closer to moving in a real environment. A Walk-In-Place (WIP) interface can be used in small rooms and gives some proprioceptive and vestibular cues. A participant walks in the same place and a device captures that movement and translates it to movement inside the Virtual Environment. This paper presents a strategy for implementing a WIP interface using only one inertial orientation sensor, placed above the knee, mainly about the calibration and real-time detection phases and the approach taken on direction changing.

Keywords: Virtual Reality, Navigation interfaces, Walk-in-place technique.

1 Introduction

Virtual Reality (VR) has been used in many fields of study, particularly in human behavior research, to examine how people behave when facing certain situations. A critical point to the effective use of this approach is to provide the users the means with which they could believe that they are in a place, even when they are physically in another, in a way to enhance the sense of presence [1].

---

* Corresponding author.

A. Marcus (Ed.): DUXU/HCII 2013, Part III, LNCS 8014, pp. 419–426, 2013.

Many aspects of the VR system can influence the immersion and the sense of presence, such as the equipment used, the narrative context, and the quality of the Virtual Environment (VE) [2, 3].

For this paper, the focus is the navigation within VEs, in a way to explore the main aspects related to a specific navigational interface and how it can improve the sense of presence in VR-based human behavior researches.

Navigation in VR is usually done by using a joystick, keyboard and mouse or a VR wand. However, these types of devices are used as mediators between the movement of the hand with the device and the dislocation in the VE which can have a negative impact on immersion and on the sense of presence.

It is important to navigational interfaces to consider proprioceptive and vestibular cues, in a manner to provide into the VE a navigational metaphor that is more similar to the locomotion in the real world. For instance, in the study of the human wayfinding behavior, VR has been used to understand how people find their way from an origin to a destination. Most of the studies in this field use the joystick as a navigational interface (e.g., [4–6]). However, the physical cost associated with walking may influence wayfinding within complex buildings [7, 8]. Additionally, the lack of proprioceptive and vestibular cues can influence the acquisition of spatial knowledge and the development of cognitive maps [9].

For that reason, different types of interfaces are been developed with the purpose to be more natural and closer to moving in a real environment. There are implementations of real-walking interfaces (requires large spaces, since it mimics the movement made in the real world to the virtual world), treadmills (it requires an extra interface to allow people to change directions), and omni-directional treadmills (requires some space but allows people to change directions). An interesting approach to bring the displacement in VR closer to the locomotion in the real world is a Walk-In-Place (WIP) interface due to the fact that it can be used on a confined space and depending on the implementation allows the participant to do a full rotation to choose direction.

Studies on human behavior using VR are done in the Ergonomics Laboratory of the Technical University of Lisbon, using the ErgoVR system [10] and focusing on behavioral compliance with signs and warnings, and wayfinding within buildings, in both everyday and emergency situations. For these types of studies, it is critical to promote the participants' behaviors which are closer to those they would have in the real world, in order to produce reliable data. So, allowing people to interact with the VE as they interact with the real world (i.e., walking and rotating as they would wandering in a real environment) could enhance the interaction quality and contributing to behavioral responses closer to those attained in real world researches.

Framework in Walk-In-Place Interfaces for VR Systems. With the growth of studies on human behavior using VR, the need of navigational interfaces that are more natural and closer to moving in a real environment increases as navigation can be considered one of the key tasks for the interaction with VEs [11]. A solution to enhance the sensation of walking in VEs is a WIP interface, which provides users with a realistic sensation of walking while moving in the VE, and without the need of large real physical space. Thus, users move up and down their foot as they were walking in the same place. This technique was introduced by Slater and colleagues [12], and since then it was used considering some different approaches (for a review see [13]).

As pointed by Terziman and colleagues [13], most of the applications consider the interaction with immersive VEs and mainly the use of Head-Mounted Displays (HMD). Studies considering WIP interfaces involve the movement acquisition and translation into the VE. Generally, motion trackers are used to capture the motions of body segments in order to be translated in movements inside the VE. First studies tracked the head movements to predict and detect the steps (e.g., [12, 14, 15]). The main disadvantage of this approach is that the movement direction is conditioned by the head direction, impeding users to look to a direction while moving in another.

To overcome this, other studies were conducted by tracking the lower body segments, such as knees [16], legs (e.g., [17]) shins and heels [18, 19]. In the study carried out by Templeman and colleagues [16], the distance and direction of the legs were tracked by 6DOF trackers attached to the knees and the motion of legs was detected by force sensors placed on shoe insoles. Yan and colleagues [17] used a hybrid acoustic-inertial 6DOF position and orientation tracking system with three sensors (two for the legs and one for the abdomen) and four sonistrips. For the Feasel and colleagues [18] study, three magnetic 6DOF sensors were used, being two positioned on the users' heels and the other one on the chest.

Motion capture cameras were used by Wendt and colleagues [19]. For their study, the user wears beacons for 6DOF trackers on his shins, which were tracked by cameras placed on the floor.

The use of the WIP technique was later adapted to be used by desktop VR [13]. For this case, head movements were captured by a webcam while users were sitting in front of the desktop and translated into lateral, vertical and roll motion.

It is important to notice that most of the WIP interfaces found in the literature use more than one sensor to track the user's displacement and rotation. Besides, they generally use magnetic sensors. This type of sensors may have high interferences with magnetic fields, which also limit the laboratory settings configuration. The use of motion capture through cameras is an alternative which can become unfeasible in small spaces and also needing a clear line of sight between the cameras and the participant.

Considering this, the objective of this paper is to provide information regarding strategies for the development process found in implementing a WIP interface using only one inertial orientation sensor (3DOF).

2   Development

A WIP interface could be the most suitable interface to be used in the studies about human behavior as it provides some proprioceptive feedback and increases the sense of presence, leading users to act in VEs as they would in the real world, requiring, at the same time, small physical space to be implemented.

The WIP interface is mostly based on allowing a person to walk on the same place, detect that motion and translate that to movement inside the virtual world. As mentioned before, a WIP interface can be implemented by detecting the motion in different manners, by using camera-based motion capture systems or using motion sensors.

The approach taken for the development of the ErgoVR's WIP interface was to use only one orientation sensor (3DOF) to control the users' displacement and direction in the VE.

2.1   ErgoVR's Walk-In-Place Interface

The ErgoVR WIP interface comprises an inertial sensor (i.e., XSens MTx) placed above the user's left/ right knee.

In a first approach, the main measure considered to translate the tracked body movement into the displacement and direction within the virtual world for the WIP interface is the amplitude differences between the rotation values given by the sensor (as can be seen on Figure 1), considering the Euler angles (i.e., yaw, pitch and roll), as shown on Figure 2. The orientation values were the ones that gave more differences in amplitude what seemed to be more appropriate to differentiate between a small, involuntary movement and a bigger, intentional movement that should represent the beginning of motion.

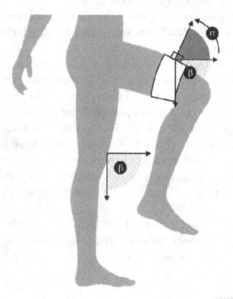

Fig. 1. The angular measurements used to translate the tracked body into the movement within the VE. α represents the difference between the rotation values given by the sensor when the leg is lifted.

Thus, the ErgoVR's WIP interface works by detecting variations on the orientation values, which are represented by the leg's movements, and determine the amount of time that passes between the moments in which the leg is lifted in order to calculate the speed value to be used in the VE.

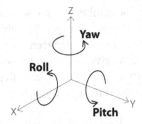

Fig. 2. The representation of the axes of the yaw, pitch and roll

The ErgoVR's WIP interface needs to be used in two modes: *Calibration* and *Real-time detection.*

Calibration Mode. Since each individual has different kinetic features, the WIP interface needs to be calibrated for each person. The approach used to do the calibration process passes by, after positioning the sensor above the participant's knee, asking him/her for making the walk movement in the same place during a controlled amount of time (i.e., five seconds). All measures recorded during this interval are processed to determine two main areas, which represent when the leg is lifted or when it is in the rest position for a specific participant, as it can be seen on Figure 3 (dimensionless data presented). A Gaussian Mixture Model (GMM) is used to determine the two areas mentioned, and an Expectation-Maximization algorithm is used for fitting the GMM to the collected data during the calibration. After fitting the GMM, the system has information on the interval of values that are considered the area of values where the leg is lifted (α) and the area of values where the leg is in the rest position (β).

It is important to refer that, due to fatigue and natural drifts in the data collected from the motion sensor, the calibration done in the beginning of the process can become inaccurate. To prevent that situation, the calibration process is re-done by the system that analyses the data, updating the calibration information (the new positions of the areas α and β) in parallel to the real-time detection, while the person is walking and interacting with the VE.

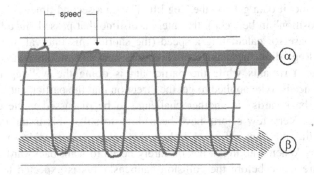

Fig. 3. The graphic model of the translated body movement tracked by the sensor with the two areas which represent the lifted (α) and rest (β) position of the leg of a specific participant (dimensionless data because it changes per participant).

Real-Time Detection. After the calibration phase, the system already has the expected intervals of orientation values for a specific subject, and can use that as a base for detecting the movement and change the current speed to the avatar in the VE. The system attributes each data that receives from the motion sensor into a category (*leg is lifted, leg is in the rest position, in between*) and depending on the previous data points, it would start counting the time until the data points return to that category for then calculate a speed value.

Since the values of speed gathered could be very different from the previous one, the speed is calculated taking that into consideration and giving a filtered value to prevent abrupt changes of speed.

The direction of the movement is given by the changes on the Yaw axis. The base direction is gathered at the calibration moment. However, during the walking movement, there are some variations of values on that axis. Therefore, to have the most correct value for the direction, a smoothing filter needs to be applied to the incoming stream of data.

3   Discussion

There are some studies (e.g., [20, 21]) that present test experiments of Walk-In-Place (WIP) implementations when compared with other types of navigational interfaces (e.g., joystick). However, no information regarding how these systems were implemented in regard to the approach taken on the development process was found in the literature.

As such, this paper presents some strategies for the development process of a WIP interface which uses only one inertial sensor, to be used in studies about human behavior, mainly considering the behavioral compliance with signs and warnings, and wayfinding issues.

One of the strategies used to detect the movement of the leg was to observe the orientation value changes during time and define two areas where we can consider the data to be on the "leg lifted" area or the "leg on rest position" area (calibration). From that, in real-time, if data gets on the "leg lifted" area a second time (being on the "leg on the rest position" in between), the interval of time that passed since the first entry is used as a base for calculating a speed (the shorter this interval, the faster is the movement). Regarding the change of direction, and due to some variations on the values on the Yaw axis while the participant is doing the walking movement, a smooth filter needs to be applied to get the direction that the participant is facing.

"Moving backwards" is another challenge to be discussed while developing a WIP interface. Very few efforts have been done to solve this issue and it was not found in the literature any reference to how this behavior is considered when using a WIP interface. When walking, a person rarely needs to walk backwards, because the corrections are made before the collision happens. This is expected to happen also when using a WIP interface. However, there might be some situations where the participant might need to make small corrections of movement and taking a step back in the VE. As a possible solution, it could be allowed that the participant positioned the leg with the sensor as it would be taking a step back and maintain in that position until it feels that the intended distance (in backwards movement) was made. Unfortunately this strategy also has a limitation which is not allowing the control of the speed of the movement, being that defined by the interface. Also, as it does not represent the real behavior, it could interfere in the immersion due to the fact that participants will have to think about the movement instead of naturally doing it.

As for future work, a full validation of the interface needs to be done. The individual movements should be validated inside a Virtual Environment by asking participants to complete specific tasks such as to follow a specific path (which has direction changes) in the middle of some obstacles that might require participants to make correctional direction changes by moving backwards. The duration of the experiment, as well as the number of those small corrections, bumps into objects are going to be taken into account. The same path should also be compared with other types of navigational interfaces for Virtual Reality (i.e., joystick). Also, a presence and immersion questionnaire should be applied. As proprioceptive and vestibular cues are linked with the development of cognitive maps, this could be also considered while comparing WIP interface with other navigational devices.

Acknowledgements. A PhD scholarship from Portuguese Science Foundation (FCT) supported this study (SFRH/BD/65216/2009), which was developed in the scope of a Research Project financed by FCT (PTDC/PSI- PCO/100148/2008).

References

1. Witmer, B.G., Singer, M.J.: Measuring Presence in Virtual Environments: A Presence Questionnaire. Presence Teleoperators Virtual Environments 7, 225–240 (1998)
2. Gorini, A., Capideville, C.S., De Leo, G., Mantovani, F., Riva, G.: The role of immersion and narrative in mediated presence: the virtual hospital experience. Cyberpsychology Behavior and Social Networking 14, 99–105 (2011)
3. Gutierrez, M., Vexo, F., Thalmann, D.: Stepping into Virtual Reality. Springer-Verlag TELOS, Santa Clara (2008)
4. Conroy-Dalton, R.: Spatial Navigation in Immersive Virtual Environments, Unpublished Thesis, University of London (2001)
5. Vilar, E., Rebelo, F., Noriega, P.: Indoor human wayfinding performance using vertical and horizontal signage in virtual reality. In: Human Factors and Ergonomics in Manufacturing & Service Industries. John Wiley & Sons, Inc. (2012)
6. Vilar, E., Rebelo, F., Noriega, P., Teles, J., Mayhorn, C.: The influence of environmental features on route selection in an emergency situation. Applied Ergonomics 44(4), 618–627 (2013)
7. Hochmair, H.H.: Towards a classification of route selection criteria for route planning tools. In: Developments in Spatial Data Handling, pp. 481–492. Springer, Berlin (2004)
8. Pingel, T.: Strategic elements of route choice, Unpublished Thesis, University of California, Santa Barbara (2010)
9. Cánovas, R., Espínola, M., Iribarne, L., Cimadevilla, J.M.: A new virtual task to evaluate human place learning. Behavioural Brain Research 190, 112–118 (2008)

10. Teixeira, L., Rebelo, F., Filgueiras, E.: Human interaction data acquisition software for virtual reality: A user-centered design approach. In: Kaber, D.B., Boy, G. (eds.) Advances in Cognitive Ergonomics. Advances in Human Factors and Ergonomics Series, pp. 793–801. CRC Press/Taylor & Francis, Ltd., Miami, Florida (2010)

11. Bowman, D., Kruijff, E., LaViola, J., Poupyrev, I.: 3D user interfaces: theory and practice (2005)

12. Slater, M., Usoh, M., Steed, A.: Taking steps: the influence of a walking technique on presence in virtual reality. ACM Trans. Comput.-Hum. Interact. 2, 201–219 (1995)

13. Terziman, L., Marchal, M., Emily, M., Multon, F., Arnaldi, B., Lécuyer, A.: Shake-your-head: revisiting walking-in-place for desktop virtual reality. In: Proceedings of the 17th ACM Symposium on Virtual Reality Software and Technology, pp. 27–34. ACM, New York (2010)

14. Razzaque, S., Swapp, D., Slater, M.: Redirected walking in place. In: Mueller, S., Stuezlinger, W. (eds.) EGVE 2002 Proceedings of the Workshop on Virtual Environments 2002, pp. 123–130. Eurographics Association, Barcelona (2002)

15. Usoh, M., Arthur, K., Whitton, M.C., Bastos, R., Steed, A., Slater, M., Brooks, F.P.: Walking > walking-in-place > flying, in virtual environments. In: Proceedings of the 26th Annual Conference on Computer Graphics and Interactive Techniques - SIGGRAPH, vol. 1999, pp. 359–364 (1999)

16. Templeman, J.N., Denbrook, P.S., Sibert, L.E.: Virtual Locomotion: Walking in Place through Virtual Environments. Presence Teleoperators and Virtual Environments 8, 598–617 (1999)

17. Yan, L., Allison, R.S., Rushton, S.K.: New Simple Virtual Walking Method – Walking on the Spot. In: 8th Annual Immersive Projection Technology (IPT) Symposium Electronic Proceedings (2004)

18. Feasel, J., Whitton, M.C., Wendt, J.D.: LLCM-WIP: Low-Latency, Continuous-Motion Walking-in-Place. In: 2008 IEEE Symposium on 3D User Interfaces, pp. 97–104 (2008)

19. Wendt, J.D., Whitton, M.C., Brooks, F.P.: GUD WIP: Gait-Understanding-Driven Walking-In-Place. In: 2010 IEEE Virtual Reality Conference (VR), pp. 51–58 (2010)

20. Peck, T.C., Fuchs, H., Whitton, M.C.: An Evaluation of Navigational Ability Comparing Redirected Free Exploration with Distractors to Walking-in-Place and Joystick Locomotion Interfaces. In: Proceedings/IEEE Virtual Reality Conference; Sponsored by IEEE Computer Society Technical Committee on Visualization and Graphics. IEEE Virtual Reality Conference, pp. 55–62 (2011)

21. Ruddle, R.A., Volkova, E., Bülthoff, H.H.: Learning to Walk in Virtual Reality. ACM Transactions on Applied Perception (2013)

Part IV

Emotional and Persuasion Design

Exhibiting Emotion: Capturing Visitors' Emotional Responses to Museum Artefacts

Genevieve Alelis, Ania Bobrowicz, and Chee Siang Ang

School of Engineering and Digital Arts
University of Kent, Jennison Building, Canterbury, Kent, CT2 7NT UK
{ga209,a.bobrowicz,C.S.Ang}@kent.ac.uk

Abstract. The museum provides the perfect setting for the convergence of culture, reflection, personal connections, and communication, and many museums supplement these visitor experiences through the use of Human-Computer Interaction (HCI) systems. While there has been past HCI research on various combinations of these four areas, the overall goal of this study is to explore the emotional links museum visitors make while encompassing all four areas through the use of engaging HCI technologies. This paper reports on the results of a study carried out at the Powell-Cotton Museum, a local ethnographic museum located in south-east Kent, UK. Using structured interviews and thematic analysis, visitors' emotional responses to museum artefacts were analysed. Findings suggest that when given the task of providing emotional responses to artefacts, visitors are motivated to find meaningful and personal connections.

Keywords: cultural artefacts, emotion, heritage, meaning-making, story-telling.

1 Introduction

While the understanding of visitors' requirements and learning has always been an important part of a museum's focus and research, recent studies on emotions have proven that designing for emotion is a valid form of learning; by integrating emotion with learning objectives, museums can create a more personal experience which can lead to repeat visits, donations in the form of time and money, and free advertising by content visitors [1,2]. Studies focusing on the emotions experienced both within and outside a museum have analyzed how objects and products affected participants; however, results thus far have not been applied to HCI systems in a heritage environment or considered the personal stories behind the connections. Due to an individual's specific background, these applications are ideal as the differences result in unique and even contrasting ways of connecting with an object.

Although previous applications allow visitors to select their emotional response through an interface, they are limited in the feedback they accept in addition to lacking the capacity to assist with understanding the cause of an emotion. Museums have increasingly invested in mobile devices and they should be utilized to their full advantage of allowing visitors to share many different configurations of responses. The aim

A. Marcus (Ed.): DUXU/HCII 2013, Part III, LNCS 8014, pp. 429–438, 2013.
© Springer-Verlag Berlin Heidelberg 2013

of this study is to determine how museum visitors emotionally engage with artefacts, the results of which will be used to develop a mobile system that supports the understanding of emotions through personal connections and stories. This paper will first present previous research on the influence of objects on emotions and the diverse HCI implementations of measuring emotions. Next, the methodology used to gather and analyse the data will be discussed, followed by the results. Finally, a conclusion will be drawn and potential applications will be suggested.

2   Related Work

2.1   Influence of Objects on Emotions

There have been prior investigations regarding emotional responses to objects both within and outside of the museum context; this includes the emotions generated solely by images of products without taking into consideration the application of the product [3], discussions on the types of situations where an object influenced emotions [4], visitors' understanding of and responses to exhibitions [5], and museums that design exhibits in order to generate a specific emotional response from the audience [1]. To date, research focusing on discovering the connections between an individual's personal history and an emotional response to an object is lacking. When an audience consists of people with different backgrounds and experiences, it is likely that they will have various opinions and interpretations of an object. Similarly, research shows that an object does not have one inherent meaning; rather, it is an individual who applies meaning to it based on personal connections made through memories, culture, and beliefs [6]. Correspondingly, recent results confirm that emotion is generated through the internal representation of an object, with assistance from its aesthetic properties and what they signify [7]. Falk and Dierking observed that "the dominant motivation for humans is meaning-making" and as such, recommend that museums combine emotion with learning into their exhibits [8]. A combination of these concepts which can be applied to objects in any environment can be found in the framework for product experience consisting of three levels: aesthetic experience, experience of meaning, and emotional experience [9]. This framework relies on the user being able to interact with the product in some way. Each of these levels overlaps to shape the experience between a user and product, allowing the visitor to be more pro-active when interacting with artefacts, whether directly or indirectly though technology.

2.2   HCI Implementations of Measuring Emotion

Within a museum, early implementations of engaging technology which let visitors reflect on their visit and share their interpretations with others were successful in encouraging interactions with the exhibits. In the PEACH project which took place in Italy's Buonconsiglio Castle, the goal of the designers was to create a guiding system that can personalize a visit through the interpretation of visitors' feelings. This implementation of a mobile device was non-obtrusive with an easy to understand interface. Several modes of emotional input were tested before deciding on one which gave the user two-degrees of freedom, either positive or negative, by requiring them to indicate their "degree of interest" through the movement of a slider either to the left towards a sad face icon or the right towards a happy face icon. This met the requirements researchers had of enabling users to easily express their approval using an intuitive, transparent system [10,11]. However, this system was bound by fixed selection choices; a better system would acknowledge the breadth and depth of potential feedback by accommodating a more unrestricted yet streamlined form of participation.

Obtaining visitors' reactions to a particular exhibit in a museum through text was one of the main elements of the ArtLinks system at the Herbert F. Johnson Museum of Art at Cornell University, which aimed to help users make connections to the exhibit as well as with other visitors, encourage reflection, and do this with transparency. It was found that for some users, using text to express their opinions to the exhibit "caused them to have a more cognitive and less emotional reaction than they otherwise would" [12].

Encompassing both tagging and navigational tools, the MobiTags system in the Johnson Museum of Art at Cornell University was a web application designed to "integrate social, spatial, and semantic navigation". Through the process of selecting or inputting tags, visitors were encouraged to find themes and understand collections but the tags were not specifically related to how the object made them feel; visitors could choose or input any tag depending on their opinion of the object [13].-

Outside of a museum setting, emotion-capturing HCI research was also being explored. In the MobiMood system, Russell's Circumplex Model of Affect [14] was used to represent the different moods available for users to select through buttons on the interface but while users can input both the intensity of each mood together with a custom mood, this system is limited in the type of engagement it gives the user [15]. Russell's Circumplex Model of Affect influenced the MoodSense interface through its use of two sliders representing the two dimensions of pleasantness and arousal, and the resulting emotion is characterized on the screen as the values change. This appears to be a more engaging system than the MobiMood system but it still not deliver diverse interaction with the system other than repeatedly moving the sliders [16]. Likewise, the Pictorial Mood Reporting Instrument (PMRI) modeled its system on Russell's Circumplex Model of Affect by creating a character with facial expressions representing nine different moods and arranging them in a two dimensional circular space, but certain expressions either overlap or are indistinguishable with another, which can cause problems when using this system for response reporting [17]. iFelt was one of the few systems that incorporates Ekman's [18], Russell's, and Plutchik's [19] emotion findings; the basic emotions were represented by different colours which were then organized into a circular spatial model. In turn, this was an engaging and interactive system. Currently, it only classifies emotional responses to movies but it shows that these three emotion models can work together to create an informative, visual interface [20].

3   Methodology

Eleven females and nine males participated in the study over the time period between July 2012 and August 2012 at the Powell-Cotton Museum. Visitors who were at least 18 years old were invited to participate. All were informed of the entire process when they were asked to participate, including the expected duration of the one-on-one interview which would take no longer than 20 minutes. Emphasis was placed on voluntary participation, freedom to withdraw from the study at any time, and agreement to have the interview audio recorded.

An Emotional Response Log was then provided to each visitor at the start of the visit along with simple instructions on how to complete it. The Emotional Response Log, an A5-sized booklet, was designed to be a portable yet informative method of capturing visitor responses. In the log, visitors were instructed to provide their initial emotional responses for up to 5 different museum artefacts to which they felt a strong reaction. The log contained the following sections: Gallery Number, Artefact Name or Number, Emotion Felt, and Additional Comments. Within the Emotion Felt section there were six emotions listed: Anger, Disgust, Fear, Happy, Sad, and Surprise, which was taken from Ekman's research on universal facial expressions of emotions [18]. Two additional options were added: "Indifferent" captured any responses that were neutral and "Other" allowed visitors to write any emotions that were not already listed. Visitors were asked to circle as many emotions as they felt in response to an artefact. After they finished their visit, they were directed to a quiet area of the museum where the interview and filling of the demographic questionnaire and consent form took place.

A demographic questionnaire of ten questions was intended to obtain an overview of the type of visitors that participated and seek information about whether or not they have access to a smartphone. Each of the five interview questions was designed to give the participants an opportunity to explain why they chose certain artefacts and felt particular emotional responses when viewing them. Further aims were to discover any personal connections and stories visitors remembered while feeling the emotions. Data was collected from visitors who completed the Emotional Response Log and participated in the interview. Information was kept anonymous and given only a number to associate the Emotional Response Log, interview responses, demographic questionnaire, and consent form to the same participant.

Overall, the interviews totaled 231 minutes, providing 26 different emotional responses to 55 unique artefacts. These interviews were transcribed, uploaded into the qualitative data analysis software NVivo, and read in order to gain an understanding of the responses. Thematic analysis was used to identify patterns in the data by iteratively creating a node in NVivo for each new theme that emerged until no further themes could be found within the interviews [21]. The themes were then organized into high-level themes and subthemes using thematic analysis techniques [22]. The coding scheme was validated by an external researcher who read a sampling of interviews and coded them according to the scheme; the results corresponded to the original coding and themes.

4   Findings and Discussion

In total, twenty museum visitors participated by completing the Emotional Response Log and one-on-one interview. A summary of the demographics is presented in Table 1.

Table 1. Participant Demographics Summary

Demographic Variables		# of Participants
Gender	Female	11
	Male	9
Age	18-24	4
	25-34	3
	35-44	2
	45-54	5
	55-64	5
	65+	1
Access to smartphone?	Yes	11
	No	9
Type of smartphone	Android	1
	Blackberry	3
	iPhone	7

4.1   Themes

The themes discovered when visitors described how the artefacts affected them can be categorized as Attitude Towards the Past, Learning Opportunity, Linking the Past with Present Equivalent, New Experience, and Personal History. Each theme represents a personal connection made with an artefact which resulted in the emotion(s) felt, with some categories overlapping to provide unique visitor experiences. More often than not, an interview consisted of several themes.

Attitude Towards the Past

The Attitude Towards the Past theme represents visitors' impressions of the time period when the artefacts were collected or created. This can be further divided into Ethics and Ingenuity, two subthemes that represent the negative and positive feelings towards the past respectively. Seventeen participants' interviews included references to ethics while 10 mentioned ingenuity when speaking about an artefact. Under Ethics, three main arguments occur: Blame, Life Unfulfilled, and Senseless Result. Participants placed blame on several different motives: Educational Purposes, Entitlement, and Ignorance. Some of the educational purposes mentioned were for scientific reasons and preservation for the future:

"[T]oday's tigers, [...] they're not many of them, so whenever you see a tiger that was shot for any purpose whatsoever, it makes you [feel] mixed feelings, sad, obviously at the time it was done, back in the 1800s, 19th century, th[is] was the done

thing because people didn't know what impact that would have on nature and the species and everything else...I suppose it was a positive thing, it was done for science [...] so that justifies some of it"

There was a sense of bitterness when visitors talked about entitlement regarding people who had the means to obtain these types of artefacts:

"I would imagine that when [hunter and collector Major Powell-Cotton] set out, at that time it was regarded as a great adventure and there was so much wildlife that they would think, ok, so you kill a couple hundred elephants, so what [...]so I think you have to accept what's in the cages is a reflection of its time [...] But I suppose if you were representative of the British Empire, you were rich, you did what you wanted to"

Ignorance was mentioned by 10 visitors, the most out of the subthemes under Blame. In particular, a few stated that in some cases, this ignorance could have led to extinction. Visitors whose emotions were linked to Life Unfulfilled claimed that the ownership of the artefact interfered with a way of life or killed a living being. Fifteen visitors had comments which fell under this subtheme.

Last, Senseless Result contains comments relating to how meaningless the resulting artefact was to them compared to the means required to obtain in, since all that was left were trophies, or as a few participants mentioned, just a head separated from the body.

Learning Opportunity
Learning Opportunity indicates that visitors either learned new information during their visit or viewed an object that made them think. A total of 19 participants had stories which were related to a learning opportunity, with some gaining knowledge and others providing commentary on why certain artefacts were thought-provoking. Some of these thought-provoking items produced meaningful reflection which connected the design of the artefact with an intended message:

"I thought it was a good play on things, first of all, porcelain, quite delicate, and the gun shape, really just contrasting between delicates and violence and stuff like that. I think it was really good because it voiced how a war would be if that makes sense, so delicate like people and stuff, them being the porcelain and the gun shape being the armies"

Other artefacts raised questions that the museum did not answer through their display or exhibit label, such as how or why an artefact was made or used:

"I was a bit dumbfounded as to how it was used. There wasn't enough for me, explanations...why, how it could be used. It was so big, if I was to pick it up I would fall over, so there must be some sort of stand or support system for it, or maybe they put it

*on their shoulder when they fired it. It's huge, so it's a slight sort-of, hmmm, that's
amazing but how do they do it"*

Visitors did not learn new information without also experiencing an additional
theme, which is understandable since learning involves the application of the new
knowledge.

Linking the Past with Present Equivalent
Linking the Past with Present Equivalent explains how visitors either associated an
artefact to a modern day equivalent object or task or interacted with a modern equivalent of the artefact viewed. Fifteen participants made this connection between the past
and present.

Associations made between the artefact viewed and a modern equivalent typically
involved ordinary objects that can be found in everyday life, such as cooking tools,
jewelry, pipes, and decorative items:

*"[I]t was called a meat cutting board, and I was fascinated to see [...] it was only
the 1900s, but I was so fascinated to see that in those countries that their meat they
used actually had a tenderizer on it as well [...] and it was being used [...]in villages
by the women to prepare dinner in the same way we would use in our modern day
kitchens"*

Interactions were usually situated in zoos or on safaris, where it is common to see
comparable animals alive in surroundings similar to the displays.

New Experience
New Experience describes the different ways visitors experienced something new in
the museum; they could have had no prior knowledge of or experience with the artefact, they might see the artefact as unexpected, or they could have had a vicarious
experience. In total, 12 participants said they had a new experience during their visit.
Of that number, most visitors felt they were seeing something they most likely will
never see in real life, particularly the animals. They also imagined themselves picking
up the artefacts or using them, which affected the way they felt about the artefact:

*"[I]n my younger years, days before going to university I did work in various jobs
in factories and so therefore I'm aware of spending hours doing a job like that at a
machine and also building up skills, so there's a part of me wondering what I would
have felt like if I would have been operating the thing and how tired I would have felt,
that's all, so there's a bit of empathy with them"*

Some artefacts were unexpected because of their size in the museum, regardless of
whether or not they were larger or smaller than expected. Other items were unexpected because visitors thought they seemed out of place within the museum, such as
a "wig for men". In addition, there were items in which visitors had never seen before

or did not know exist, meaning they either had no prior knowledge or experience with them. These unexpected and new artefacts positively affected emotional responses.

Personal History

Personal History is related to one's identity and includes factors that make each individual different. All 20 of the participants mentioned stories which fall within this theme, the only theme to involve everyone. The subthemes include Childhood, Job, Knowledge Acquired, and Sense of Self. When visitors recalled memories of their childhood, they usually viewed the artefacts positively whether the artefact was intact, such as whole animals, or whether it was just a leg bone. One's past job was also brought up by a few visitors as a connection when viewing an artefact, which affected them positively. Even if the past job was in the army and the artefact lead to death, if the deaths had a positive role in history, then the general feeling was positive:

"[I]t's a bit difficult to explain, things bring back, when I read, look up things like luger guns I think of all the people the Germans or the SS killed with lugers in the war [...] so very positive, that's why these things, I know all about these things and what effect they've had on human beings in this world, and what, guns may have a positive role in the war"

Knowledge Acquired was mentioned by 13 visitors and encompasses the following subthemes: Books, Media (as in TV or Film), Prior Knowledge in General, and School. Artefacts such as weapons and animals were predictably associated with this theme as it is not common to encounter them or learn about them elsewhere. These subthemes encouraged comparisons between what was learned and what was in front of them, prompting a wide variety of emotions. Recognizing a version of an artefact from a television show or film seemed to have a positive effect on the visitors while seeing one from a documentary or news program had a negative or neutral effect. Sense of Self was mentioned by 13 visitors and includes Family, Female or Motherhood, Opinion or Subconscious, and Residency. Since these are tied to identity, the strength of the emotions felt was strong irrespective of the type of emotion experienced.

4.2   Emotions

When specifying the emotions felt, there were those who felt many of the listed emotions, those who wrote in an unlisted emotion, and those who said they did not feel any emotions. As expected, there were artefacts that caused conflicting emotions, such as the animals in various states of totality and weapons, and others that were universally positive, such as the wig for men. There were some artefacts which produced no emotional response at all from some visitors, causing them to circle "Indifferent" on the Emotional Response Log or state that they felt nothing. However, during the interviews, it was evident that the artefacts left an impression on them. One individual said they selected "Indifferent" when viewing the dioramas because the animals were killed a long time ago but mentioned that he felt surprise upon seeing how large, detailed, and realistic the displays were.

In all, 11 out of the 55 unique artefacts chosen by visitors (20%) caused either indifference or no emotional response from the participant. These items were appreciated for their craftsmanship or simply because of object recognition, but seeing many of the same types of items grouped together or previously seeing similar items in other museums did not create a new experience. It can be surmised by the detail and variety of responses that the Emotional Response Log did not interfere with a visit and in fact, when combined with reflection through the interview, enhanced their overall visit.

This preliminary study will provide the basis needed to develop an engaging application which will enhance a museum experience and facilitate an understanding of why visitors are emotionally drawn to certain artefacts.

5   Conclusion and Future Work

In general, findings suggest that when given the task of providing emotional responses to artefacts, visitors are motivated to find meaningful and personal connections without relying heavily on curators, exhibit labels, and arrangement of objects. Future work on this research will include the development of a mobile device which will allow visitors to understand their emotions in response to viewing museum collections after carefully thinking about how an object makes them feel, recalling a related memory, or connecting it to something personal in their lives. The inclusion of a contextual visualization will allow the sharing of responses with others along with the comparison of emotions regarding the same artifacts and even view personal connections and stories. These results can be applied to various types of museums as well as mobile devices involving user-product relationships where the need for personalization and emotional connections is a fundamental part of the design.

Acknowledgements. We would like to thank the Powell-Cotton Museum and its staff for their support, along with the museum visitors who participated in this study. We appreciate the time and feedback provided for this research.

References

1. Gadsby, J.: The Effect of Encouraging Emotional Value in Museum Experiences. Museological Review 15, 1–13 (2011)
2. Suchy, S.: Museum Management: Emotional Value and Community Engagement. In: INTERCOM 2006, Taiwan (2006)
3. Desmet, P.: Designing Emotions: Delft University of Technology, Department of Industrial Design (2002)
4. Hiort af Ornäs, V.: Emotive User-Artefact Relations. Paper read at 3rd Nordcode Seminar & Workshop, Lyngby, Denmark, Technical University of Denmark, April 28-30 (2004)

5. Krmpotich, C., Anderson, D.: Collaborative Exhibitions and Visitor Reactions: The Case of Nitsitapiisinni: Our Way of Life. Curator: The Museum Journal 48(4), 377–405 (2005)
6. Weil, S.E.: The Museum and the Public. In: Making Museums Matter. Smithsonian Institution Press, Washington (2002)
7. van Gorp, T., Adams, E.: Design for Emotion. Elsevier Science (2012)
8. Falk, J.H., Dierking, L.D.: Learning from Museums: Visitor Experiences and the Making of Meaning. AltaMira Press (2000)
9. Desmet, P., Hekkert, P.: Framework of Product Experience (2007)
10. Goren-Bar, D., Graziola, I., Kuflik, T., Pianesi, F., Rocchi, C., Stock, O., Zancanaro, M.: I like it – An Affective Interface for a Multimodal Museum Guide. Paper read at In CHI Workshop on Evaluating Affective Interfaces, CHI (2005)
11. Rocchi, C., Stock, O., Zancanaro, M.: Adaptivity in Museum Mobile Guides: The Peach Experience. Paper Read at Proceedings of the Mobile Guide 2006, Turin, Italy (2006)
12. Cosley, D., Lewenstein, J., Herman, A., Holloway, J., Baxter, J., Nomura, S., Boehner, K., Gay, G.: ArtLinks: Fostering Social Awareness and Reflection in Museums. In: Proceedings of the Twenty-Sixth Annual SIGCHI Conference on Human Factors in Computing Systems. ACM, Florence (2008)
13. Cosley, D., Baxter, J., Lee, I., Alson, B., Nomura, S., Adams, B., Sarabu, C., Gay, G.: A Tag in The Hand: Supporting Semantic, Social, and Spatial Navigation in Museums. In: Proceedings of the 27th International Conference on Human Factors in Computing Systems. ACM, Boston (2009)
14. Russell, J.: A Circumplex Model of Affect. Journal of Personality and Social Psychology 39, 1161–1178 (1980)
15. Church, K., Hoggan, E., Oliver, N.: A Study of Mobile Mood Awareness and Communication Through MobiMood. Paper read at Proceedings of the 6th Nordic Conference on Human-Computer Interaction: Extending Boundaries (2010)
16. LiKamWa, R., Liu, Y., Lane, N.D., Zhong, L.: Can Your Smartphone Infer Your Mood? Paper read at in PhoneSense 2011, Seattle, Washington (2011)
17. Vastenburg, M., Herrera, N.R., Van Bel, D., Desmet, P.: PMRI: Development of a Pictorial Mood Reporting Instrument. In: Proceedings of the 2011 Annual Conference Extended Abstracts on Human Factors in Computing Systems. ACM, Vancouver (2011)
18. Ekman, P.: Universals and Cultural Differences in Facial Expressions of Emotion. University of California (1971)
19. Plutchik, R.: The Nature of Emotions. American Scientist 89(4), 344 (2001)
20. Oliveira, E., Martins, P., Chambel, T.: iFelt: Accessing Movies Through Our Emotions. In: Proceddings of the 9th International Interactive Conference on Interactive Television. ACM, Lisbon (2011)
21. Aronson, J.: A Pragmatic View of Thematic Analysis. The Qualitative Report 2, 1 (1994)
22. Ryan, G., Bernard, R.: Techniques to Identify Themes. Field Methods 15, 85–109 (2003)

Blinklifier: A Case Study for Prototyping Wearable Computers in Technology and Visual Arts

Katia Fabiola Canepa Vega[1], Patricia J. Flanagan[2], and Hugo Fuks[1]

[1] Department of Informatics, PUC-Rio
{kvega,hugo}@inf.puc-rio.br
[2] Academy of Visual Arts, HKBU
flanagan@hkbu.edu.hk

Abstract. The Cybernetic Serendipity exhibition in 1968 [1] and the Computer in Art book in 1971[2] represent some remarkable initial approaches in collaborative art-technology projects. Over the years, projects have evolved through thinking influenced by other areas such as psychology, sociology and philosophy. Much of art theory and practice is exploratory and its outcomes may be challenging. The advent of novel materials and increasingly evolution of smaller and more affordable electronic components made it possible for anyone to make their own wearable devices. Moreover, people with different skills get together and share their knowledge to create new products. This work describes our prototyping process for developing wearable computers in multidisciplinary teams. In this paper, we present the implementation of our collaborative and iterative prototyping process in the development of Blinklifier, an art and technology project that amplifies human expressions and creates a feedback loop with the wearer.

Keywords: Wearable Computers, Feedback Loops, Blank Model Prototyping.

1 Introduction

The electronic culture has being shaping how artists express their artworks. The facilities to create wearable computers have increased the number of new media artists that experiment with wearable computers and sensor technology to create electronic interfaces between bodies and their environments. At the junction between science and art, these works coincide with the refinement of contemporary post human and cyborg discourses and establishes personal interaction among the users.

Since the rinse of movements like open source hardware and do-it-yourself, people with totally to no science background are taking a proactive interest in science, technology and knowledge-sharing. Wearable computers is one of the fields that this people try to achieve but it requires a combination of multi-faceted factors like electronic efficiency, electrical safety, programming development, physical comfort and aesthetics of the garment. Thus, for successful designing of wearable computers, the traditional development process must be modifying in order to include appropriate steps for multidisciplinary creation.

A. Marcus (Ed.): DUXU/HCII 2013, Part III, LNCS 8014, pp. 439–445, 2013.
© Springer-Verlag Berlin Heidelberg 2013

We propose the use the Effective Prototyping for Software Makers [3], a prototyping process that was customized for the development of wearable computers in multidisciplinary teams. Blank Model Prototyping is presented as the method used in the early stages of the wearable prototyping. This method encourage participants to get the first impressions and ideas about the solution, either hardware or software and to process their ideas. It unleash them to go forward an illuminating step toward understanding what is going to be developed and how it will function. For exemplifying this exploration, Blinklifier [4] was prototyped, a wearable device that senses and amplifies our reflex of blinking. Blinklifier was developed by a multidisciplinary tem, combining arts and technology.

2   Related Works

The design of human computer interaction has become a new challenge due to the communication asymmetries between wearable computer and desktop users [5]. Moreover, multidisciplinary teams would need to balance of design constraints between technology, the human body, human-computer interaction, and social context [6].

Smailagic et. al [7] describes an interdisciplinary design methodology for the development of wearable computer systems. This process was used with the participation of students from electrical and computer engineering, industrial design, mechanical engineering, and computer science. This process goes from defined a product cycle which ranges from perceived customer need to initial product design through detailed design to design of manufacturing, distribution, repair processes and eventually to product disposal.

Papadopoulos D. [8] outlines her experience in creating wearable computers in a team that includes a fashion designer and an electronic engineer. She highlights the misunderstanding in communication between the team members. Since the engineer feeling intimated in not understanding the deign/patterning/cutting process and reversely the designer not understands the engineering one.

Blank Model Prototyping for prototyping wearable computers intends to close the gap between the members of a multidisciplinary team, using a physical model in the early stages of the prototyping as intended hardware/software design. This prototyping method was also used by PUC-Rio for designing of a collaborative museum [9]. The process we describe in this paper is continues by this previous work.

3   Prototyping Blinklifier

This project begins with the collaboration of three artists: a Japanese painter, a Chinese fashion designer and an Australian artist. In an overseas collaboration, the Japanese-inspired painting was turned into a fashionable wearable piece and a matching wearable head dress. From this matching wearable, a new collaboration between art and technology arises in order to create Blinklifier [4], a wearable device that displays intimate data and creates a feedback loop between the wearer and the wearable. In this way, Blinklifier enriches our emotional dialogues and manages our social relations through blinking. It follows the natural eye muscles contraction and extends the motion into a visible light array. It responds to the specific eye movement patterns of the wearer and amplifies emotions that the wearer wants to communicate by presenting noticeable, exaggerated visual compositions.

Effective Prototyping for Software Makers (Figure 1) is a repeatable process where the prototyping approach depends on the analysis of the current state of requirements as well as the current needs of the organization [3]. Thus, it uses a prototyping tool, method and process given the appropriate need. An iteration consists of the four phases of this process. They will iterate until all the requirements are established.

This section explains our experience in selecting an appropriate prototyping method for developing Blinklifier. The Effective Prototyping Process proposes the following prototyping methods: Card sorting, Wireframe, Storyboard, Paper prototyping, Digital prototyping, Blank model prototyping, Video prototyping, Wizard of Oz and Coded prototyping. Blank Model Prototyping and Coded Prototyping were chosen as the prototyping methods in our multidisciplinary team (an artist and a technology designer).

Phase 1	Plan	Step 1. Verify Requirements Step 2. Develop Task Flows Step 3. Define Content and Fidelity
Phase 2	Specification	Step 4. Determine Characteristics Step 5. Choose a Method Step 6. Choose a Tool
Phase 3	Design	Step 7. Select Design Criteria Step 8. Create the Design
Phase 4	Results	Step 9. Review the Design Step 10. Validate the Design Step 11. Deploy the Design

Fig. 1. The Effective Prototyping Process [3]

3.1 Blank Model Prototyping

Blank Model Prototyping [3] is a rapid role-playing technique similar to drawing the experience but with physical models instead of drawings. The blank models are low-fidelity prototypes often made with any kind of materials like foam, clay and wooden blocks, on which research participants draw controls. This technique facilitates to envision participant's ideas and to understand the functionality of a physical device in real world scenarios. Moreover, it exposes a basic idea for the development of wearable computers, the combination between hardware and software. Blank Model

Prototyping is used to elicit user perceptions and mental models about hardware form factors and interaction controls in conjunction with a software user interface.

In the first iterations of Blinklifier, Blank Model Prototyping was the method chosen for the multidisciplinary team understand the idea and start developing the project due to the early stage of the project, rapid speed of the iterations for obtaining a faster feedback, the prototyping was used for clarifying the project main idea and combine art and technology aspects and the low fidelity of the prototypes. Figure 2 shows the iteration activities developed in Blank Model Prototyping Sessions.

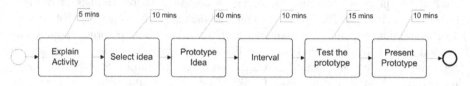

Fig. 2. Activities in the Blank Model Prototyping Sessions

The prototyping session started with an explanation of schedule and the materials to be used for the physical model. The materials used in these sessions were not only the common materials for this kind prototyping method but also conductive ink, conductive materials and other electronic components that approximate more the participants to the real model. In this way, the participants mainly discussed and understand the goal of the prototype and not just focus in the technical or design issues but also this prototyping method let them explain and discuss they own technical and artistic ideas. Then, they designed the prototype. Finally, the session was concluded with a discussion and presentation of the prototype, using the designed objects as a support.

Fig. 3. First Iteration. Prototyping conductive makeup technology

In the first iterations, the idea was to prototype conductive makeup and metalized eyelashes for amplifying human blinking. The main goal was to avoid the use of any electronic device on the wearer's face, so we prototype conductive makeup as black eyeliner and conductive false eyelashes to connect the blinking to the wearable device.

In our first iteration, the conductive makeup was prototype using conductive ink [10] (Figure 3). It was noticed that the ink is a safe material to have around the body, but it is not specifically approved for use on the skin. Even more, if the humidity of the eyes and skin could that cause issues for the wearer when the ink was dissipated.

Conductive stickers that look like makeup were created in our second iteration. A thin conductive fabric tape was used and a makeup shape was prototyped for giving it the appearance of normal makeup. The third iteration involves the prototyping of the eyelashes. We started creating false eyelashes with aluminum foils. Even the artistic results were achieved, the technical results in this iteration wasn't the desired. Also the silver color of the first eyelashes prototypes didn't match with the main goal of the project of the natural appearance of the conductive eyelashes. The eyelashes were chemically metalized with an activate and electrolysis process in order to maintain the natural black color of the eyelashes in the fourth iteration. In this iteration, the "prototype idea" activity took more time than the 40 minutes due to the time for metalizing the eyelashes with the chemical process. However, the results were achieved. All the prototypes testing included artistic aspects like the design of the eyeliner and technical aspects like the resistance of the materials on the skin.

3.2   Coded Prototyping

A coded prototype [3] is usually developed in a programming language or scripting code and should be considered as a later iteration of other forms of low and medium-fidelity prototyping. A coded prototype has the advantage of allowing the software team to productively reuse code for an actual finished product.

Blinklifier uses a multiplexing matrix of 72 LEDs to create the blinking patterns in the headpiece and is prototyped using an Arduino microcontroller [11]. This patterns were specific light arrays emitted when the wearer close the left, right and both eyes. The fifth iteration of our process was the coding of the patterns that will be shown in the LED matrix. The prototyping tool for coding was Arduino. This prototype combines hardware that displays the light arrays in the multiplexing LED matrix and software that let the technology designer to change the patterns iteratively. The artist and the technology designer evaluated the results until getting the desired patterns. Figure 4 shows the final prototype of Blinklifier.

4   Conclusion and Future Works

Our research explores the relationships between arts and technology and the implementation of a prototyping process for the creation of a wearable device for feedback loops. Blinklifier was the prototyped wearable device that amplifies human blinking, and proposes a combination of body worn objects and hidden technology to create solutions that not only appeal to our senses, but which fuse seamlessly with our everyday lives.

Even though, the multidisciplinary team faced up different barriers such as new terminology, different understandings of technological problems and different creativity processes in each area, the blank model prototyping facilitates the common perception of the main goal of the project and oriented them into a balanced understanding of how they must communicate, and the coded prototyping consolidate the ideas and made it easy to conclude the project in the last iteration.

While the participant begins to process his ideas, he begins to synthesize them and to construct a creation. During this step, the participant does not actively try a find a solution, but continues to mull over the idea. As ideas begin to mature, the participant understands how to piece his thoughts together in a manner that makes sense. The moment of illumination can happen unexpectedly. Blank Model Prototyping aims to reorganize participant's ideas and make this moment happen. Furthermore, this method encourages the participants to create a prototype collaboratively and this is a physical prototype which is more appropriate for discussing different features of wearable computers. Conductive materials and electronic components were added to the common materials of this kind of prototyping for approximating the participants to the model and get a consensus in the artistic and technical ideas.

Fig. 4. Blinklifier, a wearable computer that amplifies human blinking [4]

Acknowledgments. Patricia Flanagan was supported with the funding from Hong Kong Baptist University (HKBU) RC-NACADFLANAGAN PJ 38-40-006. Katia Vega is a PhD research candidate with grant funding by CNPq-Bazil. Hugo Fuks is the recipient of an individual grant by CNPq (302230/2008-4). This work was partially financed by UBILIFE FAPERJ/ADT1-190.116/2010,FAPERJ/INC&T (E-26/170028/2008) and CNPq/INCT (557.128/2009-9). The authors acknowledge EQA Lab for the collaboration in the development of the black false eyelashes. Blinklifier was developed in collaboration with Prof. Patricia Flanagan of the Academy of Visual Arts, Hong Kong Baptist University. Blinklifier photo by Dicky Ma.

References

1. Reichardt, J.: Cybernetic Serendipity, pp. 10–11. Studio International, London (1968)
2. Reichardt, J.: The Computer in Art (1971)
3. Arnowitz, J., Arent, M., Berger, N.: Effective Prototyping for Software Makers. Morgan Kaufmann, Elsevier, Inc. (2007)
4. Flanagan, P.J., Vega, K., Fuks, H.: Blinklifier: The power of feedback loops for amplifying expressions through bodily worn objects. In: Proceedings of APCHI 2012, The 10th Asia Pacific Conference on Computer Human Interaction, Matsue, Japan, vol. 2, pp. 641–642 (2012) ISBN 978-4-9906562-0-1
5. Billinghurst, M., Bee, S., Bowskill, J., Kato, H.: Asymmetries in collaborative wearable interfaces. In: The Third International Symposium on Wearable Computers, pp. 133–140 (1999)
6. Martin, T., Kim, K., Forsyth, J., McNair, L., Coupey, E., Dorsa, E.: An Interdisciplinary Undergraduate Design Course for Wearable and Pervasive Computing Products. In: Proc. of 15th Annual International Symposium on Wearable Computers, pp. 61–68 (2011)
7. Smailagic, A., Siewiorek, D., Anderson, D., Kasabach, C., Martin, T., Stivoric, J.: Benchmarking an Interdisciplinary Concurrent Design Methodology for Electronic/mechanical Systems. In: Proceedings of 32nd Design Automation Conference, pp. 514–519 (1995)
8. Papadopoulos, D.: Natural Language, Connectors, and Fraying Threads. In: Proceedings of the Workshop on the Role of Design in Wearable Computing, pp. 21–27 (2007)
9. Moura, H., Cardador, D., Vega, K., Ugulino, W., Barbato, M., Fuks, H.: Co-designing Collaborative Museums using Ethnography and Co-creation Workshops. In: Proceedings of VIII Simpósio Brasileiro de Sistemas Colaborativos (SBSC 2011), pp. 152–159 (2011)
10. Bare Conductive, http://www.bareconductive.com
11. Arduino, http://www.arduino.cc/

Emotional Experience and Interactive Design in the Workplace

Kuo-Pin Chen and Wen-Huei Chou

Graduate School of Computational Design
National Yunlin University of Science & Technology
123 University Road, Section 3, Douliou, Yunlin 64002, Taiwan, R.O.C
{slayer80645,cristance}@gmail.com

Abstract. The negative emotions accumulated at work are easily overlooked, and unknowingly influence our lives and health. Happy emotions, positive interactions, and pleasant experiences can all effectively provide some opportunities to prevent fatigue and mitigate negative emotions and troubles. This study uses User-Centered Design (UCD) to investigate the needs of office workers dealing with work pressure, in the hopes that improved design can improve actual working conditions. ORID and empathy maps were used to elicit relevant experience and needs from the participants. Results showed that office workers tend to a certain degree to project emotional qualities on physical aspects of their work space, including furnishings and decorations. In the second stage, the Semantic Differential Scale was used to identify research limitations and scope, and identify a clear design direction. Finally, this study presents recommendations for the appropriate application of interactive design in office environments with the aim to provide points of reference for designers working in similar areas.

Keywords: Office work stress, interactive design, emotional design, empathic design, user-centered design.

1 Introduction

Among Asian countries, people in Taiwan are known for putting in long hours at work, with workers in technology companies frequently working 12 hour days. Thus, office workers not only face rapid changes in technology and work patterns, but also face great pressure to work long hours. With workers spending more time at the office than nearly anyplace else, [10] the negative emotional effects of work pressure can accumulate unnoticed, but this does not mean they are insignificant. [9] Work pressure may affect an individual's mental and physical health, and also impact the organization's operation efficiency. The UK's Public and Commercial Services Union (PCS) reported that 67% of survey respondents work overtime, while over 25% indicated that they experience pressure not only from the office culture and work management practices, but also from other individuals, all of which can negatively

A. Marcus (Ed.): DUXU/HCII 2013, Part III, LNCS 8014, pp. 446–454, 2013.

impact the emotions of the people around them. This study examines the behavioral needs of office workers responding to workplace stress with the aim to use appropriate design to enable workers to effectively express their emotions, reduce negative feelings, reduce fatigue and improve work effectiveness. Thus, this research seeks to understand workers in office environments and identify their needs for stress relief, and thus determine the principles of interactive emotional design to reduce workplace stress.

2   Related Work

According to the World Health Organization (WHO), good physical and psychological health, along with strong social relations, are considered to be strong indicators of overall health and well-being. Good physical and mental health and happiness are all conducive to excellent work, family and living conditions and can give people a sense of security. Therefore, before investigating ways to reduce workplace stress, we first evaluate the mental health and emotional needs of workers to identify key factors in stress relief. Increased emphasis should be paid to internal factors, especially the views and thoughts of the workers themselves. Additional focus must also be put on spirit and thought, using external and internal mechanisms to provide workers with meaningful help in alleviating excessive workplace stress.

Brown [2] referred to Fromm's contention that deep emotional factors contribute to a sense of powerlessness and anxiety that people experience in their interaction with technology and society. Lasch [8] coined the term "narcissistic survivalism" to describe modern culture, suggesting that the demands of daily life and work lead people to engage in behavior that emphasizes self-protection, specifically characterized by selective apathy, emotional disengagement and lack of interest in the past or future. This can result in a "contradiction of self" reaction. When we encounter social stress in our daily life, it triggers a defense mechanism which minimizes the need for emotional engagement. Buechler [3] referenced Fromm's theory as the ideological foundation for a healthy lifestyle, suggesting that modern people have lost enthusiasm for healthy living. In The Revolution of Hope, Fromm [5] suggested that humanity is the ability of a person to express his self-realization according to his personal needs. This means that our eyes see what we need to see and our ears hear what we want to hear because our needs are generated based on our subjective views, and our spirit produces the required emotion. Buechler also believes that self-fulfillment includes rich life and emotional experience.

Our lives are shaped by technological artifacts, and science and technology have begun to mediate how people experience reality and the past. Bostrom [1] suggested that technological innovation is the main driving force for long-term economic growth, and that technological change is driving global trends such as population size, education, material living standards, and communications. Social and personal life has also been directly affected by science and technology including such aspects as entertainment, interpersonal relationships, morality and material comforts. Most technology is used to increase productivity. Thus, people are required to master new tools, no matter how complex, to continually increase their competitiveness and chance of professional success. Currently, many successfully designed modes of operation are based on natural human behavior, thus understanding human emotions and experience is extremely important to the complexity of modern technology.

McDonagh and Lebbon [11] suggest that the ultimate aim of design should be to meet peoples' emotional needs, improving quality of life, and conferring meaningful value to everyday situations or problems. Emotion is an important source of information for people. Regardless of whether one is creating or solving problems, or developing an interactive system, [13] emotions ultimately have a significant impact and designers must understand the user's experiential and emotional needs. Roy et al. [12] proposed that the continuously increasing complexity of technology raises the importance of natural interactive behavior and emotions. Stimulating user emotions through physical contact in everyday human interaction is an effective way of giving people a better sense of connectedness. Thus, we hope to use design to better allow people to see themselves and others in the process of interaction, thus bringing people closer together.

Positive emotions have many benefits – they can help people overcome stress, making them an important aspect to human curiosity and learning. Dewey [4] proposed the aesthetic as a type of experience in which beauty can emotionally move the user. Kim et al. [7] proposed that the meaning of design aesthetic lies not only in emphasizing the designer's intent but also includes the user's experience and emotional value. Triggering an emotional response in the user through aesthetics is an important aspect of design because emotion has a strong effect on the average user. Kim [6] mentioned that, to date, studies of interactive design basically focus on issues of utility and effectiveness but, to motivate sustained behavior on the part of the user, the interactive experience raised by the user's emotions is a key factor. Interest is not only an emotional reaction, but is also a holistic experience incorporating the individual's outlook, the social environment and human relationships. Interest and amusement are excellent motivators, and design elements use surprise and interest to attract the user's attention and leave a deep impression. This is a point in design which should not be disregarded.

3   Method

Empathic design methods are usually people-oriented research approaches featuring direct contact and interaction with potential users to ensure that the design adopts the user's viewpoint. The standard framework for empathic design is built on user-centered design methods, and is able to support and establish creative and comprehensible designs for users to engage with in daily life. This study uses ORIED and empathy maps to investigate the needs of office workers. The discussion revolves around their actual everyday experience and seeks to help them infer a group-wide consensus and emotions. Good design is based on a deep understanding of human needs. The two methods mentioned above can help us observe and identify unexpected viewpoints. At the outset, this research requires multifaceted development and ideas to ensure that the research and participants themselves identify solutions to problems and design requirements.

The focus group method was developed by the Institute of Cultural Affairs (ICA) as a process for exploring beneath the surface of a conversation. The hierarchical process goes through four stages: Objective, Reflective, Interpretive and Decisional, known by its acronym ORID. This kind of dialogue method can guide the formation of a decision-making consensus, thus reducing the frequency of reprimands or embarrassment, while enhancing the mutual learning experience and highlighting the value of dealing with the underlying problem. Empathy maps are a comprehensive tool that helps observers identify different viewpoints, thus facilitating the quick prototype development while identifying potential user demands. In discussions and guidance based on empathy maps, a description of the participants and key words are collected as the basis for the design direction. Observing users is the first step of empathetic design. Observing and learning the users' actions through user body language, spontaneous active responses or other non-verbal cues can overcome the limitations of traditional questionnaires for recording the expression of emotions, thus allowing users to offer innovative ideas which can be further elucidated for improvement and use.

4   Workshop

The workshop included eight participants, four men and four women with an average age of 25. Participants were all full-time office workers who indicated they were under stress at work. The workshop process lasted about 2.5 hours, beginning with ORID interaction and a ten-minute office-themed film. Watching the film encouraged participants to recall events they normally encounter at work, thus putting them in an appropriate frame of mind and mood. The ORID guidance framework includes a total of ten questions based on the content of the film and taken from the point of view of the main character of the film (see Table 1). The participants were asked to raise and discuss their own viewpoint and opinions, and to describe potential solutions. The participants' responses were recorded on stickers and placed on the discussion board (Fig. 1).

The focus group session helped create a common consciousness and personal links among the workshop participants, which facilitated the empathy map discussion where problems were categorized as belong to (1) seeing, (2) listening, (3) thinking and feeling, (4) doing, (5) gain and (6) difficulty. The items for each problem were related to the normal work conditions of each participant (Table 2). We invited a representative participant to draw portraits on paper, and categorize them as belonging to six regions for the purposes of discussion. We then asked the participants to answer the discussion questions in the context of these six regions, with the answers written on stickers and placed in the corresponding areas on the empathy map. Based on the participants' answers, we attempted to find a key element for an emotional interactive design that could be implemented in an office environment. The entire discussion process was open and free, with participants actively exchanging ideas. To avoid preconceived answers or concepts, participants were asked to answer the questions in reference to their internal needs and everyday work experience. The responses to the final questions were all items which the participants found interesting or which they felt they may need help with (Fig. 2).

Table 1. ORID questions (organized from the current research)

Question Type	Question Content
Objective	1. In the film, Peter was late to work because of traffic, and he suffered a mild electric shock. What happened to him after he got to the office?
	2. Which of his colleagues and superiors did Peter encounter?
	3. What was Nelly using that upset Peter?
Reflective	1. What emotions did Peter experience when facing his TPS report?
	2. How did Milton (the uncle listening to the radio) react to Peter's request?
	3. What adjectives can you use to describe the atmosphere at Initech?
Interpretive	1. Why do Peter Michael and Nelly feel unhappy at work?
	2. Why do Peter, Michael and Nelly slip out of the office during working hours for coffee?
Decisional	1. If you were Peter, how would you resolve the morale problems at work?
	2. If you were Peter, what kind of changes would you like to make?

Fig. 1. Workplace documentary (arranged for this research)

Table 2. Empathy map problems (arranged for this research)

Problem Type	Problem Content
See	1. Reflect on your everyday office environment. What things do you remember seeing that made you feel happy?
	2. What kinds of things do you keep at your desk for your own enjoyment?
Hear	1. At the office, what kinds of sounds make you unhappy or irritated?
	2. What do your colleagues normally say to you?
Think and Feel	1. What do you feel is most important to you in the office?
	2. What do you expect an office to look like or include?
Say and Do	1. What do you do most often at the office?
	2. What do you normally talk about at the office?
Pain	1. At present, what kinds of things do you worry about most at the office?
	2. What is the greatest frustration you've encountered at the office?
Gain	1. What goals do you hope to achieve at work?
	2. What kind of achievement do you hope to obtain at work?

Fig. 2. Workplace documentary (arranged for this research)

5   Analysis

From the experimental results we obtained 326 concepts related to office work environments. The discussion process was unrestricted, thus many items had technical limitations such as improvements to office space configurations, changes to company systems, pay raises, adding vacation days, etc. None of these items fall within the scope of discussion in this study, and thus are seen as research limitations. The data was then categorized according the psychological demands proposed by Murray's requirements theory, while the empathy map was broken down into two large areas for positive emotions and negative emotions to facilitate identifying exactly which levels were positive demands for office workers, to serve as a reference for future design stages and thus enhance the positive demands of users. These two large categories were subdivided into target needs, material needs, power needs, emotional needs and information needs to locate the participant group's demand consciousness in one of these subcategories. To determine reasonable design scope and limitations, this study used the semantic differential method to identify more detailed and well-defined emotional elements, thus confirming the technical and physical conditions restraints, along with conditions not applied to office environments. SD analysis was used to obtain a high degree of user demand strength and apply currently available techniques to resolve design elements for office morale. The X-axis is divided into technical rationality and irrationality, to increase the clarity of the design's technical goals. The Y-axis is divided into personal behavior and group behavior, which helps us identify the emotional needs of office workers. This falls under personal characteristics or, in the context of communication or interaction with others, group characteristics, thus providing indicators for design direction for personal use or group interactive use. Analysis results show that the, among the empathy map categories, items for "see", " hear", and "think and feel" are concentrated in the first quadrant (i.e., technical rationality and individual behavior), with creative desktop toys being the most frequently mentioned item (14 times) followed by music and interaction with others (Fig. 3).

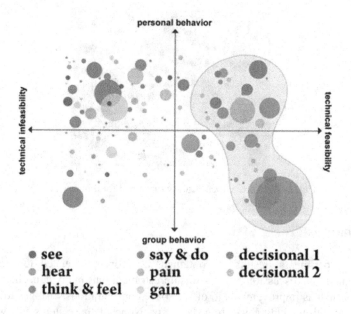

Fig. 3. Workplace documentary (arranged for this research)

The results indicate that the majority appear in the quadrant of technical feasibility and group interaction, for which the more relevant corresponding demand theory classification is emotional needs and information needs. Thus, the analysis chart message prompted us to search for more convincing information. Some future design directions are summarized as follows: (1) The importance of emotional needs extends beyond an individual's emotional catharsis to also involve the emotional influence and interaction of the group. (2) The importance of information exchange is that it helps maintain morale by connecting workers through the exchange of messages. (3) Embedding emotions in design allows objects to change and grow alongside their users, providing a type of emotional sustenance. Thus, the above mentioned data analysis primarily obtains development directions for interactive designs which can be used to in actual office environments to meet the needs of office workers.

6 Conclusion

Modern science and technology has changed our socioeconomic system, compressing us into a type of controlled, consistent, unified unit. In this type of mechanical working environment, workers lose their personal uniqueness and creativity, and even the expression of personal feelings are subject to monitoring. This study starts from the viewpoint of emotional design, using empathic methods to identify the needs of office workers in an attempt to use design to re-trigger human emotions and further allow workers to express their feelings and relieve stress. In retrospect, the key point of this research is to identify design elements and strategies which can help office workers relieve work stress, to apply emotional design principles to fit these research results, and to find the intersection of interactive design and emotional design. This study raises a few important conclusions: for workers in office environments, emotional needs are an important consideration and must be taken seriously. The research results also provide the basic requirements for future creative design.

We hope that future research efforts can identify more convincing evidence tying user needs with design requirements and, more importantly, complying with the principles of emotional design to allow provide users with improved feedback and experiences in interacting with one another. This study focuses on the stress reduction needs of office workers. Data from a workshop developed using concepts from user-centered design was organized and analyzed to obtain the daily habits and behavior patterns for office workers which revealed some requirements and directions hidden among the data. Semantic differential analysis was used to propose a design concept prototype for key user goals among office workers, producing interactive design recommendations suitable for application in office environments. Thus, future work will discuss the following points: (1) Understanding the weekday habits and stress-relieving behavior of office workers. The habits of office workers when they come under stress at work, and the characteristics of how they interact with colleagues will inform effective recommendations for the design of relevant products. (2) Inducing the core design direction and requirements for office workers. Discussion workshops for office workers can be used to obtain design requirements and directions, thus improving the proposed interactive design prototype and making it more acceptable. (3) Formulating interactive designs concepts and suggestions suitable for use by office workers in an office environment. Future work needs to focus on office workers as the users of interactive design, and emphasize the details when proposing constructive references and implementing designs.

References

1. Bostrom, N.: The Future of Humanity Future of Humanity Institute. Oxford University Press (2007)
2. Brown, W.S.: Ontological Security, Existential Anxiety and Workplace Privacy. Journal of Business Ethics 23, 61–65 (2000)
3. Buechler, S.: Why We Need Fromm Today: Fromm's Work Ethic. Productive Orientation and Mental Health (2006)
4. Dewey, J.: Arts as Experience (1934)
5. Fromm, E.: The Revolution of Hope: Toward a Humanized Technology. Bantam Books, New York (1968)
6. Kim, J.W., Kim, Y.K., Nam, T.J.: The ténéré: design for supporting energy conservation behaviors. Paper Presented at the 27th International Conference Extended Abstracts on Human Factors in Computing Systems (2009)
7. Kim, T., Hong, H., Magerko, B.: Design requirements for ambient display that supports sustainable lifestyle. Paper Presented at the 8th ACM Conference on Designing Interactive Systems (2010)
8. Lasch, C.: The Minimal Self: Psychic Survival in Troubled Times. W.W. Norton, New York (1984)
9. Leka, S., Griffiths, A., Cox, T.: Work-related stress: the risk management paradigm: Organizational Health Psychology (2005)
10. Levey, R.E.: Sources of Stress for Residents and Recommendations for Programs to Assist Them. Academic Medicine 76 (2001)
11. McDonagh-Philp, D., Lebbon, C.: The emotional domain in product design. Design Journal 3(1) (2000)
12. Roy, M., Hemmert, F., Wettach, R.: Living interfaces: the intimate door lock. Paper Presented at the the 3rd International Conference on Tangible and Embedded Interaction (2009)
13. Sas, C., Zhang, C.: Do emotions matter in creative design. Paper Presented at the 8th ACM Conference on Designing Interactive Systems (2010)

A Study on Time Differences between Actual Advertisement Viewing and Retrospective Perception

Miao-Hsien Chuang[1] and Chiwu Huang[2]

[1] Department of Visual Communication Design, Ming Chi University of Technology,
New Taipei City, Taiwan
Graduate Institute of Design, National Taipei University of Technology, Taipei, Taiwan
joyceblog@gmail.com
[2] Department of Industrial Design and Graduate Institute of Innovation & Design,
National Taipei University of Technology, Taipei, Taiwan
chiwu@ntut.edu.tw

Abstract. Upon entry into the digital age, the number and importance of images in media has increased considerably. This paper discusses the similarities and differences between implicit and explicit memory produced by the subjective perception of time when viewing images and text in advertisements. The durations involved in implicit memory were measured using scientific instrumentation (eye-tracking devices), while explicit memory was gauged via a self-administered questionnaire. Three out of ten subjects retrospectively perceived browsing times that differed from the actual times measured through eye tracking, indicating a difference between implicit observation and explicit memory. We also investigated the layout preferences of subjects with various backgrounds in terms of images, text, and logos. These results could assist advertisers to enhance the effectiveness of communication regarding content as well as brand recognition through the use of strong narrative methods.

Keywords: Eye movement, Explicit memory measurement, Psychological time, Layout.

1 Introduction

The Chinese proverb, "time is like an arrow" echoes the English saying, "time flies". Happy times often feel brief, while painful moments appear like an eternity. Most people describe the duration of their experiences according to subjective impressions. The dissemination of digital content has increased the reliance of advertisers on images and text in order to attract public attention, whether employing mass media advertising or personal pages on Facebook. The time readers spent on images and text is our main focus.

Is reading order associated with the layout of image and text? Do elements such as the time used to browse images and text, the order of the browsing, and individual perception vary from person to person? Researchers have employed eye tracking to

A. Marcus (Ed.): DUXU/HCII 2013, Part III, LNCS 8014, pp. 455–464, 2013.

investigate the order in which images and text are viewed (Rayner, Rotello, Stewart, Keir & Duffy, 2001). They have also used this technology to explore the attention and memory for advertisement of brands (Wedel & Pieters, 2000) and investigate the saccadic pathways in the layout of news articles (Tang & Jhuang, 2005). Eye tracking instruments have become fundamental tools in the field of psychology to reveal cognitive processes hidden with the function of the human brain. Although the traditional questionnaire survey method is susceptible to errors resulting from subjective introspection, it remains an effective approach for the collection of opinions, feelings, and responses from target subjects. Researchers have proposed the use of paper-and-pencil questionnaires or memory tests as a supplement for eye tracking to compensate for the inadequacies of self-reporting by experiment subjects. Nevertheless, studies have failed to verify the consistency of results derived from the two types of experimental methods.

2   Objectives

This study conducted an in-depth exploration of various issues related to print advertising, including the time required to browse images and text and the order in which layouts are browsed. We also sought to determine whether measurement methods using scientific instruments and traditional questionnaires provide complementary results. The objectives of this study were as follows:

1. Establish whether the time measured by eye tracking differs from the subjectively perceived time of test subjects;
2. Determine whether test subjects differ in their preferences and browsing time;
3. Determine whether the layout of advertisements influences when the logo of the advertised product is noticed;
4. Reveal the image and text browsing preferences of test subjects with different educational backgrounds.

3   Literature Review

3.1   Eye Tracking

Eye tracking has been widely applied in the fields of physiology, pathology, psychological cognition, and to evaluate cultural differences. Conscious eye movement is associated primarily with the shift of attention, high-level memory, and the processes of understanding and cognizing.

Constant eye movement is used to provide comprehensive visual acuity. Generally, both eyes must be fixed on the target object for approximately 200 to 500 milliseconds in order for the image to form in the clearest region on the retina, the fovea. This action is known as fixation. A series of iterative fixations and saccades form a scan path. Current eye tracking instruments can effectively record these eye movements and are believed to be able to obtain results similar to those of questionnaires.

Nodine, Locher, and Krupinski (1993) analyzed the eye movement of art-trained and untrained viewers looking at paintings. They discovered that the former focuses on structural relationships among pictorial elements that express narrative theme, while untrained viewers pay attention to representational issues (i.e., how accurately individual pictorial elements conveyed objective reality). Observing the internet viewing behavior of male and female individuals, Schiessl, Duda, Tholke, and Fischer (2002) conclude from empirical data and describe women as being text-oriented and accurate, and men as icon-oriented and loose. Eye tracking has already established that readers with different professional backgrounds and genders display different scan paths and durations.

3.2   Image and Text Layout

Images and text are essential in the planning of visual layouts, but which is more eye-catching? It is generally agreed that vivid images attract more attention. Pieter and Wedel (2004) asserted that images have the advantage in drawing attention regardless of size and that text element best captures attention in direct proportion to its surface size.

As for the reading order of image and text, Rayner et al. (2001) believed that when viewers look at print advertisements, they spend more time on the text; some viewers may give the images an initial cursory scan before reading the heading and content before looking at the images. While reading, viewers often make cross-references between the images and the text for interpretation. Yeh (2007) studied textbooks used by younger elementary students, discovering that illustrations placed before the text are better able to attract the attention of learners and increase motivation. In contrast, illustrations that placed after the text are more effective in augmenting memory and review processes.

3.3   Implicit Memory and Explicit Memory

Memory includes the processes of encoding, storage, and retrieval. External information is received, processed, combined, stored, and then called back or extracted from storage. Researchers advocating the multi-store model have proposed three types of memory storage: (1) sensory stores, such as visual and auditory, which, when noticed, is placed in a (2) short-term stores; through rehearsal, the information is then passed on into (3) long-term stores (Eysenck, 2004).

Long-term memory is divided into implicit memory and explicit memory. The greatest difference between the two lies in conscious awareness. In other words, it depends on whether consciousness is involved in the state of the memory. As for the measurement of memories, procedures such as free recall, cued recall, and recognition can be used, involving direct instruction to retrieve information related to particular experiences. These are considered the measurements of explicit memory (Eysenck, 2000). However, memory is not restricted to environmental cues; beliefs and expectations can also influence what people see and hear (Nairne, 2000). In this study, we employed questionnaires to measure explicit memory, hoping that the conscious recollections of test subjects could be used for control and testing.

3.4   Psychological Time

Aristotle proposed the "time of physics", while Augustine proposed the "time of the soul", demonstrating how subjective and objective views of time have long been argued over (Ricoeur Paul, 1984). In addition to conventional time, which encompasses the precision of clock speeds, the customary days, weeks, and months, and the socially designed segmentation of continuous time as periods, time is a conceptual existent in subjective experience. With time, a concrete form of duration, people experience the interlacing changes of events, the feelings of happiness or pain in their hearts, memories, and desires (Kramer, 1988; Pressing, 1993; Wu, 1966).

Psychological time refers to the framing of a moment of physical time in a unit of perceived time. While experiencing events, people generate perceptions of feelings and memories; the length of the time experienced is described using their feelings at the time. Hornik and Jacob (1992) mentioned time perception as the subjective judgment of consumers towards time, otherwise known as the subjective perception of time. Psychological time can be warped by psychological factors, in terms of which Levine (1997) divided influences to the psychological clock into five categories: pleasantness, the degree of urgency, the amount of activity, variety, and time-free tasks.

3.5   Summary

From the literature above, we can establish the following: Eye movement is associated with attention, high-level memory, and the processes of understanding and cognition. Eye tracking has shown that subjects with different professional backgrounds and genders display different scanning patterns. The layout influences attention and memory. Long term memory is divided into implicit memory and explicit memory; the recollection of one's behavior in a conscious state is explicit memory. Furthermore, in addition to clock units, years, and months, time is a subjective experience as well as a conceptual cognitive existence. Based on the literature above, we investigated whether gender or educational background influences browsing time and order when observing images and text in print advertisements. Moreover, we hoped to determine whether the results of scientific measurement instruments reflect those obtained from traditional questionnaires.

4   Methodology

We first employed the eye tracking method and then measured explicit memory (semi-open questionnaire). The results were subjected to tests of independence, tests of chi-square goodness of fit and chi-square test of independence.

4.1   Eye Tracking Method

Experimental Equipment and Environment. This study employed the Face Lab4 real-time face and fixation tracking device in conjunction with GazeTrail software analysis. The computer display was 38 cm in width and 30 cm in length with a resolution of 1280x1024 pixels. During the experiment, the device automatically and synchronously recorded scan paths, the time of the tests, and the time distribution involved in browsing various regions of the screen image. The experiment was implemented in an independent space; the participants were tested individually with no need for helmets or goggles, and were free to browse the screen as they normally would with other computers.

Participants. Number of participants: 36 people
Background: 18 participants with a background in design and 18 participants without a background in design (technological)
Gender: 22 males and 14 females, selected by random sampling

Experiment Samples. *Samples: Sample A was a print advertisement for Citibank.* The original copy was written in English, but for the sake of the participants, whose mother tongue was not English, and to avoid reading difficulties, we replaced the English text with Chinese text of the same meaning. Sample B contained the same content as Sample A except that it was horizontally flipped; the image was flipped so that the model in the image remained facing the center of the ad, but the heading was placed in the upper right corner rather than in the upper left corner (Fig. 1).

Sample A   Sample B

Fig. 1. Samples A and B, with the same image and text content flipped horizontally
Source: http://adsoftheworld.com/

Advertisement Heading: I don't cook. So I made my eat-in kitchen a fabulous walk-in closet.

Content: My name is Grace and I live in a small apartment in a big city. And since I enjoy a day of shopping far more than, say, cooking, I decided to do a bit of home remodeling. (inserted icons of high heels) so with my Citi card in hand, I set out to get some closet organizers. (inserted icon of organizer) I bought a shoe rack for the oven, sweater boxes (inserted icon of sweater box) for the lower cupboards, and some

12-inch baskets for handbags (inserted icon of handbag) up above, I saved room for plates, glasses, and silverware. And one large drawer stuffed with take-out menus. Whatever your story is, your Citi card can help you write it.

Experiment Procedure. Order of sample browsing: using the counterbalancing approach, we rotated the order in which the two groups of participants looked at the samples.

4.2   Measurement of Explicit Memory

The measurement of explicit memory is a form of memory retrieval in which an individual consciously acts to recall or to recognize particular information. After the participants completed the eye tracking procedure, we suggested they take a break (which most of the participants declined) before filling out the semi-open questionnaire (see Appendix 1). The questionnaire requested that the participants recall the time and order in which they browsed the image and text during the eye tracking procedure. Furthermore, it inquired as to which of the layouts looked smoother, whether the icons inserted in the text caused interference, and how soon they understood the nature of the advertising product from the image and text.

5   Results and Discussion

5.1   Eye Tracking Results

Following completion of the eye tracking procedure, we used GazeTrail software to analyze the results. Regions were marked on both of the samples in relation to the image, the right portion of the layout, the face of the female model, the heading, the text, the logo, and the icons inserted into the text. We performed independent samples t-tests on the time that the participants spent looking at these regions with respect to the background and gender of the participant. The results showed no significant differences. Participants with and without a background in design spent an average of 11.05 seconds and 7.57 seconds looking at the image on the left in Sample A, respectively. For the text on the right in Sample A, they spent 7.34 seconds and 16.96 seconds, respectively. Neither of the results reached the level of significance but conformed to the data derived in the pilot test of this study. In other words, individuals without a background in design spend more time looking at the text, while those with a background in design spend more time looking at the image.

Participants with and without a background in design respectively spent an average of 7.15 seconds and 7.52 seconds looking at the text on the left side of Sample B. They respectively spent 7.81 seconds and 6.21 seconds looking at the image on the right of Sample B. Again, the results did not reach the level of significance, but it is apparent that the participants with a background in design spent more time looking at the text in Sample B than they did on the text in Sample A. From the data above, we can infer that regardless of background or preference, an individual will spend more time looking at the content on the fore-end of their scan path (the left), in accordance with common reading habits.

5.2   Questionnaire Analysis

In terms of the first question, "Which one do I think looks smoother?", the results demonstrate that regardless of whether Sample A or Sample B was viewed first, participants with a background in design felt that Sample A looked smoother. The results of the chi-square goodness of fit test were statistically significant (test statistic: p value=.029). However, one of the participants felt that both samples looked the same in terms of smoothness, rendering the overall test results statistically insignificant (test statistic: p value=.063).

Questions 2 through 5 investigated whether the participants spent more time on the images or the text. The chi-square test of independence presented significant correlation (Pearson chi-square p value=.001), indicating that the individuals who looked at Sample A first felt that they had spent more time looking at the images. Individuals who looked at Sample B first felt that they had spent more time looking at the text.

Question 6 asked the participants whether the icons inserted in the text affected readability. The results of the chi-square test of independence indicated no significant correlation. However, participants with a background in design who looked at Sample B first tended to feel that the icons adversely affected readability.

Question 7 inquired as to when the participants realized the purpose of the advertisement, the speed at which they perceived the message, and the sample that they viewed first (A or B). These served as variables in the chi-square test of independence. In terms of the participants without a background in design, the speed at which they perceived the message was found to be significantly correlated to the in order in which they viewed the samples (chi-square value=0.037). For participants without a background in design, those that viewed Sample A first became aware of the product message early on, while those that viewed Sample B first became aware of the product message later. The data from the participants with a background in design did not present significant correlation. We infer that this is because participants without a background in design have a preference for reading the text, which helps them to naturally notice the logo in the lower right corner after reading the text on the right. Generally, this is where logos are placed in advertisements. In Sample B, however, the logo was situated on the left side, which is not a place that people customarily look. Consequently, the logo in Sample B was easily overlooked.

5.3   Analysis and Comparison of Eye Tracking and Questionnaire

This study revealed the following conclusions: 1. In terms of the time spent on images and text, three out of ten participants displayed perceptions (their own conscious memories) that differed from the time measured in the eye tracking experiment, indicating that there were indeed differences between implicit observation and explicit memory. 2. Among the participants that viewed Sample A (image on left, text on right) first, 61 % spent more time looking at the images, and 33 % displayed eye movements that were different from what they perceived. 3. Among the subjects that viewed Sample B (text on left, image on right) first, 56 % spent more time looking at the text, and 27% displayed eye movement durations that were different from what they perceived (Fig. 2).

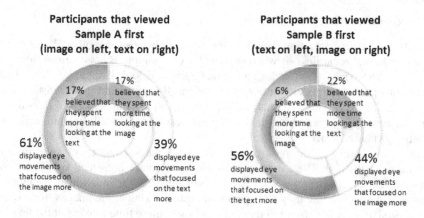

Fig. 2. The outer ring indicates the time recorded by the eye tracker, and the inner ring shows the results consciously recalled by the participants

6   Conclusion and Suggestions

This study administered eye tracking and a questionnaire to subjects with different backgrounds and genders using two samples with different layouts as to image and text. The results were compared and analyzed using chi-square tests of independence and goodness of fit tests. Our results indicate the following: 1) The measurements of time obtained from eye tracking differed from the subjectively perceived time of test participants. Three out of ten participants reported perceptions that differed from the time measured in the eye tracking experiment. 2) Participant preferences for image and text layout, browsing time, and scanning patterns showed no significant differences; however, the results presented a few trends in which most of the participants considered images on the left and text on the right to be smoother-looking. More time was spent reading text than looking at the image. 3. Participants without a background in design who looked at Sample A first noticed the product fairly quickly, indicating that the lower right corner is the optimal location for a logo. 4. Individuals with a background in design preferred images, while individuals without this training preferred text. In addition, females preferred images, and males preferred text.

This study has a number of limitations. Funding restrictions limited the number of participants in the eye tracking exercise. In addition, with only two sample types, we employed counterbalancing to switch the order in which the participants viewed the samples. Therefore, a portion of the data was split in half for analysis, creating greater difficulty in obtaining statistically significant results.

This study stressed the importance of combining research methods to investigate implicit and explicit memory in order to enhance reliability. Our results reveal the layout preferences of subjects with different backgrounds in terms of images, text, and logos, enabling advertisement designers to enhance message communication and brand information with strong narrative methods.

References

1. Eysenck, M.W.: Cognitive Psychology-A Student's Handbook, 4th edn. Wu-Nan Books, Taipei (2000); Li, S.-C.(trans.)
2. Eysenck, M.W.: Simple Psychology, 2nd edn. HungYeh Books, Taipei (2004); Wei, C.-F. (trans.)
3. Hornik, J.: Time Estimation and Orientation Mediated by Transient Mood. The Journal of Socio – Economics 21, 209–227 (1992)
4. Kramer, J.D.: The Time of Music. Schirmer, New York (1988)
5. Kress, G., Leeuwen, T.V.: Reading Images: The Grammar of Visual Design. AsiaPac Books, Taipei (1999); Ni, S. (trans.)
6. Levine, R.: A Geography of Time -The Temporal Misadventures of a Social Psychologist. Basic Books, New York (1998)
7. Nairne, J.S.: Psychology: The Adaptive Mind. Hurng-Chih Books, Taipei (2000); Li, M.-H., Chen, M.-Y. (trans.), Huang, S.-L., Kuo, C.-C. (revise)
8. Nodine, C.F., Locher, P.J., Krupinski, E.A.: The role of formal art training on perception and Aesthetics judgment of art composition. Leonardo 26, 219–227 (1993)
9. Pieters, R., Wedel, M.: Attention capture and transfer in advertising: Brand, pictorial and text-size effects. Journal of Marketing 68, 36–50 (2004)
10. Pressing, J.: Relations Between Musical and Scientific Properties of Time. Contemporary Music Review 7(2), 105–122 (1993)
11. Rayner, K., Rotello, C.M., Stewart, A.J., Keir, J., Duffy, S.A.: Integrating text and pictorial information: Eye movements when looking at print advertisements. Journal of Experimental Psychology: Applied 7(3), 219–226 (2001)
12. Ricoeur, P.: Time and Narrative. The University of Chicago Press, Chicago (1984); McLaughlin, K., Pellauer, D. (trans.)
13. Schiessl, M., Duda, S., Tholke, A., Fischer, R.: Eye Tracking and Its Application in Usability & Media Research. Humboldt University, Berlin (2002), http://www.eye-square.com/fileadmin/docs/publications/user_experience/eye_s quare-eye_tracking_research_applications.pdf (retrieved on February 25, 2012)
14. Tang, D.L., Jhuang, S.J.: Exploring Attentional Effect of Image Position on News Reading from Eye-tracking Method. The Journal of Advertising & Public Relations 24, 89–104 (2005)
15. Wedel, M., Pieters, R.: Eye fixations on advertisements and memory for brands: A model and findings. Marketing Science 19(4), 297–312 (2000)
16. Wu, K.: Henri Bergson. The Commercial Press, Taipei (1966)
17. Yeh, S.Y.: Effectiveness of Illustrations in Junior-Grade Elementary School Mandarin Textbooks under the Nine-year Integrated Curriculum (Master's thesis, National Taichung University of Education) (2007)

Appendix 1

*Background: ☐ Design: Dept of _____ ☐ Non-design: Dept of
_____

*Gender: ☐Male ☐Female

*Age:_____

*Name (Nickname):_____

1. Which one do I think looks smoother? ☐Sample A ☐Sample B ☐They look the same

(Note: For those that looked at Sample A first, please answer Questions 2 and 3; for those that looked Sample B first, please skip to Question 4.)

2. When I looked at Sample A, I think I first looked at
☐the image on the left ☐the text on the right ☐I briefly scanned the image on the left first and then read the text on the right ☐I briefly scanned the text on the right first and then looked at the image on the left ☐other:

_____

_____

3. When I looked at Sample A, I think I spent more time looking at:

_____

(For those that looked at Sample A first, please skip to Question 6.)

4. When I looked at Sample B, I think I first looked at ☐the text on the left ☐the image on the right ☐I briefly scanned the text on the left first and then looked at the image on the right ☐I briefly scanned the image on the right first and then read the text on the left ☐other:

_____

_____

5. When I looked at Sample B, I think I spent more time looking at:

_____

6. I think that inserting small icons in multiple lines of text ☐interferes with my reading ☐somewhat interferes with my reading ☐ does not interfere with my reading

7. I knew that the advertisement was introducing a credit card ☐early on ☐later ☐just now

~ Thank you for your participation ~

Semiotic Analysis for Gestural and Emotional Human-Computer Interaction

Roman Danylak

University of Technology, Sydney
roman@emotional-computing.com

Abstract. The discussion that follows describes the design of an interactive artwork *To be or not to be* using semiotics. The goal of *To be or not to be* was to create a user experience that was coherent and continuous, generating gestures and emotions - not uncommon Human Computer Interaction (HCI) objectives. The design problem was to isolate what could be elements of user experience as inputs and outputs in a multimedia interactive system. Essentially there were five parts to the process: the first was an understanding of gesture and its modeling within the framework of generating expressive gestures in theatre – defining media before simulation; the second, was to define the input and output process by which gestural interaction using HCI media might proceed; the third was to create a semiotic matrix of both the theatrical and HCI terms as *equivalences*, creating a system by which the design could follow; the fourth was evolving an experience, in this case an interactive film-game, that generated gestures and associated emotional content; the fifth was a user evaluation and statistical analysis (results summary only). The emphasis presented here is on the preparatory stage of correct process modeling, leading to the effective application of semiotic analysis. Readers are encouraged to access the URL for youtube description of the work.

http://www.youtube.com/watch?v=jKNvSpXG0Z0

Keywords: theatre, game, gesture, emotion, metaphor, metonymy.

1   Introduction

The recent rapid development of extended sensory input and output devices, including tactile and visual aids, has meant that new forms of data emerging from human experience can be processed by a computer. Bolt's work [1], *Put That There* (1980) was the first instance of gesture-based multimodal interaction where deictic (pointing) gestures would move on-screen objects. Since then, the range of human experiences as input data has continued to rapidly increase. A design question then arises: 'could the role of human communication as presented by what is commonly known as *body language*, be integrated into a human-computer

A. Marcus (Ed.): DUXU/HCII 2013, Part III, LNCS 8014, pp. 465–474, 2013.
© Springer-Verlag Berlin Heidelberg 2013

interaction? To rephrase and refocus this ambitious goal, would be to say that some useable, communicating configuration of gesture and emotion in a multi-modal computer interaction might be possible. *To be or not to be* partially realized this objective by generating gestures and emotional response in a multimedia interactive context. The success of the design was owing to the careful modeling of the expressive gesture process based on expressive gesture generation in theatre, followed by semiotic analysis of both the human and machine design elements, enabling the design in a game format.

2   The Problem of Gesture: Ambiguity and Context

The notion of language in view of the problem of gesture and emotion persists. A major difficulty with gestures and their communicated emotional content is that meaning – a key feature of language - can be ambiguous. Gestures and interpreted expressiveness is context dependent: a raised open hand could mean 'stop'; it could mean 'hello'; or 'throw me the ball!'; or it may be done to sense the air temperature and the presence of a breeze. Alternatively, what seems to be expressive content may have no meaning at all – "I was only stretching my muscles!". Most importantly gestures then, do not exist in isolation. Establishing a clear vocabulary where 'this movement means X' is very difficult to achieve. As such, an all-encompassing system of design that would harness gestural emotional human computer interaction – a means of simplifying the complexity of user experience and the design process - is as yet elusive as Oviatt and Pantic state respectively [2, 3].

3   A Five Step Design Process for *To be or not to be*.

There were five key steps in designing *To be or not to be*. Step 5 will be discussed in summary only. These steps are as follows:

1. understand gesture and its modeling within the framework of generating expressive gestures in theatre, defining the media machine *before* simulation.
2. define the input and output process that gestural interaction by which the HCI might proceed.
3. create a semiotic matrix of both the theatrical and HCI terms as *equivalences*, creating a system by which the design could follow, modifying terms as necessary.
4. evolve a user experience applying semiotic matrix, in this case a game.
5. user evaluation and statistical analysis of objectives.

3.1   Step 1 Defining Gestures, Emotion and Media in Theatrical Practice

The literature on gestural interaction displays a difficult variety of definitions, primarily arising out of its ambiguous nature. The modeling adopted was that of theatrical practice, adopted to reduce the volatility of the problem. Actors perform repeated expressive gestural sequences in the virtual space of the theatre, suggesting it to be an appropriate model. The process by which actors prepare their bodies for performance is often based on yogic exercise as exampled in the work of Grotowski [4]. In yoga, gestures are defined by stillness; this stillness allows for the examination of emotion associated with the pose. A still form is then what constitutes a gesture; the test for the presence of gesture then is a photographic still. Significantly, intention, communication, reception and potential ambiguity with this definition disappear from the user experience: bodily form equals gesture.

In terms of defining media, creating gestures in theatre is essentially a three-step process, that is, if we assume the creation of the play plans – the script – already to be in existence. The gestural and verbal expression of the play is devised by the director who interprets the text and directs actor actions on stage to create the illusion of live reality through the iteration of rehearsal; this is the case in classical Stanislavskian scripted theatre, which is still quite commonly practiced [5]. Figure 1 diagrammatically shows key steps.

1/TEXT:	**2/REHEARSAL:**	**3/PERFORMANCE:**
The play exists as script; dramatic conversations, inscribed in text, to be interpreted by directors and actors. What will the play mean? What shall be its expressions, its gestures?	Gestural and verbal iterations. Actors and directors work together to form and langauge shaping the virtual reality of the work.	Gestural and verbal iterations are now fixed. Repeatable live performance is possible with a set, expressive paradigm of language and gestures.

Fig. 1. Diagrammatic representation of the three stages in expressive gesture development for theatre: a multimedia process. Images source: Google

The process of text / rehearsal / performance is then, importantly, a *linear multimedia process,* each phase separate to the other, developed through directorial interpretation of each step. These elements underpinned the design of the gestural interface following semiotic analysis. Directors interpret text with the outcome of repeated performance in mind. The process is further summarized in Figure 2, emphasizing the separate components, highlighting the presence of elements that are fixed, such as text, versus elements that are interpreted and therefore arbitrary.

Therefore, in Step 1, the severe ambiguity of gestural meaning was reduced. What emerged is a modelled process where expressive gestures can be manufactured according to a scripted plan.

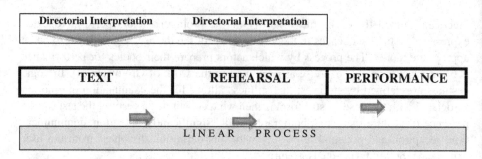

Fig. 2. The linear multimedia process used in classical theatre to create expressive gestures in a narrative context. Director's interpretation at script and rehearsal phases influences expressive content. Once performed, interpretation is complete. Scripts (text) are nevertheless static.

3.2   Step 2 Defining Multimedia HCI Inputs and Outputs

The range of input and output devices available was quite extensive and growing rapidly. The next question that needed resolution was: what combination of input and output devices would underpin a successful design where gestural and emotional human-computer interaction could proceed? The assumption that this would satisfy is that the experience was to be somehow modeled on the theatrical model. Table 1 indicates the large choice of user sensory experience; Table 2 indicates the wide choice if input devices.

Table 1. Sensory channels for potential user experience in HCI modality

Sensory perception	Sense organ	Modality
sense of sight	Eyes	Visual
sense of hearing	Ears	Auditive
sense of touch	Skin	Tactile
sense of smell	Nose	Olfactory
sense of taste	Tongue	Gustatory
sense of balance	Cochlea	Vestibular

The vast array of multimedia input / output systems was quite daunting. At this stage of development, the range of devices was seen as useful opportunities. The only design distinction that was made is that gestural interaction, that is to *touch,* was a foundational process as evidenced by Sutherland's invention of pen based interaction in 1962. The action of touching the screen was a gesture that located user presence in the matrices of the computer system. Touching is also an act of signification [6] a key semiotic process.

Table 2. Key advances of multimodal input /output devices with gestural application, adapted from Turk [7]

Attached Technological Device	Description	Date invented	Inventor / significant technical demonstration
pen based	pin pointing of light manipulated on screen	1963-5	Sutherland (1963)
tracker - based gloves	hands used as sophisticated control device	1992	Sturman (1992)
tracker based - data suits/ coda motion	continuous gesture analysis in combination with eye tracking	1994	Wexelblat (1994)
passive and computer vision gesture recognition	tracking of gestures using cameras	1870/ 1983	Muybridge([1887] 1957) Moeslund & Granum (2001)
head and face	FACS system measurement of facial movement	1978	Ekman & Friesen (1978)
hand and arms	graphic extraction of hand and arm positions	1995	Stark & Koehler (1995)
sign language (hearing impaired)	visual recognition of coded hand signals	1995	Starner & Pentland (1995)
body gestures	Pfinder system 2D representation of tracking and gesture recognition using statistical models of colour and shape	1996	Wren, Darrell, & Pentland (1996)
dance gestures	dancer generating music and graphics through body movements using Pfinder system	1999	Paradiso & Sparacino(1999)
laser based tracking			Perrin, Cassinelli & Ishikawa (2004)
floor pad systems	registers users entry into an environment and spatial coordinates through pressure sensitive pads		Hightower & Borriello, (2001)
magnetic field tracker	use of magnetic field to establish spatial coordinates		Hightower & Borriello, (2001)
Cave Virtual Automatic Environment	gestural manipulation of biological models	early 1990's	Berry, Pavlovic & Huang (1996)

Fig. 3. Ivan Sutherland's ground-breaking Sketchpad console, 1962. Sketchpad is operated with a light pen and a command button box (under left hand) [8] - evidence of gestural interaction.

3.3   Step 3 Forming a Semiotic Design Matrix

Winnograd [9] has stated that the computer is *a language machine.* Its processing of mathematical symbols, a part of its deep functions derives the term 'programming languages'; its extensive manipulation of image, text and sound representations in various combinations makes this invention a primary machine of communication. The computer then has many language systems within it. Semiotic analysis, a meta-language process that describes the symbolic and sign processes of potentially any language system, logically, would seem to offer a possible solution to design problems associated with computers - this language machine - an approach first proposed by Andersen [10]. The semiotic system here followed is that of Saussure [11], which is also Andersen's prescription. In particular, what was useful for the project at hand was Jakobson's [12] further extension into the notions of metaphor and metonymy. Significant modifications to semiotic analysis were necessary, particularly in view of the non-temporal capacity of semiotics; semiotics does not easily define dynamic, time-based systems, a key characteristic of expressive, performed gestures.

What is noteworthy is Kant's attempt to develop a system where all art forms could be represented in a schema, calling it a *System of the Arts* [13]. He begins with the premise that art is *essentially expressive,* just as language is, and for this reason language is a means by which the expressiveness of art can be understood (see Table 3). The key concepts used were *word, gesture,* and *tone.* He stated, that there are equivalent characteristics of both the execution and their function in human sensory processes. This presents something of a prototype to the process evolved. The qualities he attributed are categorized as follows:

Table 3. Kant's *System of the Arts* [14]

Word	Articulation	Thought
Gesture	Gesticulation	Intuition
Tone	Modulation	Sensation

As mentioned, the key semiotic tools used in this study were Jakobson's notions of metonymy and metaphor, to which was also added the term, utterance (see Table 4); the first two terms are characteristic of Jakobson's work on semiotics, metaphors being that which represents something else or other – from the Greek metapherein meaning 'to transfer', whilst metonymies represent the same - also from the Greek meaning 'to change name'. The third element added is utterance [15], that is, the speech act itself. This is the word as sound not as meaning. The significance of utterance is its temporal quality and that is the emanation of the word: it is ephemeral, fleeting. The 'act' itself of speaking is significant; something that happens once and once, only emphasizing the purely performative quality of language as voice. This element being ephemeral cannot be programmed whereas the metonymic, sequential

Table 4. Key Characteristics of Semiotic Terms

Semiotic Terms	Definition
Metaphor	Representation of other
Metonymy	Representation of same
Utterance	Ephemeral, not unlike speech

elements can. These terms and their key characteristics are represented in Table 4. Hence the expressive nature of the gesture is made equivalent to the expression of the word. To these three key terms abstractions are added: form, sequence, wave and world, to aid in understanding their characteristics and context - see Table 5.

Further, Table 5 shows comparisons of a number of the design elements for analysis and includes the semiotics for the final interactive film game. Most importantly, the theatrical model has within it elements that may support the HCI design in the game format. The interactive film game is then but a refiguring of the theatrical process. Andersen's [16] 'acting machine' is an analysis of a ship's multimedia system built by Andersen, highlighting the difference between two dimensional screen systems to the real action − or gestures − of users. The metonymic elements are particularly useful as they can be designed into the interaction of the system. Metaphors can be included but require interpretation. Whilst anything in the 'utterance' category is ephemeral and cannot be programmed or designed interactively.

Table 5. Semiotic Matrix of Human and Computer Elements

Abstraction	Semiotic	HCI	Yoga	Theatrical Model	Game Model	Acting Machine
Form	Metaphor	Image	Gesture	Gesture	Film content	Tool
Wave	Utterance	Sound	Emotion	Emotion	Emotions	Automaton
Sequence	Metonymy	Touch	Narrative	Text	Text/ Touch	Media
World	Linguistic	Virtual	Somatic	Stage	Ludic	Engineering

3.4   Step 4 Design of User Experience: Interactive Film Game *To be or not to be*

Users walked upon an array of a thirty-six square interactive floorpad measuring 3m x 3m connected to a Mac G5 computer which also controlled an adjacent 2m x 3m back

472   R. Danylak

4a   4b

Fig. 4. a, b. Interactor in two different gesture positions. The user is activating programmed floorpad patterns corresponding to the onscreen position map, activating film sequences to assemble a narrative. The emotional response to the assembled narrative as interpreted by the film director is essential. See http://www.youtube.com/watch?v=jKNvSpXG0Z0

projected multimedia screen with sound which the user faces when interacting with the floorpad (Figs. 4 a, b).

When interactors entered the room the work was in a steady default state displaying a title and brief description. As the interactors walked onto the floorpad this triggered the game cycle. The second screen gives a brief description of the game rules and the functions of the on-screen gesture map: green squares show a user where they are actively walking; blue squares are an indication of where users should walk to; red squares indicate that the user has hit a target, being in the right place at the right time on the programmed floorpad grid. The goal of the game – to solve all twenty-three gesture / word puzzles for full film play back – see Figures. 5 a, b, c.

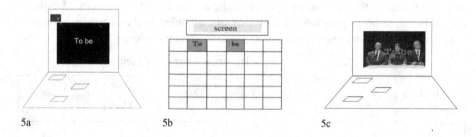

5a   5b   5c

Fig. 5. a,b,c. 5a shows the initial screen in gesture puzzle mode; 5b is a map of the floorpad programmed with positions to be found to activate the screen, the first of the twenty three such puzzles. 5c shows the system in playback of one film sequence of the Hamlet film.

Figs. 5(a) shows Step 1 of *To be or not to be*. The foreground shows some representative floor pad squares, thirty-six in total number, in a regular square configuration. The first two syllabic phrases of the *Hamlet* text appear in the middle of the screen illuminated by computer video back projection 'To be'. Interactors can see where they are standing on the active grid from the floor pad map in the upper left hand corner (green active squares). A pre-programmed blue flashing square also appears which the user must locate in the space corresponding to their position on the floorpad to activate the game goal of film playback. Having reached the target square, shown by a red square appearing on the map, a section of the Hamlet film plays. 5(b) is a map of the first two gestures to be solved on the floor pad appearing as blue square screen targets to be located on the floor pad, turning to red on activation. These have been pre-programmed along with loaded reward film sequences. Fig. 5c shows the first film sequence playback. Each sequence lasts 4-7 seconds and is evolved from the Shakespeare text that has been used in the gesture floor pad puzzle 'To be'. Multimedia text appears on the film surface reinforcing the narrative experience. Essentially, the interactor, by walking about the floor pad, assembles the Hamlet film. Once all twenty-three puzzles are solved the film plays back in its entirety as a single work, communicating specific emotional messages formed by the director's interpretation.

3.5   Step 5   Evaluation

Evaluation of the system was carried out with a number of random participants. The gestural interaction hit rate with the floorpads was recorded in the MAC G5 and showed consistent interactor learning of gestures. Verbal protocol analysis of the interactor response to the film content showed consistent emotional reaction to the film when compared to the directorial intention of the film message for the audience. Hence the interpreted film meaning was successfully communicated *emotionally* to users whilst generating a predictable *gestural response* [17].   The equation formed is: gesture sequence 'x' generated an associated emotional response to content 'y'.

4   Conclusion

As Andersen has stated, the division between the human experience and the machine process is formidable [18]. However, the careful modeling of gestures from the theatrical process set a real and workable foundation for the entire task. Defining the gesture as a 'photographic still' removed the inherent ambiguity of gestural meaning establishing an equation between gesture and computer gestural input. Furthermore, semiotics enabled the design of *To be or not to be* by offering equivalences between the human and experience and the machine design. Semiotic analysis is effective if the correct cognitive modeling is developed with adjustments to the semiotic categories to accommodate temporality. Lastly, it was the game design that refigured the theatrical process into an interactive film game, where interactors could build a narrative using walking gestures and also respond emotionally to the director interpreted narrative content. The design enabled a continuous and coherent gestural and emotional user interaction, evidenced in evaluation studies.

References

1. Bolt, R.A.: Put That There: Siggraph Computer Graphics. In: Proceedings of the 7th Annual Conference on Computer Graphics and Interactive Techniques ACM, vol. 14(3), pp. 262–270 (1980)
2. Oviatt, S.: Multimodal Interfaces. In: Jacko, J.A., Sears, A. (eds.) Human-Computer Interaction Handbook. Lawrence Erbaum & Associates, Mahwah (2003)
3. Pantic, M., Sebu, N., Cohn, J.F., Huang, T.: Affective Multimodal Human-Computer Interaction. In: Conference Proceedings, Multimedia 2005, pp. 669–676. ACM, Singapore (2005)

4. Grotowski, J.: Towards a Poor Theatre. Methuen, London (1969)
5. Stanislavsky, C.: Building a Character. Methuen and Co. Great Britain (1936, 1981)
6. Danylak, R., Edmonds, E.: Touch as the Act of Signification: naming as a Key design Concept for Gesturally Intuitive Interactive Space. In: Engage, Interaction, Art and Audience Experience. Creativity and Cognition Studios Press (2006)
7. Turk, M.: Gesture Recognition. In: Stanney, K. (ed.) Handbook of Virtual Environment Tech., p. 8 (2002)
8. Muller-Prove, M.: User Experience and Interface Design (2008), http://www.Mprove.De/Diplom/Text/3.1.2_Sketchpad.Html (viewed March 22, 2008)
9. Winnograd, T.: Scientific American. In: Rheingold, H. (ed.) Virtual Reality, p. 215, Touchstone (1991)
10. Andersen, P.B.: A Theory of Computer Semiotics: Semiotic Approaches to Construction and Assessment of Computer Systems. Cambridge University Press, UK (1990)
11. Saussure, F.: Course in General Linguistics. McGraw-Hill, New York (1986)
12. Jakobson, R.: Two Aspects of Language and Two Types of Aphasic Disturbances. In: Pomorska, K., Rudy, S. (eds.) Language and Literature, Harvard University Press, Cambridge (1956)
13. Kant, E.: The Critique of Judgement. Oxford University Press, UK (1790, 1848, 1978); Meredith, J.C.(trans.)
14. Slater, H.: The System of the Arts. The Journal of Aesthetics and Art Criticism 51(4), 611–617 (1993)
15. Greimas, A.J., Courtes, J.: Semiotics and Language: an Analytical Dictionary. Indiana Univ. (1979)
16. Andersen, P.B.: Acting Machines. In: Liestol, G., Morrison, A., Rasmussen, T. (eds.) Digital Media Revisited, pp. 183–213. MIT Press, Cambridge (2004)
17. Danylak, R.: A Semiotic Analysis of Gesture and Emotion in Artistic Human Computer Interaction. Doctoral Thesis. University of Technology, Sydney (2008)
18. Andersen, P.B.: What Semiotics Can and Cannot Do for HCI. Knowledge-Based Systems 14(8), 419–424 (2001)

Evaluating Emotional Responses to the Interior Design of a Hospital Room: A Study Using Virtual Reality

Susana Dinis[1], Emília Duarte[1], Paulo Noriega[2,3],
Luís Teixeira[2,3], Elisângela Vilar[2,3], and Francisco Rebelo[2,3]

[1] Unidcom, IADE – Creative University, Av. D. Carlos I, 4, 1200-649 Lisboa, Portugal
susana_dinis@msn.com, emilia.duarte@iade.pt
[2] Ergonomics Laboratory, Faculdade de Motricidade Humana, Universidade Técnica de Lisboa,
Estrada da Costa, 1499-002, Cruz Quebrada – Dafundo, Portugal
{pnoriega,lmteixeira,elivilar,frebelo}@fmh.utl.pt
[3] CIPER – Interdisciplinary Center for the Study of Human Performance, Universidade Técnica
de Lisboa, Estrada da Costa, 1499-002 Cruz-Quebrada, Dafundo, Portugal

Abstract. Many studies have shown the ability of interior design elements (e.g., artwork, nature, home elements) to elicit positive emotions on hospital users thereby enhancing the healing process. Nevertheless, it is not clear whether such elements can affect users' emotional responses during a VR experience. In this study we explored the influence of interior design elements (i.e., landscape poster, painting, plant and home chair), on the participants' emotional responses after being exposed to 3D virtual hospital rooms. We used a short version of Zipers scales, developed by Zuckerman, to explore participants' emotional responses regarding 28 rooms, resulting from all the possible combinations of the identified elements plus a neutral and a negative room. Our sample included 30 university students. The results show that the more elements present in the hospital room the more positive the emotional response. The landscape and artwork elements emitted positive responses, whereas the home chair did not.

Keywords: Interior Design, Hospital, Emotion, Virtual Reality.

1 Introduction

Traditionally, healthcare settings (e.g., hospitals) were conceived bearing in mind functionality and sterilization issues primarily. While failing to comply with such requisites leads to poor solutions, with obvious consequences on the quality of the health care services, their satisfaction, however, does not necessarily mean that an environment has a positive effect on patients' feelings. A clear understanding of the effect of specific features of the environment on the patients' health and well-being may help the design of more effective healthcare environments.

Studies on restorative environments have pointed out the importance of the hospital environment on patients' health and well-being, see [1, 2] for a review. Some studies

A. Marcus (Ed.): DUXU/HCII 2013, Part III, LNCS 8014, pp. 475–483, 2013.

suggest that the quality of the environment's aesthetics affects the patients' perceptions and can have an important effect on their well-being and recovery [e.g., 3, 4, 5]. Other investigators have identified nature as an element which has a positive impact on the visual aesthetics of the hospital's design [e.g., 6, 7], and has stress-reducing properties [e.g., 8] which can influence the healing process [9], as well as the patients' tolerance to pain [10, 11]. As a result, many hospitals are now privileging sights for gardens, or more commonly, are incorporating nature in the form of artwork or posters depicting the so-called "therapeutic landscapes". Such a positive effect is also extended to indoor plants, which were found to reduce the patients' feelings of stress through the perceived attractiveness of the room [7]. Furthermore, because most people associate medical devices and sterile look to "feeling unwell", home-like environments of healthcare were also found to ease psychological stress and positively affect the healing and well-being of patients [12]. Finally, artwork has also been suggested as having a positive effect on the patients' perceptions [13-15].

Interior design features (e.g., artwork, indoor plants, furniture) stand out among the features of the environment that have the power to affect the health and well-being (e.g., architectural features: layout, dimensions; ambient features: lighting, temperature) because they are a relatively easy and inexpensive way to change the environment, specially for interventions on built facilities (e.g., renovations, use changes). For this reason this study is concerned with the ability of interior design elements to elicit positive emotions on hospital users.

Many studies on this topic used photographs [e.g., 7, 11, 16] or videotape [8] to depict the environments, and participants were asked to evaluate the scenes. However, such presentation modes differ on their ability to mimic the actual real-world scene, and have limitations (e.g., lack of stereoscopic vision and interactivity, difficulties in manipulating the scene's features) that can affect the studies' both internal and external validities. To further clarify the validity of VEs for this type of studies, in the present study we used a Virtual Reality (VR) simulation to immerse the participants in a Virtual Environment (VE), in which they are not physically present but where they might feel that they were really there (sense of presence). Previous studies have shown that VR is able to simulate realistically looking environments [17, 18] which have the capacity to induct or affect the participants' moods[19, 20], especially if associated with a contextualized narrative [21].

The purpose of this paper is to report the results of a study that explored the influence of interior design elements (i.e., landscape poster, painting, plant and a home chair), on the participants' emotional responses after experiencing 3D virtual hospital rooms. In this context, this study addresses two major research questions:

1. Examine to what extent the emotional response of the hospital's room users are affected by the number of design elements (considered as positive) present in the room.
2. Assess how the category of the interior design elements (i.e., plants, landscape views, artwork, home furniture) relates to the emotional response.

Considering the conclusions reported in literature, it is proposed that:

H1: The greater the number of positive elements present in the room, the more positive the evaluation will be among the users.

H2: The emotional response is more positive in the presence of natural objects (e.g., plants) than with visually structured objects (e.g., furniture).

2   Materials and Methods

2.1   Design

A within-subjects design was used. The independent variables were: (1) type of element present in the room (i.e., plant, painting, poster, and chair) and (2) number of coexistent elements in the room (1 to 4). In addition, two other rooms were created, one with negative elements (i.e., influenza posters), and another with no-elements, as a baseline and control condition, respectively.

The dependent variables were ratings on the following Zuckerman's 6 five-point Zipers scales (Zuckerman Inventory of Personal Reactions) [22], with (1) Not at all and (5) Very Much, as anchors:

1. I felt angry or defiant.
2. I felt fearful.
3. I felt sad.
4. I felt carefree or playful.
5. I felt elated or pleased.
6. I felt like acting friendly or affectionate.

2.2   Participants

Thirty university students, 18 females and 12 males, aged between 18 and 28 years (M = 22.33, SD = 2.294) participated in the study. They had normal sight or had corrective lenses, as well as normal color vision [23]. They also reported no physical or mental conditions that would prevent them from participating in a VR simulation. Before the experiment, subjects were informed of the overall goals of the experiment but were unaware of the study's main hypotheses. All participants were asked to sign an informed consent form.

2.3   Equipment and Experimental Setup

The VE was rendered and updated by the ErgoVR system [24]. The visual scene was projected onto a wall screen, 1.72 m (59.7° of horizontal field-of-view - FOV) by 0.95 m (35.2° of vertical FOV) with an aspect ratio of 16:9, by a stereoscopic projector (Lightspeed DepthQ 3D). The observation distance (i.e., the distance between the observer's eyes and the screen) was 1.50 m. Participants were seated during the experiment. The virtual rooms were observed in stereoscopy, through active glasses

(MacNaughton Inc.'s APG6000), with a simulation of an egocentric perspective of the participant lying in bed, with freedom of head movements. Participants could visually explore the VE using a standard mouse as the input device. Moving the mouse right, left, up or down allowed the participants to control their perspective.

A sheet of paper with the Zipers scales printed with large characters was placed on the participant's table, in front of him/her. The experimenter took notes on paper, about the participants' oral responses. The experimenter's setup was located on a table, 1 m behind the participant. The room was dark so that no external light would influence the VE.

Fig. 1. Experimental setup showing a participant with the equipment (left), and the wall screen displaying the VE (right)

2.4   Virtual Environment

The VE for this experiment consisted of a square hospital room, floor area around 9 m2, with a corridor, 1.5 m wide, containing the entrance door (not visible from the participants' viewpoint). The walls and ceiling were light gray and the floor beige. The VE also contained a variable configuration of elements (independent variables), which were positioned, interchangeably, either on the front or left walls. A bed, and a window with frosted glass, on the right wall, was constant in all rooms, except for those on the negative and neutral conditions that had no window. An example environment is shown in Figure 2, in which the four elements are present.

2.5   Procedure

Participants were welcomed by the researcher and were briefed about the study, after which they were requested to sign an informed consent form. Prior to the experiment, each participant was checked for color vision deficiencies using the Ishihara Color Test [23].

Fig. 2. Hospital room with the four elements (from left to right, painting, plant, poster, and chair)

Before testing, participants were placed in a sample environment and directed to familiarize themselves with the control of the mouse and the questionnaire. They were instructed to practice until they felt completely comfortable with the equipment and the task. After training was completed, they watched a video in which a person enters an Emergency Room with a broken leg, for contextualization. At this point, the experimenter told them a cover story in which they had suffered an accident, which broke their leg, and that they were in the hospital room after having received medical care.

The participants' task was to observe each room and rate their emotional responses using the six Zipers scales. They were randomly given the 28 rooms, which they could observe for a period of 10 seconds, and were instructed to respond as accurately as possible. They could use the mouse to change their viewpoint. The order in which the rooms were presented to the participants was balanced using two randomized sequences.

After completing the task, each participant filled out a simulator sickness questionnaire and a questionnaire about the experience with the simulation. The whole experiment lasted about 30 minutes including the initial instructions, the training phase, as well as the test and questionnaire after the experiment.

3   Results

All the results from the scales were transformed in order to match: the minor value (1), being the worst emotional response to a room; and the highest value (5), being the best emotional response to a room. The results present an average of the six Zipers scales used.

3.1   Number of Elements in the Room

Figure 3 shows boxplots for emotional responses attained by the rooms with 4 to 1 elements. As demonstrated, the more elements present in the hospital room, the better the evaluation.

A Friedman test was conducted to evaluate differences in medians between the ratings for rooms with 4 elements (Median = 3.58), with 3 elements (Median = 3.17), with 2 elements (Median = 2.90), with 1 element (Median 2.64) and for negative and neutral rooms together (Median = 2.25). The test revealed a significant effect of the number of elements in the room on the emotional responses $\chi2(4, N = 30) = 99.16$, $p < .001$. Post-hoc multiple comparisons (Fisher's LSD method performed on ranks) showed that there were significant differences between all pairs ($p < .001$).

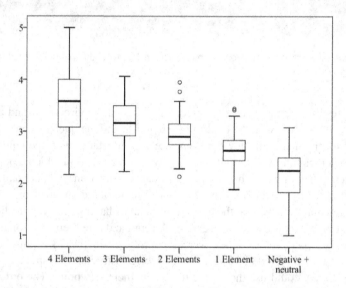

Fig. 3. Boxplot for the ratings on emotional response by rooms with different numbers and types of elements

Therefore, the hypothesis that the greater the number of positive elements presented in the room, the more positive the evaluation would be among users, was supported by the results.

3.2   Type of Elements in the Room

This descriptive analysis is based on the rooms with three, two and one element. Since in the rooms with four elements, i.e., all elements are present, it is not possible to discriminate which element is responsible for the highest positive emotional response.

For each set of rooms (rooms with 3 elements, 2 elements and 1 element) we hierarchically categorized the rooms according to the most positive emotional response to the less positive. Subsequently, we identified which elements were present in each room. Thus, it was possible to determine, in each set, which elements were responsible for the most positive and the less positive emotional responses.

In the room with three elements, the landscape and painting were responsible for more positive evaluations, followed by the plant and the furniture. In the rooms with two elements, the results were scattered. However, we can conclude that in first place, was the painting, then the plant, next the landscape and last the furniture.

In the rooms with one element, the results are clear. First the painting, second the plant, third the landscape and, again, with the less positive emotional response, the room with the furniture.

There are more powerful elements that, when present, regardless of the other elements, always cause a positive appreciation of the room. However, these more influential elements are not always the same, because they vary depending on the number of elements present in the room. The poster landscape and painting are those that relate to more positive evaluations, while the home chair presents less positive evaluations. Therefore, the hypothesis that the emotional response is more positive in the presence of natural objects (e.g., plants) than with visually structured objects (e.g., furniture) is only partially supported by the results.

4   Discussion

Preliminary data discussed in this paper provides insights, to both researchers and practitioners, about the importance of interior design decisions on the patients' evaluations of the hospital environment. This is an important topic if, following a User Centered Design approach, one wishes to create an environment with the patients' needs and expectations in mind.

The current study used a Virtual Environment to investigate the effect of several interior design elements, indicated in literature as having a positive effect on patients' perceptions and emotional responses towards a hospital room. The primary hypothesis was that positive emotional responses would be greater for rooms with more elements present. Additionally, we also hypothesized that rooms with natural elements (i.e., plants) would gather more positive emotional responses than those with home objects (i.e., chair).

This study corroborates previous findings suggesting that the presence of elements such as artworks [13, 14], natural elements such as plants [7] and landscape views [9], and home elements (e.g., furniture) in hospital rooms [13] exert a positive influence on patients' perceptions, acting as a positive influence on their recovery. Furthermore, the results suggest that the more positive elements present in the room, the more positive the emotional response gathered. The results also indicate, as expected, that people do not feel comfortable in minimal/empty rooms (i.e., without any other objects besides the bed) and rooms without windows that have negative elements (e.g., influenza posters). Thus, it seems that people feel significantly more comfortable in rooms that are decorated with plants, posters, artwork and home furniture, which we can generically describe as tasteful, colorful and warm/cozy. One possible explanation for these findings is that when patients are able to distract themselves from the reality (which can be painful and unpleasant), by looking at positive stimuli, their anxiety/stress decreases because they can think of something other than the health issue.

While the decisions regarding the interior design are an important topic to consider in research on patients' perceptions, equally important are the methodological aspects of conducting such type of studies. Is VR an adequate and viable option for evaluating people emotional responses and expectations regarding a product, in this case an environment? In order to address this question more data would be necessary besides the one reported here. However, a preliminary verification of the post-hoc responses appears to indicate that the participants experienced medium-high values of presence and immersion in the VE. Furthermore, after post-procedure interviews, the participants reported no relevant usability issues. Thus, based on this and supported by the fact that we were able to elicit responses in VR that are similar to/comparable with responses in real-world situations, we consider that VEs can provide valid outcomes for the environmental perception.

Some cautions are required when generalizing this study's findings, namely because of the study's exploratory nature, and the limitations of the reduced version of the Zipers scale used for evaluating the emotional responses and the sample of university students, who might not have had a recent hospital experience. Additional research is also needed to refine the VE and the level of interaction offered by the VR system. Future research should also replicate this study with actual patients, eventually from a senior population, who are in hospitals. Recruiting real patients may enhance results. Finally, future studies could consider the use of eye-tracking technologies in order to give further insights about the patients' perceptions.

Hospital administrators, health care practitioners, and interior designers ought to view the results of this study both as a reminder that the interior design of the hospital influences the users' perceptions, as well as that VR provides an interesting methodological opportunity for conducting this type of research.

References

1. Dijkstra, K., Pieterse, M., Pruyn, A.: Physical environmental stimuli that turn healthcare facilities into healing environments through psychologically mediated effects: systematic review. Journal of Advanced Nursing 56(2), 166–181 (2006)
2. Leather, P., Beale, D., Santos, A.: Outcomes of environmental appraisal of different hospital waiting areas. Environment & Behavior 35(6), 842–869 (2003)
3. Caspari, S., Eriksson, K., Nåden, D.: The aesthetic dimension in hospitals—An investigation into strategic plans. International Journal of Nursing Studies 43, 851–859 (2006)
4. Lawton, M.P., Van Haitsma, K., Klapper, J.: Observed affect in nursing home residents with alzheimer's disease. Journal of Gerontology 51B(1), 3–14 (1996)

5. Rubin, H.R., Owens, A.J., Golden, G.: Status report : An investigation to determine whether the built environment affects patients' medical outcomes. The Center for Health Design, Inc., Baltimore (1998)
6. Gesler, W.: Healing places. Roman & Littlefield Publishers, Lanham (2003)
7. Dijkstra, K., Pieterse, M., Pruyn, A.: Stress-reducing effects of indoor plants in the built healthcare environment: The mediating role of perceived attractiveness. Preventive Medicine 47, 279 (2008)
8. Ulrich, R., Simons, R.F., Losito, B.D., Fiorito, E., Miles, M.A., Zelson, M.: Stress recovery during exposure to natural and urban environments. Journal of Environmental Psychology 11, 201–230 (1991)
9. Ulrich, R.: View through a window may influence recovery from surgery. Science 224, 420–421 (1984)
10. Diette, G.B., Lechtzin, N., Haponik, E., Devrotes, A., Rubin, H.R.: Distraction therapy with nature sights and sounds reduces pain during flexible bronchoscopy: A complementary approach to routine analgesia. Chest 123, 941–948 (2003)
11. Lohr, V.I., Pearson-Mims, C.H.: Physical discomfort may be reduced in the presence of interior plants. Horttechnology 10, 53–58 (2000)
12. Douglas, C.H., Douglas, M.R.: Patient-friendly hospital environments: Exploring the patients' perspective. Health Expectations 7(1), 61–73 (2004)
13. Arneill, A.B., Devlin, A.S.: Perceived quality of care: The influence of the waiting room environment. Journal of Environmental Psychology 22(4), 345–360 (2002)
14. Ulrich, R.: Effects of interior design on wellness: theory and recent scientific research. Journal of Health Care Interior Design 3, 97–109 (1991)
15. Cusack, P., Lankston, L., Isles, C.: Impact of visual art in patient waiting rooms: survey of patients attending a transplant clinic in Dumfries. Journal of the Royal Society of Medicine Short Reports 1(52), 1–5 (2010)
16. Bishop, I.D., Rohrmann, B.: Subjective responses to simulated and real environments: A comparison. Landscape and Urban Planning 65, 261–277 (2003)
17. Marshden, J.P.: Older persons' and family members' perceptions of homeyness in assisted living. Environment & Behavior 31, 84–106 (1999)
18. Rohrmann, B., Bishop, I.D.: Subjective responses to computer simulations of urban environments. Journal of Environmental Psychology 22, 319–331 (2002)
19. Riva, G., Mantovani, F., Capideville, C.S., Preziosa, A., Morganti, F., Villani, D., Gaggioli, A., Botella, C., Alcañiz, M.: Affective interactions using virtual reality: The link between presence and emotions. CyberPsychology & Behavior 10(1), 45–56 (2007)
20. Gorini, A., Mosso, J.L., Mosso, D., Pineda, E., Ruíz, N.L., Ramíez, M., Morales, J.L., Riva, G.: Emotional response to virtual reality exposure across different cultures: The role of the attribution process. CyberPsychology & Behavior 12(6), 699–705 (2009)
21. Gorini, A., Capideville, C.S., Leo, G.D., Mantovani, F., Riva, G.: The role of immersion and narrative in mediated presence: The virtual hospital experience. CyberPsychology, Behavior, and Social Networking, 1–7 (2010)
22. Zuckerman, M.: Development of a situation-specific trait-state test for the prediction and measurement of affective response. Journal of Consulting and Clinical Psychology 45, 513–523 (1977)
23. Ishihara, S.: Test for Colour-Blindness, 38th edn. Kanehara & Co., Ltd., Tokyo (1988)
24. Teixeira, L., Rebelo, F., Filgueiras, E.: Human interaction data acquisition software for virtual reality: A user-centered design approach. In: Kaber, D.B., Boy, G. (eds.) Advances in Cognitive Ergonomics, pp. 793–801. CRC Press, Boca Raton (2010)

Changing Eating Behaviors through a Cooking-Based Website for the Whole Family

Marc Fabri, Andrew Wall, and Pip Trevorrow

Leeds Metropolitan University, Leeds, United Kingdom
{m.fabri,p.trevorrow}@leedsmet.ac.uk, andy_wall9@hotmail.com

Abstract. This paper reports on the results of a study investigating how nutritional eating behaviors can be improved by presenting a cooking-based website for parents to use with their children. Participants' eating behaviors were closely monitored via questionnaires and food diaries. Results show that over the course of the study, children's willingness to consume fruit and vegetables had improved and they enjoyed participating in food preparation. This was supported by the participants' food diaries, which showed a statistically significant increase in the number of portions of fruit and vegetables consumed by both children and parents. An attempt was made to place participants in a stage of change before and after the study (Transtheoretical Model). This was flawed, however, due to inaccurate measurements and the short study duration. Overall, this study provides support for the use of educational websites, in particular a cooking website, to improve nutritional eating behaviors in children.

Keywords: Obesity, Nutrition, Behavior Change, Persuasive Technology.

1 Introduction

Childhood nutrition has a significant impact on the physical and mental development of children [1]. Developing interventions to improve children's healthy eating behaviors is therefore extremely important and should be researched thoroughly. Consumption of fruit and vegetables during childhood can decrease the risk of many types of cancer [2], cardiovascular disease [3] and stroke [4], as well as diabetes and bowel disorders [5]. Furthermore, the World Health Organisation (WHO) estimated that 70% of premature deaths in adulthood can be attributed to health related behaviors learned in adolescence [6]. There has been rising concern over the increasing numbers of overweight and obese in the population globally. In developed countries in particular, childhood obesity has been seen to reach epidemic levels [7]. The UK [8] viewed the problem as so severe that they claimed that the current generation of children is the first for over a century whose life expectancy has fallen. It concluded that unless action was taken, by 2050 60% of men, 50% of women and 25% of children would be obese. Not only this, but also that the numbers of overweight in the population would reach approximately 90% of adults and 66% of children [9]. Figures such as these

A. Marcus (Ed.): DUXU/HCII 2013, Part III, LNCS 8014, pp. 484–493, 2013.
© Springer-Verlag Berlin Heidelberg 2013

have provided the impetus for the British government to develop a number of campaigns to promote healthy eating in people of all ages. These campaigns include "Healthy Weight, Healthy Lives" [10], which is a cross-government strategy to focus on the prevention and management of excess weight, and the "Change4Life" campaign [11]. The Change4Life campaign uses multiple approaches to encourage the improvement of healthy eating and a more active lifestyle. The campaign includes an informative website which features lots of ideas for improving families' diets without increasing costs, tips for lifestyle changes that would complement dietary changes, further details about what campaigns are currently taking place throughout the country and links to national partners. The campaign also features activities that are rolled out into the community at places such as schools and nurseries. For example the Games4Life campaign, which is designed to encourage physical activity in children's' everyday lives, was introduced in June 2012. Another example is the successful MoreLife residential summer camps for overweight and obese children, supported by the British National Health Service [12]. The annual program includes a daily schedule of six one-hour, skill-based, fun, physical activity sessions, moderate dietary restriction, and group-based educational sessions [12]. In a further effort to disseminate information on nutrition to the public, the government have also delivered a series of training courses to nursery and school staff called HENRY (Health, Exercise and Nutrition for the Really Young) [13]. The training not only teaches staff about current government guidelines for nutritional standards such as portion sizes and advised nutritional intake, but also how to best convey this information to community members. This approach emphasizes the need to help parents come to the appropriate conclusions themselves rather than bombarding them with information, thereby giving them the knowledge and skills to reach such conclusions without any help in the future [13].

2   Healthy Eating Behaviors

Research suggests that the primary focus of improving healthy eating behaviors should be upon children rather than adults. Obesity is difficult to reverse in adults and even older children [14]. Taveras et al [15] extended this by suggesting that healthy eating strategies should begin as early as possible, preferably when feeding practices are just beginning. Similarly, it has been found that people will continue to eat foods that they ate as children throughout their lives [16]. This was mirrored in a longitudinal study of food intake which found that children who selected the least healthy foods at the beginning of the study continued to do so throughout the study [17]. Lytle et al [18] examined eating patterns in children in American elementary, junior high and middle schools. Interestingly, they found that the consumption of breakfast, fruit, vegetables and milk decreased with increasing age. For example, fruit consumption decreased by 41% between the 3rd and 8th grades, whilst vegetable consumption decreased by 25% and the amount of soft drinks consumed more than tripled. These startling results prompted the authors to highlight the need for promotion of healthy eating behaviors both at home and at school, particularly in adolescents [19].

2.1 The Importance of Parental Involvement

The influence that parents have on their children's diet has been displayed by many researchers. Olivera et al [20] performed a study examining the food intake of preschool children and their parents concluding that parents should be the target of interventions attempting to change their children's diets. Story et al [21] found that parental practices and foods available at home were strongly influential in the dietary decisions of children. Lindsay et al [22] described parental influence as the most important influence on a child's healthy eating behavior, and that understanding the variety of influences the parent has is key to preventing poor healthy eating behaviors. This conclusion was also reached elsewhere [14] following a systematic review of interventions that target parents. In their critique they suggested that it is an area of research that is still in its infancy, but shows promise as an obesity prevention strategy. There is much research that provides evidence for the need to target childhood health through their parents. For example, a relationship was found between the quality of children's diets and their mother's health motivation [23]. Another interesting finding was that mothers did not necessarily eat the same food as their children [24]. Perhaps encouraging parents and children to eat together and to eat the same food would motivate more healthy eating behaviors. Further, children of adolescent age were found to be more likely to eat breakfast if their parents did too [25].

2.2 Using Websites to Modify Eating Behavior

Such a large proportion of the UK population, in fact 77% of households as of August 2011, now has access to the internet that it must be considered as a viable method of disseminating information [26]. Clark et al [27] developed a website used to disseminate information to childcare providers about feeding infants. Participants used the website for a 3 month period, completing surveys on knowledge of and attitudes towards nutrition before and after using the site. Results showed that both knowledge of and attitudes towards infant nutrition improved, but not to a statistically significant extent. The authors conceded that this may have been due to the extremely basic nature of the website. In the United States, the First Lady Michelle Obama's Let's Move initiative [28] is a coordinated strategy to significantly reduce childhood obesity within in a generation. It combines legislative efforts with advice on the Let's Move website and affiliated sites, offering parents advice with nutrition facts, recipes, and step-by-step action plans. However, it is mainly targeted at parents and it is too early to assess the impact of the initiative.

Our aim in the current study was to employ a fun and engaging user experience in an attempt to produce significant positive behavior change results. In particular, we considered images children would respond to as central to the experience. The use of images in learning and behavior acquisition has been found to have a positive effect, and there is a particular prevalence in the use of images in software aimed at children [15]. Research on using websites to disseminate nutritional information is still in its early stages, and more research is required to determine whether this is the most appropriate method of disseminating such information, particularly given the rise of mobile apps. In the present study, it is hoped that using a website as a behavior intervention will influence eating behaviors of participants for the better, i.e. they eat more healthy fruit and vegetables. From the discussed research, it is clear that instilling these behaviors early in life is vital in ensuring their presence and maintenance later in life. Therefore the website to be used in this study will be aimed at parents and their young children.

3   Transtheoretical Model of Change

This study uses the Transtheoretical Model (TTM) of behavior change as a basis for assessing participants' healthy eating behaviors. TTM has been used extensively to develop interventions which can be tailored to the individual's stage of readiness to change an unhealthy behavior or to adopt healthy lifestyle behaviors [29-30]. The TTM focuses on understanding how behavior changes, asserting that individuals move through 5 distinct stages of behavior change [30]:

1. The individual having no intention to change the behavior within the next 6 months (*pre-contemplation stage*).
2. They would move to the *contemplation stage* upon intending to change their behavior within the next 6 months.
3. When the individual has a serious intention to change the behavior within the next 30 days they are in the *preparation stage*.
4. The *action stage* is marked by engaging in the behavior change at the target level for 6 months or less.
5. Once this behavior change has been sustained for more than 6 months, the individual has reached the *maintenance stage*.

Before reaching the final stage individuals will often move through the five stages in a cyclical fashion [31] due to relapses of behavior whereby the individual could re-enter the cycle at any of the prior stages.

4   Website Prototype

Building on the research and government initiatives outlined above, the study reported in this paper had the overall aim to investigate whether regular usage of a cooking-based website can improve nutritional eating behaviors. The website was designed for both children and their parents to encourage healthy eating behaviors for the whole family. It contains content related to cooking and nutrition including a blog with recipes, cook-a-long videos, specially featured meals, a forum for users to discuss nutrition-based issues, information on healthy eating and links to related websites. The main tool for delivering the content and engaging users is a cuddly toy bear called Noodles. Users of the website can also find out more about the Noodles character and its back story. The decision to introduce a toy character was based on previous research which stated the importance of including a 'fun factor' in systems for children [32] as well as the 'Computers As Social Actors' (CASA) model [33-34]. CASA presumes that interfaces supported by toy characters can make technology interactions simpler and more intuitive because they are built on implicit social understandings that users already have, and hence require no extra learning or accommodation [34]. This is particularly the case for young children, who due to their stage of development generally have cognitive and motor limitations [35].

Page layout, design and richness of experience was somewhat restricted by the site's prototype nature. Figure 1 shows the homepage with navigation, image carousel, Noodles' back story and the recipe blog further down the page. The main aim of the research was to create a proof-of-concept, whilst visual design of the website is an area worthy of future consideration and research.

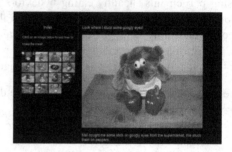

Fig. 1. Website Homepage   **Fig. 2.** Recipe blog entry and index of recipes on the left

5   Study Details

The study employed qualitative and quantitative methods to investigate changes in participants' healthy eating behaviors before and after using the website.

5.1   Procedure

Participants were recruited via opportunity sampling. Altogether 7 mothers between the age of 40 and 47 took part. Children were in the age range 5-11, attending one of three different schools. All mothers were provided with an information sheet on the investigation and gave their informed consent to participate. The sample size is small and this was due to the time of the study – during the school summer holidays. Study duration varied from participant to participant. The shortest was 17 consecutive days, the longest 20 consecutive days. Given the small number of participants available to take part in this study and the potential complexity of eating behaviors, semi-structured interviews were deemed the most appropriate method of gathering rich data. Semi-structured interviews utilize a fixed set of core questions to be covered whilst enabling the interviewee to provide clarification or elaboration on any issues that may be relevant to the study [36], thereby providing flexibility.

Participants took part in a pre-intervention semi-structured interview to provide both quantitative and qualitative data on initial eating habits. Any barriers perceived by participants to limit nutritional eating behaviors could be investigated, as well as the willingness of both parents and children to eat fruit and vegetables. The interview also involved participants completing a questionnaire to identify which TTM stage of change each participant was in at the time. The questionnaire, previously used by Green et al [30], included items that mapped directly to one of the TTM stages. The same interview structure used post-intervention so that a comparison could be made to assess any apparent changes. Additionally, the post-intervention interview contained a set of questions related to website content and usability. Interviews were transcribed and any differences in answers between the two interviews were noted. During the intervention period participants completed food diaries by recording meals and detailing the numbers of portions of fruit and vegetables consumed, to the nearest half portion. Diaries were completed on a particular weekday, once a week This frequency was regarded as the most accurate and most practical alternative to observing participants 24/7. Participants were encouraged to make records of foods consumed immediately after each meal to minimize erroneous or missing entries.

5.2   Interview Results

The pre and post-intervention interviews suggest that the intervention had a positive effect on participants' attitudes to healthy eating. All participants reported that the use of the website had made their children keener and more willing to cook with them and try new foods, but participants did not explicitly state that they had been eating more healthily in this period.

The majority of parents were always willing to consume fruit and vegetables, but in reality there were varying degrees of actual healthy eating behaviors. The most common reported barrier was *time restrictions related to working patterns*. However, participants were generally interested in their children's healthy eating behavior and seemed to make more of an effort to get their children to eat more healthy foods following the study. The amount of meals participants and their children ate together varied greatly, both between participants and on different days or times of year for each participant. Somewhat predictably, this was directly related to children's school hours. Whether participants ate the same meals as their children also varied, with some eating the same meals but later than their children, or, as one participant reported, only eating what their child leaves on their plate. These behaviors remained unchanged during the intervention period, and appeared to be derived from longstanding habits and routines. Most participants reported a gradual introduction of new recipes, attempting to find new foods that their children enjoyed. Some very actively changed their family's diet. One participant who did report making an active change stated that whilst it was difficult at first, it became much easier once a routine was established.

5.3   TTM Stages

Figure 3 shows the stages of the TTM that participants were considered to be in at the pre and post-intervention interviews. Two of the seven participants progressed forwards along TTM stages, while one participant stayed at the same stage and four participants moved backwards:

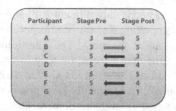

Fig. 3. TTM stage change by participant

These results were surprising, and suggest potential issues with the questionnaire and participants' judgment of their own fruit and vegetable consumption. For example, participants A and B moved from stage 3 (preparation) to stage 5 (maintenance), a behavior change that normally takes at least 12 months. Participants D and F moved backwards, which is possible but unlikely, especially in the short time period. The questionnaire, or rather the inferences taken from self-reported consumption with regards to TTM stages, are clearly flawed and require further attention.

Food Diaries. Participants were asked to complete a food diary on one day, once a week. Some participants completed their diary entries once at the beginning and once at the end of the intervention period. Therefore, to ensure consistency across all participants, we considered only the first and last entry of each food diary. Overall, participants' fruit and vegetable consumption increased during the intervention. This was the case for parents as well as children. 11% of participants reported consumption of their 5-a-day before the intervention, compared to 26% after the intervention. The overall change to healthy eating behavior was statistically significant (P(T<=t) two-tail, p=0.004).

Website Evaluation. The website was generally well received. All participants reported enjoying using it, as did their children. The majority of users found the website easy to use (100%) and navigate (71.4%). Two participants commented on the text content and wording being particularly child friendly. Participants liked the look and feel of the website, although many suggested decreasing the size of food images. The primary character 'Noodles' was highlighted as being particularly beneficial, as was the inclusion of people in the photos alongside the character, which helped make Noodles seem real. One participant specifically highlighted how the website was a "fun way of getting children interested in cooking", and that it was better than other cooking games or websites their children have used before. Regarding previous experience, all participants reported being generally computer literate and confident in using the Internet. Many use the Internet to find recipes, and all but one of the participants said they would be using the study's website more in the future for this purpose.

6   Discussion

Results from the food diaries showed a statistically significant increase in healthy food consumption, thereby meeting the main objective of the investigation. Interestingly, participants did not think their behavior had changed significantly when asked about this during the interviews. One aspect that emerged from the interviews was that participants generally saw themselves as willing to eat healthily. This increased during the trials as did participants' interest in trying out new foods. This is somewhat in line with previous findings that parental practices and foods available at home were strongly influential in the dietary decisions of children [21]. However, perceived barriers (such as time constraints) prevented participants from eating as much healthy food as they would have liked. Despite this, participants ensured that their children ate as many portions of fruit and vegetables as possible, confirming the suggestion that mothers perceived their child's health to be more important than their own [37].

There is clearly a tension here between parents wanting their children to eat more healthily than they might do themselves, whilst children are being directly influenced by their parents' eating habits. This can be further exacerbated by parents not having meals together with their children. We therefore propose that it is most effective for future interventions to involve children and parents collaboratively, thereby maximizing sustained dietary improvements for both. In addition to the motivational and nutritional benefits of 'doing it together', there is a third factor: children very much enjoyed engaging in the joint activity with their parents, and this may prove equally influential in improving, and sustaining, healthy eating behaviors.

The results of placing the participants in stages of the Transtheoretical Model of health behavior change did not support the rest of the study findings. The findings indicated that more than half of participants moved backwards in their TTM stage during the intervention. However, as pointed out previously, some of the stage movements were deemed highly unlikely given the time period involved. More attention needs to be paid to how participants approach self-reporting, and how this data is then used to place the participant in a TTM stage.

It should be noted that the use of quantitative data as well as qualitative data gave a better understanding of the results than either would have alone. The results from the interviews and food diaries did not always match up though, and whilst some of the data had been regarded as unreliable (for example the TTM stage placement), as a whole the combination of the two has led to a better understanding of the effects of the website as an intervention in healthy eating behaviors.

7   Further Work

This project has certainly opened up suggestions for further research. The intervention website could be expanded to cover additional aspects of eating behavior – something participants suggested in their feedback. These may include sections to increase knowledge on nutrition and related quizzes, questionnaires or games, previously put forward as directly affecting nutritional behaviors [38], and a questionnaire similar to that used by Oenema et al [39] so participants can assess their own healthy eating behaviors in a personalized system. Future work may also focus on educating parents in quick and healthy meals to combat the perceived time constraints. The scope of the research itself could be expanded to incorporate more detailed investigations of behavioral aspects like attitudes towards healthy eating and social aspects that affect the number of portions of fruit and vegetables consumed. Factors like these should be investigated through a more thorough set of interview questions.

Finally, we are interested in creating a mobile app version of the site, focusing on personalized content and the use of persuasive strategies where the device becomes a social companion. We believe that the 'always on' and 'always connected' nature of mobile devices make them an ideal technology to support individuals during all stages of behavior change.

References

1. Shor, R., Friedman, A.: Integration of nutrition-related components by early childhood education professionals into their individual work with children at risk. Early Child Development and Care 179(4), 477–486 (2009)
2. World Cancer Research Fund: Food nutrition and the prevention of cancer: A global perspective. American Institute for Cancer Research, Washington (1997)
3. Liu, S., Melanson, J., Lee, I., Cole, S., Hennekins, H., Willett, W., Furing, J.: Fruit and vegetable intake and the risk of cardiovascular disease. J Clin. Nutr. 72, 922–928 (2000)
4. Joshipura, K.J., Ascherio, A., Manson, J.E., Stampfer, M.J., Rimm, E.B., Speizer, F.E., Hennekens, C.H., Spiegelman, D., Willett, W.C.: Vegetable and fruit intake in relationship to ischemic stroke. JAMA 282, 1233–1239 (1999)
5. Gregory, J.: National Diet and Nutrition Survey, vol. 1. HMSO, London (2000)
6. World Health Organization: The Second Decade: Improving Adolescent Health and Development,
   http://whqlibdoc.who.int/hq/1998/WHO_FRH_ADH_98.18_Rev.1.pdf
7. Foley, L., Maddison, R.: Use of Active Video Games to Increase Physical Activity in Children: A (Virtual) Reality? Pediatric Exercise Science 22(1), 7–20 (2010)
8. House of Commons Health Committee: Obesity. Stationery Office, London (2004)
9. Department of Health: Obesity,
   http://www.dh.gov.uk/en/Publichealth/Obesity/index.htm
10. Department for Children, Schools and Families: Healthy Weight, Healthy Lives. HMSO, London (2010)
11. Department of Health: Change 4 Life, http://www.nhs.uk/change4life
12. Gately, P., Cooke, C., Barth, J., Bewick, B., Radley, D., Hill, A.: Children's Residential Weight-Loss Programs Can Work: A Prospective Cohort Study of Short-Term Outcomes for Overweight and Obese Children. Pediatrics 116(1), 73–77 (2005)
13. HENRY: Health Exercise Nutrition for the Really Young,
    http://www.henry.org.uk
14. Skouteris, H., McCabe, M., Swinburn, B., Newgreen, V., Sacher, P., Chadwick, P.: Parental Influence and Obesity Prevention in Pre-Schoolers. Obesity Review 12, 315–328 (2011)
15. Steptoe, A., Pollard, T., Wardle, J.: Development of a Measure of the Motives Underlying the Selection of Food: The Food Choice Questionnaire. Appetite 25, 267–284 (1995)
16. Taveras, E.M., Gillman, M.W., Kleinman, K., Rich-Edwards, J.W., Rifas-Shiman, S.L.: Racial/Ethnic Differences in Early-Life Risk Factors for Childhood Obesity. Pediatrics 125(4), 686–695 (2010)

17. Kelder, S., Perry, C., Klepp, K.I., Lytle, L.: Longitudinal tracking of adolescent smoking, physical activity and food choice behaviors. Am. J. Publ. Health 84, 1121–1126 (1994)
18. Lytle, L.A., Seifert, S., Greenstein, J., McGovern, P.: How Do Children's Eating Patterns and Food Choices Change Over Time? Am. J. Health Promotion 14(4), 222–228 (2000)
19. Ells, L.J., Campbell, K., Lidstone, J., Kelly, S., Lang, R., Summerbell, C.: Prevention of Childhood Obesity. Clinical Endocrinology & Metabolism 19(3), 441–454 (2005)
20. Olivera, S.A., Ellison, R.C., Moore, L.L., Gillman, M.W., Garrahie, E.J., Singer, M.R.: Parent-Child Relationships in Nutrient Intake. Am. J. Clinical Nutr. 56, 593–598 (1992)
21. Story, M., Neumark-Sztainer, D., French, S.: Individual and Environmental Influences on Adolescent Eating Behaviors. J. Am. Dietetic Assoc. 102S(3) (2002)
22. Lindsay, A.C., Sussner, K.M., Kim, J., Gortmaker, S.: The Role of Parents in Preventing Childhood Obesity. Future of Children 16(1), 169–186 (2006)
23. Contento, I.R., Basch, C., Shea, S., Gutin, B., Zybert, P., Michela, J.L., Rips, J.: Relationship of Mothers' Food Choice Criteria to Food Intake of Pre-School Children: Identification of Family Subgroups. Health Education Quarterly 20, 243–259 (1993)
24. Alderson, T., Ogden, J.: What Mothers Feed Their Children and Why. Health Education Research: Theory and Practice 14, 717–727 (1999)
25. Pearson, N., Biddle, S.J., Gorely, T.: Family Correlates of Breakfast Consumption Among Children and Adolescents: A Systematic Review. Appetite 52(1), 1–7 (2009)
26. Office For National Statistics: Internet Access – Households and Individuals (2011), http://www.ons.gov.uk/ons/dcp171778_227158.pdf
27. Clark, A., Anderson, J., Adams, E., Baker, S., Barrett, K.: Assessing an Infant Feeding Web Site as a Nutrition Education Tool for Child Care Providers. J Nutr. Educ. & Behavior 41(1), 41–46 (2009)
28. Let's Move: America's Move to Raise a Healthier Generation of Kids, http://www.letsmove.gov
29. Prochaska, J.O., Redding, C.A., Evers, K.A.: The transtheoretical model and stages of change. In: Glanz, K., Rimer, B.K., Lewis, F.M. (eds.) Health Behavior and Health Education, pp. 60–84, Jossey-Bass, San Francisco (2002)
30. Green, G.W., Fey-Yensan, N., Padula, C., Rossi, S., Rossi, J.S., Clark, P.G.: Differences in Psychosocial Variables by Stage of Change for Fruits and Vegetables in Older Adults. J. Am. Diet Assoc. 104, 1236–1243 (2004)
31. Green, G.W., Rossi, S.R.: Stages of change for dietary fat reduction over 18 months. J Am. Diet Assoc. 98, 529–534 (1998)
32. Chamberlin, B.A.: Creating Entertaining Games With Educational Content. PhD Thesis, New Mexico State University (2003)
33. Fogg, B.J., Nass, C.: Silicon sycophants: The effects of computers that flatter. Int. J. Human-Computer Studies 46(5), 551–561 (1997)
34. Fogg, B.J.: Persuasive Technology. Morgan Kaufmann, San Francisco (2003)
35. Bergman, E.: Information appliances and beyond. Morgan Kaufmann, San Francisco (2000)
36. Becker, H.: Tricks of the Trade: How to Think About Your Research While You're Doing It. University of Chicago Press, Chicago (1998)
37. Wardle, J.: Parental Influences on Children's Diets. Proceedings of the Nutrition Society 54, 747–758 (1995)
38. Van Horn, L., Obarzanek, E., Friedman, L.A., Gernhofer, N., Barton, B.: Children's adaptations to a fat-reduced diet. Pediatrics 115(6), 1723–1733 (2005)
39. Oenema, A., Brug, J., Lechner, L.: Web-based technology tailored nutrition education: results of a randomized control trial. Health Education Research 16, 647–660 (2001)

Design for Relaxation during Milk Expression Using Biofeedback

Loe Feijs[1], Jeanine Kierkels[2],
Nicolle H. van Schijndel[2], and Marjolein van Lieshout[2]

[1] Eindhoven University of Technology, Department of Industrial Design. The Netherlands
[2] Philips Research, Eindhoven, The Netherlands
l.m.g.feijs@tue.nl, {jeanine.kierkels,nicolle.van.schijndel,
marjolein.van.lieshout}@philips.com

Abstract. Many women experience difficulty expressing milk using a breast pump. A negative influence upon their success is stress, hampering the milk ejection reflex. We explore biofeedback to enhance relaxation during milk expression. We discuss context, the principles of biofeedback and the design of an experiential prototype. The effect of biofeedback on milk expression shows promising trends towards increased relaxation, shorter time to milk ejection, and more milk production. Themes that emerged are: control, distraction, endorsement, setting of milk expression session, and pragmatism.

Keywords: Breastfeeding, milk expression, stress, relaxation, biofeedback, smart environments, oxytocin, aesthetics of interaction.

1 Introduction

There is a strategic cooperation in which TU/e, the Máxima Medical Centre, and Philips Research cooperate. Our earlier projects include neonatal monitoring [1], bonding in case of premature birth [2] and delivery simulation [3]. Central in our projects is the notion of an experiential prototype: a design realised such that an experience is created, a source of knowledge and inspiration for further design steps. A second important notion is Experiential Design Landscape [4]: a context of field labs and partnerships to put designs to the test, not in a classical research lab, but in a context of high ecological validity, much closer (or identical to) the real context of use.

In this project, our university and Philips worked together on the topic of milk expression. Sometimes at-breastfeeding has to be replaced or supplemented by milk expression by the mother, so the milk can be stored and given to the baby later. We explore biofeedback for relaxation (other projects addressing the design aesthetics of the pumping equipment, notably [5]). There is a biological reason why relaxation is important, beyond the ordinary human need for balance, opportunities for relaxation, and aesthetic qualities in her environment: the very process of expressing milk is facilitated by relaxation and is hampered by stress.

A. Marcus (Ed.): DUXU/HCII 2013, Part III, LNCS 8014, pp. 494–503, 2013.

2   Breastfeeding and Milk Expression

There are several reasons why breastfeeding is replaced by pumping and storage of the mother's milk. Of course, the benefits of breastfeeding are widely recognized. Breastfeeding not only provides a baby with proper nutrition, but also helps maintain health and ward off illness during infancy as well as later on in life. At-breast feeding is therefore the first choice nutrition for every baby around the world [6]. But because of reasons such as premature birth, suckling problems, or the mother's absence from her baby (e.g. back at work), it is sometimes impossible or undesirable for a mother to solely feed the baby at the breast. In that case, the first substitute for at-breast feeding is bottle-feeding of the mother's breast milk. For this, a breast pump may be used. Figure 1 shows some typical breast pumps. The experience of using these devices is not the same experience as feeding the baby. The technicalities of the device and the milk storage ask for a lot of attention, even when the pump and milk container are ergonomically designed. No surprise many women experience difficulty expressing milk using a breast pump. A major negative influence upon their success is stress. Stress hampers lactation via responses that inhibit milk synthesis (prolactin), milk release (oxytocin) and/or maternal behaviour [7,8,9,10].

Fig. 1. Milk pump equipment by Medela and Avent

3   Relaxation

In a study on using biofeedback training for stress-related disorders [13] significant therapeutic effects were identified. Nevertheless, only limited well-controlled experimental research has been done on the effect of biofeedback on any clinical problem, because this method is relatively new in this area [14]. Rovers *et al.* [15] proposed a generic framework for designing biofeedback games. This framework was adapted to the specific context of the present study. We present two existing designs:

- Stress-eraser, a portable device, entirely based on pure HRV feedback, and bar-chart feedback on a small screen. The sensor is of the PPG type for one finger.
- Journey to the Wild Divine, which is based on both HRV and skin conductance level (SCL). It comes with special sensors with one PPG finger clip and two SCL clips. The software runs on a regular PC and displays beautiful scenery.

For our context of use, the stress eraser is quite technical and performance-oriented (the pumping equipment is already technical enough). It does not add special aesthetic

Fig. 2. Stress Eraser and screen shot of the Journey to the Wild Divine

qualities besides the gadget-style form-giving. The Wild Divine does have attractive aesthetic qualities, but the long and complicated journeys and way-finding in the gardens are not compliant with a milk expression time schedule.

4   Design of a Biofeedback System

In Figure 3 the process of measurement and interpretation is visualised. The purpose of the biofeedback stimulus is to guide the user towards a more relaxed state. Inspired by guided imagery theories (applied to women's health [16]), a choice was made for a visual that is related to nature: a flower placed against a background of scenery and sky. When relaxation increases, the flower opens more.

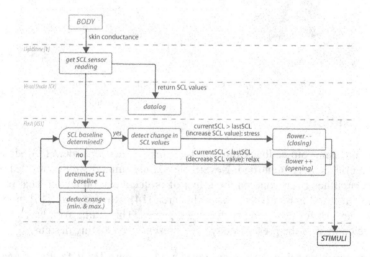

Fig. 3. Technical information flow of measurement data and feedback

The flower is purple, the scenery is green, and the sky is blue. In western society, these colors are generally considered restful and quiet [17]. These are also perceived as the colors that make a space a soothing environment [18]. In Figure 4, four screenshots of the biofeedback animation are portrayed.

Fig. 4. Screenshots of the biofeedback display

In addition to the animation, respiratory guidance could be provided, similar to that of Reyes del Paso *et al.* [19]: "Try to breathe more slowly, fewer times, and more deeply. The more the flower flourishes, the more slowly or the more deeply you are breathing." The SCL values are used as feedback signal for the stimulus. Thereupon, the stimulus will communicate with the sensory system of the user. It reacts on the bodily parameters, and makes the user aware of her current state: it will be represented in a graphical way, and evolve according to changes in the bio-signal. In essence, the stimulus should reward the user for increased relaxation (thus decreased SCL values). Besides the fact that the stimulus has a communicative functionality, it should carry at the same time aesthetic values [15].

Colors have a strong impact on our emotions and feelings [18,19] . However widely recognized this belief, it is also known that color-emotion associations are partly influenced by personal preference, one's past experience and cultural context [20,18]. Current understandings about meanings attributed to colors in the western society are described here. This information will serve as guideline for developing the stimuli graphics/aesthetics. Colors that are generally considered restful and quiet are the cool colors like blue, green and purple. Green reminds people of nature, and is found to evoke feelings of comfort and soothing emotions [18,19]: it has a retiring and relaxing effect. Blue (which is also the color most widely preferred among Europeans) is most often associated with the ocean or the sky. It is held to be sensitive, concentric and expresses tranquility, relaxation and calmness [20]. While purple/violet is often associated with royalty, it is also the color that expresses imagination, inspiration and spirituality. It refers to peace of mind. Overall, light colors are more likely to be associated with positive emotions and dark colors with negative emotions [18,19].

5   Testing the Experiential Prototype

The experiential prototype was designed in order to gain more design knowledge. This is the first question: is bio-feedback an effective way of relaxing in the given context? To answer that question, we conducted an exploratory study in which the main independent variable was the biofeedback, as designed before, which was either used (test condition) or not used (control condition). A before-and-after within-subject repeated measures study was done. To control for carryover effects, the mothers were divided into two groups. One group first had a session with the control condition and then a separate session with the biofeedback condition, and the other group first had a biofeedback session and then a control session. This first question is addressed using quantitative methods. The second question is: can we understand the context of use and how the users experience milk expression in general, and biofeedback in particular? This second question is addressed using qualitative methods. In the remainder of this section we describe the tests and a summary of the results. Then more information about the results can be found in Section 6.

5.1   Participants and Setting

The participants were mothers whose premature infants were hospitalized in the neonatal intensive care unit (NICU) of the Máxima Medical Centre, which is a hospital that is specialized in neonatal (intensive) care. Mothers with babies in a NICU are typically under a lot of stress because of anxiety and fatigue associated with the critical situation of their babies [7]. Since the babies could not drink at the breast directly, these mothers chose to express milk regularly using a breast pump. Potential participants were contacted via a lactation consultant at the hospital and received an information letter. The mothers who agreed to participate signed an informed consent agreement, which clearly explained that they could withdraw from the study at any time. Twelve participants entered the study, which was performed in the rooming-in room of the NICU. None of the participants had experience with using biofeedback before entering the study. From the 12 participants that agreed to participate, seven completed the two sessions of the experiment successfully.

5.2   Materials

The biofeedback device consisted of the SCL sensor and a regular laptop PC with the software pre-installed. Instructions for the biofeedback and the control condition were slightly different. For the biofeedback conditions, the instructions were: "Try to breathe more slowly, fewer times, and more deeply. The more the flower flourishes, the more slowly or the more deeply you are breathing." For the control condition, the instruction was only: "Try to breathe more slowly, fewer times, and more deeply."

5.3   Procedures

After a pre-set questionnaire, collecting profile information such as age, current breastfeeding pattern and number of children breastfed, the participants filled in the Spielberger *Trait* Anxiety Inventory. The experiment then proceeded with the main part of the study, which consisted of two sessions on separate days. At the start of a session the participant was asked to complete the Spielberger *State* Anxiety Inventory. Subsequently, three finger sensors were put on after which the participant started expressing milk (six participants used a double pump; one participant used a single pump). In case the session was set as the intervention session, the biofeedback method was applied during milk expression. When finished expressing, the finger sensors were taken off and again the Spielberger State Anxiety Inventory was administered.

During each session the following measurements were done: skin conductance, total duration of milk expression, time to milk ejection, and the amount of milk produced. Then, within the same week, the second session took place, as much as possible at the same time of the day, but fitting with the mothers' normal milk-expression schedule (usually every three hours). After the two sessions, the experiment was concluded with a post-test interview.

5.4   Measures

Both quantitative as well as qualitative data were gathered: milk expression performance measures (milk production, duration, time to milk ejection), a physiological measure (skin conductance), a psychological measure of stress (the Spielberger State-Trait Anxiety Inventory), and an interview.

- Milk expression performance measures: Milk production: the amount of milk expressed in the bottle. Duration: the time that is needed to express the Time to milk ejection: the time that is needed until the milk starts to flow. Time was marked by the mother and clocked by the researcher (who stayed in the background).
- Physiological measure of stress: As a physiological measure of stress, skin conductance was measured. For this, the finger sensor (resistance sensor) of a Wild Divine LightStone apparatus was used, which had a sampling frequency of 1.5 Hz.
- Psychological measure of stress: To determine the mother's perception of stress, a Dutch translation of the Spielberger State-Trait Anxiety Inventory (STAI) was used [21,22,23,24]. This validated measure determines the participant's emotional experiences of stress. It is a short questionnaire, one part measures state-anxiety and the other part measures trait-anxiety.

5.5   Interview

The interview was semi-structured to obtain rich information about how the participants experienced the use of biofeedback during milk expression. During the experiment, they were shown the biofeedback prototype. The following questions were used as starting points: "how have you experienced the biofeedback during milk expression?"; "did you pay attention to the biofeedback animation on the screen?"; "how does the visualization of (some of) your bodily parameters make you feel?"; "what is your attitude with respect to the use of such a product during milk expression?"; "what are, in your opinion, important ingredients for such a product?"; "what would be necessary for you to actually start using such a product for real?". An interview took about 15 minutes.

5.6   Results

Quantitative data were statistically analyzed with the Student's t test and the Wilcoxon signed rank test. The effect of biofeedback on milk expression showed promising trends towards increased relaxation, shorter time to milk ejection, and more milk production, but these effects were not statistically significant. By way of example we

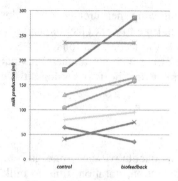

Fig. 5. Milk production

show the results for Milk production. We have similar data for State-Trait Anxiety Inventory, for Duration of milk expression, for Time to milk ejection and for Skin conductance but space limitations prevent us from including them in detail here. We plan a separate publication for all of the data. In Figure 5 the amount of milk produced during the sessions is shown for each participant.

The average amount of milk was 134±78 ml. Five of the seven participants expressed more milk when biofeedback was added to the session; one participant's milk production was the same for both conditions, and one participant showed a lower milk production with biofeedback. The average increase in milk production, however, is not statistically significant (absolute values: one-sided paired two-sample Student's t-test: p = 0.05; normalized differences: one-sided one-sample t-test: p = 0.13).

6   Interview Results and Grounded Theory

Qualitative data were evaluated by applying grounded theory, a systematic qualitative research methodology [25,26,27]. For this, all collected data (interviews, measurements, observations) were first examined systematically to discover relevant dimensions, relate (sub)categories, and track down the subtle aspects of causality. Initial findings steered the structure of the interviews, also allowing the participants to introduce new issues to the discussion. By theoretical comparisons it was investigated how often concepts emerged and how they varied according to their properties and dimensions. Grounded theory [25,26,27] was used to uncover the characteristic patterns.

6.1   Control

With the early birth of her infant and its hospitalization at the NICU, the life of the mother takes an unexpected turn. In addition, the mother is in an intensive and unfamiliar baby schedule, which includes 5 to 8 milk expression sessions a day. A recurring factor was therefore (lack of) control, which was also identified by Hauck et al. [12] for women's perceptions of using a Snoezelen room for breastfeeding and put in the theme "finding relaxation for the breastfeeding mother". Other subthemes that are associated with the theme "control" are the hectic circumstances, the mothers' inability to influence the circumstances and insecurity about milk production. The need for control was also recognized in relation to the biofeedback (see paragraph "Setting of milk expression session").

6.2   Pragmatism

Mothers associated expressing milk with performing a lot of actions and operations. A condition for the design of a biofeedback stimulus is therefore that is does not add any extra installation operations. Other properties that came forward from the collected data and fall within this category are mobility and costs.

6.3   Distraction

The phenomenon distraction emerged from the data. In this case, distraction can be divided in two different subcategories that interact with each other. First, a pleasant form of distraction was identified, which the biofeedback stimulus provided the mothers with. When a mother is consciously engaged in the breathing activity related to the biofeedback it "distracts the mind" and provides a moment of "inner rest". Second, there are also the distractive thoughts that guide her away from focusing on the biofeedback stimulus. This was also observed during the biofeedback session. Most mothers indicated that their attention was partly taken up by two other parallel actions: the milk expression activity itself, and diverted thoughts. Actions related to the milk expression requiring most attention were operating the breast pump power, holding the breast pump shields or bottles, and breast massage. Reasons for diverted thoughts away from the biofeedback exercise were related to "concentration problems", there being a lot of things on one's mind, thoughts about the infant's health (who is in the NICU), delivery pains, and the tendency to look around instead of to the screen. Most of the participants – especially the mothers that indicated to be guided away from the biofeedback exercise – would therefore prefer more guidance and practice with respect to the biofeedback.

6.4   Professional Endorsement

All mothers indicated that professional endorsement of biofeedback is extremely important, for example at childbirth classes, or breast-feeding information evenings. The condition leading to action of actual use of the product is conceptualized as "proof of concept". The mothers principally associated "proof of concept" with the consequence of an "increased milk production". While a small part of the users mentioned a more calming experience as an additional consequence, none associated the "total duration of milk expression" or "time to milk ejection" with this phenomenon.

6.5   Setting of Milk Expression Session

Milk expression takes place in different settings, for example in a hospital, at home, or at work. Two types of contexts emerged from the data influencing the mothers' attitude towards using biofeedback during milk expression. In both a hospital and work context, she experiences a low level of control; she allows herself only little time and rest for milk expression, has a limited feeling of privacy, and usually not much means of relaxation. Consequently, expressing milk is experienced as a must in between all commotion. These factors make that the mothers are open to additional relaxation tools like biofeedback. Home-like contexts (family home or temporary living like a "Ronald McDonald Huis") show an opposite pattern, making a mother less likely to use biofeedback for relaxation.

7 Conclusions

This study confirms the importance of relaxation during milk expression and shows potential for the use of biofeedback to achieve that. Several promising trends were observed with biofeedback: an increased milk production, increased relaxation, and shorter time to milk ejection. No statistically significant effects, however, could be attributed to this relaxation method. The following issues are relevant in the mothers' experiences related to milk expression and biofeedback: "control", "distraction", "professional endorsement", "setting of a milk expression session", and "pragmatism". In a setting with a low level of control (hospital, at work), which usually allows little time for milk expression, limited privacy, and not much other means of relaxation, mothers stated that they were likely to use biofeedback to promote relaxation. Statement of potential competing interests: NHvS and MvL are employed by Philips. JK was a TU/e student at the time of doing the design work and the study; she works at Philips now. Acknowledgements: We thank the participants in this study and the hospital staff of Máxima Medical Centre and M. Rauterberg for advice.

References

1. Chen, W., Bouwstra, S., Bambang Oetomo, S., Feijs, L.M.G.: Sensor integration for perinatology research. International Journal of Sensor Networks 9(1), 38–49 (2011)
2. Croes, M.J.G., Bambang Oetomo, S., Feijs, L.M.G.: Designing remote connectedness between parents and their premature newly born: a design proposal. In: Chen, W., Bambang Oetomo, S., Feijs, L.M.G. (eds.) Neonatal Monitoring Technologies: Design for Integrated Solution, pp. 386–413. IGI Global, Hoboken (2012)
3. Peters, P.J.F., Delbressine, F.L.M., Feijs, L.M.G.: Design of a Medical Simulator Hard- and Software Architecture. In: Zhang, X., Zhong, S., Pan, Z., Wong, K., Yun, R. (eds.) Edutainment 2010. LNCS, vol. 6249, pp. 235–246. Springer, Heidelberg (2010)
4. Gent, S.H., van Megens, C.J.P.G., Peeters, M.M.R., Hummels, C.C.M., Lu, Y., Brombacher, A.C.: Experiential design landscapes as a design tool for market research of disruptive intelligent systems. In: Proceedings of the 1st Cambridge Academic Design Management Conference, University of Cambridge, September 7-8, (2011)
5. Knoester, J., Djajadiningrat, T., Ross, P.: Fluenci: The expression of expressing. In: Chen, L.-L., Djajadiningrat, T., Feijs, L., Fraser, S., Kyffin, S., Steffen, D. (eds.) Design and Semantics of Form and Movement, Proceedings of DeSForM (2012)
6. World Health Organization (WHO). Breastfeeding. Health Topics Web Page, http://www.who.int/topics/breastfeeding/en/ (retrieved January 2013)

7. Dewey, K.G.: Maternal and fetal stress are associated with impaired lactogenesis in humans. Journal of Nutrition 131, S3012–S3015 (2001)
8. Lau, C.: Effects of stress on lactation. Pediatric Clinics of North America 48, 221–234 (2001)
9. Lau, C., Hurst, N.M., Smith, E.O., Schanler, R.J.: Ethnic/racial diversity, maternal stress, lactation and very low birthweight infants. Journal of Perinatology 27, 399–408 (2007)
10. Ueda, T., Yokoyama, Y., Irahara, M., Aono, T.: Influence of psychological stress on suckling-induced pulsatile oxytocin release. Obstet. Gynecol. 84, 259–262 (1994)
11. Feher, S.D.K., Berger, L.R., Johnson, J.D., Wilde, J.B.: Increasing breast-milk production for premature-infants with a relaxation imagery audiotape. Pediatrics 83, 57–60 (1989)
12. Hauck, Y.L., Summers, L., White, E., Jones, C.: A qualitative study of Western Australian women's perceptions of using a Snoezelen room for breastfeeding during their postpartum hospital stay. Int. Breastfeed. J., 3 (2008)
13. Lehrer, P.M., Vaschillo, E., Vaschillo, B., Lu, S.E., Eckberg, D.L., Edelberg, R., Shih, W.J., Lin, Y., Kuusela, T.A., Tahvanainen, K.U.O., Hamer, R.M.: Heart rate variability biofeedback increases baroreflex gain and peak expiratory flow. Psychosomatic Medicine 65, 796–805 (2003)
14. Lehrer, P.M., Vaschillo, E., Vaschillo, B.: Resonant frequency biofeedback training to increase cardiac variability: Rationale and manual for training. Applied Psychophysiology and Biofeedback 25, 177–191 (2000)
15. Rovers, A.F., Feijs, L.M.G., van Boxtel, G.J.M., Cluitmans, P.J.M: Flanker shooting game, model-based design of biofeedback games. In: Proceedings of DPPI 2009, Compiegne, France, October 13-16 (2009)
16. Bazzo, D.J., Moeller, R.A.: Imagine this! Infinite uses of guided imagery in women's health. J. Holist. Nurs. 17, 317–330 (1999)
17. Ballast, D.K.: Interior Design Reference Manual. Professional Pub. Inc., Belmont (2002)
18. Kaya, N., Epps, H.H.: Relationship between color and emotion: a study of college students. College Student Journal 38, 396–405 (2004)
19. Hemphill, M.: A note on adults' color–emotion associations. The Journal of Genetic Psychology 157(3), 275–280 (1996)
20. Gage, J.: Color and meaning: Art, science, and symbolism. University of California Press (2000)
21. van der Ploeg, H.M., Defares, P.B., Spielberger, C.D.: Zelf-Beoordelings Vragenlijst. STAI-versie DY-1 en versie DY-2. Swetz en Zeitlinger, Lisse (1979)
22. van der Ploeg, H.M.: De Zelf-Beoordelings Vragenlijst (STAI-DY). De ontwikkeling en validatie van een Nederlandstalige vragenlijst voor het meten van angst. Tijdschrift Voor Psychiatrie 24, 576–588 (1982)
23. van der Ploeg, H.M.: The development and validation of the Dutch form of the Test Anxiety Inventory. Applied Psychology 33, 243–254 (1984)
24. Spielberger, C.D., Gorsuch, R.L., Lushene, R.E.: STAI Manual for the State-Trait Anxiety Inventory. Consulting Psychologists Press, Palo Alto (1970)
25. Adams, A., Lunt, P., Cairns, P.: A qualitative approach to HCI research. In: Cairns, P., Cox, A.L. (eds.) Research Methods for Human-Computer Interaction, pp. 138–157. Cambridge University Press (2008)
26. Strauss, A., Corbin, J.: Basics of Qualitative Research Techniques and Procedures for Developing Grounded Theory, 2nd edn. Sage Publications, London (1998)
27. Glaser, B.G.: Examples of Grounded Theory: a Reader. Sociology Press, Mill Valley (1993)

Designing Ludic Engagement in an Interactive Virtual Dressing Room System – A Comparative Study

Yi Gao and Eva Petersson Brooks

Department of Architecture, Design and Media Technology
Aalborg University, Campus Esbjerg, Niels Bohrs Vej 8, 6700, Esbjerg, Denmark
{gao,ep}@create.aau.dk

Abstract. The phenomenon of creating virtual dressing room (VDR) environments has currently been widely recognized. Most of the existing VDR systems are of a goal-oriented, rather than open-ended, nature. This study is comparative and investigated two VDR solutions: LazyLazy and a new VDR user interface (UI). The systems were tested by 426 participants. The study applies a qualitative approach including video observations, questionnaires and interviews. The comparison targeted an investigation of the users' experience and behaviour when interacting with the two VDR systems. The results showed that ludic activities can be enhanced without interfering with goal-oriented desires of the user.

Keywords: Ludic activities, motivation, goal oriented, ludic engagement, virtual dressing room.

1 Introduction

A Virtual Dressing Room (VDR) is a contemporary solution, which is changing users clothes shopping habits, preferences and experiences. This type of system enables the users to "try on" clothes virtually in the privacy of their home as well as in retail shops. The purpose of the system is to offer users an overview of available clothes, give an impression of how the clothes fit, and enabling users to make a final purchase decision. The motivation for shopping clothes has a strong impact on the users' performance and behaviour while using a VDR system. The expected shopping experience when using a VDR system, directly influences the customers intentions and final purchases, including both online and offline clothes shopping [1, 2, 3].

Users' motivation for shopping clothes online and/or offline can be divided into two categories of shoppers, namely the utilitarian shopper who has a specific goal in mind, and the hedonic shopper who is simply shopping clothes for the enjoyment of the activity [4]. Utilitarian shoppers are looking for the most efficient (easiest, fastest, safest, etc.) way to reach their goal of making a specific purchase decision. They are driven by motivations such as informativeness, convenience, product selection, and control of the shopping experience [5, 6]. Hedonic shoppers are also, to some extent, motivated by these factors, but it is not their primary purpose for shopping clothes. This type of shopper enjoys browsing websites and to be immersed in a product category, fuelled by their personal interests.

A. Marcus (Ed.): DUXU/HCII 2013, Part III, LNCS 8014, pp. 504–512, 2013.
© Springer-Verlag Berlin Heidelberg 2013

Related work [7] has identified certain elements that are related to utilitarian and hedonic purchase intentions. These elements express user values which motivate such intended purchases and include utilitarian values as well as hedonic values. The hedonic value includes five key elements for shopping: (1) "Adventure/Explore", which means that the shopper is encouraged to follow their interest, and experience the enjoyment during the clothes shopping processes, as well as satisfy the needs of sensorial excitement in trying clothes; (2) "Social Interaction"which concerns the issue of being able to share the experience and this is, for some, the main joyful part of hedonic shopping; (3) "Idea" and (4) "Value" refers to what the shopper can learn about new trends in a pleasurable way; and finally (5) "Authority & Status" indicating that the shoppers can decide how they want to view the clothes and when and where to make the order [8].

Several existing VDR systems, such as FittingReality[1] and LazyLazy[2], share several similarities, for example their goal-oriented nature. The goal-oriented nature of most existing VDR solutions implies a clearly defined navigation where the user systematically can follow certain steps, for example, browsing the collection of clothes, selecting an item to try on, and finally examining the clothes on the body. On the other hand, satisfying experiences also include joyful interactions that captivates and holds the user's interest. In this regard, it can be useful to consider ludic engagement as a crucial design goal when targeting satisfying user experiences.

This paper is based on a comparison between two specific systems, the LazyLazy system (see footnote 2) and the new VDR UI. The latter is a beta version of a prototype developed within the Virtual Dressing Room[3] project. The focus of the paper addresses the question of how to advance the activity of online shopping by identifying affordances and constraints related to users' experiences and expectations on such virtual dressing room (VDR) systems. Particularly, the paper investigates how ludic engagement can be integrated in a goal-oriented system, and to explore in what way this might dissolve possible boundaries between shopping for clothes and having fun.

1.1   Ludic Engagement Designs

In order to create joyful experiences when interacting with a goal-oriented system, in this case a VDR system, include the questions of how the system processes information and, also, how the user engage with this specific system so that his/her expectations and actions correlate with computational expectations and actions [9]. This might elicit qualities in interaction through ludic engagement. The word "ludic" comes from the latin "ludus", which means "game" [10]. However, related work [11, 12, 13] has shown ludicity to be about far more than simply playing a game. It relates to the engagement of the body and mind, where a ludic activity is something that can create a good feeling for a person [13]. Rather than being useful, systems designed to support ludic values are rich, ambiguous and open-ended and differ in their

---

[1] http://fittingreality.com
[2] http://lazylazy.com
[3] Financed by the Danish National Advanced Technology Foundation.

assumptions, values, and techniques from those developed for the workplace [14]. This type of interaction is commonly referred to as "ludic engagement"; a term which was first described by Huizinga [15] who defined people as playful creatures. Thus, systems that promote ludic engagement should not be concerned with achieving clear goals, or be overly structured with defined tasks [16, 17, 18].

In the context of this paper, ludic engagement is related to the immersiveness offered by the system, which is dependent on the functionality and navigation possibilities of the system. Related work [19] investigated the intensity level of immersion and found that engagement is the basic level of immersion. Here, the affordances and constraints concern "access", "control" and "feedback", which have to be detailed and complete in order for the user to reach a higher level of immersion (engrossment). For example, the question of how fast the user can access the system, how the system can be controlled, and, finally, what kind of feedback the user will receive, constitute three fundamental points, which are crucial to captivate the user's interest. In this paper, this captivation of interest is related to having enjoyable and fun experiences. This means to being engaged and that the user is offered possible choices of action and exploration [17]. Overall, previous research has shown how a VDR system could enhance the user's exploration, social activities, self-recognition, and expression, which would provide increased hedonic value.

2   Method

In order to determine the affordances and constraints presented by current VDR solutions and investigate in what way ludic engagement can be utilised to enhance enjoyment in VDR activities, two different VDR systems were introduce in to the study.

The LazyLazy system "Webcam Social Shopper" (WSS) is a webcam-based VDR solution. The user steps in front of a camera within a certain distance. The camera tracks your position and the 2D image of a piece of clothes is applied to a real-time image of yourself on the screen. The clothes can be scaled in size to fit as close as possible to the size of the specific body measurements. The system tries to utilize the webcam similar to a mirror and "holds" a piece of clothes up in front of the user. The initial purpose of this system is to enable online users to immediately see if the style and/or colour of a piece of clothes is fitting. This to ultimately remove users' doubts about the clothes without physically trying it; benefitting sales by reducing the rate of returned items. The LazyLazy UI can be seen in figure 2.

The new VDR UI (developed by Commentor and Virtual Lab ApS) is also a camera based system. It uses the depth camera of a Microsoft Kinect to track the position of the user, and similarly to LazyLazy it placec a 3D scanned piece of clothes on them. The user interacts with the system mainly by relying on movements and gestures. The system uses two screens: One for displaying the full body image (like a mirror), and another for menu selection. This can be seen in figure 1. of the new VDR UI.

This comparative study relies on a qualitative research approach to determine the affordances and constraints for both systems. The study is based on a participatory design (PD) approach, including video observation, questionnaire and interview. In line with a PD approach [20], participants took part in a short design session followed by an interview. A total of 14 people were involved in this design process. The task for the participants was to provide suggestions on improvements for the both above-mentioned VDR systems, particularly changes they would consider to make the experience more fun, i.e. enjoyable. The data was analysed using an interpretative approach [21], in which the researchers draw on the understanding, and shared perspective of the users, as well as the domain of their actions, to determine the reality of the VDR system.

2.1 Participants

The research took place at the TV2 Beep exhibition, where 426 participants were involved in the test. They were selected randomly at the location, where each participant could choose to try either of the two systems, or both depending on how long time and personal interest that the participants had. The sample had an age range from 2 to 69 years of age and covered both genders (66% were male and 34% were female).

Of the 426 participants, 103 filled out a questionnaire afterwards. Of the participants, only 8% have had experience with similar system (the remaining 92% had never tried it before). 43% of all the participants only tried the LazyLazy system, 18% only tried the new VDR system, and the remaining 39% tried both systems. For the comparative analysis as a whole, only these 39% were included. In relation to the questionnaires, this means that 22 of the 103 are included in this study. Comments from the groups that only tried one system will be brought in where it is relevant.

2.2 Procedure

The participants were briefly introduced to the systems and the test procedure. They were then told to freely interact with the system and to try on different pieces of clothes until they felt they were done. Afterwards the participants were asked to fill out a questionnaire. Those who were willing were also invited to take part in an informal semi-structured interview and a design session directed towards possible affordances, constraints and improvement suggestions related to the two systems. Due to the limited selection of VDR-capable clothes available in both systems, the clothes were selected for the user to avoid wasting too much time while the user searches for an item.

The video observation focused on the user's interaction with the two systems targeting affordances and constraints. From the facial expressions and behaviour of the participants during the interaction with the two systems, indications of enjoyable moments were identified. The 22 questionnaires focused on general participant background and experience-based information, as well as the preference between the two VDR systems in the domains self-recognition, system control, and general cognition. The interview process focused on determining the participants' perspectives on affordances and constrains and their design suggestions for a VDR system.

3   Result

The results are based on an analysis of video observations, questionnaires and interviews. Our findings presented the usefulness of this triangulation of methods. The findings are presented in the three following sections: System performance, user preference, and design suggestions.

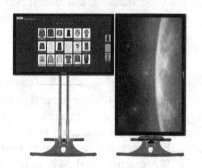

Fig. 1. New VDR UI   **Fig. 2.** LazyLazy UI

3.1   System Performance

When interacting with the LazyLazy system, users accidentally navigated to the second page (where colours can be adjusted, and pictures taken), and then became confused, as the controls are similar but not the same as the first page (where size is adjusted). Since the navigation was accidental, they also did not understand how to get back too the starting point. Some functionality has no undo or cancel option, for example, if the picture taking option is activated, there is no way to stop it, though it takes several seconds before it actually executes. The users did not immediately understand the function of the buttons, i.e. what to do with them. The system relies on the ability of the users to learn how the buttons work and where functionality is located, rather than presenting it in an easily recognizable way.

Error prevention is most clearly seen in the size adjustment, where the system will allow the user to move the clothes completely off the screen (by pressing "up" or "down" for a long time – maybe accidentally), or adjust the clothes to extreme scales.

Several interaction constraints appeared in the LazyLasy system such as the user using one hand for pointing at side buttons on opposite side of the screen. Users also had difficulty in judging distances the system does not support multiple users, and browsing the clothes collection. The clothes adjustments take time and effort.

In the new VDR system, the menu auto hides right after the user clicks on it. This confuses the users, complicating access to for example the clothes-browsing page. They may also accidentally jump to the detailed information page, leading to further confusion. However, the users can freely explore the system. They did not immediately understand what the images and icons on the menu do, and asked for assistance in understanding each function. Clothes is automatically scaled and positioned, eliminating the possibility of mistakes, but also reducing the ability to make fine adjustments. The users were confused about button activation, which was evidenced by random pointing, clicking, flipping, and cycling with the buttons. When confused the users also occasionally accidently hit other buttons, complicating the navigation.

A common constraint in both systems was the fact that many users required help and advice from the observers during the tests, since this is not available through the systems as such. For example, if the user is confused about which buttons do what, there is no help immediately available on the screen. Furthermore, lag in tracking and system operation was also common.

Overall average performance time in the LazyLazy system was over 2 minutes, while in the new VDR system it was less than 2 minutes.

3.2   User Preference

The questionnaire inquired the preferred control method (using body movement) for each participant. The options where: Using a smartphone as a remote, voice control, foot touch (e.g. a dance pad), a touch screen, or regular body motion as in the systems tested. Of the people trying the LazyLazy system, 64% preferred body motion, compared to 72% of the ones trying the new VDR system. For comfortableness in using body movement for control, a 7-point Likert scale was used. In this, the most selected value was 5, which was at 26% for both systems. Overall, for the LazyLazy system, 71% selected 5 or higher, while in the new VDR system 68% selected 5 or higher.

In mirroring, 69% of the participants trying the LazyLazy system preferred a mirror image of themselves, compared to 72% in the new VDR system. The second most common choice was a self-like 3D model with the same figure as the user, which was wanted by 26% of the LazyLazy participants and 18% of the new VDR system participants.

When asked about intentions to purchase after using a system, the most common value on a 7-point Likert scale was 4 for both systems, meaning neither for nor against.

Overall, 58% of the participants that tried both systems preferred the LazyLazy system in favour of the new VDR UI.

3.3   Design Suggestion

The participants generally wanted more functionality in the LazyLazy system, such as recommendation of clothes size, and clothes collection browsing. In regards to the system performance, they wanted a friendlier user interface; the clothes should follow the body movements, the system should be more sensitive, and react faster. In the new VDR system, the participants wanted the image of the piece of clothes to be presented in a more realistic way. They would also like a bigger selection of clothes, and to be able to adjust the clothes size and colour. More detailed information about the clothes should be provided.

For both systems, the users would like to be able to view the clothes in 360 degrees (by being able to turn around).

4   Discussion

The five elements of hedonic shopping values [7] are used as a framework to discuss the results of the study, particularly focusing on the aspect of ludicity related to the VDR systems included in the study.

For access, the results showed that the participants use a longer time for the Lazy-Lazy system, and a step-by-step control process is required for the user to go through. The new UI provided the user with quicker access time, by simply requiring them to stand in front of camera, after which the clothes were somewhat auto-scaled and applied to the image of the user. Due to not having a clear navigation sequence, the system could provide the user with more hedonic adventure and exploration activities.

The LazyLazy system's distance judgement constraint meant that the user could not stand too close or too far away from camera. This limited the group of users that could access the system properly, such as people of shorter stature (e.g. young children, or a person in a wheel chair). By using the Microsoft Kinect, the new UI prevented the distance issues, which increased accessibility and provided more freedom to move back and forth.

Both systems provided movement based interaction. In general the users appeared to prefer using one hand to control the system. The button placement in the LazyLazy system meant that these users had to perform awkward movements to activate the buttons in the side opposite to whichever hand they preferred using. Furthermore operation errors continuously occurred when the user moved any part of their upper body and accidentally activated the buttons. The new UI menu was designed to be on one side of the system exclusively, and as a result the confusion regarding which hand to use was solved. Since the system was designed to only be activated by hand movements, this also allowed the user more freedom to move around in front of the camera.

In the new UI system, users showed their enjoyment by dancing a little in front of the system or turning to check the sides and back of the clothes. The LazyLazy system does not support either of these types of interaction. These results also show that the users consider that their body can be used to directly manipulate the system in a fun and interactive way.

Self-recognition and expression was facilitated mainly by both systems being camera based, which enables users to directly recognize themselves by the mirror image presented on the screen. A limitation in the LazyLazy system is the fact that it can only show half of the user's body, while the new UI shows a full body image. The users of both systems confirm that they could easy and immediately recognize themselves with the clothes on. The view of the entire body, in the new UI, encourages more movements from the users as they try to express themselves with different clothes. Interestingly, the second most popular choice for the users would be to see the clothes on an avatar made to look like them.

Social activity is one of the hedonic shopping experience activities [7]. LazyLazy does not support multiple users, which means that the user need to be alone and no one else can be even within a range of the camera's view. If so, the motion of the second person will interfere with the tracking.

The new VDR UI supports multiple users. For example, a mother brought her 3 years old son to try the new system. During the process the mother tried to pick up the virtual clothes, which were placed on her body, and pass it to her son. Both mother and child appeared to enjoy doing this. Two male participants did something similar. In this way, the system supports interaction not only between the user and the system itself, but also between users. It provided a shared social behaviour which enhanced the user's feeling of it being more fun to play with.

Overall, the new UI offers more ludic activities compared to the LazyLazy system. However, generally there is not a significant preference for the new UI.

In terms of authority, the main constraint of the LazyLazy system is the fact that it did not allow the user to browse different clothes, which is refers to one of the important hedonic clothes shopping experience: Browsing the clothes collection. The participants mentioned the inclusion of this affordance as something positive in the new UI. On the other hand, the main constraint for the new UI is in the lack of ability to control the choice of colour, shape, size, etc., on the part of the user.

5   Conclusion

This study focused on investigating how ludic engagement could be involved in a VDR system, by comparing user behaviour in two such systems, namely LazyLazy and the new VDR UI. The affordances and constraints that were determined for both systems had a strong impact on the system performance.

The performance differences between the systems in terms of constraints can be related to the five fundamental ludic activities: Access, movement based interaction, social activity, self-image recognition, and authority. These factors should be enhanced to provide a more hedonic shopping experience to the users. The freedom to freely move was a required affordance, which enabled expressions of self and fostered ludic engagement. However, since the navigation of the systems was not clear and the user, thereby, had difficulties to find the boundaries of the system, this constrained the ludicity and the qualities in the interaction.

The LazyLazy system only provides a 2D front image of the clothes, while the new UI provides a low quality 3D model of the clothes. Both systems have strong latency issues in the tracking (and positioning) of the clothes. The user experience of being involved with the product is reduced by these two limitations. Progress in image quality and tracking technology is required for future development. The location of the test, the TV2 Beep exhibition, was a limiting factor in the participant sample. A majority of the participants were male, and can be assumed to be familiar or interested in new technology (due to their presence at the exhibition). Future research should involve locations where a more broad range of interests can be found.

Acknowledgements. The Danish National Advanced Technology Foundation funds this work, as well as the entirety of the Virtual Dressing Room project. The authors would also like to thank Virtual Lab ApS and Commentor for the new VDR user interface developments

References

1. Cordier, F., Seo, H., Magnenat-Thalman, N.: Made-to-Measure Technologies for an online clothing store. IEEE Computer Graphics and Applications, 38–48 (2003)
2. Liu, X.H., Wu, Y.W.: A 3D Display System for Cloth Online Virtual Fitting Room. In: Proceedings from Computer Science and Information Engineering, 2009 WRI World Congress on Computer Science and Information Engineering. IEEE Computer Society, Los Angeles (2009)
3. Holte, M.B.: The Virtual Dressing Room: A Perspective on Recent Developments. In: Shumaker, R. (ed.) VAMR/HCII 2013, Part II. LNCS, vol. 8022, pp. 241–250. Springer, Heidelberg (2013)
4. Wolfinbarger, M., Gilly, M.C.: Shopping online for freedom, control and fun. California Management Review 43(2), 34–55 (2001)
5. Sorce, P., Perotti, V., Widrick, S.: Attitude and age differences in online buying. International Journal of Retail and Management 33(2), 122–132 (2005)
6. Perea, T., Pikkarainen, K., Karjaluoto, H., Pahnila, S.: Consumer acceptance of online banking: An extension of the technology acceptance model. Internet Research 14(3), 224–235 (2004)
7. To, P.-L., Liao, C., Lin, T-H.: Shopping motivations on Internet: A study based on utilitarian and hedonic value. Technovation, pp. 774–787. (2007)
8. Parsons, A.G.: Non-functional motives for online shoppers: Why we click. The Journal of Consumer Marketing 19(5), 380–392 (2002)
9. Murray, H.J.: Inventing the Medium. Principles of Interaction Design as a Cultural Practice. The MIT Press, Cambridge, Massachusetts (2012)
10. Almeida, A.: Ludicidade como instrumento pedagógico (2009), http://www.cdof.com.br/recrea22.htm
11. Cook, G.: Language Play, Language Learning. University Press, Oxford (2000)
12. Leventhal, L.I.: Inglês é 10! O ensino de Inglês na Educação Infantil. Disal, São Paulo (2006)
13. Luckesi, C.C.: Ludicidade e atividades lúdicas uma abordagem a partir da experiência interna (2005), http://www.luckesi.com.br/textos/ludicidade_e_atividades_ludicas.doc
14. Gaver, W., Boucher, A., Pennington, S., Walker, B.: Evaluating Technologies for Ludic Engagement. In: van der Veer, G., Gale, C. (eds.) Proceedings of the 2005 Conference on Human Factors in Computing Systems, p. 1. ACM, Portland (2005)
15. Huizinga, J.: Homo Ludens: A study of the Play-Element in Culture. Beacon Press, Boston (1971)
16. Gaver, W., Bowers, J., Boucher, A., Gellerson, H., Pennington, S., Schmidt, A., et al.: The Drift Table: Designing for Ludic Engagement. In: CHI EA 2004 - CHI 2004 Extended Abstracts on Human Factors in Computing Systems, pp. 885–900. ACM, New York (2004)
17. Petersson, E.: Non-formal Learning through Ludic Engagement with in Interactive Environments. Doctoral dissertation, Malmoe University, School of Teacher Education, Studies in Educational Sciences (2006)
18. Petersson, E.: Editorial: Ludic Engagement Designs for All. Digital Creativity 19(3), 141–144 (2008)
19. Brown, E., Cairns, P.: A grounded investigation of game immersion. In: Proceedings CHI 2004, pp. 1297–1300 (2004)
20. Muller, M.: Participatory design: The third space in HCI. In: Sears, A., Jacko, J. (eds.) The Human-Computer Interaction Handbook, 3rd edn., pp. 1051–1068. CRC Press, Boca Raton (2002)
21. Walsham, G.: Interpreting Information Systems in Organizations. Wiley, Chichester (1993)

Humor Illustration Design,
a Summary of Illustrations, Designs, and Projects

Jochen Gasser

Bahnhofstraße 10, 39040 Vahrn (Bz), Italy
info@jochengasser.com

Abstract. This paper summarizes my work as an illustrative designer; it covers details of my inspiration, ideas, final works, and specific projects that I have worked on throughout my career. This paper is organized in parts; Humor Illustration Design as a Solution Mechanism for Various Problems describes my view on how humor functions in the world today and how it alleviates issues. Illustration as a Tool is where I explain the workings behind and the outcome of an ongoing project and the goals I'm aiming for as a designer in terms of reaching my audience. I then show how I incorporate my work into marketing strategies in Humor Illustration Design as Marketing Strategy. Finally I focus on the project that I will present in Las Vegas in July.

Keywords: Humor Illustration Design, Humor, Andreas Hofer, Humanity, Emotional Connection, Gondola.

1 Humor Illustration Design as a Solution Mechanism for Various Problems

In a powerful and function-oriented world, it is more important than ever not to come short on emotions and humanity when it comes to design and illustration. The motto "Sex sells", is an evident example of how humor functions in our society; at first the directness of this motto seems crude and grabs our attention, then it eases and brings about a laugh. Humor is a concept that can be used to reach audiences within seconds, and draws them in through amusement and emotional connection. Illustration is a way to depict humor; it is an ideal means of expression as themes can be apprehended and understood with no specific boundary. In other words, illustration allows individual opinions and views on certain themes through imagination.

2 Illustration as a Tool

Since the beginning of my career as a freelance illustrator in 2008, I have been interested in innovative ways to apply the concept of "Humor Illustration Design". I worked together with a historian named Norbert Parschalk on my first project. It was based on the idea of historical story telling through a new style. The main idea was to

A. Marcus (Ed.): DUXU/HCII 2013, Part III, LNCS 8014, pp. 513–519, 2013.

create "comics", in which history and humor were combined, without questioning the significance and plausibility of a given storie's contents.

The first story I transformed into a comic was the biography of "Andreas Hofer", a local freedom fighter and hero in the South Tirol (a small region of Italy, far north in the Alps)(Fig.1 shows an exerpt from the book). In this region of Italy – in my homeland –, the status and importance of Andreas Hofer can be compared to that of Abraham Lincoln in the USA. I designed the illustrations and Norbert Parschalk helped me formulate the texts.

Fig. 1. Exerpt from the Andreas Hofer book

But there were consequences that came with animating this historical figure and things went through the roof when the storybook was first published and released; as quoted, one cannot make "Serious historical figures into comical heroes." However the book was soon accepted and became a best seller. It also serves as an educational tool for many middleschool students and a number of others in general.

The concept of this project was simple and came down to one question and goal: How could I get people from each age group who were historically 'uninterested', to want to experience and learn history? The solution lay in the combination of texts and matching cartoons and comicstrips; I recreated each story based on this combination, with the intention of finding a way to give people no option but to learn the history; they would have to read the texts in order to understand the illustrations they were looking. And this worked!

I designed the humorous elements of my story books with the purpose of "rewarding" the reader, who had been "forced" to do something undesireable (i.e. to read) in order to understand the story. This concept takes after the motto: "You can learn and also laugh!". I didn't want to undermine or question the seriousness of the biographies however, and so, I only chose scenes that are either proven or unverifiable. This is how the subtitle of my book series, "An Illustraded History", was founded. Based on this subtitle, my books can be considered "subjective history" rather than as "joke" or "satire".

My work focuses on and is demonstrated through the concept of "humanity", which is the central theme and a crucial building block in the thoughts and procedures that go into my ideas, texts and illustrations. In these re-created stories, my intention is for heroes to be seen as humans that have strengths and weaknesses! With this method, which is not always met with sympathy or understanding, I aim to convey these characters not as dismantled or lesser heroes, but rather as heroic figures to whom readers of any age group can relate. The simplicity of the combination of the illustrations and texts, allows readers to have a better understanding of these heroes and the things that led them to the honorable and heroic decisions they made.

Every product, every service and every action is, when it comes down to it, based on "humanity" and can be communicated as just that. Consider times when you have viewed a situation or experience, a conversation, or an emotion, from another person or friend's perspective. You probably discovered the different possibilities of meaning or intention and were able to feel what might be felt "under one's skin" rather than only seeing the what's on the surface.

This concept plays an important role in my approach of communicating humor; in my illustrations, heroic figures become happily-seen and read about companions because people see that these figures once existed in the real world and therefore feel that they can relate and connect to the heroe's achievements, struggles, enjoyments, etc. on a more personal level. Thus, these humorous illustrations and texts allow the "gray and serious every day life" of the reader to be forgotten for a short time and bring a smile to his or her face. I've come to see this as the best medicine for anything and everything!

In describing my experience with readers I've shown my take on the importance of being able to relate to a person or a character in order for success. For a story to succeed, it's important that the readers can relate to its contents. For business (in my case), this type of connection is equally important. In my opinion when it comes to design, possibility is created through the simple method of studying one's customers; learn about their products and services, and know, understand and then focus precisely on their weaknesses. Here is a phrase that I believe to be quite relevant: "Only a person who can laugh about oneself, shows one's 'true colors' and thus one's true greatness". I have learned to follow this method: get to know customers on a deeper level and gain their interest by working with not only what you think they are looking for, but also what they believe they will benefit from.

Something that I find important in my work and that sets my ideas apart from a great deal of illustrators like myself, is that I disagree with the idea that maintaining the 'character' of a product is a "no go", a popular idea in the general efficiency-oriented business philosophy. In fact, on a maybe slightly emotional level, I think that maintaining the character of a product is a "must do" and that putting an emphasis on the difference of a product and distinguishing it from competing products while simultaneously maintaining success, is an actual possibility.

As an example of Humor Illustration Design and my method, I'd like to describe the evolution of the design that is currently on my car. In this case the product was the vehicle and the client or customer was myself. I was looking for a different way to show my illustrations and decided that I wanted to print a design on a large object. I had to begin by asking myself what this 'object', with which I would like to show off and promote my work could be. I chose my car! This seemed like a good idea, since everyone sharing the road with my car would of course also see my work. But what difficulty did I find when it came to putting a print on my car...? Well, due to the specific model, the Materia Daihatsu which has a high vertical 'snout', thousands of flies and insects would encounter a fatal end every summer, smooshing and splattering against the front of my car.

This led me to establish an animated illustrations of a 'gentle'-looking, oversized flyswatter that is stretched across the hood of the car, counting it's 'victims' in a very unfazed manner. I found the backside of my car to be the ideal advertising surface for the targeted onlooker, which is, of course, whoever drives behind me.

Every car has a 'rear' part. Mine however, is decorated with a "Buttface" with the phrase "Please don't rear me in the butt" (translated from Italian). This phrase, to many people, has a double meaning... and is another example of where humor and illustration work well together in portraying a certain meaning. In this case, one of the two interpretations of the phrase serves as a request to watch out for the back of my car.

The quickly successful effects of this advertising method were due to and achieved by numerous photographs (especially of the 'rear') and resulted in an additional 'side-effect': Being stopped by the police has become a very rare occurrence since the installation of the design on my car, in fact, police encounters have since only ended with a friendly goodbye. And this I'd like to assume, happens because even Policemen and other figures of authority are, when it comes down to it, also just "human". This is further proof of a common appreciation for humor that can have a positive influence on anyone.

3   Humor as a Marketing Strategy

So far in my career as an designer the fact that humor functions independently from product or service has become clear to me. When properly combined with "customary" marketing strategies, a product can become a popular item or idea, and thus can lead to an emotional connection with the customer. My illustrated characters create a sense of connection and understanding for my clients and allow them to dive into a somewhat realistic comic world that really doesn't seem too unbelievable.

I have displayed my illustrations and work in various ways, from simple T-shirt designs to interior designs of entire facilities. The range of possibilities seems to be endless. As an example, I have incorporated my work in restaurants where humorous details have found their place on anything from beer barrels to napkins and from bathroom walls to garden furniture.

Another example of a 'Humor Illustration Design' project that has come about in last few years in an entertainment performance based project called, in German, "die Zupprmandor", which combines music and drawing. In a performance, a projection appears on a large screen in front of an audience. Before their eyes appears an illustration, which I draw live, accompanied by a matching and timely coordinated song, which is written by a local song-writer (Markus Dorfman). This is a new type of live-performance that leads the audience on a journey of discovery with it's captivating creation process. The "Zupprmandor" entered into the Austrian television talentshow, 'die große Chance' (in English, The Big Chance), similar to the show 'x-factor', and even made it to the semi-finals!

Regardless of whether it comes to marketing, entertainment, or simply amusement, my personal desire for challenge remains to be the driving force of Humor Illustration Design, especially when it comes to opportunities in which one would not expect work like mine to appear. And with this, I would like to introduce my project-in-process.

4 Project in Las Vegas

In searching for a perfect project for the Las Vegas event, I came across and interesting object in Las Vegas which is currently being established. This object is called The High Roller Observation Wheel, an enormous ferriswheel at Caesar's Palace on the Las Vegas strip. This is the world's largest observation wheel at 550 feet, with large round cabins, or gondolas, that each fit up to 40 people and allow for a 360 degree view of the city. One regular ride on this ferriswheel ride lasts 30 minutes, but a gondola can also be booked for groups and parties for much longer rides.

This is not the average 'object' for a Humor Illustration Design project. I think that I found this object appealing for this very reason; trying to find a way to connect my work with and object like the High Roller Observation Wheel would be a completely new and interesting undertaking. So I set to thinking about ideas that could combine my humor and illustration with this object. In my opinion the most stand-out aspect of this object is the large scale gondola. So I started to think of ways to transform these gondolas into my own version of gondolas with my Humor Illustration Design. In accordance with Las Vegas' attempt to become a more family-friendly destination, my idea of illustrating a variety of themed gondolas was established. I will elaborate on my first idea, which is the 'wedding-gondola'. In this gondola, a couple can exchange their "I do's" in a heavenly setting above Las Vegas' famous strip. This idea is simple and maybe a little less than exciting for this city, given its well-known wedding and marriage possibilities. However my personal focus and challenge lies in the execution of my idea. Since my illustrations take place within a gondola, the surface space and portrayal of my ideas are confined to the inside and facade of the gondola, a small area.

This illustration is a 3-D comic strip that tells the stories of a couple in love and concludes with a happy ending upon exiting the gondola; a funny depiction of love, as all of us have at one time or another experienced it, that will show the path towards finding 'true' love with amusing images of both past, unsuccessful relationships and a future of happiness. With few written words, the illustrations will communicate the story of the comic strip, which allows for an international understanding as well as an opportunity for self-reflection for the observer who is looking at 'Gondola number 9' (based on cloud number 9).

The facade of the round gondola resembles a 'Cloud # 9' on which a welcoming 'Amor' sits and greets guests. The couple enters their Cloud # 9 through the, entrance of the gondola, which looks like Heaven's gate. Upon arrival, the illustration expands left and right and tells both of the character's stories on the way to their final happiness, which they simultaneously find on the opposite side of the gondola. The illustration symbolizes both the helplessness the main characters experienced when it came to falling in love and the love they each find as it comes to their wedding day. This comic strip resembles relationship situations in which love must first be stumbled upon before becoming a possibility!

This illustrations incorporates many details, like depictions of blind love, high flying emotions, hesitations towards the "I do's", the heavy back pack of loneliness, which all resemble experiences faced on the path towards finding true love. As the motto goes, "Everything happens for a reason", the two characters travel on their own, with butterflies in their stomachs, on the path to each other. (Figure 2. Shows an example of my illustrations).

Fig. 2. Example of my 'Love' illustrations

The ride in the wedding gondola shows a funny and emotionally exciting romance, a happiness and love that is shadowed by the less happy past. At the end of the ride and at the exit of the gondola, the illustration suggests a 'typical' situation where the wife is in the lead, dragging the husband behind her. In summary of this project, Humor Illustration Design transforms the function of a transportation device and creates an experience, as we see in this wedding-ride that is full of amusing highs and lows (laughing, crying, suffering and loving).

Themed gondolas of this type are by no means a must have unsuccessfully securing this project , however, the individual elements of my illustrations can shine a new light on the overall awareness and experience of the High Roller Observation Wheel.

Regardless of the theme, whether it is a wedding-gondola, a football-gondola, or a casino-gondola, there is no limit when it comes to imagination and production of these illustrations. My illustrations act as an imaginative High Roller Observation Wheel for those who observe my project. In seeing each imaginary gondola, they experience different 'gondola rides', which becomes their own experience, and strengthen the appeal to 're-enter' the ferris wheel on a different gondola in order see yet another comic world.

To summarize what I've written, projects like the ferriswheel project can probably be viewed as luxury items since they are sure to succeed just as well without illustration design. However, illustrations like mine provide humor and character to an object and allow for yet another aspect of the object and experience to be engrained in ones memory, which is of course very important for every designers work.

Like so often in life, the most important thing is not 'what' but 'how'. Humorous, illustrated designs are no ground stone for success, but are a great addition to any project and enhance the memories that one will have in walking away from an experience with almost anything. My illustrations offer customers and observers a a chance to smile or laugh for a moment and also creat a connection to an object or a place by shining a positive and humorous light on whatever it is.

Increasing Trust in Personal Informatics Tools

Luis G. Jaimes, Tylar Murray, and Andrew Raij

Department of Electrical Engineering
University of South Florida, Tampa, Florida
{ljaimes,tylarmurray}@mail.usf.edu, raij@usf.edu

Abstract. Personal Informatics (PI) systems help individuals collect
and reflect on personal physiological, behavioral and/or contextual data.
Typically, these systems offer users interactive visualizations that allow
meaningful exploration of the data. Through this exploration, PI systems
have great potential to facilitate self-reflection and encourage behavior
change.

One of the challenges facing PI systems is a general lack of transparency about the uncertainty, noise or measurement error in the information they display. Data acquisition, processing/inference, and wireless
transmission, can each inject errors into the data. However, most PI systems do not provide a way to help users understand what types of errors
could be in the data, where these errors come from, and to what extent
they can trust the data they see is correct. This paper describes how
errors can affect the perception and use of PI data and discusses ways
to integrate more transparency into PI systems.

Keywords: personal informatics, data provenance, information visualization, transparent user interfaces.

1 Introduction

The combination of wearable sensors and ubiquitous computation (e.g., smartphones) is creating a self-surveillance society, where individuals can track a
variety of personal behaviors and states to improve their mood[1], health[2],
productivity[15], and ecological footprint[6], among others (Figure 1). Comple-
menting these sensing and computation tools are user interfaces that support
reflection on such behaviors and states. Taken together, these components - self-
tracking sensors, self-report tools, computation, and self-reflection user interfaces
- are often called personal informatics (PI) systems [8]. PI systems have emerged
as powerful tools in facilitating reflection on behaviors and ultimately, changes
in behavior.

While PI systems are powerful tools for behavior change, they generally
present opaque user interfaces. More specifically, they process, filter, and aggregate data before it is presented to the user, with the goal of hiding details
that may not facilitate reflection on a behavior of interest. This is generally a
good practice, as it reduces the complexity of the data and makes it more accessible to the end-user. However, this paper argues there is one category of data
hidden by PI user interfaces that should be made more transparent: uncertainty.

A. Marcus (Ed.): DUXU/HCII 2013, Part III, LNCS 8014, pp. 520–529, 2013.

Uncertainty (noise or measurement error) can be injected into PI data at several places, including data acquisition, processing, and display. This error or uncertainty, if left hidden from the user, can present two important challenges to the long-term adoption of PI systems. First, if the behaviors presented by a system do not match the user's memory, the user may feel the system is too inaccurate to be useful, and thus may lose trust in the system, and perhaps abandon its use. Second, errors in the data can skew the story the data is supposed to tell users. If users are not aware that errors, and by extension skew, exist in the data, then they could make inappropriate behavior changes based on the data.

This paper aims to address these challenges by proposing two forms of transparency for PI systems: data acquisition transparency (DAT) and data uncertainty transparency (DUT). DAT involves presenting users with the provenance, or history of the data, including the source of the data, and any processes that alter or transform the data until it is presented to the user. By presenting provenance data, we aim to help users identify sources of data errors and better understand the weaknesses of their PI systems. DUT involves modifying PI user interfaces to juxtapose known error or uncertainty with the data itself, allowing end-users to evaluate the quality of their PI data in context. By adding transparency to PI systems, we aim to increase user trust in PI systems and improve decision-making based on observations of noisy PI data.

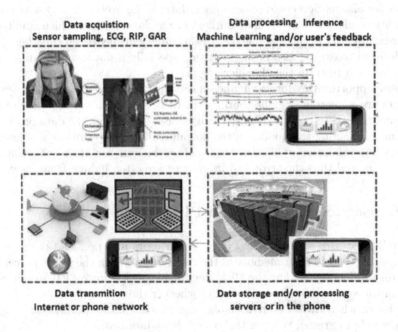

Fig. 1. A generic architecture for personal informatics systems

2   Sources of Error in PI Systems

The path from the acquisition of raw data to the presentation of the data in a PI tool requires several transformations and interpretations of the data, and thus presents several opportunities for error to be injected into the PI data. To demonstrate this problem, we present *Corredor*, a PI system designed to provide feedback on physical activity.

Corredor processes smartphone accelerometry to identify one of three user activities: standing, walking, and running. First, data is sampled from an accelerometer built into the user's smartphone. Second, before passing this data to *Corredor*, the smartphone may apply additional filtering algorithms to reduce the effects of noise. The filtered data is then passed on to *Corredor* for classification. Third, *Corredor* starts the classification process by applying data reduction and smoothing algorithms, eliminating outliers, and imputing missing values. Fourth, frequency-based features are extracted from the signal. Fifth, these features are then passed to a J48 decision tree classifier, which transforms input features to the specific activity the user is performing.

Error can be injected into *Corredor's* data processing pipeline at several places. Amplifiers and ambient temperature changes add noise when the accelerometer is sampled. Filtering and smoothing is critical to making the data useable, but valuable features of the data could be lost in the process. Overzealous outlier elimination could remove good data, while overly conservative outlier elimination might leave too many outliers in the data, both of which could skew classification later in the pipeline. Lastly, machine learning based classifiers (e.g., J48 decision trees) are also prone to error, especially if not enough data of each class was used to train the classifier.

Thus, opportunities for error and uncertainty to play a role in PI system outputs are numerous. Furthermore, as in Li et al's stage-based model of personal informatics [8], errors in earlier stages cascade through the data processing pipelining, affecting the quality of the output at later stages in the pipeline. All of these potential sources of error occur before the user has any interaction with the system, and thus the error and its sources are often hidden from view.

3   Consequences of Error in PI Systems

Figure 2 illustrates scenarios that occur when users interpret and compare the displayed PI data to their memory of their activities. When the user's perception of history differs from what the PI system displays (Figure 2 - left side in red), trust in the system falls (independent of whether the system is correct). On the other hand, when the PI system display matches the user's perceptions (Figure 2 - right side in green), trust in the system is maintained.

In the latter case, we note that trust in the system is maintained even when the data presented by the PI system is inaccurate, because the user has no reason to suspect its inaccuracy. Adjusting behavior based on inaccurate data could have significant negative consequences. For example, if a PI system incorrectly

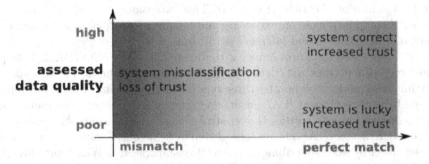

Fig. 2. User Perceptions vs. PI System Display vs. PI System Accuracy

tells a user that his/her stress level is generally low, and the user believes this assessment is correct, the user will not take action to reduce daily stress, even though he/she may need to do so to avoid heart disease later in life.

In previous work, a lack of trust in a PI system led users to quickly lose interest in the system [9]. Dzindolet et al [4] and Kulesza [7] point out that the frequent occurrence of data errors tends to erode the confidence of users and eventually users abandon the system. Users are often skeptical of black-box systems [3] and may often discount important data, rather than adapt their conceptions and change behaviors. Authors such as Lim and Dey [3] [10] and Kulesza [7] hypothesize that explaining the system behavior to end users will enable them to form better judgments and increase their trust in the system. Their proposals include self-explanatory algorithms to give users a better understanding of the system outputs.

Building on these ideas, we propose two approaches to increasing the transparency of, and trust in, PI systems: 1) data acquisition transparency and data uncertainty transparency. In data acquisition transparency, users are shown provenance models describing how the data is collected and derived. In data uncertainty transparency, information about the accuracy of the data is integrated into the PI system's visualizations.

4   Data Acquisition Transparency

Data provenance refers to metadata describing the derivation history or chronology of a data product [11]. Providing the user with a data provenance model would make the data acquisition history, and by extension the sources of error, more transparent. Users could then determine the causes of error and take appropriate action. The appropriate action could be to abandon the PI system because the error is unacceptable, to continue using the system as is, or perhaps make changes to the system or his/her behaviors to reduce errors (based on their understanding of the model).

The challenge then is choosing the right model and model visualization that can convey the data flow and possible sources of error clearly. We use an extended Open Provenance Model (OPM) proposed by Riboni and Bettini [14] to model the provenance of *Corredor* (Figure 3). This extension is specifically designed to model components of context-aware and ubiquitous systems, such as sensors, context, smartphones, and inference algorithms.

OPM represents data provenance with directed acyclic graphs (DAGs). Graph nodes represent entities and edges represent causal dependencies. The Riboni and Bettini OPM model incorporates three types of nodes: *artifacts* (i.e., data) represented by ovals; *processes* (i.e., sensors and inference algorithms) represented by rectangles; and *agents*, entities that control processes (e.g., smartphones controlling onboard sensors). Agents are represented by hexagons. Entities are connected to each other by edges describing causal relationships, such as *Was-Controlled-By*, *Used*, *Was-Generated-By*, and *Was-Derived-By*.

Several of these relationships are shown in Figure 3: a *Was-Controlled* edge from the smartphone (agent) to sensors (processes); a *Used* edge from segmentation algorithms (processes) to accelerometer data streams (artifacts); a *Was-Generated* edge from activity predictions (artifacts) to inference algorithms (processes); and a *Was -Derived* edge that relates acceleration features (artifacts) to raw streams of acceleration data (artifacts).

Figure 3 represents a specific moment in the use of *Corredor*, when an individual named John Doe takes a morning run. The model shows that the prediction of John Doe's 7:00am activity (running) was generated by the J48 activity inference process. That prediction was derived from features generated by the Fast Fourier Transform (FFT) process. The FFT process received as input a set of accelerometer magnitudes computed in the time domain by a segmentation process. The segmentation process derived those magnitudes from streams of 3-axis acceleration data provided by the accelerometer sensors on John Doe's smartphone.

While we believe the extended OPM is a useful model to describe provenance, it is not clear if a visual representation of the model (similar to Figure 3) would help end-users understand the sources of error in PI systems. Perhaps collapsing nodes of the graph to reduce its complexity would provide a simpler, more useful view of the data. For instance, we could collapse the FFT and segmentation processes into one process to create a more direct presentation of the relationship between streams of raw data and features.

5   Data Uncertainty Transparency

Data uncertainty transparency refers to integrating uncertainty or error measurements directly into the PI system user interface. This allows users to visually assess the quality of the data they rely on to make behavior change decisions. A critical assumption is that the PI system is capable of assessing the quality of every data point it produces. In the rest of this section, we present several example uncertainty visualizations that could be integrated into PI systems to provide transparency.

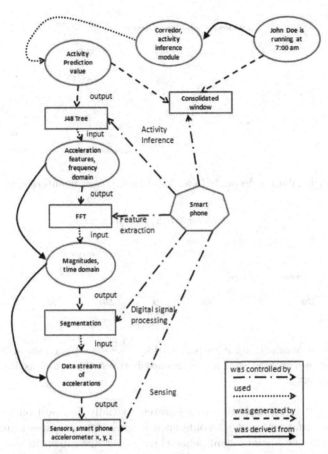

Fig. 3. *Corredor's* OPM extension graph describing detection of John Doe's 7:00am running episode

Figure 4 is a time-series visualization of sample stress predictions from AutoSense [12] [5], a suite of sensors and a smartphone that infers a user's stress level from physiological data. A value of 1 indicates the user is not stressed, 2 indicates the user is stressed, and 3 indicates there is not enough information to make a prediction. However, in the intervals in which predictions are uncertain, the time series is plotted with a dashed line. The size of the dash is inversely proportional to the uncertainty in the data. Larger dashes mean the uncertainty is low, smaller dashes mean the uncertainty is high, and no dashes (a continuous line) mean there is no known error in the data. The user can then interact with this visualization to selectively query the data. Figure 4 shows the result of querying an interval (shown in red) for precise accuracy data.

We present another time-series visualization in Figure 5, this time using data collected by *Corredor*. As in Figure 4, the horizontal axis is a time span (800 seconds), and the vertical axis represents different activities *Corredor* can classify: standing, walking, and running. The three activities are shown in red, green,

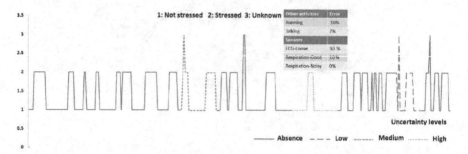

Fig. 4. Visualizing data uncertainty in a PI system for stress monitoring and reflection

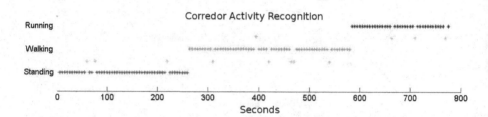

Fig. 5. 800 seconds of activity data produced by *Corredor*. Uncertain activity classifications are shown in gray, and are positioned between the two classifications most likely to be correct.

and blue, respectively, and are also separated spatially. In addition to the three activities, *Corredor* assesses its confidence in each activity classification. Only those classifications above a confidence threshold σ are shown in red, green, or blue. The remaining uncertain classifications are shown in gray. They are positioned spatially between the two activities that are most likely to be correct. By reviewing Figure 5, a user can see the frequency of uncertain classifications for each activity, and thus better understand what types of activity are likely to confuse the system.

Figure 6 uses a pie chart to present an aggregated version of the *Corredor* data in Figure 5. The pie chart shows the percentage of data classified into each activity and the percentage of data for which confidence in the classifications was low. The latter are spatially positioned between two activity classes to indicate which two activity classes are most likely to be correct in these low-confidence situations. One piece of information present here that is not in Figure 5 is the distribution of low-confidence classifications among the two possible correct classes. These distributions are demonstrated visually by subdividing the low-confidence sections of the pie chart proportionally to the percent that fall in each class. For example, in Figure 5, 12% of the classifications are considered low-confidence. Of those low-confidence classifications, 8% could either be classified as walking or standing. Furthermore, 5% is more likely to be walking and the remaining 3% is more likely to be standing.

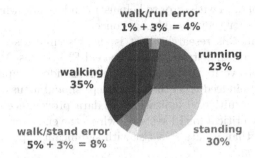

Fig. 6. A pie chart summarizing the percentages of activities classified by *Corredor* with high and low confidence

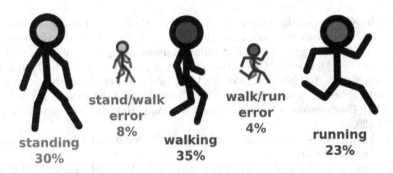

Fig. 7. An avatar-based iconographic visualization of the activities detected by *Corredor*

Lastly, Figure 7 presents a third approach to presenting *Corredor's* data to the end-user, using avatars as icons that demonstrate the three activity classes. Percentages of each activity detected are shown below the activity's corresponding avatar icon. Visual aggregations of low-confidence classifications are positioned between the two corresponding activity icons and are depicted as the two activity icons layered on top of each other. Transparency and color blending are used to indicate the extent to which each low confidence classification could be one class or the other.

6 Conclusion and Future Work

In this work, we presented an approach to increasing the level of transparency, and by extension trust, in personal informatics (PI) systems. We introduced data acquisition transparency as the use of provenance model visualizations to explain how data is produced by a PI system and help users pinpoint sources of error in PI data. We also introduced data uncertainty transparency as the integration of error and uncertainty measures directly into the UI elements already presented in many PI systems. This integration of error and uncertainty into the UI leverages the juxtaposition of data with error to help users understand what types of errors can occur and whether they should be a concern.

The next step in this research effort is the systematic study of both data acquisition and uncertainty transparency in real PI systems. Most importantly, these studies need to verify that transparency does indeed improve user trust in PI systems. If this is indeed true, then next steps should focus on identifying the most transparent, intuitive visualizations of data provenance and uncertainty. This is particularly critical for PI systems, where the end-user is often the 'average' person rather than a data scientist with significant experience interpreting visualizations [16,13].

References

1. Church, K., Hoggan, E., Oliver, N.: A study of mobile mood awareness and communication through mobimood. In: Proceedings of the 6th Nordic Conference on Human-Computer Interaction: Extending Boundaries, pp. 128–137. ACM (2010)
2. Consolvo, S., McDonald, D.W., Toscos, T., Chen, M.Y., Froehlich, J., Harrison, B., Klasnja, P., LaMarca, A., LeGrand, L., Libby, R., et al.: Activity sensing in the wild: a field trial of ubifit garden. In: Proceedings of the Twenty-Sixth Annual SIGCHI Conference on Human Factors in Computing Systems, pp. 1797–1806. ACM (2008)
3. Dey, A.K.: Understanding and using context. Personal and Ubiquitous Computing 5(1), 4–7 (2001)
4. Dzindolet, M.T., Peterson, S.A., Pomranky, R.A., Pierce, L.G., Beck, H.P.: The role of trust in automation reliance. International Journal of Human-Computer Studies 58(6), 697–718 (2003)
5. Ertin, E., Stohs, N., Kumar, S., Raij, A., Al' Absi, M., Shah, S.: Autosense: unobtrusively wearable sensor suite for inferring the onset, causality, and consequences of stress in the field. In: Proceedings of the 9th ACM Conference on Embedded Networked Sensor Systems, pp. 274–287. ACM (2011)
6. Froehlich, J., Findlater, L., Landay, J.: The design of eco-feedback technology. In: Proceedings of the 28th International Conference on Human Factors in Computing Systems, pp. 1999–2008. ACM (2010)
7. Kulesza, T.: An explanation-centric approach for personalizing intelligent agents. In: Proceedings of the 2012 ACM International Conference on Intelligent User Interfaces, pp. 375–378. ACM (2012)
8. Li, I., Dey, A., Forlizzi, J.: A stage-based model of personal informatics systems. In: Proceedings of the 28th International Conference on Human Factors in Computing Systems, pp. 557–566. ACM (2010)
9. Lim, B.Y.: Improving trust in context-aware applications with intelligibility. In: Proceedings of the 12th ACM International Conference Adjunct Papers on Ubiquitous Computing-Adjunct, pp. 477–480. ACM (2010)
10. Lim, B.Y., Dey, A.K.: Investigating intelligibility for uncertain context-aware applications. In: Proceedings of the 13th International Conference on Ubiquitous Computing, pp. 415–424. ACM (2011)
11. Moreau, L., Clifford, B., Freire, J., Futrelle, J., Gil, Y., Groth, P., Kwasnikowska, N., Miles, S., Missier, P., Myers, J., et al.: The open provenance model core specification (v1. 1). Future Generation Computer Systems 27(6), 743–756 (2011)

12. Plarre, K., Raij, A., Hossain, S.M., Ali, A.A., Nakajima, M., Al' Aabsi, M., Ertin, E., Kamarck, T., Kumar, S., Scott, M., et al.: Continuous inference of psychological stress from sensory measurements collected in the natural environment. In: 10th International Conference on Information Processing in Sensor Networks (IPSN), pp. 97–108. IEEE (2011)

13. Pousman, Z., Stasko, J.T., Mateas, M.: Casual information visualization: Depictions of data in everyday life. IEEE Transactions on Visualization and Computer Graphics 13(6), 1145–1152 (2007)

14. Riboni, D., Bettini, C.: Context provenance to enhance the dependability of ambient intelligence systems. Personal and Ubiquitous Computing, 1–20.

15. Santos, J.L., Govaerts, S., Verbert, K., Duval, E.: Goal-oriented visualizations of activity tracking: a case study with engineering students. In: Proceedings of the 2nd International Conference on Learning Analytics and Knowledge, pp. 143–152. ACM (2012)

16. Shneiderman, B.: Session 2 infovis for the masses. IEEE Transactions on Visualization and Computer Graphics 13(6)

Feed-In Tariff Personal Carbon Allowance: A Case Study of Psychological Change

Takayoshi Kitamura, Asao Takamatsu, Hirotake Ishii, and Hiroshi Shimoda

Graduate School of Energy Science, Kyoto University, Kyoto, Japan
{kitamura,takamatsu,hirotake,shimoda}@ei.energy.kyoto-u.ac.jp

Abstract. The scheme of Personal Carbon Allowance (PCA) system which has been under discussion in United Kingdom is one of the innovative policies which have the potential to solve energy and climate issues. The authors have been proposed Feed-in Tariff PCA (FIT-PCA) as a suitable policy for Japan. The main purpose of this scheme is to encourage citizens to manage their CO_2 emissions from their daily lives, furthermore, it is expected to improve their attitudes to global environmental issues. In the psychological model to express their behavioral changes, it is assumed that the experience of FIT-PCA causes loss aversion, goal setting and eudaimonia, and they change their life styles to pro-environmental ones. In this study, a case study has been conducted for half a year in cooperation with 30 households to investigate the validity of the model and the change of their energy reduction behaviors and attitudes to global environmental issues.

Keywords: social system, case study, personal carbon allowances, energy issues, psychological changes.

1 Introduction

In Japan, reduction of CO_2 emission towards realization of a low-carbon society has been progressing in the industrial sector. On the other hand, in the household sector, it has not progressed enough [1]. Personal carbon allowances (PCA) system is the policy in which the government distributes the right to emit CO_2 to citizens and manage them [2]. The PCA system has been studied mainly in the UK and it is expected not only to reduce CO_2 emissions but also to improve our environmental attitudes as a non-economic effect [3]. Japanese government however has no experience to introduce CO_2 emission management system when using energy. It is therefore difficult to adapt the research results in the UK directly to Japan.

The authors have proposed Feed-in Tariff PCA (FIT-PCA) suitable for Japan, which has employed the idea of German feed-in tariff rule of electricity trading [4] where the government purchases and sells the excess allowance at a fixed price. This idea can avoid the decrease of their motivations for CO_2 emission management caused by the price instability in the conventional PCA systems and encourages the investment in housing equipment for reducing CO_2 emission

A. Marcus (Ed.): DUXU/HCII 2013, Part III, LNCS 8014, pp. 530–539, 2013.

because they can easily design their future energy management plan. In order to investigate the public acceptance and problems of the FIT-PCA, the authors conducted a questionnaire survey [5]. As the result, the total support rate of FIT-PCA compared with an assumed down-stream Carbon Tax was 60.5%. It was also found that the presentation of the average CO_2 emissions of general public affects their attitudes of energy consumption. However, it has not been revealed yet about what has the effect of promoting their pro-environmental attitudes and behaviors when actually introducing FIT-PCA. The purpose of this study is to conduct a case study of FIT-PCA and to examine the effects based on the psychological model which assumes that it promotes their pro-environmental behaviors caused by the effects of loss aversion, goal setting and eudaimonia.

2 Feed-In Tariff Personal Carbon Allowance (FIT-PCA)

2.1 Proposal of FIT-PCA

Since the PCA systems studied in the UK and Nordic countries allow the citizens to trade their allowances between themselves or in the market, the management effect of CO_2 emission is greatly affected by the price of allowance deals. In addition, the lives of the people who have to consume much energy may be pressured when the price becomes high. On the contrary, when the price becomes low, the motivation to reduce energy consumption and CO_2 emission may be discouraged. This instability may spoil the effect of improving their pro-environmental attitudes and behaviors by managing their own CO_2 emissions. In addition, such as a policy of downstream carbon tax which is the direct economic burden to the consumers has not existed in Japan until now. To solve these problems, FIT-PCA has been designed based on three principles which are simplicity, effectiveness and fairness. The details of the principles will be described as follows;

Simplicity: FIT-PCA mechanisms must be comprehensive and the procedure must be simple. Because the ideas of imposing a constraint on CO_2 emissions is relatively new and current emission trading system is applied only to companies, it is unfamiliar to the public at present.

Effectiveness: FIT-PCA should be effective for the citizens to improve their pro-environmental attitudes and behaviors. This is the main purpose of this policy. It is also expected to give a good influence to solve other social issues because its affected fields can be broad.

Fairness: FIT-PCA should not cause the feeling of unfairness because it is applied to various kinds of people who live in various areas and situations such as ages, number of family members, climates of residential areas and house forms, and these varieties affect the amount of CO_2 emissions. FIT-PCA needs compensatory rules to reduce such unbalance caused by the varieties.

2.2   Rule Details

Figure 1 shows the basic flow of FIT-PCA.

 (i) Government distributes free personal carbon allowance (PCA) to the citizens periodically and equally. Here the PCA means how people have the right of CO_2 emission when they consume energy in their daily lives.

 (ii) They have to redeem the PCA when they purchase or consume energy such as electricity, gas, gasoline, light oil and heating oil which originate in fossil fuels.

(iii) If they don't have enough PCA when purchasing the energy, they have to also purchase the shortage of PCA for a fixed price.

(iv) They can sell the excessive PCA to the government for a fixed price if they don't need it. In this system, they have to manage their CO_2 emission by their energy consumption and it is expected not only that they reduce their energy consumption and CO_2 emission but also that their pro-environmental attitudes and behaviors are fostered.

The PCA is transferred to all the individual PCA accounts equally without charge at the beginning of each month. The amount is one-twelfth of annual amount decided based on the annual average of CO_2 emission per person. The account is allowed to be kept for 12 months including the distribution month (banking system). The PCA which exceeds 12 months will be expired and disappears from the account. Due to this rule, the government would be able to prevent from weakening the effect of PCA management after the next fiscal year. The PCAs which are distributed to children should be managed by their parents or protectors. And the transfer and integration of PCA inside the same household is allowed because the energy consumption of their daily lives is often managed by their household units.

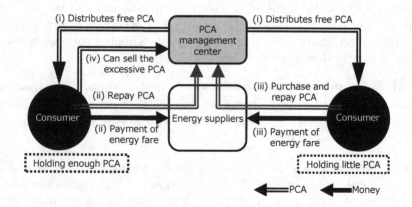

Fig. 1. Flow of FIT-PCA

2.3   Psychological Model of FIT-PCA

In order to examine whether FIT-PCA encourages eco-friendly behaviors and attitudes or not, this study have assumed a model of its psychological effect as shown in Figure 2. This model is based on four theories: loss aversion, goal setting, eudaimonia and self-perception.

Loss Aversion

The loss aversion is employed from the prospect theory [6]. It refers to their strong tendency to avoid losses comparing with to make profit. This tendency is influenced by the price or a length of time. Although the price of PCA is not so expensive in the FIT-PCA, the authors expect that the loss aversion would play an important role to improve their CO_2 management.

Goal Setting

Locke claimed that the goal setting affects their motivation and performance [7]. In the FIT-PCA, the amount of distributed PCA is set considering the average of CO_2 emission from their daily lives. Therefore, the following effects can be expected.

1. Rational target: The target performance is better if there is a difficulty. However, it requires the rational reason.
2. Clear goal: A clear and specific goal can foster high motivation.
3. Effect of feedback: When the feedback is combined with the target setting, it improves their motivation.

Eudaimonia

The gEudaimoniah is a Greek word associated with Aristotle. This is the highest human good state of well-being and prosperous [8]. You will feel the eudaimonia when you are living well in our society. In the FIT-PCA, the authors expect the person who makes an effort to reduce CO_2 emission would feel the eudaimonia.

Self-perception

This is one of the theories on behavior mechanism. Bem claimed people develop their own attitudes, beliefs, and other internal states by observing their own behaviors [9]. Therefore, in the FIT-PCA, participants may have developed their attitude by observing their own behaviors reducing CO_2 emissions. And they maybe perceive their own behaviors in connection with global environmental issues. This expectation can be also explained by cognitive dissonance theory[10].

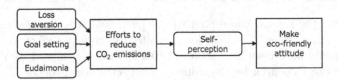

Fig. 2. Psychological model of FIT-PCA

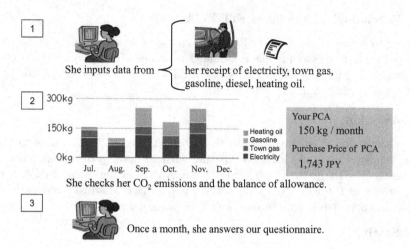

She inputs data from her receipt of electricity, town gas, gasoline, diesel, heating oil.

She checks her CO_2 emissions and the balance of allowance.

Once a month, she answers our questionnaire.

Fig. 3. Overview of case study

3   A Case Study of FIT-PCA

3.1   Purpose of Case Study and Its Outline

The purpose of this study is to examine the effects which improve their attitudes and behaviors to reduce CO_2 emission when FIT-PCA is introduced in their lives. In this study, therefore, a case study has been conducted for a half year in cooperation with 30 households to investigate how they have changed their energy saving behaviors and attitudes on global environmental issues when FIT-PCA has been marginally introduced. Figure 3 shows an overview of this case study. In the case study, a web system has been developed which realizes PCA accounts virtually. The participants cansee the information about not only their balance of PCA but also bar graphs of CO_2 emissions with general average line (this is a distributes PCA/month) in this web system. The overall procedure of the case study is shown below;

1. The participants input their energy consumption data which they used in the household to the web system when they pay for the energy.
2. They check their CO_2 emissions and the balance of PCA.
3. They answer the questionnaire once a month in order to examine the change of their attitudes and behaviors.
4. The above 1-3 is repeated for six months (From July to December 2012).

In this study, the reward to be paid to the participants is changed depending on how they trade their PCA in order to realize its economic effect. In addition, the participants have been divided into two PCA price groups, 1 JPY/kg-CO_2 and 10 JPY/kg-CO_2 in order to examine the effect of loss aversion.

3.2   Methods of Case Study

The participants of the case study participants can understand their balance of CO_2 emissions and PCA of the month by inputting the amount of their consumed energy to FIT-PCA account inventory (FAI). In this case study, the amount of PCA which was distributed to the participants was set 150 kg- CO_2/month. It is because the average of CO_2 emissions by Japanese household per capita is 167 kg-CO_2/month approximately [11] and the distributed PCA should be a little lower than the average to promote their CO_2 emission reduction. Formula (1) shows a calculation of CO_2 emissions G in FAI.

$$G = \frac{p_i c_i E_i}{n} \tag{1}$$

Where p is the proportion of energy use in their household against their business, c is the emission factor by energy source, E is the energy consumption, n is the number of people per household and i is the type of energy. Table 1 shows the CO_2 emission factors of energy [12].

Table 1. CO_2 emission factors by energy types

Type of energy	CO_2 emission factor	
Electricity $[kWh]$	@0.559	$[CO_2\text{-}kg/kWh]$
Town gas $[m^3]$	@2.23	$[CO_2\text{-}kg/m^3]$
Gasoline $[l]$	@2.32	$[CO_2\text{-}kg/l]$
Light oil $[l]$	@2.58	$[CO_2\text{-}kg/l]$
Heating oil $[l]$	@2.49	$[CO_2\text{-}kg/l]$

In this case study, the questionnaire surveys have been conducted at beginning of each month. In the questionnaire, the authors have set the questions about the each element of FIT-PCA psychological model and the change of attitude to the global environmental issues. The participants answered each question as a five grade likert-scale for later quantitative analysis. In addition, the sixth choice of gdo not knowh is set in some questions where there is a possibility that the participants cannot understand the meaning of the questions. Furthermore, interviews to the participants will be carried out at the end of the case study period in order to confirm their detail psychological changes and their reasons.

3.3   Results of the Case Study

In order to examine whether there is a difference of the loss aversion by the different price of PCA or not, the participants were divided into two groups of 1 JPY/CO_2-kg and 10 JPY/CO_2-kg as the price of PCA. Table 2 shows the result of independent t-test which shows the difference between the 1 JPY/CO_2-kg and 10 JPY/CO_2-kg groups' answers about loss aversion gI want to reduce the loss by purchasing PCA as much as possibleh. In the questionnaire of all case studies' period, there is no significant difference between these groups. In other

Table 2. Result of t-test which shows the difference of the loss aversion between 1 JPY/CO_2-kg and 10 JPY/CO_2-kg groups

Questionnaire period	Group	mean value	SD	t-statistic	df	Two-sided P value
Early August	1 JPY	4.07	1.15	0.35	25	0.73
	10 JPY	4.20	0.95			
Early September	1 JPY	4.27	0.80	0.94	26	0.35
	10 JPY	3.93	1.17			
Early October	1 JPY	4.07	1.18	0.61	26	0.55
	10 JPY	4.27	0.58			
Early November	1 JPY	4.33	1.07	0.39	26	0.70
	10 JPY	4.20	0.86			
Early December	1 JPY	4.07	1.08	0.59	25	0.56
	10 JPY	4.20	0.80			

Question: Do you want to reduce the loss by purchasing PCA as much as possible?
This questionnaire uses a likert scale. 1:No, 5:Yes

words, it was found that loss aversion has not been affected by the difference of PCA price. And this result can increase the feasibility of FIT-PCA because it is easier to obtain public acceptance when introducing low price FIT-PCA.

In order to examine whether FIT-PCA has led to the participants' efforts to reduce CO_2 emissions by the loss aversion, the goal setting and the eudaimonia as shown in Figure 2, a multiple regression analysis was made. Figure 4 shows the path diagram based on the results. As shown in the figure, it was found that the efforts to reduce CO_2 emissions has significantly affected by the goal setting or the eudaimonia. Table 3 shows the number of the participants who perceived their own attitude to global environmental issues. This result shows the people who made efforts to reduce CO_2 emissions tended to perceive their own attitudes to be eco-friendly. Table 4 shows the changes of the attitudes to the environment which are their risk perception, effectiveness and responsibility attribution. This result shows their attitudes to global environmental issues have been improved comparing with before the case study.

3.4   Discussion

As shown in Figure 4, the results of multiple regression analysis show the goal setting or eudaimonia have improved the gmake efforts to reduce CO_2 emissionsh. It is supposed that the loss aversion have not affected it directly because the participants have not been able to imagine which activity saves a loss in daily lives from FAI. In summer and winter, they tended to be conscious of their goals because they have consumed more energy and PCA in these seasons and they have been forced to be aware of the rest of their PCAs. On the other hand in autumn, it is supposed that they could feel endaimonia because they have enough margins of their PCAs.

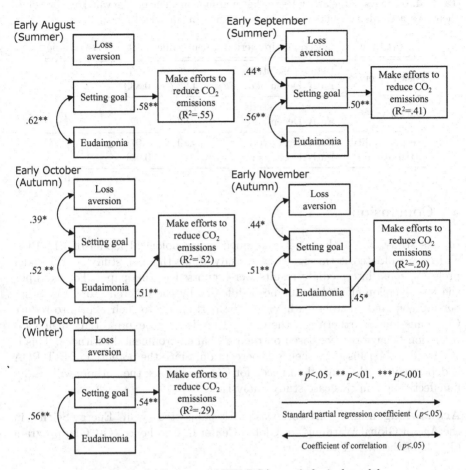

Fig. 4. Path diagrams of FIT-PCA psychological model

Table 3. The number of the participants who perceived their own behaviors in connection with global environment

Questionnaire period	Make efforts to reduce CO_2 emissions $[n]$	Perceive their own attitude to global environment issues $[n]$
Early August	10	6
Early September	11	8
Early October	11	7
Early November	12	8
Early December	10	9

Table 4. Changes of the attitudes to the environment (The people who have perceived their own attitude to global environmental issues in early December)

Attitude	Questionnaire period	Mean value	SD	df	t-statistic
Risk Perception	Before case study	3.22	1.09	8	2.26*
	Early December	4.22	0.833		
Effectiveness	Before case study	1.22	0.441	8	2.00*
	Early December	1.89	0.928		
Responsibility attribution	Before case study	3.00	1.07	7	1.69
	Early December	2.13	0.991		

$^*p < .05$

4   Conclusion

In this study, the authors have assumed a psychological model of FIT-PCA and have validated it through a case study. Since the case study is still under progress, some intermediate results were reported in this paper. For example, the loss aversion effect has not been different by the difference of PCA price. Setting goal and eudaimonia have led the participant to their efforts to reduce CO_2 emissions. Furthermore, there was a tendency to express that their CO_2 reduction behaviors were based on their global environmental attitudes. This is supposed to be caused by their self-perception. Since the potential of FIT-PCA is dependent on the individual needs for CO_2 emissions, the authors will clarify its effectiveness in this case study analysis.

Acknowledgement. This work was partly supported by an "Energy Science in the Age of Global Warming" of Global Center of Excellence (G-COE) program (J-051) of the MEXT of Japan.

References

1. Ministry of Environment: Japan's National Greenhouse Gas Emissions in Fiscal Year 2010 (Final Figures) (2012),
   http://www.env.go.jp/en/headline/headline.php?serial=1763
   (accessed February 20, 2013)
2. Howell, R.: Living with a carbon allowance: The experiences of Carbon Rationing Action Groups and implications for policy. Energy Policy 41, 250–258 (2012)
3. Fawcett, T.: Personal carbon trading: A policy ahead of its time? Energy Policy 10(4), 369–384 (2010)
4. Huenteler, J., et al.: Japan's post-Fukushima challenge-implications from the German experience on renewable energy policy. Energy Policy 45, 6–11 (2012)
5. Kitamura, T., et al.: A Proposal of Feed-in Tariff Personal Carbon Allowance (FIT-PCA) and its Evaluation. In: Symposium on Socially and Technically Symbiotic Systems (STSS 2012), Okayama, Japan, pp. 281–288 (2012)
6. Kahneman, D., Tversky, A.: Prospect Theory: An Analysis of Decision under Risk. Econometrica 47(2), 263–291 (1979)

7. Locke, E.: Toward a theory of task motivation and incentives. American Institutes for Research 3(2), 157–189 (1968)
8. Waterman, A.: Two conceptions of happiness: Contrasts of personal expressiveness (eudaemonia) and hedonic enjoyment. Journal of Personality and Social Psychology 64, 678–691 (1993)
9. Bem, D.: Self-perception theory. Advances in Experimental Social Psychology 6, 1–62 (1972)
10. Festinger, L.: A theory of cognitive dissonance. Stanford Univ. Press, Stanford (1997)
11. Greenhouse Gas Inventory Office of Japan: The GHGs Emissions Data of Japan (1990-2010) (2012), http://www-gio.nies.go.jp/aboutghg/nir/nir-e.html (accessed February 20, 2013)
12. Ministry of Environment: The system of reporting of carbon dioxide equivalent greenhouse gas emissions (2006), http://ghg-santeikohyo.env.go.jp (accessed February 20, 2013)

Positive Design:
New Challenges, Opportunities,
and Responsibilities for Design

Anna Elisabeth Pohlmeyer

Delft University of Technology, Faculty of Industrial Design Engineering,
Delft Institute of Positive Design
Landbergstraat 15, 2628 CE Delft, The Netherlands
A.E.Pohlmeyer@tudelft.nl

Abstract. In recent years, there has been an increasing interest in the scientific study of happiness and wellbeing. However, so far, there has been only little discussion about the relevance and applicability for design. This paper provides a brief overview of related developments in the field of psychology and user experience, before it introduces and illustrates the emerging field of positive design. Positive design builds on insights from positive psychology to create and improve products and/or services that increase human flourishing.

Keywords: Positive Design, Human Flourishing, Subjective Wellbeing, Experience Design.

1 Introduction

In 2011, a resolution of the United Nations (UN) on happiness was adopted unanimously in a General Assembly meeting [1] and a UN high-level meeting on happiness and wellbeing followed in 2012, emphasizing its importance for public policy and associated development measures. The resolution not only regards the pursuit of happiness as a fundamental human goal, but also recognizes that happiness captures the spirit of the Millennium Development Goals. In other words, the focus on happiness is motivated by personal aspirations of individuals as well as by challenges that affect society as a whole.

In a way, these two go hand in hand. Happiness has been positively associated with health, productivity and success at the workplace, as well as prosocial behavior, e.g. acts of kindness and charity (for overviews see [2, 3]). It can be seen as an *"emotional capital we can spend in the pursuit of other attractive outcomes"* ([2], p.20).

Consequently, plenty reasons suggest it might be worthwhile – perhaps even necessary – to explicitly focus on happiness in the discipline of design as well. In the end, we all strive for happiness in our lives. The focus in this paper will be on *subjective* wellbeing and happiness and the following definition will be used as a reference to ensure a shared understanding: *"I use the term 'happiness' to refer to the*

A. Marcus (Ed.): DUXU/HCII 2013, Part III, LNCS 8014, pp. 540–547, 2013.

experience of joy, contentment or positive well-being, combined with a sense that one's life is good, meaningful and worthwhile." ([4], p. 32). As indicated by this quote, happiness (in the following also referred to as subjective wellbeing) is a multi-faceted concept that comprises an affective component (a hedonic balance of high positive and low negative emotions) as well as a cognitive component (life satisfaction) [2]. According to Seligman, one of the founders of positive psychology, elements of subjective wellbeing that contribute to human flourishing are positive emotions, relationships with others, engaging activities that optimally challenge one's skills, meaningful contributions for a greater good, and achievement [5].

This paper will introduce and illustrate the newly arising field of positive design. Positive design builds on insights from positive psychology to create and improve products and/or services that increase human flourishing.

2   Recent Developments

Two research streams of recent years are indispensable for this future challenge: *User Experience (UX)* and *Positive Psychology*. Firstly, from a technological point of view, UX has advanced the field of HCI by moving beyond mere task-oriented approaches and encompassing emotional and more pleasure-oriented aspects [6-9] as well as shifting the focus from products to experiences [10].

In parallel, a movement within the scientific community of psychologists entitled positive psychology emerged that studies the underpinnings as well as consequences of positive human development [11].

Both disciplines have undergone two major developments: a focus on the positive (1) and on activities (2).

2.1   Seeking the Positive

In Positive Psychology. The logic behind positive psychology is that reducing and preventing pain is no guarantee for wellbeing. A solely problem-oriented approach might succeed in offering a state of neutrality (e.g. drying one's tears), but moving into the positive zone (e.g. laughing) requires a different strategy. Thus, in contrast to more traditional approaches in psychology that center around human weaknesses and their treatment, positive psychologists investigate optimal human functioning and the promotion of subjective wellbeing to reach a point beyond the neutral.

Already in 1946, the World Health Organization defined health as *"a state of complete physical, mental, and social well-being and not merely the absence of disease or infirmity"* [12]. This definition is noteworthy in two ways: for one, it acknowledges a holistic understanding of health and secondly, it recognizes that being healthy is more than simply not being ill.

Antonovsky [13] coined the term 'salutogenesis', which stands for an approach highlighting the promotion of health and wellbeing as an alternative to the dominant pathogenic model that focuses on the cure of illnesses. It is important to note, that positive psychology and the salutogenic model are not meant to replace the pathogenic model, but rather to function as a valuable extension.

In UX. A positive, possibility-oriented approach in addition to a mindset of fixing problems could also be of benefit to the world of design and engineering [14]. Furthermore, as mentioned above, UX has achieved the integration of hedonic aspects of human-product interactions in the respective design, development, and evaluation (e.g. [6, 8]). In particular, these days interactive products focus not only on the pragmatic value in terms of efficiency and effectiveness as has been the emphasis for many years of usability research, but consider also emotional aspects and pleasurable experiences [6, 9]. Hence, in addition to the outlook of a possibility-oriented culture in design and innovation, positive emotions have been embraced as important elements in the field of UX.

2.2   Towards Activities and Experiences

In Positive Psychology. What determines our level of happiness? To some extent, the level of people's happiness is genetically determined [15]. We tend to fluctuate within a given range of happiness ups and downs in everyday life. However, there is reason to believe, that other factors can be influenced to reach a sustainable increase in happiness: Lyubomirsky, Sheldon, and Schkade [15] argue that 50% of individual differences in happiness can be explained by a genetic set point, surprisingly only 10% by circumstantial factors (e.g. demographic variables such as age, gender, marital status, region of residence, income), and substantial 40% by intentional activities. In other words, we have better chances to enhance our wellbeing if we change our behavior than by trying to change our circumstances. Lyubomirsky [4] identified and empirically validated twelve activities and cognitive strategies that can lastingly increase subjective wellbeing, e.g. increasing flow experiences, expressing gratitude, and cultivating optimism.

We rise and fall back to our individual set point upon changes in affect if these are not complemented by constructive activities (or thoughts). This automatic habituation process, or hedonic adaptation, is nothing bad per se – to the contrary, it helps us recover from unfavorable experiences in life [2]. However, if we try to increase our happiness without putting effort into it by adopting positive activities, we might get trapped in a 'hedonic treadmill' [4, 16, 17]. A hedonic approach of seeking positive emotions and pleasures while avoiding negative emotions and reducing displeasure certainly contributes to one's wellbeing. However, to avoid hedonic adaptation, a second approach to wellbeing, called eudaimonia can be pursued. Eudaimonia relates less to a specific outcome, but more to a way of (virtuous) living and flourishing, e.g. pursuing intrinsic values and goals as well as meeting basic psychological needs of relatedness, competence, and autonomy [18]. Simply put, the two approaches to wellbeing – hedonia and eudaimonia – can be differentiated as feeling good vs. living well [18]. In sum, there is no shortcut to happiness, in fact, it should not be seen as an 'end state' at all, but rather as a way of living [2, 4, 5].

In UX. A new emphasis on experiences over products can be observed in the design world. User experience emerged in the field of HCI focusing on experiential aspects of technology use from the user's perspective [7]. In experience design, the experience evoked receives a higher priority than the product itself [10], or put differently, a positive experience is the aim, while technology is simply the means to reach it. Hassenzahl [10] illustrates in a three level hierarchy of goals that motor-goals in a human-product interaction are most basic and relevant in terms of *how* to use a product, while do-goals guide *what* we can actually do with the product, and be-goals motivate *why* this is of interest to the user's self. Someone might want a car to *be* independent while someone else might desire it to *be* connected to a loved one. While efforts in HCI oftentimes center on practical issues of the *what* and the *how*, experience design incorporates all three levels. If a product is able to meet a psychological need, it can enable personally meaningful experiences. Instead of referring to positive experiences, Hassenzahl [10] suggests to use the term 'worthwhile' or 'valuable' as some negative experiences can result to be worthwhile in a long-term perspective, if they serve a higher goal.

3   Positive Design

Positive psychology studies the elements of wellbeing and strategies that support the pursuit to live not only a good – but also a fulfilling life. Positive design translates these into actionable design solutions.

Creating means for human flourishing offers numerous opportunities for innovative design. Apart from minimizing sources of displeasure, design can also proactively target the promotion of subjective wellbeing by evoking valuable experiences [14]. In the following, some design examples from the field of HCI will be given to exemplify this approach. It is important to note that design should not be seen as merely a direct source of pleasure, but rather as a medium that can address different components of wellbeing in multiple ways. Technology can, but does not have to be, center-stage in this endeavor – instead, prior attention is devoted to the activities supported and experiences evoked.

A Design Wellbeing Matrix has been proposed [19] that illustrates the diversity of Design for Subjective Wellbeing touch points. It comprises two dimensions: (1) roles that design can play and (2) elements of subjective wellbeing ('ingredients'). Noteworthy, multiple role-ingredient combinations can be integrated simultaneously. The matrix is intended to provide an overview of possible starting points, strategies, and classification criteria for a wellbeing-oriented design process.

Firstly, design can have multiple roles. It can be the direct *source* of happiness, both as a source of hedonic pleasure as well as manifestations of eudaimonia. Furthermore, as noted earlier, our activities are pivotal for our wellbeing and by shifting the focus from the product itself to the activities and experiences it enables, many more possibilities to enhance wellbeing open up. *Enablement* is an indirect approach to design for wellbeing; the effect on our happiness level is the result of an activity, which in turn is mediated through a product or service. *Symbolic* representations of what is important to people is a third role that design can play. Diener and Biswas-Diener [2] emphasize the influence of attention, interpretation, and memory on how we perceive the world and consequently appreciate our lives. By attracting attention and acting as a reminder, symbolic artifacts serve as a cognitive strategy to strengthen subjective wellbeing. Design as a means of *support* is an approach to coach the user in happiness-enhancing activities. Thus, it is neither something that makes the user happy by itself, nor does it enable an activity that would do so, but it can motivate, consult, and guide the user in living a healthy and fulfilling life. Hence, it can support initiation, maintenance, and commitment to happiness-enhancing activities and reflection. For example, Jane McGonigal [20] is a forerunner in the field of gaming, in particular of alternate reality games that interconnect online tasks with real-life challenges. She shows that games can be used to improve wellbeing holistically by incorporating physical, mental, emotional, and social challenges, e.g. one of the multi-player, online games she invented, 'SuperBetter', helps people build resilience, i.e. persistence even in the face of obstacles.

The four roles of design presented above widen the scope of possibilities from a mere product focus to enablement of activities, cognitive cues, as well as to supervisory support [19].

On the second dimension of the matrix, different elements of subjective wellbeing can be targeted in combination as well as in isolation, exemplified by Seligman's proposed five elements – positive emotions, engagement, relationships, meaning, and accomplishment (PERMA) [5]. Preferably, the profile matches the values and talents of the user as not all elements of subjective wellbeing are of equal importance to everyone and because the person's strengths should be recognized [4, 5] in order to facilitate and amplify the design's impact.

Positive emotions are likely to appear in all elements in some form and at some point in time or another. For example, having achieved a personal goal will evoke pride, intimate relationships involve love and affection, and committing to a project for a greater cause is accompanied by hope. However, the activities related to these situations are not sought for merely the sake of experiencing positive emotions. On the other hand, pleasurable experiences can indeed also be pursued for their own sake, e.g. taking a warm bath, riding a rollercoaster, watching a comedy, appreciating the beauty of a painting. To give a design example, The Happiness Cube [21] is an installation that was created, explicitly aimed to evoke happiness through pleasurable, multi-sensory experiences. Light, sound, odor, and video were orchestrated to please the senses. Hence, the Happiness Cube is a *source* of positive emotions.

The past years of UX research have shown that non-instrumental attributes can be vital in human-product interaction [7]. This also holds for positive design and should be considered in all cases. However, please note that to be delighted, motivated, or even inspired by hedonic features of an artifact is very different from basing one's happiness on hedonic gratification. Such an approach to happiness bears the risk of getting into a hedonic treadmill [16, 17]. In sum, despite the undeniable value of feeling good, there is more to life that makes it worthwhile and that can increase the level of subjective wellbeing. Design will need to address these factors to have a lasting effect.

Engagement refers to Csikszentmihalyi's concept of flow experiences [22], thus, being fully immersed in an activity that is engaging and self-actualizing. The activity is intrinsically motivated and rewarding, which means that it is performed for its own sake and because the person wants to do so, and not because of external incentives. It is not about the activity's outcome, but about the activity itself and about the possibility to improve one's skills. The perceived challenge of the activity should be high, but still realistic with regards to the skills of the performer; ideally the task fits the person's talents and strengths. Interestingly, the feeling of happiness might only arise afterwards, but not in the moment of flow, as the person has devoted undivided attention to the activity at hand.

Playing a musical instrument is a good example of a potential flow experience. Unfortunately, some people might not be able to play an instrument due to a disability. With the 'MotionComposer', Wechsler [23] created a musical environment for people with disabilities that allows them to artistically express themselves. The system tracks their movement and generates sounds based on musical algorithms.

In contrast, achievement, success, winning, and accumulation of wealth can be a driving force of its own [5]. Put differently, satisfaction is not necessarily derived from the activity performed, but based on the end result. In this case, design can function as a *source* and *symbol* of accomplishment. However, it can also *enable* an optimization of performance, for instance, by providing appropriate tools (e.g. climbing equipment) or (sensor-based) feedback of the progress.

Meaning is attained by belonging to or serving something that is greater than the self is [5]. For instance, many find a sense of purpose in life through spirituality or religion [4]. However, it can also be derived by, for example, investing in a better future (e.g. environmental, political) or by being active in the neighborhood. Many designed artifacts related to meaning are *symbolic* representations (e.g. religious symbolism), but they can also *enable* meaningful behavior. For example, the web-based platform kiva.org enables people around the world to support entrepreneurs in developing countries or otherwise challenged regions to build their business via microloans.

Finally, according to Seligman [5] and others (e.g. [4, 18]) relatedness is a pivotal element of wellbeing. We are social beings and much of our happiness is derived through social relationships. Even sharing life's experiences with other people often make these events worthwhile in the first place. However, relationships also need to be nurtured [4]. In this line, Hassenzahl et al. [24] recently collected and classified 143 examples of technologies that were designed to mediate intimate and co-located relationships. The six strategies of awareness, expressivity, physicalness, gift giving, joint action, and memory were identified [24] and demonstrate different possibilities of *enablement* (e.g. joint action) and *symbolic* representations (e.g. memory).

Design holds the potential to contribute in meaningful ways to people's happiness once it is freed from the constraining view of material value and mere hedonic pleasures. In particular, HCI has the capability to globally interconnect people, to provide means and tools for living an engaged and meaningful life as well as to persuade behavior change for a personal and societal good.

The following Positive Design Manifest by the Delft Institute of Positive Design [25] highlights the core aims of this discipline and captures the key points of this paper:

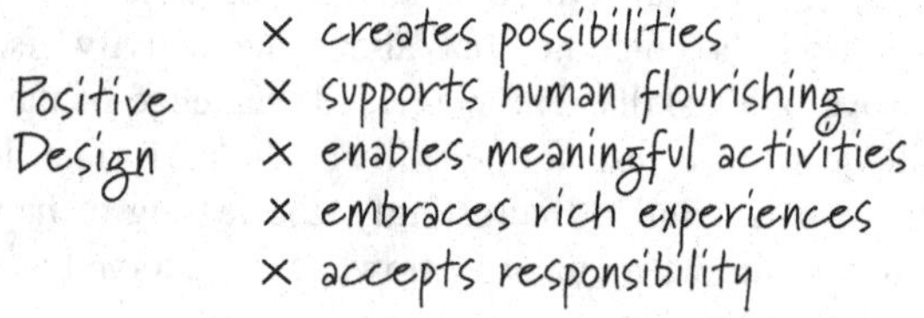

Positive Design

× creates possibilities
× supports human flourishing
× enables meaningful activities
× embraces rich experiences
× accepts responsibility

Fig. 1. Five Headings of the Positive Design Manifest [25]

4   Concluding Remark

What are the responsibilities of design? What do we design for? Functional tools can amplify our physical capabilities, and with the progression of smart technologies even cognitive limitations can be compensated. In this paper, it is being argued that the possibilities and the resultant responsibilities of design go even further: design holds the potential of empowering people to thrive intellectually, socially, and emotionally.

In the critical words of Daniel Fallman ([26], p.305): *"To continue to be relevant, it is important for HCI to understand that it is also leaving the comforting moral aimlessness of traditional usability."* Fallman calls for a philosophy of technology, that dares to raise the question of what is "good design" and thus also the question of the associated responsibility in design. This not only entails crucial issues of what not to design, but also what to design (for).

Instead of limiting itself to the classic approach aimed solely at achieving user satisfaction, the design community is invited to join the current momentum of research on happiness and wellbeing, and to accept the challenge to design for lasting wellbeing by targeting eudaimonic elements of products, services, or the activities they enable. Positive design offers the framework for this endeavor.

Acknowledgments. I would like to thank Pieter Desmet and our colleagues from the Delft Institute of Positive Design for fruitful discussions and for co-creating the Positive Design Manifest.

References

1. UN General Assembly, 65th session. Resolution A/RES/65/309 [Happiness: Towards a Holistic Approach to Development] (2011)
2. Diener, E., Biswas-Diener, R.: Happiness. Unlocking the Mysteries of Psychological Wealth, Blackwell Publishing, Malden (2008)

3. Lyubomirsky, S., King, L.A., Diener, E.: The Benefits of Frequent Positive Affect: Does Happiness Lead to Success? Psychological Bulletin 131(6), 803–855 (2005)
4. Lyubomirsky, S.: The How of Happiness. Piatkus, London (2010)
5. Seligman, M.E.P.: Flourish. Free Press, New York (2011)
6. Desmet, P.M.A.: Designing Emotions. PhD thesis, Delft University of Technology (2002)
7. Hassenzahl, M., Tractinsky, N.: User experience – a research agenda. Behaviour & Information Technology 25(2), 91–97 (2006)
8. Jordan, P.W.: Designing Pleasurable Products. Taylor & Francis, London (2000)
9. Norman, D.A.: Emotional Design: Why We Love (or Hate) Everyday Things. Basic Books, New York (2004)
10. Hassenzahl, M.: Experience Design: Technology for all the right reasons. Morgan Claypool, San Francisco (2010)
11. Seligman, M.E.P., Csikszentmihalyi, M.: Positive Psychology: An Introduction. American Psychologist 55(1), 5–14 (2000)
12. World Health Organization. Preamble to the Constitution of the World Health Organization as adopted by the International Health Conference, Official Records of the World Health Organization, New York, June 19–22, vol. (2), p. 100 (1946)
13. Antonovsky, A.: Health, Stress, and Coping. Jossey-Bass, San Fransisco (1979)
14. Desmet, P., Hassenzahl, M.: Towards happiness: Possibility-driven design. In: Zacarias, M., de Oliveira, J.V. (eds.) Human-Computer Interaction. Studies in Computational Intelligence, vol. 396, pp. 3–28. Springer, Heidelberg (2012)
15. Lyubomirsky, S., Sheldon, K.M., Schkade, D.: Pursuing happiness: The Architecture of Sustainable Change. Review of General Psychology 9, 111–131 (2005)
16. Brickman, P., Campbell, D.T.: Hedonic relativism and planning the good society. In: Appley, M.H. (ed.) Adaptation Level Theory: A Symposium, pp. 287–302. Academic Press, New York (1971)
17. Diener, E., Lucas, R.E., Scollon, C.N.: Beyond the Hedonic Treadmill. Revising the Adaptation Theory of Well-Being. American Psychologist 61(4), 305–314 (2006)
18. Ryan, R.M., Huta, V., Deci, E.L.: Living Well: A Self-Determination Theory Perspective on Eudaimonia. Journal of Happiness Studies 9, 139–170 (2008)
19. Pohlmeyer, A.E.: Design for Happiness. Interfaces 92, 8–11 (2012)
20. McGonigal, J.: Reality Is Broken: Why Games Make Us Better and How They Can Change the World. The Penguin Press, New York (2011)
21. Giannoulis, S., Verbeek, F.J.: The Happiness Cube Paradigm; Eliciting Happiness through Sound, Video, Light and Odor. Assessment of Affective State with Non-Invasive Techniques. In: 4th International Workshop on Emotion and Computing, 32nd Annual Conference on Artificial Intelligence (KI 2009), Paderborn (2009)
22. Csikszentmihalyi, M.: Beyond Boredom and Anxiety. Jossey-Bass, San Francisco (1975)
23. Wechsler, R.: Applications of Motion Tracking in Making Music for Persons with Disabilities. In: Proceedings of the 4th Workshop Innovative Computerbasierte Musikinterfaces, Mensch&Computer. Oldenbourg Wissenschaftsverlag, Konstanz (2012)
24. Hassenzahl, M., Heidecker, S., Eckoldt, K., Diefenbach, S., Hillmann, U.: All you need is love: Current strategies of mediating intimate relationships through technology. ACM Transactions on Computer-Human Interaction 19(4), 4 (2012)
25. Delft Institute of Positive Design. Positive Design Manifest, http://www.diopd.org (accessed January 22, 2013)
26. Fallman, D.: Persuade Into What? Why Human-Computer Interaction Needs a Philosophy of Technology. In: de Kort, Y., IJsselsteijn, W., Midden, C., Eggen, B., Fogg, B.J. (eds.) PERSUASIVE 2007. LNCS, vol. 4744, pp. 295–306. Springer, Heidelberg (2007)

Tassophonics: Nanotechnology as the Magical Unknown

Audrey Samson[1] and Kristina Andersen[2]

[1] City University of Hong Kong, School of Creative Media, 18 Tat Hong Ave., Hong Kong
[2] Center for Mathematics and Computer Science, Science Park 123, Amsterdam,
The Netherlands
Gerrit Rietveld Academy, Fred. Roeskestraat 96, Amsterdam, The Netherlands
mail@ideacritik.com, kristina@tinything.com

Abstract. This paper outlines a set of experiments designed to explore how we can embed memories in objects augmented with non-discernable nanotechnological interfaces. It explores whether the object can successfully embody a wish or fear and how the participant experiences living with a physical reminder of these secrets. As such the experiments draw on more traditional paper-prototyping and body-storming techniques. The goal is to assess if the introduction of nanotechnology as a magical unknown can be used to seed and affect our relationships to objects and archived memories.

Keywords: Magical unknown, Nanotechnology, probe, secret, desire, archaeoacoustics, archive, performative consultation.

"The objects which surround us do not simply have utilitarian aspects; rather they serve as a kind of mirror which reflects our own image."
-Ernest Dichter in *The Strategy of Desire.*

1 Introduction

Tassophonics investigates different techniques of embedding information and emotive attachment onto an object and the ability of that object to continue to hold on to this meaning over time. In order to do this we introduce nanotechnology as what we term a *magical unknown*, which allows us to imagine new possibilities for a recognizable object. New technologies can often be perceived as magic, or even haunted, because we do not understand how they work [1]. With technologies shrinking to become only barely visible, or invisible, their function is now largely 'believed' or assumed by the uninitiated rather than observed. As a consequence these technological advances and the science they implicate require a certain suspension of disbelief from the layman, a reframing of perception in the spirit of Hayes' naive physics [2]. The *Tassophonics* project makes active use of this suspension of disbelief to introduce the potential for an everyday object to hold and embody a secret and to signify the secret's underlying fear and desire.

A. Marcus (Ed.): DUXU/HCII 2013, Part III, LNCS 8014, pp. 548–557, 2013.

The experiment reported in this paper takes the form of performative consultations that probe the participant's feelings towards nanotechnology and imagine ways in which data can be embedded into a physical vessel in the form of a porcelain cup. Semi structured interviews were conducted with sixteen university students and followed up via sms messaging over the course of five days. During the interview we invite the interviewee to consider a personal wish or regret and draw it as a private symbol onto a porcelain cup. The symbol *represents* the embedding of the secret and serves as a reminder of that secret. A stranger may drink from the cup not knowing what the symbol refers to. As such the cup can be imagined as the holder of both emotional and technological secrets.

The experiment was inspired by well-established user research methods such as the Cultural Probes [3] and the Placebo Project [4] as well as the experimental theatre work of Boal [5] and the art practice of estrangement as described by Shklovsky [6]. The content choices deliberately reference the myth of archaeoacoustics [7],[8], gift exchange [9], and the role of souvenirs [10], with regard to the potential for mapping fears and desires onto objects.

The aim of the project is to ask questions that address the underlying drivers such as fear and desire as well as consider the overall emotional impact of a secret being made visible, and external to the subject, but encoded and unreadable in the form of a symbol. How does the secret embodied by the object change the relationship towards that object itself? Does it affect the wish or fear expressed? How does the extended interaction with the object affect the participant's experience? We attempt to map how the experimental techniques affect our relationship to the object, the secret, and the level of intimacy that can develop from such an encounter. If indeed, as Jean Baudrillard postulated in *The System of Objects*, an "object's function is the mediation of a wish... the voice of desire",[1] then, could an object also hold the inherent fear and desire of the technological unknown, in this case, nanotechnology?

This paper explicates the notion of the technological unknown, the concepts that frame the project: the relationship between desire and objects and the power of the myth in creating a relationship to that object. We then describe the sets of experiments that were conducted, the data we collected and offer an analysis. Finally we suggest some conclusions and directions for future iterations of the project.

2   The Technological Unknown

New technologies have considerable magical potential until they become commonplace and well understood. Nikola Tesla understood this phenomenon very well and acted the part of a magician when he made his demonstrations of 'electricity' at fairs [11]. The intent was to present the raw and awe inspiring power of electricity as a tamable magic trick, so that it would not be seen as an unnatural development that messed with God's natural order (rather than for example a fairly non-dangerous technology that could bring light to all homes). The fear of the unknown can lead to perceiving new technologies as an abomination, and often the simplifications offered

---

[1] Jean Baudrillard. The System of Objects. J. Benedict (Trans). Verso Books, London and New York 1996 (1968) p.97.

can take the form of a de facto 'against' position towards the technology itself. This uncritical stance shuts out the possibility of imagining not only the future implementation of the technology but also the boundaries and conditions of that implementation. In contemporary culture, bio art often skirts this taboo terrain of the 'culturally unacceptable' in order to incite reflection upon emerging biotech practices. Critical Art Ensemble (CAE)[12], a group working with bioart interventions, sets up temporary labs inviting non-scientists to enter the space of the laboratory, to familiarize themselves with its tools and terminology to make simple experiments, effectively demystifying new advancements in the biotech industry. These artists present themselves as scientists, just like Tesla played the magician, to build a contextual narrative that can frame the participant's perspective of the *technological unknown*. Such experiences creates a space in which partial technical understanding, scientific wonder, (dis)belief and sometimes fear allow us to probe how a new technology embodies our fears and desires. The *Tassophonics* project was created to investigate these questions specifically with regards to nanotechnology.

What are our feelings towards this barely perceptible and largely unknown technology? We cannot see how it works, so how do we really understand what it does? Nanotechnology is commonly discussed as having potential applications as diverse as the miniaturization of electronics, the development of strong new building materials, medical implants, targeted drug delivery and tissue engineering. It seems that nanotechnological elements will eventually become part of our bodies. How do we imagine this experience, and what are our feelings towards it? Rather than asking this question directly *Tassophonics* contextualizes it by introducing it in the form of a questionnaire and then inviting the participants to engage in an experiment designing to probe their emotional response to a suggested nanotechnological object. We then explore if this context amplifies or influences the participant's relationship to the object. For example, could a fundamental mistrust in nanotechnology transform the relationship to the object, to one based on fear?

Desire and Objects: Our desires are situated in objects, or rather, objects can be seen to point to our desires. They evoke emotion in relation to the desire we map to them. In *The System of Objects*, Baudrillard argues that we construct the/our world through objects [13]. He defines 'objects' as only those that are abstracted from their function. These everyday objects transcend functionality and become property and passion, echoing the consciousness of the owner. The object's function becomes the mediation of a wish, the voice of desire. *Tassophonics* deliberately makes use of an everyday 'functional' object, the teacup, as object. We investigate if the object can become 'an object of passion' through the ritual of embedding a secret or wish onto the cup through the invocation of imaginary nanotechnology.

The Power of the Myth: The overall project is executed in the cultural context of the myths of archaeoacoustics, the rituals of formal gift exchange, the meaning attribution of souvenirs, and the broader fundamental potential for mapping fears/desires onto objects. In *The Strategy of Desire* Ernest Dichter argues that emotional attachment is strongly linked to old myths [14]. In this experiment we use the myth of archaeoacoustics to trigger a 'belief' that the object could indeed record sound through nanotechnology. Archaeoacoustics refers to the myth of ambient sound being accidentally recorded in the grooves of ancient pottery. The idea being that the clay might hold the soundtrack of the past, like a piece of vinyl imprinted by a phonograph [7], [8]. Simultaneously, the cup in the experiment functions like a souvenir as described by Susan Stewart in *On Longing: Narratives of the Miniature, the Gigantic, the Souvenir, the Collection* [10]. It is a mass produced object that only becomes meaningful when *activated* through an embodied experience. In that sense it serves as a physical bookmark, deliberately acquired and kept as a way to *remember this moment*. The cup is *activated* in a similar way through the experimental experience which can be said to exploit the mechanics of gift exchange as described by Marcel Mauss in *The Gift* [9]. We give the cup to the participant and they are then potentially bound by the ritual of this exchange to continue in their relationship with the experiment.

3   Experiment Setup

The experiment is constructed as a contextually situated interview followed by a five day long embedded experience where the users are probed with a daily question via text messaging. The experiment itself runs through five stages: recruitment, baseline questionnaire, recording and encoding of message, embedded probe, and transition and closure.

Recruitment: The experimenters wear lab coats and are holding clipboards (holding the interview questionnaire). They recruit potential participants as they walk out of the City University of Hong Kong campus. The experimenters approach walkers-by by asking if they would like to participate in an experiment about nanotechnology.

Baseline Questionnaire: An interview is conducted with each participant. They are asked the following questions:

— What do you study?
— Have you ever heard of nanotechnology?
— Do you know what nanotechnology is?
— Can you explain what you think it is?
— Do you think nanotechnology is 'good' or something to be feared?
— How do you think you could use nanotech?
— Do you think nanotechnology can keep a secret forever?

The last question is meant to probe how permanent or secure the participant feels nanotechnology is, or in what capacity could it serve as an archiving tool. Nanotechnology is not usually referred to in this manner. In asking this question that invokes the secret, we both stretch the usual boundaries of perceived uses of nanotechnology and make a bridge to the following phase of the experiment.

Recording and Encoding of Message: Participants are asked to close their eyes and think of a wish or regret. Once they have thought of it, they open their eyes. They are handed a small teacup and an indelible marker and then asked to draw a secret symbol representing that wish or regret onto the cup (a symbol that only they would recognize).

Embedded Probe: A photo is taken of the participant with her/his cup. They are then asked if they wish to participate in the second part of the experiment in which participants are prompted every day for five days about how they feel about the cup. If they agree, contact details are exchanged and the participants are told that the cup is theirs to keep for the next five days. During this phase, 'living with the cup', the following questions are asked:

Day 1: Drink from the cup. How does it feel? Will it make you strong or weak?
Day 2: Look at the cup in your kitchen. What do you think when you look at it?
Day 3: Serve a drink from the cup to someone else. How does that make you feel?
Day 4: Do you feel you have to hide the cup? Do you hate it? Do you love it?
Day 5: a) You must now say goodbye to the cup. You can give it away or you can destroy it. Send us a picture of your choice. b) How do you feel now?
All questions were sent in both Cantonese and English, here for simplification, only the English version is included.

Transition and Closure: On the fifth day, participants are given two options on how to end the process. They can either give the cup away, or destroy it. They are asked to send documentation of their choice. We surveyed 21 people in total. The experiment was divided into two selection groups. The first experiment was conducted outside a university campus in Hong Kong with 16 out of the 21 participants. The latter were mainly studying at the Bachelor level in a range of fields (except one MA and one PhD student). The age group was 18-22 with the exception of the PhD student who was 31. The second group was surveyed in a street market famous for its cheap electronics, as well as being the birthplace of bootlegs, Sham Shui Po (a district of Hong Kong). It was much more difficult to find willing participants in the latter context. We interviewed five people with varying backgrounds and ages. None of these participants made it to stage five (transition and closure), we therefore chose to only consider their answers to the baseline questionnaire. As a result, we consider 16 as our base number of participants in the second part of the experiment 'living with the cup'. It is worth mentioning that in the first group from the university, those conducting the experiment were wearing lab coats. In the second group, we began with the lab coats, and later dropped the idea fearing it lowered our chances to find participants as the area is known for bootlegs and might not respond well to the authority of the lab coat. Though that proved inconclusive because not using the lab coats did not end up increasing the number of participants.

4   Data Collected

4.1   Baseline Interview

1. Everyone had heard of nanotechnology
2. Most participants could cite an example of how nanotechnology was used and were uncritical about its potential uses.
3. Most participants also imagined very practical and existing ways of using the technology when asked what it *could* be used for.

4. When asked if they thought if the technology could 'keep a secret forever', the answers were more divided. Little less than half said yes, around half said no, and a small portion was undecided.

The baseline interview was largely conducted to set the stage for the second part of the experiment, 'living with the cup'. By framing the discussion around nanotechnology, the participant can imagine what it could be like if there were nanotechnology, such as a miniaturized electro-mechanical recording/storage device, embedded in the cup by the time it is given to them. Therefore, the collection of data in the questionnaire is almost incidental and though it says something about participants' exposure to the subject of nanotechnology, and their reaction towards it, we will not discuss the data any further, as the focus of this experiment is on the embedded probe, and the transition and closure phases. The following are a selection of images taken of the participants holding their cup showing the symbol they drew on it.

Fig. 1. A participant holding their cup, showing the symbol they drew. The symbol is abstract

Fig. 2. A participant holding their cup, showing the symbol they drew. The symbol resembles a sound wave

Some participants drew representational symbols such as a robot, others abstract shapes or line strokes, and the later could be said to resemble a sound wave, a representation of the whispered secret?

4.2   'Living with the Cup'

Ten out of sixteen participants answered question one of 'living with the cup'. Five out of sixteen answered up to and including question four (on day 4). Three documentation pieces were sent back to us as a final answer to question five (on day 5, two images and one video).

Day 1: Half the participants reported it either makes them feel strong, weak, or mysterious. The other half reported 'no feeling' or 'nothing special' after drinking from the cup.

Day 2: Three people mentioned the secret. Out of the 8 who answered this question, 5 participants thought of the cup as a metaphor or as some sort of representation of their secret.

Day 3: Six people felt differently than they would have serving tea from a random cup (e.g. "quite weird", "awkward yet amused"). One participant reported that he thought the person he served the cup to would know his secret by drinking out of the cup ("I thought he would know my secret"). 7 people answered this question.

Day 4: Two people felt like they should hide the cup. One person answered that they had no special feeling towards it. The others reported that they do not want to hide it.

Day 5: Only four of the participants answered this question. One participant was totally shocked by the thought of parting with the cup. He first answered: "really?! no!! i really like the cup! i put it on my bookshelf and i think it is really delicate and beautiful!!". When he was told he *must* either destroy or give it away, he answered: "oh my god!" and never sent a photo of his choice nor a response. The three others chose to destroy the cup, two by smashing it (see figure x and y), and the third by attempting to burn the cup until it broke (he sent video documentation of this process). After having destroyed their cups, the participants reported relief, sadness, a sense of loss, and "stimulation".

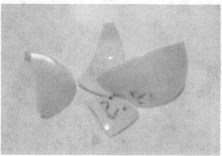
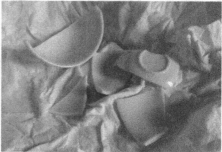

Fig. 3. An image sent by one of the participants in response to the last question. The participant reports feeling: "a tad sense of loss" after smashing the cup.

Fig. 4. An image sent by one of the participants in response to the last question. The participant reports feeling: "Kind of... relieved xd but feel sad for the cup (sic)" after smashing the cup.

5   Analysis

To our surprise, 6 out of the 8 participants who answered beyond day 1 of 'living with the cup' had an overall emotional response to the cup. We did not expect such a high response. The responses of many of the participants seem to indicate that they imagine a secret is embedded in the cup. Moreover, they feel that this object can even have an effect on them, such as making them strong or weak. The object becomes symbolic of their wish or regret in some cases, and in others it is endowed with magical powers. Sometimes this is expressed literally: "It's like a mugic gobbet (sic)" and others metaphorically such as: "i feel cool and stronger... (sic)" or "I feel weak and relaxed after drinking". One respondent reports that making others drink from the cup makes him feel: "Warm, kind and take care of other people's happiness". Some participants think of the cup as a metaphor of their secret, or an embodiment of it. The fact that some feel that the cup should be hidden, for fear of divulging the secret, possibly also relates to the cup embodying their wish or desire, therefore having to hide it to effectively hide the secret. It also could indicate a lack of belief in the capacity of the technology to keep a secret. This could be related to a perceived weakness in 'digital security' for example. Those that felt that they have to hide the cup answered differently to the baseline questionnaire section asking if they think nanotechnology can keep a secret forever. It is therefore impossible to make a correlation on that level at this stage. The sense of relief, sadness or loss reported by the participants after destroying the cup might suggest that they feel that they are parting with the secret, or that the object has successfully been embedded with meaning. It certainly indicates that the cup is no longer trivial to them. The cup has become special through the experience of the experiment. It is important to note that not all responses support this theory, many answered: "no feeling" and not all respondents had an emotional response to the cup. To some it remained a purely functional object, a cup to serve tea in, with no special meaning whatsoever. It is interesting that the three respondents that sent an image back to us chose to destroy the cup (either by smashing it or by burning it), rather than giving it away. This might signify that they imagined giving the cup to someone would be like giving away their secret. Perhaps by destroying the cup they would rid themselves of the commitment to that secret or wish. At this stage no follow up questions were designed in the experiment. Therefore any conclusions would be purely speculative. Future experiments should be designed to probe the significance of the destruction of the object for the user in relation to their secret wish or regret.

6   Some Conclusions and Directions for Future Work

Tassophonics is meant to be understood as the first step towards an experimental method to explore the relationships between memory/object, emotion/object and technology/object. Our findings are modest and are meant as an initial test, to see whether there is anything interesting to further explore, and if so in what direction. We feel that this initial iteration of the *Tassophonics* experiment was successful in creating, and providing evidence for, an emotional connection between the object and the participant. Some results were quite compelling with regards to levels of attachment, projection and embodiment. We set out to explore the emotional value of a secret being made visible but 'unreadable'. We posit that as the secret is imagined and made visible and physical onto an object exterior to the self, it can be contemplated, manipulated or even destroyed. This suggests that we can use future experiments to explore not only the specifics of nanotechnology, but more broadly the manipulation of memory and security of data in technological objects. In this regard, the documentation sent by the participants was particularly poignant; the broken shards in combination with comments about their relief and sadness at its destruction. One of the goals of the *Tassophonics* experiment was to assess how nanotechnology as a *magical unknown* affects our relationships to objects and archived memories.

As all of the participants that took part in the 'living with the cup' phase had positive (and mostly uncritical) perception of nanotechnology, it is impossible to assess whether that positive feeling affected their relationship with the cup as we have no negative cases to compare with. Had they feared the technology, would they have also feared the cup? With the set of questions posed, we are also not able to assess whether it was the experiment's framing with nanotechnology, or the symbols drawn on the cup that are responsible for creating the emotional response to the cup. Would it have been the same had we talked about another *sufficiently advanced* [1] technology? How would it have been different had the technology really been embedded in the cup? Also, since we did not ask the respondents to reveal their secret, it is difficult to assess how the symbol they drew on the cup relates to it, and its importance as a symbol. In this iteration of *Tassophonics* we used nanotechnology as a *magical unknown* to explore the participant's engagement with the object. In future iterations of the project we will deepen our investigation of this engagement by making our method and questions more precise. We will conduct the re-designed experiment again but this time with a much broader range of age and cultural backgrounds. The main project remains to unpick the influences of the suggestion of the technology and it's potential power as a *magical unknown*. We believe that the *Tassophonics* project seen in context with our broader body of work, the OWL project [15], the Magic Machine Workshops [16] and threads/ [17], can mature to become a new type of user investigation with wide implications for the HCI community. The work to design scenarios-of-use, interfaces and experiences in the age of the disappearing computer must increasingly rely on matters of emotional responses and systems of belief as we are given less physical constraints and technically dictated specifications. It should be noted that these methods are not primarily designed to brainstorm new developments of the scientific base of these new technologies themselves, but rather to develop experiences and use-cases that allow users to access and co-design the ways that a technology might manifest in their everyday life. By exploring the use of a technology as a *magical unknown* to seed and incite the user's imagination (or creative thinking about potential/future uses) we might not only be able to begin to democratize the creation of ethical and cultural responses to new technologies, but ultimately be creating tools to generate the user scenarios and experiences of the objects these technologies may bring.

Acknowledgments. Thanks to Linda C.H. Lai and Jane Prophet. In addition, we would like to thank our student volunteers Chen Haoyuan and Harry Hon Yuet Hei, as well as all those who kindly participated in the *Tassophonics* interviews.

References

1. Clarke, A.C.: Profiles of the Future. Holt, Rinehart & Winston (1984)
2. Hayes, P.: The naive physics manifesto Systems in the Micro-Electronic Age. University Press, Edinburgh (1978)
3. Gaver, W., Dunne, A., Pacenti, E.: Cultural Probes. In: Interactions, vol. 6(1), pp. 21–29. ACM Press, New York (1999)

4. Dunne, A., Raby, F.: The placebo project. In: Verplank, B., Sutcliffe, A., Mackay, W., Amowitz, J., Gaver, W. (eds.) Proceedings of the 4th Conference on Designing Interactive Systems: Processes, Practices, Methods, and Techniques (DIS 2002), London, England, pp. 9–12. ACM Press, New York (2002)
5. Boal, A.: Games For Actors and Non-Actors. Routledge, London (1992)
6. Shklovsky, V.: Art as Technique. In: Russian Formalist Criticism: Four Essays, 1965. Trans. Lemon, L.T., and Reis, M.J., University of Nebraska Press, Lincoln (1917)
7. Woodbridge, R.: Acoustic Recordings from Antiquity. In: Proceedings of the IEEE, pp. 1465–1466. IEEE Press, New York (1969)
8. Kleiner, M., Åström, A.: The Brittle Sound of Ceramics - Can Vases Speak? In: Archeology and Natural Science, Scandinavian Archaeometry Center, Göteborg, vol. 1, pp. 66–72 (1993)
9. Mauss, M.: The gift: Forms and functions of exchange in archaic societies. Cohen&West, London (1954)
10. Stewart, S.: On Longing: Narratives of the Miniature, the Gigantic, the Souvenir, the Collection. Duke University Press, Durham (1993)
11. Cheney, M.: Tesla: man out of time. Simon & Schuster, New York (2001)
12. Critical Art Ensemble (CAE): http://www.critical-art.net/
13. Baudrillard, J.: The System of Objects Benedict, J (Trans). Verso Books, London and New York (1996, 1998)
14. Dichter, E.: The Strategy of Desire. Doubleday, New York (1960)
15. Andersen, K., Wilde, D.: Circles and Props - Making Unknown Technology. In: Interactions, pp. 60–65. ACM Press, New York (May 1, 2012)
16. Andersen, K. (publication pending): Making Magic Machines in Proceedings of Crafting the Future. In: 10th European Academy of Design Conference, Göteborg (2013)
17. threads/ project: http://ideacritik.com/threads/

Engineering Awareness™: An e-Service Design Approach for Behavioral Change in Healthcare and Well-Being

Alberto Sanna, Sauro Vicini, Sara Bellini, Ilaria Baroni, and Alice Rosi

eServices for Life and Health, Fondazione Centro San Raffaele - Milano, Italy
{sanna.alberto,vicini.sauro,bellini.sara,
baroni.ilaria,rosi.alice}@hsr.it

Abstract. Personalized interventions that empower users through pertinent and reliable information alongside ubiquitous and user-friendly services can provide them with the opportunity of adopting healthy lifestyle choices which improve quality of life and help prevent a vast number of chronic diseases. The eServices for Life and Health research unit alongside the City of the Future Living Lab strives to apply an e-Service Design approach to deploy innovative ICT and multi-device based services, aimed at truly responding to user needs and aspirations – both inside and outside hospital walls.

Keywords: Design philosophy of HCI and UX, heuristics, healthcare and well-being.

1 Addressing Lifestyles: Transforming a Prescription into an Experience

An OECD-WHO's analysis [1] of a wide spectrum of strategies addressing issues such as unhealthy diets, sedentary lifestyles and obesity for the prevention of chronic diseases, unveils that the more interventions are personalized and directly involve highly skilled medical experts, the higher their success compared to the impersonal interventions of mass media communication campaigns.

This means that Healthcare systems must adopt a more proactive approach by providing Individuals with comprehensible information and education to raise awareness on health and well-being, as well as build a vast network of services that can sustain them in their choices towards healthier lifestyle choices and behaviors.

The underlying concept behind this new proactive approach that Healthcare is indeed already widely tested and used in the old "reactive" approach: once a disease/condition is identified, a (set of) drug(s) is prescribed and administered, and this prescription's compliance is monitored together with the development of the patient's clinical picture. There is wide evidence in literature that regular physical activity and a correct diet can have the same effect of a drug, and in many cases can be used to reduce/substitute the drug prescribed. Adopting proper "behaviors" (not only limited

A. Marcus (Ed.): DUXU/HCII 2013, Part III, LNCS 8014, pp. 558–567, 2013.

to physical activity and nutrition, but for example also sleep, etc.) and, more in general, proper lifestyles is a matter of what we can call "culture of health", which implies the strong need to educate the patient. The "extended prescription" concept thus uses the following three assumption:

– Physical activity is medicine
– Nutrition is medicine
– Education is medicine

With these assumptions in mind, it becomes evident the importance of both a correct prescription (which should be personalized and tailored to the specific patient's needs), and a correct administration (and compliance monitoring) of these three "medicines". As a further generalization of this concept, we should consider physical activity, nutrition and education as three of many behaviors (e.g., sleeping, working, etc.) which impacts strongly on the health of people, and which needs to be constantly prescribed, administered and monitored. Administration and monitoring of behaviors is possible only through ICT, as will be explained in the following subsection.

2   ICT as Healthier Ecosystem Enabler

Such a proactive approach described above will lead to a dramatic expansion of evidence-based medical knowledge domains due to the intrinsic need of an interdisciplinary approach to care. At the same time, the etiology of the single clinical case implies that doctors and their teams will have to deal with an exponentially higher quantity and types of Patient's data (e.g., physiological data and information collected by wearable sensors, data and information on patient's behavior in nutrition, physical activity, medication regimens, education, awareness, etc. collected by mobile apps). These will in turn drastically change the present concept of Electronic Healthcare Record (EHR), which will evolve towards the much broader paradigm of Personal Health Record (PHR): both aspects imply levels of 'Big Data' storage and analytics that only ICT can provide.

On the patient side, doctors' prescriptions will need to turn into comprehensible, practical and actionable advices that help guide them towards making informed choices in everyday life (while shopping, cooking, dining out, exercising, etc.). In this way, a lifestyle prescription becomes actionable and adaptive to Individual and context, raising the Healthcare System-Citizen relationship to a higher level of mutual collaboration.

As this new paradigm involves several aspects of the patient's daily life as a whole, it is clear that this new paradigm will require new players, which implies more market opportunities also in companies/sectors that traditionally do not belong to healthcare. These new players have been thoroughly described in the PREVE project [2], called with the name of Co-producers of Health (CPH). A CPH is an actor who, pursuing its own business opportunities, is in parallel improving the health of the citizens, or it is contributing to create the conditions for the persons to have an healthier lifestyle.

The fact that the Co-production of Health model is citizen-centric doesn't mean that it is restricted to the person only. Of course to realize this vision, different levels in the society should be involved, from the individual level (single citizens), to the interpersonal level (friends, family, co-workers, etc.), to the organizational level (policies and practices of civic, religious, social, political, and related organizations), to community level (attributes, resources and norms of the person's communities, such as neighborhoods, markets, restaurants, etc.), to public policy level (laws and regulations that affect the person).

All these actors, institutions, public bodies, companies, etc. can participate to improve the personal health of the Individual, if properly engaged through ICTs.

From a medical perspective, a Personal Health Record and a new Lifestyle Personal Guidance Systems model of care is suitable both for primary and secondary prevention and leverages on Patient/Consumer empowerment at every life stage. From a market perspective, the introduction of a health-trusted third party acting as a demand-driven broker in the Consumer market, enables disruptive business models to take place in the form of healthier lifestyle-related added value networks that aggregate and offer personalized bundles of education, media, entertainment, food & beverage, consumer electronics, sport & fitness, leisure & tourism products and services according to Individual's needs and preferences.

3   Engineering Awareness: An e-Service Design Model

In order to respond to this r-evolution in healthcare, the e-Services for Life and Health research unit has developed a unique Service Design model that synchronizes Emotions (a trigger to an Individual's psychological reaction in context with his/her preferences) and Relations (a trigger for a social interaction with other Individuals physically present or not, and/or with a proximity or remote environment in context with his/her preferences) to Functions (an Individual's practical need addressed by the service) delivered. This Service Design model is called Engineering AwarenessTM.

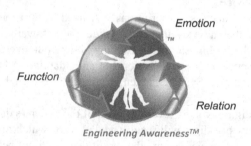

Fig. 1. Engineering AwarenessTM process

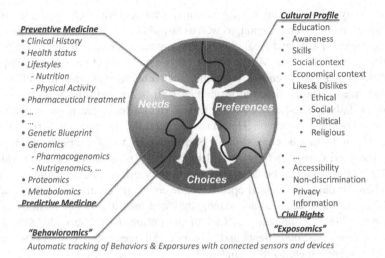

Preventive Medicine
- Clinical History
- Health status
- Lifestyles
  - Nutrition
  - Physical Activity
- Pharmaceutical treatment
- ...
- ...
- Genetic Blueprint
- Genomics
  - Pharmacogenomics
  - Nutrigenomics, ...
- Proteomics
- Metabolomics
Predictive Medicine

Cultural Profile
- Education
- Awareness
- Skills
- Social context
- Economical context
- Likes& Dislikes
  - Ethical
  - Social
  - Political
  - Religious
  ...
- ...
- Accessibility
- Non-discrimination
- Privacy
- Information
Civil Rights

Needs   *Preferences*   *Choices*

"Behavioromics"   *"Exposomics"*
Automatic tracking of Behaviors & Exporsures with connected sensors and devices

Fig. 2. Engineering AwarenessTM description

Designing for Individual's awareness and behavioral change is the primary ethical objective of any personalized service developed within the eServices for Life and Health. The mission of this research unit is not to manipulate Individuals (i.e., making them doing a supposed "right thing/healthy thing" as decided on behalf of them by a knowledgeable third party) but provide them with an unbiased understanding of the impact that a given decision/action implies. Each Individual is characterized by his/her own digital profile which is a complex, dynamic and progressive repository of personal data, information and events which is split into three parts as illustrated on the right of the Figure:

- needs, i.e. the medical part of the profile: the genetic blueprint and the meaningful biochemical/physiological parameters of an Individual that are considered relevant for a statistical health risk assessment at the state of the art knowledge in primary/secondary preventive medicine and predictive medicine;
- preferences, i.e. the personal preferences part of the profile: the unique cultural resources of an Individual, that include his/her likes and dislikes and ethical beliefs;
- actions, i.e. the health-related actions part of the Individual's profile: the unique (and constantly evolving) series of meaningful health-related actions performed by an Individual ("Behavioromics") and exposures to environmental factors ("Exposomics") in his/her daily life.

4   eServices for Life and Health Research Pilots in the San Raffaele City of the Future Living Lab

There is an array of definitions used to define what is meant by Smart Cities[3] or Intelligent Cities[4] in contemporary literature, but all of them stress the important role technology plays in improving communication, creativity, business, urban growth, social and relational capital, as well as social and environmental sustainability [5,6]. e-Services for Life and Health[7] in this context is a research unit at the Scientific Institute San Raffaele in Milano (Italy), whose mission is to design, develop and demonstrate the ethical, scientific, economic and technological feasibility of innovative personalized services aimed at promoting well-being and informed choices and behaviors in daily life. e-Services for Life and Health has three main research and innovation streamlines - Smarter Hospital, Smarter Life and Smarter City - that are managed within the unique context of the San Raffaele City of the Future Living Lab (ENOLL member, European Network of Living labs[8]): i.e., an ecosystem within an area of 300,000m2 that can be described as a tertiary urban area or a compact urban district where all daily and typical operations.are concentrated in a reduced space and its structures allows to access, understand, study and measure the interactions among an estimated 27,000+ community of City of the Future daily Users (20,000+ a day turn-over of inpatients, outpatients and visitors of all ages and needs; 5000+ on site employees, researches, etc.; 1700+ students).

4.1   City of the Future Living Lab Methodology

The Living Lab follows along the conceptual framework presented by ESoCE-Net, in which user-driven innovation is fully integrated within the co-creation process of new services, products and societal infrastructures. [9] The Living Lab process is focused on four concurrent phases: co-creation, exploration, experimentation, and evaluation. There isn't a real starting point because the approach is iterative and reflective, so the LL process can take live in any stage of each activity.

In the City of the Future Living Labe the target is to gain the access to the users' needs, knowledge, ideas, desires, and anything else could be a support to improve services, products or applications. The involvement of the stakeholders and users from the early stages of the products is to take advantage of their support in each activities of the production, in order to implement and define realistic, useful, desirable and effective artifacts.[10]

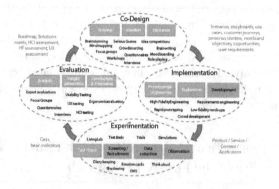

Fig. 3. Living Lab methodology

4.2   European and Italian Projects

Such a unique environment has been field of international ICT research projects in 5th, 6th and 7th European Commission Framework R&D Programs and Italian/Lombardy Region R&D Programs since year 2000, nurturing intense cross-disciplinary collaborations between medical and healthcare professionals, designers, engineers, scientists, policy makers, and entrepreneurs across a number of well-being, life and health-related fields. The following 5 cases better represent the efforts of this research unit and its users:

M3 (Mobile Medical Monitoring). M3 is a project funded by the Italian Region of Lombardy. It consists of a wearable patch, a Smartphone and tablet app and web portal. It is a service where users (both professional athletes as well as the average individual) can monitor different biological parameters (e.g., heart rate, breathing, METS) and share this data as well as other data with their trainers, doctors, nutritionists and so on, in order to receive from them personalized help via both the app and the web portal. The service is integrated with individuals' PHR. The current state of this work, at the time of the writing of this paper, is that the relevant technologies have been selected, the PHR was deployed on a Cloud and is now ready to be used. The evaluation saw two fases: the first was the Co-Design phase consisted in the participation of a group of expert users (including nutritionists, cardiologists, biomedical engineers and professional athletes) alongside a team of City of the Future researchers (including engineers and designers) to a focus group. Throughout this activity, the different actors were guided through a phase of analysis (questions were asked such as who could the end user of the service be, what are the user requirements of this user, in what context could the service be used on a day-to-day basis, what other similar products and services already exist, and so on) as well as through a phase of brainstorming. The insights gathered from the phase of co-design (and which include the Engineering Awareness[TM] Model) were used as base for the phase of Implementation, where ideas and user and service requirements were translated by City of the Future's tech team into a series of rough prototypes for the Smart Patch. In the second phase, some end users (N=10, 5 males and 5 females, ages 25-34) were involved in the usability tests: they were requested to create an account on the web portal, to fill life-style related questionnaires and then to use the M3 system for at least 3 days. The system includes a smart patch (equipped with sensors for heart rate monitoring, temperature monitoring, breath rate monitoring, ECG and caloric consumption) and an Android mobile phone, with an application to visualize the data coming from the sensors. Users were of course also properly instructed and trained in the use of the devices and the web-portal. The tests were run during November 2012. Most of the usability concerns were of course related to the smart patch (e.g., about recharging, wearing it, etc.), and some of them related to the Android application (e.g., graph readability, etc.). All the users' feedbacks were taken into account to improve the devices and services, as foreseen in the Living Lab methodology. The department of Physical Activity and Sport Medicine is now ready to enroll more patients to experiment the system.

Fig. 4. M3 devices

Well-Being on the Go. It's a service that falls into the ELLIOT (Experiential Living Lab for the Internet Of Things) European Commission FP7 project. It is composed by a set of real interactive vending machines [11] deployed within the City of the Future Living Lab. The service offers not only healthy food options in non-places, but also personalized and pertinent information on health, nutrition, well-being, mobility, entertainment and socialization via different identification mechanism. It will soon be integrated with PHR. The vending machines have been deployed and are currently being used by employees and external users. Statistics are under collection and they will be analyzed soon to understand/improve the usability of the system.

Fig. 5. Vending machine details

ALIZ-E - Adaptive Strategies for Sustainable Long-Term Social Interaction. This is a European Commission FP7 R&D project. The ambitious aim of this project is to create a companion for hospitalized children that plays with them, supports their learning of health-related behaviors (such as nutrition, physical activity, and specifically diabetes management), and motivates them to follow healthy behaviors in their daily life. Currently 200+ children have interacted with the robotic companion, in several small scale experiments to understand how children perceive this technology, how they react to it, and thus how it can be used to create an additional channel toward the child to convey useful information [12].

Fig. 6. Pictures from Aliz-e project

Feed for Good. This is also a project funded by the Italian Region of Lombardy. It rides the current trend of TV food shows and web platforms, combining their entertaining and social aspects with information on food culture, nutrition and healthy eating. A set of semantically coded video recipes can be viewed by users alongside personalized information on one's eating habits and health status. The main support system consists of a web portal and an application for mobile devices (especially for tablets and smartphones), which provides an easy and immediate access to services, with the advantage of specific applications developed to support the user in the various daily contexts (e.g., during the purchase as Shopping Assistant, or during the preparation of specific dishes as Cooking Assistant, etc.). This project is still in the prototyping phase, however there is a plan for users' involvement to validate/improve the software interface, usability and functionalities.

Fig. 7. Feed for Good interface

5 a Day. The program started some years ago as a nutritional and technological training to motivate children to eat more fruits and vegetables. In a first step we carried out the 5 a day program in four primary school classes for a total of 76 children. Fruits and vegetables consumption was measured before and after a classroom intervention, with the purpose to educate children about the importance of healthy eating habits. The experiment underlined an increase of the 12.7% in the consumption, with the most significant increase in vegetables intake.

In a second step the program was moved into the hospital, with the aim to create an environment able to satisfy patients' needs and dedicated to well-being promotion. In this case an Interactive Totem was placed in the pediatric ward, with educational services created to entertain and empower the hospitalized children. This platform is part of an Internet of Things system that is used to understand the impact of the services offered, achieve fine-tuning from the collaboration of children, and explore the role of an Internet of Things System in the Living Lab process [13]. In particular, the Totem is able to communicate information, educational and motivational contents, related to the importance of fruit and vegetable daily consumption, that are provided to children at the meals booking time (reservation for lunch and dinner). This second step is still going on in the pediatric ward, with periodic co-creation activities.

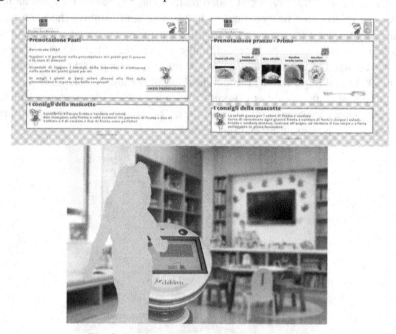

Fig. 8. 5 a Day interface and Interactive Totem

5 Conclusions and Future Developments

The main strategic prerogative for the growth of City of the Future Living Lab is without a doubt to strengthen relationships with partners that the eService for Life and Health unit has been able to create over time, as well as to create new partnerships and business models that reflect the changes in action.

From a technical and scientific point of view, there is the strive to refine even further the methodology adopted and the implementation of new tools, methods and competences able to sustain the Living Lab's evolution and ability to foster innovation.

The experiences made so far were related to heterogeneous activities (education, physical activity, nutrition, etc.), for sure a future evolution of the City of the Future Living Lab will be related to the integration of different kind of services, pervasively surrounding the patients in the different aspects of their daily life. At that point the full potential of the City of the Future Living Lab will be exploited, and it will be really able to design integrated, useful, and usable applications, interoperating data and services to seamlessly improve the health of the patients.

References

1. Healthy Choices OECD Health Ministerial Meeting, Paris, October 7-8 (2010)
2. PREVE project, http://www.preve-eu.org
3. Santoro, R., Conte, M.: Living Labs in Open Innovation Functional Regions (2010), http://www.esoce.net/Living%20Labs%20in%20Functional%20 Regions%20-%20White%20Paper.pdf
4. Vicini, S., Bellini, S., Sanna, A.: How to Co-Create Internet of Things-enabled Services for Smarter Cities. In: SMART 2012, The First International Conference on Smart Systems, Devices and Technologies, Stuttgart, Germany, pp. 56–61 (2012)
5. Caragliu, A., Del Bo, C., Nijkamp, P.: Smart cities in Europe. Serie Research Memoranda 0048, VU University Amsterdam, Faculty of Economics, Business Administration and Econometrics (2009)
6. Komninos, N.: The Architecture of Intelligent Cities. In: Conference Proceedings from the 2nd IET International Conference on Intelligent Environment (2006)
7. eServices4Life unit, http://www.eservices4life.org
8. European Network of Living labs, http://www.openlivinglabs.eu
9. Steventon, A., Wright, S.: Intelligent spaces: The application of pervasive ICT. Springer, London (2006)
10. Giffinger, R., Fertner, C., Kramar, H., Kalasek, R., Pichler-Milanovic, N., Meijers, E.: Smart cities – Ranking of European medium-sized cities. Centre of Regional Science, Vienna (2007), http://www.smartcities.eu/download/ smart_cities_final_report.pdf (retrieved in February 2013)
11. Vicini, S., Sanna, A., Bellini, S.: A Living Lab for Internet of Things Vending Machines. In: Uckelmann, D., Scholz-Reiter, B., Rügge, I., Hong, B., Rizzi, A. (eds.) ImViReLL 2012. CCIS, vol. 282, pp. 35–43. Springer, Heidelberg (2012)
12. ALIZE project, http://www.aliz-e.org/
13. Vicini, S., Bellini, S., Rosi, A., Sanna, A.: An internet of things enabled interactive totem for children in a living lab setting. In: ICE 2012, 18th International Conference on Engineering, Technology and Innovation, Munich (2012) ISBN: 978-1-4673-2273-7

Designing a Product Satisfaction Model Using Customer Segmentation and Information Consolidation

Meng-Dar Shieh

Department of Industrial Design, National Cheng Kung University, No.1,
University Road, Tainan City 701, Taiwan (R.O.C.)
mdshieh2012@gmail.com

Abstract. This study proposes a prediction model, based on Kansei Engineering, which applies the concept of consumer segmentation and information consolidation. When constructing a mutual satisfaction model for each cluster, the extracted parameters showing different levels of consumer influence were then treated as retrieval data by applying Ordinal Regression (OR). This study also tried to construct a satisfaction model for a cluster of consumers instead of just focusing on an individual satisfaction model, which is less valuable in real-life situations. The combined application of Fuzzy C-means and Ordinal Regression are considered worth using as the data needed. The combined application is less complicated compared to other forms of numerical regression analysis. It is a great benefit to designers as it lessens the time required to explore consumer satisfaction data at the early stages of the design process.

Keywords: Consumer Satisfaction, Kansei engineering, Ordinal Regression, Information consolidation.

1 Introduction

The keen competition of markets and the increasing demand for various products has pushed the development of industrial design far beyond just focusing on function and cost of production. We must now consider the physical factors of a product including esthetics. Maslow's Hierarchy of Needs has determined that the needs of humans can be categorized into several classes. Many of these needs are instinctive. Since the User-Centered and User-Oriented concepts are highly promoted these days (Donald A. Norman, 1986), consumer focus groups are playing a greater role in the effort to ensure that an upcoming product or service is successful. Difficulty in gaining consumers' confidence increases as market competition becomes more intensive. Consequently, it is essential to capsulate consumers' preferences to predict their purchasing choices. Researchers have used many methods in an attempt to predict how a product may appeal to a consumer in the market place.

One of the most useful is called Kansei-Engineering from Japan, which translates people's emotional reactions to physical design elements into a quantitive format (Nagamichi,1995). Researchers are able to determine the cause-and-effect relationship

A. Marcus (Ed.): DUXU/HCII 2013, Part III, LNCS 8014, pp. 568–577, 2013.

between people's emotions and the design elements of an object (product). This study focuses on the opposite case where a scheme contains a unified result to certain groups of people. This is called collaborative recommendation (Cheung, Kwok, Law, & Tsui, 2003).

Previous studies have shown that averaging operators are not suitable for data expressed in bipolar scales, which appear frequently in consumer preference studies. The application will not deal well with real work problems if it neglects minority data (Dubois & Prade, 2004). Another critical issue when dealing with information aggregation is determining the relative importance of different sources. If not handled properly, it may lead to incorrect results. Fuzzy integral has been proved to be a better method than the classical aggregation operator as it is a non-additive set function on the power set of all information sources (Grabisch, 1995). This research is inspired by these ideas. The density and distribution of the information sources, obtained from fuzzy-clustering based consumer segmentation, can be used to aggregate the affective satisfaction of consumers.

There is still a lot of improvement required to combine individual single consumer/ multiple product forms into a coherent suggestion model as previous researches did. They usually averaged individual consumer's data and then incorporated them into the calculations. To deal with nonlinearity, "black-box" methods including neural networks (NN) (Tsai, Hsiao, & Hung, 2006) and SVR (Yang & Shieh, 2007) are offered as good candidates for building the prediction model. In addition, NN and SVR, endowed with numerous highly evolving techniques developed in machine learning, have great potential for constructing real-world applications rather than for laboratory research alone.

This study proposes a Kansei-Engineering prediction model that combines consumer segmentation and information consolidation. At the first stage, fuzzy c-means clustering is applied to a list of selected study participants. Some representative products are chosen as segmentation variables by related experts. Participants are required to express their preferences towards the representative products and then are separated into different groups that reflect their responses. Next, there is some membership grading showing to what extent they belong to a group. There are other interactions between every two pairs of participants, which are determined by their position in a multidimensional scaling space. These variables will later be used as retrieval parameters in the final stage, which will be explained later. A method called Ordinal Regression is then used to construct the affective satisfaction model by treating the form features, obtained from morphological study, as input and the participants' preferences as output. When the combined satisfaction is calculated, the parameters gained from FCM clustering are then integrated into the Ordinal Regression results by inputting the weight parameter that describes the extent of belonging to a particular group. The satisfaction level of each cluster can be appropriately adjusted to fit the real situation. An expected final application can obtain an entirely satisfactory product form. The combined satisfaction results can also be saved for further study & use.

2   Research Framework

A classic prediction model is illustrated in Figure 1. It demonstrated a traditional Kansei-Engineering approach that does not pay too much attention to handling the variations among each individual; the problem becomes more obvious when a group of people instead of a single individual is addressed. In fuzzy clustering, data elements can belong to more than one cluster, and associating with each element is a set of membership levels. These indicate the strength of the association between that data element and a particular cluster. Fuzzy clustering is a process of assigning these membership levels, and then using them to assign data elements to one or more clusters.

Typical prediction models often ignore this condition and consider every piece of data as having the same importance. As a result, minority satisfaction is sacrificed, which leads to an over-fitting or inappropriate united satisfaction calculated from the aggregation operator. Besides, it is believed that most people are not as capable as an expert in giving a sophisticated score when it comes to expressing their preferences towards a product; so a ranking form would be more appropriate for the estimation. The proposed prediction model is constructed with the expectation of overcoming these drawbacks by applying consumer segmentation and information consolidation, which is illustrated in Figure 2.

This hybrid prediction model is constructed in three main parts: consumer segmentation, individual affective satisfaction model, and the united unanimity prediction model (Figure 2). The details steps are listed in Figure 3.

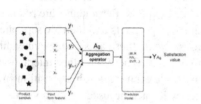

Fig. 1. Typical Kansei-engineering prediction model

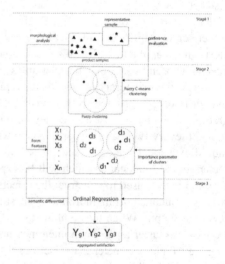

Fig. 2. Proposed Kansei-Engineering prediction model

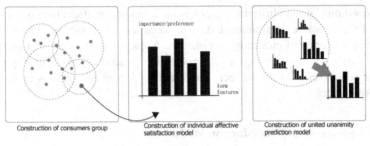

Construction of consumers group | Construction of individual affective satisfaction model | Construction of united unanimity prediction model

Fig. 3. Three main stages of proposed affective satisfaction model

The research framework can be divided into three parts:

1. Collect the study samples and related adjectives and determine the suitable adjectives for further use. Analyze morphologically the design elements of a bicycle's form, and choose representative samples with the help of experienced experts.
2. Establish the relationship between the adjectives and the bicycle's design elements, build up an individual preference model, and calculate the different weightings of every consumer in the group.
3. From the above steps, aggregate the information collected to obtain the synthetic conclusions according to the different clusters of consumers.

3 Experimental Procedures

3.1 Construction of Consumer Segmentation

Choosing Representative Samples. Three design experts were asked to choose representative samples from the 70 samples. When choosing the representative samples diversity was the main concern. Finally, 15 samples were chosen, as shown in Figure 4:

Fig. 4. 15 representative samples chosen by related experts

3.2 Applying Fuzzy C-Means to Consumer Segmentation

To apply FCM clustering, all our proxy consumers are separated into clusters with others with similar preferences. Each consumer is considered as a data point. Assessing the validity of the clustering results is most important after checking the significance of the structure of preference data imposed by the clustering algorithm and determining the optimal clustering parameters. A questionnaire designed using Macromedia Flash was used to capture the subjective preferences without relying on any bipolar adjectives. Fifteen subjects are asked to choose the options nearest to their own preferences.

3.3   Construction of Satisfaction Model

Choosing representative adjectives. The initial selection of related adjectives describing bicycle features was 100 bipolar adjectives in Chinese, which were too many to study. There are no principle or set of rules prescribing the suitable number of adjective for a similar study, but according to Miller, the optimum number of adjectives to apply to semantic differential evaluations is from five to seven, the so-called "magic numbers". Our three experts mentioned previously were required to choose five pairs of bipolar adjectives from the 100 pairs by using the **KJ** Method (Table 1).

Table 1. Five bipolar adjectives are chosen for further study

1	2	3	4	5
modern	light	professional	passion	male
classical	steady	casual	cool	female

Capturing Design Elements. In this step, Morphological Analysis is applied to capture the design elements of the bicycle. Morphological analysis was developed by Fritz Zwicky -- a Swiss astrophysicist and aerospace scientist based at the California Institute of Technology in the 1940s and 50s -- as a method for systematically structuring and investigating the total set of relationships contained in multi-dimensional,

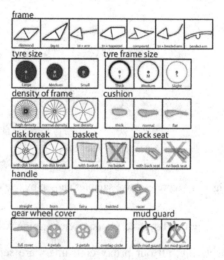

Fig. 5. Components and attributes of a bicycle

usually non-quantifiable, complex problems. Morphological analysis decomposes the form features into simple components; each component may have several attributes. For example, bicycle forms are decomposed into 11 components having 36 attributes in total as shown in Figure 5. The color information of the product can actually be decomposed to an RGB (or other colors formats like CMYK, depending on usage) format as one of the components, but in this study the color information is ignored in order to focus on the influence of the product form.

3.4   Construction of Aggregation Satisfaction

Capturing Individual Satisfaction. A digital questionnaire was designed to capture each consumer's personal preferences. The subjects were required to register their feeling by utilizing a 5-point Likert scale: most disagree, disagree, normal, agree and most agree, for every randomly shown sample. To calculate the individual satisfaction of the survey participants, the collected data was then sent for statistical analysis using SPSS software. A panel of design experts chose five pairs of bipolar adjectives: *modern-classical, light-steady, professional-casual, passionate-cool, and masculine-feminine*. However, only the first half of the five adjective pairs: *modern, light, professional, passionate, and masculine*, were used for semantic differential evaluation when calculating individual satisfaction, to simplify the later aggregation.

Obtaining the Important Parameters. From the clustering result calculated by FCM, we can obtain the level of importance and interaction of the consumers. The relative importance of each consumer is calculated according to the membership grade of each, indicating what degree the consumer belongs to a certain cluster. The procedure followed for obtaining the relative importance of consumers from the FCM clustering result is:

1. The higher the membership grade the closer to the center of the cluster. Firstly, we establish a suitable threshold to pick up any remarkable data. n consumers, near the center of the cluster are preserved for further use.
2. The most important consumer, the one having the highest score in the cluster, is given the largest membership grade, μ_{max}. This consumer is assigned a weight value of $r_{max} = 1$.
3. We compare the remaining consumers with the most important consumer and assign them a relative weight of r_i, $i = 1, ..., n-1$ according to the proportion of the membership grade to μ_{max}. In this way, these weights satisfy the conditions that $\max\{r_1, ..., r_n\} = 1$ and $\min\{r_1, ..., r_n\} > 0$.

4. Normalize the value of r_i and obtain the relative weight value

$$w_i = r_i / \sum_{i=1}^{n} r_i, \ i = 1,...,n$$ to satisfy the condition $\sum_{i=1}^{n} w_i = 1$. If the importance

of each consumer is equal, then $w_1 = ... = w_n = 1/n$.

3.5   Aggregation of Satisfaction in a Cluster

After grading the importance of every consumer in the cluster, we set apart the consumers having the most dominant influence for analysis. The regression equations in the five adjectives are compared with others in the same cluster according to their different levels of importance, thereby obtaining the overall satisfaction aggregate of each cluster. As Figure 6 shows below, both consumers four and five show remarkable importance to the cluster after the calculation, the semantic differential result is aggregated depending on their importance to the cluster and will be applied to the mutual satisfaction model later.

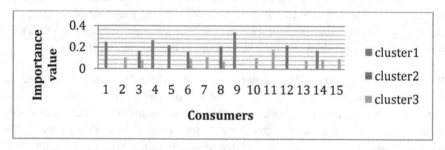

Fig. 6. Importance of each cluster

The next step is to aggregate the data we have obtained so far into SPSS and calculate the mutual satisfaction model through Ordinal Regression. For every calculation, one adjective was treated as a dependent variable while the data obtained from morphological analysis was treated as a factor.

4   Results and Discussion

Figure 7 shows the clustering results after applying Fuzzy C-means. One can notice that each consumer actually belongs to all three clusters by having different membership grades. This result shows that not every data point has a different level of influence on the overall preference trend of the cluster. In the later part of this case study the most dominant, remarkable data point is calculated to construct the aggregation satisfaction of the cluster.

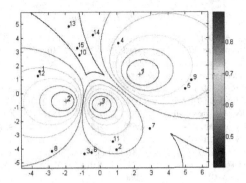

Fig. 7. Clustered result in c=3

A digital questionnaire was designed to collect affective responses from 15 test consumers to five adjectives: modern, light, professional, passionate, and masculine, using a 5-point Likert scale. The collected results were then analyzed with the statistical tool SPSS together with data from samples obtained from morphological analysis. Using Ordinal Regression calculations it is possible to obtain a regression equation that shows the cluster's satisfaction model for any given adjective, so there are five regression equations for every cluster. Before we capture the regression results so that we might write the mutual satisfaction of every cluster, we must first see if the data is suitable for analysis and if the model is capable of analyzing the given data. In this study, we proposed three validations to test the results.

The Model Fitting Information, Goodness-of-Fit and Pseudo R-Square all show that there is a significant result for cluster one for the adjective light, so we looked further for the parameter estimation. As Table 2 shows, the regression equation of cluster one for the adjective light is:

$$Light = -53.617 + (-93.079)\mathbf{a6} + (-8.499)\mathbf{d1} + (-7.951)\mathbf{e1} + (-16.872)\mathbf{f1} + (-8.312)\mathbf{g1} + (-71.967)\mathbf{i2} + (-19.730)\mathbf{j3}$$

The variables **a1** to **k1** are actually replacements of the design elements obtained from morphological analysis as shown in Table 2.

Table 2. Parameters Estimation for cluster one in adjective *light*

		Estimate	Std. Error	Wald	df	Sig.	95% Confidence Interval Lower Bound	95% Confidence Interval Upper Bound
Threshold	[light = 2.00]	-53.617	30.260	3.140	1	.076	-112.925	5.691
	[light = 3.00]	-25.896	26.407	.962	1	.327	-77.653	25.860
Location	**a1** [main_frame=1.00]	-48.755	36.819	1.753	1	.185	-120.918	23.408
	a2 [main_frame=2.00]	-59.909	36.417	2.706	1	.100	-131.284	11.466
	a3 [main_frame=3.00]	-35.077	22.594	2.410	1	.121	-79.361	9.207
	a4 [main_frame=4.00]	-45.809	31.773	2.079	1	.149	-108.083	16.465
	a5 [main_frame=5.00]	-36.578	24.510	2.227	1	.136	-84.616	11.461
	a6 [main_frame=6.00]	-93.079	51.291	3.293	1	.070	-193.609	7.450
	a7 [main_frame=7.00]	0(a)	.	.	0	.	.	.
	b1 [tyre_size=1.00]	11.100	24.871	.199	1	.655	-37.646	59.846
	b2 [tyre_size=2.00]	28.984	32.160	.812	1	.367	-34.048	92.016

Table 2. (*Continued*)

b3 [tyre_size=3.00]	0(a)	.	.	0	.	.	.
c1[tyre_frame_size=1.00]	29.593	20.374	2.110	1	.146	-10.339	69.524
c2[tyre_frame_size=2.00]	34.736	16.228	4.582	1	.032	2.931	66.542
c3[tyre_frame_size=3.00]	0(a)	.	.	0	.	.	.
d1 [disk_break=1.00]	-8.499	16.831	.255	1	.614	-41.488	24.490
d2 [disk_break=2.00]	0(a)	.	.	0	.	.	.
e1[density_of_frame=1.00]	-7.951	20.327	.153	1	.696	-47.791	31.888
e2[density_of_frame=2.00]	-1.632	20.774	.006	1	.937	-42.348	39.085
e3[density_of_frame=3.00]	0(a)	.	.	0	.	.	.
f1 [cushion=1.00]	-16.872	45.494	.138	1	.711	-106.038	72.293
f2 [cushion=2.00]	12.749	8.014	2.531	1	.112	-2.958	28.457
f3 [cushion=3.00]	0(a)	.	.	0	.	.	.
g1 [basket=1.00]	-8.312	12.529	.440	1	.507	-32.869	16.246
g2 [basket=2.00]	0(a)	.	.	0	.	.	.
h1 [backseat=1.00]	28.117	40.731	.477	1	.490	-51.715	107.948
h2 [backseat=2.00]	0(a)	.	.	0	.	.	.
i1 [handle=1.00]	-41.093	20.166	4.152	1	.042	-80.617	-1.569
i2 [handle=2.00]	-71.967	37.179	3.747	1	.053	-144.836	.902
i3 [handle=3.00]	-14.673	672.311	.000	1	.983	-1332.378	1303.031
i4 [handle=4.00]	-53.513	25.339	4.460	1	.035	-103.177	-3.849
i5 [handle=5.00]	0(a)	.	.	0	.	.	.
j1[gear_wheel_cover=1.00]	15.568	671.975	.001	1	.982	-1301.480	1332.615
j2[gear_wheel_cover=2.00]	21.396	13.665	2.452	1	.117	-5.387	48.178
j3[gear_wheel_cover=3.00]	-19.730	12.716	2.407	1	.121	-44.653	5.194
j4[gear_wheel_cover=4.00]	0(a)	.	.	0	.	.	.
k1 [mud_guard=1.00]	27.333	14.572	3.518	1	.061	-1.228	55.893
k2 [mud_guard=2.00]	0(a)	.	.	0	.	.	.

For the adjective professional, the calculation of ordinal regression has shown a significant result. Model Fitting Information, Goodness-of-Fit and Pseudo R-Square all show a significant result for cluster one, for the adjective professional has gained a remarkable value proving that the result is reliable.

Consequently, we can generalize the satisfaction of cluster one with four regression equations as listed in Table 3:

Table 3. Aggregated satisfaction of cluster one

Light	-53.617 +(-93.079)a6 + (-8.499)d1 + (-7.951)e1 + (-16.872)f1 + (-8.312)g1 + (-71.967)i2 + (-19.730)j3 (-71.967)i2 + (-19.730)j3
Professional	15.196 + (23.968)a5 + (1.309)b1 + (6.902)d1 + (13.055)j1
Passion	85.580 + (55.141)a6 + (13.323)c1 + (24.001)d1 + (6.758)e1 + (3.347)g1 + (20.297)i3 + (47.030)j3
Male	-12.249 + (-3.603)a6 + (-4.462)b1 + (-3.133)e1 + (-20.912)f1 + (-2.560)i4 + (-4.291)j3 + (-4.823)k1

Note that, the coefficients are shown as a negative value in some of the regression equations, such as those for the adjectives *light* and *male*. This is because the satisfaction of cluster one of the mentioned adjectives shows the image of the opposite value, the negative coefficient in the adjective *light* shows that members in cluster one actually prefer the opposite adjective *steady*, and the negative coefficient for the adjective *male* tells us that members in cluster one prefer the opposite adjective *feminine*. Conclusion and Suggestions.

This study explored consumers' mutual satisfaction towards bicycle forms to capture trends and consumers' preferences quickly. The concept of taking account of the differences among consumers had been proposed using the bicycle as a case study. We applied Fuzzy C-means to capture consumers' subjective preferences as the variable of segmentation. The parameters extracted from the clustering results have been treated as retrieval data when constructing the mutual satisfaction model. A semantic differential method was applied to measure consumers' attitude towards 40 bicycles using five bipolar sets of adjectives. The chosen five bipolar sets of adjectives proved to be valuable when exploring the bicycle form and should be treated as reference material for further study. We proposed a modified framework by considering the differences among consumers as a retrieval parameter to gain a deeper understanding of the object under study. The combined application of Fuzzy C-means and Ordinal Regression are considered worth using as the data needed are less complicated compared to other forms of numerical regression analysis. The results show that different clusters within the same group of consumers actually produce different satisfaction models.

References

1. Cheung, K.W., Kwok, J.T., Law, M.H., Tsui, K.C.: Mining customer product ratings for personalized marketing. Decision Support Systems 35, 231–243 (2003)
2. Dubois, D., Prade, H.: On the use of aggregation operations in information fusion processes. Fuzzy Sets and Systems 142, 143–161 (2004)
3. Grabisch, M.: Fuzzy integral in multi-criteria decision making. Fuzzy Sets and Systems 69, 279–298 (1995)
4. Jindo, T., Hirasago, K., Nagamachi, M.: Development of a design support system for office chairs using 3-D graphics. International Journal of Industrial Ergonomics 15, 49–62 (1995)
5. Maslow, A.H.: A theory of human motivation. Psychological Review 50(4), 370–396 (1943)
6. Nagamichi, M.: Kansei Engineering: A New Ergonomic Consumer-Oriented Technology for Product Development. Int. J. Ind. Ergonom. 15(1), 3–11 (1995)
7. Norman, D.A., Draper, S.W.: User-Centered System Design: New Perspectives on Human-Computer Interaction. Erlbaum, Hillsdale (1986)
8. Norman, D.A.: The Design of Everyday Things (1988) ISBN-10: 0465067107, ISBN-13: 978-0465067107
9. Tsai, H.C., Hsiao, S.W., Hung, F.K.: An image evaluation approach for parameter-based product form and color design. Computer-Aided Design 38, 157–171 (2006)
10. Yang, C.C., Shieh, M.-D., Chen, K.-H., Lin, P.-J.: Product Form Feature Selection for Mobile Phone Design Using LS-SVR and ARD. Journal of Convergence Information Technology 6(2) (February 2011)

Design Matters: Mid-Term Results from a Multi-Design Fuel Economy Feedback Experiment

Tai Stillwater[*] and Kenneth S. Kurani

UC Davis PH&EV Center, University of California, Davis,
1590 Tilia Street, Davis, CA 95616
tstillwater@ucdavis.edu

Abstract. Energy feedback to drivers is one method to engage drivers in energy saving driving styles. In contrast to the occasional broadcasting of general driving tips, in-vehicle energy feedback gives drivers access to accurate information about their specific driving situation on an ongoing basis. The increasing prevalence of such feedback in new vehicles suggests a belief that ongoing, in-vehicle feedback is better. However, there is little reliable evidence of the effectiveness of energy feedback in real-word driving in passenger vehicles. This study begins to fill this gap. Participants are given a commercially-available fuel consumption display and recording device to use in their personal vehicle for two months. For the first month the display is blank as the device records a baseline of driving and fuel consumption. For the second month the display is switched on to show drivers one of three feedback designs. This paper presents preliminary results (N=75) of a larger study that will include 150 drivers along the California-Nevada Interstate-80 corridor. Using a mixed-effects linear model, we find an average driving efficiency improvement of between 1.5% and 6% (gallons/100 miles) between the without- and with-feedback months, depending on the feedback designs. Categorizing trips into types based on distance and multiple speed characteristics, there are differences in the apparent effectiveness of feedback across trip types. Finally, an overall decrease in fuel consumption of 10% between periods was observed. While approximately 3% of that is explained by changes in driving behavior, the remaining 7% is due to reduced VMT.

Keywords: Driver Behavior, HMI, Human Machine Interface, Behavior Change, Energy Conservation, Ecodriving.

1 Introduction

Past research indicates the influence drivers can have on passenger vehicle fuel economy (1–3). A suite of energy-saving behaviors has come to be known as ecodriving—including moderating top speeds and acceleration and increased coasting (especially approaching stops). However, the potential improvements from eco-driving are mediated or structured by roadway design, traffic levels, competing norms about driving styles, and drivers' own interest and knowledge regarding eco-driving.

---

[*] Corresponding author.

A. Marcus (Ed.): DUXU/HCII 2013, Part III, LNCS 8014, pp. 578–584, 2013.

In this paper, we focus on the impact of in-vehicle fuel economy feedback on fuel consumption, using a framework of driver attitudes, interest, and knowledge to help explain driver behavior. To make precise measures of the effectiveness of feedback, we test the effectiveness of three common feedback styles on ecodriving behaviors on-road fuel consumption using a large sample size and two months of recorded driving per observation. The experiment will eventually reach a sample size of 150 drivers in cities and towns along the I-80 corridor from San Francisco, CA to Reno, NV, for a projected total of 25 driver-years by the end of the project (of which only ¼ has been completed to date). Here, we present preliminary results based on the first 36 drivers from Davis, CA, representing six driver-years of study.

2   Description of the Experiment

This study extends the current body of knowledge of ecodriving feedback efficacy by testing multiple versions of fuel economy feedback in a two month natural driving experiment. To make the best possible estimate of the efficacy of the three tested designs, thirty to forty participants will be enrolled in each four distinct regions in two states, for a total of 150 individual drivers and 25 vehicle years in the experiment (12.5 baseline vehicle-years and 12.5 treatment vehicle-years).

2.1   Study Regions and Household Selection Process

To ensure that the estimates of fuel savings can be generalized many driving situations, four distinct metropolitan regions along the I-80 corridor were selected for study, comprising San Francisco, Davis, and Sacramento, CA as well as Reno NV. This paper details the preliminary results from Davis, CA.

A household sample was selected with the participation of the North American American Automobile Association (AAA). The recruitment criteria included ownership of at least one non-hybrid post-1996 model year vehicle, AAA insurance of $100,000 in accident coverage, $300,000 per occurrence, and $50,000 in property damage. A letter stating the general outline of the study was sent to a sample of 3-500 qualifying drivers in each region. The letter included a link to a recruiting survey which would enter the participant into our pool of possible participants. Participants and interested co-insurees were then enrolled in the study.

Each participating household was given a display to use for one month without receiving feedback to record a baseline driving period. After one month a researcher would return to the household to reprogram the device to enable the fuel economy feedback feature. The household would then use the updated device and view energy feedback for the following month, until a researcher would return to the household a final time to interview the participants about their experience using the display as well as to uninstall the display from the household vehicle and retrieve the driving data.

2.2   Screen Selections

Three feedback display designs were selected that span the range of designs tested for user comprehension and satisfaction in the 2010 NHTSA Fuel Economy Driver Interface Report (4).

Table 1. Feedback Designs used in the Experiment

Screen Name	Description	Image of Feedback Screens as Deployed
Numbers	Real-time MPG (1) , trip average MPG (2), current value shown by a green bar chart(A) the mean value is set to the EPA combined cycle fuel economy rating for that vehicle (B) the current value is also shown in numeric form (C).	
Accelerator	Instantaneous acceleration bar (2) and trip-level leaf representation of fuel economy (1) where the center point (A) represents the EPA combined cycle Fuel Economy Rating.	
Shrubbery	Short term (1A) and trip-level (2) leaf representations of fuel economy. The mean value of the bars is set to the EPA combined cycle fuel economy rating for that vehicle (B).	

The implications for the design and sample size of the field test are discussed below. The selection of three screens from the NHTSA report's seven representative screens is based on three factors: reducing cognitive load by reducing the number of different screen types we will have any of our drivers view (measured by user response time), improving comprehension (measured by a user task with a binary correct/incorrect result), and increasing user satisfaction (measured by user self-reports). The three screens are implemented nearly as shown in the NHTSA report, although higher-contrast colors are used to increase visibility in the vehicle.

2.3   Data Recording Details

To estimate the influence of the three feedback designs on fuel consumption as closely as possible, detailed data were recorded from each vehicle. The study used the DrewTech DashDaq display and data logger to retrofit participant's own vehicles with a graphical feedback display. Fuel-consumption related data were recorded from the On Board Diagnostic (OBD-II) port at an average of 20hz (twenty records per second) for the duration of each recorded trip. Standard conversions were used to calculate fuel consumption from recorded MAF (Mass Air Flow) sensor readings, and distance traveled from the VSS (Vehicle Speed Sensor). For vehicles using the speed-density engine control strategy, which do not include a MAF sensor, synthetic MAF values were calculated in the DashDaq using the vehicle engine displacement, intake air temperature, engine RPM, and an assumption of 80% volumetric efficiency. When available, the Lambda sensor was also recorded to adjust the fuel consumption values in periods of rich or lean fuel-air mixtures. In addition to the OBD-II engine data, a GPS receiver attached to the DashDaq was used to log altitude at a 1hz rate for estimates of elevation and road grade.

To enable proper estimation of the effect of the interface in vehicles with multiple drivers, the display was programmed to allow each driver to enter a personal driver identification number, allowing up to three drivers per vehicle to be recorded.

3   Data Treatment and Analysis

The summary data for each trip was collected in a single R data set for analysis. First, the trips were clustered into distinct types as described in the Trip Type section below to test for differences in effectiveness of the feedback based on the driving pattern (e.g. city and highway trips). The data analysis then proceeded in order of model complexity to determine the true effect of the devices. Fuel consumption and distance were then used to calculate an overall GP100M (Gallons per 100 Miles) fuel consumption measure for each trip.

An overall T-test was used to make an estimate of un-adjusted driving data (wherein the fuel consumption was not controlled for factors such as the vehicle or driver, temperatures, or trip types). Then a T-test for each feedback design was performed to make an unadjusted estimate for each design.

To adjust for changing drivers, vehicles, temperatures, and driving patterns a mixed effects linear regression model was fit to the data. The regression model includes a consumption offset for each driver-vehicle combination to account for the different intrinsic efficiency of various vehicles. The model then includes multiple explanatory factors besides the experimental treatment to disentangle changes in efficiency due to temperature changes, changes in trip patterns, and changes in driver or vehicle during the course of the experiment. Two regression models were fit to the data, the first to test the average effect of the feedback on different driving patterns, and the second regression tested the differential effect of the three feedback designs. The models and interpreted output are shown in Tables 4 and 5 and Figures 1 and 2.

Trip Types
To reduce drive-cycle variance in the model, and to assess the effectiveness of feedback in varying drive-cycles, trips were clustered using the K-means methodology to identify trips that have distinct drive-cycle characteristics. The four dimensions used for clustering are the trip distance, mean speed, maximum speed, and number of stops.

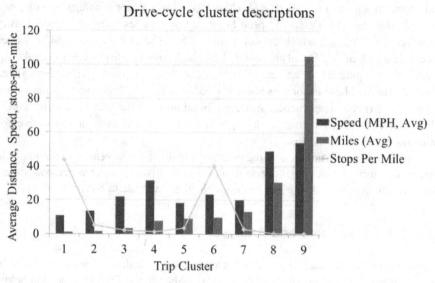

Fig. 1. Trip Types

4   Results

The overall t-test between experimental periods shows a statistically significant decrease in fuel consumption per mile of 10% (p = 0.007), a value that generally fits within previous estimates. However, this effect is not primarily due to driving behavior. Only 3% (on average) decrease in fuel consumption is due to driving behavior as given by the model methodology. The remaining 7% decrease is due to reduced driving. A further analysis with the final dataset will hopefully clarify if those changes were seen by chance, or if they are an effect of the interfaces as well.

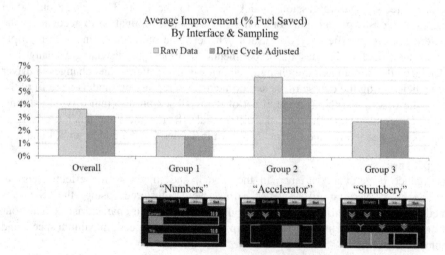

Fig. 2. Trip Type Model Testing Effectiveness of Feedback in Varying Driving Circumstances

To provide realistic estimates that control for vehicle differences, driver, drive-cycle and temperature, a mixed-effects linear model was used to estimate the average changes in on-road fuel consumption by each driver due to the feedback. The model results are shown below in graphical format.

The trip model (Table 4 and Figure 1) dependent variable is GP100M (Gallons/100 Miles driven). Trips below 0.25 miles are excluded, N=6103 Trips, 47 vehicle-driver combinations, R2 = 0.49. Trip type 1 (she category with the shortest trips) is used as the model baseline. Explanatory variables include temperature difference from 72F (to account for heating as well as cooling), average road grade, and experimental phase*trip type interaction term. Unique driver-vehicle combinations are included as the random-effect grouping to control for differences in average fuel consumption between vehicle types.

The driving behavior model shows changes of 1.75% (p = 0.006) for the Numbers display, 6% (p = .018) for the Accelerator display, and 3% (p = 0.3) for the Shrubbery display (a net increase in consumption).

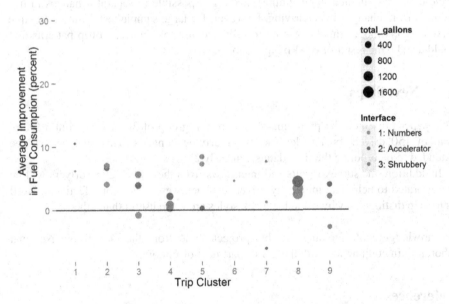

Fig. 3. Average Fuel Consumption and Reduction in Fuel Consumption across Trip Categories. Results are shown for a trip with 72° ambient temperature, 0% grade.

The Trip Model shows that there is a significant decrease in fuel consumption in almost all trip types and interface designs. A number of trends in this analysis are worth noting for future design studies: the most effective design changes between shorter trips (1-4, the shrubbery display was the most useful) and longer trips (8-9, where the accelerator display was the most useful). This suggests that different information is more valuable during different driving periods.

5   Conclusions

The ecodriving experiment conducted here examines 1) the efficacy of in-vehicle feedback to drivers on energy consumption outcomes, and 2) the differential efficacy of three different designs of such feedback, i.e., what information is provided through what graphical representation. Results from the first set of drivers indicate that energy consumption is reduced in the presence of feedback. Controlling for contextual differences between the without and with feedback phases, the presence of three feedback designs are correlated with reductions in fuel consumption of 8%, 4% and 2%, respectively, for a median trip of the Short Arterial type. The type of driving appears also to be important; feedback had little or no impact on energy consumption for long-distance highway driving (Regional type). All other trips showed reduction in energy consumption of between 4 and 6%.

A mixed-effects linear model was found to be better than a direct t-test of fuel consumption because it controls properly for vehicle effects and trip factors (e.g., drive-cycle and ambient temperature), making it possible to separate changes in trip patterns from changes in ecodriving. However, for large sample tests, a more flexible mixed effects model should be used to fully account for changes in trip patterns that could also be the result of ecodriving feedback.

6   Next Steps

This paper presented the preliminary data from a group of 36 drivers from a future total of 150 drivers in a wider variety of driving contexts. This analysis will be extended to incorporate the final data set in early 2013.

In addition, the survey results and interviews from the participating drivers will be incorporated to help determine why driver feedback was or was not effective, as well as to help distinguish why some feedback styles are more useful than others.

Acknowledgement. Funding for this project came from the Oak Ridge National laboratory in conjunction with the US Department of Energy.

References

1. Greene, D.L.: Driver Energy Conservation Awareness Training: Review and Recommendations for a National Program, Oak Ridge National Laboratory (1986)
2. Ando, R., Nishihori, Y., Ochi, D.: Development of a System to Promote Eco-Driving and Safe-Driving. In: Balandin, S., Dunaytsev, R., Koucheryavy, Y. (eds.) ruSMART 2010. LNCS, vol. 6294, pp. 207–218. Springer, Heidelberg (2010)
3. Barkenbus, J.N.: Eco-driving: An overlooked climate change initiative. Energy Policy 38(2), 762–769 (2010)
4. Jenness, J.W., Singer, J., Walrath, J., Lubar, E.: Fuel Economy Driver Interfaces: Design Range and Driver Opinions Report on Task 1 and Task 2 (2009)

Running to Behavior Change

Pip Trevorrow and Marc Fabri

Leeds Metropolitan University, Leeds, UK
{P.Trevorrow,M.Fabri}@leedsmet.ac.uk

Abstract. Levels of overweight and obese individuals have been seen as rising across the globe. This has caused concerns with regard to how active individuals are and realization that a high percentage of the population do not meet the weekly requirement of physical activity. Current focus has been on the capabilities that new technologies can offer as an intervention technique. This paper offers an initial investigation into one such technology, namely the iPod Nike+ kit, which acts as a tracker for running behaviors. This scoping study was conducted via a questionnaire and analysis of customer reviews. Participants were assessed on their stage of change for physical activity behavior, based on the Transtheoretical Model of Change (TTM), before and after using the technology. The results from this study showed that the technology was received positively from those who used it and the predominant outcome was that individuals were more enthusiastic about running.

Keywords: Behavior change, physical activity, iPod Nike+ kit, Transtheoretical Model of Change.

1 Introduction

Levels of overweight and obese individuals have been seen as increasing across the globe. The World Health Organisation [1] has identified obesity as being the fourth highest contributor to premature death. Numbers of obese children have also been seen as increasing in developed countries [2]. Being overweight or obese can lead to a number of health related diseases, such as diabetes, heart disease and musculoskeletal disorders; these have all been seen to be reduced through physical activity [1, 3, 4].

In the UK the Government have commissioned reports and White Papers specifically related to improving healthy lifestyles [5-7]. In addition campaigns such as Everyday Sport and Change4Life have been promoted as part of the Government initiative to get more people active and aware of healthy behaviors [8, 9].

Being physically active is seen to have benefits for all groups of society, in addition to reducing the costs that health related diseases can accrue [3, 10]. The recommended level of physical activity has been set as [1]:

- **5-17 year olds**: at least 60minutes of moderate to vigorous intensity on a daily basis. Vigorous intensity should be incorporated at least three times per week
- **18-64 year olds**: at least 150minutes of moderate intensity throughout the duration of the week; or at least 75minutes of vigorous intensity throughout the week; this

A. Marcus (Ed.): DUXU/HCII 2013, Part III, LNCS 8014, pp. 585–593, 2013.
© Springer-Verlag Berlin Heidelberg 2013

should also include muscle strengthening activities on two or more days throughout the week
- **65+**: as for 18-64 year olds but with some adjustments based on the frailty of the
individual.

However, despite the many benefits that being physically active can provide an increasing number of the population are largely sedentary [3] and do not meet the stated
recommendation for activity levels [8, 11]. Sedentary lifestyles, amongst other factors
have been seen as contributing to the rise in weight levels [2]. The activity habits of
children have been seen as particularly affected by the increase in technology entertainment through activities such as video games and playing on computers [2, 12].

More recently researchers have been investigating whether technology could become part of a solution rather than a contributing factor [2, 12, 13]. Technologies such
as pedometers, mobile phones and heart rate monitors are being used to encourage
participation and performance in physical activity [13]. Interactive games such as
Nintendo Wii and Dance Dance Revolution have entered the market, requiring some
form of body movement to play the game. Whilst not deemed to be as high in energy
expenditure as actually participating in some form of sport or exercise, they have the
potential to increase activity levels for some [2].

With an increase in the capabilities of technologies related to healthy behaviors,
the authors looked into the potential to utilize them in order to change behaviors with
regard to physical activity. The focus of the research collected for this paper was on
the activity of running; obviously there are other forms of exercise that have similar
related new technologies to potentially encourage behavior change to activity habits,
however, running is something that perhaps is more available to the majority of the
population. Running is potentially one of the cheapest, most accessible forms of exercise to get involved in; a good pair of trainers is all the equipment that is really required.

2   Use of TTM

The Transtheoretical Model (TTM) of change has been used extensively with regard
to behavioral change for health and physical activity [14, 15]. The TTM arose from a
need to understand how individuals change behavior rather than the more popular
topic at the time of its development of why people do not change [4, 16, 17]. The
TTM includes four concepts that are crucial to the ultimate aim of behavioral change;
these are stages of change, processes of change, self-efficacy and decisional balance
[15]. The stages of change are identified as follows [16, 18]:

1. Precontemplation – the individual is not ready for change and has not considered
   change
2. Contemplation – the individual is thinking about changing but has not started anything
3. Preparation – the individual has decided to change their behavior and is getting
   ready for the change

4. Action – the individual is actively partaking in changing the problem behavior
5. Maintenance – the individual has adopted the behavioral change and has sustained this for more than 6 months.

The model is cyclical in nature as individuals can relapse and re-enter at any one of the previous stages [16].

The processes of change must be accomplished in order for the individual to progress from one stage to the next. The processes required are dependent on the stage that the individual is currently within. Ten processes were identified from investigating specific techniques of behavior change in other theories, the most important ones were identified and applied to the TTM [16]. The processes can be divided into experiential processes, which relate to personal awareness of how the change in behavior will help, and behavioral processes, which involves actual activity by the individual [14].

Decisional balance involves the individual being aware of the advantages of changing their problem behavior and believing that these advantages outweigh the disadvantages. Self-efficacy is the personal belief that the individual can avoid temptation and can maintain the change to their behavior [18].

The TTM will be applied to the pilot study data in order to ascertain the impact of the iPod Nike+ kit technology on the participants with regard to behavior change.

3   Encouraging Physical Activity

Whilst not the main focus of the paper, it was deemed appropriate to include a brief discussion of potential factors that have been seen to help individuals to start or continue physical activity. These are not specifically related to technology as they stand but can be used to help inform the design of such technologies for the use of behavioral change.

Social support has been seen as having an impact on continuing physical activity, although it is claimed to be more influential on women than men [19].

Goal setting is perceived to have an impact on change with regard to physical activity [20]; for example, setting a particular step count for the day or week. If the individual combines goal setting with monitoring their performance this is believed to enhance behavioral change with regard to physical activity [21].

Receiving messages that are specific to the individual is considered to increase the likelihood that the message is read and also then applied to personal behavioral change [12, 21]. However, literacy is something that may need to be considered when targeting a wide proportion of the population, spoken messages are thus considered as beneficial for such groups or indeed for those who may prefer such communication techniques rather than the written word [12].

Obviously there are many barriers to getting involved in physical activity, to name but a few, other demands, tiredness, potential costs, safety and lack of interest are just a few that can inhibit the uptake of exercise [22]. With regard to running specifically the environment can be a big issue especially if running alone, the weather and daylight hours can impinge upon running in public spaces [22].

The focus of this paper is on the potential of new technologies, specifically the iPod Nike+ kit, to enhance and overcome the above points and ultimately encourage individuals to become or continue being physically active.

4   Technology Used for Behavior Change with Regard to Physical Activity

With the increase in weight levels and sedentary behavior across the globe, the entertainment industry was highlighted by the Department of Health and Human Services as a potential area for increasing activity levels and hence reduce weight issues [11, 23].

By utilizing the ever increasing capabilities of technology to act as interventions for physical activity, the time and cost pressure such processes can place on health care organizations can potentially be alleviated. Further, technology can have a wider, faster reach than conventional interventions. Recruitment and delivery of such interventions can be highly increased through the use of technology [12]. Technologies such as mobile phones, personal digital assistants (PDAs), websites and many other formats have the potential to provide such interventions [3].

Recruitment can be considered as proactive, where participants are contacted directly, or reactive, where participants act on the basis of advertisements. The use of technology feeds into recruitment via the proactive method on a potentially large scale [12]; thus reaching those who may be in the pre-contemplation stage of the TTM, in addition to the other stages of behavioral change, which a reactive approach may miss.

Mobile phone technology, namely the use of SMS texting, was used as an intervention method for encouraging physical activity amongst postnatal women [24]. The intervention was focused on increasing walking and intensity of activity for the participants. The study found an increase in self-efficacy and goal setting; however physical activity did not significantly change.

Cavallo et al [19] conducted an intervention study using Facebook as a potential social support mechanism to encourage physical activity uptake and maintenance. The study showed that although there was no immediate increase in social support perceptions or physical activity in the participants, the medium of social networks such as Facebook had great potential for delivering interventions to young people.

A review of research on active video games conducted by Foley and Maddison [2] showed that the level of intensity and time attributed to such activities did not add up to the recommended physical activity levels. However, it was by far an improvement on purely sedentary activities. Such games have the potential to improve levels of physical activity in those who are predominantly partaking in sedentary technology based activities.

Sports trackers such as the iPod Nike+, Endomondo, Run Keeper, are just a few of the devices available to use whilst exercising. Some of these started their life specifically focused on running but have since opened up to other activities such as cycling, skiing, mountain climbing. Trackers enable sharing and analysis of workouts [25] in addition to recording information such as calories burnt, distance and speed travelled [10]. These trackers do require carrying a GPS enabled device which can be off-putting to some [10].

In using new technologies to help increase activity levels, it is believed that they must be "inexpensive, easy to use, comfortable to wear, durable and reasonably accurate" [21 p.157]. Accuracy is key in order for the user to view a true recording of their efforts and not blame the technology for poor performance. Introducing some form of automated coach with the capability of detecting a decline in the users performance was deemed as a potential solution to keeping users on track and motivated [21]. Working as teams was also believed to be more encouraging than working alone, which is in line with the idea of social support helping to maintain physical activity levels [19].

Endomondo, just one of the trackers available, enables data to be viewed via maps in addition to sharing the information with friends encouraging a competitive arena through formalized competitions and general social competition amongst peers [25]. The use of a GPS tracker enables high accuracy of distance and duration.

The key is to make the technology something that the user will continue to use, rather than discard once the novelty of it has worn off [21].

5   Scoping Study

The aim of this pilot study was to investigate, at a low level, the potential for new technologies to help encourage individuals to become active through the activity of running. The iPod Nike+, the focus of the pilot study for this paper, was launched in the US in 2006, this has since become more sophisticated but the initial device, described in more detail below, was the one used for the initial scoping project.

The iPod Nike+ kit allowed runners to track miles, speed and duration via a small receiver which fit into their trainer and linked to their iPod. At the end of the run a voice would report the information to the runner in addition to displaying the overall outcome on the screen. The runner could upload their personal data to a website in order to track and monitor performance, they could also partake in competitions and challenges posed by the Nike+ team [26, 27].

Working within the Leeds Metropolitan University ethics code of practice the pilot study explored two different data sets with the intention of gaining some initial idea of the potential for the iPod Nike+ kit to encourage individuals to start or continue running.

Data collected via a questionnaire (Data Set 1) was explored with the main aim of collecting TTM related information. Data collected from a set of customer reviews (Data Set 2) was investigated to investigate wider issues related to the technology. The customer reviews were posts placed on the Apple iPod Nike+ website [26]. The data sets were reviewed separately and then combined to give an overall perspective of the use of the new technology to support running behavior.

5.1   Data Set 1 Procedure

Free iPod Nike+ kits had been distributed to two universities in Leeds, UK, in April 2008 as part of a promotion by Apple and Nike. Kits were distributed from a bus on campus on a first come first served basis. Each person who received a free kit also received a free t-shirt, was registered to the Nike website and also automatically signed up to a Facebook group (376 members in August 2009). The likelihood of the individuals spanning all stages of the TTM was high and this group was therefore deemed suitable to try and recruit participants from. The potential participants were not contacted until a year after the distribution of the kit, thus allowing time for any changes to behavior to occur; the TTM states 6 months before movement to a new stage can occur [28].

The Facebook group was contacted with a questionnaire link, set up using survey monkey. The questionnaire investigated stage of change for prior to receiving the kit and a year after receiving the kit in addition to information about use of the kit itself.

Ideally a pre and post-test would have been preferred, but due to the nature of the launch, this was not possible.

5.2   Data Set 1 Results

Unfortunately only 14 respondents answered the questionnaire which whilst very disappointing will still be used to give some insight into the study but with no statistically significant results being claimed.

Nine of the participants claimed that they had noticed an impact on their running behavior, with the remaining 5 claiming that it had no effect. Using the TTM data, 5 respondents showed a change of stage, with one respondent moving up two stages. No one showed a relapse or reduction in stage of change with regard to running behavior.

Receiving the data on their performance was highlighted as the most encouraging factor to take the kit with them on their run, followed closely by having a set goal to meet. One of the main reasons for not taking the kit with them was having nowhere to put the iPod.

5.3   Data Set 2 Procedure

Customer reviews (298) posted on the Apple iPod Nike+ website [26] were accessed in January 2010. The posts were completed by people who had already purchased the kit and were therefore likely to be in stage 2 of the TTM or above.

Each review was coded via a phrase by phrase technique and then codes were grouped under theme headings. The reviews were treated with caution as it was possible they could have been posted by the company to help promote the kit, however, upon reading the reviews it was deemed unnecessary to be cautious as many contained negative points as well as positive which were unlikely to have been posted by company representatives.

5.4   Data Set 2 Results

An overarching element that was clear from all of the comments made in the reviews was that they all had a motivation for running already. The comments ranged from wanting to take up running and using the kit as an encouragement to do so, to using the kit as a tool for maintaining their current running habits, and improving upon already existing running activities.

"[The device] compelled me to run more frequently and with greater purpose than ever before" (Customer Review ID 21)

The comments reviewed verified the initial assumption that those posting comments would all have been in at least stage 2 of the TTM.

Receiving data about their performance through written data in addition to the personalized messages received at the end of the workout were all reported as positive features of the kit.

"During the workout the feedback was great, the voice was nice, and being able to hear my pace/distance/time/calories at the touch of a button was cool. My favourite part has been the Nike+ site which visually shows your runs as a graph over time" (Customer Review ID 182)

Despite some negative comments made throughout the reviews, predominantly with the very poor battery life of the sensor, no one claimed that they were going to stop running or had found that this had reduced their activity levels, if anything the reviews were stating ways around the problems or recommending other similar products that did not have this negative element included.

6 Discussion

Overall the data collected showed a positive report with regard to improvement in running behaviors as a result of the technology. Individuals who answered the questionnaire had claimed that they had moved up at least one stage of change. In some cases respondents from both data sets who were already active runners stated that they had increased the frequency and/or duration of their workouts. Other individuals from data set 2 had purchased the device with the specific aim of using it to help them to start running. This is a positive outcome for using the device to encourage behavioral change. Information from individuals in stage 1 was lacking, which was to be expected from the data that was available to the researchers at the time. This is perhaps an area worthy of future study.

The iPod Nike+ kit offers social support as discussed by Cavallo et al [19] via the Nike website where results and challenges can be exchange via formal competitions and social forums. This adds a community aspect to something that could otherwise be viewed as a very solitary activity.

Goal setting and monitoring performance are obvious features of the device as workout statistics such as duration, distance, and pace are reported back on screen and via a voice message at the end of each workout. The data is also available for viewing as individual runs and as overall performances dating back to the start of using the tracker via the website. Both of these elements were mentioned in both data sets as factors that encouraged the use of the device. The participants saw great benefit in being able to see if they were improving and meeting goals. This fits with research conducted by Rhodes and Pfaeffli [20], Richardson [21] and Nigg [12].

Personalized feedback of data was included in the technology via a sports star reporting when the individual had improved the time for their fastest mile or run a new distance. This aspect was considered an appealing feature by respondents from both data sets which fits with information raised in the literature [12]. The participants enjoyed the idea of being able to hear, from a famous person, how they were improving.

Some of the barriers to the uptake of physical activity, such as tiredness, and other demands [22] cannot immediately be overcome by this specific technology. However barriers such as cost can be addressed by such technologies.

This scoping study shows a positive outcome of using technology such as the iPod Nike+ to help motivate and encourage activity levels with regard to running. Long term effects and any influence on individuals portraying characteristics of stage 1 in the TTM require further investigations.

7   Further Work

Taking into account the number of activity led technologies now in existence the authors would like to explore other devices than the iPod Nike+ kit. Whilst the kit has improved since this study was conducted it still has some limiting factors such as the individual requiring an iPod device. Endomondo, a tracker mentioned earlier in the paper, has a wider reach as it is a free app to download to a wide variety of GPS enabled devices. This emphasizes the availability to all aspect that was the emphasis behind the idea of looking at running as an activity.

Factors such as long term impact of the technology on activity behaviors and the capacity to reach individuals in all stages of the TTM need careful consideration in any future research.

References

1. World Health Organization: Global Recommendations on Physical Activity for Health. Who Press, Switzerland (2010)
2. Foley, L., Maddison, R.: Use of Active Video Games to Increase Physical Activity in Children: A (Virtual) Reality? Pediatric Exercise Science 22, 7–20 (2010)
3. McPhail, S., Schippers, M.: An evolving perspective on physical activity counselling by medical professionals. BMC Family Practice 13, 1–8 (2012)
4. Jackson, R., Asimakopoulou, K., Scammell, A.: Assessment of the transtheoretical model as used by dietitians in promoting physical activity in people with type 2 diabetes. Journal of Human Nutrition and Dietetics 20, 27–36 (2007)
5. Department of Health: At least five a week. Evidence on the impact of physical activity and its relationship to health. A report from the Chief Medical Officer. Department of Health (2004a)
6. Department of Health: Choosing Health: making healthy choices easier. Public Health White Paper (November 16, 2004), (2004b)
7. Department of Health: Health benefits of physical activity in childhood and adolescence. At least five a week: Evidence on the impact of physical activity and its relationship to health (April 29 2004), 31-35 (2004c)

8. PublicTechnology.net: Sport England uses web as a prime comms tool in its Everyday Sport campaign (2005)

9. http://www.nhs.uk/change4life/Pages/change-for-life.aspx

10. Gil-Castineira, F., Costa-Montenegro, E., Gonzalez-Castano, F.J., Lopez-Bravo, C.: Experiences inside the Ubiquitous Oulu Smart City. IEEE Computer 44, 48–55 (2011)

11. Cummings, J., Duncan, E.: Changes in affect and future exercise intentions as a result of exposure to a regular exercise programme using the Wii Fit. Sport and Exercise Psychology Review 6, 31–41 (2010)

12. Nigg, C.R.: Technology's influence on physical activity and exercise science: the present and the future. Psychology of Sport and Exercise 4, 57–65 (2003)

13. Hall, T.: Emplotment, Embodiment, Engagement: Narrative Technology in Support of Physical Education, Sport and Physical Activity. Quest 64, 105–115 (2012)

14. Kennett, D.J., Worth, N.C., Forbes, C.A.: The Contributions of Rosenbaum's model of self-control and the transtheoretical model to the understanding of exercise behaviour. Psychology of Sport and Exercise 10, 602–608 (2009)

15. Callaghan, P., Eves, F.F., Norman, P., Chang, A.M., Yuk Lung, C.: Applying the Transtheoretical Model of Change to exercise in young Chinese people. British Journal of Health Psychology 7, 267–282 (2002)

16. Grimley, D., Prochaska, J.O., Velicer, W.F., Blais, L.M., DiClemente, C.C.: The Transtheoretical Model of Change. In: Brinthaupt, T.M., Lipka, R.P. (eds.) Changing the Self: Philosophies, Techniques, and Experiences, pp. 201–228. SUNY Press, New York (1994)

17. Prochaska, J.O., DiClemente, C.C.: The transtheoretical approach: Crossing the traditional boundaries of therapy. Krieger Publishing Company, Melbourne (1984)

18. Pro-change behaviour systems inc, http://www.prochange.com/ttm

19. Cavallo, D.N., Tate, D., Ries, A.V., Brown, J.D., DeVellis, R.F., Ammerman, A.S.: A Social Media-Based Physical Activity Intervention. American Journal of Preventive Medicine 43, 527–532 (2012)

20. Rhodes, R.E., Pfaeffli, L.A.: Mediators of physical activity behaviour change among adult non-clinical populations: A review up-date. International Journal of Behavioural Nutrition and Physical Activity 7, 37 (2010)

21. Richardson, C.R.: Objective monitoring and automated coaching: a powerful combination in physical activity interventions. Physical Therapy Reviews 15, 154–162 (2010)

22. Burton, N.W., Turrell, G., Oldenburg, B.: Participation in Recreational Physical Activity: Why Do Socioeconomic Groups Differ? Health Education and Behavior 30, 225–244 (2003)

23. Department of Health and Human Services: Physical activity and health: A report of the Surgeon General. US Department of Health and Human Services, Centres for Disease Control and Prevention. National Centre for Chronic Disease Prevention and Health Promotion, Altanta (1996)

24. Fjeldsoe, B.S., MIller, Y.D., Marshall, A.L.: Social Cognitive Mediators of the Effect of the MobileMums Intervention on Physical Activity. Health Psychology (2012)

25. Kjaergaard, M.B.: Location-Based services on Mobile Phones: Minimizing Power Consumption. IEEE Pervasive Computing 11, 67–73 (2012)

26. http://www.apple.com/ipod/nike/

27. http://nikerunning.nike.com/nikeplus/?sitesrc=GBLP

28. Cardinal, B.J., Lee, J.-Y., Kim, Y.-H.: Predictors of Transitional Shifts in College Students' Physical Activity Behavior. International Journal of Applied Sports Sciences 22, 24–32 (2010)

Well-Being on the Go: An IoT Vending Machine Service for the Promotion of Healthy Behaviors and Lifestyles

Sauro Vicini, Sara Bellini,
Alice Rosi, and Alberto Sanna

City of the Future Living Lab, Fondazione Centro San Raffaele - Milano, Italy
{vicini.sauro,bellini.sara,rosi.alice,sanna.alberto}@hsr.it

Abstract. Vending machines are often considered mere dispenser facilities that elicit only low engagement in their users. Instead, it is a market that is not only growing and expanding, but also evolving from a technological as well as service point of view. The City of the Future Living Lab in Milan has designed alongside its users an interactive Internet of Things vending machine based service which has been successfully deployed and is being tested in a public space within the Living Lab. This paper would like to present this as a case studies of designed experiences for behavior change.

1 Introduction

It is widely recognized that healthier nutritional behaviors are a powerful means for the prevention of numerous chronic disease such as obesity, type 2 diabetes mellitus, cardiovascular diseases and one third of cancers [1]. Therefore eating healthy has direct consequences on an individual's state of health and quality of life. Nonetheless, people still decide (more or less conscientiously) to eat in an unhealthy manner. But how can society's eating habits be affected in a positive and constructive manner in order to bring about long lasting change?

City of the Future Living Lab is a real and virtual research environment and community that embodies a Smart and Intelligent City, run by the e-Services for Life and Health department of the San Raffaele Hospital in Milan (Italy). The unit is specialized in the application of Information Technology to healthcare, and its aim is to develop and deliver services for everyday life and well-being that are designed by the user and that can empower the user to live better lives.

The researchers of the eServices for Life and Health believe that building a common knowledge of nutrition that is delivered in a context-driven, personalized and entertaining manner through an interactive eService can be a solution to help Individuals adopt healthier eating habits and lifestyle behaviors, and for this reason have developed an innovative IoT-enabled vending service which has been deployed in the City of the Future Living Lab entitled Well-being on the Go. This paper presents the case for this eService, the process behind its implementation, and the results which are being collected from its instantiation.

A. Marcus (Ed.): DUXU/HCII 2013, Part III, LNCS 8014, pp. 594–603, 2013.
© Springer-Verlag Berlin Heidelberg 2013

2   The Context

This section will provide a description of the context in which the vending machine based service was developed, and the fundamental approach used by the eServices for Life and Health Unit.

2.1   Nutrition Knowledge as One of the Solutions for Changing Society's State of Health

In his review of the studies executed by his peers in the realm of nutrition and health [2] Worsley states that nutrition knowledge, or a person's knowledge of the nutritional content of food and its effect on a person's state of health (e.g., the necessary number of fruit and vegetable daily servings that guarantee a correct intake of vitamins and minerals), is significantly associated with 'healthy eating'. Worsley cites numerous works to uphold his claim: a study by Wardle et al. [3] shows that those individuals who possess this nutrition knowledge eat healthier (knowledgeable individuals are 25 times more likely to consume adequate amounts of fruit and vegetables daily), whilst a study by the USDA' s Economic Research Service [4] shows that the more mothers know about food and nutrition the better the quality of their children's diets, especially younger children's diets.

Nevertheless, an individual's knowledge of nutrition is not the sole trigger for adopting healthier eating and lifestyle behaviors. Information can help build common beliefs and values that the individuals of a society can refer to, but providing information alone is not the only answer.

There are a list of factors which complement and enhance nutrition knowledge, which have been verified by the eServices for Life and Health research unit in past clinical and user research and which are very well summarized in Worsley's article. In order to stimulate a new consciousness of what is meant by health and how behaviors have a direct consequences on one's state of health, nutrition knowledge must be supported by a set of perceived consequences, based on the Expectancy value model [5]. Promoting skills related to nutrition, such as learning how to shop and how to cook, are also important, as well as building an individual's confidence in being able to perform the desired behavior is also key, based on self efficacy in models such as the Social Learning Theory [6]. Repetition and entertainment are also factors that play into the acquisition and use of knowledge, where the former refers to the act of repeatedly receiving information or perpetuating a behavior until it has become acquired and spontaneous, whilst the latter refers to the act of learning through entertainment (also called edutainment or serious gaming) [7].

The environment and its properties where food is purchased and consumed also influence an individual's behaviors towards eating and health (the smell of freshly baked bread, for example) as well as a vast multitude of motivators. These can range from the individual's personal attitudes and beliefs (such as the perception of good value for money), to his or her cultural values, to his or her psychogenic needs (such as the need to feel rewarded), to social or peer influence, all of which are present in Grunert's Food Lifestyle Model [8].

From the above paragraphs, it emerges that nutrition knowledge must be supported and delivered alongside a series of elements in order for it to have an impact on an individual or a society. For nutrition knowledge to be meaningful, it must be easy to understand and implement, contextualized, personalized, relevant and fun to acquire and put into practice. These elements formed the basis for eServices for Life and Health's vending machine service.

2.2   New Emerging Behaviors

It is estimated that almost 8 million people consume a meal outdoors [9] every day in Italy. If one considers also the snacks individuals consume throughout a typical day, the percentage rises, and indeed it is estimated that outdoor food consumption amounts to almost 50% of the average food shopping of an Italian [10].

According to a report by Censis (the main Italian research Institute for socio-demographic research) and Coldiretti (the Italian agriculture association), Italians eat outdoors not only for work or leisure reasons, but also to transgress: indeed, consideration of nutritional values plays a much less important role in the choice of what to eat outdoors as to when at home (29,7% at home as oppose to only 14,9% outdoors) [11].

The World Health Organization has selected Food Security and Food Safety as the two main areas within the realm of Nutrition that are in need of interventions in order to preserve and promote society's health. The aims of future actions are those of ensuring a correct consumption of foods that are safe, healthy and sustainable, especially in public spaces such as schools, workplaces, healthcare institutions and so on. For this reason, food businesses including cafés and restaurants, as well as vending machines, must abide by the same diet guidelines [12]. The Italian Ministry of Health has developed a plan that is in line with WHO's directives in order to promote healthy lifestyles and behaviors in Italy, through a series of actions whose aim is to spread a culture of healthy eating and virtuous lifestyles [13], especially in public spaces such as schools and hospitals.

It is for these reasons that the eServices for Life and Health Unit decided to tackle the concept of vending machines – not only are they a controversial topic but the potential is huge considering the number of people who everyday depend on them for their nutrition.

3   The Process

The City of the Future Living Lab strongly believes in involving the end user in the innovation process of successful and truly user-centric products, interfaces and services, and for this reason has developed a revised Living Lab methodology based on co-creation. This section describes the process adopted by the City of the Future Living Lab that generated the Well-being on the Go eService.

3.1   Understanding Behaviors – The Living Lab Co-creation Method

Living Labs are innovation environments that focus on user communities embedded within 'real life' situations and environments. The fundamental concept at the base of a Living Labs [14] is to gain direct and unfiltered access to users' ideas, experiences, and knowledge, based on their daily needs and desire of feeling supported by products, services, or applications. City of the Future Living Lab, as the name suggests, is a miniature version of a city (with a hospital, a university, a hotel, stores and offices, a supermarket and a post-office, an automatic metro rail and bus service as well as streets and parks) and it articulates itself in numerous scenarios where a multitude of stakeholders and partners can work alongside each other, sharing knowledge and experiences whilst interacting with a wide variety of ICTs. Its aim is of understanding, studying and measuring the interaction dynamics among users and services offered and the potential of Internet of Things technologies.

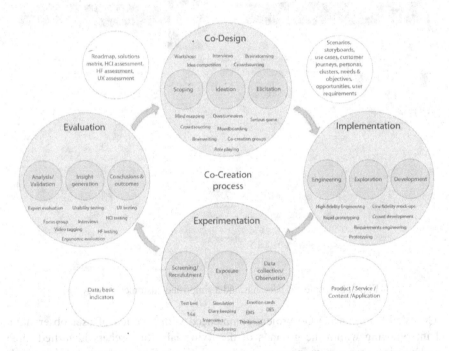

Fig. 1. The Co-Creation methodology ideated and adopted by City of the Future Living Lab

The City of the Future Living Lab has decided to push this concept of user involvement and active participation even further by adopting a methodology that is entirely based on co-creation, thus inviting volunteers from its living lab to freely participate and contribute to all the steps of the design process that is illustrated in the following image (Figure 1). The methodology consists of four main phases, each composed of a set of sub-phases: Co-Design (a phase in which users are observed interacting with existing services or products in the identified scenario, where they are questioned in order to gain a 360° understanding of their needs and aspirations, and where they are involved in generating ideas and concepts that can drive the innovation process), Implementation (where users are involved in developing, personalizing and fine-tuning prototypes), Experimentation (when the final concept is deployed in a real-life context and users are observed interacting with it) and Evaluation (where the data collected throughout the Experimentation phase is analyzed by a team of experts in order to evaluate whether the concept developed fully responds to users' require-ments). Since the Co-creation process is iterative and reflective, there is no real start-ing point and not all sub-phases must be carried out necessarily, making it a very adaptable, scalable and easy to personalize according to a project's aims and re-sources.

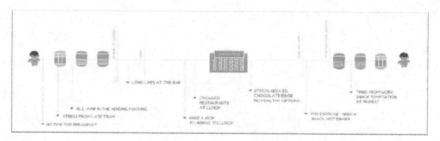

Fig. 2. Examples of personas and a simplified customer journey

The Well-being on the Go project commenced with a period of user observation and interviewing within the grounds of the living lab. Researchers identified three main behaviors: consumers increasingly depend on vending machines for their feed-ing throughout the day (which can involve breakfast, mid morning snacks, lunch, afternoon snacks, and in some cases dinner), and this translates into needs which are becoming more articulate than in the past regarding the type, range and quality of products supplied by vending machine. At the same time, users are increasingly more careful about what they eat, interested in learning how to eat better but without dis-rupting their everyday lives. The third insight is that users are becoming more tech savvy, across all age groups, which means that they have expectations towards vending machines are able to communicate with 'things' and not only supply goods but also services. These three main behaviors, alongside the demographic data collected, were translated into a set of persona profiles and corresponding customer journeys, which helped guide the project throughout its course (Figure 2).

The previously described information collected during the Co-design phase was used to develop a first concept of an interactive vending machine during the Implementation phase. The idea proposed consisted of using an existing vending machine and integrating it with an ad hoc IoT system that could make it capable of offering more of a service rather than just sell food. Three evolutionary steps were identified for this concept: the first consisted in equipping the machine with a touch screen, video camera, proximity sensor, internet connection and speakers, so that the machines could not only dispense healthy foods but also edutaining content regarding the food offered as well as the most basic and vital nutrition knowledge (in the form of digital art, videos and music) and practical information (such as a map of the hospital grounds as well as the schedule of the shuttle line and local bus service). The second step would be to integrate an NFC reader or Smart Card reader so that the vending machine is able to recognize its user and therefore administer personalized information and content that can therefore offer targeted motivational strategies. The third step would involve the vending machine being able to communicate in a secure manner with the hospital's database so that each user can monitor over time his or her state of health and correlate it to what he or she eats, how much physical activity he or she does every day, and so on – in particular it could offer those individuals with a health condition or illness additional support in order to correctly manage them, and provide pertinent information to those who instead are at risk of developing a health condition.

Such variegated and personalized content would allow the vending machines to become a point of reference for visitors, employees and patients, not only elevating the common attitude towards these machines but also offering an extremely innovative 360° service that integrates nutrition, healthy behaviors, illness prevention and management, edutainment and socialization.

Throughout the implementation phase, engineers, technicians, programmers and UI and product designers from the City of the Future Living Lab worked together in order to develop a first concept of the vending machine that responded to user requirements (Figure 3). At the same time, a team of healthcare specialists (including nutritionists, psychologists and biomedical engineers) from the San Raffaele Hospital collaborated with the design team to develop a set of menus as well as key nutrition information and knowledge to integrate with the concept, in order to align the Well-Being on the Go project to the Italian Ministry of Health guidelines and to the elements described in the first few paragraphs of this paper. Throughout this phase, volunteers recruited across the Living Lab grounds were asked to comment on the vending machines and suggest changes or improvements, specifically on the services offered, the graphics and the information supplied.

The refined concept of the vending service was then deployed in a space of the living lab during the experimentation phase, next to the shuttle line service and stores since the customer journeys developed from the co-design phase showed the potential of this specific space (it is indeed a busy area where many people grab a bite to eat either before or after work, or during coffee breaks and lunch whilst they visit the local shops).

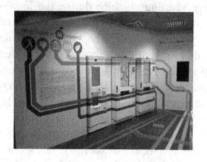

Fig. 3. The vending machine concept deployed in the Living Lab

For a period of five months, the vending machines were exposed to the public of the hospital and Science Park. Data was collected via the IoT system, the vending machine's software and direct user observation on behalf of a team of researchers in accordance with the Italian privacy laws and regulations. The project finds itself in the evaluation phase, where the qualitative and quantitative data collected during the experimentation is being analyzed to produce a series of insights which will determine whether or not the existing concept responds to the user needs and aspiration identified in the co-design phase and in what way the concept can be tweaked and fine-tuned before moving on to the next vending machine concept and new Living Lab cycle. More of these initial results will be discussed in section 3.3 below.

3.2 Supporting Behavior Change: An e-Service Design Model

Alongside the Co-creation methodology previously described, an e-Service Design Model was adopted, ideated and developed by the research unit e-Services for Life and Health which operates within the City of the Future Living Lab. This model consists of merging user needs, preferences and behaviors to produce a virtual profile that can be combined with the individuals Personal Health Record. Such a pairing produces a 360° vision of a person so that he or she can be provided with pertinent, contextual and actionable guidance from healthcare professional in order to stimulate them towards adopting healthy lifestyle choices and behaviors. This unique Service Design model synchronizes an Individual's three most important facets: Emotions (a trigger to an Individual's psychological reaction in context with his/her preferences), Relations (a trigger for a social interaction with other Individuals physically present or not, and/or with a proximity or remote environment in context with his/her preferences), and Functions (an Individual's practical need addressed by the service) delivered. This Service Design model called Engineering Awareness™ [Figure 4].

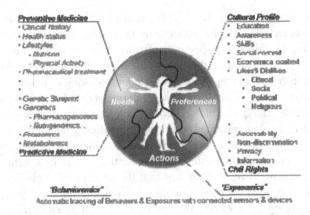

Fig. 4. The Engineering Awareness™, an e-Service Design model

Designing for an Individual's awareness is the primary ethical objective of any personalized service developed within the eServices for Life and Health unit. Individuals should not be manipulated or pushed to adopt a specific lifestyle or behavior, rather they should be provided with unbiased and personalized information so that the Individual is empowered to make informed choices. With a complete understanding of an Individual, the service provided can respond to all of his her needs, expressed and unexpressed, physical as well as emotional, biological as well as sociological, and therefore truly bring about long lasting and widespread change [Figure 5].

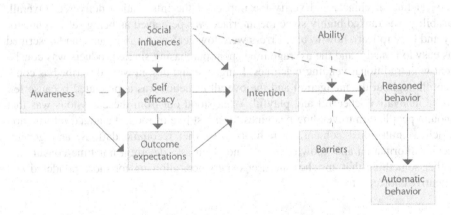

Fig. 5. How awareness can influence behaviors

4   Initial Results of the Project

As previously mentioned, the Well-being on the Go project finds itself in the experimentation phase of the living lab cycle. In order to evaluate the impact of the project on users of the City of the Future Living Lab, a series of questionnaires, interviews and thinkaloud exercises were carried with walkers-by who fitted the personas identified during the co-design phase. This evaluation phase is still occurring and not all results have been collected. Feedback from these initiatives was coupled with data from the vending machines' sensors and software in order to depict a clearer picture of the user experience. Attention throughout the evaluation phase was focused on: the usability of the interface; perception of the space; monitoring of behavior changes.

At the moment a total of ten people were interviewed and asked to participate in a thinkaloud exercise. The questionnaires consisted of a series of closed and open questions, aimed at collecting information on the Individual's demographic details, attitudes towards vending machines in general, feeling of the way the space was designed and the initiative was communicated, and perception of the new vending machines proposed. What emerged from them was that the mission of Well-Being on the Go was successfully decoded by users, for they felt that the initiative promotes healthy eating and well-being as a whole, in a relaxing as well as energizing space where people on the move can enjoy nutritionally correct food that fits their preferences. The majority of individuals interviewed stated also that having screens on the interactive vending machines added to their everyday experience of vending machine elements of playfulness, but also intuitiveness, and that the music, media, games and videos often attracted them to the space but also made them return to the space with others and talk about health and well-being related issues.

The thinkaloud sessions consisted in three sets of exercises, where Individual's were asked to buy a product, followed by a combo and then obtain the directions to a point of interest on the other side of Milan. The aim of these sessions was to gain feedback on the usability, efficacy and satisfaction of the user interface designed for the vending machines, and verify the impact of the information delivered. Overall, usability was ranked highly since the interface was perceived as being self explanatory and easy to learn how to use. Errors were low across all age groups, and described as easy to remedy, and the average time spent purchasing single products was consistent with traditional vending machines. Language and design were described as coherent throughout the navigation and the overall esthetics was appreciated because felt to be innovative, cheerful and playful. What stood out from these sessions was that though people turn to vending machines for a fast bite of food, the added information (such as nutritional content, ingredients lists, diet recommendations, and general health information and knowledge) was not seen as a deterrent nor time-consuming, rather something that enriches the user experience, allowing for more pondered and attentive choice of food.

5   Conclusions

The healthy food option isn't always perceived as the most appealing one, especially when dispensed by a vending machine. A healthy food choice can be made more interesting and attractive not by imposing it through strict policies or rigid regulation, but rather by promoting awareness in Individuals on a widespread scale so that they can appreciate the effect of choosing a healthy food option on their health and well-being. By empowering Individuals through pertinent, personalized, contextualized and fun information which they can retrieve at any point of their busy day, they can appreciate the impact of their everyday lifestyle choices and make informed decisions that can promote long-term behavioral change. Nevertheless, a 360° understanding of the Individual, in all of its facets, must be gained and the user must be involved in all the phases of the development of a concept (be it a product, an interface or a service) so as to design solutions that truly respond to their functional, social and behavioral needs and therefore successfully permeate everyday life.

The next steps of the Well-being on the Go project will be to continue the interviewing phase to include the remaining personas, and move on to the next concept evolution where the remaining sensors for the identification of users will be implemented in order to provide a fully personalized and truly innovative user-centric and user-driven eService.

Acknowledgements. City of the Future Living Lab and the eServices for Life and Health research unit would like to thank Rhea Vendors group for having shared with us their vending machines and knowledge.

References

1. Robertson, A., et al.: Food and health in Europe: a new basis for action. WHO Regional Publications, European Series No. 96 (2004)
2. Nutrition knowledge and food consumption: can nutrition knowledge change food behaviour? Asia Pacific Journal of Clinical Nutrition 11(supp. 3) S-579–S-585
3. Wardle, J., Parmenter, K., Waller, J.: Nutrition knowledge and food intake. Appetite 34, 269–275 (2000, 2002)
4. US Department of Agriculture Economic Research Service. Mother's nutrition knowledge is key influence on the quality of children's diets. J. Am. Diet. Assoc. 100, 155 (2000)
5. Feather, N.: Human values and the prediction of action: an expectancy value analysis. In: Feather, N.T. (ed.) Expectations and Actions: Expectancy Value Models in Psychology, pp. 263–289. Erlbaum, Hillsdale (1982)
6. Bandura, A.: Social Learning Theory. General Learning Press (1977)
7. Baranowski, T., Buday, R., Thompson, D.I., Baranowski, J.: Playing for real: video games and stories for health-related behavior change. Am. J. Prev. Med. 34(1), 74–82 (2008)
8. Grunert, K.G., Brunso, K., Bisp, S.: Food-related life-style: Development of a cross-culturally valid instrument for market surveillance, MAPP Working paper no. 12. The Aarhus School of Business, Aarhus (1993)
9. Elaborazione Centro Studi Fipe su dati Istat (2011)
10. Primo rapporto sulle abitudini alimentari degli italiani. Censis e Coldiretti s.l. (2010)
11. Primo rapporto sulle abitudini alimentari degli italiani. Censis e Coldiretti s.l. (2010)
12. European Action Plan for Food and Nutrition Policy 2007-2012. WHO, s.l.
13. Schema di piano sanitario nazionale 2011-2013. Ministero della Salute s.l.
14. Santoro, R., Conte, M.: Living Labs in Open Innovation Functional Regions, ESoCE-NET White Pap (2010)

Author Index